Teaching Young Children

Teaching Young Children
An Introduction

Third Edition

Michael L. Henniger
Western Washington University

PEARSON

**Merrill
Prentice Hall**

Upper Saddle River, New Jersey
Columbus, Ohio

Library of Congress Cataloging-in-Publication Data

Henniger, Michael L.
 Teaching young children: an introduction/Michael L. Henniger. — 3rd ed.
  p. cm.
 Includes bibliographical references and index.
 ISBN 0-13-113529-5
 1. Early childhood education. I. Title.
LB1139.23.H45 2005
372.21—dc22

2004042581

Vice President and Executive Publisher: Jeffery W. Johnston
Publisher: Kevin M. Davis
Acquisitions Editor: Julie Peters
Editorial Assistant: Michelle Girgis
Production Editor: Linda Hillis Bayma
Production Coordination: Amy Gehl, Carlisle Publishers Services
Design Coordinator: Diane C. Lorenzo
Text Designer: Ali Mohrman
Photo Coordinator: Valerie Schultz
Cover Designer: Ali Mohrman
Cover image: Getty One
Production Manager: Laura Messerly
Director of Marketing: Ann Castel Davis
Marketing Manager: Autumn Purdy
Marketing Coordinator: Tyra Poole

This book was set in New Baskerville by Carlisle Communications, Ltd. It was printed and bound by Courier Kendallville, Inc. The cover was printed by The Lehigh Press, Inc.

Photo Credits: Scott Cunningham/Merrill, pp. 2, 9, 14, 56, 61, 107, 183, 206, 211, 222, 241, 276, 311, 340, 396, 400, 420; Karen Mancinelli/Pearson Learning, p. 12; Anthony Magnacca/Merrill, pp. 25, 60, 62, 82, 132, 140, 164, 288, 291, 296, 328, 358, 393, 426, 437, 439; Corbis/Bettmann, p. 32; Courtesy of the Library of Congress, pp. 35, 44; American Montessori Society, p. 38; Bill Anderson/Photo Researchers, Inc., p. 43; Eddie Lawrence/Dorling Kindersley Media Library, p. 75; Elizabeth Crews/The Image Works, p. 100; Robert Brenner/PhotoEdit, pp. 102, 129; Richard Hutchings/PhotoEdit, pp. 105, 229; Silver Burdett Ginn, pp. 114, 168; Myrleen Ferguson Cate/PhotoEdit, pp. 120, 334; Michelle D. Bridwell/PhotoEdit, p. 125; Jo Browne/Mick Smee/Getty Images Inc. – Stone Allstock, p. 145; George Dodson/PH College, pp. 155, 157; Bob Daemmrich/Stock Boston, p. 173; Laima Druskis/PH College, pp. 190, 409; Pearson Learning, p. 194; Michael Newman/PhotoEdit, p. 197; Tom McCarthy/PhotoEdit, p. 198; Laura Dwight/PhotoEdit, p. 218; David Young-Wolff/Photo Edit, pp. 248, 360; John Bulmer/Dorling Kindersley Media Library, p. 255; Dana White/PhotoEdit, p. 257; John Paul Endress/Modern Curriculum Press/Pearson Learning, p. 262; Tom Prettyman/PhotoEdit, pp. 268, 304, 381; Michal Heron/PH College, p. 282; Tony Freeman/PhotoEdit, p. 308; Will Hart/PhotoEdit, p. 315; Doug Menuez/Getty Images, Inc. – Photodisc, p. 319; Mary Kate Denny/PhotoEdit, pp. 336, 428; Edouard Berne/Getty Images Inc. – Stone Allstock, p. 343; KS Studios/Merrill, p. 350; Ray Ellis/Photo Researchers, Inc., p. 365; John Paul Endress/Silver Burdett Ginn, p. 370; Tom Watson/Merrill, p. 376; Paul Conklin/PhotoEdit, pp. 388, 416; Patrick White/Merrill, p. 405; Courtesy of IBM Corporation, p. 435.

Pearson Education Ltd.
Pearson Education Singapore Pte. Ltd.
Pearson Education Canada, Ltd.
Pearson Education—Japan

Pearson Education Australia Pty. Limited
Pearson Education North Asia Ltd.
Pearson Educación de Mexico, S.A. de C.V.
Pearson Education Malaysia Pte. Ltd.

10 9 8 7 6 5 4 3 2
ISBN: 0-13-113529-5

PREFACE

Educators involved in teacher preparation occasionally hear students make statements such as, *"I wasn't successful teaching fourth grade, but I know I can do better with younger children. They're great fun to be around and so easy to teach."* Although it is true that young children are exciting and enjoyable, teaching them is far from easy. Students new to the field of early childhood education need to develop an awareness of both the challenges and the joys involved in working with young children. This book presents both perspectives, providing a comprehensive, balanced overview of early childhood education.

This text is designed to be reader-friendly and uses a clear, well-organized, informative, and personal writing style. Throughout the text, the reader encounters concise overviews of important topics and current references for further study. Vignettes of children and teachers, as well as questions presented throughout the chapters, encourage readers to understand young children, reflect on teaching and learning, and discuss with others the topics presented.

Unique Features

Teaching Young Children: An Introduction is unique in several ways:

- **Five essential elements of early education**—understanding child development, play, guidance, working with families and communities, and diversity— are clearly identified. They are explored in the prose, through boxed features in every chapter, and in one chapter devoted to each essential element in the book.

- **Curriculum and play**—The book emphasizes appropriate curriculum for young children in six chapters and play in two chapters, which is unique in this market.

- **Concrete applications**—helpful classroom strategies—were deliberately added to boxed features in this edition. Opportunities for students to practice applying knowledge are available in activities on the Companion Website, thereby making readers better prepared to apply theory in early childhood settings.

This textbook provides a framework for understanding how to teach children from birth through age 8 by clearly identifying and discussing five essential elements of early childhood education. Each element is a critical component of quality programs for young children and is woven repeatedly throughout the text. Each element is highlighted and explored in every chapter by a special feature box:

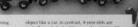

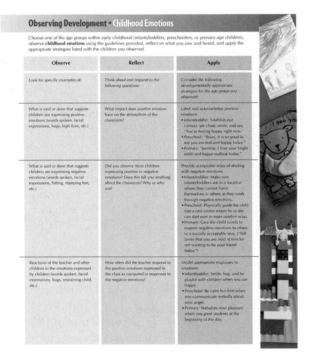

Observing Development

An understanding of children and their development. Educational experiences for young children need to be based on children's developmental abilities and interests. An understanding of child growth and development is a necessary starting point for early childhood education. The "Observing Development" features list traits and behaviors to observe, factors to consider and reflect upon, and specific applications and strategies to use to support and enhance development for children in *three age groups:* infant/toddler, preschool, and primary.

Celebrating Play

Opportunities to play. Young children need times during their school day to engage in quality play experiences, both indoors and outdoors. Play is one of the most important ways for young children to learn about the world around them. "Celebrating Play" features appear in each chapter to illustrate how play can be used to promote development in all domains.

Celebrating Play . . .
Puzzles in the Preschool Classroom

Puzzles are a traditional and important part of learning in the preschool classroom. The first puzzles for children were produced in 1760 by John Spilsbury, an Englishman (Maldono, 1996), and have been part of teaching and learning since that time. However, what is the attraction of these manipulatives for young children? When you watch them working with puzzles, children are often intensely focused and will often complete the same puzzle over and over again. Maldono (1996) explains it this way:

> Children are interested in puzzle making because they can be active as observers, problem solvers, and learners, with little or no assistance from adults and others. The intrigue involved in puzzle making is that fragments come together to complete an image. Through puzzle making, young children experience satisfaction by putting things together where they belong. Contentment is achieved by the mere fact that things that look broken are fixed. (p. 4)

Good puzzles should have the following characteristics (Maldono, 1996):

1. *Puzzles should match the child's developmental abilities.* For example, most 2-year-olds need puzzles that have knobs and depict a single whole object like a car. In contrast, 4-year-olds are typically ready for knobless puzzles of 12 to 18 pieces.

2. *Puzzles should be attractive and durable.* They should be colorful and include clearly recognizable items. Because of high usage, they also must be sturdy.

3. *Puzzles should reflect items that are familiar to children.* They should be of items that children have seen or had experiences with, such as foods, vehicles, and animals.

4. *Puzzles should be solvable.* While being challenging, they should be something the child is motivated to complete and be successful with. Some children may be ready for more complex puzzles of 100–150 pieces (Barron, 1999), while others are more typically challenged by puzzles with fewer pieces.

1. Do you enjoy doing puzzles as an adult? If so, what do you find attracts you to this activity?

2. Take the time to read one of the two articles referenced in this feature. In terms of overall development, what can children potentially learn from puzzle use?

Into Practice

Guiding young children. Assisting with the social and emotional development of young children is another key element of early education. Guidance in these areas requires a strong knowledge of child development and sensitive interactions between adults and children. Many "Into Practice" boxes identify specific ways that teachers can use guidance in their daily practice. Look for the strategies in the bulleted and numbered lists.

REVISED!

Into Practice . . .
Guiding Children Who Have Difficulty Sharing

Although young children are capable of many things at an early age, it is also important to keep in mind what they are unable to do . . . yet. As with 3-year-old Mario on pp. 101–102, one example of this is that many young children have difficulty sharing toys and equipment in the classroom. Teachers of preschool children need to be prepared to deal with the problems that this may bring. The following strategies are commonly used to help students who are struggling with sharing:

- **Have two or more of the most popular toys.** It is not always possible to do this, but when you have two or more toy trucks, popular dolls, magnifying glasses, floor pillows, or shovels to use for gardening, make sure to have them available for children. This will not eliminate problems, but may make it easier to share a popular item among several children.
- **Set time limits with toys and equipment.** If, for example, three children want to use the two toy trucks available in the block center, give each child a time limit (perhaps 10 minutes), set a timer so that you do

not forget, and then try to get the child without the desired toy involved in another activity for the next few minutes.
- **Identify ways in which children can use the equipment together.** For example, if three children want to play the same game on the computer, see if you can set them up so that all three can be seated around the screen with specified roles. The additional benefits of playing together may well outweigh the challenges of getting them involved in a cooperative activity.
- **Give children words to use in sharing situations.** Because of their more limited language skills, preschool children often use physical actions in their place. If a child wants a stapler but one is not available, many young children will simply take one away from someone else. You can help them with the language they will need to share. "Rather than taking the stapler away from Lise, ask her if you can use it to staple your pages together. Tell her you will return it when you are done."

Family Partnerships . . .
Working with Teen Parents

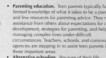

It may surprise you to learn that the number of teen parents in this country is high. While there was an overall decline in teen parents during the last decade of the 20th century, America still has one of the highest teen pregnancy rates among developed countries. Four of every 10 young women in this country become pregnant at least once before their 20th birthday (Annie E. Casey Foundation, 2003). These statistics make it clear that, as a teacher of young children, your partnerships with families will probably include working with teen parents.

Because of these probable connections, it is important for you to be aware of the many challenges faced by very young parents and be prepared to assist them when possible. Teen mothers tend to drop out of school and live in poverty more often than their peers. In addition, they have children with increased health problems, more frequent developmental delays, and a greater likelihood for future difficulties in school (Shore, 2003). As society struggles to reduce the incidence of teen pregnancy, your job will be to work cooperatively and effectively with these very young parents in whatever ways you can.

In addition to interacting with teen parents in your classroom, you will want to be aware of other resources within the schools and local community. Teen parents are receiving services in several important ways:

- **On-site child care.** Many high schools now provide on-site child care so that teen parents can continue their own schooling while their young children receive quality care. These programs are often cooperative schools (see Chapter 3) and teen parents are expected to spend time as aides in the classroom, where they learn parenting skills as they interact with other trained early educators.

- **Parenting education.** Teen parents typically have limited knowledge of what it takes to be a parent and few resources for parenting advice. They need assistance from others about expectations for child development, strategies for parenting, and help in managing complex lives under difficult circumstances. Teachers, schools, and community agencies are stepping in to assist teen parents in these important areas.
- **Alternative schooling.** Because of their life situations, teen parents may find it difficult to be successful in a regular middle school or high school program. Most school districts provide alternative schooling options for teen parents and others that offer learning experiences to better meet their needs.
- **Counseling and career education.** School districts and community agencies also provide teen parents with counseling and career education opportunities to help them cope with challenging life circumstances and take advantage of local resources.
- **Health care.** Because teen parents are often in low-income family situations, they frequently qualify for free or low-cost medical care. Taking advantage of these services can have a major positive impact on the health and well-being of children.

1. Have you had experiences with teen parents in either your family or home community? What do these experiences tell you about the challenges they face?
2. How do you think you will feel about working with teen parents? How will your attitudes and beliefs influence your interactions?

Family Partnerships

NEW!

Working with parents, families, and communities. The development of mutually supportive relationships with parents, families, and the community is another essential element of teaching at this level. Strong relationships help ensure maximum opportunities for growth and development in young children. "Family Partnership" features present ways that teachers can team up with other important people in children's lives.

REVISED!

Celebrating Diversity

Diversity and young children. An understanding of, and respect for, diversity is the final essential element of early education. Differences due to culture, gender, and physical and/or mental capabilities influence each of the other four essential elements and must be studied, understood, and discussed in the early childhood classroom. The "Celebrating Diversity" features present issues that teachers need to be aware of in today's diverse classrooms.

Celebrating Diversity . . .
Supporting English Language Learners

Growing numbers of young children come to the early childhood classroom speaking languages other than English at home. Data from the U.S. Census Bureau (2000) indicate that nearly one in five American families speaks a language other than English at home, with Spanish, Chinese, Tagalog (Filipino), Korean, Vietnamese, Arabic, Hindi, and Russian being the most common (Banks, 2002). Teachers of young children must be prepared to support these English Language Learners as they work to master a new language.

Lake and Pappamihiel (2003) identify four main components of a developmentally appropriate language environment for young English Language Learners (ELL):

1. *Conversation.* Teachers must make time to engage English Language Learners in direct conversation to stimulate their understanding and use of oral language. While avoiding overcorrecting and judging these children, regular and natural conversations help children practice and build confidence in their English speaking abilities.
2. *Understanding and acceptance.* Much has been written about the process of second language acquisition, and teachers will need to understand and accept the additional steps children must take. Lake and Pappamihiel (2003) emphasize that even though young children take only 1 to 2

years to develop basic interpersonal communication skills, it often requires 5 to 8 years to reach the point where they have the language competence needed for academic success.
3. *Experience.* As with all children, English Language Learners need meaningful experiences that they can then use as the basis for productive oral language communications. Teachers should plan a variety of meaningful experiences with these English Language Learners in mind.
4. *Children's literature.* Quality children's literature that values the differences between children can help young English Language Learners feel good about themselves and stimulate oral language learning. A collection of books like *Someone Special, Just Like You* (Brown, 1991) will add important insights for the whole class.

1. Think about the positive aspects of having English Language Learners in the classroom. How will these children enrich your life and the lives of other children?
2. Read an article about English Language Learners and then think about the implications for your future teaching. What changes will you need to make in how you teach when you have English Language Learners in your room?

Each of these five essentials is discussed in an individual chapter dedicated to the topic (see Part II). To emphasize the importance of these themes, however, a discussion of child development, play, guidance, family and community partnerships, and diversity is also integrated within each chapter of the book.

The text's emphasis on curriculum in six chapters familiarizes students with the content areas and domains that they will need to understand and learn to integrate when creating enjoyable, playful, educational experiences for young learners. The two chapters on play are especially unique.

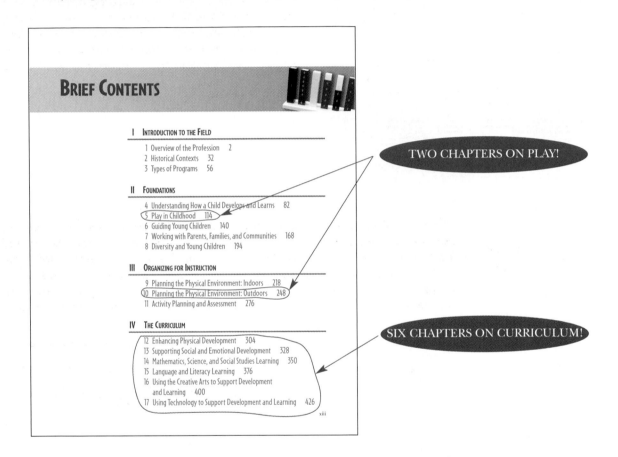

- *Six chapters on curriculum.* As one of six chapters devoted to curriculum in early childhood settings, the concluding chapter on technology is unique in its description of play-oriented, developmentally appropriate computer experience.

- *Two chapters on play.* Although several other texts present information on planning outdoor play environments, this text provides a complete chapter (Chapter 10) identifying the outdoor play area as a significant component of early education. A second chapter on play (Chapter 5) offers a strong rationale for including play in the classroom.

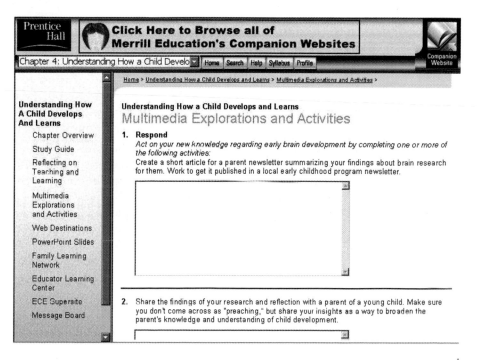

Into Practice...
Examples of Developmentally Appropriate Practice

When teachers of young children plan programs that are developmentally appropriate, they are using an understanding of child growth and development to plan activities that take advantage of children's abilities and interests. Developmentally appropriate practice, in addition to being used to plan appropriate activities, also influences the materials used, organization of the classroom, guidance strategies, and the daily schedule. The following examples are intended to highlight the many different facets of developmentally appropriate practice in classrooms for infant/toddlers, preschool children, and those in the primary grades:

Infant/Toddlers

- Routines in the day, such as diaper changes, are made as enjoyable as possible by adults when they play simple games like Peek-a-Boo, smile and talk to children, and have a positive attitude about these parts of the child's day.
- Pictures of infants and their families are hung on the walls so that children can see them. Adults take the time needed to talk to children and show them the pictures on a regular basis.
- Rattles, balls, squeeze toys, stuffed animals, and chewing toys are all available for children to grasp, drop, shake, chew, and manipulate.

3-, 4-, and 5-Year-Olds

- Each week, teachers take materials out of each center and replace them with other interesting and developmentally challenging options. For example, in the manipulative center, five new puzzles of differing complexity are added to replace the ones that have been out for the past week. LEGO bricks

are removed and Lincoln Logs are added in their place. Playdough is added as a new option for children to explore.
- Over the past week, two children who normally are friendly started to call each other names. Knowing this, the teacher first talks to both sets of parents to find out if they are aware of any problems or issues. Then the teacher plans to read a story at group time that brings up the topic of name-calling and discuss the issue with the class.
- The schedule each morning has been constructed to allow children to have 45 minutes in the morning for center time. During this period, children can choose the center they wish to attend and the activities that they want to engage in.

6-, 7-, and 8-Year-Olds

- Knowing that most young children have difficulty sitting still for any length of time, teachers organize the schedule so that children have short breaks in an academic period to sing a song or get up and "get the wiggles out" by doing some simple stretching exercises.
- Children have the opportunity to work in groups several times each day so that they can learn from each other in a social context. In some instances the teacher identifies the small groups, while in others the children themselves decide on groupings.
- Children are encouraged to engage in long-term projects that interest them. For example, three second-grade students may have a fascination with spiders and are encouraged to develop a science report on this topic that they can share with the rest of the class.

To help students bridge the gap between theory and practice, **concrete strategies** are listed in many of the five boxed features. These strategies give students a real-world flavor for what teaching in early education settings requires. Applications are culturally and developmentally appropriate, research-based, and classroom-tested. Opportunities for students to think of and report their own ideas for application are available on the Companion Website in "Multimedia Explorations and Activities."

The **"Multimedia Explorations and Activities"** feature located at the end of each chapter uses the ABC News/Prentice Hall Companion Video Series and Web links to articles to engage students in activities that help them apply what they have learned in each chapter. Students research, reflect, and respond on the Companion Website at **www.prenhall.com/henniger,** providing students with practice opportunities in *applying* their knowledge of early education and care.

Other Book Features

Vignettes

Short vignettes opening each chapter and located throughout the chapters are designed to give readers a mental image of early childhood classrooms and issues related to the content of the chapter. These real-world images help the content come to life and stimulate interest in the chapter discussion.

Margin Notes for Concept Exploration

The margin notes are designed as ways to get students to expand their understanding of such topics as Head Start, multiage education, diversity, block centers, and portfolio assessment, to list a few. Links to these topics are located on the Companion Website (**www.prenhall.com/henniger**) in the Web Destinations module. Look for the computer icon in the margins.

Ancillaries and Supplements

Several additional materials are available for instructor and student use to support additional learning and instruction:

NEW! PowerPoint Slides

PowerPoints of key concepts from the text are available to instructors on the Companion Website at **www.prenhall.com/henniger**. Easily accessed and organized by chapter, they are colorful, simple, and straightforward, and may be customized to fit instructors' needs.

Videos

The ABC News/Prentice Hall Companion Video Series includes three cassettes, *Current Issues in Early Childhood Education, Volumes 1, 2,* and *3.* Free to professors upon adoption of this textbook, these cassettes feature 12 thought-provoking video segments of varying lengths chosen from award-winning news programs on *ABC News.* These segments are integrated into the text via selected "Multimedia Explorations and Activities" boxes featured at the end of each chapter. Look for the *ABC News* icon.

Companion Website

The Companion Website accompanying this text (**www. prenhall.com/henniger**) has been updated and expanded for this third edition. For each chapter there is a "Chapter Overview," a student "Study Guide" that includes sample multiple-choice, true/false, and essay questions, "Reflecting on Teaching and Learning" essay questions, "Multimedia Explorations and Activities," and "Web Destinations." In addition, there is a *message board* and a link to the *Early Childhood Education Resources* website created by Merrill/Prentice Hall. Instructors also have access to the Website's *Syllabus Manager* tool. Look for the CW icon in the margins of the text and in the "Multimedia Explorations and Activities" boxes.

Instructor's Manual and Test Bank

This updated manual includes suggestions for teaching, additional instructional resources, and multiple-choice, true/false, and essay test items for each chapter. It also includes handouts and overhead transparency masters that match the content of the PowerPoint slides. Two new sections have been moved from the text to the *Instructor's Manual.* "For Discussion and Action" offers prompts for in-class activities. "Building Your Personal Library" provides key reference books related to chapter content.

Electronic Test Bank

Test items are available to instructors in the *Instructor's Manual* or in electronic format in the Prentice Hall TestGen, which allows instructors to create customized exams on a personal computer.

Acknowledgments

No book of this complexity can be completed without the assistance of a great many competent and supportive people. Grateful thanks are given to Amy Gehl, senior project editor at Carlisle Communications, and to the following staff at Merrill/Prentice Hall: Julie Peters, acquisitions editor; Linda Bayma, senior production editor; and Valerie Schultz, photo coordinator. Their support and assistance throughout this process have been invaluable.

I also thank the reviewers of the previous editions of this text for their thoughtful commentary and helpful suggestions: Beverly B. Dupre, Southern University of New Orleans; Eleanor Duff, Southeast Missouri State University; Elizabeth Engley, Jacksonville State University; Richard Fiene, Pennsylvania State University; Pat Hofbauer, Northwest State Community College; Carol S. Huntsinger, College of Lake County, Illinois; Peg A. Ketron-Marose, NAEYC; Lynn Lessie, Atlantic Cape Community College; Sima Lesser, Miami Dade Community College; Kevin J. Swick, University of South Carolina; and Elizabeth Walker-Knauer, Cuyahoga Community College. Third edition reviewers include Barbara F. Boyd, Radford University; Tena Carr, San Joaquin Delta College; Phyllis Gilbert, Stephen F. Austin State University; Bernadette Haschke, Baylor University; and ReJean A. Schulte, Cuyahoga Community College.

On a personal note, I want to say a special word of thanks to my wife, Lisa, for all her support throughout this writing project. During this revision process, she has adeptly managed a busy home with four children who currently range in age from 3 to 16. She spent many an evening or weekend with this very active and tiring group of youngsters so that I could have the time I needed to revise this text. Her willing attitude and ready smile helped me through many difficult days. Thank you, Lisa, for your continued flexibility, for your encouraging words, and for the understanding you displayed throughout the process.

Michael L. Henniger

EDUCATOR LEARNING CENTER: AN INVALUABLE ONLINE RESOURCE

Merrill Education and the Association for Supervision and Curriculum Development (ASCD) invite you to take advantage of a new online resource, one that provides access to the top research and proven strategies associated with ASCD and Merrill—the Educator Learning Center. At

www.EducatorLearningCenter.com you will find resources that will enhance your students' understanding of course topics and of current educational issues, in addition to being invaluable for further research.

How the Educator Learning Center Will Help Your Students Become Better Teachers

With the combined resources of Merrill Education and ASCD, you and your students will find a wealth of tools and materials to better prepare them for the classroom.

Research

- More than 600 articles from the ASCD journal *Educational Leadership* discuss everyday issues faced by practicing teachers.
- A direct link on the site to Research Navigator™ gives students access to many of the leading education journals, as well as extensive content detailing the research process.
- Excerpts from Merrill Education texts give your students insights on important topics of instructional methods, diverse populations, assessment, classroom management, technology, and refining classroom practice.

Classroom Practice

- Hundreds of lesson plans and teaching strategies are categorized by content area and age range.
- Case studies and classroom video footage provide virtual field experience for student reflection.
- Computer simulations and other electronic tools keep your students abreast of today's classrooms and current technologies.

Look into the Value of Educator Learning Center Yourself

A four-month subscription to Educator Learning Center is $25 but is **FREE** when used in conjunction with this text. To obtain free passcodes for your students, simply contact your local Merrill/Prentice Hall sales representative, and your representative will give you a special ISBN to give your bookstore when ordering your textbooks. To preview the value of this website to you and your students, please go to **www.EducatorLearningCenter.com** and click on "Demo."

Brief Contents

CONTENTS

II   FOUNDATIONS

III ORGANIZING FOR INSTRUCTION

IV THE CURRICULUM

NOTE: Every effort has been made to provide accurate and current Internet information in this book. However, the Internet and information posted on it are constantly changing, so it is inevitable that some of the Internet addresses listed in this textbook will change.

SPECIAL FEATURES

Into Practice

Multimedia Explorations and Activities

*These features incorporate ABC News/Prentice Hall *Current Issues in Early Childhood Education* video segments.

Teaching Young Children

1

OVERVIEW OF THE PROFESSION

In this chapter you will

- Develop an understanding of the foundations for early childhood education.
- Learn about the many different types of programs for young children.
- Identify the sources of funding for early childhood programs.
- Determine the roles, responsibilities, and skills needed for teachers of young children.
- Investigate the current training typical of teachers in early childhood education.
- Become familiar with the resources for professional development available to early childhood educators.

Adrienne has just been offered the job she interviewed for last week. After spending several years at home caring for her children, she decided to reenter the workforce.

One of the first challenges she faces, however, is finding quality child care for her daughter and son: 4-year-old Alyssa and 2-year-old Mark. During the past few months, Adrienne and her husband have been exploring the many different early childhood programs available in their community.

Adrienne knows how important it is to her children's growth and development that they continue to be stimulated and well cared for when she is not with them. Therefore, she and her husband have been visiting preschool and child care centers in her area, meeting with teachers, talking with other parents, touring classrooms, and observing the children enrolled in these different programs. They have also been collecting information on teacher-to-student ratios, staff qualifications and turnover rates, and the approach to early childhood education in each program.

Finding affordable, high-quality programs where Alyssa and Mark will have plenty of personal attention and many opportunities to learn and play will take careful planning, but with so many possibilities, the right option is sure to present itself.

Perhaps, like Adrienne, you have had some exposure in one form or another to early childhood education. Alternatively, this may be your first introduction to working with children from birth to age 8. In either case, this book will help you begin to explore a most interesting and challenging profession. Because this is an introductory text, however, a great many issues are only briefly described. You will need much more study and practice before you have the knowledge and skills necessary to teach at this level. As you read through the chapters of this book, discuss what you are learning with others, and observe children and teachers in the classroom, you will develop a deeper understanding of the field of early childhood education.

This first chapter introduces you to the many different types of programs associated with early childhood education and describes the professional aspects of becoming an early childhood educator. Before discussing these issues, however, the chapter begins with an overview of the five essential elements of early childhood education.

Essentials of Early Childhood Education

Early childhood education is a unique field of study and practice organized around five key elements. Understanding these foundational components and their interrelationships will help you develop a clear understanding of what is needed to work with young children. Early childhood teachers and caregivers must understand each of these elements and deal with their implications in their classrooms. None of these components can be implemented without the understanding, commitment, and hard work of the classroom teacher.

Understand Children and Their Development

The first of these essential elements is an understanding of child development and learning. Early childhood educators believe that educational experiences are based first on children's needs and interests. To know these needs and interests, adults must understand children, both individually and collectively. By studying child development, teachers of young children know the normal patterns of behavior for children at specific ages. They also realize that individual differences exist between children, and they can identify those variations. This knowledge helps early childhood teachers select materials and activities that will create optimal learning opportunities in the classroom. The "Observing Development" feature at the end of each chapter of this text will help you to understand children and how they develop. The feature at the end of this chapter (see p. 29) prompts you to look at aspects of child development—such as language development, physical skills, social interactions, and understandings of concepts—reflect on what you observe, and consider how you might apply your understanding to children of various ages to maximize their development.

The following vignette illustrates how one effective teacher applies her understanding of child development with her students:

> *Lavelle Peters is preparing for the coming week in her kindergarten classroom. She remembers overhearing Noell and Jaleen talking excitedly about the recent class field trip to the zoo. The Primate House was particularly interesting to several members of the class. Planning some activities centering on this interest seems appropriate and fun. Lavelle uses her general knowledge of child development and individual differences to select books, computer software, and discussion topics about monkeys, baboons, and gorillas for the coming week.*

The approach described in this example is very different from the typical procedures used to develop the curriculum in many primary classrooms. Textbooks used by teachers carefully organize and structure the content taught in elementary schools and present it in a specific sequence. In science, for example, the textbook may call for the study of insects first, followed by birds, and later still, the investigation of primates. Rather than considering children and their developmental needs and interests first, teachers who use this more structured approach with their primary-grade students allow the teaching materials to dictate the sequence and appropriateness of learning activities.

Provide Opportunities to Play

A second essential ingredient found in early childhood programs is the provision of times during the school day in which children can engage in play. Play is one of the major ways in which young children learn about the world around them. Rather than having adults *tell* children what they need to know (an efficient strategy for many adult situations), children need the chance to manipulate real materials and learn for themselves important information about their environment. When children have large blocks of time to choose their own materials and play-mates, the learning that takes place can be quite amazing.

> *Lattice and Malcolm are in the block area in their preschool classroom. They are working together building a road, schoolhouse, and a parking garage. Lattice is struggling to find just the right block for her portion of the roadway. Malcolm suggests she try the "long, long one like mine," and Lattice discovers that his idea solves her problem nicely. As these children continue their play together, they solve additional problems, practice the important skill of cooperation, and indirectly learn about the mathematical properties of their play materials.*

While most parents and teachers recognize play as an enjoyable experience for children, many fail to see the learning potential of this important activity. Consequently, play is often viewed as frivolous and is excluded from the more meaningful work experiences in the classroom. Early childhood educators, however, believe that play is a crucial way in which children learn about language, develop intellectual concepts, build social relationships and understandings, strengthen physical skills, and deal with stress. In short, play enhances every aspect of child development and is an essential ingredient in early education (see Figure 1–1).

Figure 1–1 *Essentials of Early Childhood Education*

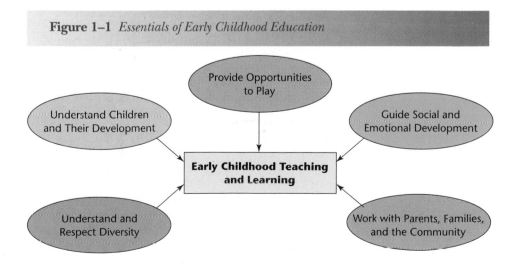

Provide Opportunities to Play

Understand Children and Their Development

Guide Social and Emotional Development

Early Childhood Teaching and Learning

Understand and Respect Diversity

Work with Parents, Families, and the Community

Guide Social and Emotional Development

The third key element of early childhood education emphasizes the importance of guiding the young child's social and emotional development. Although educating the mind is critical during the early years, teachers of young children find it equally important to help children develop a strong sense of self, learn to relate in positive ways with adults and peers, and work through the many positive and negative emotions they experience. Guiding young children in these areas requires a solid background in child development and a sensitive, insightful adult.

> *Carly is a quiet but capable second grader in Ingrid Siegelman's classroom. Lately, however, her behavior has been less than desirable. Carly seems distracted and stares out the window much of the day. Ingrid has noticed that Simone, Carly's best friend, has been playing with other children more often during recess and decides to discuss this with Carly. During free choice time, she takes Carly aside and brings up the issue of Simone's friendship. Ingrid's concern and interest have the desired effect, and Carly opens up about her sadness at having to share her best friend. They discuss several ideas that could help Carly feel better about her situation. With follow-up, Ingrid feels that she has made important progress in understanding and helping Carly.*

Some adults may downplay this activity as tangential to the main mission of education, yet Ingrid and other early childhood teachers recognize it as a critical component of their teaching role. The development of effective social skills and the promotion of emotional health are essential elements of the early childhood curriculum. While this makes the teacher's role more complex, the overall benefits to children are immense.

Work with Parents, Families, and the Community

The fourth essential element of early childhood education is the development of mutually supportive relationships with parents, families, and the community. Although this concept has just recently gained support among educators in general, teachers of young children have had a long tradition of working closely with families and community members. Effective two-way communication, a climate of caring, and the involvement of parents and others in the educational process all provide early childhood teachers, parents, and their children with many benefits.

> *Larry Marshall is in his second year of teaching third-grade children. He tried to communicate with parents and get them involved last year, and he has worked even harder this term to build stronger relationships with families and community members. The results have been truly surprising. Larry expected to see greater student progress and satisfaction and is pleased to find these results. An unanticipated result, however, is the value that parents have found in the informal conversations and observations they have during their time in the classroom. One parent confided that she was learning some very helpful discipline tips from watching Larry in action. She was using similar techniques at home with good success and feeling much better about this aspect of her parenting. Larry also finds that he is personally benefiting from his work with parents. When they share their special talents in the classroom, for example, Larry is challenged and invigorated by the experiences along with the children.*

Celebrating Diversity...
America's Growing Religious Diversity

While American religious beliefs are still primarily Christian, there are many diverse traditions and practices within the subgroups that consider themselves Christian. For example, the beliefs of Mormons, Seventh-day Adventists, and Jehovah's Witnesses differ significantly from Protestant groups such as Lutherans and Presbyterians.

In addition, there are growing numbers of other faiths present in most schools and communities across the nation. As greater numbers of immigrants from non-European countries have found their way to America (U.S. Census Bureau, 2000), they have brought with them a growing diversity of religious beliefs. In the United States, the Jewish, Muslim, Buddhist, and Hindu religions are the largest non-Christian groups (Largest Religious Groups, Adherents.com, 2002). Diana Eck (2001) makes a startling pronouncement about religious diversity in America today when she says, "The United States has become the most religiously diverse nation on earth" (p. 4).

With this growing religious diversity come many opportunities for teachers of young children to help themselves and their children to understand and respect the various belief systems that exist within their classrooms. Teachers need to become aware of the religious diversity within their schools and classrooms, understand the differences in traditions and practices that exist between religions, and make sure to plan activities and discussions that respect this diversity of beliefs.

1. How do you feel about respecting the religious beliefs of the children and families you will be working with? Will this be easy for you or something that will require considerable effort on your part?

2. At this point, can you identify ways in which religious diversity will change the ways in which you will work with young children and their families? For example, how would you celebrate holidays such as Ramadan and Hanukkah in your classroom if you have children for which they are important?

Understand and Respect Diversity

The final essential element of early education is an understanding of, and respect for, the many elements of diversity that have an impact on the lives of young children. Cultural backgrounds, variances due to gender, and physical/mental differences among children all influence development and learning. Furthermore, each of the other four essentials of early childhood mentioned earlier is impacted by diversity. The following examples help highlight the importance of diversity and its interrelatedness with the other essential areas:

- *Child development and diversity.* Two-year-old Sabrina has a hearing loss. After being fitted for a hearing aid next month, she will start attending an early learning program designed to help her catch up with her peers in oral language development.

- *Guidance and diversity.* At group time, you are introducing Corinne, a new Asian American student, in your preschool classroom. Four-year-old Andy says: "Teacher, why does her skin look different than mine?"

- *Play and diversity.* After school, 7-year-old Audrey likes to get out her paint set and create imaginative pictures using a variety of vibrant colors. Her twin brother, Darian, prefers racing around the cul-de-sac on his bicycle, weaving around a self-constructed obstacle course.

- *Parents and diversity.* At the open house, 5-year-old Franklin has just introduced you to Denise and Angela, his two parents. They mention their interest in occasionally helping out in the classroom.

The Scope of Early Childhood Education

Although quality early childhood programs have the five elements just described in common, they also have many differences because of the children these programs are designed to serve. The "Observing Development" feature at the end of the chapter outlines some differences that may be identified. In this section, we will identify and discuss these options.

Infant/Toddler Programs

For more information about infant/toddler programs, go to the Companion Website at www.prenhall.com/henniger, select Chapter 1, then choose Web Destinations.

The fastest growing segment of early childhood programming is the infant/toddler component (birth to 2 years of age). Until fairly recently, most very young children were cared for by family members in the home. Recent research in the United States, however, has found that 44 percent of babies in their first year of life and 53 percent of 1-year-olds are cared for outside their homes (Erle, Adams, & Tout, 2001). Statistics on the family suggest that this trend will likely continue. As these numbers continue to grow, the impact on low-income families is particularly strong. The need for quality infant/toddler care is especially important for this group of children and their families (Paulsell, Nogales, & Cohen, 2003). Although most current infant/toddler programs operate in a home environment with small groups of children, the number of center-based programs caring for larger groups of very young children is increasing. In either setting, the major challenge for a teacher is to form a close relationship with each child in his or her care. Consistently and lovingly meeting the physical and emotional needs of very young children is an extremely important and challenging task (Edwards & Raikes, 2002).

Preschool Programs

Traditionally, preschool programs were designed for children between the ages of 3 and 5 as a way to enhance social and emotional development. These nursery school options became popular in the 1920s and continue to be highly valued by middle-class families. More recently, prekindergarten programs have been promoted as a way to help children identified as at-risk of failing in the K–12 system develop the skills they will need to be successful in later years. Many preschool programs today have also expanded their age range downward to include 2-year-olds.

Rather than being full-day programs, most preschool classrooms operate halftime or less. A common model is to enroll children for three to five half-day sessions per week. With the increasing numbers of single parents and dual-career families, however, these partial-day sessions are often combined with the chance to participate in child care as well. This blending of preschool and child care options often makes it difficult to separate the two programs.

A major challenge for infant and toddler caregivers is to consistently meet children's physical and emotional needs.

Child Care Programs

For more information about child care programs, go to the Companion Website at www.prenhall.com/henniger, select Chapter 1, then choose Web Destinations.

Child care programs are designed to provide children with quality care and education for full days. With more parents working full-time, the need for child care options for young children has grown. Typically, child care programs provide care for children from the beginning to the end of the parents' workday. It is not uncommon for some children to be in a child care setting from 7:00 AM until 6:00 PM. As indicated earlier, other children may attend part-days as a preschool experience.

A variety of child care options are available. The most common type is called the **family home child care.** These programs operate out of the caretaker's home and enroll only a small number of children. **Child care centers** are programs located in buildings either designed for, or remodeled to be used with, young children. More children are typically enrolled in these programs, with several teachers hired to work with different groups of children. **School-based child care** is becoming a more popular option in many locations. Public and private schools are setting aside space in their elementary school buildings for child care programs under their direction. **Corporate child care** is also growing in popularity. An increasing number of businesses are offering on-site child care as a convenience and service to their employees. **Before- and after-school care** is a final option available in many settings. These programs may be provided at the elementary school, or children may travel to other sites to receive this care.

Programs for Children with Special Needs

For more information about programs for children with special needs, go to the Companion Website at www.prenhall. com/henniger, select Chapter 1, then choose Web Destinations.

Early childhood programs designed for children with special needs are also available in most communities. Federal legislation over the past two decades has

Into Practice...
A Special Needs Preschool

With the school year about to begin, Monica, the head teacher for the special needs preschool, is getting ready for her new group of students. She is reviewing the written information she has on each of the children with special needs in the class. There will be nine students: seven children with special needs and two "typical" children to serve as peer models. While Patti and Kara, her two classroom aides, are busy setting up centers and the speech therapist and occupational therapist are down the hall reviewing last year's Individualized Education Plans (IEPs) for returning students, Monica considers the challenges she will face in meeting the needs of such a diverse group of students: Evan is a quiet 4-year-old boy with Down syndrome who has delays in his language, physical, and intellectual development. Stephanie is 3 and has very limited spoken English because she comes from a migrant family that does not speak English in the home. Angie has mild cerebral palsy and slower speech and motor development. Brian is in his second year in the preschool and has significant problems in his social interactions with adults and other children. Mark is a 4-year-old with speech delays of unknown origins. Esther has a birth defect known as spina bifida and spends her time at the preschool in a special wheelchair/bed. Sam has significant vision problems and is considered legally blind. In addition, he has sensory integration difficulties.

Each of the children just described will eventually spend most of his or her time in "regular education" classrooms.

As it is likely that you will have special needs children in your future classrooms, it is important for you to begin thinking about the following:

- **Emphasize commonalities first.** Every child with special needs shares much in common with other children in your classroom (likes, dislikes, positive/negative personality characteristics, strengths/weaknesses, etc.). Make sure to find those similarities and build on them in your teaching. Mark, for example, despite his speech delays, loves to construct with blocks; he can build complex structures and engages in creative play in that center.
- **Define what the child can do.** Rather than focusing on what the child cannot do, work on identifying and building on the child's capabilities. Esther, despite spending her time in a wheelchair, has a great love of books and is beginning to read some simple beginning children's books on her own.
- **Include the child in classroom life.** Make a special effort to find ways in which a child with special needs can be included in all aspects of the activities planned each day. One of the characteristics of children with Down syndrome, like Evan, is that they tend to stand back and watch rather than actively participate in many activities. But when Monica works to include him at group time, he interacts well with her and other students.

mandated these important options. **Public Law (PL) 94–142,** enacted in the mid-1970s, requires that all children with special needs beginning at age 3 be provided a free and appropriate public education. The availability of these programs was extended to birth by **PL 99–457.** The intent of both these laws has been to educate children with special needs in classrooms with their normally developing peers. This integration effort has led to early childhood special education programs that are blended with other options for young children.

While many educational efforts for children with special needs are integrated with other early childhood programs, **early intervention programs** for children with special needs are also available (U.S. Department of Education, 2001). These programs are designed to help identify children's disabilities and assist them in growth and development. Options for infants and toddlers are most common and often combine limited small-group experiences with home visits where the parent and home visitor work together to support the young child's development.

Kindergartens

It may surprise you to know that publicly funded programs for 5-year-old children are a relatively new option in many states. Many public schools either did not provide kindergarten or offered it only for parents who were able to pay for the service. Currently, only 40 states mandate kindergarten education for all students. In the remaining states, school districts are encouraged to offer this option, but are not required to do so (Griffith, Kauerz, & McMaken, 2003).

Traditional kindergartens in the United States were half-day programs designed to help children develop social, emotional, and cognitive skills through a play-oriented experience. Despite the many benefits of this focus, many programs today are more academic and present a curriculum that looks much like that of the first-grade classroom. In addition, many kindergarten classrooms are now full-day programs that typically meet two or three days a week. Research on this option suggests that the longer school day is beneficial when teachers provide a curriculum that allows children time to learn playfully about their world (Clark & Kirk, 2000).

Celebrating Play...
In the Primary Grades

While most preschool teachers include many opportunities for children to play, most primary classrooms are organized around tasks that exclude play as an option for learning (Stone, 1995). With the heavy emphasis on teacher-directed learning found at this level, little time is left for this valuable activity. Yet play can provide many opportunities for primary children to create, problem solve, and learn about the world around them.

Wassermann (2000) has clearly identified ways in which children in the primary grades use play to enhance language development, learn concepts, and build social relationships. She is considered one of the leading advocates for play at this level. She gives the following example of a second-grade classroom in which play is effectively used:

As I walk through the door, the sight dazzles me. Five groups of children are working in investigative play groups with dry cells, buzzers, low-wattage light bulbs, and switches. They are carrying out inquiries with these materials. Bob (the teacher) has used the following activity card to guide them:

Use the materials in this center to find out what you can about electricity and how it works.

- What can you observe about the dry cells? The buzzers? The light bulb?

- Talk together about your observations and make some notes about what you did. (p. 21)

Wassermann describes the intensity and enthusiasm of the children involved in this playful activity. Everyone is busy exploring the materials provided. Many choose to continue the science activity rather than go outside for recess. No discipline problems arise. This playful task has created an ideal situation for creatively learning about science.

1. Earlier in this chapter (page 5), you read about the importance of play for children during the early childhood years. Based on Wassermann's description, what are three or four benefits of play in the primary classroom?

2. From what you know of play so far, do you think it should be included in the primary classroom? If you were a primary teacher, would you encourage your children to play? Why or why not?

Primary Education

Grades 1 through 3 in elementary schools are referred to as *primary education* and have been a part of American schooling from colonial times. For most of this period, the methods and materials for teaching at this level have mirrored those used with older elementary students. Instruction was teacher-directed and included mostly small- and large-group teaching combined with independent work for students.

Beginning in the 1960s and 1970s, the popularity of theorists such as Piaget (Flavell, 1963), Bruner (1966), and Dewey (1929) led to new teaching strategies for this level. Educators began to view primary-age students as more like preschool and kindergarten children in their thinking rather than older elementary students. More opportunities to learn through hands-on manipulation of objects and interaction with peers were implemented. Although instruction at the primary level remains teacher-directed in a majority of classrooms, many primary teachers are starting to engage in a variety of interesting teaching and learning strategies. The **multiage classroom,** in which two or three grades are grouped together for instruction, is one option being tried. For example, rather than having separate groups of 5-, 6-, and 7-year-old children, students are mixed together in the same room. Multiage classrooms can be traced back to the one-room schoolhouses that existed in America until the early part of the 20th century. A renewed interest in this option began in the 1980s. In these classrooms, younger children learn from their interactions with older classmates, and older students reinforce their own understandings as they work with younger students. Because teachers have many of the same students for more than one year, there tend to be stronger teacher–student relationships in multiage classrooms. Research also suggests that

These second graders learn many valuable concepts with manipulative materials.

these classrooms enhance socioemotional development (Kinsey, 2001). Multiage classrooms produce students who have more positive attitudes toward schooling, demonstrate stronger leadership skills, have greater self-esteem, and engage in fewer aggressive behaviors.

Other creative options being tried include **looping,** in which the teacher remains with the same students for several years. Using an **integrated curriculum,** in which mathematics, reading, science, and social studies are all learned simultaneously through the teaching of specific themes, is another example of this effort (see Chapter 11 for more information). Creating **classroom centers** where children can independently explore materials and activities of their own choosing in playful ways is yet another strategy being implemented. (Chapter 9 provides further details on centers for the early childhood classroom.)

For more information about looping, go to the Companion Website at www.prenhall.com/ henniger, select Chapter 1, then choose Web Destinations.

Funding: Who Pays for Early Education?

Another way to conceptualize programs for young children is to look at who pays for the services. In general, it is either the public (through local, state, or federal funds), the families involved in the early childhood program, or some combination of these two. In this section, we will look at this issue in more detail.

For-Profit Programs

Approximately 60 percent of all child care programs are run as businesses to generate profits for their owners (Administration for Children and Families, 2001). The revenue generated from parent fees is the major source of income for these programs. This money is used to pay for teacher salaries, space/housing costs, and the expenses for toys and equipment used in the program. Most for-profit programs are locally owned child care centers and family child care homes. These community entrepreneurs may or may not have expertise in early education. Because of this variance in knowledge and training, some programs offer excellent education and care while others leave much to be desired. National corporations also are making money in the child care business. KinderCare is the largest of these options, with over 1,250 franchised centers nationwide. In addition to child care, some preschool programs are operated for profit as well.

Cooperative Programs

An important option that began in the 1920s is often referred to as the **parent cooperative.** Parents in these programs are usually responsible for paying their children's educational costs. These expenses are kept low by involving parents as assistant teachers in the classroom. Each family unit is expected to spend a specified number of hours each month helping out in the classroom. This allows the program to operate with fewer paid adults and makes the overall costs to parents lower. Many community colleges and universities operate cooperative programs for their students. High school child care programs for teen parents may also follow this cooperative model and require parent participation to reduce overall program costs. In addition to keeping the educational expenses low, early childhood cooperatives are excellent parent–education experiences. By participating in a school environment with specially trained adults, parents have many opportunities to learn about children and gain experience in positively interacting with them. Discussing common problems with other parents whose struggles are similar is also helpful to many parents.

Federally Funded Programs

For more information about Head Start, go to the Companion Website at www.prenhall.com/henniger, select Chapter 1, then choose Web Destinations.

The federal government spends a relatively small amount of its budget on programs for children in their early years. However, the support it does provide meets some important needs. The most well-known early childhood program funded by federal money is the **Head Start** program. Begun in 1964 as an attempt to help low-income 4-year-olds catch up academically with their more advantaged peers, Head Start has withstood the test of time as an important program for young children. Typically educating children who are 3 to 5 years old, the Head Start program is considered comprehensive because of its emphasis on all aspects of the child's development. In addition to focusing on social, emotional, intellectual, language, and physical development, Head Start emphasizes good health and provides resources and assistance with medical, dental, nutritional, and mental health needs. Although not all children who are eligible are served because of underfunding, approximately 830,000 participate nationwide. Head Start has four major components (U.S. Department of Health and Human Services, 2003):

- *Education.* In addition to providing learning experiences to stimulate intellectual development, the Head Start program emphasizes social and emotional growth as well. Children participate in indoor and outdoor play experiences and engage in more structured learning.

- *Health.* Head Start places a strong emphasis on early identification of health problems, because many children served have never seen a doctor or dentist. This comprehensive health care includes medical, dental, mental health, and nutritional services.

Federal funds help support programs for children with special needs.

- *Parental involvement.* Parents are viewed as the single most important influence on the child's development. It is therefore essential for parents to be involved in parent education, in the classroom, in program planning, and in operating activities.
- *Social services.* This component of Head Start is an organized method of assisting families in assessing their needs and then guiding them to resources to help meet those needs.

The **Early Head Start** program, which focuses on children younger than 3, is a more recent option that has become available because of the successes experienced in Head Start and due to the growing awareness that working with even younger children pays big dividends in the long run. Approximately 10 percent of the overall Head Start budget is used to serve children in Early Head Start programs operating across the nation. Because research results indicate that this early intervention option is effective, it is likely that the Early Head Start program will continue to grow (Zero to Three Policy Center, 2003).

A second group of programs receiving federal money is designed for **children with disabilities.** Options integrating children into regular classrooms and those providing separate services are funded in part by government dollars. Generally, the level of federal support is less than what it actually costs to educate children with special needs. State or local assistance is used to make up the difference.

Elementary schools benefit from additional federal support authorized by 2001's **No Child Left Behind Act.** This act provides substantial funds to help elementary schools improve the academic achievement of disadvantaged children and those identified as at risk for future failure in school (U.S. Department of Education, 2003). Realizing the importance of the early years, many elementary schools spend many of these federal dollars on literacy, mathematics, science, and social studies programs for kindergarten and primary-age children.

Another early childhood program option funded through federal sources is called **Even Start.** With goals similar to the Head Start program, Even Start provides money for educational experiences for young children from low-income families. In addition, however, the program promotes the development of literacy skills in parents. As they improve their own abilities, parents are better able to assist and encourage their children in school-related tasks (Rimdzius, 2003).

State and Locally Funded Programs

In recent years, despite funding some important educational options, the federal government has cut back other types of assistance to children and families. As a result, state and local governments have had to either increase their financial support or cut programs for children and families. In addition to providing for public K–12 education, state and local agencies help fund a variety of other options. Some states, for example, supplement the federal money designated for Head Start so that more children from low-income families can be served. Washington State's Early Childhood Education and Assistance Program (ECEAP) is one such example. State and local support for the inclusion of children with special needs is also common. Local governments and philanthropic organizations, such as United Way, also give money to nonprofit programs for children and families.

Into Practice...
Family-Friendly Corporations

Eli Lilly and Company, a major manufacturer of pharmaceuticals, is also a great example of a family-friendly corporation. Lilly recognizes that when it supports the health and well-being of its employees it creates a win-win situation that leads to greater productivity and employee loyalty. Their web site (Eli Lilly and Company, 2003) lists several benefits that the company offers to help employees meet the many challenges of parenting and family life:

- **Resource and referral service for child care.** Employees with children can use this service to find options for after-school programs, summer camps, emergency back-up care, and sick child care.
- **On-site child development centers.** Employees may choose to have their infants through kindergarten-age children cared for at a center located right at the work site. These centers also provide back-up care when regular arrangements are not available.
- **Maternity and parenting leaves.** The first few months of parenting are particularly stressful. Lilly recognizes this and provides parents with opportunities to take time off to make this important adjustment.
- **Nursing mother stations.** Access to quality electric breast pumps and children on-site allows nursing mothers to easily continue to breast-feed their young children.

You can make your future classroom more family friendly by having:

- **Resources for children and families.** Arrange to have pamphlets available providing information on such things as public library times, community agencies that provide services to families (counseling, housing, low-cost medical care, etc.), and local options for after-school and back-up child care.
- **An open-door policy.** Make sure families know that they are always welcome in your classroom by regularly inviting them to participate. Welcoming family involvement as you communicate with them via letters, newsletters, telephone calls, and e-mail messages helps ensure that they will become more involved in the life of your classroom.
- **Parent-to-parent interactions.** Provide a directory (after receiving permissions from families) that includes parent/guardian and child names and contact information, plan an evening parent meeting to address a topic of interest to parents (such as ideas on encouraging language development), or host a lunch or dinner potluck social activity to bring parents together.

For more information about corporate child care, go to the Companion Website at www.prenhall.com/henniger, select Chapter 1, then choose Web Destinations.

Corporate Child Care

A small but growing number of businesses are providing on-site child care for their employees. These programs are usually jointly funded, with corporations partially subsidizing the costs and parents paying the balance. Businesses that have implemented child care programs cite many important benefits (Seefeldt, 1990):

- Lower employee absences, tardiness, and turnover
- Improved productivity, morale, and health
- Enhanced community and public relations

Although these are powerful benefits, many corporations still find it difficult to provide this option for its employees. The investment of time, energy, and resources is difficult for even large corporations to manage. Rather than taking full responsibility for a child care program, many businesses are contracting with private child care corporations to provide on-site care. For example, Bright Horizons (2003) promotes itself as the world's largest provider of employer-sponsored child care, with over 480 centers worldwide. Despite many challenges, on-site corporate child care should continue to grow in the years ahead.

College- and University-Supported Programs

Many colleges and universities have child care programs for students and employees that provide similar benefits to those stated previously for corporations. Generally, the expenses for these child care options are shared. Some support is provided by the college or university, with parents who use the service paying the balance.

In addition to the obvious child care benefits, college and university programs are often designed to serve as research and training sites. Faculty who want to study child development or examine the effectiveness of a specific teaching strategy can use the child care facility for this purpose. In addition, early childhood teacher preparation programs often use campus child care centers as sites for their students who need direct experiences with young children.

Teaching Young Children

Now that you have had some initial exposure to the field of early childhood education, take a more personal look at what teaching young children is like. This will help you to understand the training and skills needed to work in the field. Look at your own personal characteristics and motivation and compare them with the descriptions of programs being presented. Is there a good match? If so, your interest in early childhood education could lead to a productive career choice. If not, you may need to think carefully before committing to this profession.

The Power of Teaching

Most of us can remember one or more teachers who have had a powerful impact on our lives. Perhaps it was an act of kindness, a belief in you as a person, or the excitement this person brought to the classroom. Unfortunately, others may remember teachers who callously or carelessly hurt the students around them through their words or actions. Teachers have great power to do either much good or considerable harm.

Haim Ginott (1972), a famous child psychologist, had the following to say on this important topic:

> I have come to a frightening conclusion. It is my personal approach that creates the climate. It is my daily mood that makes the weather. As a teacher, I possess tremendous power to make a child's life miserable or joyous. I can be a tool of torture or an instrument of inspiration. I can humiliate or humor, hurt or heal. In all situations it is my response that decides whether a crisis will be escalated or de-escalated, a child humanized or de-humanized. (p. 13)

The power of teaching is real at all levels, but perhaps more so when adults work with young children. How do you see yourself using this power? Would you use it to positively assist child growth and development? If so, then you should continue to consider teaching as a potential career choice.

Roles of the Early Childhood Educator

Teachers of young children serve in many roles as they assist students in their development. The most obvious role is that of facilitator of learning. Helping students know more about the world around them has been a time-honored expectation for teachers. Because young children are naturally curious about nearly everything, it is also an exciting role. Teachers also serve as counselor to the children in their care. Obviously, early childhood personnel do not have specific training as counselors, but they use many of the same skills as they guide children in their social and emotional development. For example, helping Alanna recognize she is mad at Derrick for taking her toy truck and helping her to learn ways to manage her anger are important forms of early counseling.

More routine tasks also are expected of teachers, especially those who work at the prekindergarten level. The role of janitor, for example, may be shared among preschool teachers. While larger programs may hire a specialist, many teachers of young children also serve as a cook for their children as they prepare nutritious snacks and possibly meals. Although it is very important to get children involved in the basic chores of the school, it is often necessary for the teacher to go beyond the basics in providing these services.

Early childhood teachers also serve as educational specialists. Because of the integrated nature of the early childhood curriculum, it is necessary for teachers to be comfortable with and to lead children in music, art, and physical education experiences. While these specialists may be available at the elementary level, the best early childhood teachers add to the limited opportunities provided by others.

In summarizing many of these roles, teachers of young children may also become a parent substitute for their students. Most parents fulfill their responsibilities well while children are in the home. However, young children continue to need parenting in the school environment even when their own parents are not around. Love, guidance, encouragement, assistance, and modeling are all needed by young children and are essential components of the early childhood teacher's role.

For more information about the roles of early childhood teachers, go to the Companion Website at www.prenhall.com/henniger, select Chapter 1, then choose Web Destinations.

Responsibilities of the Early Childhood Educator

In addition to their specific roles, early childhood teachers also assume important responsibilities. Overall, the early childhood educator's foremost responsibility is to be an advocate for children and their families (Jensen & Hannibal, 2000). **Advocacy** simply means promoting the causes of children and families. Taking leadership in helping meet the needs of children and families is an important responsibility early childhood educators must assume. While the challenges are great (Wiechel, 2003), every individual interested in the well-being of children and families must get involved. Following are several important reasons why early childhood educators should make advocacy for children and families a high priority:

For more information about advocacy, go to the Companion Website at www.prenhall.com/henniger, select Chapter 1, then choose Web Destinations.

- *Importance of the early years.* It is critical that young children and their families receive the best possible education and care because the early years are such a critical period in overall child development. Decision makers at all levels need to repeatedly hear this message.

- *Powerless children and families.* It is virtually impossible for children to speak for themselves about their educational, emotional, and physical needs. Many families also need the support of articulate, dedicated professionals advocating on their behalf.

Figure 1–2 *Summary of the NAEYC Code of Ethics*

Section I: *Ethical Responsibilities to Children*

Our paramount responsibility is to provide safe, healthy, nurturing, and responsive settings for children. We are committed to support children's development, respect individual differences, help children learn to live and work cooperatively, and promote health, self-awareness, competence, self-worth, and resiliency.

Section II: *Ethical Responsibilities to Families*

Families are of primary importance in children's development. Because the family and the early childhood educator have a common interest in the child's welfare, we acknowledge a primary responsibility to bring about collaboration between the home and school in ways that enhance the child's development.

Section III: *Ethical Responsibilities to Colleagues*

In a caring, cooperative workplace, human dignity is respected, professional satisfaction is promoted, and positive relationships are modeled. Based upon our core values, our primary responsibility in this arena is to establish and maintain settings and relationships that support productive work and meet professional needs.

Section IV: *Ethical Responsibilities to Community and Society*

Our responsibilities to the community are to provide programs that meet its needs and to cooperate with agencies and professions that share responsibility for children, and to develop needed programs that are not currently available. Because the larger society has a measure of responsibility for the welfare and protection of children, and because of our specialized expertise in child development, we acknowledge an obligation to serve as a voice for children everywhere.

Note. Excerpted from "NAEYC's Code of Ethical Conduct and Statement of Commitment: Guidelines for Responsible Behavior in Early Childhood Education" by the National Association for the Education of Young Children, 1996. Reprinted with permission.

- *Low priority of early education and care.* The lack of program support for young children and families at the state and federal levels is painfully obvious. Early educators and others must work hard to raise the priority of young children and families in the eyes of others.

An additional responsibility of early childhood educators is continuing education. Research by scholars in the discipline as well as innovations by educators in the classroom contribute to our understandings of how best to educate young children. To keep up with this growing body of knowledge, teachers of young children should continue to take classes, attend workshops, and read the professional literature available to them. The closing sections of this chapter focus on opportunities for continuing education and professional development.

A final responsibility of early childhood professionals is that they must know and follow a shared code of ethical conduct, based on a set of core values with deep historical roots in the field of early childhood education. The code of ethical behavior developed by the **National Association for the Education of Young Children (NAEYC)** provides guidelines for responsible behavior in relation to students, families, colleagues, and society (see Figure 1–2). Members of NAEYC agree to engage in conduct that demonstrates high standards and commit to monitoring the behavior of others in the profession. This Code of Ethical Conduct was first adopted by the organization in 1989, has been revised twice, and is under consideration for

Into Practice...
A Day in the Life of Jan Nelson

At the end of the 2003–2004 school year, Jan Nelson is preparing to wrap up her 18th year of teaching. Jan is currently teaching 25 kindergarten children in a half-day program operating Monday through Friday mornings at Larrabee Elementary School in Bellingham, Washington. The following schedule overviews the many different tasks she engages in during a typical day. Try to imagine yourself in Jan's place as you read about her morning's activities. Think about the extensive planning and preparation needed for the tasks described.

7:15 AM **Staff meeting** with principal and teachers (twice a month is usual).

7:30 AM **Normal arrival time.** Check phone messages and e-mail. Have a brief conversation with the principal regarding a recent meeting with a parent. Finalize plans for the day. Prepare materials and equipment needed. Create sign-in sheet with a survey question to be used for graphing activity during group time. Make sure notes home to parents are ready to go. Prepare tasks for the parent helper of the day.

8:25 AM **Students can enter classroom.** Greet individual children as they arrive, have them sign in, and talk to parents when possible. Talk to parent helper about tasks for the day. Students find a book to read, while music is playing in the background.

8:50 AM **School bell rings.** Children who chose to play outside come indoors. Greeting parents and children continues. Students finish signing in.

8:55 AM **Large-group time.** Children recite Pledge of Allegiance and greeting song. Introduce adult helpers, present phonemic awareness activities, and read book about frogs (current theme). Stretch break to get the wiggles out. Model writing for the day, prepare students for journal writing (this is the end of the year; much work led to these more mature writing tasks).

9:25 AM **Small groups.** One group receives specialized assistance from a reading teacher. Two groups are writing/ conferencing with Jan. One group is working independently. Parent helper works with additional small group. As students finish tasks, they review the planning board for follow-up activities such as listening center, magnetic letters, or playing with

---

further revisions (Freeman, Feeney, & Moravcik, 2003). By continually refining and strengthening this document, NAEYC is demonstrating its strong commitment to professionally responsible behavior on the part of all early childhood educators.

Skills Needed to Teach Young Children

The responsibilities and challenges of teaching make it one of the most difficult of occupations. The best teachers are successful in taking advantage of their personal strengths and in building their teaching ability through many interactions with children and others. Good teaching requires skills in three main areas: interacting with children, preparing the environment, and working with other adults.

Interacting with Children. The early childhood teacher spends much of her day engaged in informal interactions with children. "Kelly, please put the puzzle back on the shelf before you get out another toy." "Adrian, that must have really hurt. Tell Mark how that makes you feel." "I'm not sure what ants eat, Ariel, but we can

alphabet blocks they can choose to do with their "study buddy." Math activities are substituted for the reading and writing tasks on selected days.

10:05 AM ***Rug time.*** Students share published works. Others ask questions and give compliments. Sing another song.

10:20 AM ***Recess.*** Early in the year, Jan goes out with the children. At this point, a playground supervisor is in charge as Jan prepares for the remaining activities and takes a short break.

10:35 AM ***Snack time.*** Children wash their hands, then eat a snack (a math-related activity such as a counting or sorting task is also included). Adult-child and peer conversations are encouraged.

10:50 AM ***Choice time.*** Children engage in play activities. They can choose blocks, art, housekeeping, the listening center, puzzles, computer activities, or the ABC center.

11:15 AM ***Closing activities.*** Clean-up of centers. During group time, children evaluate their day. Children share through the "Mystery Box," which goes home with one child each

evening. Child writes three clues so that others can guess what is in the box.

11:25 AM ***Lunch time.*** Children can stay or leave for home. Bus leaves after lunch for those riding. Jan regularly eats lunch with her children. This time may also be used to meet for a debriefing with her teacher leader who has observed her during the school day. Planning for the next day, making telephone calls, and attending committee meetings also begin at this time.

Consider the following when you create a schedule for your future classroom:

- **Time to greet parents.** Plan experiences for children at the beginning and/or end of the day so you have the opportunity to spend time talking briefly with parents.
- **Balance teacher-directed times with child choice.** Planned group activities should be balanced with plenty of opportunities for activities children choose.
- **Plan for outdoor time.** Children need and want to spend time outdoors. Make sure that this is a part of your daily routine.

probably find some information on the computer." Times like these provide many opportunities to assist child growth and development. Sensitive teachers learn the right times to step in and communicate with individual children and times when it is best to simply stop and observe what is taking place.

Teaching also requires skills in working with both small and large groups of children. Getting their attention, maintaining students' interests in a project or topic, making smooth transitions from one activity to the next, and presenting information in an exciting way are just some of the skills a teacher must use to be successful in working with a group of young children. Often, teachers must use several skills almost simultaneously to make sure everything moves along smoothly.

Preparing the Environment. Early educational experiences are best when children actively manipulate materials. This process of learning by doing allows the young child to build stronger understandings of the world around her. This requires that the teacher carefully plan and prepare the materials in the learning environment. Knowing about student interests and needs, the early childhood

Family Partnerships...
Communication Is the Key

KINDERGARTEN NE

As with all healthy relationships, the key to effective partnerships with parents and other adults is to engage in effective communication. You will need to know about and use several key elements of good communication, including:

- **Use of voice.** The loudness, pitch, speed of delivery, and tone of one's voice all help determine the message received by someone else. A calm, moderately pitched voice makes it more likely that parents and others will be able to hear and respond to the messages you send.
- **Body language.** Body posture, hand gestures, and facial expressions all send important messages to others. For example, leaning forward while communicating with parents indicates interest and a desire to engage in effective communication. You will want to be sure to send this kind of positive nonverbal message as you interact with parents.
- **Word choice.** Because words individually and collectively convey so much meaning, it is important to think carefully about the words you use when communicating with parents. While it is important to be honest with parents, saying that their child is outspoken rather than belligerent may lead to a more productive conversation.

- **Situational variables.** Such things as the clothes you wear, the choice of chairs for seating, and the location in which you communicate all influence the interactions you have with parents. For example, when choosing the clothes to wear for parent-teacher conferences, make sure to select items that are professional without appearing too elitist.
- **Listening skills.** Because good communication requires both speaking and listening, it is important for you to take care to truly listen when parents are speaking so that their messages are being accurately heard. It takes concentration and practice to be a good listener, but making the effort will pay big dividends in relationships with parents.

1. Based on your life experiences to date, how important are good communication skills in human relationships? Would you expect the same to be true for relationships with parents and other adults?

2. Do a self-assessment of your communication skills at this point in time. What do you see as your personal strengths and weaknesses as a communicator and listener?

teacher must organize and plan for materials that can stimulate the young child's understanding. By regularly rotating new materials in and out of the classroom and playground, teachers can continually challenge children to learn from their surroundings.

Ramona has just finished her week with eighteen 4-year-olds. Before heading home, however, she plans on spending the next few hours getting the classroom ready for next week. Ramona will spend much of her time setting up a new dramatic play center with a post office theme. In addition, there are new books to be added to the reading corner, art materials to organize, manipulative toys to exchange for new items, some interesting rocks to put out at the science table, and new props to add to the block center. The time Ramona spends in preparing the classroom today will help make next week another great learning experience for her students.

Working with Other Adults. Most people enter teaching to work with children, but teachers often find themselves interacting with other adults. Communicating and working effectively with other teachers, aides, and administrators will make the many tasks associated with teaching more manageable. In addition, strong relationships with parents and community members are essential for good teaching in an early childhood classroom. Many teachers are surprised to learn about the importance of these adult relationships. Furthermore, making interactions with other adults work is not easy for many teachers. They require the use of different strategies and a new mind-set to be successful.

Should I Teach?

Take a careful look at the roles, responsibilities, and skills described here. Can you envision yourself as a teacher of young children? The challenges of teaching are very real. The rewards are also clearly identified. Only one question remains: Is teaching in the early childhood classroom a career you should pursue? While *you* must make this decision, others can assist in this process. Consider doing any or all of the following as you reflect on teaching as a possible career:

- *Observe early childhood teachers at work.* If possible, observe several teachers so that you see a variety of teaching styles. Try to critically analyze all that the teachers are doing while interacting with children. Can you see yourself doing the same sorts of things?

- *Spend time working with children.* The more time you can spend interacting with children, the better your chances of determining if there is a good match. Try seeing yourself as a teacher and putting on all of the roles (facilitator of learning, counselor, etc.) discussed earlier.

- *Ask for feedback from others.* Teachers who can observe you working with young children are probably the best source of information about your teaching ability. Ask them to be honest with you. Everybody has both strengths and weaknesses. Find out about both.

- *Analyze your potential.* Although self-analysis may be a struggle, it is often helpful to critique your own skills. Identify your personal strengths and weaknesses. How do they match the roles and skills of teachers?

As you investigate early childhood education as a career option, you will realize that you are stronger in some roles and more skilled in certain areas than others. Which aspects of the job might be more difficult for you? What could you do to make the difficult roles more workable for you? Fortunately, quality educational programs can help guide and train you in these areas.

Making the decision to become a teacher is often a difficult one that requires careful reflection and considerable time. It is important to begin this process now as you initiate your study of early childhood education. As you read each succeeding chapter and discuss with classmates issues related to its content, continue to reflect on how well you fit in the role as a teacher of young children. It may even be useful to stop at the end of your introductory course in early childhood education and take another look at the ideas presented in this chapter. After several opportunities to evaluate these issues, you will be much better prepared to make a realistic appraisal of your potential as an early childhood teacher.

Into Practice . . .
Am I Right for Teaching?

While self-reflection is only one of many ways to develop a better understanding of your capabilities and motivation to teach, it is often a good starting point for exploring the issue. Prior experiences, personal strengths, and weaknesses all influence our ability to become an effective teacher. With this in mind, for each of the roles and responsibilities of the early childhood educator defined in this chapter, spend some time thinking about personal experiences, strengths, and weaknesses that will influence your potential as an early childhood teacher. The organizing questions that follow are designed to help you get started with this process of reflection. It may be beneficial for you to do this exercise more than once. Try it out now as you begin to read and study about early childhood education and then reflect again on these same issues as you complete the text.

- **Past experiences.** What experiences with people or children have you had that would influence your ability to manage the roles and responsibilities of an early childhood educator?
- **Personal strengths.** What personal strengths do you think would help you effectively engage in the roles and responsibilities of an early childhood educator?
- **Potential weaknesses.** What personal traits do you have that you think may decrease your effectiveness in carrying out the roles and responsibilities of an early childhood educator?

Professional Preparation of Early Childhood Caregivers

For more information about professional preparation, go to the Companion Website at www.prenhall.com/henniger, select Chapter 1, then choose Web Destinations.

Teacher education programs are clearly defined for those preparing for K–3 classrooms, but not so for prekindergarten education. In many cases, a high school diploma is the only requirement for beginning work in these settings, despite the many complex roles and responsibilities that skilled early childhood educators must assume. Increasingly, a 2-year college preparation program or a 4-year degree is required for teaching prekindergarten children.

Teaching within the early childhood classroom occurs at a variety of levels. Assistant teachers, associate teachers, head teachers, and supervisors all play important roles. Because these different levels of teaching exist within the early childhood classroom, the training required to prepare for these roles varies. Most teachers of young children follow one of three main routes for their initial training: the Child Development Associate (CDA) credential, 2-year teacher preparation programs at the community college, or 4-year-degree programs in colleges and universities. Master's and doctoral programs are also available for those interested in continuing to increase their knowledge of early education.

The CDA Credential

The CDA credential, a national program designed to improve the qualifications of those who teach in prekindergarten classrooms, is a nondegree option that is based on demonstrated competencies in six areas: (a) maintaining a safe and healthy learning environment, (b) advancing physical and intellectual competence, (c) supporting social and emotional development, (d) establishing positive relationships with families, (e) ensuring a well-run program meeting individual needs, and (f) maintaining a commitment to professionalism (Parris, 2001).

Two-Year, or Associate Degree, Programs

Many community colleges offer 2-year programs preparing interested students to teach in prekindergarten programs and serve as administrators at this level. NAEYC (2003) has developed professional preparation standards for associate degree programs. Providing a combination of child development course work, early childhood instructional methods, and practical experiences with young children, these programs generally provide excellent preparation for teaching in infant/toddler and preschool classrooms. The following content summary is an example of a 2-year program in early childhood education (semester system):

Introduction to early childhood education	3 credits
Practicum experiences	10 credits
Curriculum development	3 credits
Creativity and play	3 credits
Working with parents	3 credits
Special needs children	3 credits
Child development	5 credits
Language and literacy	3 credits
Cognitive development	3 credits
Social and emotional development	3 credits
Infant and toddler care	3 credits

Practical, hands-on experiences with young children are an important component of both 2-year and 4-year programs.

Four-Year Programs

To teach at the elementary level, prospective teachers must complete a 4-year degree in elementary education from an accredited college or university. Traditionally, these programs have emphasized the preparation of elementary and secondary teachers. This is in part due to the fact that in most states there is no required teacher certification before kindergarten; however, more states are developing teaching certificates that either specialize in preparation at the primary (K–3) level or that also include the prekindergarten level (birth through grade 3). NAEYC (2001) has developed professional preparation standards for those completing a 4-year degree.

Coordinating Efforts

Unfortunately, for many years little effort has been made to have 2-year colleges and 4-year institutions work together to articulate student course work and to help students move to the next step in the educational sequence. Students seeking training in early childhood education have often been blocked from making smooth transitions by colleges and universities who battle over issues of quality and comparability of course work.

These roadblocks are slowly beginning to erode (Marshall, Morrison, & Davis, 2000), and national professional organizations are working to ensure that students can move through a continuum of educational experiences leading to increasingly advanced early childhood training (NAEYC, 2003). Furthermore, No Child Left Behind has provided additional incentives to have highly qualified teachers in every early childhood classroom.

Advanced Degrees

Master's degree programs in early childhood education are commonly found at most 4-year colleges and universities across the nation. Some offer advanced preparation for teaching at the primary level, while others provide graduate training in prekindergarten education, and a third group addresses the entire early childhood age range from birth to age 8. In addition to programs for practicing teachers, other master's degree options lead to advanced knowledge of topics such as child development, parent education, and special education. A master's degree is also the minimum educational level needed for teaching college students at 2- and 4-year colleges and universities.

If you are interested in eventually teaching full-time at the college level, you should plan on completing a doctoral degree program in early childhood education. These options, while available in every state, are more limited in number than programs at the master's level. Normally, one or two public universities and a similar number of private institutions in each state offer course work and degree programs at the doctoral level in early childhood education.

Resources for Professional Development

Although professional development begins with initial teacher training, this process will continue throughout your teaching career. As you gain experience in the classroom, make careful observations of children, have conversations with other educators, and attend professional conferences, your growth as a teacher continues. By actively participating in professional organizations, subscribing to professional journals, and being aware of other sources of information on early childhood education, you can continue to grow in your ability to meet the needs of children and families.

Professional Organizations

For more information about ECE professional organizations, go to the Companion Website at www.prenhall.com/henniger, select Chapter 1, then choose Web Destinations.

Two major professional organizations emphasize early childhood education. By far the largest and most influential is NAEYC. With a membership of approximately 100,000, NAEYC promotes quality education and care for children from birth to age 8 and their families. Members receive the journal *Young Children*, which provides teachers and others with many practical ideas for the early childhood classroom. More recently, NAEYC began publishing the *Early Childhood Research Quarterly* for those interested in studies of children, families, and curriculum. In addition to publishing an important list of books for early educators, NAEYC holds an annual conference that attracts approximately 25,000 national and international participants. State and local affiliates of NAEYC provide additional opportunities for workshops and professional growth for early childhood educators.

The second professional organization for early educators is the **Association for Childhood Education International (ACEI).** Although the focus of this organization is broader, with an emphasis on children from birth through adolescence, the early years have been a major interest of many members. Smaller in size than NAEYC, ACEI has nonetheless had a significant influence on the directions of early childhood education. Members receive the journal *Childhood Education* and have the opportunity to participate in national and regional conferences. Books and other publications are also available through the national headquarters. Finally, ACEI offers a research publication titled the *Journal of Research in Childhood Education.*

Other professional organizations are also available that have special interest groups or that focus on aspects of early childhood education. Some examples of these groups include

- American Montessori Society
- Council for Exceptional Children
- Association for Supervision and Curriculum Development
- International Reading Association
- National Council of Teachers of Mathematics
- Society for Research in Child Development

Journals

In addition to the journals from NAEYC and ACEI mentioned earlier, many professional publications are helpful to those involved in early childhood education. These can be divided into two broad groups: (a) research publications emphasizing child development and family issues and (b) journals that focus primarily on ideas useful to the practitioner. Some examples of research journals dealing with child development and family issues are

Child Development

Developmental Psychology

Early Child Development and Care

Merrill Palmer Quarterly

Monographs of the Society for Research in Child Development

Journals published for practitioners include

The Arithmetic Teacher

Child Care Information Exchange

Day Care and Early Education

Dimensions of Early Childhood

Early Childhood Education Today

The Reading Teacher

Reference Materials

One set of tools that early educators use as they work to increase their knowledge of children and teaching is a rich collection of reference materials. In addition to journals, many books provide insights on issues relating to early childhood education. For example, numerous texts are available that describe in more detail the importance of play in child development. These resources provide a more in-depth understanding of issues of interest to caregivers and teachers.

The **Educational Resources Information Center (ERIC)** is another very important reference system that can provide quick and detailed assistance in locating information on children and families. This computer-based information retrieval system is free of charge to users. Funded by the U.S. Office of Education, ERIC can help educators locate articles, books, and microfiche on topics of interest. The ERIC system provides an abundance of information and resources relating to young children and families.

A third reference option that is growing rapidly with the expansion of materials on the Internet is the availability of web sites with information on children and families. Most colleges and universities, professional organizations, and government agencies now have web sites with links to other useful Internet options. Keep in mind, however, that not every web site has accurate information based on current research and best practices. The following are examples of some of the many quality sites that are available:

- National Association for the Education of Young Children: http://naeyc.org
- Children, Youth and Family Consortium: www.fsci.umn.edu/cyfc
- ERIC Document Reproduction Service: http://edrs.com/
- National Board of Professional Teaching Standards: www.nbpts.org
- National Center for Education Statistics: www.nces.ed.gov/

Observing Development • General Developmental Abilities

Choose one of the age groups within early childhood (infants/toddlers, preschoolers, or primary-age children), *observe* **general developmental abilities** using the guidelines provided, *reflect* on what you saw and heard, and *apply* the appropriate strategies listed with the children you observed.

Observe	Reflect	Apply
Look for specific examples of:	*Think about and respond to the following questions:*	*Consider the following developmentally appropriate strategies for the age group you observed:*
Language/communication strategies used by children (gestures used to communicate, sounds, words, sentence structure)	Was there anything surprising or interesting that you heard or saw children doing to communicate with others?	Include toys that encourage language • Infant/toddler: mirrors, rattles, musical toys • Preschool: dolls, transportation toys, toy animals • Primary: blocks, toy people, electronic toys
Physical skills (sitting, crawling, standing, walking, grasping with fingers, etc.)	Based on this one observation, what did you learn about general developmental abilities at this age level?	Provide play options that support physical development • Infant/toddler: rattles, mobiles, textured balls, inclined ramps • Preschool: play dough, scissors, large balls, climbing equipment • Primary: writing materials, music/movement activities, beanbag toss game
Social interactions with other children and adults (plays alone, aware of others but does not interact, engages others in conversation/play)	Were there more similarities or differences between children in terms of the quality of their social interactions?	Promote social interactions • Infant/toddler: talk and sing to children, position children so they can see and touch one another • Preschool: model positive interactions, assist children with words needed for social interactions • Primary: allow opportunities for social problem solving, encourage group experiences with sharing activities
General level of conceptual understanding (knows names of objects, colors, numbers, letters, words, etc.)	What were the actions and words children used that helped you make decisions about their general level of conceptual understanding?	Build conceptual understandings • Infant/toddler: toys that children can shake, chew, touch, and look at • Preschool: blocks, books, puzzles, sorting games • Primary: computer games, math manipulatives such as Cuisenaire Rods, long-term projects that children choose and research

Summary

To test your knowledge of this chapter's contents, go to the Companion Website at www.prenhall.com/henniger, select Chapter 1, then select Study Guide. Also see Chapter Overviews, Reflecting Essay Questions, Multimedia Explorations, and relevant Web Destinations.

Essentials of Early Childhood Education

This chapter has provided you with a broad introduction to the field of early childhood education. The five essential foundations include understanding child development, providing quality play experiences, guiding children's social and emotional development, working with parents and families, and understanding the importance of diversity in child growth and development.

The Scope of Early Childhood Education

The different types of early childhood programs include infant/toddler programs, preschool education, child care, programs for children with special needs, kindergarten, and primary education.

Funding: Who Pays for Early Education?

The issue of who should pay for early education is significant; the various options include programs for profit, federally funded programs, state and locally funded programs, corporate child care, and college/university-supported programs.

Teaching Young Children

This chapter also addressed teaching in the early childhood classroom. An understanding of the teacher's roles and responsibilities and of the skills needed for teaching at this level will help you to decide whether teaching is a good career choice for you.

Professional Preparation of Early Childhood Caregivers

Different educational paths are available to those wanting to enter the field, including the CDA credential, an associate of arts degree in early childhood education from a community college, and a 4-year bachelor's degree in early education. In addition, resources are available to assist teachers of young children in continued professional development.

Resources for Professional Development

Early childhood educators have numerous professional organizations, journals, and reference materials available to assist them in professional development.

Multimedia Explorations and Activities . . .

Quality Child Care

Because of the high numbers of single and working parents in America today, increasing numbers of children need quality care outside the home. Literally millions of young children are spending at least 30 hours each week outside the home being cared for by someone other than a parent. Statistics indicate that approximately 70 percent of all preschool children in the United States are enrolled in child care (U.S. Census Bureau, 1999). Parents are scrambling for the limited number of high-quality child care options available, and often must settle for settings that are less than ideal and providers that have minimal qualifications for the job. Children who are placed in these settings are receiving less than they need or deserve and end up suffering the consequences.

Research

Child care is a growing concern for many American parents. Just finding openings can be a problem in many locations. In addition, the high cost of care make it a heavy burden for many families. Another major issue is determining the quality of the child care programs available. This multimedia exploration is designed to help you become more informed regarding this issue and participate in improving these options.

1. View the ABC News video segment titled "Finding Consistent and Quality Child Care."

2. Go to the Companion Website at www.prenhall.com/henniger and click on the Multimedia Explorations and Activities button for Chapter 1 for additional information on quality care. Review at least two of the web sites found there for different perspectives on this issue.

Reflect

Based on the previous information, think about the following issues:

- What innovation does the video segment promote as a key to improving the quality of child care? What would need to happen to make this option more commonly available?
- What do others say is needed to improve the quality of child care available to young children? Do you agree or disagree with their conclusions? What would it take to get the needed innovations implemented?
- Who do you believe should pay the costs of quality care? Parents? Community members? Your state? National funding? Some combination of these? Why?

Respond

Become an advocate for children and their families regarding the importance of quality child care options. An advocate is someone who is well informed and willing to speak out or write in support of others. In this case, it means being informed about the importance of quality child care and sharing this knowledge with others. Consider one of the following options for advocacy:

1. Speak up when others complain about the quality of child care options. Share what you have learned about the changes needed and the obstacles that make change difficult. Involve others in the change process.

2. Make up a one- or two-page checklist of components needed for quality child care and share it with interested parents and others.

3. Write a letter to a community, state, or national politician making a case for improving the quality of child care in your area and outlining what is needed for this to happen.

2

HISTORICAL CONTEXTS

In this chapter you will

- Learn about the early European influences on early childhood education.
- Study the beginnings of early education in the United States.
- Review historical events that have influenced directions in early education.

It is a beautiful spring day, and Ms. Gregory's kindergarten class is excitedly exploring the outdoors. Marta and Gina are digging contentedly in the garden in preparation for some later planting. Erik and Daniel have discovered an anthill and are down on their hands and knees carefully observing the scurrying workers. Nateesha and Elizabeth have taken two tires and are building their own pretend bird's nest by collecting twigs and grass for the base of the nest. Several children are playing a loosely organized game of tag and are running gleefully around on the grassy field. Still others are playing on the climbing structure in the middle of the playground, while three children swing and chat on the swing set nearby.

While everyone is so actively engaged, Ms. Gregory has taken the opportunity to carefully observe her children's actions. She is particularly interested in their social interactions and is focusing on the friendship patterns and general communication strategies children use as they interact with their peers. Ms. Gregory is pleased with the skills she is seeing her students use.

Although the preceding scene is typical of many early childhood classrooms, it may surprise you to know that these options have not always been available to children. For most of recorded history, for example, boys were the only ones to receive formal education. Playing outdoors and learning from nature were not promoted until the 18th century. Toys and equipment designed specifically for young children appeared around the middle of the 19th century, and formal playground equipment became available near the beginning of the 20th century.

This chapter examines the historical roots of current practice in early childhood education. By examining the people and events from the past that have shaped early childhood education, you can develop a deeper understanding of this exciting field.

Historical Figures Influencing Early Childhood Education

Having introduced the scope of early education today in Chapter 1, key people from the past who have had a major impact on directions in early childhood education will be identified and discussed here. Understanding the contributions of these individuals provides insight into the theory and practice of programs for young children.

Some of the people discussed next are **theorists.** Although they identified and discussed important issues related to children and teaching, they did not actually put these ideas into practice working with children. Others were **practitioners** who, in addition to presenting new and interesting ideas about child development and learning, actually worked in the classroom teaching young children.

European Contributors

For the past several centuries, Europe in particular has been the leader in promoting innovative educational theory and practice. Many of the key methods and materials used in early childhood classes today can be traced to these European theorists and practitioners (see Figure 2–1).

Martin Luther (1483–1546). While Martin Luther is best known for his impact on Christian religious reformation, he also had a significant impact on educational thinking and practice. Because of his conviction that the Bible was the key to Christian reform, Luther began to promote improved education, particularly the ability to read, as an essential element in German society. In order to establish a personal relationship with God, he felt that everyone needed to be able to read the Bible.

As an early educational theorist, Martin Luther suggested many revolutionary ideas for his time (Braun & Edwards, 1972):

- *All towns and villages should have schools.* This was not common in Luther's time, but leaders of the day began to take the idea seriously.

Figure 2–1 *Europeans Influencing Early Childhood Education*

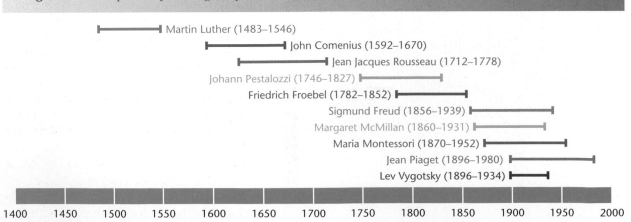

- *Both girls and boys should be educated.* Up until this time, education was almost exclusively for boys. Luther's emphasis on everyone reading the Bible, however, required that all children be taught basic academic skills.

- *Schools should foster intellectual, religious, physical, emotional, and social development.* This concept of educating the whole child is an essential element of early childhood education today.

For more information about Comenius, go to the Companion Website at www.prenhall.com/henniger, select Chapter 2, then choose Web Destinations.

John Amos Comenius (1592–1670). Comenius was another early educational theorist who presented many new and important ideas about children and learning. Although his interests were broader than early childhood education, one of his books in particular addressed issues that dealt with teaching young children. Titled *School of Infancy* (Comenius, 1896), this text describes many ideas that are very much a part of early education today. He suggested, for example, that the first years of life are crucial to overall development and that adults must take advantage of this time to assist the child's growth. Comenius also believed that movement and activity were sure signs of healthy learning experiences. Young children, he stated, learn best from natural, real-world experiences.

In other writings, Comenius also made clear his views on the teacher's role in learning and identified who he felt should be educated. He said this about the goal of education: "To seek and find a method by which the teachers teach less and the learners learn more, by which the schools have less noise, obstinacy, and frustrated endeavor, but more leisure, pleasantness" (Braun & Edwards, 1972, p. 31). Comenius advocated for enjoyable educational experiences and for students who could take charge of their own learning. He also was one of the first to promote the idea that all children should be educated. Rather than teaching just the sons from wealthy families, Comenius wanted all boys and girls, bright and dull, rich and poor, to receive an education.

Jean Jacques Rousseau (1712–1778). Although Rousseau lived a tumultuous and undisciplined life, which included the abandonment of all five of his children, his educational writings have had a significant influence on the direction of early childhood theory and practice. Rousseau's most well-known book, titled *Emile*, describes the ideal early education of an imaginary child (Rousseau, 1762/1979). From his writings, it is clear that Rousseau was advocating educational experiences that were very different from what children of his day were receiving. He proposed:

- *Negative education.* By this, Rousseau meant that formal educational experiences should be postponed until children are 12 years old.

- *Learning from nature.* Young children could learn all they needed to know from the natural world around them. Books should be forbidden during this period.

Jean Jacques Rousseau

- *Education should focus on sensory experiences.* Touching, tasting, and experiencing new sights and sounds were Rousseau's building blocks for early learning.

- *Children need to choose their learning experiences.* Rousseau believed that when left to their own devices children would select the best tasks for developmental progress.

- *Childhood is a stage in development.* One of the first to make this claim, Rousseau recognized that children can be distinguished from adults in more ways than just size. They think differently, reason differently, and require different ways of learning.

Rousseau's educational theory, although idealistic and naive as presented in *Emile*, significantly impacted the thinking of many later theorists and practitioners. Often referred to as a *naturalist,* his belief in the innate goodness of children and allowing development to simply happen has strongly influenced current thinking and practice in early childhood education. Much like a flower grows with water and good soil, young children often do well when adults prepare a quality environment for learning, step back, and watch for the results.

Johann Pestalozzi (1746–1827). Pestalozzi, an early childhood practitioner, was inspired by the writings of Rousseau and was determined to apply Rousseau's principles in raising his own children. While he quickly learned that the unlimited freedom proposed by Rousseau needed to be tempered with adult guidance and limits, Pestalozzi continued to believe in Rousseau's basic ideas and worked to refine their implementation.

In 1799, Napoleon invaded Switzerland and left the town of Stanz with a great many homeless and destitute children. Pestalozzi took charge of an orphanage there, and his educational career took root. Working with children whom others had written off as incapable of learning, Pestalozzi was able to demonstrate remarkable progress within a few short months. Gradually, other educators learned of his programs and spent time studying his methods.

Pestalozzi's most well-known publications were actually novels written for the general public of his day. Although the characters in these books portrayed many of his educational thoughts through their actions, most of what we know about Pestalozzi's methods and theories comes from the writings of others (e.g., Guimps, 1890). Pestalozzi has been described as a great teacher who made every effort to love and care for his students in addition to educating them. He modeled much of what we currently do in early childhood education:

- *Careful observation of children.* Pestalozzi was a perceptive observer of children and used what he saw to plan learning experiences for them.

- *Recognizing the potential in each child.* He saw every child as having the ability to learn, given the right circumstances. He believed in their potential, when others had given up on them.

- *Importance of teacher–student relationships.* Pestalozzi felt that before children could learn they needed a strong relationship with their teacher. Once the confidence and affection of each child had been won, learning was a much simpler process.

For more information about Rousseau, go to the Companion Website at www.prenhall.com/henniger, select Chapter 2, then choose Web Destinations.

Into Practice . . .
Guiding Children Begins with Strong Relationships

Pestalozzi was one of the first early childhood practitioners to emphasize the importance of strong teacher–student relationships. Since that time, many others have reinforced this concept and see these relationships as key to the guidance process. Here are some suggestions for building relationships with young children (Jones & Jones, 2004):

- **Be a good role model.** Make sure that you are engaging in the same behaviors you want for your children. For example, if you want them to sit in chairs, rather than on the tables, be sure you do the same thing yourself. "Please" and "thank-you" should be your verbal responses if you want those replies from students.
- **Make time for positive interactions.** When you have a high number of positive interactions with students, it

makes it easier to work through the more difficult times together. Be sure to make a conscious effort to take the time needed to have quality interactions with your students by doing such things as spending time talking with them, sharing snacks or lunch together, and periodically playing games with them.
- **Demonstrate high expectations for children.** When children know that you think positively enough of them to have high expectations, they know that you believe in them and want the best for their lives. Continually reinforce your high expectations with both words and actions.
- **Show children you care.** A hug when a child is feeling sad, a pat on the back for a job well done, and positive words of encouragement are all examples of ways in which children come to know that you care about them as individuals.

- *Strengthening peer relations.* Pestalozzi encouraged older children to tutor younger students and in general promoted good relations among his students.
- *Sensory learning.* Pestalozzi recognized the importance of learning experiences that took advantage of young children's natural interest in using their senses.

Friedrich Froebel (1782–1852). After discovering he had an interest and aptitude in teaching, Froebel spent time studying the techniques of Pestalozzi. Although he liked much of what he saw, Froebel eventually developed his own approach to teaching. His educational interests were broad: Froebel wanted to remake all of education. Needing to begin somewhere, however, he focused initially on working with 5-year-old children. Froebel named his program the *kindergarten* (meaning "children's garden" in German); this approach gradually spread throughout Germany, and later moved to the United States.

Froebel wrote two books that outline much of his approach to teaching young children. In *Education of Man* (Froebel, 1886) he describes his teaching materials and techniques. *Mother-Play and Nursery Songs* (Froebel, 1906) emphasizes the role of mothers in the young child's development. Froebel's contributions to early childhood education were many. One important idea was his emphasis on the benefits of childhood play. Froebel extolled the virtues of play throughout his writings:

> It gives, therefore, joy, freedom, contentment, inner and outer rest, peace with the world. It holds the sources of all that is good. A child that plays

For more information about Froebel, go to the Companion Website at www.prenhall.com/henniger, select Chapter 2, then choose Web Destinations.

thoroughly, with self-active determination, perseveringly until physical fatigue forbids, will surely be a thorough, determined man, capable of self-sacrifice for the promotion of the welfare of himself and others. (Braun & Edwards, 1972, p. 67)

Froebel also emphasized the value of singing at home and in school as a pleasant way to learn. He encouraged mothers to spend time singing with their children and also incorporated songs and musical experiences into his kindergarten classroom. Froebel felt that music helped build teacher-student and parent-child relationships, was an excellent tool for teaching young children concepts, and was also fun for both children and adults.

During observations of young children engaged in play, Froebel was intrigued by the number of times they joined hands and made a circle. He incorporated this natural tendency into his teaching, and what we now call **circle time** was born. Froebel recognized that seating children in a circle for group experiences brought them together in a setting that was easy to manage while creating a more personal atmosphere that helped improve interactions. The "Observing Development" feature at the end of this chapter highlights some characteristics of play you might observe in classrooms today, reflections on how children learn from play, and some specific ways you can enhance play and, ultimately, children's development.

Maria Montessori

Maria Montessori (1870–1952). The courage and determination of Maria Montessori are exemplified by her initial choice of careers. Near the end of the 19th century, despite many obvious and other more subtle challenges, she became the first female physician in Italy.

Montessori's first educational interest was in mental retardation. She felt that institutionalized children were eager for learning experiences and could, if given appropriate instruction, grow more normally. Like Pestalozzi before her, Montessori took up the cause of young children whom the rest of society had rejected. After careful observations of children classified as retarded and the study of earlier educators such as Itard (1801/1962), Seguin (1907), and Froebel (1886), Montessori was ready to begin her educational career.

In 1898, Montessori assumed the directorship of a school for "defective" children. Her reputation as an educator began to grow when she prepared these "idiot" children to successfully pass examinations for primary certificates. At the time, these examinations were typically the highest educational accomplishment of most Italians.

Montessori's most well-known educational program opened in 1907 and was called the **Casa dei Bambini** (Children's House). Located in the slums of Rome, Casa dei Bambini was where Montessori further developed her theories about children and refined her teaching techniques. Montessori detailed her fascinating ideas in several books (e.g., Montessori, 1949/1967), and other writers also have summarized her work (e.g., Lillard, 1972, 1996). A more detailed discussion of her practice and theory can be found in Chapters 3 and 4.

 For more information about McMillan, go to the Companion Website at www.prenhall.com/henniger, select Chapter 2, then choose Web Destinations.

Margaret McMillan (1860–1931). Margaret McMillan and her sister Rachel had a significant impact on early education in England at about the same time Montessori was gaining popularity in Italy. The McMillan sisters were early activists concerned about the health problems of children growing up in low-income areas in London. To help correct the health issues they identified, the McMillans founded the **Open-Air Nursery.** After Rachel's untimely death, Margaret continued to refine their program for young children.

The Open-Air Nursery was designed for children from 1 to 6 years of age and, as the name implies, emphasized outdoor play. The McMillans felt that the health benefits of outdoor activities were just what their children needed. The McMillans provided opportunities for gardening, playing in a sandbox, and building with scraps of materials in the "rubbish heap." Baths, clean clothes,

Into Practice . . .
Singing in the Kindergarten

Froebel, the father of the modern kindergarten, was an early proponent of singing in the classroom. For example, Froebel created songs that helped young children understand the properties of each of the new play materials he introduced during circle time. The songs also helped children to understand how to use these materials in appropriate ways.

If you have ever spent time observing or participating in a kindergarten classroom, you know that most teachers use singing for a variety of purposes. Four of the most important of these include:

- **Singing for the pleasure of the activity itself.** Songs such as "The Wheels on the Bus" for young children are engaging and fun. When done right, singing is an activity that most children find highly pleasurable.
- **Breaking up work periods.** In addition to simply singing for fun, many kindergarten teachers find that a lively song with accompanying movements is a good way to break up a more academic work period. It provides a pleasurable break in the routine while allowing students to move, stretch, and momentarily change their focus.

- **Using songs to enliven routines.** Another common strategy is to use a good song to help make daily routines more enjoyable. For example, while cleaning up is a chore that most children recognize as important, it is not a very exciting task. Many teachers sing a simple repetitive clean-up song during the actual clean-up time to alert children to this part of the daily schedule and help make the activity a more playful part of the school day.
- **Teaching concepts.** There are many wonderful cassette tapes and CDs that contain a variety of songs that teachers can use to teach concepts to young children. Ella Jenkins and Hap Palmer are two classic examples of performers who have long been involved in producing tapes and CDs that teach many concepts to young children. Songs (see Chapter 16 for more details) teach such things as mathematical concepts ("Five Little Speckled Frogs"), principles of language ("ABC Song"), understanding feelings ("It's All Right to Cry"), and body parts ("Head, Shoulders, Knees and Toes"). Many children can learn more quickly and well with the assistance of a good song.

Into Practice...
Inexpensive Outdoor Play

When Margaret McMillan allowed her children to play outdoors, she discovered that students tended to gravitate to several inexpensive materials that they found there:

> More than any other place our children love the great heap of stones and builders' rubbish that the masons have left behind them after building our extension. To put up some kind of house, to fix some kind of tent, and to sit inside—that is the aim and desire of all the children of five and over. And the making of this house is a more popular occupation than any other, except of course the making of mud hills and trenches and the filling of dams and rivers. (McMillan, 1919, p. 106)

Children today can enjoy the same experiences that McMillan described when some simple and inexpensive play materials are available to them (Frost, Wortham, & Reifel, 2001):

- **Loose parts.** Teachers can collect an assortment of boards, bricks, tires, and donated building materials so that children can construct their own play spaces for hours of inexpensive fun.
- **Natural materials.** The availability of water, dirt, sand, and pea gravel can provide many hours of creative play for young children. While these materials are messy and may present storage problems, they are a low-cost and attractive alternative to the expensive playground equipment typically found on playgrounds.
- **Garden area.** A small area for digging and planting can provide many opportunities for creative play experiences outdoors. A few shovels, trowels, hoes, and buckets are all that are needed once the garden space has been initially prepared for use.
- **Shrubs and plants.** With some planning and preparation, a few carefully placed shrubs and plants can be used to form natural play spaces and quiet areas for children. These plantings can also be used for engaging science experiences as children observe flowers, fruits, seeds, and new growth.

healthy meals, medical and dental care, and learning experiences were additional components of the program. Margaret McMillan emphasized several important concepts in her program that are considered important in early education today:

- *Facilitating emotional development.* McMillan recognized that young children need more than physical health and intellectual stimulation to develop normally. Emotional well-being was equally important and needed to be addressed by teachers.

- *Parent involvement.* Monthly parent meetings, home visits, strong parent–teacher relations, and support for families during crises were all emphasized in the Open-Air Nursery.

- *Children's art.* McMillan considered children's spontaneous drawings and artwork important to their overall development and made sure they were encouraged.

Lev Vygotsky (1896–1934). Vygotsky was a Russian scholar who began his study of developmental psychology and education in the 1920s. Unfortunately, his death from tuberculosis at age 37 prematurely ended a brilliant career. Nonetheless, Vygotsky's contributions have been substantial (Charlesworth, 2004). Three important concepts from Vygotsky's work have significantly influenced early childhood education. First is the **zone of proximal development,** the most well-known of his ideas (Vygotsky, 1978). The zone of proximal development is the gap between the child's independent performance of a task and that which he can perform with the help of a more skilled peer or adult. Children who are functioning in their zone are being challenged and growing with the assistance of others at a maximum rate. Second, Vygotsky's thinking about the relationships between language and thought in childhood have also influenced teaching and language learning in the early years. Third is the value of play in the development of symbolic thinking and the overall growth of children. These ideas are discussed in more detail in Chapter 4.

Sigmund Freud (1856–1939). Near the start of the 20th century, Freud began his study of human personality and emotional development. He created a complex

Celebrating Play . . .
Vygotsky's Thoughts on Play

Although Vygotsky's ideas on play do not really qualify as a theory, his writings about play have become very influential in our thinking about its importance (Berk, 1994). In particular, he felt that make-believe (dramatic) play was a major contributor to the child's social, language, and cognitive development. Vygotsky's high regard for play can be seen in the following quote:

> Play creates a zone of proximal development in the child. In play, the child always behaves beyond his average age, above his daily behavior; in play it is as though he were a head taller than himself. As in the focus of a magnifying glass, play contains all developmental tendencies in a condensed form and is itself a major source of development. (Vygotsky, 1978, p. 102)

Kara is a fearless 5-year-old who loves to climb to the top of the jungle gym on the playground. Her close friend Aleesha, however, is more timid. As the two climb, Kara tells Aleesha where to place her hands and feet and constantly reinforces her efforts. With this help, Aleesha nearly climbs to the top of the play structure. She is playing in her zone of proximal development.

Vygotsky felt that imaginary play has two critical features that help make it so influential in the child's development:

1. Play creates an imaginary situation that allows the child to work through desires that are unrealizable.

   Andrew is learning as a 3-year-old that he must wait for his turn many times in the preschool situation. He does not want to do this, and his imaginary play allows Andrew to work through these feelings.

2. Play contains rules for behavior. If children are to successfully complete a play scene, they must follow the accepted rules for social behavior in the situation they are enacting.

   Kathryn wants to be the mommy and must conform to the rules of maternal behavior for the play sequence to work.

---

1. Earlier in this chapter Froebel was quoted as saying that play gave children joy, freedom, and contentment. Are Vygotsky's ideas on play compatible with those of Froebel? What do you see as the similarities and differences between the two perspectives?

2. Choose an age/grade that currently appeals to you as a future teacher. For that level, identify two or three specific examples of ways in which play could be beneficial for children at that age.

theory that is often referred to as *psychoanalysis*. In relation to early childhood education, perhaps the most important aspect of Freud's theory is his psychosexual stages of development. Freud believed that personality was strongly influenced by the ways in which children learned to expend what he called sexual energy from one stage to the next (Thomas, 1985). He defined five major stages that children pass through as they develop their personalities:

- *Oral stage (0–1)*. The mouth is the location of satisfying or frustrating experiences. Exploring objects by sucking on them and nursing at the mother's breast are examples of a positive release of what Freud called sexual energy.
- *Anal stage (1–3)*. The child is developing sphincter and bladder control, which allows parents to begin work on toilet training. While the child receives pleasure from eliminating the bowels and bladder as needed, parents want the child to delay until a toilet is available.
- *Phallic stage (3–5)*. The child's genitals become important objects of pleasure during this period. Children want to touch themselves while parents often try to discourage this behavior.
- *Latency stage (5–11)*. The genitals remain the focus of sexual energy, but children work to suppress their wants. They tend to work and play with others of the same sex partly to control their sexual energies.
- *Genital stage (11+)*. At puberty, the child enters this final stage. While the focus of sexual energy remains on the genitals, the means of satisfaction now becomes sexual orgasm. Young people become very interested in others of the opposite sex.

While many today disagree with Freud's heavy emphasis on sexual energy and its gratification in childhood, his theory had a major influence on child-rearing practices during the 20th century. Rather than rigidly excluding what Freud termed pleasurable sexual activity at each stage, parents and child care providers were encouraged to relax a little and allow children to experience gratifying experiences (Schickedanz et al., 2001).

Jean Piaget (1896–1980). Piaget is another theorist who has had a major impact on early education. A true scientist from an early age, Piaget published his first research investigation at the age of 10. He began his lifelong investigation of humankind's acquisition of knowledge shortly after completing his doctoral studies. Piaget took a job analyzing responses to standardized intelligence tests and was intrigued by children's incorrect answers. After carefully questioning and observing many different children (including his own), Piaget published his theories concerning intellectual development. These theories are often labeled *constructivist* (Kamii & Ewing, 1996) because they suggest that individuals actively construct knowledge on an ongoing basis. In other words, Piaget theorized that we are all constantly receiving new information and engaging in experiences that lead us to revise our understanding of the world.

In a constructivist learning environment, the child creates rather than receives knowledge, and the teacher guides or facilitates this process of discovery. Unlike a traditional classroom where the teacher might lecture or perform demonstrations in front of a group of passive students, children in a constructivist environ-

Jean Piaget

ment actively learn by doing. For early childhood educators, this approach makes good sense. After all, children learn a great deal without being formally taught. They are able to understand, communicate, move, and function in the world around them long before they encounter schoolteachers, handouts, tests, homework, and report cards. They learn all these things by simply interacting with their environment.

Some characteristics of a constructivist learning environment include:

- Learning is a social and collaborative endeavor rather than a solitary activity.
- Activities are learner-centered rather than teacher-centered.
- Activities are often cross-disciplinary, encouraging students to make connections and integrate information, rather than compartmentalize it.
- Topics for inquiry are driven by students' interests rather than strict adherence to a fixed curriculum.
- Emphasis is on understanding and application rather than rote memorization or copying.
- Assessment is through authentic measures rather than traditional or standardized testing.

Piaget's studies of children continue to influence contemporary educators in many ways. The best-known component of his research was a definition of stages of intellectual development (Piaget, 1950). Less well known is Piaget's research

John Dewey

on moral development in children (Piaget, 1965). Piaget also studied play in childhood (Piaget, 1962) and found that child development was enhanced through these experiences. His work is discussed in more detail in Chapter 4.

American Influences

The 20th century ushered in a period of rapid growth and improvement in American education. Several theorists and practitioners from the 1900s have had a significant impact on the direction of early childhood education today. They relied heavily upon the European leaders described previously while at the same time striking out in new directions to influence young children and their development. The American theorists will be described first, followed by key early childhood practitioners (see Figure 2–2).

John Dewey (1859–1952). Dewey's career began as a teacher of philosophy at the university level. After time at several institutions, he settled at the University of Chicago in 1894. It was here that Dewey began to apply his philosophical ideas to the study of education. As his concepts took shape, Dewey's fame spread, and the **Progressive Movement** in American education was born.

The last half of the 19th century was a period of rapid growth in the availability of education in America. Although this was a major step forward, at the start of the 20th century many were questioning the generally accepted methods and content of schooling. Dewey's ideas were a catalyst for the reform efforts of progressive education in the 1920s and 1930s.

Figure 2–2 *Americans Influencing Early Childhood Education*

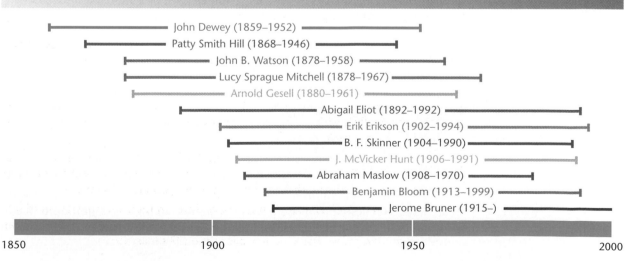

Although his philosophy was embraced by many educators of his day, Dewey was also often misunderstood by his supporters. Braun and Edwards (1972) summarize the major ideas associated with Dewey as follows:

- *Education should be integrated with life.* To make education meaningful, it must be associated with real-life events.
- *Education should preserve social values.* The common values of the culture need to be taught and supported by the schools.
- *True education occurs in social situations.* Dewey felt very strongly that learning was strengthened through social interactions with peers and adults.
- *Children's instincts and powers create starting points for education.* An understanding of child development and individual needs and interests is necessary for teachers planning learning experiences for children.
- *Active learning is essential.* Children must be intellectually and physically involved in their classrooms to truly learn from their experiences.

Erik Erikson (1902–1994). Erikson was a German-born psychoanalyst who came to the United States after having internalized much of the Freudian theory described earlier. While accepting much of what Freud developed, he worked to extend and refine the psychoanalytic theory of personality development. Thomas (1985) proposes three main additions that Erikson made to Freud's earlier work:

- *Emphasis on the healthy personality.* While Freud was often perceived as having studied neurotic personalities, Erikson's theory helps us understand how healthy personalities develop.
- *The epigenetic principle.* Erikson proposed that growth in personality, like other aspects of development, follows a clearly defined plan that is primarily determined by genetics. It develops according to steps "predetermined in the human organism's readiness to be driven toward, to be aware of, and to interact with a widening radius of significant individuals and institutions" (Erikson, 1968, p. 92).
- *Psychosocial stages of development.* Erikson defined eight stages in the development of the personality. These stages begin at birth and end in old age. The first four of these stages are described in Chapter 4.

Abraham Maslow (1908–1970). Maslow is considered a key advocate of what is called *humanistic psychology.* Humanists propose an optimistic picture of children that emphasizes:

- *The basic "goodness" of the child.* Human needs, emotions, and capacities are seen as basically positive. Life experiences are what lead to such things as cruelty and destructiveness.
- *Human needs.* Behavior is seen as motivated primarily by the person's efforts to fulfill a series of needs. Successfully meeting needs leads to healthy development; conversely, those who have unmet needs will face difficulties.
- *The importance of self.* Although humanists differ in their interpretation of self, it is seen as the integrator of human experiences and the "central core" of an individual that grows and changes over time (Thomas, 1985).

For more information about Maslow, go to the Companion Website at www.prenhall.com/henniger, select Chapter 2, then choose Web Destinations.

Maslow's major contribution to humanistic theory was the development of a **hierarchy of needs.** He proposed that basic needs such as food, shelter, and clothing must be satisfied before higher-level needs such as belongingness and affection can be met. His theory is presented in more detail in Chapter 4.

J. McVicker Hunt (1906–1991). As Piaget's theory of development grew more popular in the 1950s and 1960s in the United States, people like J. McVicker Hunt began writing about the implications for working with young children. Hunt (1961) argued that young children learn a great deal as they interact with the people and things in their environment. He was one of the first to suggest that children from low-income families could improve their intelligence (IQ) if provided with quality experiences in their early years. Rather than being determined at birth through heredity, intelligence was influenced by environment as well. Providing excellent educational experiences early in life could provide lasting benefits to children from less privileged homes. This idea was at the heart of the War on Poverty discussed later in this chapter and influenced the beginnings of programs such as Head Start and Project Follow Through.

Benjamin Bloom (1913–1999). Like J. McVicker Hunt, Bloom's writings led to an increased interest in early childhood education. He did much to popularize the importance of development during the early years of life. Bloom also promoted the idea that human intelligence was strongly influenced by environmental factors. In his book, *Stability and Change in Human Characteristics* (Bloom, 1964), he stated:

> . . . the data suggest that in terms of intelligence measured at age seventeen, about 50 percent of the development takes place between conception and age four, about 30 percent between ages four and eight, and about 20 percent between ages eight and eighteen. . . . The evidence from studies of identical twins reared separately and reared together as well as from longitudinal studies in which the characteristics of the environments are studied in relation to changes in intelligence test scores indicate that the level of measured general intelligence is partially determined by the nature of the environment. (p. 88)

For more information about Bruner, go to the Companion Website at www.prenhall.com/henniger, select Chapter 2, then choose Web Destinations.

Jerome Bruner (1915–). At the same time that Hunt and Bloom were identifying the early years as critical to intellectual development, Bruner published his influential book, *The Process of Education* (1960), in which he challenged educators at all levels by stating that the "foundations of any subject may be taught to anybody at any age in some form" (p. 12). In other words, he felt that young children can and should be taught the basic concepts and methods of studying such subjects as mathematics, science, and social studies. These early experiences could then be built upon in later years to enhance intellectual understandings even further. Bruner also promoted what he called *discovery* (or *inquiry*) *learning*, in which students are encouraged to discover for themselves the important elements of a given discipline. In this approach to learning, teachers guide their students as they discover meaningful understandings of the world around them.

Arnold Gesell (1880–1961). With medical training and a doctorate in psychology, Arnold Gesell had unique qualifications for his work in early childhood education. Gesell used his education to research the developmental patterns of childhood. Interested in studying children's maturational characteristics, he spent 30 years as director of the Yale Clinic of Child Development. In this position, he created a comprehensive collection of data describing normal child development. For children from birth through adolescence, Gesell identified observable changes in growth and behavior categorized into 10 major areas. Gesell authored or coauthored several books (see, e.g., Gesell & Ilg, 1949) that summarized for readers the typical or normative behaviors of children. This information became very popular with both parents and teachers who needed clear descriptions of normal child behaviors. Gesell's descriptions continue to be used and are discussed further in Chapter 4.

Patty Smith Hill (1868–1946). Hill, an important early childhood practitioner, was trained in Froebel's methods of kindergarten education. In addition, she was strongly influenced by the work of John Dewey. By blending the thinking of these two different but compatible theorists, she was able to create a strong curriculum for young children. Hill's educational efforts became the foundations of kindergarten practice in the United States.

Hill is credited with two important innovations. First, she helped found the laboratory nursery school at Columbia University Teachers College in 1921. This model program helped train many fine teachers of young children while providing a research site for faculty at the college. Her second contribution was to help organize the National Association for Nursery Education. This group was later renamed the National Association for the Education of Young Children (NAEYC), which is currently the largest and most influential organization of early childhood educators.

Lucy Sprague Mitchell (1878–1967). While Patty Smith Hill worked at Columbia University Teachers College, Lucy Sprague Mitchell labored under similar circumstances, also in New York. Mitchell is credited with helping start the laboratory nursery school at the Bureau of Educational Experiments in 1919. She initiated an excellent model program for young children where researchers could study children and their development. She also trained prospective teachers who left to start their own nursery school programs in other locations. The Bureau of Educational Experiments was later renamed the Bank Street College of Education. This program has been influential over the years in defining important directions for early childhood education (see Chapter 3 for more information).

Abigail Eliot (1892–1992). Abigail Eliot made important contributions to early childhood education through her work with nursery school children from low-income families. After working with the McMillan sisters in their Open-Air Nursery in London, Eliot served as director of the Ruggles Street Nursery in Boston beginning in 1922. In many ways, this nursery school became an early model for the Head Start program.

The Ruggles Street Nursery had the following characteristics:

- Child-sized equipment
- Comprehensive program (including health care, to meet the needs of the whole child)
- Variety of materials (Froebelian, Montessori, and McMillan materials)
- Full-day program (including nap)
- Work with parents (communicating with and involving them in education)

Family Partnerships . . .
Letters to Parents and Guardians

Just as Abigail Eliot was a strong proponent of effective relationships with parents, you will need to plan for a variety of positive interactions with parents and guardians. An effective and commonly used strategy is to regularly send home letters to parents and guardians. These letters are generally one or two pages in length and describe happenings in the classroom. Although the content of these letters varies between classrooms, some typical components would be such things as information about projects being worked on in class, notice of upcoming field trips and special productions that would be of interest to parents and guardians, and ideas about what families can do at home to support the activities in class.

If you choose to do a letter to families, consider the following in developing them:

- **Use your best writing skills.** Parents expect the teachers of their children to be good written communicators. If you send home a letter with even a few spelling, grammar, or punctuation errors, parents and guardians may well think less of your teaching abilities. Make sure to write, edit, and rewrite whatever you send home.
- **Consider the first languages of parents and guardians.** In many homes today, the language spoken and read by parents and guardians is not English. If you find this to be the case in your classroom, you may need to get a translator to rewrite your letter in the appropriate language/languages so that these families can also have the benefit of your communications.
- **Develop a strategy for making sure the letters get home.** After spending time writing a great letter, you want to make sure that it reaches parents and guardians. Some teachers create a folder for parent communications and make sure that these folders go home on the same day each week so that parents and guardians can be expecting them.

---

1. Do you remember any teachers in your schooling that used letters home to parents and guardians? Did your family appreciate this form of communication?

2. What do you see as the advantages and disadvantages of this form of communicating with families? Can you see yourself regularly using letters to communicate with parents and guardians?

Historical Events Influencing Early Childhood Education

The insights of many early educators have enriched the teaching and learning of young children over the past several centuries. However, historical events as well as people have influenced the directions of early childhood education. During the 20th century in America, several key events significantly shaped the ways in which we teach and care for young children.

Child Study Movement

The end of the 19th century and beginning of the 20th century brought a rapidly growing interest in studying children and their development (Weber, 1984). This period is known as the Child Study movement. It may surprise you to know that the main reason for this newfound urge to understand children was the realization that children are qualitatively different from adults. Although we accept this today as common knowledge, for much of the history of humankind, children were viewed simply as miniature adults (Aries, 1962). As teachers and researchers began to recognize that differences existed between children and adults, they were forced to investigate these variations. The Child Study movement was born.

This research effort was important to early childhood education for two main reasons. First, the interest in studying children generated a great deal of very useful child development information. People like Arnold Gesell were observing children and carefully documenting data about typical development and the variations between children. This information is still very much in use as an initial planning guide for teachers of young children.

The Child Study movement was also an important catalyst in the growth of laboratory nursery schools. To better understand young children, colleges and universities throughout the nation created nursery schools as research sites for faculty (Braun & Edwards, 1972). Some key programs begun during this period include:

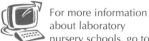

For more information about laboratory nursery schools, go to the Companion Website at www.prenhall.com/henniger, select Chapter 2, then choose Web Destinations.

- *Bureau of Educational Experiments:* Lucy Sprague Mitchell was the guiding force behind this program, which began in 1919. Eventually, this became the Bank Street College of Education in New York.

- *Columbia University Teachers College:* This program, under the direction of Patty Smith Hill, began in 1921.

- *Merrill–Palmer Institute:* Edna Noble White was this program's first director, beginning in 1922.

- *Yale Guidance Nursery:* Arnold Gesell was instrumental in this nursery program, started in 1926.

In addition to providing research sites for the Child Study movement, the laboratory nursery schools were models of excellence in early education and also stirred interest in prekindergarten programs. As adults learned of these opportunities and recognized the benefits for the development of children, more options became available across the country. Preschool programs for disadvantaged children and cooperative nursery schools are two examples of this increased interest.

The Great Depression

Surprisingly, the U.S. Great Depression of the 1930s had an important impact on early childhood education. Major federal efforts to put people back to work ended up promoting the cause of prekindergarten education. The Works Progress Administration (WPA) took unemployed schoolteachers, custodians, cooks, and nurses and gave them jobs in government-sponsored preschool programs (Steiner, 1976). The main benefit of these efforts was that nursery education became more widely recognized, which led to acceptance by the American public. Early efforts at parent education were another important spin-off of the WPA programs. Unfortunately, significant problems also surfaced as a result of the WPA nursery schools. The unemployed educators put to work teaching in the nursery programs were given little or no training for their new roles. The assumption (a false one) was that because they knew how to teach older students, they could easily manage younger children. Teachers were also paid very low wages for their services. The WPA was able to pay teachers only a fraction of their prior salaries. The perception that began to develop during this period was that teachers of young children did not need much training or salary for the work they were doing.

World War II

As America reluctantly became involved in World War II, those left at home were called upon to keep the economy running. The government gave special priority to war-related industries to make sure the equipment needed for the war effort was produced on time. Both government and industry encouraged many women with young children to work in these industries, creating a temporary need for child care. The Lanham Act made federal money available to provide this care.

The most well-known child care program from this period was located at the Kaiser Shipyards in Portland, Oregon (Hymes, 1978). Under the guidance of James Hymes, this program implemented many innovations:

- *Specially designed building.* While most child care facilities today are remodeled business sites or portions of church facilities, the Kaiser program had a carefully designed building with many innovative design features.

- *Located at the work site.* Because the building was at the work site, there were opportunities for mothers to nurse during break times, have lunch with their children, and participate in center activities.

- *Open 24 hours a day.* To accommodate workers around the clock, the center was open 24 hours a day.

- *Special attendance times.* Parents could occasionally leave their children for an extra session so that they could have some time to enjoy a special event or recreational activity.

- *Infirmary for sick children.* A special room was available for children who were sick. Parents could be assured that their child was receiving good care even during times of illness.

- *Family consultant.* An adult was available to assist parents in finding needed community resources.

- *Home food service.* Parents could use the child care food service to order a hot meal to take home with them.

At the war's end, programs such as the one at the Kaiser Shipyards were simply closed as women returned to their traditional roles as homemakers. Quality options for child care virtually disappeared for several decades and are just now beginning to reemerge. The innovations in child care implemented during World War II continue to be a model for present-day child care programs.

The Launching of *Sputnik*

In 1957, the launching of Russia's first satellite created a great uproar in America. *Sputnik* represented to many our decline as a society. We were behind the Russians in the race to conquer this new frontier. Something must be done, people said, to reverse this truly alarming situation. The consensus among these people was that we needed to do a better job of educating children so that American scientists could eventually catch up with their Russian counterparts (Braun & Edwards, 1972).

This attitude led to both positive and negative results. One clear benefit was a renewed interest in preschool education. The general thinking seemed to be that if we started earlier, we could better educate our children. The early years began to be recognized as an important developmental period that needed to be taken advantage of and carefully studied. Another positive result was the increased public support for early education. People were more willing to provide financial assistance for programs that showed promise. More federal money, in particular, was available during the 1960s and 1970s to demonstrate new models of early education and for research on teaching and learning at this level.

Unfortunately, there were also negative outcomes in education stemming from the launching of *Sputnik*. One of the most problematic was an overemphasis on intellectual performance. The concern over lagging abilities in mathematics and science in particular led many early educators and the general public to place too much importance on the intellectual activities of young children. While the traditional preschool emphasized all aspects of the child's development, the growing expectation was for programs that could demonstrate improved intellectual performance. A second problem associated with *Sputnik's* launch was the demand for quick and lasting results. The American public, while providing support for new educational efforts, anticipated speedy solutions that would rapidly help us catch up with the Russians—a wholly unrealistic expectation.

Celebrating Diversity...
Leaving No Child Behind

No Child Left Behind, signed into federal law by President George W. Bush on January 8, 2002, has a noble purpose: to make sure that all children have the opportunity to obtain a high-quality education so that they can be successful in life (*No Child Left Behind,* 2002). All children, regardless of socioeconomic status, disability, race, or gender, should have access to quality education. While this is an admirable sentiment, there are many who say that this act cannot attain its goal without addressing several other important factors (Children's Defense Fund, 2002). They include:

- **Health insurance coverage.** More than 9 million children in America lack adequate health coverage. Children in poor health find it more difficult to learn.
- **Parent education.** Because parents are the most influential people in children's lives, they need to receive training and assistance to do their jobs well.
- **Greater access to quality preschool education.** While No Child Left Behind recognizes the importance of having children come to school ready to learn, no provisions are made to increase the opportunities for preschool learning for those children who need it most.
- **Addressing the conditions of poverty.** Poverty can lead to homelessness, poor nutrition, and environments that are unsafe for children. Abuse, neglect, and violence are frequently associated with poverty. Children in these circumstances have much greater difficulty being successful in school.

1. Do you think children can be successful in school when one or more of the previous risk factors are present? Why or why not?

2. What can and should you do as a future teacher to help children and families who face the kinds of problems previously identified?

The War on Poverty

The presidencies of John F. Kennedy and Lyndon B. Johnson saw a marked increase in the federal government's efforts to help low-income families break free from the grip of poverty. The cornerstone of this "War on Poverty" was the provision of national monies to fund early childhood programs designed for young disadvantaged children (Hymes, 1978). The thinking of policy makers was that the cycle of poverty could only be broken by providing quality educational experiences for children from low-income families. These children would then end up in better-paying jobs, and all of society would benefit. Beginning in 1964, the federal government provided money to local sites for preschool-age children from low-income families.

The most well-known option for disadvantaged children to come out of this period was the Head Start program (see Chapter 1). The early research conducted on the effectiveness of Head Start was disappointing (Coleman, 1966), with minimal initial success in improving children's intelligence scores and with the gains made eventually washing out by the time children reached the third grade.

However, Head Start survived the criticisms that came with these results by reemphasizing the comprehensive nature of the program. Over the years, it has been effective in serving the needs of the children from low-income families enrolled. Head Start's emphases on developing the whole child and working closely with families are important elements to be modeled by others in early education and care.

Other federally funded compensatory education programs for disadvantaged children were also initiated during the War on Poverty. These programs were each designed to assist children from low-income families to catch up with their more advantaged peers in intellectual functioning. Like Head Start, however, gains in intelligence test scores were minimal and disappeared by the time these children were in the third grade (Bronfenbrenner, 1974). Despite these initially disappointing results, the model programs developed during this period still continue to influence thinking and practice today (see Chapter 3).

The inability of Head Start and other compensatory education programs to produce long-term IQ score gains in their students led many to believe that a more concentrated effort over a longer period of time was needed. Project Follow Through, begun in 1969, was funded by the federal government as a way to continue this assistance to children from low-income families in the primary grades. A variety of model programs were funded at sites across the country, and others conducted research to determine their effectiveness. Although the research results continued to be disappointing, Project Follow Through had a significant impact on early education. Most importantly, these programs created a stronger link between preschool and primary education. Most of the Follow Through models used many of the same techniques that had been successful at the preschool level to assist primary-age children in their development. Early childhood educators began to view children from birth through age 8 as similar in many ways and started planning educational experiences that reflected this perspective.

No Child Left Behind Act

One of the most significant recent events to impact the lives of children and their families is 2001's No Child Left Behind Act, designed to provide schools and teachers that allow all children to have a quality education. The act states: "The

Observing Development • Childhood Play

Choose one of the age groups within early childhood (infants/toddlers, preschoolers, or primary-age children), *observe* **childhood play** either indoors or outdoors using the guidelines provided, *reflect* on what you saw or heard, and *apply* the appropriate strategies listed with the children you observed.

Observe	Reflect	Apply
Look for specific examples of:	*Think about and respond to the following questions:*	*Consider the following developmentally appropriate strategies for the age group you observed:*
What children play with (toys, equipment, found objects, etc.)	How did children use toys and equipment in their play?	Include creative play materials that children can explore and enjoy • Infant/toddler: texture balls, musical rattles, water-play materials • Preschool: sandbox activities, simple art materials like crayons, paper, and scissors • Primary: Large collection of blocks for construction play, book-making materials for creative story writing
What children are doing when they play (simple repetitive movements, pretending, games, etc.)	What could children potentially be learning (language, concepts, social skills, emotional understandings) from the activities you observed?	Provide open-ended activities • Infant/toddler: finger painting, pouring/mixing cornmeal, playdough • Preschool: music and scarves for movement to music, dress-up clothes • Primary: flannelboard materials for storytelling, tape recorder
Social interactions during play (none, some awareness of others, playing alongside others, playing with others)	How important were the social interactions to the actual play activities observed? Could the play have continued without the social interactions or were they an essential component?	Promote social play • Infant/toddler: simple games like "Peek-a-Boo" • Preschool: pretend play materials such as props for camping • Primary: writing and performing a puppet play

purpose of this title (act) is to ensure that all children have a fair, equal, and significant opportunity to obtain a high-quality education and reach, at a minimum, proficiency on challenging state academic achievement standards and state academic assessments" (No Child Left Behind, 2002).

Three provisions of this act have particular relevance to early childhood education. The first of these provisions is that renewed efforts are being made to ensure that all children can read. The federal government has tripled its funding of reading instruction in support of this goal. Secondly, the act is intended to strengthen teacher quality by requiring states to put a highly qualified teacher in every classroom by 2005. Finally, No Child Left Behind strongly promotes English proficiency for limited-English-proficient (LEP) students. The federal agencies responsible for assisting non-English-speaking students have been consolidated, and federal money is available to help these children to quickly and effectively learn English.

Summary

To test your knowledge of this chapter's contents, go to the Companion Website at www.prenhall.com/henniger, select Chapter 2, then select Study Guide. Also see Chapter Overviews, Reflecting Essay Questions, Multimedia Explorations, and relevant Web Destinations.

Historical Figures Influencing Early Childhood Education

This chapter introduced key historical figures who have had a significant impact on early childhood education. Major figures from Europe are Martin Luther, John Amos Comenius, Jean Jacques Rousseau, Johann Pestalozzi, Friedrich Froebel, Maria Montessori, Margaret McMillan, Lev Vygotsky, Sigmund Freud, and Jean Piaget. In the United States, John Dewey, Erik Erikson, Abraham Maslow, J. McVicker Hunt, Benjamin Bloom, Jerome Bruner, Arnold Gesell, Patty Smith Hill, Lucy Sprague Mitchell, and Abigail Eliot had a significant impact on early education.

Historical Events Influencing Early Childhood Education

The Child Study movement, America's major economic depression of the 1930s, World War II, the launching of *Sputnik*, the 1960s War on Poverty, and the No Child Left Behind Act were all important events influencing early education.

Multimedia Explorations and Activities...

A Closer Look at History

In order to talk about the good life, we have to talk about the good society; and in order to talk about the good society, we have to talk about the kind of education that will bring that society into existence and sustain it. Hence, there is no vision of the good life that does not imply a set of educational policies; and conversely, every educational policy has implicit in it a vision of the good life. . . .

Plato, The Republic

Since the time of Plato, philosophers and educators have been aware of the importance of education in society and have proposed many diverse ideas about what it takes to have good teaching and learning. In this chapter we have briefly addressed the key historical figures that have had a major impact on early childhood education. Much more can be learned from an in-depth investigation of the information available on the Internet concerning these theorists and practitioners. This activity is designed to get you involved in doing just that.

Research
While additional information on virtually every person described in this chapter can be found through a careful search, some names are easier to find and are more thoroughly reviewed. The following historical figures in early childhood education fit this latter category: John Dewey, Jean Piaget, Lev Vygotsky, Sigmund Freud, Arnold Gesell, and Maria Montessori.

1. After selecting the historical figure of your choice from this list, go to the Companion Website for this text at www.prenhall.com/henniger and click on the Multimedia Explorations and Activities button for Chapter 2 to find initial web sites to get you started in your research. Try a variety of search options to make sure you are locating the sites you need.

Reflect
After you have collected all the information you can regarding the historical figure you selected, think about the following issues:

- What did you learn about this person's life that may help you or others understand the directions of his/her work?

- What were the main contributions of this person to the theory or practice of early childhood education?

- Did you find evidence of this person's influence on current practices in early childhood education? What are those influences?

Respond
Share the results of your investigation with others. Consider one of the following options:

1. Write a paper on your historical figure, including a brief biographical sketch, a description of the key ideas/contributions of this person, and a discussion of the influence on current practices in early education.

2. Lead a class discussion of the historical figure you have chosen. Include the same three elements described in option 1 and be sure to use handouts, overheads, activities, or other options to actively engage your audience in what you want them to learn.

chapter

3

TYPES OF PROGRAMS

In this chapter you will

- Identify the diverse program models associated with early education.
- Study the Montessori program and its implications for teaching young children.
- Investigate the High/Scope curriculum for preschool and primary classrooms.
- Review the behaviorist approach and its application to young children.
- Consider the Bank Street model for early education.
- Identify the elements of the Reggio Emilia program and its applications in the United States.

Amanda is taking her first course in early childhood education and is trying to make sense of all that she is learning. The issue she is currently struggling with concerns early childhood program models. Amanda has learned about Montessori education, the High/Scope model, the Bank Street program, and the Reggio Emilia approach. Is one better than the others for young children?

The programs that she has studied share many similarities, which makes it more difficult to sort out her thoughts. Amanda's thinking is further complicated by the fact that she likes different elements of each model. Additional information would be helpful to her as she evaluates the options. It would be nice, for example, to see each of the programs in action, but the local early childhood centers do not clearly identify themselves with the specific models Amanda has studied.

The issues you will face as you read this chapter will probably mirror those that Amanda identified in the preceding scenario. Several clearly defined models for early childhood education are currently in practice; making conclusive judgments about them without in-depth study, however, is difficult. Also, pure models of the different approaches are hard to find, making it unlikely that you can compare each of the models in action. While it is difficult to find examples of the models described here, you need to be aware of the different program options used to educate young children and understand their similarities and differences. Also, take time to think about which models appeal to you personally, and plan to learn more about them later. Remember, this is just the beginning point for your understanding of early childhood education.

This chapter presents an overview of five major program models for early childhood education, and discusses the key elements of each. These options significantly influence the philosophy and teaching in early childhood programs across the country. Figure 3–1 summarizes the key features of each approach.

Figure 3–1 *Key Feature of Five Early Childhood Programs*	

PROGRAM	KEY FEATURES
Montessori education	Work experiences rather than play. Special materials for specific learning tasks. Carefully prepared classroom environment.
High/Scope program	Based on the theory of Jean Piaget. Use of a plan-do-review sequence. Classroom organized into centers. Emphasis on cognitive development.
Behaviorist approach	Based on theory of Watson and Skinner. Emphasizes extrinsic motivation. Three techniques for modifying behavior. Not developmentally appropriate.
Bank Street model	All aspects of child development are addressed in the curriculum. The work of Freud, Erikson, Piaget, and Dewey all influence the model. Commercial equipment is supplemented with teacher-made and child-made materials. Emphasis is on an integrated curriculum.
Reggio Emilia approach	Emphasis is on in-depth projects to facilitate learning. A special workshop area is used to record in visual form what is learned. Parents are expected to share responsibilities in educating children. Strong collaboration among staff members is encouraged.

The Montessori Program

The teaching and writing of Maria Montessori led to a unique model for early learning that has had a significant influence on early childhood education. The Montessori approach has both strong supporters and vocal critics (Roopnarine & Johnson, 2000).

Montessori education began as a program for children from 4 to 7 years of age in low-income families. Today, the principles of this approach are being used with preschool through high-school-age students. Although most of these options are private schools for predominantly middle-class students, some public school programs are using the Montessori method (Chattin-McNichols, 1992).

Montessori programs in the United States are generally associated with one of two major associations. The American Montessori Society is a group dedicated to implementing the ideas of Montessori in the United States. This association has adapted Montessori's methods and materials for use in American schools in an attempt to make the approach more widely accepted here. The more traditional methods and materials Montessori developed are promoted through the Association Montessori Internationale. Montessori programs throughout Europe, India, and the rest of the world generally associate themselves with this organization. Some American programs also affiliate with the international association.

 For more information about Montessori associations, go to the Companion Website at www.prenhall.com/henniger, select Chapter 3, then choose Web Destinations.

Celebrating Play...
Encouraging Divergent Thinking

While the work tasks described in this section by Montessori can definitely benefit children and their development, many early childhood educators emphasize the values of play experiences for young children. For example, Doris Fromberg (2002), in her book *Play and Meaning in Early Childhood Education,* describes astrophysicist Michio Kaku's projections for the kinds of thinking needed by adults in the 21st century. Adults need to do three important things:

1. envision more than one answer to a question;

2. take imaginary leaps and act on them;

3. adapt to rapid change.

The world will need people who can think flexibly, collaborate with others, and feel comfortable with the predictably unpredictable. (p. 3)

Fromberg goes on to say that play is the vehicle that young children use to develop these skills. When children play, rather than engaging in the convergent thinking associated with Montessori tasks, they are engaged in a process of divergent thinking that allows them to resolve the dilemmas they face in daily life. Take, for example, Irina, a 4-year-old preschool child playing in the art center. She has been working on her painting for the past 20 minutes and is carefully painting with red, blue, and yellow colors to fill her easel paper. Irina accidentally mixes colors and finds that when she does it leads to new and interesting options. As she gets excited about her discovery, she experiments with new combinations to find out the colors that result. Through her play, Irina is developing the skills she will need to be a creative, problem-solving adult.

1. Reread the sections in this chapter describing Montessori's work tasks and play experiences. Compare and contrast work tasks and play. What are the similarities and differences?

2. As a future early childhood teacher, would you promote work tasks as defined by Montessori or play? Is there room for both in the early childhood classroom? Why or why not?

One major difference between Montessori education and many other early childhood programs in the United States is the emphasis on work experiences rather than play times. Although these concepts share similarities, the differences are significant.

Montessori's Work Experiences

Montessori described children's interactions with materials in the classroom as **work tasks** (Montessori, 1965). Although children are free to choose the materials they want to spend time with, these items are used in very specific ways. Before the child is allowed to work on a task, the teacher demonstrates how the materials are to be used. Precise steps are clearly presented, and any deviations from these procedures result in a new demonstration of the task by the teacher or redirection into a different work activity by the adult.

An example of a work task used in Montessori classrooms is the spooning of dried peas. On a child-sized tray, the Montessori teacher organizes two bowls (one filled with dried peas) and a spoon. When a child shows interest in these materials, the teacher carefully demonstrates how the child should place the bowls, hold

This Montessori teacher shows students how to trace letters made from sandpaper.

the spoon, and move the peas from one bowl to the next without spilling. The child is then free to engage in this work task as often as he wants.

Very different from Montessori's work tasks are the **play experiences** found in most preschool programs. Play tends to be much more open-ended than the learning opportunities designed by Montessori. Children have many choices of interesting materials and use those toys and equipment in their own unique ways. Play materials usually do not require demonstration by the teacher. Children understand their use and simply take them from their storage location and engage in play. A set of wooden blocks, for example, is an excellent play material that leads to building castles, roads, towers, or anything else that comes to mind. Chapter 5 provides a more thorough description of play and its importance.

Montessori Materials

Montessori's ideas of work and play and her views of child growth and development (discussed in Chapter 4) provide a clear rationale for the materials in the Montessori classroom. Because of her work with poor children in the slums of Rome (see Chapter 2 for a brief biographical sketch), Montessori felt very strongly that the materials used in her classrooms should be beautiful (Lillard, 1996). They were constructed with care from only the finest woods and other materials and carefully finished to look and feel good to children. For many of her students, this equipment was one of very few contacts with truly beautiful materials. Montessori designed her equipment with other specific characteristics in mind as well (Standing, 1962):

- *Careful attention to concept development.* Each piece of equipment was designed to teach specific concepts to children as they used them.
- *Graduated difficulty/complexity.* As children develop, they need increasingly challenging materials to stimulate their continued growth.

Given an exciting environment that can be freely explored, children will actively engage in learning about the world around them.

- *Self-correction.* Whenever possible, Montessori-designed materials are self-correcting, eliminating the need to consult an adult.
- *Sensory orientation.* Montessori considered all the senses to be important, and she designed her materials to stimulate their use as part of the learning process.

One popular Montessori work task is the cylinder block. Several different types are used, some varying only in the depth of the cylinder, others only in the diameter (see Figure 3–2a). The more difficult ones require the child to differentiate both depth and diameter. Children take the cylinders out and place them carefully on the table and then replace them in the appropriate holes.

Another common material found in Montessori classrooms is the buttoning frame (Figure 3–2b). There are several variations of these wooden frames, all of which have two half-sheets of fabric attached. Some have buttons, while others have tying materials that children use to connect and disconnect the two pieces of fabric. This task develops fine motor skills and prepares children to dress themselves.

Classroom Organization

Montessori carefully organized her materials and equipment in her classroom so that children could easily and effectively use them (Lillard, 1996). One characteristic of this organization is the child-sized equipment she used. Montessori designed tables and chairs with young children's bodies in mind. She also constructed storage shelves, sinks, drinking fountains, toilets, and other equipment at the appropriate height for young children. Montessori wanted children to independently and easily use the available equipment.

Precise organization is another characteristic of the work spaces in a Montessori classroom. The teacher stores each activity in a specific place and carefully

Figure 3–2 *(a) Montessori Cylinder Blocks; (b) An Example of a Buttoning Frame*

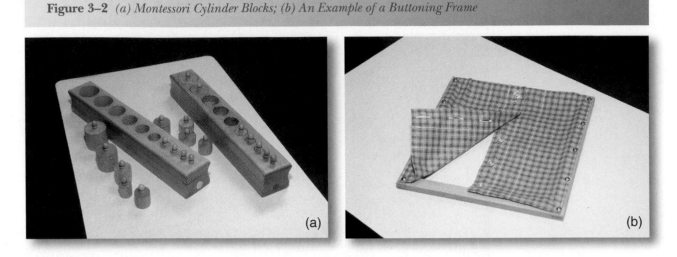

organizes the materials for easy use by students. The teacher organizes many of the work tasks on trays so that children can take them to their own work space, use the materials, and return them to their proper storage spot. The washing-up tray, for example, is stored on a shelf in the home living center and typically contains a child-sized pitcher, bowl, washcloth, soap, soap dish, and apron, all neatly organized for children's use.

A third characteristic of organization in the Montessori classroom is the use of individual work spaces for each child. Typically, a small rug or mat defines the personal space children need for their work tasks. During work time, children bring out their rug, place it on the floor or at a table, and then select the task they want to use. These mats encourage children to focus their energies on the work before them rather than being distracted by the activities of others.

Montessori classrooms are loosely organized into centers that differ somewhat from the typical early childhood classroom. Lillard (1972) identifies four categories of materials that are used in each of these centers:

- *Daily living materials.* This equipment allows children to engage in activities associated with their own physical well-being or provides opportunities for them to manage the classroom environment. Materials for washing up and a child-sized dustpan and broom are examples of these options.

- *Sensorial materials.* Montessori saw the development of all the senses as an important way to help young children learn. These materials help enhance sensory awareness while assisting in intellectual development. Montessori's sound cylinders, which the teacher uses to help children discriminate between sounds of different objects placed in wooden cylinders, are examples of this type.

- *Academic materials.* Children use this equipment to learn language arts, mathematics, geography, and science. There is a natural progression from sensorial to academic materials. An example of an academic material is the collection of metal shapes that students use for tracing. These shapes help develop the physical skills children need for later writing tasks.

- *Cultural and artistic materials.* This equipment helps prepare children for later artistic expression. For example, Montessori teachers believe that children

Celebrating Diversity . . .
Programs for Children Who Are Gifted and Talented

Although none of the program models described in this chapter are designed exclusively for students who are gifted and talented, each can accommodate these students and provide quality educational experiences for them. Most programs for gifted and talented students begin in the primary grades. Three approaches to gifted education are commonly found in the United States (Piirto, 1999):

- **Separate education.** In this option, children who are identified as gifted and talented are isolated from other students and taught in a separate classroom within the school. While providing potential benefits, this option runs counter to the current emphasis on integrating children with special needs into the regular classroom.
- **Accelerated education.** In this type of program, children who are gifted and talented either skip grades in the public school system, work with older children and their teacher to learn more advanced topics, or use accelerated materials more independently in their regular classroom. Although it moves gifted and talented children more rapidly through required subjects, this approach may fail to stimulate and challenge these students.

- **Enrichment education.** Children in this program type remain in their regular classroom and receive experiences that extend and expand learning through special projects and activities. This option allows children who are gifted and talented to socialize and interact more normally with their peers while still receiving the stimulation they need for exciting learning experiences. Enrichment programs support the effort to integrate all children with special needs in the regular classroom.

1. During your schooling, did you know someone you would consider gifted or talented? What options did the school provide to support this student? Do you think this person received the assistance needed to develop to his or her potential?

2. Identify the potential strengths and weaknesses of each of the approaches to gifted education described here for primary-age children.

3. Do you think primary-age children can and should be identified as gifted or talented? What are the benefits and potential problems?

need practice in walking a line on the floor as they prepare for future music and dance expression. As children develop their sense of balance and gain better control over their hands and feet, they develop the skills needed for rhythm and dance experiences.

Role of the Teacher

The formal training of Montessori teachers is extensive. Prospective candidates must thoroughly study child development, understand the educational values of all the materials used in the classroom, become sensitive to the appropriate times to present work tasks to students, and gain experience in interacting with children.

Teachers in a Montessori classroom operate on three basic principles (Roopnarine & Johnson, 2000):

- *A carefully prepared environment.* The first and most important task of a Montessori teacher is to thoroughly prepare the classroom environment. When children can work with materials that meet their developmental needs, they

For more information about Montessori teacher preparation, go to the Companion Website at www.prenhall.com/henniger, select Chapter 3, then choose Web Destinations.

spend many productive hours engaged in work tasks that enhance learning and development.

- *An attitude of humility.* Montessori teachers recognize that children's inner needs are very difficult to understand. At the same time, adult attempts to assist in meeting these needs are often misguided. Therefore, truly effective teachers must approach their roles humbly, while constantly evaluating their own motives and the needs of children.

- *Respect for the child's individuality.* A thorough understanding of child development and individual differences is essential for the Montessori teacher. Knowing and respecting these differences within and between children helps the teacher focus on the positive characteristics each child possesses.

Montessori's ideas, materials, and teaching strategies have a relatively small but loyal group of supporters both in the United States and around the world. The strong emphasis on highly structured work tasks, however, is generally in conflict with the play orientation of most American early childhood classrooms. In America, Montessori's approach is most popular with parents who seek a more structured learning environment in which to stimulate child development.

The High/Scope Curriculum

The High/Scope curriculum model has had a major influence on early childhood education for over 40 years (Bredekamp, 1996). David Weikart and others created the Perry Preschool Program in the 1960s as a model approach designed to help disadvantaged preschool children develop the skills needed to succeed in the public school system. The program emphasizes the importance of teaching the cognitive understandings needed for academic success in reading and mathematics (DeVries & Kohlberg, 1987).

After initially receiving federal support in the 1960s, a private organization called the High/Scope Foundation took over responsibility for continuing to promote the model. This curricular approach, although originally designed for preschool-age children, has been successfully used with primary-age children in more recent years (Bredekamp, 1996).

Theoretical Basis

The High/Scope curriculum is grounded in the theoretical perspectives of Jean Piaget, who believed that children learn best when they build understanding through direct experiences with people and objects in the world around them. The application of Piaget's theories to life in classrooms has led to the development of several programs that are collectively called *constructivist* in their approach. The High/Scope curriculum is the best-known example of this type. DeVries and Kohlberg (1987) and Kamii and DeVries (1978) have each described their thoughts on constructivist education in separate books. Studying the perspectives presented in these resources will add further insights into the High/Scope model.

While emphasizing the development of the whole child, High/Scope focuses on strengthening cognitive skills through active, hands-on learning experiences.

For more information about the High/Scope program, go to the Companion Website at www.prenhall.com/henniger, select Chapter 3, then choose Web Destinations.

This cognitively oriented curriculum is founded on the belief that children cannot understand themselves without first being able to place themselves in time and space and to classify and order objects and events (Weikart, Rogers, Adcock, & McClelland, 1971, p. 6).

The High/Scope program is designed to help children develop logicomathematical and spatiotemporal understandings of the world around them (Hohmann & Weikart, 1995). **Logicomathematical relationships** include organizing objects into groups according to common characteristics and ordering items from smallest to largest. These tasks are based on Piaget's studies of logic and number. **Spatiotemporal relationships** focus on helping children understand relational concepts such as up/down, over/under, and inside/outside. Event sequences and cause-and-effect relationships are also emphasized.

The Plan-Do-Review Sequence

To help children develop stronger conceptual understandings, the High/Scope curriculum uses a procedure called the **plan-do-review sequence** (Hohmann & Weikart, 1995). The teacher encourages children to plan the tasks they want to accomplish during free-choice time, engage in those activities, and then spend time later in the day reflecting on what they learned.

Children typically engage in planning time in small groups of four or five, while working with a teacher. Children identify activities they would like to try during work time, and the teacher helps them refine their thinking to produce a clear, structured plan for the work period ahead. The teacher uses a variety of motivational strategies to assist children in making decisions about their school day. For example, a set of pretend walkie-talkies could be used to help children communicate their plans to others.

Teachers often refer to the "do" time in the High/Scope curriculum as *work time;* it directly follows the planning period. In this model, teachers organize classroom space into areas where children spend their work time with blocks, art projects, quiet activities, and dramatic play. Teachers provide children with a large block of time (usually 40 to 60 minutes) to carry out their planned activities.

Review time is the last of the three components of the plan-do-review sequence and typically follows the work period. Teachers can conduct this recall time either in small groups or as a whole class. Again, teachers assist the children in reviewing their work experiences in a variety of developmentally appropriate ways. Drawing a picture of the block structure built, discussing who children spent time with, and reviewing the plans made earlier in the day are examples of the techniques used during this period.

The Curriculum

Teachers in the High/Scope program emphasize eight **key experiences** as they plan for their time with children (Weikart et al., 1971):

1. *Active learning.* Teachers expect children to initiate and carry out their own tasks in the classroom. They encourage manipulation of materials in all areas of the High/Scope classroom.

2. *Using language.* Teachers emphasize oral and written language. They encourage children to talk with others about their experiences and feelings as they go through the school day.

3. *Experiencing and representing.* Children need many opportunities to experience through their senses and represent those activities through music, movement, art, and role-playing.

4. *Classification.* The ability to notice similarities and differences among objects grows during the early childhood years. Teachers provide many opportunities for children to grow in their understanding of classification because of its importance in later mathematical learning.

5. *Seriation.* Another important foundation for mathematics is the ability to order objects from smallest to largest on the basis of some criteria such as length, weight, or width.

6. *Number concepts.* Understanding, for example, what *fiveness* means is another mathematical concept that High/Scope teachers promote.

7. *Spatial relationships.* Children gain understandings of concepts such as under/over, up/down, and in/out as they interact with materials in their environment.

8. *Time.* Although an understanding of time develops slowly, children gradually learn concepts about seasons, past and future events, and the order of activities as they work with tasks and communicate their results to adults and others.

Structure of the Class Day

The High/Scope model emphasizes that the best learning experiences occur when children have a consistent classroom routine. Teachers carefully plan special events such as field trips and discuss them with children ahead of time. This adherence to a planned sequence of events helps give children the control they need to learn successfully from the people and materials in their environment (Hohmann & Weikart, 1995).

A typical half-day classroom schedule in the High/Scope program includes the following elements:

- *Planning time.* The day begins with time in small groups where children plan their work experiences with the assistance of a teacher. Children have consistent opportunities to share their ideas and plans with teachers and then learn to act on their choices.

- *Work time.* This period is generally the longest time children spend in any one activity during the day. Children select their activities for this time based on the planning conducted earlier and engage in the tasks at their own pace. During this time, teachers observe and assist where needed.

- *Clean-up time.* This period offers an opportunity to restore order to the classroom environment following work experiences. It also becomes additional learning time as children sort and return materials to their proper storage locations.

- *Recall time.* Children have the opportunity each day to summarize what they have learned during the work period. This recall period helps bring closure to the earlier planning and work times and assists children in building stronger conceptual understandings.

- *Small-group time.* Teachers carefully plan structured activities and conduct them with four or five children in a small-group setting. They encourage children to participate in activities that build upon their backgrounds and experiences and add new cognitive understandings.

- *Large-group circle time.* This component of the class day consists of 10 to 15 minutes of games, songs, finger plays, sharing, and a short story. Circle time helps children develop group social skills as they engage in a variety of motivating experiences.

A full-day High/Scope program includes several additional elements (Hohmann, 1996). One of these is the opportunity for outside time. Being outdoors provides children with additional opportunities for play and work experiences in that setting. Full-day programs also include mealtimes where further occasions for learning are presented. Most full-day programs provide both breakfast and lunch for students. Finally, a nap/quiet time gives children the chance to rest and prepare for further learning later in the day.

The Teacher's Role

Teachers in a High/Scope program work with children to strengthen their overall development, while specifically emphasizing cognitive skills. Roopnarine and Johnson (2000) identify four key components to these interactions with young children:

- *Teachers as active learners.* High/Scope teachers are active learners themselves as they work with children. By modeling excitement and interest in learning, they encourage children to do the same. This attitude also helps teachers prepare more interesting activities and materials for use in the classroom.

- *Careful observers.* Good teachers need to make thorough, detailed observations of children to understand their developmental abilities and plan motivating activities for them. The High/Scope program has developed an observation guide called the Child Observation Record (COR) to assist teachers in this effort (Schweinhart, 1993).

- *Environmental planning and organization.* A key role for teachers is preparing the classroom for students' work and play activities. Although teachers maintain overall consistency in the environment, students need new materials to stimulate their growth and development. Minor modifications each week help keep children involved in their school day.

- *Positive interactions with children.* High/Scope teachers work hard to communicate effectively with children. These positive interactions include being a good listener, asking challenging open-ended questions, and motivating children to reach higher levels of understanding.

Research on the High/Scope Model

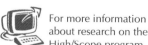

For more information about research on the High/Scope program, go to the Companion Website at www.prenhall.com/henniger, select Chapter 3, then choose Web Destinations.

From its beginnings as the Perry Preschool Project, the High/Scope program has conducted research on program effectiveness. Because of the diligence of the program founders, some of the best long-term research on the effectiveness of early childhood programs for children from low-income families comes from High/Scope. Having kept track of former students for over 30 years, the program research provides convincing evidence of the values of early education.

Into Practice . . .
Planning with Children

The planning component of the plan-do-review sequence in the High/Scope program is considered essential for both children and teachers. It helps children make good decisions about the activities they choose during play-times. The following hypothetical dialogue between a teacher of 4-year-old children and one of her students highlights the planning process taking place in a typical small-group session:

Teacher: Miranda, here is Muppet the Puppet. Can you tell her what you plan on doing today during work time?

Miranda (puts puppet on her hand and speaks to it): Muppet, I think I'll go to art today.

Teacher: Tell Muppet what you plan to do when you get there, please.

Miranda: Well, probably paint at the easel.

Teacher: That's a good choice, Miranda. You haven't painted at the easel for several days. Anything else you want to tell Muppet?

Miranda: . . . Nope.

Teacher: Remember at group time I mentioned that there were both wide and narrow brushes to use at the easel? Do you want to use one or the other, or both?

Miranda: I think I will try the wide one first and then maybe the narrow one.

Some options you could consider using to help young children plan include:

- **Tape recorder.** Have students speak into a microphone attached to a tape recorder, telling their choices of activities for the play period. Play back what the child has said to reinforce the choice(s) made.
- **Spyglass.** Use the cardboard cylinder from an empty paper towel roll as a "spyglass." Ask each child to look through the spyglass and find a center in the classroom that he or she would like to visit during playtime and describe the activities to engage in.
- **Camera.** If you have a digital camera, you could ask the children to take a picture of the center they want to visit and then describe the activities they want to engage in there. Or, you could simply ask children to look through the camera viewfinder and identify the center they are interested in visiting.

Schweinhart (2003) summarizes these findings from interviews with former students who are now young adults:

- A higher percentage of High/Scope students had completed high school than non-program students.
- Fewer students had been arrested.
- More young adults from High/Scope had a job at age 19 than those not attending the program.
- A greater percentage of these young people were self-supporting as young adults.
- Nearly three times as many former students owned their own homes.
- Fewer students had been classified as special education students.

These results translate into considerable savings to the public. Lower costs for special education, jails, and police interventions; higher income levels; and less reliance on welfare services all mean that early intervention programs can be highly cost-effective. Schweinhart (2003) estimates a savings of approximately $7.00 for every dollar invested in early intervention programs.

The Behaviorist Approach

For more information about the behaviorist perspective, go to the Companion Website at www.prenhall.com/henniger, select Chapter 3, then choose Web Destinations.

Dewey's progressive movement (see Chapter 2) began as an alternative to what is referred to as the *behaviorist perspective*. Based on the theories of people such as Watson (1924) and Skinner (1974), this approach continues to be popular in elementary and secondary schools across the country. In early childhood education, many primary and a few prekindergarten classrooms base their approach on behavioristic principles. While behaviorism can be useful when used sparingly in classrooms for young children, it is generally not compatible with developmentally appropriate practice and should be avoided as the primary method for teaching and learning at these ages.

Theoretical Perspectives

John B. Watson is usually credited with being the "father of modern behaviorism." Sharply critical of the research methods that Freud and other psychologists used in studying human behavior, Watson wanted psychology to be viewed as a science and gave his approach the name **behaviorism** (Schickedanz et al., 2001). He emphasized the importance of studying and understanding the data obtained from observable human behavior.

Probably the most influential behaviorist was B. F. Skinner (1904–1990). He promoted the concept of **operant conditioning,** in which the frequency of a behavior's occurrence can be increased by the presentation of a reinforcing event immediately following the desired behavior. If, for example, 5-year-old Margaret likes chocolate chip cookies (the reinforcer) and is given one after she remains in her seat working quietly for 10 minutes (the targeted behavior), she is more likely to remain seated in the future. Skinner believed that virtually all human behavior is a result of this kind of operant conditioning.

Implications for Teaching

Behaviorism has some important implications for teaching. Perhaps the most basic is that behaviorists believe all learning is externally motivated, which is further explored in the "Observing Development" feature at the end of this chapter. For example, a behaviorist would believe that 8-year-old Randy is motivated to learn science at school because his father (himself a scientist) is constantly rewarding him at home. Randy's dad spends extra time with him and verbally praises Randy when he reads a science magazine for children or wants to watch a science-oriented program on television. Randy, according to behaviorists, does not engage in scientific discovery because he is interested in what he is learning for its own sake, but because he is rewarded in a variety of ways by others when he studies science. While there is no doubt that external motivation can be a powerful factor, most early educators also believe that children are frequently inspired to learn because they are interested, curious beings. The other major implication of behaviorism for teaching is that behaviors can be encouraged or eliminated through the use of three basic tools: positive reinforcement, punishment, and ignoring. According to behaviorists, learning in all subject-matter areas, social interactions, and appropriate classroom behavior can be controlled through the use of these three techniques (Kameenui & Darch, 1995):

- *Positive reinforcement.* Anything that immediately follows a behavior and *increases* the likelihood that the behavior will occur again is called a positive reinforcer.

These reinforcers will vary among children, but some common examples include smiles, a pat on the back, verbal praise, a sticker on an assignment, or a piece of candy.

- *Punishment.* Anything that immediately follows a behavior and *decreases* the likelihood that the behavior will occur again is called a punishment. Just as with positive reinforcement, effective punishers vary between children, but often include time taken away from recess, a verbal reprimand, or spanking (against the law for teachers to use in many states).

- *Ignoring.* Not giving any response to a child's inappropriate behavior is referred to as ignoring, or *extinction.* While this may sound easy, it is actually the most difficult technique to implement. The teacher and other children must completely ignore a child's inappropriate behavior if this technique is to work. If ignoring is consistently used for a given behavior that previously received a response, the undesired activity will eventually end.

Relationship to Developmentally Appropriate Practice

The behaviorist perspective is generally considered to be at odds with the developmentally appropriate approach emphasized in this book. Teachers who operate from a behaviorist perspective look considerably different from those who use developmentally appropriate practice. Some examples include the following:

The behaviorist teacher:

- Deals only with observable behaviors.
- Breaks a learning task down into its smallest components and teaches them to children in a predefined sequence.
- Plans the curriculum (what is to be taught) first and then matches children with those plans.
- Spends most of her time engaged in direct instruction: sharing information with children in small- and large-group settings.
- Uses positive reinforcement, punishment, and ignoring as primary tools of management and discipline.

The developmentally appropriate teacher:

- Deals with observable behaviors and also with feelings and motives for behaviors.
- Often allows children to discover appropriate steps in learning.
- Understands each child's developmental abilities and plans the curriculum based on this understanding.
- Spends much of her time facilitating children's hands-on learning through playful experiences.
- Uses a variety of techniques for guidance and discipline, many of which emphasize counseling and communication strategies.

 The Bank Street Model

A fourth important model for early childhood education is called the **Bank Street approach** and was developed at the Bank Street College in New York. Initially designed in the 1930s at what was then called the Bureau of Educational Experiments, this model continues to have a strong influence on theory and practice in the field.

Although this program also promotes a constructivist approach similar to that of the High/Scope curriculum, Bank Street is best described as a **developmental interactionalist model** (Weber, 1984). The Bank Street curriculum addresses all aspects of child development in a setting that encourages both interpersonal interactions and learning experiences that integrate intellectual, social, and emotional understandings.

For more information about the Bank Street program, go to the Companion Website at www.prenhall.com/henniger, select Chapter 3, then choose Web Destinations.

Theoretical Underpinnings

The Bank Street approach identifies three major theoretical perspectives that form the foundation for the model (Mitchell & David, 1992):

- *The psychoanalytic perspective.* The writings of Freud and others, particularly Erik Erikson (see Chapter 4 for further details), clearly describe children's psychological, social, and emotional development. This information guides the Bank Street teacher's planning for these aspects of development.

- *Piaget's cognitive developmental theory.* Piaget's ideas on how human intelligence changes during the early childhood years are the basis for this component of the Bank Street curriculum (Chapter 4 provides additional information).

- *John Dewey and progressive education.* Dewey (see Chapter 2) emphasized the importance of social learning experiences and the value of active involvement of children in the educational process. Both of these ideas strongly influence the Bank Street model.

Program Goals

The Bank Street program has four broad goals (DeVries & Kohlberg, 1987). The first of these is to *enhance competence.* This goal includes building not only children's knowledge and skills but also the more subjective elements of competence, such as self-esteem, resourcefulness, and resilience.

A second broad goal of the program is to *develop individuality,* or identity. Teachers encourage children to develop qualities of selfhood. Teachers assist children in the process of learning what makes them unique and build on their individual strengths. The program fosters an attitude of independence by allowing children to make choices, develop preferences, and learn from their mistakes.

A third goal is to *positively influence socialization.* Young children need considerable practice and assistance as they work through the complex process of becoming social beings. Learning to recognize and respond appropriately to the points of view of others is one major challenge they face. The ability to use a variety of communication strategies to interact positively with adults and other children in work and play situations requires much additional practice.

The final goal of the Bank Street model is an *integration of functions.* Children are guided in understanding the interrelatedness of things and people in the world around them. For example, rather than compartmentalizing the teaching of mathematics or science, the Bank Street program integrates these subjects into the study of topics such as recycling or aging.

Governing Principles

Understanding child development and then using that information in the planning of activities for young children is essential in the Bank Street model. Mitchell and David (1992) identify six general developmental principles that guide the program:

- *Child development is a complex process.* Some general concepts are helpful in describing this process, such as stages of development and moving from simple to more complex behaviors. It is important to realize, however, that each child differs from the average and that development varies among children.

- *Behavior varies and is often unpredictable.* Although it would be nice to have a checklist that allows us to predict what children will do next, many factors may cause children to engage in more mature behavior today and in less-advanced interactions tomorrow.

- *Developmental progress includes both stability and instability.* Periods of stability allow children the opportunity to consolidate their understandings and refine concepts. As children approach developmental milestones and are challenged to develop new understandings, they face times of uncertainty and instability in their knowledge. Both are necessary for healthy development.

- *Motivation to learn about the world lies within each child.* Given an exciting environment that can be freely explored, children will actively engage in learning about the world around them.

- *Developing a sense of self is essential.* Critical to overall development is the process of learning about capabilities and understanding one's uniqueness. Children who develop a positive self-concept become active, independent learners.

- *Conflict is necessary for development.* As children mature, their ideas and wants come in conflict with others. Children need strategies for dealing with these natural conflicts in positive ways.

Curriculum and Materials

The activities and materials found in a Bank Street classroom reflect the goals and principles previously described. One essential characteristic is a learning environment that allows children to choose their preferred activities and materials (DeVries & Kohlberg, 1987). Areas for building with blocks, dress-up, sand and water play, books, and art are typical in this model. During much of the class day, children are allowed to choose the activities and materials that they want to use for play and work experiences.

Although commercial toys and equipment are common in Bank Street programs, classrooms also use teacher-made and child-made materials (Mitchell & David, 1992). Some simple rhythm instruments made by the teacher, for example, could be selected by children during choice time for exploration and use. In addition, teachers in the Bank Street program encourage children to make their own books, read them to others, and then place them in the book area for others to enjoy.

Another important characteristic of the Bank Street model is its emphasis on an integrated curriculum (Weber, 1984). Rather than attempting to separate mathematics, science, and literacy topics, for example, teachers work hard to integrate these content areas into experiences that focus on thematic studies of interest to children. A field trip to a local park for a group of second-grade children might lead to a discussion of the problems associated with litter and the broader

Into Practice...
Integrating the Curriculum Through Woodworking

Teachers implementing the Bank Street approach to teaching and learning might well include woodworking in the classroom as a means of encouraging learning in several subject-matter areas. The following example highlights how woodworking could be used to promote an integrated curriculum in a second-grade classroom:

It is springtime and Mr. Hanson's second-grade class has just returned from a nature hike around the school neighborhood. As students reflect on what they observed at group time, many mention the birds they saw and heard. They ask questions about what birds eat and where they live. It is evident that this is a good topic for future study. After further discussion, children begin to show an increased interest in birdhouses. Several were seen on the walk through the neighborhood.

Mr. Hanson agrees to set up an area in the classroom in 2 weeks where children can build their own birdhouses from scraps of wood. In preparation for this opportunity, interested children are to collect information about local birds and their natural habitat. Others will research the design features of different birdhouses and the construction challenges of each. During independent work time over the next several days, children excitedly locate information on the Internet, check books out of the school library to read, interview parents and neighbors who have birdhouses, sketch their plans, and complete step-by-step directions for constructing their birdhouses.

At a later class meeting, the children decide that once the construction process is complete, they

will work on donating the birdhouses to interested groups around the community. The local senior citizens center, community churches, and the city parks department are mentioned as possibilities. These organizations will need to be contacted once the birdhouses are finished.

As students prepare for and complete their woodworking activities, they are engaging in an integrated curriculum. With the assistance of Mr. Hanson and other students in the class, children are reading, writing, learning about their local community, engaging in scientific inquiry, and using a variety of mathematics skills. These learning opportunities flow naturally from the tasks of preparing for and building the birdhouses.

Some other possible integrated learning experiences using woodworking that could be included in a primary classroom include:

- **Putting on a class play.** In addition to constructing the props needed for the play, students can practice reading and writing and engage in dramatic activities.
- **Building a scale model of a local building or landmark.** Students can research local architecture/history, practice measuring and computational skills, learn about proportion, and better understand building principles as they construct their model.
- **Constructing classroom gardening boxes.** If students are interested in gardening activities, constructing gardening boxes that can be filled with soil and kept in the classroom will allow opportunities to engage in scientific inquiry as they observe, record, and make hypotheses about the growth of plants over time.

topic of what happens to our garbage. The teacher could develop this theme into several activities that combine mathematical, science, and literacy skills.

Strong two-way communication with parents is yet another valued component of the Bank Street program (Mitchell & David, 1992). Parents are important allies in the educational process. They provide teachers with much useful information about attitudes, feelings, and stressors while assisting in essential ways with developmental progress. Effective communication between home and school is the foundation needed for taking full advantage of all that parents have to offer.

The Reggio Emilia Program

For more information about the Reggio Emilia program, go to the Companion Website at www.prenhall.com/henniger, select Chapter 3, then choose Web Destinations.

In recent years, the preschool programs of Reggio Emilia, Italy, have captured the imaginations of early childhood educators in the United States. Using what is referred to as a **project approach** because of the emphasis on in-depth investigations of topics of interest to children and teachers, the educational experiences these preschools provide are truly remarkable (Hendrick, 2003). With adult help, children in Reggio Emilia schools document their learning through insightful and detailed conversations, photographs, and artwork.

An exhibit that includes photographs and projects completed by children in the Reggio Emilia schools and titled "The Hundred Languages of Children" has been touring the United States for the past several years and provides many examples of experiences in the Reggio Emilia classroom.

> Few walk away unmoved by its visual impact. They remember the carefully selected photographs, most often grouped in sequences, that serve as vibrant records of children's experiences and explorations as they investigate various aspects of a particular theme. Even more beguiling are the extraordinary pictures and objects made by the children themselves. (Hendrick, 1997, p. 28)

What makes the Reggio Emilia model so remarkable? According to program founders, it is a combination of fundamental ideas that must all be present for the model to be successful (Gandini, 1993). Many of these components are present in other programs for young children. The difference may be in the intensity with which they are applied in Reggio schools (Bredekamp, 1993). The following sections describe the key elements of this unique program.

The Environment

The physical space in a Reggio Emilia school is designed to foster communication and relationships. Children are encouraged to learn from each other, the teacher, and parents in a setting that is discovery-oriented and attractive to them. The basic message teachers attempt to convey as they set up the environment is that learning is a pleasurable, social activity (Hendrick, 2003).

Reggio Emilia classrooms are full of children's own work. Although this is true of many early childhood programs in the United States, the differences are in the breadth and depth of these representations by children of what they have learned. Paintings, collages, sculptures, drawings, mobiles, and photographs are present in every nook and cranny of the classroom. They are displayed so that parents, teachers, and other children can better understand the process of children's thinking.

One special space found in Reggio classrooms is called the **atelier.** The teacher sets aside this special workshop area for recording in visual form what students learn as they engage in projects of their own choosing (Edwards, Gandini, & Forman, 1998). The atelier contains a wealth of tools and resource materials that children can use for their documentations. Under the direction of a trained specialist, children work cooperatively to construct summaries of their learning experiences.

Children, Parents, and Teachers

Reggio Emilia teachers view children as active, curious, and eager learners. When interesting materials and activities are present and when adults give children thoughtful guidance, children can engage in quality educational experiences.

In the Reggio Emilia model the atelier, *with its tools and art materials, is the site where the* atelierista *guides teachers and children in documenting learning.*

Parents are considered essential in the Reggio Emilia approach and are expected to share responsibilities in educating children (Hendrick, 2003). Some parents participate regularly in the classroom, while others are involved in special events or engage in parent education activities. Strong parental support and communication help maximize child growth and development in the early years.

Reggio Emilia teachers are partners with children and parents in the educational process. Careful observation and strong communication skills allow teachers to develop plans for assisting the learning experiences for each child in the classroom. In addition, teachers see themselves as learners and continue to grow in understanding along with children.

Cooperation, Collaboration, and Organization

Additional key elements of the Reggio Emilia model are the cooperation and collaboration between staff members in each school and throughout the system (Gandini, 1993). Teachers work in pairs in Reggio classrooms and view themselves as equal partners in gathering information about children and making plans to enhance students' growth and development. Through active cooperation, teachers and administrators make it possible for students to achieve the lofty goals of the program.

Cooperation and collaboration are more effective in a system that is highly organized. Reggio Emilia teachers work within a structured system that is designed to make planning and discussions about children more effective. The program sets aside a minimum of 6 hours each week for teacher meetings, preparing the environment for children, parent meetings, and in-service training (Hendrick, 2003).

Family Partnerships . . .
The Importance of Parent Education

For much of American history, new parents could rely on their own parents and/or extended family members to help them learn the many complex tasks associated with raising children. Families lived close to one another, and it was relatively easy to get advice and support.

As families have become more mobile, however, this support system is available less often. Assume, for example, that it is midnight and your infant daughter is coughing and crying from what is apparently a new cold. You would like some ideas about medicines that would be safe for her to take or things you could do to make your daughter more comfortable. Although you might call your parents or a favorite aunt for advice if they were living in the same community, it is less likely that you would do so if they are living in a different part of the country and in a different time zone. The advice and support you need and want is just not as readily available.

Parenting is a very difficult job that can be made easier with the assistance of others who have experienced or are experiencing similar challenges. Because extended families are not as able to manage this task, you should consider taking time as a teacher of young children to create opportunities for parent education. There are a variety of ways in which this could happen:

- **Informal sharing opportunities.** Parent education can be as simple as having parents come together for dinner and then gather in groups of four or five to take some time to get to know one another, share their parenting concerns, and receive advice from others.
- **Parenting network.** You could also help set up a parent telephone/e-mail exchange network so that interested families could seek advice from others when needed.
- **Community parenting expert.** Every community has professionals whose job includes helping parents be more effective in their many roles. You could invite an expert to come and share with your parent group.
- **Parenting book or videotape.** Another parent education option would be to use a chapter from a well-known parenting book or a videotape on a topic of interest to parents as the discussion starter for a parent meeting.

1. How do you think you will feel about helping future families deal with their parenting concerns? Do you think this is something you will enjoy or find a burden? Why do you feel this way?

2. Do you think teachers and schools should be involved in parent-education activities? What makes you think this way?

The Atelierista

A specialist trained in the visual arts referred to as the **atelierista** is hired for each Reggio Emilia school and works with the other teachers and children to develop projects summarizing learning experiences (Edwards et al., 1998). The atelier (workshop/studio area), with its tools and art materials, is the focal point for the atelierista's efforts. By guiding teachers and children as they proceed through several refinements of their projects, the atelierista contributes significantly to the work efforts in the Reggio Emilia classroom.

The Importance of Documentation

A critical part of schooling in the Reggio Emilia model is the process of **documenting learning experiences** (Hendrick, 2003). Students are expected to describe for others the work they have accomplished and the processes they have used in discovering new knowledge. This documentation can take a variety of forms, including

- *Transcriptions* of children's remarks and discussions.
- *Photographs* of activities in and around the classroom.
- *Art media representations* of experiences (group murals, sculptures, paintings, drawings, etc.).

Documentation serves several important functions (Hendrick, 2003). First, it helps parents become more aware of children's learning and development. In addition, teachers use these representations of learning to better understand children and to assess their own teaching strategies. Reviewing documentation with other teachers also encourages a sharing of ideas among adults and promotes professional growth. Children benefit as well, seeing that their efforts are valued by adults and consolidating their understandings by being able to communicate them to others.

Projects

A project is an extended study of a topic usually undertaken by a group of children, sometimes by a whole class, and occasionally by an individual child. The

Into Practice...
Documenting Project Work

A well-known project from the Reggio Emilia program dealt with the topic of dinosaurs (Rankin, 1993). After teachers realized that their children had an interest in dinosaurs and suggested taking it up as a project, several children chose to participate in an investigation that lasted for 44 separate sessions over a 4-month period. The teachers and the atelierista first determined students' beginning level of knowledge about dinosaurs, then helped them find more information to broaden their understanding. After investigating the topic for several sessions, children were ready to begin some initial documentation of their learning. By vote, children selected the Tyrannosaurus Rex as the dinosaur they wanted to create using materials available to them in the atelier. A group of four girls handled this step in the following manner:

The girls chose styrofoam as their medium. This material turned out to be rather easy to work with as it was easy to handle and the shape and size of the styrofoam pieces often suggested to them different parts of the dinosaur. They had to ask for Roberta's (the Atelierista's) help only at specific

times; she did some things they were unable to do, such as attaching pieces of foam in a stable way with a piece of wire. A satisfying, three-dimensional, approximately four-foot high, highly decorated Tyrannosaurus Rex resulted, along with a stronger friendship among these particular girls. (Rankin, 1993, p. 198)

Some other possible ways of documenting learning in this dinosaur project might include:

- **Drawings.** Students could draw their understanding of the Tyrannosaurus Rex, giving dimensions, naming parts, providing skeletal diagrams, and depicting such things as sleeping and eating habits.
- **Slide show.** Students could download clip art from the Internet and combine them into a slide show to share with others.
- **Videotape.** Students could create a script (much like a play) in which they described what they had learned about the Tyrannosaurus Rex. By videotaping their efforts, they could document their learning and share it with others.

study is an investigation into various aspects of a topic that are of interest to the participating children and judged worthy of their attention by their teachers. (Roopnarine & Johnson, 2000, p. 209)

Although the Reggio Emilia program is the most recent example of the project approach in early education, the methods have been a part of educational experiences since at least the 1920s and the work of John Dewey. More recently, the "open education" movement in the United States in the 1960s and 1970s relied on project work.

Four key steps are involved in implementing project work (Roopnarine & Johnson, 2000):

- *Selecting a topic.* This is a very important step that generally requires considerable guidance from the classroom teacher. The topic possibilities are limited only by the imaginations of children and teachers but should be based on children's own firsthand experiences. They should also be topics that children can investigate in the school setting.

- *Beginning the project.* Teachers encourage children to share their own understanding of the topic through drawings, writings, or dramatic play. This helps everyone involved start with a common understanding of the issue being studied.

- *Doing the project.* Children and teachers engage in gathering new information on the topic primarily through real-world experiences. Taking field trips, carefully observing and manipulating objects, and talking directly with people who have additional information on the topic can all be productive ways of collecting new knowledge.

- *Ending the project.* Children need procedures for consolidating the new information they have gathered. Children can summarize what they have learned through artwork, photographs, displays, or a discussion with others not involved in the project.

In-depth projects often last several weeks and captivate the interests of both children and adults. Ideas for these projects come from the experiences of both children and adults and lead children to advanced understanding of the world around them.

Hendrick (1997) describes how children and teachers in a Reggio Emilia classroom developed a project related to birds on the playground. Teachers remembered how children during the previous school year were very interested in promoting birds visiting the playground and had built a small lake and birdhouses as projects. The teachers then prepared questions and possibilities to present to children to see if the students were interested in following up on these earlier efforts.

> Then they had the first meeting with the children. The children's conversation was full of ideas and surprises as, in the course of it, they became more and more involved. First, they explored the idea of repairing what had been constructed the previous year, and then they thought of improving the area by adding several amenities for the birds to make them feel welcome in their playground. Finally, they became very enthusiastic about the idea expressed by one child of constructing an amusement park for the birds on the school's playground (Hendrick, 1997, p. 23).

Observing Development • Internal versus External Motivation

Choose one of the age groups within early childhood (infants/toddlers, preschoolers, or primary-age children), *observe* **internal versus external motivation** using the guidelines provided, *reflect* on what you saw or heard, and *apply* the appropriate strategies listed with the children you observed.

Observe	Reflect	Apply
Look for specific examples of:	*Think about and respond to the following questions:*	*Consider the following developmentally appropriate strategies for the age group you observed:*
Situations in which adults or other children provided *external motivation* for a child to engage in an activity (words of encouragement, telling a child to do the activity, smile or pat on the back)	What is the difference between external and internal motivation? How can you tell if a child is externally motivated or internally motivated? During your observation time, what kinds of things did the adults provide for children to do? What were the external motivators, if any, used to help make this happen?	Include teacher-led experiences • Infant/toddler: teacher-initiated games like "Pat-a-Cake" • Preschool: group times with singing and a story • Primary: discussion of a famous painting, organized trip to the fire station
Situations in which the child was *internally motivated* to engage in an activity (child chose the activity, interest shown through verbalizations or body language, etc.)	Did children have many opportunities to make choices about what they were doing in the classroom? What might be the reasons for the number of choices children were given? What are some ways children's internal motivation can be encouraged and supported?	Promote child-directed learning • Infant/toddler: allow free exploration of safe toys and equipment • Preschool: encourage play during center time • Primary: expect small groups to plan and implement projects they choose

This discussion led to several children drawing what they thought should be included in the amusement park for birds. The teachers discussed the idea further and presented more questions and suggestions to the children, and gradually the idea began to take shape. A project was born and eventually implemented by children and adults in the Reggio Emilia classroom.

Summary

To test your knowledge of this chapter's contents, go to the Companion Website at www.prenhall.com/henniger, select Chapter 3, then select Study Guide. Also see Chapter Overviews, Reflecting Essay Questions, Multimedia Explorations, and relevant Web Destinations.

The Montessori Program

In Montessori education, children engage in self-selected work experiences in an environment that is carefully prepared by the classroom teacher. Montessori materials are designed to be used by students in specific ways that are first demonstrated by the teacher.

The High/Scope Curriculum

The High/Scope program is based on Piaget's theory and emphasizes the importance of learning through direct experiences with people and objects. Teachers help students develop deeper cognitive understandings through the plan-do-review sequence.

The Behaviorist Approach

The behaviorist approach is seen in limited numbers of prekindergarten and many primary classrooms. Based on the writings of people such as B. F. Skinner, it emphasizes that virtually all learning is externally motivated. Most people suggest that behaviorism does not support the basic tenets of developmentally appropriate practice.

The Bank Street Model

The Bank Street approach stresses the interrelatedness of all aspects of the child's development and the importance of enhancing the development of the whole child. This approach emphasizes the use of an integrated curriculum that is created by the teacher based on the needs and interests of individual children.

The Reggio Emilia Program

In the Reggio Emilia program, students engage in extensive project work that allows them to study topics of interest in great depth. Students document the results of their studies through detailed artwork or another form of media to summarize what was learned so that they can share this knowledge with others.

Multimedia Explorations and Activities . . .

Early Head Start

Dr. Ron Lally has been studying young children for over 30 years. He believes that very young children learn a great deal during the first few years of life. When adults and caregivers provide infants and toddlers with a variety of stimulating activities, they learn more readily and end up performing better in school. Since 1970, Dr. Lally has been studying two groups of infants from Syracuse, New York. One group was placed in a quality child care program where they were provided with a creative and highly stimulating environment in the first few years of their lives. The second group of infants and toddlers stayed at home with their own families. This long-term study has yielded important results that verify Dr. Lally's original assumptions. The children who were provided a stimulating child care environment were found to be more successful in school, had fewer problems with the law, and were generally more successful in their lives.

Research

You have already learned that the Head Start program is a national effort to provide low-income children from 3 to 5 years of age with the opportunity to participate in a quality program to prepare them for the K–12 educational experience. Early Head Start has the same goals—it simply begins at an earlier age. This activity is designed to make you more aware of the importance of the first 3 years of life and give you the opportunity to explore in greater detail a successful program option for this age.

1. View the ABC News video segment titled "Early Head Start."

2. Go to the Companion Website at www.prenhall.com/henniger and click on the Multimedia Explorations and Activities button for Chapter 3 for more information on Early Head Start and other programs for children 0–3.

3. See if you have an Early Head Start program in your area. Spend some time observing in the program or talking to someone who works there about the strengths and problems they have seen.

Reflect

After reviewing the video clip and visiting the Companion Website, think about the following issues:

- What evidence did you find that substantiates the importance of the first 3 years of life?

- What do you see as the strengths of the Early Head Start program? Did you discover any problems?

- Do the benefits of Early Head Start and other similar programs outweigh the cost of providing them? Why or why not? Should these programs be expanded and made available to more low-income children and their families? What about middle- and upper-class children?

Respond

Find out what programs are available within your community and state to meet the needs of low-income children from birth through age 3 and their families. Share the results with your classmates. You could consider one or more of the following options:

1. Check with your local school district office to find out if they house any programs of this type. If so, find out where they are located, whom they serve, and what the programs are like.

2. Contact local child care centers to find out which ones serve children ages 0–3. For those that work with this age, determine how many low-income children are served by each and who pays for those children to attend. Also ask for details about the program itself.

4. Ask the state office for public instruction or another state agency to give you information about the location of programs that serve low-income children from birth to age 3. Contact one program for more information.

4

UNDERSTANDING HOW A CHILD DEVELOPS AND LEARNS

In this chapter you will

- Learn about developmentally appropriate practice.
- Gain insight into the relationships between child development, learning, and teaching.
- Study differing perspectives on development.
- Review characteristics of children at different ages and stages of development.
- Identify strategies for learning about children and their development.

It is time for another school year to begin, and you sit down to study the class list for your second-grade students. Patrick's name is a familiar one to you. Other teachers have warned that he is a handful and that you should be prepared for a very busy, bright, sensitive, easily excitable child. Patrick has been tested and qualifies for the school's gifted program, yet often is off-task and gets into trouble. But Patrick's name is not the only one you recognize. From the additional 25 names on the list, 3 are on medication for attention-deficit/hyperactivity disorder, 2 others are receiving special education assistance, and 4 more students on the list come to you with very low reading scores. Oddly enough, this is considered a normal classroom. As their teacher, what can you do to prepare for this diverse mix of children? How will you meet Patrick's need for challenging experiences while working effectively with the children in your class who have special needs? The remaining students on the roster also have diverse abilities that require your teaching expertise. This is shaping up to be another challenging and exciting year.

A s difficult and challenging as the preceding scenario appears, this classroom experience is manageable. Good teachers across the country face these dilemmas each year and consistently find creative ways to deal with them. One essential ingredient for success in this process is an understanding of the overall patterns of child development and learning. The more you know about normal child development and variations from these typical patterns, the better able you will be to plan appropriate learning experiences for your class. In the same way, an understanding of different theoretical perspectives on how children learn and develop allows you to see children through new eyes and create lessons and activities that meet the needs of all your students.

The Developmentally Appropriate Classroom

For more information about developmentally appropriate practice, go to the Companion Website at www.prenhall.com/henniger, select Chapter 4, then choose Web Destinations.

Basing the curriculum on an in-depth understanding of child development and learning is often referred to as **developmentally appropriate practice.** Rather than focusing first on what is to be learned, the teacher in a developmentally appropriate classroom begins by working hard to understand the developmental abilities of his class and then makes decisions about what should be taught. This philosophical approach to teaching and learning is at the heart of most early childhood classrooms. The National Association for the Education of Young Children (NAEYC) has published two editions of a book outlining the characteristics of developmentally appropriate practice (Bredekamp, 1987; Bredekamp & Copple, 1997) for children birth through age 8.

Developmentally appropriate practice has two dimensions. The first is referred to as *age appropriateness,* or what is appropriate for the age of the child based on developmental averages (called *norms*) for that age. When a kindergarten teacher selects a game that requires the child to count to 10, she is using knowledge of age appropriateness to choose a game within the developmental abilities of the typical 5-year-old. The second dimension to developmentally appropriate practice is called *individual appropriateness.* This aspect takes into account what is appropriate for each child based on her unique personality and experiences. When Sarah's mom shares with you her daughter's interest in collecting rocks, and you decide to have some books in your third-grade classroom about different kinds of rocks, you are using individual appropriateness as you plan your curriculum.

Developmentally appropriate classrooms have many other characteristics (Bredekamp, 1987) (see Figure 4–1). An essential one is that *learning is viewed as an active process.* Children in a developmentally appropriate classroom are busy exploring their indoor and outdoor environments and interacting with other children and adults. Play is considered a vital element of this active learning: "child-initiated, child-directed, teacher-supported play is an essential component of developmentally appropriate practice" (Bredekamp, 1987, p. 3).

Another characteristic of developmentally appropriate practice is that it *considers all aspects of the child's development.* The child's physical, emotional, and so-

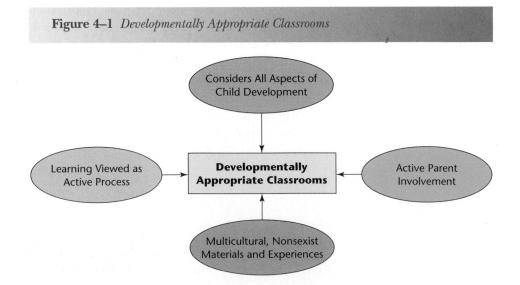

Figure 4–1 *Developmentally Appropriate Classrooms*

cial development are valued just as highly as cognitive development. All areas of development are integrated into the activities planned for the early childhood classroom (Kostelnik, Stein, Whiren, & Soderman, 2002).

Active parent involvement in the education process is also considered critical to developmentally appropriate practice. Parents can contribute time and talents both at home and in the classroom to assist the teacher in the learning process. Parents' knowledge of their own children's developmental histories provides the teacher with invaluable information to assist in planning individually appropriate activities (Gestwicki, 2004).

Teachers should provide *multicultural, nonsexist materials and experiences* in developmentally appropriate classrooms. Citing a variety of research studies, Banks (1993) identifies the early childhood years as critical to the development of multicultural and nonsexist attitudes. Chapter 8 provides specific advice on how teachers of young children can empower their students in this important area.

NAEYC (Bredekamp & Copple, 1997) has identified 12 key principles of child development that help teachers make decisions about developmentally appropriate practice:

1. All areas of development (physical, social, emotional, and cognitive) are closely related and influence each other.
2. Child development is a relatively orderly process, with new skills and abilities building on those previously learned.
3. Development proceeds at different rates for individual children and varies for different aspects of development within the same child.
4. Early experiences can either positively or negatively influence the child's later development. Key periods lead to optimal growth in many aspects of the child's development.
5. Development is predictable and proceeds toward increasing complexity.
6. Development occurs in, and is influenced by, social and cultural contexts.
7. Children are active learners who construct their own knowledge of the world around them.
8. Both heredity and environment influence child development.
9. Play is essential for healthy social, emotional, physical, and cognitive development.
10. Development is enhanced when children can practice newly acquired skills and when they are challenged just beyond their current ability level.
11. Children have different learning modes and also vary in the ways in which they represent what they know.
12. Children who feel safe, secure, and valued will develop and learn at their highest level.

Key Perspectives on Learning and Development

Many attempts have been made over the years to explain child development and learning. It should come as no surprise that there are no easy answers to these complex issues. However, armed with the insights from a variety of theorists, early educators can have a much better understanding of developmental processes in

Into Practice . . .
Examples of Developmentally Appropriate Practice

When teachers of young children plan programs that are developmentally appropriate, they are using an understanding of child growth and development to plan activities that take advantage of children's abilities and interests. Developmentally appropriate practice, in addition to being used to plan appropriate activities, also influences the materials used, organization of the classroom, guidance strategies, and the daily schedule. The following examples are intended to highlight the many different facets of developmentally appropriate practice in classrooms for infant/toddlers, preschool children, and those in the primary grades:

Infant/Toddlers

- Routines in the day, such as diaper changes, are made as enjoyable as possible by adults when they play simple games like Peek-a-Boo, smile and talk to children, and have a positive attitude about these parts of the child's day.
- Pictures of infants and their families are hung on the walls so that children can see them. Adults take the time needed to talk to children and show them the pictures on a regular basis.
- Rattles, balls, squeeze toys, stuffed animals, and chewing toys are all available for children to grasp, drop, shake, chew, and manipulate.

3-, 4-, and 5-Year-Olds

- Each week, teachers take materials out of each center and replace them with other interesting and developmentally challenging options. For example, in the manipulative center, five new puzzles of differing complexity are added to replace the ones that have been out for the past week. LEGO bricks are removed and Lincoln Logs are added in their place. Playdough is added as a new option for children to explore.
- Over the past week, two children who normally are friendly started to call each other names. Knowing this, the teacher first talks to both sets of parents to find out if they are aware of any problems or issues. Then the teacher plans to read a story at group time that brings up the topic of name-calling and discuss the issue with the class.
- The schedule each morning has been constructed to allow children to have 45 minutes in the morning for center time. During this period, children can choose the center they wish to attend and the activities that they want to engage in.

6-, 7-, and 8-Year-Olds

- Knowing that most young children have difficulty sitting still for any length of time, teachers organize the schedule so that children have short breaks in an academic period to sing a song or get up and "get the wiggles out" by doing some simple stretching exercises.
- Children have the opportunity to work in groups several times each day so that they can learn from each other in a social context. In some instances the teacher identifies the small groups, while in others the children themselves decide on groupings.
- Children are encouraged to engage in long-term projects that interest them. For example, three second-grade students may have a fascination with spiders and are encouraged to develop a science report on this topic that they can share with the rest of the class.

---

childhood. Several key theorists stand out as sharing perspectives that are essential for those who work in the field of early childhood education. The works of Bowlby, Maslow, Gardner, Gesell, Montessori, Vygotsky, Erikson, Piaget, Bruner, and Bronfenbrenner provide a wealth of insights into child development and learning.

John Bowlby (1907–1990)

Early in his work in child guidance, British researcher John Bowlby became concerned about the ability of children raised in institutions to form lasting relationships with others. He developed an explanation for these behaviors that is referred to as an *ethological theory* (Schickedanz, Schickedanz, Forsyth, & Forsyth, 2001) because he studied relationship building within an evolutionary context. Bowlby proposed that children who grew up in orphanages were unable to love because they had not had the opportunity to form a solid attachment to a mother-figure early in life (Bowlby, 1969). This **attachment** is an emotional bond that occurs between two people and is essential to healthy relationship building. Bowlby's work led him to suggest that this bonding process begins at birth and is well under way by about 6 months of age. During this time, infants typically attach themselves to their primary caregiver. From about 6 to 18 months, a young child separated from an attachment figure (often the mother) will be quite upset and frequently engage in much crying. Fear of strangers is another common behavior during this period.

Damon (1983) identifies four stages in the attachment process:

For more information about attachment, go to the Companion Website at www.prenhall.com/ henniger, select Chapter 4, then choose Web Destinations.

- *Preattachment (Phase I)* lasts from birth to approximately 12 weeks of age. During this time, children make little distinction between people in their vicinity. They turn toward them, follow them with their eyes, and are generally more content when others are around.

- *Attachment-in-the-making (Phase II)* is the period from about 12 weeks to 6 months of age. At this point, children continue to be interested in people around them. They do not express concern when strangers are introduced during this period. The main change at this phase is that infants become more enthusiastic in their responses to their primary caregivers. They begin to clearly prefer that key person who is providing for their basic needs.

- *Clear-cut attachment (Phase III)* begins around 6 months of age and continues to about 2 years. Now, the young child clearly discriminates between people who provide primary care and others. As children begin to explore the world around them, they use the attached person as a secure base from which they move out to interact with people and things. The bonds between primary caregivers and the child are strong, and it is hard for the child to be separated from these attachment figures. Strangers produce more anxiety and concern for children during this phase as well.

- *Goal-corrected partnership (Phase IV)* finds the 2-year-old beginning to develop relationships with attached persons that are more complex and that start to recognize the goals and plans of the attached adults. Up to this point, the child has focused on having needs met, and the attachment bond is a rather one-sided relationship. Slowly, these partnerships mature, and the increased opportunities for reciprocal interactions benefit both the child and the adult.

Although infants develop a primary attachment to one caregiver, other attachment bonds can also be significant. Fathers, siblings, relatives, and other important caregivers can be attachment figures to the young child. Mary Ainsworth, a key American researcher to study attachment, describes these as *secondary attachments* (Ainsworth, 1973) and discusses the importance of these bonds in her work.

Bowlby (1969) also describes the more positive aspects of this attachment relationship. As the infant/toddler becomes more confident in his caregiver bonding, he becomes more able to use the attached person as a base from which to explore. If, for example, a mother and her 1-year-old son go to the park for the afternoon, the strongly attached child will typically remain close for a short time and then move off to briefly explore his new surroundings. This sense of confidence and competence allows young children to learn more about the world around them and continue to grow emotionally and intellectually stronger.

Clearly, the attachment relationship has important implications for the early childhood classroom. Teachers of infants/toddlers in particular need to be aware of the importance of attachment and be prepared to deal with the separation problems that many children will face when attached caregivers leave. Another issue is the effect of high turnover rates in child care centers on secondary attachments. Raikes (1993) found that children who spent at least 9 months with a high-quality teacher were more likely to develop a secure relationship and that attachment security was enhanced.

Abraham Maslow (1908–1970)

Maslow's ideas about human development are often referred to as a *humanistic theory* (Schunk, 2004) because of the emphasis on the development of self. He proposes that people have needs that must be met in order to become and stay healthy. Maslow's **hierarchy of human needs** is depicted as a pyramid in Figure 4–2, with the most basic needs starting at the bottom and progressing up the pyramid to higher-level needs. The first two levels of needs are often referred to as **deficiency needs** (Maslow, 1968) because their absence causes physical illness. Healthy growth requires that physiological, safety, and security needs be met. The top three levels of needs are called **growth needs** and are the individual's attempts at becoming a more satisfied and healthy person.

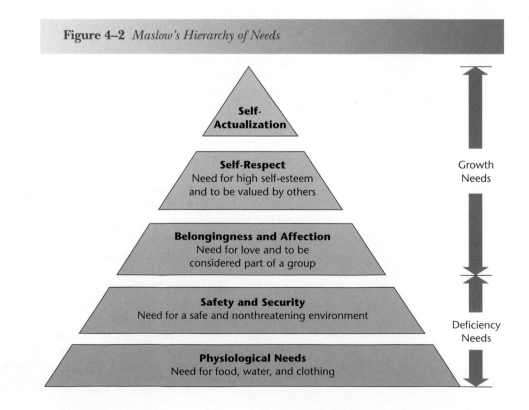

Figure 4–2 *Maslow's Hierarchy of Needs*

Maslow emphasizes the fact that the lower-level deficiency needs must be met before the higher-level growth needs can be addressed. The traditional role of nurturing the child's intellect may be difficult if other more basic needs are not being met. Because lower-level needs must be met before higher-level needs, the child who comes to school without breakfast is unlikely to be excited about the learning process. Once deficiency needs are met, academic learning helps meet the growth needs of self-respect and self-actualization.

Maslow's theory provides hope for children who come from difficult circumstances. He suggests that when unmet basic needs are met, the child can move ahead and develop more normally. Clearly, the child who lives in a physically abusive home is under incredible stress and is likely to experience many difficulties in school. Yet, if this child is removed from the abusive environment or if the abuse is eliminated, healthy growth is again possible. This encouraging perspective has support in the research literature (Skeels, 1966) and should help teachers be more optimistic toward even the most difficult circumstances.

Maslow's theory makes it clear that teaching is much more complicated than many people believe. Rather than focusing solely on academics, teachers must also be concerned with children's needs and must do their best to make sure these needs are consistently being met. Although it is not possible for any one teacher to meet all of the needs of each student, it is necessary to work to meet as many needs as possible. Teachers must begin by being aware of any needs that children have that are unmet.

Howard Gardner (1943–)

 For more information about multiple intelligences, go to the Companion Website at www.prenhall.com/henniger, select Chapter 4, then choose Web Destinations.

As a faculty member at Harvard University, Howard Gardner has been promoting in his many writings a new view of intelligence. Rather than seeing intelligence as a single, general capacity that each of us possesses, he suggests that we have at least eight distinct types of intelligence. This **theory of multiple intelligences** (Gardner, 1993) has prompted many to rethink the ways in which learning takes place and the techniques used to measure intelligence.

Gardner identifies eight intelligences that people possess to greater or lesser degrees (Gardner, 1983, 1999). *Linguistic intelligence* is seen in people who speak or write creatively and with relative ease. A person with strengths in *logical-mathematical intelligence* can reason effectively and engage in mathematical and scientific inquiry. *Spatial intelligence* allows people like engineers and sculptors to form refined mental models of the spatial world around them. Other people are especially talented in singing or playing a musical instrument and have strong *musical intelligence. Bodily kinesthetic intelligence* helps people solve problems and fashion products using their body or body parts. Athletes and dancers have high bodily kinesthetic intelligence. Two additional intelligences are referred to as the personal intelligences: *Interpersonal intelligence* is the ability to understand other people, while *intrapersonal intelligence* allows a person to understand himself. Finally, *naturalistic intelligence* was recently added to the original seven categories (Gardner, 1999). The person strong in this intelligence has special abilities in recognizing differences in the natural world. Gardner's notion of multiple intelligences reminds us that children come to the classroom with many different talents and skills and that we as teachers need to recognize and respect these abilities. Too often, schools prize linguistic and logical-mathematical intelligences and overlook the rest (Gardner, 1999). When we are sensitive to the other intelligences, children see themselves as more successful and competent.

Recognizing a variety of intelligences also means that teachers must plan their curriculum differently. Campbell (1992) describes his efforts to implement thematic learning centers designed to take advantage of the different intelligences in his third- through fifth-grade multiage classroom.

Arnold Gesell (1880–1961)

Through 37 years as director of the Yale Clinic of Child Development (later renamed the Gesell Institute of Child Development), Arnold Gesell pursued the task of observing and recording the changes in child growth and development from infancy through adolescence. Gesell is a **maturationist;** his descriptions of developmental patterns in childhood emphasize physical and mental growth determined primarily by heredity. By carefully observing children in his campus school, Gesell established norms or typical behaviors of children throughout childhood. He categorized these **gradients of growth** into 10 major areas (Gesell & Ilg, 1949):

1. *Motor characteristics:* bodily activity, eyes, and hands
2. *Personal hygiene:* eating, sleeping, elimination, bathing and dressing, health and somatic complaints, tensional outlets
3. *Emotional expression:* affective attitudes, crying, assertion, and anger
4. *Fears and dreams*
5. *Self and sex*
6. *Interpersonal relations:* mother-child, child-child, groupings in play
7. *Play and pastimes:* general interests, reading, music, radio, and cinema
8. *School life:* adjustment to school, classroom demeanor, reading, writing, arithmetic
9. *Ethical sense:* blaming and alibiing; response to direction, punishment, praise; response to reason; sense of good and bad; truth and property
10. *Philosophic outlook:* time, space, language and thought, war, death, deity

Gesell and his staff created an extensive list of normative information that remains popular with and useful to parents and teachers. A parent or teacher concerned about what is normal behavior for a given age can refer to Gesell's growth gradients for specific information. In his books, he summarizes the statistical data into statements of what a child is like at a given age. For example, here is his statement about 2-year-olds and their eating:

> Appetite—Fair to moderately good. Breakfast is now relatively small. The noon meal is usually the best, but with some the one good meal is supper. (Gesell & Ilg, 1943, p. 164)

Maria Montessori (1870–1952)

Maria Montessori is another maturationist. Through her teaching of young children in Italy, she developed an intriguing theory and many practical strategies that have significantly influenced early childhood education. Based on her readings and observations of children, Montessori believed that children pass through numerous **sensitive periods** during their progress to adulthood (Montessori, 1949/1967). She viewed these periods as genetically programmed blocks of time when young children are especially eager and able to master certain tasks. For example, Montessori suggested that there is a sensitive period for walking when the infant/toddler spends considerable time and effort in learning to walk. As most parents can attest, it becomes almost an obsession for children as they struggle to master this important task.

Another important idea that Montessori promoted was the concept of the unity of the mental and physical (Lillard, 1996). Until Montessori, Western educational thought had been influenced by Descartes, who viewed mankind as divided into two parts: the intellectual and physical. Her readings and work with children led Montessori to the opposite conclusion. That is, full development of the intellect is not possible without physical activity. Learning through doing is a cornerstone of Montessori's educational approach.

Montessori also believed that during the first 3 years of life children have absorbent minds (Montessori, 1949/1967). Because children's minds are not fully formed during these years, she reasoned that they must learn in ways different from adults. Montessori believed that children unconsciously absorb information from the environment around them and, like a sponge, simply soak up information into their developing minds. This information also forms their minds in preparation for later, more advanced thought.

Montessori also felt that children pass through stages in their growth and development. She described five specific periods of growth:

- *Birth to age 3.* During this period, children unconsciously absorb information from the world around them.

- *Age 3 to 6.* Gradually, children bring the knowledge of the unconscious to a conscious level.

- *Age 6 to 9.* Children build the academic and artistic skills necessary for success in life.

- *Age 9 to 12.* A knowledge of the universe gradually opens up to children during this period.

- *Age 12 to 18.* Children explore areas of special interest in more depth (Lillard, 1972).

Lev Vygotsky (1896–1934)

For more information about Vygotsky, go to the Companion Website at www.prenhall.com/henniger, select Chapter 4, then choose Web Destinations.

Although he lived a short life, Vygotsky's theory of development has had a significant impact in his homeland of Russia and more recently in the United States. Often referred to as a *sociocultural theorist* (Schunk, 2004), Vygotsky believed that development is primarily influenced by the social and cultural activities in which the individual grows up. Interactions with other children and adults are the primary vehicles children have for learning about the world around them. Language becomes a crucial tool for learning because it is the primary way we communicate and interact with others. It allows us to talk about our social interactions and is essential in the thinking process.

The major focus of Vygotsky's research was the relationship between language and thought. He concluded after much study that this relationship changes over time. Initially, there is little connection between the two. They are like two circles that do not touch. Over time, however, language and thought partially overlap to form verbal thought. The child now learns concepts that also have word labels (Thomas, 1985). Language and thought never totally

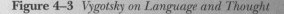

Figure 4–3 *Vygotsky on Language and Thought*

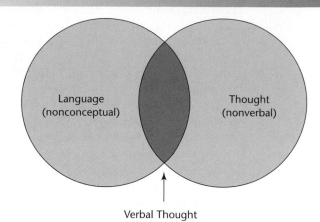

merge, however; both children and adults continue to use nonverbal thought and nonconceptual speech. Figure 4–3 diagrams these relationships.

Vygotsky (1962) is perhaps best known for a concept referred to as the **zone of proximal development.** This is the gap between the child's independent performance of a task and that which he can perform with a more skilled peer or adult's help. The child builds knowledge of the world when he is in this zone of proximal development and receives assistance from a more skilled peer or an adult. Vygotsky felt that educational tasks should be planned to challenge each child at the top of his zone of proximal development.

As with the other theorists identified, Vygotsky's ideas have many practical implications for the classroom teacher. First, if the child's social and cultural experiences play such a major role in development, it is critical to understand and build on the experiences children bring to the early childhood classroom. Also, because relationships with peers and adults are so critical to development, the classroom teacher must work hard to foster strong teacher–student and peer relations. Teaching strategies such as project learning in which small groups of peers work together to attain a common goal (see Chapter 3 for more information) are also compatible with Vygotsky's theory.

Erik Erikson (1902–1994)

Erikson's theory of human development is one of the few to describe human behavior from birth through old age. It is often called a *psychosocial theory* because of its emphasis on psychological development through the person's interactions within his social environment (Schickedanz et al., 2001). Erikson proposes that humans pass through a series of eight stages from birth to old age. Each stage has a major issue that must be addressed, which Erikson refers to as a *psychosocial crisis* for that time of life (Erikson, 1963). Successful resolution of the psychosocial crisis of the current stage provides a stronger foundation for approaching the next crisis.

The first four of Erikson's stages are important for early childhood education and are briefly discussed next. The title for each stage identifies the psychosocial

Into Practice...
Supporting Psychosocial Development in Young Children

Each of Erikson's stages of psychosocial development has important implications for how teachers interact with young children in the classroom. Ideas for supporting positive outcomes for the first four stages of this theory are presented below:

Stage 1: Trust versus Mistrust

- When the same adult provides primary care for individual infants and toddlers, very young children begin to trust that their basic needs will be met. Consistent and competent care for daily routines such as changing diapers, providing meals, and engaging in play help very young children develop a greater sense of security and trust in the adults in their lives.
- A dependable daily schedule also helps develop a sense of trust in very young children. When they know that play time in the morning is followed by clean-up, snack time, and a story, they feel more secure and are able to interact more positively with people and their environment.
- While the toys and equipment in an infant/toddler program should be changed on a regular basis, the location and use of the basic classroom spaces should remain as consistent as possible. So, for example, the quiet corner of the classroom set up with rocking chairs and used for rocking/soothing crying infants and for feeding times should be the same space used for this purpose over the next several months.

Stage 2: Autonomy versus Shame and Doubt

- An initial sense of autonomy is developed when teachers encourage children to actively participate in tasks such as dressing themselves, washing hands, toileting, cleaning up the classroom, and eating.
- Beginning independence is promoted when children are allowed to make appropriate choices for themselves. Choosing between grapes and apple slices at snack time, making choices about the play centers they want to participate in, and selecting a book for adult reading are all examples of this type.

- Adults also promote autonomy when they clearly identify both acceptable and unacceptable child behaviors. For example, a teacher must regularly remind children that hitting is not allowed in the classroom and provide them with the words they need to tell others of their anger or frustration. When this occurs, children can be more independent in their interactions with peers.

Stage 3: Initiative versus Guilt

- Providing larger blocks of time for projects of interest to children is an important strategy for developing initiative. Teachers know that it often takes 30 minutes or more for preschool and kindergarten children to begin a task, explore and create, and then prepare to move on to the next part of the day.
- When teachers know that children have the social skills to work out problems that come from such things as changing friendship patterns, it is often effective to try and let children work out their dilemmas first without adult intervention. When they are successful in these efforts, they are more likely to work out similar problems in the future.

Stage 4: Industry versus Inferiority

- During the primary school years, it is important for teachers to give children accurate feedback about their developing skills. This should be done privately and with sensitivity. "Miguel, you read that passage more smoothly today. You are recognizing many more words now and it is making a real difference. Keep up the good work!"
- Teachers also need to let individual students know when they are making progress. It is often hard for children to realize that they are growing academically and socially. Emphasizing progress helps children feel good about themselves and continue to develop their sense of industry. "Keneesha, I am so proud of you for working quietly at your table for this math activity! It has been hard for you to focus on your work lately, so thank you for your efforts today."

crisis for that stage, with the first descriptor representing the positive resolution of the crisis:

- *Stage 1: Trust versus Mistrust.* For the first year of life, children are dealing with the trustworthiness of their primary caregivers. If parents and others provide consistent care and meet the child's physical and emotional needs, a sense of trust begins to develop and the young child can start to trust others.
- *Stage 2: Autonomy versus Shame and Doubt.* From approximately 1 to 3 years of age, young children make initial attempts at doing some things for themselves. Wanting to dress and feed themselves helps give them a sense of independence. When not allowed to engage in these activities, children may develop a sense that they are not capable and experience what Erikson calls shame and doubt.
- *Stage 3: Initiative versus Guilt.* During the preschool and kindergarten years, children are developing a sense of initiative by making plans, setting goals, and working hard to accomplish tasks. Parents and teachers need to encourage the child's natural curiosity to allow this growing initiative to blossom.
- *Stage 4: Industry versus Inferiority.* The elementary school years (ages 6 to 12) are spent in Erikson's fourth stage of psychosocial development. A child develops a sense of industry through learning the skills necessary to be successful in society. Children begin comparing themselves with others and identifying their own particular strengths and weaknesses (Schickedanz et al., 2001).

Teachers and parents play key roles in assisting children with successful resolution of each of these psychosocial crises. Adults must be constantly aware of the impact of their words and actions on young children. Demonstrating trustworthiness, allowing some independence, encouraging planning and exploration, and praising children's accomplishments help ensure positive resolutions to each of these stages of psychosocial development.

Jean Piaget (1896–1980)

Piaget's long and productive career is difficult to summarize, because of the breadth of his writing and research. In general, Piaget was interested in studying how knowledge develops in human beings. Through careful observations and ingenious experiments with children, he proposed that we all pass through a series of four stages in gaining knowledge about our world.

Regardless of age, Piaget suggests that people form mental concepts about our world that he refers to as *schemas*. These schemas are general ways of thinking about or interacting with things in our environment. As we take in new information from the world around us, we can assimilate that information into already existing schemas to strengthen our understanding of that mental concept. A 3-year-old, for example, may already have a schema for *dog* that includes experiences with short-haired dogs such as Dalmations, Labradors, and boxers. Upon meeting a new breed of short-haired dog such as the dachshund, the child can assimilate that new information into his schema for dog. When new information does not fit already existing schema, however, the schema must then be modified to accommodate this new knowledge. The same 3-year-old, upon meeting a curly haired poodle, must change or modify his schema for dog to accommodate this new bit of information.

The best-known and most influential aspect of Piaget's work is his four **stages of intellectual development** (Flavell, 1963). Piaget states that everyone passes through each of these stages at approximately the same ages and that ways of knowing about the world vary significantly from one stage to the next:

- *Sensorimotor intelligence.* From birth to about age 2, children are in Piaget's stage of sensorimotor intelligence. During this time, children learn about the world through sensory experiences and motoric activity. The infant's sucking and shaking of various objects are examples of early ways of learning about things in his environment through physical manipulation and sensory exploration.

- *Preoperational intelligence.* Children from approximately 2 to 7 years of age (most of the early childhood years) engage in preoperational thinking. During this stage, children begin to use symbolic thinking rather than exclusively learning through sensory and motor interactions with the world. Preoperational children make initial attempts to be logical but are unsuccessful by adult standards. Since they are **egocentric** in their thinking, children have a difficult time seeing things from any perspective other than their own. Taking things literally is another characteristic of this stage.

- *Concrete operations.* From 7 to 12 years, children engage in concrete operational thinking. The child becomes more successful in thinking logically and systematically, especially when dealing with concrete objects. At this stage, the child understands **conservation,** recognizing that matter does not change in quantity or mass when moved or manipulated. Children are less egocentric and more able to see the perspectives of others.

- *Formal operations.* Piaget suggests that from adolescence on we enter the stage of formal operations. At this point, the abstract and logical thinking necessary for scientific investigation are possible.

Piaget's constructivist approach has had a significant impact on education in general and on early childhood education specifically. Although he spent little time in defining the educational implications of his theory, others have suggested many connections. Piaget's theory implies active learning during the early childhood years. Hands-on manipulation of materials and objects in the world provides the child with much information to assimilate and accommodate. Understanding how children gain knowledge about their world is essential to planning for future learning (Kamii & Ewing, 1996). The learning environment must allow for manipulation of objects and interactions with other children and adults.

Jerome Bruner (1915–)

Bruner, like Piaget, studied the child's cognitive development through investigations of perception, thinking, memory, and classification. His research led him to conclude that children learn as they try to make sense of the objects, events, and people in their lives. They discover meaning through playful interactions with their world. Bruner emphasizes the importance of what he calls **discovery learning,** in which students learn through active physical and/or mental manipulations of materials or problems.

Bruner's research (1966) led to the conclusion that there are three stages in cognitive growth:

- *Enactive stage.* From birth to about 18 months, children come to know their world through their senses. Through these sensory interactions, young children discover more about the world around them.

For more information about preoperational thinking, go to the Companion Website at www.prenhall.com/henniger, select Chapter 4, then choose Web Destinations.

For more information about discovery learning, go to the Companion Website at www.prenhall.com/henniger, select Chapter 4, then choose Web Destinations.

- *Iconic stage.* From about 18 months through age 6 children are in the iconic stage, where they combine sensory interactions with concrete images to make sense of the world.

- *Symbolic stage.* At about age 6 children begin to use abstractions, language, and thinking to construct knowledge of their world. These capacities are less well developed than those of an adult, but the move toward more symbolic thinking and understanding has begun.

Urie Bronfenbrenner (1917–)

Bronfenbrenner (1979) created an influential theory of human development called the **ecological model** to describe the many different systems that contribute to the overall development of the child. He proposes four major systems that influence children's growth (see Figure 4–4):

- *Microsystem.* This includes close relationships within the home, school, neighborhood, and church. These are the earliest and some of the strongest influences on the young child's development.

- *Mesosystem.* Surrounding the microsystem, these factors include the interactions and relationships between home, school, neighborhood, and church.

Figure 4–4 *Bronfenbrenner's Ecology of Human Development*

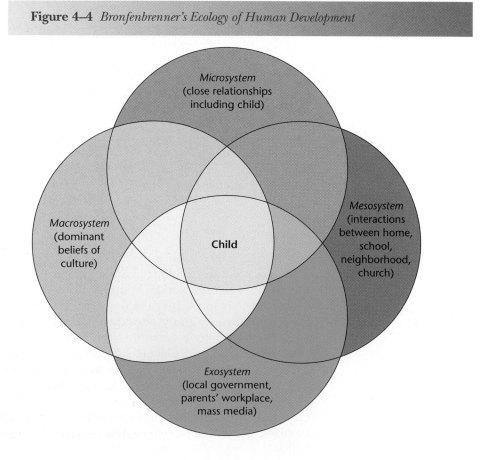

Family Partnerships...
Benefits of Family and Community Relationships

The Mesosystem described by Bronfenbrenner (see pp. 96–97) includes the family and community as significant influences on the lives of young children. But, what are the benefits to you as an individual teacher of establishing strong relationships with families and community members? Because it takes considerable effort to have positive home/school/community interactions, there need to be obvious benefits to you and your students in order for this to become a priority activity. Kowalski (2004) identifies several important benefits:

- **Enhancing student learning.** Family and community members can strengthen student learning when they volunteer in the early childhood classroom. For example, retired members of the community have a wealth of experiences and talents that they may enjoy sharing with students. Conversely, taking young children out into the community for field trips (such as one to the fire department) also provides many valuable opportunities for learning.

- **Celebrating accomplishments.** Family and community members can provide significant financial and emotional support for the work that teachers do in the classroom. For example, when they are invited to watch the class play developed by children, family and community members have a clearer understanding of the learning that is taking place and are more supportive of the teacher's efforts.

- **Support change.** With the involvement of family and community members, positive changes are more likely to occur. For example, a group of interested parents and community members could work with school personnel to plan for and build a more creative playground for young children.

1. Do you think the benefits listed for strong family and community relationships make it worth the effort it will take to develop them? Why or why not?

2. How do you think you will feel about working to have strong family and community relations? Is this something you think you will be good at doing? Will you enjoy this part of your job?

For example, the communications and interactions between parents and teachers have an impact on the child's development.

- *Exosystem.* The exosystem consists of local governmental agencies, the parents' workplace, mass media, and local industry. Although the influences of these elements are less direct, it should be clear that they all impact the overall development of children.

- *Macrosystem.* Encompassing all of the other systems is the macrosystem, which includes the dominant beliefs and ideologies of the culture. These beliefs also influence the child's development.

Children: Developmental Similarities and Differences

Imagine for a moment the process a creative chef uses for cooking a culinary delight. Although the process may not be conscious, the knowledgeable cook understands the characteristics of each of the foods used in a recipe. Length of time needed to cook, properties when mixed with other ingredients, consistency, color, and aroma are just some of the bits of information the creative chef relies on before beginning the process of cooking. In much the same way, a creative teacher must know a great deal about children and their typical developmental patterns before beginning the teaching process. This information becomes the basis for the planning and teaching that will follow. Unfortunately, there are few recipes to follow for success in the classroom.

From study and experience working with children, the best teachers know what is normal for a group of young children. A kindergarten teacher, for example, knows that a typical 5-year-old child should be able to string a set of 10 beads and has the fine motor skills to begin to enjoy the writing process (Charlesworth, 2004). Preschool teachers have learned that many young children have difficulty separating from their parents when they arrive at school (Hendrick, 2003). The tears and clinging are normal reactions to the stress of leaving loving parents. Third-grade teachers understand the importance of peer relationships and work hard to encourage positive interactions among students. In these and many other similar ways, teachers use their knowledge of child development to begin the process of planning and teaching.

Knowledge of what is typical for a given group of children must be supplemented with an understanding of the variations that exist among children of the same age. Children develop at different rates. The reasons for these deviations are complex but are some combination of genetic factors and environmental influences (Charlesworth, 2004). Finding and using this information about individual differences among children is very useful to the teacher in planning the curriculum. Talking to a 3-year-old child's parents, for example, could help a teacher to understand that this child's delay in climbing may be partially due to a broken leg

Celebrating Play . . .
Infant and Toddler Play

When most people think about children playing, the image that comes to mind is probably one of preschool or elementary children engaged in playful interactions. Those writing about children's play, however, also make it clear that even the very youngest of children engage in play. Doris Fromberg (2002), for example, provides the following examples of infant/toddler play:

The six-month-old lay on a carpet under a table. A mirror was attached to the underside of the table. The teacher had attached a knitted ribbon loop to the infant's ankle. When he moved his leg down, the ribbon pulled down a soft, red stuffed toy. His entire body shook with excitement as his legs and arms waved in the direction of the toy. When he raised his leg, the toy moved higher. With repeated play, he began to pull his toes closer to his mouth. (p. 16)

As individual toddlers finished their meal, they began to pull playthings from a low shelf.

Several children walked around the open, low-pile carpeted space with pull toys. Several children sat with a teacher in a construction activity with miniature animals. The children piled animals into a central "zoo" and alternately walked toward the shelf of pull toys. Four other children stood at a table on which the teacher had taped paper. The teacher commented, "Jenny's using a red crayon; Hal is writing with a brown crayon. . . ." (pp. 16–17)

1. On page 102 a play sequence for preschool children is briefly described. Compare that description with those above. What are the similarities and differences?

2. With your current level of understanding, do you think that play for infants and toddlers is as important for growth and development as play for older children? Why or why not?

at age 2. Observing kindergarten children at play, a teacher may discover that a child needs help in making friends. Or the second-grade teacher who analyzes a fairy tale that her student has written may learn of the child's special writing talents.

The longer a teacher works with children, the more sensitive he becomes to the general patterns of development and the subtle variations between children. These building blocks of knowledge and understanding form the foundations for good teaching and learning.

Infants and Toddlers

The first 3 years of life are characterized by rapid growth. The young child moves from being totally dependent on others to someone able to walk and talk and begin to interact with others. This period is also a critical foundation for all of the development that is to follow. Parents and caregivers need to understand the developmental patterns of this period (see Figure 4–5).

Infant Development. Newborn Jenny has just arrived home and is already causing quite a stir in the household. She seems so helpless and unaware of her surroundings. Yet, Jenny is quickly learning about her parents and the world around her. Although her first movements are reflexive, she quickly begins to develop more purposeful activities. Nursing is quickly mastered, and Jenny's cries take on a variety of meanings from "I'm wet" to "feed me!" She is learning about her world through her senses and motor activities, so dropping, squeezing, sucking, seeing, and hearing are some of the many ways in which Jenny is making sense of her world. By the middle of her first year, Jenny is sitting up when propped, grasping objects, and rolling over. Her understanding of language is growing rapidly, and she is babbling the sounds used to make up words. At this point, Jenny is also attached to her significant caregivers and becomes upset when they are not with her.

Figure 4–5 *Infant and Toddler Development*

The following characteristics describe typical behaviors of infants and toddlers. They are meant as a guide in understanding the patterns of development at these ages.

Physical
Grasps objects (4 months)
Sits and crawls (6–7 months)
Feeds self (10 months)
Walks (12 months)
Up and down stairs (toddlers)
Scribbles (toddlers)

Language
Cries to express needs (0–1 months)
Babbles sounds (3 months)
Understands words (8–10 months)
First words (12 months)
Two-word phrases (toddlers)
Knows up to 50 words (toddlers)

Cognitive
Smiles of recognition (4 months)
Object permanence (8 months)
Plays pat-a-cake (12 months)
Block towers, 3–4 (toddlers)
Identifies book pictures (toddlers)
Follows one direction (toddlers)

Social-Emotional
Recognizes familiar faces (3 months)
Attachment begins (6 months)
Stranger anxiety begins (6 months)
Does things by self (toddlers)
Plays by self (toddlers)
Active, curious (toddlers)

Infants explore their world by touching, tasting, and shaking objects within their reach.

As Jenny's first birthday approaches, she is taking her first steps and speaking her first words. These are major milestones that dramatically change her interactions with others. No longer dependent on others to get from one place to another, Jenny is free to explore her environment more independently. Words open up a new and more precise way of communicating with others, and Jenny is using this tool to her full advantage. Jenny's total dependence on caregivers has changed significantly over the past 12 months.

One-Year-Olds. Matt has just turned 1 and is already off exploring his environment. From his first shaky steps just a few weeks ago, he is now becoming more confident and stable in his gait. By the end of his second year of life, he is able to run and effectively navigate up and down stairs. This newfound mobility allows Matt to expand his horizons and learn even more about his growing world.

Matt's language is also growing by leaps and bounds. Beginning the year with just a few words that were understandable mostly to parents, Matt's vocabulary will expand to approximately 300 words by year's end. He is also now able to put together words and form simple two-word sentences. Matt understands much more of the verbal communications from others than he is able to repeat himself.

Toward the end of this year, Matt will be able to mentally represent objects and events as symbols. Although he still learns much from his senses and motor activity, he can now engage in symbolic thought. Matt can now imitate the actions of others and get involved in simple make-believe play.

Matt's push toward more independence can be difficult for his parents and caregivers. Although he wants to do as much as he can by himself, he still needs and wants closeness and assistance. Finding that delicate balance between independence and assistance is often difficult for both Matt and his parents. Patience and calmness are virtues for adults at this point.

Two-Year-Olds. As a 2-year-old, Serena is making the transition from babyhood to childhood. She continues to gain body control, with improved walking and run-

For more information about infant/toddler development, go to the Companion Website at www.prenhall.com/henniger, select Chapter 4, then choose Web Destinations.

ning and small muscle development. Serena spends considerable energy in refining her skills by repeating over and over again the things she is learning. For example, she will put together a simple puzzle many times before she is ready to move on to the next activity.

Serena's language continues to grow exponentially. Her vocabulary will triple by year's end to approximately 1,000 words. Serena's sentences have grown as well, with many including three or more words. Conversations with others become more interactive, with Serena able to listen and talk in appropriate contexts.

Along with her growing language abilities, Serena is developing deeper conceptual understandings of her world. She remains curious and excited about exploring the natural world around her. Serena has a lively imagination and enjoys using it in her play with others.

Although Serena's social skills are growing, she is still likely to play side by side, rather than with, other children. And rather than ask for a toy, Serena may well just take it. Her newly acquired ability to communicate more effectively is often not enough in many situations to avoid conflict, and Serena reverts to throwing a temper tantrum.

Children Age 3 Through 5: The Preschool Years

The years from 3 to 5 are often referred to as the *preschool years*. Many young children are entering a school-like setting for the first time. Although growth has slowed somewhat from the frantic pace of the earlier years, development is still rapid during this period. A 3-year-old is very different developmentally from his 5-year-old friend, and each year brings new milestones (see Figure 4–6).

Three-Year-Olds. Mario is very much a child and no longer a baby. He has lost most of the baby fat that gave him that chubby look of younger children. Mario's physical skills have grown, and he is able to balance on one foot, unbutton and

---

Figure 4–6 *Development of Children Age 3 Through 5: The Preschool Years*

The following characteristics describe typical behaviors of children ages 3 through 5. They are meant as a guide to understanding the patterns of development at these ages.

Physical

Losing baby fat (3 years)
Can ride a tricycle (3 years)
Hops and skips (4 years)
Draws stick figures (4 years)
Ties bow knot (5 years)
Rides a bicycle (5 years)

Language

Three- to four-word sentences (3 years)
Correctly uses past tense (3 years)
Plays with words (4 years)
Uses talk to solve some conflicts (4 years)
Knows up to 5,000 words (5 years)
Dictates stories (5 years)

Cognitive

"Why?" questions common (3 years)
Names basic colors (3 years)
Understands concept of three (4 years)
Curious about how things work (4 years)
Calendar has meaning (5 years)

Social-Emotional

Often imitates adults in play (3 years)
Sex-role stereotypes form (3 years)
Can work in groups of two or three (4 years)
Has special friends (4 years)
Sorts by color, shape (5 years)
Feelings can easily be hurt by others (5 years)
Likes group games (5 years)

button clothing, and ride a tricycle. He has achieved bowel and bladder control and can use the toilet with limited supervision.

Mario's language continues to develop, with increased vocabulary and sentence structure. He is better able to engage in a real conversation with others, talking *with* rather than just *to* others. Mario is full of questions about his world and constantly asks for information about the people and things around him.

During this year, Mario is developing conceptual understanding through playing with people and things. His pretend play has become more complex, and Mario can now include two or three other children in the scenarios he creates. Although his attention span is still relatively short, Mario can use his lively imagination to play out complex themes, especially those in which he imitates adult roles. In the block corner, Mario often constructs and then names what he has made.

Socially and emotionally, Mario continues to make significant progress. He can now establish and maintain short-term friendships with others and begins to enjoy playing *with* rather than *near* his buddies. Mario is learning to use social skills such as taking turns, but he finds it difficult to use these emerging skills consistently. His imaginary friend, Buffy, is often included in play themes around home and in school. Mario is often frightened by large dogs and horses and needs comforting when he encounters these animals.

Four-Year-Olds. Mary is an active and confident 4-year-old. Having mastered the basics of movement, she is constantly testing her physical limits to improve upon her skills. Mary climbs higher, runs faster, and pumps vigorously on the swing to challenge her motor skills.

Mary's language has now matured to the point that she can communicate with others using fairly sophisticated words and sentences. Language becomes a plaything for Mary, and she loves rhyming and nonsense words. Bathroom talk, tall tales, and swearing are also parts of her experimentation with language.

Highly interested in how things work, Mary is constantly asking questions that challenge the adults who work with her. Her interest in the concepts of life and

Most 4-year-olds enjoy dressing up as part of their play.

death lead her to explore the world of insects and small animals. Mary will often name her artwork and begins to draw and paint objects that represent things and people in the world. Number concepts are beginning to develop, and Mary enjoys games and songs that incorporate them. Mary understands time as a sequence of events and appreciates a consistent routine to her day.

For more information about developmental patterns from ages 3 to 5, go to the Companion Website at www.prenhall.com/ henniger, select Chapter 4, then choose Web Destinations.

Mary's friendships are becoming stronger, and she has clear preferences for playmates. These special friends change regularly, however. Play has now become a truly social activity during most times with others. Occasionally, however, Mary still likes to go off by herself for some quiet time. Turn taking and sharing are becoming easier for Mary because she is beginning to recognize the value of cooperation. However, her growing skills and confidence often lead Mary into confrontations with others. She wants to be the leader and is bossy and assertive in her relationships with peers.

Five-Year-Olds. Abdul has calmed down a bit from a few short months ago. He is now much more interested in fine motor activities and spends considerable time building with Legos, cutting paper, making artwork, and engaging in beginning writing activities. Abdul's interest in swinging, climbing, and running is still strong, and he engages in these activities in a fluid, coordinated, confident manner. He also has fun throwing and catching from short distances.

Abdul's language use is now fully developed, with a vocabulary of several thousand words. He can construct complex sentences and accurately use grammatical forms in communicating. Abdul eagerly learns new words that give him labels for

Into Practice...
Guiding Children Who Have Difficulty Sharing

Although young children are capable of many things at an early age, it is also important to keep in mind what they are unable to do . . . yet. As with 3-year-old Mario on pp. 101–102, one example of this is that many young children have difficulty sharing toys and equipment in the classroom. Teachers of preschool children need to be prepared to deal with the problems that this may bring. The following strategies are commonly used to help students who are struggling with sharing:

- **Have two or more of the most popular toys.** It is not always possible to do this, but when you have two or more toy trucks, popular dolls, magnifying glasses, floor pillows, or shovels to use for gardening, make sure to have them available for children. This will not eliminate problems, but may make it easier to share a popular item among several children.
- **Set time limits with toys and equipment.** If, for example, three children want to use the two toy trucks available in the block center, give each child a time limit (perhaps 10 minutes), set a timer so that you do

not forget, and then try to get the child without the desired toy involved in another activity for the next few minutes.
- **Identify ways in which children can use the equipment together.** For example, if three children want to play the same game on the computer, see if you can set them up so that all three can be seated around the screen with specified roles. The additional benefits of playing together may well outweigh the challenges of getting them involved in a cooperative activity.
- **Give children words to use in sharing situations.** Because of their more limited language skills, preschool children often use physical actions in their place. If a child wants a stapler but one is not available, many young children will simply take one away from someone else. You can help them with the language they will need to share. "Rather than taking the stapler away from Lise, ask her if you can use it to staple your pages together. Tell her you will return it when you are done."

the increasingly widening world he is exploring. Socially, Abdul has solidified his friendships at school and in the neighborhood. Although he will play with others, his strong preference is to be with his special friends. Cooperative play themes, in which children take on roles, is a common component of Abdul's activity. He is aware of rules and begins to enjoy simple games.

Abdul's conceptual knowledge is expanding rapidly. His understanding of numbers has improved, and he can now accurately count 10 objects and count by rote to 20. Abdul can sort objects by either color or shape. He knows the purpose for a calendar and can tell time by the hour. Abdul also understands the concepts of *tomorrow* and *yesterday*.

Children Age 6 Through 8: The Primary School Years

Although the life of a primary-age child has changed dramatically with the introduction of formal schooling, developmental characteristics through this period closely resemble those of earlier years. Children are still working hard to understand and construct social relationships, deal with their emotions, and learn about their world through hands-on manipulation of objects and interactions with peers and adults (see Figure 4–7).

Six-Year-Olds. Christy is a normal, busy 6-year-old who enjoys practicing newly acquired skills. Although her physical growth has slowed, she likes to test the limits of her body with challenging activities such as acrobatics and jump rope. Christy just got a new bicycle and is working hard to master two-wheeling. Other activities that require good balance such as skating and skiing are also fun for her.

Christy has many friends, most of whom are other girls. Her playmates change regularly, however, with new friends being added and old ones set aside. Christy

Figure 4–7 *Development of Children Age 6 Through 8: The Primary School Years*

The following characteristics describe typical behaviors of children age 6 through 8. They are meant as a guide in understanding the patterns of development at these ages.

Physical
Permanent teeth appear (6 years)
Likes rough-and-tumble play (6 years)
Works at mastery of physical skills (7 years)
Growth slows (7 years)
Body proportions more adult-like (8 years)
Healthier, less fatigued (8 years)

Language
Learning to write (6 years)
Understands conventions of conversation (6 years)
Likes to write own stories (7 years)
Spelling lags behind reading (7 years)
Masters reading (8 years)
Written stories more complex, detailed (8 years)

Cognitive
Interested in reading (6 years)
Enjoys collecting (6 years)
Able to sequence events (7 years)
Understands beginning arithmetic skills (7 years)
Eager to learn about happenings around the world (8 years)
Games with rules popular (8 years)

Social-Emotional
Nightmares common (6 years)
Same-sex friendships (6 years)
Compares self with peers (7 years)
Wants more time to self (7 years)
Special friendships develop (8 years)
Most fears conquered (8 years)

is making comparisons between herself and her peers, which is leading her to recognize personal strengths and weaknesses.

Although Christy still has some minor articulation errors, she is eager to talk with adults and others. It is hard to get her to be quiet long enough to enter the conversation. Christy is making significant progress in putting her thoughts into writing and enjoys practicing this newfound skill.

Christy's school days are filled with learning to read and developing early math skills. She is making steady progress with these very complex tasks.

Christy collects rocks and enjoys sorting and classifying them. Although she enjoys simple games in school and at home, winning and losing are very difficult for Christy, and she is happier when they are deemphasized.

Seven-Year-Olds. At 7, Gordon values his and others' physical competence. Sports figures like Michael Jordan and Ken Griffey, Jr., are important to him. Gordon is a typical boisterous 7-year-old and enjoys rough-and-tumble play with his friends. He needs daily opportunities to engage in active play. Sitting still does not seem to be a part of Gordon's makeup.

Gordon's rate of vocabulary development has slowed, but language learning remains significant. Gordon is learning Spanish in an after-school enrichment program and is finding this a fun activity. His ability to communicate in writing is improving steadily, and Gordon enjoys writing long, fantasy-oriented stories to share with his friends and parents. Although Gordon likes to work alone, his overriding desire is to be part of the group. Peer pressure to conform to the in-group expectations is growing. Mood swings are common for Gordon, as well as complaints of not being liked and concerns over competence when he compares himself to peers. Gordon's thirst for knowledge about the world around him appears boundless. He wants to know how the real things he encounters work, and he spends considerable energy on tasks that interest him. Gordon has mastered the basics of reading and has learned the arithmetic operations of addition, subtraction, and multiplication.

Eight-Year-Olds. Marissa is beginning to look more adult-like in her physical appearance. Her body proportions are subtly changing in preparation for the more dramatic changes of puberty just ahead. Marissa's movements are now quite fluid and graceful, and she uses good posture when seated. She is in general healthier and less easily fatigued than she was as a 7-year-old.

Marissa is very aware of the differences between herself and the boys in her class, and she works hard to separate herself from "those geeks." Her friends are all girls, and she likes it that way. Her group of friends is becoming more exclusive, and it is difficult for them to add new members. Although closeness with her parents at home is still important to her, Marissa is beginning to separate herself from her teacher and finds this relationship less important than it was a year ago.

Participating in peer group activities is very important to most 7-year-olds.

Marissa's hungry mind is eager to know more information about her expanding world. In addition to her desire to know more about people and relationships in her family and neighborhood, Marissa can conceptualize nations around the world and is curious about life there. She has an Internet pen pal in Australia and enjoys learning about school and family life there. Marissa is beginning to show an interest in historical events and can conceptualize and discuss future events.

Children with Special Needs

Every early childhood classroom is filled with a wonderful diversity of students. One of the major reasons for this diversity is the growing trend to place children with special needs in the regular classroom. It is important to understand these students and be prepared to deal with them. Children with special needs can be categorized as either disabled, at-risk, or gifted.

Children with Disabilities. A child who is **disabled** is unable to do something or has difficulty with a specific task (Hallahan & Kauffman, 2003). Seven-year-old Angela uses a wheelchair and is unable to walk. She is considered physically disabled. All other aspects of Angela's development are normal, however. Other disabilities can influence more than one aspect of development. Brian has a significant hearing loss and is delayed in his oral language development. Because he has difficulty hearing others and communicating with them, Brian also struggles with social relationships. The types and severities of disabilities children possess are many and varied. Some children experience mild disabilities, while others are faced with moderate to severe ones. For example, at age 7, Aretha has trouble distinguishing between letters such as *b* and *d* as she reads. She has been diagnosed as having a mild learning disability. Jason has Down syndrome, congenital heart defects, and severe mental retardation. His disabilities are much more damaging to his overall development. Wolery and Wilbers (1994) have suggested the following categories of disabilities often encountered by teachers of young children:

- *Speech and language:* hard-of-hearing, deafness, stuttering, cleft palate, chronic voice disorders, learning disabilities
- *Physical-motor:* visual impairment, blindness, hearing impairments, orthopedic disabilities (cerebral palsy, loss of limbs, muscular dystrophy, etc.)
- *Intellectual:* mental retardation, brain injury, brain dysfunction, dyslexia, learning disabilities
- *Social-emotional:* self-destructive behavior, severe withdrawal, dangerous aggression, noncommunicativeness, attention-deficit/hyperactivity disorder, depression, phobias, autism
- *Health impairments:* severe asthma, epilepsy, hemophilia, congenital heart defects, malnutrition, diabetes, cystic fibrosis, Down syndrome, sickle-cell anemia

Two categories of disabilities currently receiving considerable attention by educators at all levels are **learning disabilities** and **attention-deficit/hyperactivity disorder (ADHD).** Children with learning disabilities are found in almost every classroom. Although they have no outward signs of problems, these children struggle with one or more basic learning tasks. Educators are attempting to define, identify, and remediate children with learning disabilities. Allen, at age 8, has considerable difficulty remembering his basic computational facts. Addition,

Early childhood classrooms typically contain many children with a variety of special needs.

subtraction, and multiplication facts all seem to go in one ear and out the other. He has a learning disability relating to memorization skills. Allen shows normal developmental patterns in other aspects of his schoolwork.

ADHD is characterized by a short attention span and a tendency to be restless and impulsive.

> *Rasheen is a very likable 5-year-old who seems to be in constant motion. At group time in his kindergarten classroom, he finds it difficult to focus on what the teacher is saying and often needs another adult next to him to remain seated and involved in the group activity. Rasheen's family doctor diagnosed him as having ADHD, and Rasheen is taking a drug called Ritalin to help him deal with his disability.*

Although treatment with Ritalin and other medications is common for ADHD, many educators are concerned that we are overmedicating children and that other options may be more helpful in working with these children.

At-Risk Children. Children who are **at-risk** may experience developmental delays due to negative genetic or environmental factors such as poverty, low birth weight, or maternal diabetes. These children have not been identified as having disabilities, but they may develop problems without adequate intervention. For example, Joy, who is only a few days old, is experiencing neonatal abstinence syndrome because of her addiction to cocaine. She became addicted during the prenatal period and is at-risk in her future development. Joy needs to receive special assistance to help her through this difficult beginning.

Early childhood education has long been involved in helping at-risk children prepare for success in the formal schooling process. Head Start and other similar programs, for example, were created to meet the needs of young at-risk children.

Particularly during the prekindergarten years, educators are reluctant to classify children as having particular disabilities. Developmental patterns at these early ages vary greatly. Yet, children who have experienced early risk factors often need assistance to develop more normally and avoid later intervention. Either biological or environmental factors can lead to the child being identified as at-risk. Biological risk factors may occur either during pregnancy or after birth. Premature birth, low birth weight, maternal diabetes, and severe illnesses are all biological factors that may place children at-risk in their development.

> *At age 2, Monica got into the cleaning agents under her mom's sink and swallowed samples of several types. After an emergency visit to the hospital for a stomach pump, she has been recovering nicely. Her child care center has been asked to carefully watch for signs of longer-term problems associated with this traumatic event. Monica is considered at-risk for at least the short term.*

Environmental factors play a major role in creating at-risk conditions for children. Poverty, homelessness, child abuse, and poor parenting are all key factors that can cause children to be at-risk in their development.

> *Andrew is 3 years old and has just begun to attend the local Head Start program. His mother is 18, a single parent on welfare who is struggling to get her life together. Andrew's overall development is lagging behind his peers', and he is considered at-risk.*

> *Five-year-old Bonnie has just been placed in temporary foster care. Her parents are suspected of neglect. Bonnie frequently comes to school dirty, unkempt, hungry, and tired. The school staff has been notified, and she is being watched for signs of problems in her overall development.*

Gifted Children. Children who are **gifted** demonstrate excellence in an aspect of development well beyond most children of the same age. For example, Armon taught himself to read at 4, and at age 6, he is reading long chapter books found challenging by many 10- to 12-year-olds. He is enrolled in a gifted program at his elementary school.

Traditionally, IQ tests have been used to identify giftedness, and very high intellectual functioning is seen by many as the true mark of a gifted person. More recently, people such as Howard Gardner (Gardner, 1999) have suggested that intelligence comes in many forms, and high levels of expertise in music, art, sports, and relationships are also evidence of giftedness. Taylor began piano instruction at age 3, and now at 5 is reading and playing classical music for pleasure. Her musical giftedness is obvious to all who listen to her play.

Giftedness is a complex concept that is difficult to define. One popular description follows:

> Gifted and talented children are those identified by professionally qualified persons who, by virtue of outstanding abilities, are capable of high performance. These are children who require differentiated educational programs and services beyond those normally provided by the regular program in order to realize their contribution to self and society. Children capable of high performance include those with demonstrated achievement and/or poten-

Celebrating Diversity . . .
Attention-Deficit/Hyperactivity Disorder

Children who used to be classified as hyperactive are now described as having attention-deficit/hyperactivity disorder (ADHD). Statistics indicate that up to 5 percent of all children under 18 may be affected by this disorder (Wallis, 1994). Boys tend to be diagnosed more often as having ADHD than are girls. For those diagnosed with this disorder, a drug called Ritalin is frequently prescribed by physicians to counteract the problems of this behavior pattern (Dunn, 2002).

Unfortunately, significant side effects are associated with Ritalin, and its overuse is questioned by many. Appetite and sleep disturbances, increased heart rate and blood pressure, and growth retardation have all been associated with Ritalin use. Newer medications with fewer side effects are also available to help children with ADHD. Teachers who recognize and understand the implications of ADHD are better able to meet the needs of these children.

Characteristics of Children with ADHD

- Impulsive (acting without thinking of the consequences)
- Short attention spans (difficulty concentrating on a task or activity)
- Difficulty in organizing thoughts and work
- Easily distracted from the task at hand
- In constant motion (find it hard to sit still and refrain from fidgeting)

Guidance Considerations

- Provide consistent routines in school day.
- Keep children away from distracting noises and active areas.
- Make eye contact while giving clear directions.
- Create a signal that reminds children to get back on task.

1. Have you known someone who has been diagnosed with ADHD? What were some characteristics of this person's behavior? Did he or she take Ritalin?

2. Can you see some problems associated with classifying children with ADHD? What are your concerns? What are the benefits?

tial ability in any of the following areas: (1) general intellectual ability; (2) specific academic aptitude; (3) creative or productive thinking; (4) leadership ability; (5) the visual and performing arts; and (6) psychomotor ability. (Marland, 1972, p. 10)

For more information about gifted education, go to the Companion Website at www.prenhall.com/henniger, select Chapter 4, then choose Web Destinations.

No one list of characteristics describes children who are gifted. Certain traits and abilities, however, do seem to be common to many (Hallahan & Kauffman, 2003). Unusually strong language skills may indicate giftedness. These children frequently have a large and complex vocabulary and are able to use their words to create elaborate oral stories, songs, and rhymes. Early reading and writing are often demonstrated as well.

Strong skills of observation enable gifted children to pay attention to details that allow them to master concepts more quickly. Four-year-old Amy, for example, notices many differences in the colors and body parts of the ladybug caught on the playground this morning. She asks her teacher many questions and is eager to look through the book in the library center that describes bugs.

These children are often more willing to take risks and problem solve as they learn about their world. Curiosity and a willingness to explore the possibilities make these children eager to grow in their understanding of people and things. Eight-year-old Aaron is constructing a castle out of blocks after reading a story about medieval times. He is having difficulty constructing a roof that meets his expectations and tries several possibilities before getting it the way he wants it.

Learning About Children

The task of understanding children and their development is definitely an important one. It is not, however, an easy process. A teacher must study a great deal and consider many factors in learning about children. How, then, does the busy teacher work this task into an already overcrowded life? The answer lies in beginning now and in working hard to become more knowledgeable over time. As you read about and study child development, make careful observations of children, use developmental and health assessments, and work closely with parents, the task becomes more manageable.

Studying Development and Learning

This chapter has provided a brief overview of child development and learning. However, it is merely a beginning point for further study and investigation. You will need to understand the work of each theorist presented and every developmental milestone in more depth in preparation for working with children. Acquiring a thorough understanding of Vygotsky's theory, for example, requires more in-depth reading, study, and discussion with others. Similarly, the concept of attachment is more complex than presented here. Most teacher preparation programs generally require courses in child development and learning, and these are an important component of the learning process for understanding these issues. In addition to this more formal learning process, most teachers continue to refine their knowledge of these topics through advanced readings and discussions with others.

Observation: Tool for Understanding

Another essential avenue for learning about children and their development is to spend time carefully observing them. After reading each chapter, take time to use the **Observing Development** feature at the end of each chapter to further your understanding of child growth and development. This feature prompts you to observe young children, reflect on what you saw, and consider how to apply these new understandings in the early childhood classroom. As you make other observations, look for, and work to understand, the actual behaviors children engage in rather than your interpretations of their behaviors. This time-honored technique can provide the insightful teacher with a great deal of useful information about children individually and collectively (see Chapter 11 for more information on observations). The energy invested in observing students at play and work pays big dividends.

Developmental and Health Assessments

As a teacher of young children, you will be expected to know about and potentially use a variety of developmental and health assessment instruments. Developmental assessment tools help teachers identify children who are either delayed or advanced in some aspect of development when compared to the norm or average for that age. They provide information to teachers, which is very helpful in planning for and teaching young children. Health assessment instruments give teachers and others information about the physical and emotional health of individual students. The topic of assessment is discussed in greater detail in Chapter 11.

Observing Development • Adult–Child Interactions

Choose one of the age groups within early childhood (infants/toddlers, preschoolers, or primary-age children), *observe* **adult-child interactions** using the guidelines provided, *reflect* on what you saw or heard, and *apply* the appropriate strategies listed with the children you observed.

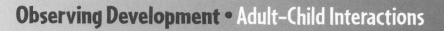

Observe	Reflect	Apply
Look for specific examples of:	*Think about and respond to the following questions:*	*Consider the following developmentally appropriate strategies for the age group you observed:*
What adults say or do as they initiate interactions with children and the responses from children (words spoken, facial expressions, body language, eye contact, physical touch, etc.)	How would you summarize the adult-child interactions initiated by the adults you observed? What do you think were the intended purposes? Were they positive interactions? What makes you feel this way?	Plan positive adult-initiated interactions with children • Infant/toddler: sing and talk to young children while changing a diaper or cleaning up after snack • Preschool: greet each child as he or she enters the classroom at the start of the day • Primary: eat lunch with children periodically
What children say or do as they initiate interactions and the responses from adults (same descriptors as above)	How would you characterize the interactions children had with adults? How many and of what type were child-initiated interactions?	Encourage children to interact with adults • Infant/toddler: get close to the young child, smile, and establish good eye contact • Preschool: sit, kneel, or bend down so that you are at the child's level for good communication • Primary: establish times when you are available to communicate with children on topics they choose

Communicating with Parents

There are many good reasons for working with parents (see Chapter 7). One important purpose is that parents know a great deal about their own children and can often share their insights with interested teachers. Although parents usually are not experts in child development, they have a wealth of knowledge about their own children that is frequently useful in the classroom.

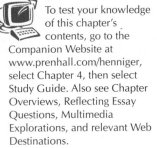

Tenesha's parents meet with you for the fall parent–teacher conference. You learn that this bright, capable 4-year-old has been struggling to get to sleep at night, fearful that there are alligators under her bed. It is clearer why Tenesha has been tearful and easily stressed this past week in child care.

Brian has been diagnosed as having autism and struggles to interact socially with other children in your third-grade classroom. In talking to his parents, you discover that he is gifted musically and that opportunities to express himself on the piano help him engage in more appropriate social behaviors.

With strong parent-teacher relationships, it is possible to learn and use parents' valuable insights regarding their own children's learning and development.

Summary

To test your knowledge of this chapter's contents, go to the Companion Website at www.prenhall.com/henniger, select Chapter 4, then select Study Guide. Also see Chapter Overviews, Reflecting Essay Questions, Multimedia Explorations, and relevant Web Destinations.

The Developmentally Appropriate Classroom

The characteristics of developmentally appropriate practice are a cornerstone of early childhood education. Early educators must understand its dimensions, characteristics, and principles.

Key Perspectives on Learning and Development

Teachers need to understand the theories and concepts of John Bowlby (attachment), Abraham Maslow (hierarchy of needs), Howard Gardner (multiple intelligences), Arnold Gesell (gradients of growth), Maria Montessori (maturationist theory), Lev Vygotsky (sociocultural theory), Erik Erikson (psychosocial theory), Jean Piaget (stages of intellectual development), Jerome Bruner (cognitive development), and Urie Bronfenbrenner (ecological theory).

Children: Developmental Similarities and Differences

An understanding of the developmental characteristics of children from infancy through 8 years of age allows teachers to successfully prepare materials and activities for young children. Children with special needs (disabled, at-risk, and gifted) are an important part of early education; teachers need to understand and prepare for educating these children.

Learning About Children

Academic study, observation, developmental and health assessments, and communication with parents are all important ways of learning about children.

Multimedia Explorations and Activities . . .

Building Brains

The minds of young infants are incredibly capable. Just as a sponge quickly and effortlessly soaks up liquids, the infant's mind takes in a complex array of stimuli and begins to make sense of it. Infants and young children are capable of tremendous intellectual growth over a very short period of time. This great potential for learning during infancy must be taken advantage of by caregivers and their families. Providing very young children with experiences that allow them to "soak up" information from the world around them helps ensure that these young minds can be developed to their fullest potential.

Research

Recent discoveries regarding the human brain support the notion that we should begin at birth to stimulate its development. This activity is designed to help you learn more about this topic and consider its implications.

1. View the ABC News video segments titled "Building Brains" and "First Three Years of Life."

2. Go to the Companion Website at www. prenhall.com/henniger and click on the Multimedia Explorations and Activities button for Chapter 4 and study additional information on this topic.

3. If you know a parent with a child who is 3 years old or younger, interview the parent to see what he/she knows about brain development during the first 3 years of life. Don't probe for technical information, but rather practical examples of what these parents are doing to stimulate brain development. Do you get a sense that the parent is aware of how crucial these beginning years of life are when it comes to brain development?

Reflect

Based on your research, consider the following issues:

- From the information gathered, what did you find most interesting about brain development?
- What aspects of brain development do you think will most directly influence the ways in which you interact with your future students?
- What specific things can professionals do to help all children from birth to age 3 have a stimulating environment that encourages brain development?

Respond

Act on your new knowledge and understandings regarding early brain development by completing one or more of the following activities:

1. Write a letter to the editor of a local newspaper summarizing your findings about brain research. Propose a way that families and/or the community can help children under the age of 3 maximize their brain development. Persuade readers to make a difference in the life of a child.

2. Share the findings of your research and reflection with a parent of a young child. Make sure you don't come across as "preaching," but share your insights as a way to broaden the parent's knowledge and understanding about brain development.

3. Write a letter to your local school board superintendent describing to him/her the importance of this topic and what the school district can do to support early brain development.

4. Contact a child care center or early childhood development center to see if they will allow you to display a poster that informs parents and employees about early brain development. Create a poster that is eye-catching and informative. Keep the print to a minimum—make your point with graphics and key words and phrases. Include specific strategies and daily activities that adults can do with children.

5

PLAY IN CHILDHOOD

In this chapter you will

- Study definitions of childhood play.
- Review theories explaining why children play.
- Reflect on cognitive and social play types.
- Understand the benefits of play to all aspects of the child's development.
- Identify the adult's role in facilitating childhood play.

Your kindergarten children *have just been dismissed for their morning recess. However, rather than heading down to the teacher's lounge today, you spend a few minutes watching your students engage in play just outside your classroom windows. It is amazing how busy they have become. Two minutes ago, they were listening quietly to the story you had chosen, but now the playground supervisor has her hands full. Phillip and John are already rolling around on the grass, enjoying the spring weather and the chance to engage in rough-and-tumble play. Maria and Chelsea are laughing and talking as they swing back and forth with their friends. Charlie and Andy are playing cops and robbers and chasing several girls excitedly around the playground. Joe is new to your class and is currently just observing the actions of others. The sandbox has attracted Albert and Amy, who are planning the castle they intend to build. Eric and Austin are climbing and swinging from the monkey bars, trying to outdo one another. The excitement and enthusiasm are evident. What is less obvious is all the learning that is taking place through the varied play experiences. If only others knew how valuable play can be during childhood, it would be much easier to include it as part of your school day. Just yesterday, a parent was quizzing you about the importance of play in the classroom, and once again you were explaining the many benefits of this natural part of childhood*

Unfortunately, the most common perception of play is that it is a fun but rather frivolous activity. Many parents, the general public, and some teachers and administrators view play as a nice treat for children who have spent time engaged in more serious learning tasks. However, should it be included as an important part of the early childhood curriculum? That is a more difficult task to accomplish. This chapter is designed to provide you with a solid understanding of the benefits of childhood play. It will also help you develop a strong rationale for including play in the early childhood curriculum and clarify others' misconceptions about this important activity. Hopefully, as research continues to identify its many benefits (Fromberg, 2002; Saracho & Spodek, 1998), childhood play will be accepted for its important role in development and learning.

Defining Play

It may be surprising to realize that childhood play is actually a difficult term to define. Garvey (1990) helps us understand the challenges of defining play through the following imaginary dialogue between a mother and her son:

> "Tom, I want to clean this room. Go out and play."
>
> "What do you mean, 'go out and play'?"
>
> "You know what I mean."
>
> "No, I don't."
>
> "Well, just go out and do whatever you do when you're having too much fun to come in to dinner."
>
> "You mean toss the tennis ball against the garage? Finish painting my bike? Practice standing on my head? Tease Andy's sister? Check out the robin eggs?" (p. 2)

The broad category of activities called play also includes a great variety of other behaviors, such as swinging, sliding, running, digging in the dirt, building with blocks, dancing to music, making up nonsense rhyming words, dressing up, and pretending. Because of this variety, no one definition of play can adequately describe its many facets. Understanding and using several different definitions helps you to better understand the complexities of play.

Characteristics of Childhood Play

One approach frequently used to define play is to list common characteristics of these experiences. Four such attributes stand out as essential to our understanding of the term. First, play is *active*. When children play, movement often involves both large and small muscles. Children are using their bodies and manipulating the natural and human-made materials that they find in their play environments. Rather than passively taking in information, children involved in play are engaged in learning about the world by constructing knowledge through active interaction with people and things (Chaille & Silvern, 1996).

For more information about characteristics of play, go to the Companion Website at www.prenhall.com/henniger, select Chapter 5, then choose Web Destinations.

Another characteristic of childhood play is that it is *child selected* (Bredekamp & Copple, 1997). Quality play experiences are those in which the child chooses to participate. Consider, for example, a parent who tells her 6-year-old child to clean her room. For most children, that request to clean something would be met with groans and protests, and it would not be thought of as a playful event. This child, however, could choose to clean her bike in preparation for an upcoming ride and find the task enjoyable and generally playful. When the child chooses the task, it becomes fun and rewarding and is more likely to fit a broad definition of play.

Play is also *process oriented* rather than product oriented (Bruner, 1972). Four-year-old Michael is constructing a road out of blocks. He makes it wide enough for the truck he is using and includes several intersections and curves. Once the road is built and he has used it for his truck play themes, Michael will be ready to dismantle it and move on to other projects. This process orientation gives children in play the freedom to explore and experiment without fear of failure. There is no right or wrong way to play, so children can try a variety of play options,

Into Practice...
Games from Other Cultures

Orlick (1978) suggests that one good way to better understand different cultures is to play childhood games from around the world. Games provide young children with enjoyable ways to indirectly learn about the attitudes, values, and interests of different cultures. The following examples are just two of the many possibilities that early childhood teachers can consider for use in their classrooms.

Pin

This game of cooperation is played by Native American children in Guatemala. A wooden pin is set up at a moderate distance from a throwing line. (The group can decide the length.) The object is for the team to work together to get the first ball that is rolled (lead ball) to touch the pin without knocking the pin over. The first player rolls her ball, and the subsequent team members try to roll their balls so that they nudge the lead ball closer to the pin. The game is won when the lead ball is touching the pin. If the pin is knocked over, the player who knocked it over starts a new game by rolling the first ball (Orlick, 1978, p. 76).

Muk (Silence)

This game comes from the Inuit people in Alaska and centers around laughter. Players begin by sitting in a circle. One player moves into the middle of the circle. She then chooses another player, who must say "Muk" and then remain silent and straight-faced. The person in the middle uses comical expressions and gestures to try to

"break the muk." The player to break the muk is dubbed with a comical name and replaces the person in the middle (Orlick, 1978, p. 81).

Because of the current interest in multicultural education, there are many publications that present options for games from other cultures. Some are excellent activities, while others should not be used with young children. Games chosen for use from other cultures should:

- **De-emphasize competition.** While it is often difficult to eliminate competition entirely, it is important for young children to have games that involve minimal competition. The game *Pin*, described previously, has a competitive element but emphasizes more the need for children to cooperate for a common goal.
- **Be developmentally appropriate.** When games are too advanced for either a child's physical or mental development, they should not be used. For example, *Mancala* is an excellent African board game for use with older primary children but it requires cognitive skills that most preschool children do not possess and should not be used at this age level (Orlick, 1978, p. 78).
- **Be enjoyable.** Clearly, there is little benefit to having children play a game they will not enjoy. It is important for them to laugh, have fun, and be successful with the activities you choose. The game *Muk*, described previously, should meet these criteria for primary children.

knowing that it is the road traveled rather than the destination that is the most important aspect of this activity.

A final characteristic of play is that it usually requires a *suspension of reality*. When children play, they set aside the realities of their world and enjoy activities that are often silly but fun. For example, the child who makes up nonsense rhyming words knows that they are not "real" words, but she still enjoys the process of creating them. Piaget (1962) calls this a *ludic set*. This ludic (or playful) mind-set allows children to suspend their knowledge of reality and engage in activities that are creative, spontaneous, and fun. Children who pretend to be astronauts or characters from their favorite movies are creating a ludic set to engage in this play.

Definitions of Play

 For more information about Froebel on play, go to the Companion Website at www.prenhall.com/henniger, select Chapter 5, then choose Web Destinations.

Other attempts at defining play have been more traditional descriptions of this broad set of activities. Definitions from key historical and modern figures provide additional insights into the complexities of childhood play. Friedrich Froebel, described in Chapter 2 as the father of the modern kindergarten, defines play as "the natural unfolding of the germinal leaves of childhood" (Mitchell & Mason, 1948, p. 103). Although this description gives few specifics, Froebel gives us a beautiful metaphor for childhood play. He characterizes it as an essential and necessary component of childhood. Play is part of the fabric of children's lives and leads to healthy growth and development.

John Dewey suggests that play consists of activities not consciously performed for the sake of any result beyond themselves (Dewey, 1929). When children play, they do so because the process is meaningful to them. The doing of the activity gives it value. The end product, if any, holds little meaning for the child. A child painting at the easel often has a goal in mind as she covers the page with vibrant colors, but the real joy of the activity is just engaging in the painting process itself. Once the painting is completed, she is ready to move on to the next challenge.

Several writers have defined play by contrasting it with work. One such definition comes from Erik Erikson (1963), who suggests:

> When man plays he must intermingle with things and people in a similarly uninvolved and light fashion. He must do something which he has chosen to do without being compelled by urgent interests or impelled by strong passion. He must feel entertained and free of any fear or hope of serious consequences. He is on vacation from social and economic reality—or as is most commonly emphasized: he *does not work*. (p. 212)

Another well-known psychologist, Jerome Bruner (1972), writes the following about childhood play:

> Play appears to serve several centrally important functions. First, it is a means of minimizing the consequences of one's actions and of learning, therefore, in a less risky situation. . . . Second, play provides an excellent opportunity to try combinations of behavior that would, under functional pressure, never be tried. (p. 693)

Play, according to Bruner, can be seen as a prime opportunity for children to take risks without fear of failure. Bruner's definition also suggests that childhood play and creative activity are closely linked. When fear of failure is low and children can explore and experiment in their play, the possibilities for creative outcomes are greatly enhanced. For example, a young girl building with Legos can creatively explore and experiment without fear of failure. There is no right or wrong way to build with these materials.

Russian theorist Lev Vygotsky (1978) provides additional insights into childhood play with his identification of two unique aspects of imaginative play. In pretend play, the child creates an imaginary situation that allows him to:

- *Deal with unreachable wants.* In some instances, he must postpone the satisfying of his desires to a later time (for example, wanting to be strong, tall, and powerful). In other cases, the imaginary situation helps the child realize that some wants will never be met (for example, a child with divorced parents wanting her dad back).

- *Engage in rule-bound behavior.* While play is often viewed as free of rules and direction, Vygotsky proposes that even the simplest of pretend play sequences require the child to engage in behaviors that follow social rules. A child pretending to be a mother, for example, must conform to the rules of maternal behavior in order to maintain the play sequence (Berk, 1994).

Vygotsky views imaginative play as a key to the overall development of the child. Challenging the child to increasingly higher levels of functioning:

> Play creates a zone of proximal development in the child. In play, the child always behaves beyond his average age, above his daily behavior; in play it is as though he were a head taller than himself. As in the focus of a magnifying glass, play contains all developmental tendencies in a condensed form and is itself a major source of development. (Vygotsky, 1978, p. 102)

One final definition of play comes from the work of David Elkind (1981b), who states, "Basically, play is nature's way of dealing with stress for children as well as adults" (p. 197). This perspective may be initially surprising, in part because it does not describe all play behaviors. But for a significant portion of children's activities, stress reduction is an important part of the play experience.

 *Four-year-old Robert's mother is pregnant. Getting ready for a new brother or sister is stressful for him. Mom and dad are busy making preparations, there is less time and energy for the other children, and just making sense of the upcoming changes takes considerable time and energy. Robert's play in the dress-up corner at preschool reflects his attempts to make sense of these changes and work through the stresses of this coming event.*

Children today are faced with a great many stressful situations. Play provides them with many opportunities to understand and work through these stressors.

It is important to emphasize again that none of the definitions presented here is sufficient, in and of itself, to fully explain this complex phenomenon we call play. However, each provides additional insight to help us in our understanding of play. Collectively, they paint a clearer picture of this important concept.

Why Children Play: Theories

Just as there are a variety of definitions of play, many different theories have been proposed to explain why children engage in this activity. Although no one theory is fully satisfying, together they add much to our understanding of a child's motivation to play. Ellis (1973) organizes theories of play into two categories: classical and contemporary. The classical theories are older and generally less complex in their explanations of why children play. Contemporary theories are more recent and provide a detailed rationale for this childhood activity.

Classical Theories

An early explanation for why children play is the **surplus energy theory,** based on the notion that each of us generates a finite level of energy that must be expended. Our first priority is to use that energy on survival. What is left over accumulates

Children of all ages engage in meaningful play.

until it reaches a point where it must be used up. Play becomes the vehicle for expending that extra energy. This theory suggests that children play more than adults because they are not burdened with survival tasks. This theory has considerable appeal. Mothers and fathers often tell their children something like, "You need to go outside and burn off a little of that extra energy." Teachers play games with their children to "get the wiggles out." Many times, children seem to need to use up their surplus energy. Yet, there are other times when children clearly are operating on reserve energy but still very much want to continue in their play.

A second classical explanation of play is the **relaxation theory.** In essence, it is the opposite of the surplus energy theory and suggests that people play because of a deficit of energy. When we engage in tasks that are relatively new to us or that are demanding in some way, fatigue sets in and relaxation is needed to replenish our energy. Because children encounter more new tasks and challenges than adults do, they need to spend more time relaxing in play.

This theory clearly has application for children in the elementary school years. With the many new academic tasks they face, play becomes an important opportunity for rest and recuperation. Recess and indoor play breaks give children much-needed opportunities to get away from work-like experiences and reenergize. At the same time, this theory seems to be less effective in explaining the play of preschool-age children. At this age, children have few work-like tasks from which to escape. New and demanding tasks are generally encountered *in* play during these years.

A final early explanation for play is the **preexercise theory.** Play is seen as an opportunity to practice the skills necessary for adult life. When puppies engage in play fighting, for example, they are practicing survival skills they need in adult life. A young boy who pretends to be a daddy is also developing abilities for his future role as a parent. This theory proposes that through their play children practice dealing with such things as fear, anger, curiosity, assertion, and submission. Although this may provide a rationale for a limited scope of childhood play behaviors, this theory seems less helpful in explaining much of what children do in their play.

Contemporary Theories

A more recent description of why children play is the **psychoanalytic theory** of play. Many have contributed to this perspective, but it is based primarily on the work of Sigmund Freud. He suggests that play is motivated by what he calls the *pleasure principle* (Freud, 1938). Pleasure is achieved, according to Freud, through wish fulfillment in play. When 7-year-old Maya pretends to be an astronaut, she is gaining pleasure by becoming that important person for a short period of time. Play provides an opportunity for children to bend reality and gain gratification.

This theory also suggests that play has significant therapeutic value. When children encounter unpleasant situations or stressful circumstances, play becomes the child's vehicle for mastering them. By playing out mom and dad fighting, 5-year-old Brent can begin to make sense of this unpleasant event and eventually set it aside and move on to other play themes. A specific branch of therapy for children who have experienced severe stress is based on this premise and is called *play therapy* (see, e.g., Axline, 1947). Trained therapists use this approach to help victims of child abuse and other traumatic events come to grips with difficult and complex experiences.

Other theorists have expanded upon Freud's ideas concerning childhood play. One such person is Waelder (1933), who added the concept of the *repetition compulsion.* He identified the almost compulsive way in which many children will repeat an unpleasant experience in their play over and over again. Waelder states that children may find some events too difficult to assimilate all at once. They often need to play it out over and over again, until finally diminishing the intensity of the experience. For example, Brown, Curry, and Tittnich (1971) describe an event in which several kindergarten children observed a man who was critically injured on the street adjacent to their playground. In observations of later play experiences, it was clear to the writers that these children needed to repeat this very unpleasant and difficult event over and over in order to make better sense of it. Throughout the school year, this accident-related play theme reappeared regularly as children worked through their feelings.

Another more recent theory that has been proposed to explain why children play is called **play as arousal seeking.** Ellis (1973) developed this theory from a number of research studies that make a case for a new drive—the drive for optimal arousal. In an attempt to avoid boredom on the one hand and overstimulation on the other, people strive to reach just the right level of excitement. Each of us is engaged in behavior that can be called *stimulus seeking.* Play is a major opportunity for most of us to be stimulated. Not all stimulus seeking, however, is play. When 5-year-old Angie challenges herself to climb one level higher on the climber or 4-year-old Jamal jumps off a three-foot-high box, each is doing a bit of thrill seeking. These behaviors are somewhat risky and therefore more exciting for the children engaged in them. Although this theory again does not explain all types of children's play, it applies readily to many childhood activities.

A final theory about childhood play comes from the work of Piaget (1962). He explains this activity in terms of children's **cognitive structures.** As children learn about the world, they are adding to their *schema* or conceptual understandings. These schema are strengthened through the dual processes of assimilation (taking in information from the environment and fitting it into an already existing schema) and accommodation (adjusting schema to take into account new input from the environment that does not fit existing structures). Piaget suggests that when children play they are engaging primarily in the process of assimilation. As children take in information during play, they are unconsciously growing in their understanding of the world. The "Observing Development" feature at the end of this chapter highlights some aspects of play and cognitive development you might observe in children, reflections on how children interact with play materials, and some specific ways you can enhance these interactions.

Piaget also proposes that the play children engage in is strongly influenced by their intellectual stage of development. For each of his first three stages (see

Into Practice...
A Pretend Grocery Store

When given the time and appropriate materials, young children can have great fun pretending as they play out a theme you have prepared as the classroom teacher. One example of this type of activity is to set up a grocery store in the classroom. The basic ingredients needed are

Grocery bags
Empty food containers such as soup and vegetable cans
    and cereal boxes (use your imagination)
Pictures or posters of food items
Telephone
Assorted baskets
Plastic foods
Play money (coins and paper)
Notepads for making out grocery lists
Sticky notes for pricing groceries

Writing utensils
Cash register
Adding machine
Shelves for storing foods
Checkout table

Although this is just a starting point for collecting materials for this play theme, it should be clear that with some work by the teacher, some very creative play can take place. Children who are provided with these materials can take on the roles of shoppers, grocery checkers, and clerks. Some can price the groceries while others shop for bargains on a budget. As they do so, they are having fun while they practice prereading and writing skills, counting, learning more about money, and interacting with others in a social setting.

Chapter 4), there is a corresponding type of play the child primarily exhibits. For example, Piaget suggests that, during the sensorimotor stage of intellectual development, children engage primarily in functional play. These simple, repetitive muscle movements match the cognitive functioning of the child during the sensorimotor period. Piaget's play stages have been expanded upon by Smilansky (1968) and are described in more detail in the next section of this chapter.

Cognitive Play Types

People who have studied childhood play often categorize it according to either its cognitive or social elements. **Cognitive play** categories identify the intellectual functioning of children during play. **Social play** types describe how children gradually become more able to relate effectively with others as they play.

As suggested earlier, Piaget (1962) developed cognitive play categories that match each of his first three intellectual stages of development. Smilansky (1968) modified this approach slightly by defining a fourth cognitive play category. Her cognitive play stages have been widely accepted as an effective way to understand and study childhood play. From birth to about age 2, children engage in **functional play.** Characterized by simple, repetitive muscle movements, this play develops physical skills and is done because the activity is pleasurable. The toddler who is learning to walk spends considerable time practicing the muscle movements necessary to get from one spot to the next. An infant shaking a rattle is also engaging in functional play. This play type is the predominant one during the first two years, but it does not end at that time. Elementary children swinging on swings or running happily across the playfield are participating in functional play.

Smilansky suggests that children from about 2 to 3 years of age are involved primarily in **construction play.** This play type is characterized by the child actually making something out of the materials available. For example, when using a set of blocks, Alyssa can begin to create simple structures such as towers. The intellectual skills needed for building are a step above those required for functional play. Older children also engage in construction play, but it is the 2-year-old's primary cognitive play type.

When the child enters what Piaget calls the preoperational stage of intellectual development, **dramatic play** becomes the preferred play type. From about age 3 to 7, children pretend that one object is something else or take on a role other than being children. For example, 4-year-old Lisa pretends to be a teacher and imitates what she has seen her preschool teacher do by encouraging her playmates to try new pretend foods in the housekeeping center. She must use considerable intellectual skill to imagine the sequence she plays out with her peers. Research indicates that this play type is crucial as a foundation for later academic learning (Smilansky & Shefatya, 1990) and should be encouraged both at the preschool and early elementary levels.

For more information about dramatic play, go to the Companion Website at www.prenhall.com/henniger, select Chapter 5, then choose Web Destinations.

At approximately 7 years of age, children enter Piaget's stage of concrete operations and begin to engage in **games with rules.** These activities require children to agree to a set of rules before beginning play and accept the defined penalties for breaking the rules. Piaget spent considerable time observing children playing marbles and learned much not only about this particular game with rules but also about children's social and moral development (Piaget, 1965). Although the game of marbles is less common today, other organized games such as basketball and soccer are popular with children of all ages.

Social Play Types

A number of researchers and writers have suggested different categories to describe children's social play. The work of Mildred Parten (1933), however, has stood the test of time as one of the best and most descriptive summaries of the development of children's socialization skills in play. Parten states that, until about two-and-a-half years of age, children engage in **solitary play.** They play alone, with toys that are different from those of children playing nearby. Children at this stage make no attempt to get close to or interact with others. Clearly, the level of social interaction at this point is very low. It is important, however, to realize that, despite its lack of social value, solitary play should be encouraged as a part of the young child's activities. Much of an elementary child's day, for example, is spent in independent seat work. Children who have learned to be comfortable in solitary play are more likely to succeed in working independently.

Parten defined the next social play category as **parallel play.** From about two-and-a-half to three-and-a-half years, children continue to play independently, but now they are among their peers and use toys that are similar to those of the children around them. Just as parallel lines run side by side, children in this play stage play beside, but not with, others. There is an awareness of the children nearby but little interaction. Andre and Kelly are playing with play dough at the art center in their

Celebrating Play . . .
Children's Invented Games

After their second-grade teacher's discussion of the procedures for creating a board game, Rebecca and Latoya decide to give it a try. During free time, they begin the process of planning a board game around the theme of horse racing. For the next week, these girls spend all of their spare moments avidly constructing their game and then sharing it with the rest of the class. Given the opportunity, primary children seem to love the chance to invent their own games. Castle (1990) describes several benefits of this activity:

- **Practice academic skills such as writing, reading, and mathematics.** Children use writing skills, for example, to label game parts and create game instructions.
- **Develop organizational skills like having a plan and putting it to work.** Planning the game sequence requires the use of organizational abilities.

- **Cooperate with other children and adults.** Through the planning and construction process, children must take into account the perspectives of others and learn to adjust their game accordingly.
- **Solve problems as children encounter differing opinions about how the game should proceed.** Once a prototype is constructed, children practice problem solving as they debug the difficulties they encounter when playing.

1. Based on the discussion of cognitive play types on pages 122–123, do you think that this activity would be appropriate for preschool children? Why or why not?

2. Try constructing your own game to discover the challenges this task may require of children. Share your game with others, and then modify it based on the feedback you get.

preschool classroom. They occasionally glance at each other's efforts but spend most of their time just molding their chunks of dough. They are engaging in parallel play.

As children continue to mature, they begin to engage in **associative play** at about three-and-a-half years. This play type is characterized as one in which children truly play with others. Children borrow and loan play materials, and the group members are engaged in similar activities. Parten suggests that, at this point, the associations are more important than the play activity itself. Children begin to form small play groups and spend considerable time moving from one activity to the next, with playmates remaining together. Watch children of this age swinging on swings, for example. They enjoy the swinging but spend more of their efforts talking and laughing with their friends. When a group leader decides it is time to move on, others make the move as well. Being with the other children has become more important than the activity itself.

Parten called the final social play type **cooperative play,** which begins to appear at about four-and-a-half years of age. Parten describes this as the highest level of social play; it is characterized by children playing in groups as they did in associative play. But now, the children demonstrate division of labor, working on a group project or cooperating to attain a common goal. When four kindergarten children decide to build a town with blocks, and each takes a specific part of the town to build, play has become cooperative. It is important to note that although cooperative play requires practicing important social skills, it is not always a desired play type. Think about three preschool children who decide to torment a fellow

In parallel play, children play beside, but not with, others.

classmate. Although each takes on a separate role and the children are working toward a common goal, the play is unpleasant for the targeted child.

While Parten observed preschool-age children, others have studied the social play of older children. Seagoe (1970), for example, identified a social play type for children beginning at about age 7 or 8 that she called **cooperative-competitive play.** It involves activities that are formally patterned toward team victory. Organized team sports such as soccer and baseball are examples of this play type. The social understanding needed for cooperative-competitive play is more advanced than that required for the cooperative play described by Parten.

Benefits of Play

Jay and Aaron are excitedly rummaging through the junk pile used for play outdoors at their preschool. This collection of bricks, boards, old tires, and assorted building materials has them thinking of the many different structures they might construct. There is no thought in their minds of the learning potential of these tasks. These two young boys are merely playing. Yet, mathematics, language usage, social skills, basic physics principles, and more may all be enhanced as they play out their fantasies.

Unfortunately, it takes a thorough educational effort for parents, other teachers, administrators, and the general public to recognize the many benefits of play. Every aspect of the child's development is enhanced through play. It is just not obvious to many people at first glance. Figure 5–1 summarizes the benefits of play.

Figure 5–1 *Benefits of Play*

Intellectual growth

Engage in multisensory experiences.
Have opportunities for problem solving.
Master abstract symbolism.

Build social skills

Learn social roles.
Decrease egocentrism.
Understand the rules of social interaction.

Language and literacy development

Play with language.
Engage in metacommunication.
Engage in pretend communication.

Physical development

Develop gross motor skills.
Develop fine motor skills.
Integrate large and fine muscle movements.
Become aware of body, space, and direction.

Emotional development

Master emotional issues.
Feel good about themselves.

Play and creativity

Have opportunities to be creative.

Intellectual Growth Through Play

Because many people assume that the primary goal of schooling is to feed the intellect, this discussion on the benefits of play begins with information on how play enhances cognitive development. Using Piaget's terminology, *cognitive development* is the process of building more elaborate schema or concepts about the workings of the world. Both Bruner (1966) and Piaget (Piaget & Inhelder, 1969) stress that multisensory experiences with things and people in the child's environment lead to conceptual development. Play provides the most natural and enjoyable opportunities for these experiences and therefore is a major tool that children use to understand their world. When 7-year-olds David and Jessica construct cardboard castles during free choice time, they are internalizing the information they read in their social studies text. Their play has expanded and solidified several existing schema.

The ability to effectively problem solve is a major asset in intellectual development. Children who can make sense of the problems they face and work through them are adding greatly to their understanding of the world and their ability to work through future problems. Evidence points to a clear link between play and problem solving. Children who engage in creative play experiences are better at convergent (Vandenberg, 1980) and divergent (Pepler & Ross, 1981) problem solving. Play frees up children to explore and experiment in ways that lead to important intellectual understanding.

When 4-year-olds Kelly and Sarah play in the dramatic play area, they discover that they do not have the props they need to become pilots. After yesterday's field trip to the airport, they are very excited about this play theme. Kelly discovers a headset from the listening center and decides it can be used "for one of those things pilots listen and talk through." Sarah arranges several child-sized chairs into rows for the passengers. After several minutes of preparation, they have created the basic props they need for their play, and they begin the process of acting out their respective roles.

During play, children encounter and master new problems as well. Play provides many chances for practicing problem solving.

A third major way in which play assists in intellectual development is by help-ing children master abstract symbolism. This is especially true when children en-gage in dramatic play. As they pretend, children arbitrarily assign meaning to objects they are using in their play. A block is temporarily viewed as a door to the castle, child-sized chairs in rows become passenger seating on an airplane, or a magnifying glass becomes "that thing doctors use." Objects become arbitrary, ab-stract symbols for real things needed for dramatic play. Nourot and Van Hoorn (1991) state this same concept as follows: "In its complex forms play is character-ized by the use of symbols to represent objects, ideas, and situations not present in the immediate time and place" (p. 41).

Children who are able to manipulate abstract symbols in their play are more likely to succeed in managing symbols in school. Both reading and mathematics are fundamental components of formal education that require frequent manip-ulation of arbitrary and abstract symbol systems. Smilansky and Shefatya (1990) emphasize that children who are good at dramatic play are going to be more suc-cessful with these and other academic tasks.

Building Social Skills

In addition to its role in cognitive development, play is an important tool for strengthening social skills. As they play, children have many opportunities to learn about the social world in which they live. The give and take that occurs as children interact helps them learn about social roles. Following a trip to the fire station, for example, a group of first graders try out this role in their play outdoors. They are consolidating and integrating their understandings of this important work situation. Piaget describes children in the preoperational stage of intellectual de-velopment (approximately 2 through 7 years of age) as egocentric. By this he means that it is difficult for children this age to see things from another person's perspective. Play provides children with many opportunities to decrease egocen-trism (Piaget, 1962). To maintain a play sequence, children are forced to ac-knowledge other viewpoints and modify or adapt the activity accordingly. For example, Ariel and Reetha are playing train conductors. Ariel is upset because "only boys wear the conductor's hat." Reetha, however, feels that girls can, too. These two will need to recognize their differing perspectives and work our a so-lution to continue the play sequence. Gradually, as children experience a variety of perspectives through their play, egocentrism becomes less of a factor in relat-ing to others.

Play also allows children to understand the rules of social interaction. While playing with others, children learn and practice the principles that underlie all social exchanges (Hughes, 1999). Such tasks as listening, speaking, taking turns, leading, and following are all guided by commonly understood rules. For exam-ple, we all understand that if several people in a group have something to con-tribute to the conversation, only one can speak at a time. To do otherwise would lead to mass confusion. Children learn this and other similar rules for social in-teractions as they become involved in their many play experiences.

 For more information about social development and play, go to the Companion Website at www.prenhall.com/henniger, select Chapter 5, then choose Web Destinations.

Chantel and Marta both want to be teacher as they play during free time in kindergarten. As they realize that it works best to have only one teacher at a time, the girls practice the art of negotiation and compromise so that the play may continue. They learn social rules in a safe and enjoyable way as they proceed.

Into Practice...
Toys for Language Learning

During the preschool and primary years, young children are growing daily in their understanding of language. One thing that teachers can do to help stimulate language learning is to provide a variety of toys that children can use in their play. While virtually every piece of play equipment has the potential to stimulate language learning, some seem to be used most productively by young children. Four examples of this type are:

- **Puppets.** Hand-held puppets are fascinating to many children. As soon as they pick them up, they begin a running dialogue with others as they speak through the puppet. Even many shy children find this an easy way to engage in social communications with others.

- **Telephones.** By their very nature, telephones encourage young children to pretend they are calling and talking to someone else. These conversations with peers and teachers give children many opportunities to speak, listen, and learn more about the rules that govern social interactions.

- **Tape recorders.** Children are often amazed to hear themselves on audiotape. Once instructed on the proper use of a tape recorder, they can enjoy making endless recordings of communications with others.

- **Electronic toys.** Many of the "talking" electronic toys available today (such as those from the LeapPad® company) provide numerous opportunities for young children to hear sounds and words spoken and then practice repeating them in a game-like format.

Language and Literacy Development

Through play, children also enhance oral and written language skills. Garvey (1990) suggests that every aspect of language can be better understood through play. Phonology (sounds of language), grammar, and meaning are all playfully explored as children engage in their free choice activities. Garvey proposes four different types of play with language:

1. *Play with sounds and noises.* Children explore the sounds used to form words and experiment with putting them together in creative and fun ways.

2. *Play with the linguistic system.* In their play, children begin to understand how sounds combine to form words and recognize the structure and ordering of words in sentences.

3. *Spontaneous rhyming and word play.* Through simple rhyming games, children learn about the structure of words and their meanings.

4. *Play with the conventions of speech.* By using and breaking the rules for conversation, children learn how to effectively communicate.

In addition to playing with language, children use language in and around their play experiences. **Metacommunication statements** are used to structure and organize play. "Let's pretend this rope is a snake." "First we'll go to the market, then the toy store." **Pretend communication statements** are appropriate to the roles children have adopted. "Hush, baby! Mom is on the telephone!"

During the preschool and primary school years, children learn about the written language around them as well. Play can provide many opportunities to facilitate literacy development.

"Would you like to come to my house for dinner?" "Yes, that would be loooovvvely."

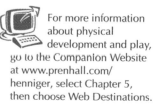 *Cindy and Erik, both age 4, are playing in the restaurant set-up in the dramatic play area at their child care center. Erik takes orders by scribbling on a notepad and passing the orders on to Cindy, who cooks up some imaginary foods. Anook has built a town out of blocks modeled after the story he has just read in his second-grade classroom. Once the town is completed, he writes an imaginary tale describing life in his town.*

When appropriate props are available, play becomes a rich resource for literacy learning (Owocki, 1999).

Physical Development

For many, play is epitomized by children running, climbing, jumping, and moving. The pure joy of these simple physical activities is warmly remembered. Children using their large muscles in these activities are strengthening their **gross motor development** (Gallahue, 1982). Beginning in infancy, children improve neuromuscular coordination through repeated use of their large muscles. Batting at a mobile as an infant, walking during early toddlerhood, running and climbing at the preschool level, and swinging and skipping in the primary years are all examples of how play enhances gross motor development.

Play activities also include use of smaller muscles for a variety of tasks. **Fine motor development** is refined through cutting, lacing, buttoning, painting, and writing experiences in play. Building with Legos, putting together puzzles, sand and water play, woodworking projects, play dough, and dressing dolls are additional examples of play activities that promote fine motor development.

As children mature, they use their muscles in continually more complex ways, integrating large and fine muscle movements with visual perception. Play allows

For more information about physical development and play, go to the Companion Website at www.prenhall.com/ henniger, select Chapter 5, then choose Web Destinations.

frequent practice of these complicated actions. Hitting and catching a ball, jumping rope, playing hopscotch, and using the monkey bars are all examples of these more difficult coordinated movements. In addition, play allows children to develop a better awareness of body, space, and direction. As they move their bodies, children learn about up, down, in, out, over, under, left, right, and more as they climb, swing, crawl, and run. Playing in the gym or outdoors is particularly good for body awareness learning.

Emotional Development

Play is an excellent vehicle for helping children with their emotional (also called *affective*) development (Johnson, Christie, & Yawkey, 1999). In their play, children can master emotional issues such as anxiety, frustration, normal developmental conflicts, traumatic situations, unfamiliar concepts, and overwhelming experiences.

> *Four-year-old Raul just had a very exciting trip to the museum, although his initial experience was a bit overwhelming. Just inside the door to the museum was a huge skeleton of a Tyrannosaurus rex. When his father told Raul that this was once a living animal, he was shocked. How could anything that big ever have lived? During the days and weeks that follow in preschool, Raul plays out his wonderment by making dinosaurs with play dough, drawing dinosaurs, building dinosaur cages with the blocks, and fighting dinosaurs on the playground. It will take him many weeks to play through this interest, but when it is completed, Raul will have mastered a complex emotional issue.*

Another major emotional benefit of play is that it gives children numerous opportunities to feel good about themselves. Because there is no right or wrong way to play, children have successful experiences that positively influence their self-concept.

> *Annette, age 18 months, is playing with a set of nesting blocks in her toddler class, experimenting with building a tower. Although this was not the intended use for this toy, Annette has managed a stack of three blocks—her tallest yet. Her success is evident in the huge smile that seems to fill her whole face. She is feeling good about herself right now.*

Play and Creativity

Sometimes, thoughts of the creative process bring to mind those rare individuals who invent marvelous new products or play a musical instrument better than anyone else. These truly gifted individuals certainly add richness to the lives of those around them. Yet, each of us has creative potential that can be expressed in different and enjoyable ways. Teachers of young children need to look for and nurture this aspect of each child's personality.

During the early years, play provides many opportunities to express and develop a child's creative talents. In free play, children experiment with things and ideas and create new combinations not experienced before. Wasserman (1992) states it this way: "The creation of new ideas does not come from minds trained

Family Partnerships . . .
Encouraging Play at Home

Because of the importance of childhood play, one of your roles as a future teacher of young children is to make sure that, in addition to including play in the classroom, play is encouraged as an option in the home environment as well. Unfortunately, many families are either unaware of play's importance or simply do not provide children with the encouragement they need to get involved in creative play experiences. With the incredibly fast pace of life today for families, many children are not engaging in much creative play at home. There are several steps you can take to help encourage play at home:

- **Share the values of play.** Your first task will be to make sure that parents know how valuable play is in the overall development of children. You will need to share this message repeatedly and in as many different ways as possible so that there is no mistake about its importance.
- **Encourage parents to turn off the television and computer.** In many homes, most of a child's free time is spent watching television and using the computer. While both of these activities have their place, when they take away opportunities for creative childhood play they are being misused.
- **Provide time to play.** Turning off the television and computer are two important ways to provide time for play. In addition, however, the busy nature of family life also makes it difficult for children to engage in this important activity. If valuable structured activities such as swim lessons, dance classes, and music lessons take up most of a child's

free time, there will be few opportunities for creative play experiences. It is important for children to have a balance of structured and unstructured time.
- **Find play partners.** Many of the richest play experiences are ones that occur in small groups. But children today typically do not simply wander outside or next door for some quality play experiences. For a variety of reasons, parents and guardians must now spend time and effort to bring children together for play. While this is an extra commitment on the part of adults, it pays rich dividends for the quality of play experiences for children.
- **Supply play materials.** While they need not cost a great deal of money, families should make sure that creative play materials are available for young children to use at home. For example, collecting some old adult clothes, shoes, jewelry, and hats for dress-up play is a relatively simple and inexpensive option for creative play at home.

1. Think back to your own childhood and the play experiences you remember having at home. What were the things you remembered? Can you see yourself encouraging families to have similar opportunities for their children? Why or why not?

2. Do you think children engage in fewer play experiences at home today than they did 20 or 30 years ago? Do you think it is important to encourage more play at home?

For more information about creativity and play, go to the Companion Website at www.prenhall.com/henniger, select Chapter 5, then choose Web Destinations.

to follow doggedly what is already known. Creation comes from tinkering and playing around, from which new forms emerge" (p. 134).

Goertzel and Goertzel (1962) studied the early years of 400 famous adults and discovered that a common thread for these creative individuals was the opportunity to explore their areas of interest and play with things and ideas. For example, Frank Lloyd Wright was encouraged by his mother from an early age to play with colored papers and cubes of wood. She felt that these play experiences would stimulate his intellectual development.

Clearly, play will not make a creative genius out of every child. However, it does help stimulate each person's creative talents.

Gared is having fun painting in his second-grade classroom. As he deftly strokes paint on the paper, he gains a sense of control over the elements he is working with. Gared feels good about himself and his artwork. When he gets positive feedback from his classmates and the teacher, his pleasure increases even further. Gared's continued success in art will bolster his attitude about school and increase his willingness to try out his skills in other aspects of school life.

Facilitating Childhood Play

Play seems such a natural part of childhood that it is difficult to imagine children needing help with this part of their lives. However, the many hours spent in front of the television, the overscheduling of children's lives, and a reluctance of many parents to let their children go outside and play for safety reasons have all taken their toll on many children's play abilities. In addition, many adults fail to recognize the importance of play in children's lives. Children today often need the help and support of caring adults to engage in quality play experiences.

Preparing the Play Environments

One important role teachers have in facilitating play is to prepare the places where children play. Teachers and administrators need to make materials and

Teachers should change materials in the students' environment regularly so that children have opportunities to play with new materials often.

spaces available for play both indoors and outdoors if quality experiences are to take place there (Johnson, Christie, & Yawkey, 1999). Time and energy must be spent in carefully planning these environments. Materials should change regularly, so that children have opportunities to play with new toys and equipment often. A variety of challenges should be available for the diverse abilities that children bring with them to their play. As a general rule of thumb, there should be at least one-and-a-half play options per child, both indoors and outside. For a class of 25 kindergarten children, this means that between 40 and 50 play options should be available so that each child has a variety of choices.

Creating a Climate for Play

Another important role for the teacher is to create a classroom atmosphere that lets children know that play is valued. One way in which this can be accomplished is to allow plenty of time for play (Ward, 1996). Quality play experiences can seldom be completed in 10 or 15 minutes. A minimum of 30 minutes (more is better) is needed for creative indoor and outdoor play.

> *As Meesha begins her second-grade art project, she first needs a few minutes to see what is available today in the way of materials, time to settle on an idea, and then additional opportunity to do her art activity. Once her project is complete, Meesha needs time to share ideas with others in the art center and clean-up before moving on to the next activity.*

A teacher's responses to children as they play also strongly influence the climate for play. Making encouraging statements to children for sharing, commenting on the positive uses of play materials, and just being nearby to assist as needed all help children know that play is valued. "Philip, thank you for sharing the blocks with Cheri! The two of you are creating some amazing structures!" "Cassandra, I like the way you combined the blue and yellow paints in this part of your picture. It makes an interesting contrast to the rest of your work." A teacher's comments and actions are essential in promoting quality play experiences.

Promote the Importance of Play

Parents and other adults are often unaware of the tremendous potential for learning through play. Particularly in the primary classroom, these skeptics must be helped to understand the rationale for including this activity. When parents and others come to value play, children will have more and better opportunities to spend their time playing.

Wasserman (2000) has written an excellent book that emphasizes the importance of play in the primary grades. She clearly describes how children who engage in creative play experiences are building cognitive and linguistic skills that are invaluable in the schooling process. They are also gaining confidence in their abilities to be creative problem solvers.

Stone (1995) provides additional reasons for promoting play, particularly in the primary grades. In addition, she provides concrete suggestions for becoming an advocate for childhood play. Some of her suggestions include;

For more information about the importance of play, go to the Companion Website at www.prenhall.com/henniger, select Chapter 5, then choose Web Destinations.

- *Understanding the values of play.* This is an important first step for teachers. They need to be clear about the many benefits of play before promoting it with others.

Celebrating Diversity . . .
Engaging All Children in Play

Play can be considered the "universal language" of childhood. All children, regardless of their cultural heritage, gender, ability, and socioeconomic status, engage in play. It is important for you to realize that the similarities in play experiences between diverse groups of children are much greater than the differences. Having said that, here are some important thoughts about the play you will observe among the diverse children you will have in your future classrooms:

- **Culture and play.** There are many games that are very similar across cultures. For example, variants of "hide and seek" games are found in nearly every cultural tradition (Kirchner, 1991). It is important for teachers to emphasize these similarities as they engage children in play activities.
- **Gender and play.** Boys and girls, while engaging in many similar activities, tend to play somewhat differently. Boys are more often engaged in active/aggressive play while girls tend to spend more time in play that develops language and relationships (Fromberg, 2002). Both sexes need to be encouraged to participate in activities that are outside their normal preferences.

- **Disabilities and play.** Children with special needs enjoy play experiences as much as any other child. While disabilities may delay the typical developmental patterns of play, when appropriate activities and materials are provided, quality play experiences result (Frost, Wortham, & Reifel, 2001).
- **Socioeconomic status and play.** Children from low-income families tend to have fewer opportunities for play than their more advantaged peers. Consequently, their play skills are often less well developed (Smilansky & Shefatya, 1990). However, because of the importance of play in children's development, children from low-income families need even more opportunities for creative play.

1. Given the importance of childhood play (see pp. 133–134), should every single child in your future classroom be encouraged to engage in play? Why or why not?

2. Based on what you now know about childhood play, what can you do to encourage all children to participate in meaningful play experiences. Identify two or three specific ideas that you could implement.

- *Posting the values of play prominently in the classroom.* Both children and parents can be visually reminded of the importance of play.

- *Providing evidence of how learning is enhanced through play.* By displaying examples of things children have invented or problems they have solved through play, others can see concrete evidence of the value of play.

- *Sharing good articles on play with others.* Provide articles from experts on the benefits of play to parents on a regular basis. The web site for this chapter lists some good examples of this type of article.

Adult Involvement in Play

Many children experience times when the teacher needs to become more directly involved in play to enrich the experience or move it in a different direction. This is not something the teacher should take on lightly, because an adult's participation can actually undermine the child's creativity, spontaneity, and choices for play. After carefully assessing the need for involvement in play, the teacher should participate at the lowest level possible. Figure 5–2 summarizes several techniques to consider when intervening in children's play.

Figure 5–2 *Adult Interventions in Play*

Parallel playing	Adult plays beside children, using similar materials.
Co-playing	Teacher enters children's play but lets children lead.
Play tutoring	Adult takes brief control of play and gives directions/suggestions.
Artist apprentice	Teacher removes clutter from play environment and adds needed props.
Peacemaker	Adult helps children resolve conflicts.
Guardian of the gate	Teacher works to get new children involved in an ongoing sequence.
Matchmaker	Adult encourages specific children to play together.

Note. Adapted from *Play at the Center of the Curriculum* by J. Van Hoorn, P. Nourot, B. Scales, and K. Alward, 2003 (3rd ed.), Upper Saddle River, NJ: Merrill/Prentice Hall, and *Play and Early Childhood Development* by J. Johnson, J. Christie, and T. Yawkey, 1987, Glenview, IL: Scott Foresman.

Johnson, Christie, and Yawkey (1987) describe three levels of adult involvement in children's play. They call the lowest level of intervention **parallel playing.** When an adult plays beside, but not with, children and uses the same materials as the other participants, she is engaging in parallel play. This play type allows children to see the teacher model positive play behaviors without directly intervening in the children's activities.

 Hermione notices that several toddlers in her program are having difficulty finding productive ways to use the play dough in the art center. She sits down at the table, tears off a piece of dough, and begins to roll it out into long snakes while quietly humming to herself.

The next level of adult involvement is referred to as **co-playing.** In this instance, the teacher actually enters the children's play but allows them to control the activities. By taking on a needed role and, again, modeling appropriate play responses, the adult can subtly influence the direction and complexity of the play.

As Antoine watches the play in the dress-up corner of his kindergarten classroom, he notices that children are struggling with the role of patient at the doctor's office. Walking into the center, he volunteers to be the next patient and helps children see how this person should interact with the doctors and nurses by playing out the role.

The highest level of involvement in play by the teacher is called **play tutoring.** Taken from the work of Sara Smilansky (1968), this form of participation requires the adult to take at least partial control of the play situation. The teacher now gives children directions or suggestions that lead the play into new areas. It is possible to engage in play tutoring while participating in the children's play or to guide them from outside the play sequence. In either instance, the teacher must be sensitive to intervene in such a way that children can learn from the suggestions being made and reinitiate their own leadership of the play events.

✏️ *As Ellen passes by the block center in her third-grade classroom, she notices that Awesta and Carrie are struggling with the castle they are trying to build. She states: "Before you two go any further in your building, perhaps you should review the book you have and then sketch the castle you would like to construct. That may give you the ideas you need to continue your project."*

Van Hoorn, Nourot, Scales, and Alward (2003) suggest additional roles for adults in guiding play. Again, the authors suggest using these strategies with care so that adult direction is kept to a minimum. Their proposed roles include:

- *The artist apprentice.* The adult guides play through the subtle removal of clutter in the physical space and the provision of props needed to continue the theme, much like a set assistant would do for a theatrical production.
- *The peacemaker.* Adults assuming this role help children resolve conflicts over toys and equipment, suggest alternatives when disputes over roles occur, and invent new roles to extend the play.
- *Guardian of the gate.* Teachers can also help children enter an existing play episode. By introducing an accessory that requires a new player or suggesting an additional role, the adult can involve other children without violating the rights of those who initiated the activity.
- *Matchmaker.* Adults may also choose to group players in pairs or small groups to stimulate more involved play sequences. Matching more skilled players with those who need assistance may encourage children to help one another as they play.

It is important to emphasize once again that, ideally, play should be child-initiated and child-directed. Only when the play is faltering should adults intervene. Heidemann and Hewitt (1992) suggest beginning first with the least-intrusive intervention strategies and working toward more active involvement as needed. Figure 5–3 summarizes this approach.

- *Watching and verbally reinforcing* is the least-intrusive intervention. Teachers who simply observe children at play or who verbally reinforce positive play behaviors are intervening at a low level to extend and strengthen play.
- *Informative play statements* give children ideas for strengthening their play without directly asking them to do so. (Example: "Doctors usually work with one patient at a time so they can help each one with their problems.")
- *Leading questions* are somewhat more intrusive since they often require a verbal or physical response by the child. Their intent is to give children ideas for

Figure 5–3 *Level of Adult Intervention in Play*

Least Intrusive				Most Intrusive
Watching and verbally reinforcing	Informative play statements	Leading questions	Play directions	Involvement in play

Observing Development • Play and Cognitive Development

Choose one of the age groups within early childhood (infants/toddlers, preschoolers, or primary-age children), *observe* **play and cognitive development** using the guidelines provided, *reflect* on what you saw and heard, and *apply* the appropriate strategies listed with the children you observed:

Observe	Reflect	Apply
Look for specific examples of:	*Think about and respond to the following questions:*	*Consider the following developmentally appropriate strategies for the age group you observed:*
Materials used in play (toys, equipment, natural materials)	What is the role of toys and equipment in learning new concepts?	Provide play materials that have "built-in" cognitive learnings • Infant/toddler: texture balls that have different textured surfaces for children to explore • Preschool: blocks that are sized proportionally for building number concepts • Primary: plants for measurement and observation
Ways in which children manipulate or use the play materials (shake, explore, construct with materials, etc.)	Were there differences between children in the ways they used play materials?	Intervene when needed to help children play more effectively • Infant/toddler: show a child how to hold a rattle or manipulative toy • Preschool: verbally guide the movements of a child struggling to put a puzzle together • Primary: give child suggestions about equipment to use to complete a desired project
Interactions between children in play (awareness of others, constructing beside, pretending with others, etc.)	How do social interactions in play provide opportunities for cognitive development?	Guide social interactions in play • Infant/toddler: model appropriate play behaviors as you play with child • Preschool: suggest play roles when children are struggling in their interactions • Primary: thoughtfully organize students in small groups for project work

To test your knowledge of this chapter's contents, go to the Companion Website at www.prenhall.com/henniger, select Chapter 5, then select Study Guide. Also see Chapter Overviews, Reflecting Essay Questions, Multimedia Explorations, and relevant Web Destinations.

extending and enriching the play sequence. (Example: "Where will you go when you have finished your grocery shopping?"

- *Play directions* inform children of actions they should take to strengthen their play. (Example: "Phillip, while you are waiting for a turn on a trike, you can be the police officer and tell the cars which way to go.")

- *Involvement in play* is the most intrusive, but may be needed to get children who are struggling with a theme to engage in quality play behaviors.

Summary

Defining Play

The characteristics and definitions of childhood play help clarify the meaning and value of this complex concept. An understanding of theories, both classical and contemporary, adds further insights into why children play.

Why Children Play: Theories

Because of the complexities of childhood play, no one theory can adequately explain its occurrence. Theories are generally classified as either classical (surplus energy, relaxation, preexercise) or contemporary (psychoanalytic, play as arousal seeking, cognitive structures).

Cognitive Play Types

One way to think about childhood play is to consider the cognitive or intellectual functioning that takes place during this activity. The four cognitive play stages of Smilansky describe increasingly complex intellectual activities during play.

Social Play Types

A second way of categorizing play is to look at the level of social interactions that children engage in as they play. Mildred Parten identifies four increasingly complex levels of social interactions in childhood play.

Benefits of Play

Play provides opportunities to enhance all aspects of child development. The intellectual, social, linguistic, physical, and emotional benefits of play define a strong rationale for including play in the early childhood classroom.

Facilitating Childhood Play

The adult's role in facilitating play includes preparing both the indoor and outdoor environments, creating a climate for quality play, and using techniques for constructive adult intervention/involvement.

Multimedia Explorations and Activities . . .

Making Play a Reality for Young Children

This chapter has emphasized the many important benefits of play in the lives of young children. These benefits can only be realized, however, when teachers fully understand the importance of play and carefully prepare the classroom environment with materials and activities that stimulate each child's playful nature. You will need to begin now to search for quality materials and activities that can be productively used by children in their play.

Research

Much has been written about the importance of children's play and how adults can help facilitate this important activity. This exploration is designed to give you more information about the importance of play and introduce methods of getting children involved at home and at school.

1. Go to the Companion Website at www.prenhall.com/henniger and click on the Multimedia Explorations and Activities button for Chapter 5 for further information on this topic.

2. Talk to a teacher of young children about the importance of playful activities and what she or he does to implement them in the classroom.

3. Interview a parent regarding childhood play.

Reflect

- What new information did you discover about the importance of childhood play?

- What exciting play activities did you locate in your search and discussions with others? How would you implement these activities in a classroom for young children?

- Do all teachers and parents value play in the early childhood classroom? How can you convince the "unbelievers" about its importance?

- Are toys and materials critical to the level and complexity of children's play? What are the connections?

Respond

Based on the information you have gathered thus far, consider one or more of the following options:

1. Write a short article for parents about the importance of childhood play. Include some simple play activities that parents could do at home with their children. Work to get the article communicated to a group of parents.

2. Based on your readings, gather materials and prepare an activity for your classmates that demonstrates the importance of childhood play. Do the activity with them and then encourage a critique of the planning, implementation, and value of the activity.

3. Work with classmates to create a play day for children in your community. Use this activity to promote the importance of play in the lives of children.

6

GUIDING YOUNG CHILDREN

In this chapter you will

- Define guidance and differentiate it from discipline.
- Study basic principles of guidance.
- Understand the importance of routines in the early childhood classroom and learn how to deal with them.
- Develop strategies to assist children in understanding and responding to their feelings.
- Identify techniques for guiding social interactions.
- Learn about guiding groups of young children.

Free choice time has just begun in your preschool classroom. Nineteen 4-year-olds are busily engaged in play in the different centers, and things are moving along nicely. Suddenly, you hear Tasha and Ariel arguing over an accessory in the block center. Going over to investigate, you discover that they both want to use the same toy elephant in their separate block-building activities. Just as you finish helping them work through this dilemma, you notice Hector standing near the edge of the manipulative center watching the other children playing there. After bending down and resting a hand on his shoulder, you suggest some play options that you think might help him get involved in the classroom activities. Moments later, Christa is screaming and pounding the floor in the art center. She has accidentally mixed the blue and yellow tempera paints on her easel paper and she is very upset. Christa is so angry that your only option is a brief time-out so that she can get herself back together and continue playing. Group time is next on your schedule, and everything is going well until you mention your new pet cat. Now everyone wants to talk at once, and it takes several minutes to get the discussion back on track. This is proving to be another typical day, with many opportunities to practice your guidance skills.

Although the preceding scenario might sound unusual, it is really a pretty average day in the life of an early childhood teacher. Young children are learning a great deal more than just conceptual knowledge as they grow and develop. The guidance skills needed by teachers of young children are many. These skills do not come naturally to most people and require both understanding and practice. This chapter is designed to help start you on the road to understanding and using these techniques.

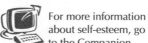

What Is Guidance?

Sometimes, the words you use make a big difference in the message others hear. Think about the words *guidance* and *discipline*, for example. When you hear the word *discipline*, what comes to mind? For most people, it brings thoughts of what you do when children have done something wrong. Guidance, however, often conjures up images of helping and assisting children in their growth and development. Although both words have much in common and in many contexts can be used interchangeably, **guidance** is generally considered a broader concept, incorporating all the adult does or says to influence the behavior of the child (Hildebrand & Hearron, 1999). **Discipline** is an important component of the guidance process in which the adult is dealing with children who misbehave.

Building Self-Esteem

For more information about self-esteem, go to the Companion Website at www.prenhall.com/henniger, select Chapter 6, then choose Web Destinations.

One important aspect of guidance is the process of helping young children strengthen their feelings of self-worth. Kostelnik, Stein, Whiren, and Soderman (2002) identify three dimensions to self-esteem: competence, worth, and control. They define **competence** as the belief that you can accomplish tasks and achieve goals. **Worth** can be viewed as the extent to which you like and value yourself. **Control** is the degree to which people feel they can influence the events around them. In many ways, the development of self-esteem is a lifelong venture. The teacher plays a critical role in the child's early efforts in esteem building.

> *Aretha is new to your preschool program and hesitates when it is her turn to pour juice for snack time. When you encourage her to do so, she can serve herself without spilling. Aretha has added a bit to her sense of competence and will likely continue to expand her horizons as she becomes more involved in preschool activities.*

> *Although Mica struggles with mathematics in your third-grade classroom, you know that he does excellent artwork. You have just complimented him for the clay pot he has made. The ready smile and obvious pleasure he displays help you know that Mica's sense of competence has been enhanced.*

Dealing with Social/Emotional Issues

Learning to relate socially to other people is a difficult and complex task. Children in the early childhood years are constantly struggling with appropriate ways to interact with others (Trawick-Smith, 2003). Teachers must regularly take time to assist children in this important process.

> *As Darla enters the block center in her kindergarten classroom, Mark blurts out, "Go away, Darla! We don't want any girls in the block area!" Clearly, the classroom teacher will need to help Mark develop better ways to communicate with Darla.*

For more information about dealing with social/emotional issues, go to the Companion Website at www.prenhall.com/henniger, select Chapter 6, then choose Web Destinations.

Emotionally, children are also just beginning to make sense of the many different feelings they experience. Children during the early childhood years need help from adults to identify their feelings and then learn appropriate ways in which they can deal with them (Reynolds, 2001).

Two-year-old Randall has just fallen off the climber on the playground, scraped his elbow, and is crying. The classroom teacher sits down, holds Randall, and says, "That must have hurt and scared you when you fell off the climber. It's okay to cry. I'm just going to hold you for a minute before we go in for a bandage."

Adults provide critical guidance when they give children labels for the feelings they see them express and then suggest effective ways for children to manage their emotions.

Growing Toward Independence and Self-Control

Another important goal of the guidance process is to help children make good decisions and interact with others without adult assistance. Good guidance should eventually create within children the ability to guide themselves (Hildebrand & Hearron, 1999). This independence and self-control develop slowly and painfully in most people over a long period of time. Yet, these elements are important to becoming healthy, fully functioning adults. For example, the influence of peers becomes strong during the middle school years. It is essential that we help young children become more independent so that they can resist the negative push to experiment with drugs and other potentially harmful activities that present themselves during these years. We also need children to be able to demonstrate self-control as they manage their anger and frustrations in positive ways rather than resorting to the increasingly more common aggression and violence, which many are using to deal with feelings (Marion, 2003).

Teachers of young children need to create an atmosphere that encourages independence. Sometimes that means stepping back and letting children work things out themselves. It may take longer and be a more difficult task,

Into Practice . . .
Rules for the Classroom

Creating rules for the classroom is an important task that will help establish the atmosphere of the learning environment and assist children in their independence and self-control. Having a short list of clear, positively stated rules that both children and teachers understand and agree with makes the start to the school year more positive. As much as possible, it makes good sense to involve children in the process of making the rules they are to follow.

The following guidelines should be helpful as you develop rules for your classroom:

- Keep your list of rules short. Only four or five broad, clearly stated rules are needed.
- Make your rules positive statements, rather than negative ones. Change "don'ts" to "do" statements.

- Use rules to preserve each child's dignity by being supportive rather than harsh.
- Apply all rules to adults as well as children. Be sure to model appropriate behaviors for students.
- Make sure students understand the rules and your specific expectations for each.
- Identify the consequences for breaking the rules so they are clearly understood by students.

A list of rules for a primary classroom may include:

1. Always do your best.
2. Cooperate with others.
3. Stay on task during work times.
4. Raise your hand to speak during group times.

but when children learn that they can do it on their own, they gain independence (Trawick-Smith, 2003).

> *Armondo and Dee are two members of a cooperative learning group in your second-grade classroom that is working on gathering information on sea life. They have just asked you for assistance in learning about whales, a special interest of yours. It would be easier (and probably more fun) to spend some time helping them with this task, but since you know that they can find this information in the resources you have provided, you direct them to the books and computer software you have in the science center.*

Self-control can also be encouraged in the early childhood classroom. One important way in which teachers do this is by demonstrating their own methods for managing difficult situations (Fields & Boesser, 2002). When the teacher remains calm in dealing with his feelings and shows children constructive ways to express them, he is inviting children to engage in similar activities.

> *Two 4-year-olds in the block area need your assistance. Briana just hit Rory with a block. After placing Briana in time-out and comforting Rory, you return and say, "Briana, I am angry with you right now. You hit Rory with that block and it really hurt him! I'm too angry to discuss it right now, so we will talk about this when the others leave for lunch in five minutes."*

Gradually, with continued verbal guidance and appropriate modeling, children begin to learn appropriate options for self-control.

Principles of Guidance

As indicated earlier, guidance is everything the teacher does or says either directly or indirectly to influence the behavior of the child. Therefore, planning and organizing the physical space in the classroom, the materials available to children, the activities and lessons for learning, and the teacher's verbal instructions and actions are all included under the broad heading of guidance. Here are some basic principles that will help conceptualize and define guidance (see Figure 6–1).

Initial Considerations

Before becoming more specific about what is involved when the teacher engages in guidance, some reminders about children and teachers are needed. First, it is essential to remember that *each child is unique.* Just look around any early childhood classroom, and you can see many of the more obvious differences between children. What may not be quite so clear are the varying responses they have to guidance techniques.

> *Two-year-old Marissa is quite happy to have you take her by the hand and gently lead her to the next play event when she struggles to get involved. Four-year-old Greg, however, is more likely to respond positively when given two options from which he can choose.*

Adding to the complexity of guidance decisions is that *every situation is unique.* Good teachers must have a variety of guidance options available so that they can

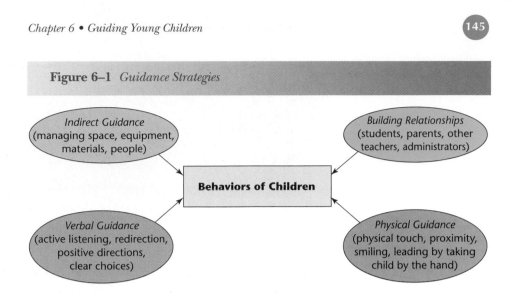

Figure 6–1 *Guidance Strategies*

meet the needs of each child and the unique situations they create in their day-to-day interactions.

> *Today, Talia and Pam are fighting over the paints available at the easel. Because of their relative maturity levels, you decide to remind them that they need to share and ask them to try to work it out themselves. Yesterday, when Craig and Ilyia were having trouble using one of the manipulative toys together, you stepped in and helped them work through their conflict. You decided that they needed your help to work through the issues involved.*

Not only are guidance techniques different because children and situations vary, but it is also important to remember that *every teacher is unique.* There is no one right way to teach and no one ideal teacher. Excellent teachers come with all sorts of different personalities and techniques that work for them.

> *Raelean is a new second-grade teacher who spends many extra hours organizing her class day. By carefully planning her activities, Raelean finds that she is more confident and her students are actively engaged in learning. Mary, however, is more spontaneous and gets really excited about her teaching. She is always coming up with crazy (but fun) ways to get her third-grade students involved in the learning process. Both are highly capable teachers with very different strengths that they bring to their classrooms. It should not be surprising to find that these two teachers tend to use a different mix of guidance strategies as they teach children.*

Indirect Guidance

For more information about indirect guidance, go to the Companion Website at www.prenhall.com/henniger, select Chapter 6, then choose Web Destinations.

Much of what a teacher does to influence children's behaviors is indirect. The behind-the-scenes work and planning help prevent problems in the first place. By managing the space, equipment, materials, and people in the child's environment, teachers can eliminate many potential conflicts. Hildebrand and Hearron (1999) provide several principles of indirect guidance:

• Carefully plan the daily schedule to meet the interests and abilities of the children.

The teacher placed this water table where the contents would not splash other children or surrounding materials and left enough space around the table for student movement.

- Arrange classroom spaces so that there are clues to help children know what to do there (pictures on the wall, pillows for reading, etc.).
- Plan activities and lessons that are varied and exciting to children and that motivate them to learn.
- Arrange activities in an interesting way that invites children to participate.
- Prepare materials so that children can use them safely and with a minimum of adult help.
- Store those materials you do not want children to use out of sight (dangerous materials should be stored outside the classroom).
- Observe children to develop a basic understanding of each child's behavior and needs.
- Talk to parents to gain a deeper understanding of each child and learn ways to effectively relate to them.

Time spent in indirect guidance helps create a smooth-running and pleasant classroom. By reducing the number of misbehaviors, it frees up the teacher for more positive interactions with children. Indirect guidance is well worth the required effort.

Building Relationships

For more information about relationship building, go to the Companion Website at www.prenhall.com/henniger, select Chapter 6, then choose Web Destinations.

An important key to effective guidance and discipline is the relationships teachers establish with students, parents, and other teachers and administrators throughout the school building. Glasser (1990) talks about the importance of building a friendly workplace. If teachers are to create what Glasser calls a quality school, it must begin with the many key relationships that teachers establish

Family Partnerships...
Building Relationships Through Potluck Socials

An enjoyable strategy used by many teachers of young children to build relationships with families is the potluck social. As the name implies, this event centers around a meal or dessert time and is designed to bring families and teachers together for good food and provides an opportunity for getting to know one another. When sharing a communal meal is combined with strategies for helping adults get to know each other better, stronger relationships are created. Here is an example of a plan for a successful evening potluck social:

5:00–6:00	Set up for social (tables, chairs, plates and eating utensils, napkins, coffee, etc.)
6:00–6:30	Families arrive (teacher greets, name tags, etc.)
6:30–7:00	Potluck meal
7:00–7:15	Children are dismissed to play area (gym or playroom for playtime with adult supervision)
7:15–7:45	Getting acquainted activity (adults find someone they do not know, interview that person using questions provided by the teacher, and then introduce this person to the large group)
7:45–8:00	Families pick up children and leave for home

1. Have you and your family participated in potluck socials as part of your schooling experiences? If so, what did you like and not like about these events?

2. Do you think potluck socials are a good investment of time and energy? Are they useful in building teacher/family relationships?

with others. Student-teacher interactions head the list in terms of importance. Teachers who want to succeed in guiding their students must establish strong working relations with their students. This can be accomplished in part through the positive interactions with children that teachers have throughout the school day. A pat on the back for a job well done, an engaging smile when greeting each child in the morning, and words of encouragement are all examples of relationship-building interactions. Sometimes, however, it is important to plan contrived situations to get better acquainted with students. Name-game activities at the start of the school year to get better acquainted with students are examples of this type of interaction.

Establishing quality relationships with parents is also important to good guidance in the early childhood classroom (Hildebrand & Hearron, 1999). When parents know the teacher and support the activities occurring in the classroom at home, children develop a stronger sense of the importance of education. This helps make guidance easier to implement in the classroom. Good communication is the key to strong home-school relationships and is thoroughly described in the next chapter.

When an entire school works to create an atmosphere of cooperation and support as a staff, children once again benefit (Glasser, 1990). When the school has created a friendly workplace, students are much more likely to want to be there. Children who are motivated to be in school and learn are less likely to create discipline problems for teachers. Furthermore, when problems do occur, the school staff can work together to address the issues and help children move forward in positive directions.

Physically Guiding Children

Teachers at all levels are becoming much more cautious about touching children in their classrooms. Many are avoiding physical contact entirely, even at the preschool level (Lewis, 1994). From one perspective, it is understandable why teachers are taking this stance; they are scared. The threat of lawsuits and possible job loss are strong deterrents. Despite these complications, however, and despite all that has been written recently about the inappropriate ways in which teachers and other adults touch young children, it is important to use good touch as a guidance strategy. What better way is there to let children know that we care about them and want to help them deal with the many problems they face? One expert writes:

> A scraped knee, a bruised ego, or a lost lunch box each brings on the same reaction: a fountain of tears. And even though the school nurse doles out bandages liberally and kindly, the act of healing is seldom complete without an additional "it'll be all right" kind of hug. Nothing kinky. Nothing amorous. Just a quick, reassuring connection that indicates our link as two human beings, one who needs comfort and another who is willing to give it. (Delisle, 1994, p. 33)

Physically guiding young children involves much more than the important hug. It also includes such things as being close to a child who is struggling to stay on task. Physical proximity of the teacher often calms and redirects children to more positive behaviors. Gesturing and body language are other aspects of physical guidance. We send children many messages about what we expect when we smile, raise an eyebrow, or point with a finger. Taking them by the hand and leading them to a more positive activity is an effective strategy for many children. Physically turning a child gently at the shoulders and redirecting him toward a desired activity also work well during the early childhood years.

Teachers and children vary in their comfort levels with physical touch. Not every adult wants to hold children close in an embrace or encourages children to sit on his lap. However, a gentle pat on the shoulder, "high fives," and handshakes all communicate to children that we care. Children also differ in their need for touch. Teachers must be sensitive to these variances and respond accordingly.

Verbal Guidance Strategies

Verbal communication is a major element of child guidance. The words we use as adults strongly influence the behaviors of young children. An excellent beginning for effective verbal communication is the ability of the adult to be a good listener. **Active listening** is a technique that helps the adult be more effective in the communication process (Reynolds, 2001). The teacher begins by being open and approachable and listens carefully to what the child is saying and doing. Then, in his own words, the teacher repeats back what he has heard the child say. "Damion, it sounds like you are mad at Ian because he took the truck you wanted to use." When the teacher uses active listening, he lets children know he is trying hard to help them identify the feelings they have and respond to those emotions in appropriate ways.

Another form of verbal guidance is called **redirection.** Two-year-old Andrew is fascinated by climbing and is preparing to move from his chair to the nearby table. His teacher, knowing Andrew's love of books, takes him by the hand and says, "Andrew, let's go find a book to read." Marion (2003) suggests that for the youngest children, redirection becomes a way to divert or distract the child from an undesirable behavior into a more appropriate activity. For older children, teachers can verbalize a substitute for the problem behavior. "Rachelle, you will need to get your own blocks from the shelf. Martin is using those."

When teachers initiate verbal messages, they should use positive directions, telling the child what to do, rather than what *not* to do (Miller, 2004). When an adult says "Don't jump off the table!" it is almost as if the child does not hear the "don't" and is further encouraged to engage in the inappropriate behavior. In addition, *don't* statements fail to tell the child what it is you would rather have him do. The statement "Climb down off the table, please" clearly identifies what it is you expect and makes it easier for most children to comply.

For more information about developmentally appropriate guidance, go to the Companion Website at www.prenhall.com/henniger, select Chapter 6, then choose Web Destinations.

Teachers can also strengthen verbal communication by making it clear when children have choices (Marion, 2003). Many times, choices are appropriate and useful to children in developing independence and decision-making skills. "Gary, would you like to use the computer now that Carla has finished, or are you interested in continuing with your math project?" Other times, however, adults inadvertently give children choices when they really do not mean to do so. Young children think more literally than adults do, so when they hear phrases like, "Would you like to sit down now for group time?" they may well assume that you have given them a choice. Another common problem many teachers have is ending their statements with "okay?" "Philip, it's clean-up time now, *okay?*" Without meaning to do so, adults have given children an implied choice by the words they have used. Hildebrand and Hearron (1999) give additional suggestions for making verbal guidance more effective with young children:

- Get down on the child's level and speak quietly and directly as you make eye contact.
- Place the action part of your guidance statement at the beginning ("Hold tight, or you might fall out of the swing").
- Give directions at the time and place you want behavior to occur.
- Give logical and accurate reasons for your requests.
- Keep competition to a minimum in your verbal guidance.

Discipline Strategies

Despite the best intentions of the teacher to prevent problems from occurring, children will still engage in behaviors that require some form of discipline. Teachers can use a variety of strategies to deal with these issues as they arise. The appropriate option depends not only on the situation and children involved but also on the teacher's personality. Knowing about, and being able to effectively use, several discipline options allows the creative teacher to make good choices in many different situations. Figure 6–2 summarizes the discipline techniques described next. In addition, the "Observing Development" feature at the end of this chapter considers child misbehaviors you might observe, reflections on the causes of these incidents, and some methods that can be applied to reduce those misbehaviors.

Figure 6–2 *Discipline Options*

I-message	I, followed by feelings experienced by the adult, ending with what behavior caused the feelings
Natural consequences	A naturally occurring result of the child's behavior
Logical consequences	The teacher establishes a consequence that has a logical link to the child's behavior
Positive reinforcement	Anything that follows a behavior and increases the likelihood it will occur again
Punishment	Anything that follows a behavior and decreases the likelihood it will occur again
Ignoring	Avoiding verbal and nonverbal responses to attention-seeking behavior
Problem solving	Using techniques of counseling, the teacher and student work together to resolve difficulties

One strategy recommended by Thomas Gordon (1974) is to use what he calls an *I-message*. This communication statement includes the personal pronoun *I*, the feelings experienced by the adult, and the actions that caused those feelings. The *I-message* itself is frequently followed by a brief explanation from the adult to help explain why the feelings are important.

> *Kelsey has just come in late from recess for the second time this week and you decide to use an I-message. "Kelsey, I get frustrated when you come in late from recess. You distract the rest of the class and miss many of my directions for the next lesson."*

Rather than criticizing a child for an undesirable behavior, an I-message identifies the feelings of the teacher and helps the child see how his behavior influences others. If the relationship between teacher and student is strong, many children will voluntarily change their behavior and act more responsibly in the classroom.

Dreikurs, Grunwald, and Pepper (1982) propose the use of natural and logical consequences as an effective discipline strategy. Both options make a clear link between the child's inappropriate behavior and the consequence for that activity. With natural consequences, the teacher simply lets the inherent outcomes for certain actions take place.

> *On a cool, fall day, you remind your kindergarten children to put on their coats before heading out to the playground for recess. Larissa hears your reminder but decides to ignore it. After discussing the situation with her individually, you allow her to experience the natural consequence of going outdoors for a few minutes without her coat—she is cold.*

A major drawback to natural consequences is that many times they either do not occur or are potentially dangerous to the child. In those instances, a logical

Celebrating Play . . .
Noise and Messiness:
Part of the Play?

It is choice time in your second-grade classroom, and Mrs. Hanson, your elementary school principal, has just walked in the door. Children are actively engaged in creative play in the three centers you have set up, but the noise level is rather high. Matt, Carolee, and Arlene are busy talking and constructing a southern plantation based on their social studies unit. Norm, Sandy, Molly, and Kareena are animatedly discussing their play options in the art center. Several others are engaged in productive but noisy tasks throughout the room. You can tell that Mrs. Hanson is distracted by the sounds of busy players. She is probably wondering, "Is all this noise really necessary?"

Hakeem and Albert have just asked your permission as their preschool teacher to get a bucket of water and make mud pies in the sandbox. It is a beautiful spring day and you have just consented. But now you are beginning to wonder about your decision. Both children are having a great time but are covered from head to foot with wet sand. You are very hopeful that no parents drop by before you can get the boys cleaned up. It always seems to be a

challenge to keep children from getting too messy when they are involved in creative play experiences.

These are not isolated incidents but are fairly typical of many play situations. Noise and mess do seem to be a normal part of children's play. That does not mean, however, that there are no limits. Noise levels can become too high, and children may need to be reminded of appropriate voices for play indoors and out. A certain amount of messiness is also typical of most play. Creative art projects, block structures in progress, and manipulatives being used all create a cluttered environment. Children learn rather quickly, however, that at the end of a play sequence, things can and should be picked up before they begin the next activity. The mess from play should be temporary and manageable.

1. What could you say to Mrs. Hanson to help her understand the need for some noise as children play?

2. How do you feel about noise and messiness? Do you think your attitudes may influence children's play activities?

consequence is needed. The teacher establishes the consequence and makes a logical link between the child's behavior and the resulting discipline strategy. For example, if Karma runs down the hallway as students go to music class, a logical consequence would be to have her start over and walk down the hall at the teacher's side. If possible, it is best to discuss these consequences before they are implemented with a child. Furthermore, stating logical consequences in a choice format helps students make stronger connections between their behavior and its results. In discussing Karma's behavior with her before the next music class, the teacher could say, "Karma, you need to walk down the hallway to music or you can walk next to me. You choose."

Many educators use a group of discipline strategies referred to as **behavior modification.** Based on the theoretical perspectives of behaviorists such as B. F. Skinner (1974), three basic techniques are associated with this approach (Kameenui & Darch, 1995). These are positive reinforcement, punishment, and ignoring.

Positive reinforcement is anything that follows a behavior and increases the likelihood that it will occur in the future. Smiles, high fives, and positive comments are all considered positive reinforcers for children when they increase behaviors that precede them. Sometimes, things that adults would normally consider negative interactions may actually be reinforcing to some children. A stern verbal response by the teacher may be reinforcing to certain children who really need to get any kind of attention from adults. However, a typically reinforcing action like a pat on the back may not be viewed as such by some children. Carefully watching the child's reactions to our interactions will help us know whether or not they are reinforcing.

Punishment is another strategy associated with behavior modification and is defined as any event or action that follows a behavior and decreases the likelihood that the behavior will occur again. A common punishment used by many early educators is **restitution** (Kameenui & Darch, 1995). When a child engages in an inappropriate behavior, the teacher insists that the child engage in activities that correct or "make up for" the problem.

> *Angie is an active first-grade student who tends to write on her desk instead of doing her project work during small group time. As her teacher, you notice that Angie is daydreaming and scribbling with her pen while others in the group are working to complete their portions of a long-term project. You immediately take Angie aside and tell her that she needs to go into the bathroom, get some paper towels and soap, and clean her desk. She is making restitution for a problem behavior.*

Some forms of punishment are widely viewed by early childhood experts as inappropriate in working with young children. Most agree that corporal punishment (spanking) is harmful to teacher–student relationships and creates a classroom atmosphere of fear and anxiety (Paintal, 1999). Although spanking is a traditional approach in some homes, early childhood educators should never resort to corporal punishment in disciplining children. Humiliation and intimidation are two other punishments that are extremely harmful to relationships and self-esteem. They, too, have no place in the early childhood classroom.

The third strategy typically associated with behavior modification is **ignoring.** Many times when children misbehave, they are seeking attention from adults. The class clown is typically engaging in attention-seeking behavior. Ignoring can be a powerful strategy if the teacher can refrain from giving any verbal or nonverbal feedback for the inappropriate behavior. When both adults and children can consistently ignore attention-getting behaviors that are not too disruptive to the rest of the class, these children rather quickly learn that what worked in the past is no longer effective.

Another set of discipline options available to teachers is often referred to as **problem-solving strategies.** These are very different from the behavior modification techniques just described. Rather than being initiated and directed by the teacher, the problem-solving approach is a cooperative effort that engages both the student and teacher in working through the issues of concern together. Similar problem-solving approaches are presented by both Glasser (1969) and Gordon (1974). The basic approach used in problem solving is to work with children much as a counselor interacts with his clients. Built on a strong foundation of good communication and positive relationships, the teacher and student

- Work together to identify the problem behavior.
- Discuss the implications of the behavior.

For more information about discipline strategies, go to the Companion Website at www.prenhall.com/henniger, select Chapter 6, then choose Web Destinations.

Into Practice...
Guidance Using Problem Solving

Problem-solving strategies can be effectively used either for issues related to individual children or problem behaviors that impact the whole class. In either case, it is important to spend time planning the problem-solving meeting and then spend a portion of the school day to work through the steps outlined on pages 152–153. The following example of an individual problem-solving meeting should help you understand both the challenges and benefits of this guidance technique:

> *Habib, one of Chelsea Evan's second-grade students, is what many people would call a "class clown." He regularly engages in silly actions to bring attention to himself. Yesterday, he "accidentally" tipped over his chair and fell noisily to the floor. Today, during quiet reading time, he burped loudly and then laughed self-consciously, causing several other children to giggle and disrupting the concentration of others. Having tried several other simpler strategies, Chelsea decides to hold a problem-solving meeting with Habib. After asking the class to return to their reading, she walks over and quietly asks Habib to stay in from recess for a few minutes so that they can discuss his behavior. The following dialogue highlights the key points of this meeting:*

Teacher: Habib, I want you to know that I really enjoy having you in my class. You are smart, contribute to class discussions, and are fun to be around. But there are times when the things you do disrupt the class. Can you tell me what you did earlier today that was disruptive?

Habib: Yeah, I burped and then laughed.

Teacher: Right, and do you know why that was a problem?

Habib: I guess it made it hard for the rest of the class to keep on reading.

Teacher: Yes, that's it. I've been thinking about why you do things like tip over your chair and burp during quiet time and I think you're trying to do things so that others will notice you and like you. And even though everyone wants to be noticed and liked, it should not get in the way of others learning. We need to think of some better ways for you to get some attention from the class. One thing I thought of was for you to spend a few minutes during group time sharing something you like to do. Is that something you would like to try?

Habib: Well . . . I guess so. But what would I share?

Teacher: I heard you talking recently about your baseball card collection. Would you be interested in telling us about it?

Habib: That would be cool! I have a collection that my brother gave me and I've added to it. That would be fun.

Teacher: Okay, let's plan to have you share at group time on Thursday. We'll start with that and then talk again next week to see if there are other things we should do.

- Brainstorm possible solutions.
- Agree on a plan.
- Check periodically to make sure the plan is working.

The process is relatively time-consuming and requires a private space and time to work through the issues, so teachers should reserve this technique for more problematic behaviors that cannot be resolved in other ways.

Guiding Routines

During the early childhood years, children's routines are an important part of their daily experiences. As they move through the school day, they encounter a variety of regularized events that often require adult assistance to successfully manage. When these components of the day are consistently managed and children know what to expect, they are more comfortable and relaxed in school (Hildebrand & Hearron, 1999).

Arrival and Departure

The beginning and end of the day are important times for children. Teachers need to plan for these times carefully to reduce problems during these transitions. For many children in the infant/toddler and preschool years, leaving the security of their parents for the school setting can be a frightening experience. Greeting children at the door and guiding the less secure ones through a consistent routine help make the arrival time more positive. Even with older children, a consistent beginning to the school day helps ensure a productive start to the day. Similarly, at the end of the day, it is important to take time routinely to summarize what has taken place in the classroom and bring closure to the many things children have accomplished in a predictable and recognizable way. Helping children leave with a good feeling about the day also increases the chances for beginning the next class session on a positive note.

Transitions

At first glance, the times between the activities of the school day may seem unimportant. Often, however, they can be a prime time for problem behaviors if teachers fail to plan for them. Children need clear directions and procedures for transitioning from one event to the next. Think about a group of kindergarten children getting ready to move from group time to recess. If the classroom teacher were to say, "Okay, children, recess is next. Go get ready," children would likely respond in a variety of ways, many of which may be problematic. Several might head to the bathroom at the same time, making for crowded conditions there. Others could line up for a drink, while yet another group could head to their tables to finish up an art project before moving to the coat area. If expectations are not clearly explained, these transition times can be very confusing and frustrating to both children and adults. Good teachers know what they want children to do at transition times and clearly describe their expectations.

Snack/Meal Time

Another important routine that requires clear adult guidance is snack/meal time. For the infant/toddler, eating is a frequent and essential part of the day. Caregivers must work carefully with parents to understand each child's eating schedule, food preferences, and routines. In addition to regular meal times, preschool and primary children need a nutritious snack both midmorning and midafternoon to ensure high energy levels and involvement in classroom activities. Whether these snacks are prepared by school staff or brought from home, children need clear expectations for how snack time is to proceed. Should children sit together in small groups and visit with peers and an adult? Or do students

Teachers must make sure children understand what behavior is expected of them at snack time.

pick up a snack, return to their desks, and continue working? What are the expectations for children serving themselves and cleaning up afterward? The teacher must address and the children must understand all these issues (and more) to have a consistently pleasant snack time. Snack time should foster independent student behavior and create a relaxed atmosphere for eating and visiting with others.

Toileting

For the youngest children, toileting in the early childhood classroom means diaper changing. Until approximately 2 years of age, most children have not developed the bladder and bowel control to use a toilet. Adult caregivers at the infant/toddler level must simply accept this aspect of young children as normal and natural and work to make these times as pleasant as possible. Talking, singing, and playing games as diapers get changed help make this time more interesting and enjoyable for all. As children begin the toilet-training process, teachers must work carefully with parents to consistently use similar toileting procedures and communicate about issues and problems as they arise. Well after toilet training has ended, some children will occasionally have accidents. How the teacher reacts to these situations will make a big difference in how the child feels about himself. A casual, calm approach will help minimize the embarrassment the child will likely feel.

Rest Times

The younger the child, the more significant the rest-time routine is in the child's life. Infants and toddlers need frequent nap times throughout the day. Each child will be different, with routines learned at home and differing sleep needs. Consistent communication with parents helps make this routine more successful with the youngest children. During the preschool years, rest/nap times are usually found only in full-day programs and occur in the early afternoon. Generally, it is best to have all children spend some quiet time on a mat or cot. During this time, some will actually nap while others rest. Caregivers must work hard to create an atmosphere in which sleep is possible for those who need it and rest time is pleasant for the rest. Back rubs, soft singing, reading a book, and quiet conversations all may help children during this time.

Dealing with Feelings and Emotions

Throughout the early childhood years, children are beginning the lifelong process of recognizing and appropriately responding to their feelings. This difficult, yet extremely important, task requires insightful interventions by the adult. By helping children recognize and deal with their feelings, the caregiver is laying the groundwork for mature coping mechanisms in adulthood. Opportunities to deal with feelings come up regularly, as Furman (1995) indicates in the following example: Two policemen arrive at the door of a preschool lunchroom with a 4- or 5-year-old boy in tow. The officers had found the child wandering around near the school and had assumed he belonged there. After being told that he did not, the policemen went on their way, leaving behind many young children who had mixed emotions about this event. Rather than ignore this experience, teachers then spent time discussing children's concerns, making the visit a learning opportunity for them.

Accept Feelings as Valid

An important starting point in guiding children through the emotions they experience is to help them realize that feelings themselves are valid responses to life situations (Miller, 2004). A preschool child who is saddened by his father's departure at the beginning of the school day is not going to be helped by an adult attempting to talk him out of those feelings. Feelings are just that—feelings. They are neither right nor wrong, good nor bad. Feelings simply exist. Helping children recognize this important concept makes it easier to deal with feelings.

> *Seven-year-old Ingrid has just described to you through her tears the anger and frustration she feels because of an incident on the playground. Two of her friends have decided to exclude her from their play activities because of a perceived slight. Ingrid is angry and hurt. Your response as her classroom teacher could begin with some variation of the following: "Ingrid, I can understand your feelings of anger right now. It hurts when others treat you that way."*

Be Calm and Direct

In many circumstances, emotions lead to turmoil. In childhood, that may mean such responses as tears, hitting, or screaming. Whether those reactions are directed toward the adult, other children, or are merely expressed, it is helpful for the teacher to remain calm and deal with these emotional responses as directly and simply as possible (Fields & Boesser, 2002). When the adult is calm, the child is more likely to regain control and begin to work through his emotions. Body language, words spoken, and tone of voice all contribute to an appropriate adult re-

For more information about dealing with temper tantrums, go to the Companion Website at www.prenhall.com/henniger, select Chapter 6, then choose Web Destinations.

Informal conversations provide opportunities for teachers to assist children in dealing with feelings.

sponse to children's emotional outbursts. Even when the child does not initially express a problem behavior, a calm demeanor will help ensure a better resolution to the feelings being experienced.

Help Child Verbalize Emotions

Although children experience emotions from a very early age, it takes considerable practice for them to identify and label these elusive feelings (Furman, 1995). For younger children, the basic feelings of sadness, fear, anger, excitement, and happiness need to be given names by caring adults.

> *Four-year-old Latoya is smiling broadly as you discuss the upcoming field trip at group time. "Latoya, your face is telling me that you are excited about going on the field trip to the farm this afternoon!" By giving her feeling a name and describing what you are observing, you are helping Latoya to gain experience in identifying her feelings.*

Older children continue to benefit from this assistance, when adults verbalize the emotions children experience. Those children who have succeeded in identifying the more basic feelings can be assisted in identifying more subtle emotions such as loneliness, annoyance, and worry. This verbalization process is an important beginning point for eventual mastery and control of feelings.

Suggest Alternatives

Inappropriate responses to negative emotions are common in childhood. It is easier and perhaps more natural to strike out either physically or verbally rather than

Celebrating Diversity . . .
Non-English-Speaking Children and Their Families

The United States is currently experiencing the largest influx of immigrants since the early 1900s (Olson, 2000). With this increase comes a growing diversity in the languages spoken by children and their families. Spanish, Chinese, Tagalog (Filipino), Korean, Vietnamese, Arabic, Hindi, and Russian are among the most common non-English languages being spoken (Banks, 2002). Data from the U.S. Census Bureau (2000) indicate that nearly one in five families speaks a language other than English in the home and that most of the children in these settings have limited English proficiency. This means that as a future teacher of young children it is highly likely that you will be working with children and families who speak languages other than English at home.

While working with non-English-speaking children and their families will have its challenges, it is also a rich learning opportunity for all. For example, non-English-speaking children bring a wealth of cultural traditions that make exciting learning experiences. The similarities and differences in foods, holidays, and clothing across cultures are better understood by children when they can talk to families that have lived in other countries. In addition, learning some simple words and phrases in the native languages of students in the class can create opportunities for meaningful learning experiences.

Not only do students learn and grow from having non-English-speaking students in the classroom, but you as the classroom teacher can also benefit. As you interact with children and their families, you will learn about the diverse life experiences these families have had and increase your understanding of different cultures. For example, hearing about the general level of poverty in India from an immigrant family would broaden your comprehension of worldwide hunger and bring to life the challenges of trying to address this issue in a way that would be difficult to do in any other setting. The potential for personal growth as a teacher is greatly enhanced by working with non-English-speaking immigrant families.

1. In the community or region in which you are currently living, are there fairly large populations of non-English-speaking families? What do you know about the culture and language of these families? How can you learn more?

2. Do you see working with non-English-speaking families as an opportunity for growth or as an added burden as a future teacher? Why do you feel the way you do?

work through these feelings in a more mature way. Children need considerable help and practice in dealing with their emotions. In addition to serving as models for appropriate responses, teachers need to give children concrete suggestions for dealing with feelings (Hildebrand & Hearron, 1999).

Two-year-old Meesha has just taken a toy truck away from Ben and caused him to cry. You suggest, "Meesha, I know you wanted that truck, but Ben was playing with it. When you want something Ben is using, you need to ask him for it." Most children will need many reminders from caring adults before they begin to understand that there are better ways to get what they want.

As children get older, the teacher may try to get students more involved in this process of selecting appropriate alternatives for dealing with feelings. Rather than making a direct suggestion, the adult may ask the student for his ideas (Gordon, 1974).

Eduardo has just called his third-grade friend Allen a "geek" for not wanting to work together on a writing project. Allen's feelings are hurt, and Eduardo is mad at him. You respond to Eduardo, "Allen was hurt when you called him a 'geek.' Can you think of a better way to tell him that you are mad because he did not want to work on the writing project with you?"

Of course, it may still be necessary to help children at this age select appropriate strategies for dealing with their feelings.

Guiding Social Interactions

Throughout the early childhood years, children learn to relate socially to one another and to adults. Becoming social beings is a complex process that also requires considerable adult guidance for success. Good teachers make strong relationships a high priority for their early childhood classrooms.

Goals for positive social interactions include:

- Showing sympathy and kindness
- Demonstrating helping
- Accepting food or toys
- Engaging in sharing
- Showing positive verbal and physical interactions
- Comforting others in distress
- Exhibiting concern
- Taking the perspective of others
- Demonstrating affection (Wittmer & Honig, 1994)

Teachers can use many strategies to help facilitate these goals. While it takes time and energy to promote positive social interactions, teachers can expect significant progress on the part of students and as a result have classrooms in which conflict and frustrations are kept to a minimum.

Be a Careful Observer

An excellent starting point for dealing with many issues in education is to make thorough and regular observations of children. The more you know about children and their typical patterns of interaction, the better able you will be to help them in their social development (Miller, 2004). When direct observations are supplemented with information provided by other teachers and parents, the chances for success in guiding social interactions dramatically increase.

Many times, these observations can be informal and require little preparation. As preschool children play during center time, for example, the teacher can focus her attention on small groups of children and make brief notes about the ways in which they interact socially. With older children, the teacher may not have as many opportunities to stop and observe, but when important behaviors occur, the teacher can make a mental note and then record a short written statement at a later, more convenient time.

Juan's interruption during reading group today is something you want to remember, but you do not have time to stop during the lesson. Later, after announcing snack break, you take a minute to jot down a note about his behavior for future reference.

On other occasions, more formal observations may be necessary to clarify the behaviors about which you are concerned. Techniques such as anecdotal records, running records, and checklists are described in Chapter 11. By choosing the appropriate observation method and creating an accurate picture of the child's activities, the teacher has taken the first step to help children improve their social interactions.

Can Children Solve Their Own Problems?

A major reason many people enter the teaching profession is that they like children and want to assist them in their growth and development. That desire to help is strong in good teachers and in most instances is a real asset. At times, however, this helping attitude actually can be harmful to children. It is useful to remember that even at very young ages, a major goal of guidance is to help children grow toward independence. This may mean stepping back a bit and allowing children to at least try to work issues through themselves. Gordon (1974) suggests that teachers should

Into Practice...
Dealing with Teasing and Bullying

Teachers of young children are increasingly finding that they must address the issues of teasing and bullying, especially in the primary grades. Children are seeing family members, neighbors, and television actors engaging in teasing and bullying behaviors and are trying out similar tactics in their interactions with peers. And while boys tend to initiate the majority of these incidents, both boys and girls are recipients of these negative behaviors (Gropper & Froschl, 1999).

Froschl and Sprung (1999) provide several suggestions for teachers in dealing with teasing and bullying behaviors:

- **Address the teasing and bullying early and often.** Many teachers tend to ignore a large percentage of these problem behaviors. While it is important to let children work things out on their own when possible, teasing and bullying are not a natural or necessary part of childhood. When intervention takes place regularly, children learn that teachers expect more positive interactions between children.

- **Talk about teasing and bullying.** Children need the chance to talk about what makes them uncomfortable in the classroom and on the playground. Several good books are available (such as Tomie dePaola's *Oliver Button Is a Sissy*) to use as discussion starters.

- **Develop classroom rules that discourage teasing and bullying.** Children can participate in rule-making activities that help them learn what teasing and bullying behaviors look and sound like and what consequences will be implemented when they occur.

- **Promote noncompetitive games.** Games that promote cooperation and friendship can be used both in the classroom and outdoors to help children develop more positive ways of interacting with each other.

- **Involve parents in the process.** Parents need to be active participants in understanding the problems with teasing and bullying and discouraging them both in the classroom and at home. Teachers who work to communicate with parents on this topic will gain valuable assistance in dealing with the problems.

mind their own business more often and see what children can do to resolve their own problems. Perhaps just hesitating briefly before stepping in will allow children the time they need to successfully work through their social conflicts. It is sometimes difficult to do, but pausing before you intervene could pay big dividends in terms of encouraging more independent behavior among your students.

Define the Limits of Acceptable Behavior

Clearly, children do need help in many social interactions. Hurting others either physically or emotionally, for example, cannot be allowed. When the teacher recognizes the need for intervention, he needs to step in and provide assistance. Frequently, problems with social interactions create strong emotions, and the teacher can begin by following the strategies outlined in the previous section for helping children deal with their feelings. In addition, however, it is often useful for teachers to clearly define for students the limits of acceptable behavior (Hildebrand & Hearron, 1999).

One way in which this can be accomplished is through the setting and consistent application of classroom rules (see "Into Practice . . . Rules for the Classroom," earlier in this chapter). As surprising as it may first seem, children actually are far more comfortable in an environment where rules are clearly understood and consistently enforced. Their need to test the limits decreases, and they are then free to explore and experiment within the known boundaries. With a few well-chosen and easy-to-understand rules, the teacher can create a consistent and fair classroom climate. More effective social interactions are one positive result of these clearly defined rules.

Another aspect of defining limits is to help children understand through examples which social behaviors are acceptable and which are not. Children learn rather quickly the clearly inappropriate social interactions. They know that hitting, biting, kicking, and swearing are unacceptable. Unfortunately, many interactions are not so easily categorized as right or wrong. Take, for example, talking back. Although it is certainly acceptable for children to ask the teacher for clarification on an assignment or task, many other responses the child might make would be considered talking back.

Yolanda's second-grade teacher has just told her to clean up her desk and get ready for recess. If she responds by saying: "No, I'm not ready yet!" that would be talking back to her teacher. However, if she said: "Can I finish my story first?" that would be acceptable. The gray areas need to be carefully defined for students so that they clearly know what is acceptable and what is not.

Help Children Become More Prosocial

Honig and Wittmer (1996) have reviewed extensive research that suggests that child-sensitive, high-quality care will promote more positive social interactions in early childhood classrooms. Specifically, teachers who engage in the following activities will help children become more prosocial:

- Emphasize cooperation rather than competition.
- Teach cooperative and conflict-resolution games and sports.
- Set up materials and spaces that facilitate cooperative play.

For more information about building social skills, go to the Companion Website at www.prenhall.com/henniger, select Chapter 6, then choose Web Destinations.

Group Guidance

- Use children's literature that promotes prosocial behaviors.
- Lead discussions that deal with positive social interactions.
- Include class projects that provide opportunities for children to help others.
- Invite adults who have helped others in the community to talk about their experiences with your children.

When you gather young children together in groups, new guidance strategies need to be considered to ensure that these experiences are positive. Children must learn many new behaviors for small- and large-group times to go well. Taking turns speaking, listening while others are talking, and sitting without disturbing neighbors are all important social skills that require considerable practice and discussion before children can successfully manage them. With careful planning and preparation, the early childhood teacher can successfully manage these group experiences.

Consider the Physical Setting

The physical space used for group times is important (Marion, 2003). If children are too crowded or uncomfortable, they will be less likely to cooperate and enjoy the experience. Normally, a carpeted area with students seated on the floor is the best arrangement for a large-group meeting. Placing children in a circle also allows for better eye contact and a more intimate setting for communication. Some teachers find that, for younger children, taping a circle on the rug is helpful to remind students visually of the approximate size of the group circle. Removing unnecessary distractions also increases the likelihood that children will be able to focus their attentions on the teacher's agenda.

Small-group experiences are often held at tables seating four to six students. In some instances, the purpose for the small group may make it more appropriate for children to sit on the floor in a carpeted area of the classroom. The classroom teacher should position himself so that he can periodically scan the activities occurring in other areas. While his primary responsibilities are to the small group, taking the time to look up briefly to notice what is happening in the rest of the room will help improve the teacher's understanding of total classroom functioning.

Careful Planning and Organization

The group experience requires thorough preparation and thought (Mitchell & David, 1992). The group time should include active and quiet components, times for children to participate, times for them to listen, and a fairly consistent routine to add stability. The length of time should be tailored to the age of the children, with 10 to 15 minutes being an adequate group time for 3-year-olds and 20 or 25 minutes more workable for second graders. The actual activities will vary according to the purposes of the group time (see Chapter 11 for more information on this topic).

An opening group time for a first-grade classroom might look like this:

8:30	Greetings and opening song
8:35	Lunch count, weather, calendar
8:40	Action songs/story
8:45	Dismiss to desks for daily oral language

Into Practice...
Helping Children Deal with Trauma

Although it is often difficult for adults to admit, many children experience periods of significant trauma. It may be a world event such as the terrorist attacks on New York's World Trade Center on September 11, 2001. While young children may have great difficulty understanding such events, they can see and feel the hurt and anguish of parents and others. Young children may also experience trauma associated with the community in which they live. Natural disasters like floods and tornadoes, drive-by shootings, and auto accidents are all events that may directly impact children and their families. Finally, there are situations within the family itself that can produce trauma for children. Severe financial difficulties, child or spousal abuse, the death or disability of a family member, and parental divorce are some of the more common traumatic events children experience. Teachers of young children need to be prepared to provide children with support and guidance as they work to cope with traumatic events. Some strategies for assisting children and their families include:

- **Be a good listener or observer.** Some children may be able to verbalize to you or other children the challenging situations they face. If so, take the time needed to listen carefully and draw out from what they know and believe. Most young children,

however, will not be able to talk about traumatic events because they have neither the language nor cognitive understanding to do so. In these situations, the teacher needs to carefully observe for telltale changes in child behaviors and/or the introduction of new play themes that may signal the occurrence of traumatic events.

- **Provide support to children and families.** The support provided by teachers is very individualized, depending on both the traumatic event itself and the time and energy commitment possible on the part of the teacher. It might include a special parent-teacher conference to brainstorm strategies that could be used both at home and at school to support the child. Support might also mean spending extra time with a troubled child to show him or her you care. Support could also take the form of volunteering for periodic after-school care so that other family members can have more time to work through the issues they face.

- **Seek professional advice and assistance.** Many traumatic events experienced by children and families require the help of trained professionals with expertise that goes well beyond the natural abilities of most teachers. These professionals should be called on early and often to provide the strategies needed to be of significant assistance to families.

Although this seems to be a rather simple group experience, each individual component needs careful planning for productive use of the time.

Mixing Active and Quiet Times

The activity level of young children is definitely high, making it difficult for them to sit still and listen to an adult for any length of time. Moving, touching, and talking to others are natural ways for children to learn about the world around them. Although it is important for students to learn to manage their wiggles and listen for short periods to the teacher, these are not easy things for most children to do.

Teachers can help this process along by making sure to allow for active involvement of children in group experiences (Dodge, Colker, & Heroman, 2002).

This can be accomplished in many good ways. Having students share their thoughts during group time can be one involvement technique. By asking appropriate questions and allowing time for children to respond, teachers engage

Placing children in a circle usually results in more cooperation because it allows for better eye contact and a more intimate setting for communication.

students' minds in the issues being discussed. Singing active songs is another favorite of many early childhood teachers.

Movement and music mesh very well in the classroom and allow children to participate physically during group time. Simple games and exercises also add movement and interest to group times. The traditional Simon Says is a time-honored favorite that can be added to a group experience to break up longer stretches of quiet sitting times. The best teachers have a long list of these fun activities that they can use as needed to add spice to group times throughout the day. Some examples include:

- *Songs.* The Eensy Weensy Spider; Head, Shoulders, Knees, and Toes; The Hokey Pokey; The Wheels on the Bus
- *Activities.* Follow the Leader, stretching, clapping to music, marching in place to music, rolling a ball inside the circle of children
- *Games.* Duck, Duck, Goose; Be My Mirror; Simon Says; Heads-Up, Seven-Up

Guidance for Children with Special Needs

In most cases, the problem behaviors exhibited by children with special needs are no different from those of other students. Although the frequency and intensity of their reactions may be greater, these children struggle with the same issues that other students their age face. For this reason, the guidance strategies described in this chapter for all students can also be effectively used with children with special needs (Hildebrand & Hearron, 1999).

Even though the techniques remain the same, it is important for teachers of children with special needs to plan carefully for the implementation of these

Observing Development • Child Misbehaviors

Choose one of the age groups within early childhood (infants/toddlers, preschoolers, or primary-age children), *observe* **child misbehaviors** using the guidelines provided, *reflect* on what you saw and heard, and *apply* the appropriate strategies listed with the children you observed.

Observe	Reflect	Apply
Look for specific examples of:	*Think about and respond to the following questions:*	*Consider the following developmentally appropriate strategies for the age group you observed:*
Language that has a negative social connotation (angry vocalizations, name calling, etc.)	Was the negative language observed disruptive to classroom activities or hurtful to other children or simply an emotional outburst by the child involved?	Discourage hurtful language • Infant/toddler: "Serena, I can't let you scream at Adrienne. Let's find you another toy for you to play with." • Preschool: "T. J., calling Hannah a weasel hurts her feelings. Tell her you are mad at her for not wanting to play with her." • Primary: "Rashaad, try thinking of something good about Kerrie's picture rather than telling her you don't like it."
Negative physical actions toward others (hitting, pushing, biting, etc.)	Do you think any of the problem behaviors observed could have been prevented? Why or why not?	Intervene early to avoid physical harm • Infant/toddler: Take hold of the block a child is swinging wildly and redirect his actions in a more appropriate direction. • Preschool: Sit next to a child who shows signs of physical aggressiveness. • Primary: "Jenna, I can tell you are getting angry. Take some deep breaths and calm down, or I will need to move you to another activity."
The teacher's verbal and physical responses to the child misbehaviors observed (using words to give the child more appropriate ways of dealing with the situation, taking the child by the hand and leading to a new area/activity, etc.)	Did you observe teachers using guidance strategies discussed in this chapter to deal with negative behaviors? How effective were they in managing the problem behaviors observed?	Use a variety of guidance techniques • Infant/toddler: Plan the physical environment so that children have many play options to avoid conflicts. • Preschool: Physically take a child by the hand and lead him or her to a new activity when potential conflicts arise. • Primary: Give children the words they need to share with others how they are feeling and why.

strategies. Working closely with parents can provide educators with the knowledge they need to better understand the child's motivation for engaging in inappropriate behaviors. Teachers of students with special needs can add further insights and work cooperatively with the classroom teacher in implementing effective guidance techniques. Other teachers who work with special children may suggest new options. When the teacher spends the extra time necessary to discuss and plan guidance strategies for the child with special needs, this component of a comprehensive management system can be effectively implemented.

Summary

To test your knowledge of this chapter's contents, go to the Companion Website at www.prenhall.com/henniger, select Chapter 6, then select Study Guide. Also see Chapter Overviews, Reflecting Essay Questions, Multimedia Explorations, and relevant Web Destinations.

What Is Guidance?

The major components of child guidance include nurturing each child's self-esteem, helping children develop skills in dealing with social-emotional issues, and allowing children to grow toward independence and self-control.

Principles of Guidance

Planning the physical environment and building relationships are important components of the guidance process. Physical and verbal guidance strategies help teachers deal effectively with young children. Discipline procedures such as I-messages, natural and logical consequences, behavior modification techniques, and problem-solving strategies are all useful in the early childhood classroom.

Guiding Routines

It is important to develop procedures for dealing with routines such as arrival and departure, transitions, snack/meal time, toileting, and rest times.

Dealing with Feelings and Emotions

Children are better able to deal with emotions when adults accept children's feelings as valid, are calm and direct in dealing with feelings, assist children in verbalizing their emotions, and present alternative ways of dealing with emotions.

Guiding Social Interactions

Careful observation, allowing children to resolve at least some of their own problems, defining the limits of acceptable behavior, and helping children become more prosocial are all important in guiding social interactions.

Group Guidance

Guidance of children in groups is another important task for teachers of young children. The physical setting, careful planning and organization, and mixing active and quiet times all help make these experiences more effective.

Guidance for Children with Special Needs

The problem behaviors exhibited by children with special needs are often no different from those of other students and usually can be dealt with using the same techniques described throughout this chapter.

Multimedia Explorations and Activities . . .

To Delay or Not Delay Kindergarten?

Many parents across the country have faced the difficult choice of placing their children in kindergarten early or delaying entrance for another year. This primarily occurs when children's birth dates are within a month or two of the typical cutoff point for entering kindergarten. In this instance, parents may have the option of either early entry for their children or holding them back so that they are older and more developmentally advanced than many classmates. Parents often choose the second option so that children gain an extra year of maturity. However, under certain circumstances, this may not be the best choice.

Research

Both parents and teachers struggle with making good decisions about children whose birthdays fall near the cutoff date for admission to kindergarten. The option chosen has the potential to significantly influence a child's schooling experiences. Since every child is unique, there is never an easy formula that can be used to make the decision. This activity is aimed at making you aware of the issues surrounding early and late kindergarten admissions.

1. View the ABC News video segment titled "To Delay or Not Delay Kindergarten?"

2. Go to the Companion Website at www. prenhall.com/henniger and click on the Multimedia Explorations and Activities button for Chapter 6 for more information on this topic.

3. Find parents who either elected to have their child enter kindergarten early or late and discuss with them the reasons for their choice.

Reflect

Based on the information you have collected, think about the following issues:

- As a parent, what information would you use to determine the benefits and drawbacks to either entering kindergarten early or late? Would your decision-making process as a teacher be any different? Why or why not?

- Although there is always a problem associated with overstating positions on issues such as this, in general, what would you advise parents of children who are struggling with the kindergarten admission issue? Why?

- Would the philosophy and practice of a particular school influence your decision regarding kindergarten admission for certain children? Why or why not?

Respond

Armed with this new knowledge, consider one or more of the following responses:

1. Create a handout for parents regarding this issue. Simply and clearly outline for them the rationale for each position (early and late admission to kindergarten). Make sure you also include a statement to remind parents that each child is unique and that the guidelines you developed are only beginning points in the decision-making process.

2. Share your thoughts with a group of preschool teachers or parents of preschool children. Make sure to include handouts and visual aids to make your presentation more valuable.

3. Organize a class discussion of this topic, with clearly defined statements of rationale for both early and late admission to kindergarten.

WORKING WITH PARENTS, FAMILIES, AND COMMUNITIES

In this chapter you will

- Learn about the diversity of family situations and their impact on education.
- Understand the importance of parent and community involvement.
- Study the elements of effective communication.
- Identify tools for quality communications with parents.
- Clarify the role of community members in early education.

Your third year of teaching first grade has just begun. The content and materials for teaching are well organized. You are feeling comfortable with your guidance and discipline strategies. Perhaps this is the year to begin involving parents more consistently in their children's learning. You are already sending home a weekly letter, making telephone calls with positive comments, and holding parent-teacher conferences in the fall and spring, but you know that much more could be done. Having parents volunteer in the classroom is rather scary, but it is clear from what you have read and heard from others that this type of involvement has many benefits. Providing ways for parents who cannot come in during the school day to participate at home would also be of significant value to you and your students. If parents are interested, you could plan to have a social event such as a potluck to get families better acquainted. And you have been thinking about collecting and organizing information about community resources to assist parents with their many needs. It looks like this will be another busy and productive year.

Teachers must recognize that although they have a major influence on children's lives, their impact pales in comparison to the significance of parental interactions. For one thing, parents have spent, and will continue to spend, far more time with their children than teachers can ever do. In addition, the bonds created between parents and children are hard to match in the classroom setting. Teachers need to recognize this fact and work with parents and families to make sure that children have the best opportunities for growth and development. As teachers understand family situations and plan strategies for working with them, everyone benefits.

It is essential to involve parents and family members who might be the child's primary caregivers in the educational process. Neglecting this important element will definitely influence the quality of early education. Parents and family members have much to offer the schools in terms of support, insights, and skills. The effort expended in establishing strong working relationships with children's primary caregivers will pay big dividends.

Family Life Today

For more information about family involvement in education, go to the Companion Website at www.prenhall.com/henniger, select Chapter 7, then choose Web Destinations.

It does not take too much insight to realize that families today look much different from the way they did just a generation ago. The idyllic picture of mom, dad, and two or three children living happily down the street in the house with the white picket fence is just not likely today. Family situations vary widely, and educators not only must know what those possibilities look like but must be ready to work effectively with diverse family patterns (Hildebrand, Phenice, Gray, & Hines, 2000).

Margaret Smith's third-grade classroom has parents who had children as young teens and others who waited until much later in life. There is a homeless family, several who qualify for food stamps, and a few who are upper middle class. Several single-parent families, remarriages, and one gay couple add variety to her family configurations. Ethnic and religious differences create an even more diverse mix of values, attitudes, and traditions among her families.

The Missing Extended Family

Not too many years ago, it was fairly common to find families and their relatives living in the same community or general area. Aunts, uncles, and grandparents were available to help with child care and give advice on how to parent. This support system was often helpful, especially to new parents as they struggled with the many challenges of raising children. Although some of these extended families still exist, they are now the exception rather than the rule. Despite the fact that many parents still need and want the support the extended family provided, few have found an adequate replacement (Berger, 2004). Teachers and schools can assist in this process by helping parents create a network with other families in similar situations to provide one another with support.

Divorce and Single-Parent Families

One of the most significant family situations that teachers will encounter is the single-parent family. National statistics indicate that more than 28 percent of children under 18 are living in families with only one parent (Forum on Child and Family Statistics, 2003). These families are also far more likely to be living at or below the poverty level (Annie E. Casey Foundation, 2003). It is estimated that approximately 39 percent of all single-parent families headed by women are poor, compared to only about 8 percent of two-parent families (Forum on Child and Family Statistics, 2003). Single parents tend to be busy with work commitments and child-rearing responsibilities, leaving less time for things like parent–teacher conferences and helping out in the schools. Teachers need to be sensitive to these time constraints and find ways to creatively work with single parents and their children.

Blended Families

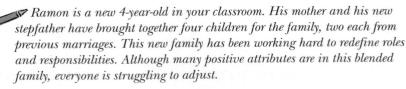

Ramon is a new 4-year-old in your classroom. His mother and his new stepfather have brought together four children for the family, two each from previous marriages. This new family has been working hard to redefine roles and responsibilities. Although many positive attributes are in this blended family, everyone is struggling to adjust.

Celebrating Diversity . . .
Gay and Lesbian Families

A small but growing number of children in America have either two moms or two dads. In some cases, these children were born into a heterosexual family that later dissolved when one of the partners discovered his or her homosexual inclinations. Others were either adopted by their gay or lesbian parents or were conceived through artificial insemination (American Psychological Association, 2003). Although gay and lesbian families currently make up only a small percentage of family totals, there is every indication that teachers and schools will see increasing numbers in the future. As state and federal laws continue to become more supportive of gay and lesbian couples and society in general grows more accepting of this family configuration, it becomes increasingly likely that you will be working with gay and lesbian families in your future teaching career.

As you begin to think about working with these families, it is important to realize that in most respects gay and lesbian parents are just like all the other parents you will work with. They have the same hopes and aspirations for their children, experience the same feelings of frustration and anxiety toward parenting, and want to support their children in whatever ways they can so that they will be successful. Having said this, however, the presence of gay and lesbian families in your classroom may well mean further modifications in the ways in which you interact with parents and children. For example, you will need to think about how you will respond to the inevitable curiosity of children: "Teacher, why does Marcus have two moms?" It may also mean that you will need to modify slightly the way in which you prepare for celebrations like Mother's Day and Father's Day. It will be important for you to be sensitive to the needs and interests of both parents and children in these situations.

1. In what other ways may you need to adapt communications and interactions as you work with gay and lesbian families?

2. How do you feel about working with this group of parents? Do you think that your religious beliefs or family values will make it more difficult to work with gay and lesbian parents? Why or why not?

Divorce leaves children without one of their parents and creates many stresses for children as well as their parents; the eventual remarriage that frequently occurs leads to other challenges. Approximately 15 percent of all families include a stepchild or stepparent (Hildebrand et al., 2000). While adults are learning to mesh parenting styles and combine efforts to manage complex households, children are adjusting to a variety of new relationships (Berger, 2004). Careful observation and sensitive interactions may be required of the teacher to assist children and families with these complex changes.

Two-Career Families

Today's economic realities find a great many intact families in which both parents must work outside the home for financial reasons. In other two-parent families, both husband and wife have career aspirations and are therefore also employed full-time outside the home. Because of these circumstances, children in recent generations tend to have less time to spend with their parents (Berger, 2004). In addition to less family time, when both parents work outside the home, parents may have fewer opportunities to be actively involved in school activities. Teachers of young children need to understand the complexities of this family type and make adjustments in their involvement strategies to ensure that busy lifestyles and limited flexible time can be managed.

Older and Younger Parents

Another change in family composition that impacts schools for young children is the age of the parents themselves. People are having children at both older and younger ages. Teen pregnancies and birthrates among unmarried women remain high in the United States as compared to other industrialized nations, despite many efforts to make young people aware of the major challenges facing teen parents (Annie E. Casey Foundation, 2003).

 Becky is a young single mother of 6-year-old Brian. She got pregnant at 15 and has worked hard to complete high school, keep a part-time job, and be a good mother to Brian. Becky has lived at home to make ends meet and is just now beginning to get herself together both financially and emotionally.

At the same time, many couples are choosing to wait until later in life to begin families. This older group of parents tends to be well educated and brings a diversity of life and work experiences to their interactions with schools.

Lisa and Mike postponed children for several years while getting established in their careers. Both returned to graduate school to strengthen their career mobility. At age 38, they decided to have their first child. Now in their mid-forties, they have two children, busy professional lives, and a secure financial outlook.

Into Practice . . .
Involving Parents in the Classroom

There are many good reasons to involve parents in your classroom. One of the most important is that children benefit from more adult help and a richer curriculum. Here are some suggestions for ways in which parents and families can effectively contribute to your classroom:

- Read books to individual children or small groups.
- Play an appropriate educational game with children.
- Prepare and organize materials for an upcoming classroom activity.
- Share a talent or interest with the class. An example might be a cooking activity.

- Assist the teacher in a planned field trip into the local community.
- Spend time with children on the playground as they engage in activities in that setting.
- Talk about their work world. Demonstrate the use of specialized equipment or talents needed for the job.
- Help children engage in an interesting science experiment that requires lots of helping hands.
- Tutor an individual child who needs assistance in mathematics.

Teachers should expect to work with parents of all ages, interests, and cultural backgrounds.

With young parents, older parents, and every possible age combination in between, teachers find less common ground on which to base their interactions and communications with parents. Working with parents becomes a more individualized event, with more emphasis on the needs, interests, and abilities of the diversity of parents found in each classroom.

Ethnic/Cultural Diversity

Another fact of life today in the United States is that families continue to grow more diverse in terms of ethnic/cultural background (Hildebrand et al., 2000). It is estimated, for example, that the non-Hispanic White population in this country will decrease from nearly 75 percent in 1980 to approximately 55 percent by the year 2020 (Forum on Child and Family Statistics, 2003). During this same period, the Hispanic and Asian American populations will increase significantly. Furthermore, the ethnic/cultural diversity of families is also growing due to an increase in multiracial families (U.S. Census Bureau, 2000).

In addition to modifications that need to occur in the curriculum because of these changes in demography (see Chapter 8), this increasing diversity will also influence the kinds of interactions that teachers have with parents and families. For example, Asian American parents tend to have high academic expectations for their children but also feel that the school should have considerable autonomy in dealing with academic and discipline-related issues (Olsen & Fuller, 2003). Consequently, they may be less likely to get involved in some aspects of school life. Adults working with young children and their families need to be aware of these cultural/ethnic differences and adjust to them as plans are made to involve parents and families in the educational process.

Family Mobility

Another characteristic of families today that significantly impacts teachers is the relocation of families in new communities (Gestwicki, 2004). In some cases, this movement is brought about when parents are promoted to a higher position in a corporation or relocate to find a better job in a new community. Members of the American military community also move frequently. However, for other families, moving may be the only way to keep one step ahead of creditors. Migrant workers who move around the country taking low-paying agricultural jobs are yet another reason many families are on the move. Regardless of the reason, family mobility frequently leads to stress and can impact the family's willingness to be involved in school.

Homeless Families

For more information about homeless families, go to the Companion Website at www.prenhall.com/henniger, select Chapter 7, then choose Web Destinations.

Each night in the United States, approximately 100,000 children are homeless (Berger, 2004). They may spend the night in a shelter, an abandoned building, or the family car. While statistics on homelessness are sketchy, it appears that the number of homeless families with children is continuing to grow (National Coalition for the Homeless, 2001) and that these families make up nearly 40 percent of the homeless (Berger, 2004). Clearly, the stress levels of these families is high, and interactions with the schools tend to be a low priority. In many instances, homeless children either do not attend school at all or participate only sporadically. Teachers should make a special effort to assist these families by directing them to community agencies that can provide them with services.

Is Involvement Worth the Effort?

Given the family situations described here and the complications they present, you may be wondering whether or not this whole task of involving parents is worth the effort it clearly will take. Despite the added time commitments, teachers and schools that take the time to work with families find the experience a richly rewarding one for all involved (Wright & Stegelin, 2003). The insight and support that parents can provide the schools simply have no substitute. Conversely, parents often find that they desperately need the support and assistance schools can offer. Parenting is an extremely difficult and complex task requiring much guidance and assistance. Children, too, benefit when parents and teachers work together. Working with families becomes a win-win situation where all participants benefit.

Benefits to Teachers

Mrs. Andreson teaches second grade at Northwest Academy. She has worked hard to involve parents in the educational process. Although it means some extra effort on her part, she clearly sees many advantages. Involved parents are important aides in the classroom and helpmates for field trips. In addition, parents who participate in their child's education extend learning into the home and are generally more supportive of the schools.

For more information about benefits of involvement, go to the Companion Website at www.prenhall.com/henniger, select Chapter 7, then choose Web Destinations.

When teachers make the effort necessary to involve parents and community members, they find that other adults have a greater appreciation of the challenges of working with young children. Parents and community members come to value and respect teachers' efforts and are more likely to speak positively with others about early education (Gestwicki, 2004). With added assistance, teachers can also do a better job in their teaching (Berger, 2004). While a parent or community member is busy with a small-group art project, for example, the teacher is freed up to work with other children in the classroom. Bringing in other adults with unique talents and abilities also adds to the excitement of the classroom and often leaves teachers feeling more satisfied with their work (Gestwicki, 2004). As teachers work to involve parents and community members, their relationships with children also tend to improve. With more time for each child, increased understanding, and a more exciting curriculum, children respond more positively to teachers.

Into Practice...
Involving Parents at Home

It is important to have parents involved in your classroom so that they can assist with teaching and learning. However, because of the high number of working parents and the complexities of life today, many parents cannot participate in classroom activities during the school day. They can, however, support you in the home. The following list of possible activities is meant to get you thinking about the many possibilities that exist. You should consider creating your own list of options.

- Read good books to children regularly.
- Talk with children about the positive and negative influences of television while viewing it together.

- Create a space at home for children to do projects related to school, and work with them to make sure they get done.
- Prepare the classroom newsletter for mailing to other parents and families.
- Prepare a game or activity that the teacher can use in the classroom.
- Call other parents to remind them of the upcoming field trip, and find volunteers to help with transportation.
- Let children know you think school is important and discuss how they need to be active, positive participants.

Benefits to Parents and Families

The difficult task of parenting is often a struggle for many adults. When parents are involved in the schools, they find opportunities for support that make this task a little more manageable (Powell, 1998). Just knowing that other parents are struggling with the same issues is reassuring to many. Talking through parenting challenges with others gives parents new ideas and renewed motivation to manage their struggles with children.

Conversations with teachers and opportunities to see them deal with similar issues in the classroom also provide parents with good options to try with their children at home (Gestwicki, 2004). Parents who get involved also gain new insights into their own children's lives in a different setting. All of this tends to strengthen their self-esteem and hone parenting skills. The Head Start program has many examples of parents who have gotten involved in school activities and gone on to improve their lives in a variety of ways (Administration for Children and Families, 2002).

Benefits to Children

Kendra has been struggling with reading in her first-grade classroom. After conferencing with her parents, Kendra's teacher has asked two parent volunteers to spend time each week listening to her read. At home, Kendra's parents have set aside 20 minutes each evening for family reading time. This combined effort is beginning to pay dividends, and Kendra's reading skills are slowly improving.

When parents, community members, and teachers work together, children's lives are improved. Children who see a variety of concerned adults working to help them improve their school performance respond positively, leading to increased achievement (Olsen & Fuller, 2003). This involvement makes it clear to children that schooling is important, and as a result, their motivation to succeed is strengthened. Just as with parents, children also tend to have improved self-concepts when parents, community members, and teachers combine efforts on their behalf. It feels good to know so many important people care. Participation also benefits children by providing an enriched classroom environment (Gestwicki, 2004). When parents get involved in the classroom, more hands-on activities (which simply could not be managed without additional help) become possible. A trip to a local grocery store, for example, to learn about an important community business would not be possible without parents and others to assist along the way.

Family Partnerships . . .
Working with Difficult Parents or Family Members

While it would be ideal if every parent you worked with was pleasant, positive, and easy to work with, the reality is that some parents will find fault with nearly everything you do. There are many possible explanations for these challenging parents. Some may have had poor school experiences themselves and come to your classroom with many negative associations. Others will have educational beliefs different from your own and challenge your teaching methods and what you want to teach. Parents may also have parenting styles that are in direct conflict with the ways in which you communicate and interact with children. Another alternative is that there may be personality differences between you and some parents that make it difficult to work together.

Regardless of the reason, you will need to develop strategies to help you improve your interactions with these difficult parents. The following options should be considered:

- **Increase communications.** While the human tendency is to step back from difficult interactions, it is important to increase these communications. For example, make it a point to regularly send a positive note or e-mail message telling difficult parents about something good that has happened with their child.

- **Listen calmly and carefully.** Difficult parents may say things that are hurtful and make you defensive. By being a calm and careful listener, you are more likely to be able to identify the problem the parent is having and begin to work toward a solution.

- **Build on parent strengths.** Just as it is important to look for the positive characteristics of every child and build on them as you teach, make sure to identify the positive attributes of difficult parents so that you can use these qualities for the betterment of children in your classroom. For example, a difficult father who experienced failures as a student himself may be an excellent carpenter that could help you design and build a flowerbox planter for your classroom. While allowing the parent to contribute in a positive way to the school, it also has the potential to strengthen his relationship with you as the classroom teacher.

1. Given the information in this chapter on the benefits of parent involvement, how important is it to work effectively with all parents, including difficult ones?

2. How do you typically deal with confrontations? Do you welcome the challenges or try to avoid them? What does this tell you about your future interactions with difficult parents?

Building Strong Two-Way Relationships

Healthy human relationships of all sorts have as a foundation strong communication. Friendships, marriages, and parent–child relationships all require regular and effective interactions to remain strong. This same basic premise is true for parent–teacher relationships as well. When teachers and parents engage in frequent verbal and/or written interactions, their relationships can grow and prosper (Powell, 1998).

Providing Mutual Support

When you think about the friendships you have with other adults, do you recognize the mutual give and take that is necessary to make these relationships work? Strong friendships require mutual support if they are to remain healthy. This same idea applies to parent–teacher relationships. If we are to work with parents as partners in the educational process, we need to see our interactions as providing support for one another (Grossman, 1999). When parents spend time in the classroom, they are providing us with support in the educational process. Other parents support teachers when they assist their children with school-related projects at home. The options for parental support of teachers are many. Creative teachers will find a number of ways to find and use this support. It is important, however, for teachers to support parents as well (Gestwicki, 2004). When we share parenting information with a concerned parent, listen to the struggles families face, or help locate a community resource to meet a parental need (Wright & Stegelin, 2003), we are providing valued assistance that will strengthen our relationships with parents. This does not imply that teachers can meet all or even most of the needs of parents and families. Many times, the teacher's role is to simply know of resources available within the community and refer families to them when needed.

Communication: The Key

Without question, the key element needed for effective parent–teacher partnerships is strong communication. It is the beginning point and a continuing need in these relationships (Gestwicki, 2004). Calling Mrs. Jackson to mention the extra effort Zachary put into his mathematics today, a brief note to Jennifer's father to thank him for coming on the recent field trip, and just taking the time to say hello to Shaquille's mom when she drops him off for class are all simple, but important, relationship-building communications. Effective understanding and positive interactions result from spending time getting to know one another via thoughtful, quality communications.

Epstein (1995) suggests that the best schools work to create partnerships between teachers, families, and communities. When members of these partnerships work together, children have the greatest opportunities for learning and development. These partnerships lead to six different types of involvement:

- *Parenting.* Help all families establish home environments to support children as students.
- *Communicating.* Design effective communication strategies to connect home and school.

- *Volunteering.* Recruit and organize parent and community volunteers.
- *Learning at home.* Provide parents with ideas that they can use to help their children at home.
- *Decision making.* Give parents and community members opportunities to participate in decisions about how the school operates.
- *Collaborating with community.* Identify and use community resources to strengthen school programs.

Although only one of these six categories of involvement specifically addresses communication and its importance in home, school, and community relations, it is not difficult to see that each type requires strong communication to be effective. The partnerships we seek with parents and community members are just not possible without good communication. The "Observing Development" feature at the end of this chapter takes a look at parent-teacher-child interactions, reflects on methods to enhance these interactions, and provides some applicable ways to enhance them.

Family-Friendly Schools

For more information about family-friendly schools, go to the Companion Website at www.prenhall.com/henniger, select Chapter 7, then choose Web Destinations.

Building strong relationships with parents also means creating classrooms and schools where families are welcomed. Family-friendly schools:

- *Welcome parents visually and emotionally.* Banners, bulletin boards, and display cases are developed to help parents feel wanted and needed. Reaching out to parents and families as they arrive also helps them feel emotionally welcomed.
- *Accommodate diverse family situations.* Scheduling conferences at convenient times, communicating with custodial and noncustodial parents, being aware of and supportive of family living situations, and adjusting involvement strategies to meet the needs of different families are all examples of this effort to accommodate diverse families.
- *Make it easy to get involved.* Rather than creating obstacles that make it more difficult to get involved, family-friendly schools do things like providing child care during parent–teacher conferences to make it easier for parents to participate.
- *Demonstrate that parental opinions and involvement are important.* Family-friendly schools make sure that parents get involved in meaningful ways and that their opinions are viewed as important in the decision-making process. For example, a parent who participates on a hiring committee for a new staff person should have all the privileges and responsibilities of the other members.
- *Create spaces for parents.* While space is always at a premium in school settings, it is important to create areas where parents can spend time when in the schools. A parent room for the entire school may be one option. Providing a small area in individual classrooms with parenting materials and a comfortable chair might be another possibility.
- *Provide assistance and resources.* One almost universal need of parents during the early childhood years is assistance with parenting. Teachers can serve as a resource by providing articles and pamphlets on parenting or through the development of parenting classes on topics of interest to the group. Teachers should also be ready to provide parents with information about community resources that can assist them with a variety of family needs.

Effective Communication Methods

Given the importance of quality interactions between parents and teachers, it is critical for teachers of young children to be aware of a variety of communication techniques and the potential strengths and weaknesses of each. No one technique will meet all of a teacher's needs for communicating with parents. Several methods, used appropriately, will be necessary to build and maintain the partnerships between parents and teachers (see Figure 7–1).

Telephone Calls

One simple but effective communication tool that teachers can put to good use is the telephone. It is a quick and easy way to communicate simple, positive messages to parents (Berger, 2004). A 2-minute call to share with a parent something positive her child did today in school will pay big dividends in terms of relationship building. Every parent wants to hear these positive messages, so if you decide to use this communication strategy, make sure you contact all families with a positive message about their children.

Using the telephone in communicating with families has several other important benefits (Gestwicki, 2004). In general, the telephone is inexpensive and provides for two-way communications. Most parents are also more comfortable in communicating with teachers when they can do it from the comfort and convenience of their own homes. Teachers can fit in short telephone calls around already busy schedules, making it more likely to be something that gets done.

Despite the many benefits, telephone use has some potential drawbacks. Because a phone call does not have nonverbal cues, the phone is not appropriate for more difficult messages that may need to be shared with parents. Remember, also, that you do not know what you may be interrupting when you call. It is always best to ask if you are calling at a convenient time. You may need to give the parent the chance to talk with you at a later time. Although the old-style party lines, where more than one family shared the same telephone line, are rare today, the tele-

For more information about communicating with parents, go to the Companion Website at www.prenhall.com/henniger, select Chapter 7, then choose Web Destinations.

Figure 7–1 *Effective Communication Methods*

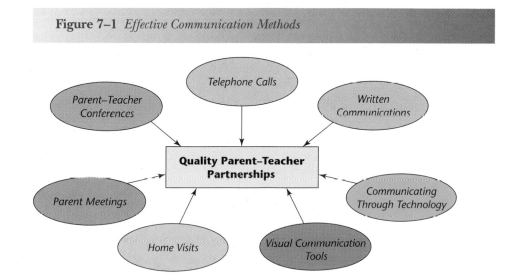

Into Practice . . .
A Letter of Introduction

One form of written communication that you may want to use as a future teacher is a letter home to parents at the beginning of the school year. This letter can be used to tell them something about you as a person, begin the process of building good relationships, and welcome their participation in the life of your classroom. The following is an example of an introductory letter for a second-grade classroom:

Dear Parents and Guardians:

It is hard to believe that the summer is nearly over and school will begin again in just two short weeks! I have enjoyed a marvelous vacation in which I tended my garden, took short trips for hikes and bicycle rides, and played with my two daughters. This was the first time I have been able to take significant time off over the summer to relax with my family. What a pleasure!

Despite this nearly perfect summer, I am truly excited about the coming school year. Teaching second grade has been a great source of pleasure to me, and I expect this coming year to be another similar experience. It will be a privilege to get to know you and your child in the coming weeks. To begin this process, I would like to invite you to our school Open House on Friday, September 28, from 6–8 PM. Bring your family for any part of that time so that you can browse through my classroom and get acquainted with me and Angie Hanson, my Educational Assistant.

Parents and guardians are always welcome in my classroom. I hope you will be able to find the time to participate in some way. If you cannot assist during the school day, there are other ways for you to get involved. Just let me know of your interest and I will make sure your talents are put to good use. Your participation will be much appreciated.

Again, I look forward to meeting you and your child in the near future.

phone is still not a secure communication system. Others may listen when you talk, so the nature of the communications shared must again be carefully considered.

One final issue should be mentioned regarding telephone use. Consider whether or not you will want to give out your home telephone number so that parents can contact you outside school hours. Some teachers feel very strongly that their home life should not be interrupted by work-related business. Others, however, want parents to know that they have the opportunity to call when they have a need. If you choose to give out your number, you may want to let parents know the appropriate times to call.

Written Communications

A common strategy that teachers use to exchange information with parents is written communications. A wide variety of options are appropriate (Barbour & Barbour, 2001).

The simplest method may be the handwritten notes sent home with individual children. Much like the telephone calls mentioned earlier, these brief notes are simply a little pat on the back for the parent and child through sharing a positive event from the classroom day. Teachers also find many opportunities to send home written notices to all parents about an upcoming event such as a field trip to the zoo. One- or two-page letters home to parents are another possible written communication tool. An introductory letter sent home to parents before the school year begins is one effective use of this strategy. A newsletter is a longer, more complicated written document that usually goes home to parents less regularly. It may contain several pages of information to parents, including such things as a calendar of events, articles of interest to parents, samples of student work, ideas for parents to use at home, and a wish list of materials that parents could collect for the classroom.

A final category of written materials are those that are prepublished through other sources. Many public agencies prepare brochures or other written materials that might be useful to you in working with parents. Articles in newspapers and magazines (remember to comply with copyright laws if you make multiple copies) are also helpful in communicating important information to parents.

As you think about using written communications with parents, consider the following issues. One of the difficulties many teachers face with any written material intended for parents is how to make sure it gets home. Children of any age need assistance in getting these messages to their parents. Another issue with written communications is that, although they provide parents with good information, they seldom encourage a response from the home. When this can be built in, the connection between home and school is stronger.

Perhaps the most important consideration when developing written communications is to make sure that your writing is of the very best quality. What kind of response would parents have to a letter from the teacher that had several spelling and grammatical errors? Often, the reaction is surprise, followed by frustration. Teachers are expected to be good models. Punctuation, grammar, and spelling errors send a negative message home that may be stronger than the more positive intent of the written communication. If writing is something you have to work hard to do well, plan on spending the necessary time to ensure a well-written message.

Communicating Through Technology

As more homes and schools invest in computer technology, electronic communications may well become a more common communication strategy for parents and teachers. Electronic mail is one such rapidly growing option. Teachers can send messages directly to individual families or create a simple listserv with families' e-mail addresses and quickly send the same message to everyone on the list.

Another popular strategy is for either schools or individual teachers to create a home page on the Internet that allows for sharing of written materials, pictures, and video segments with families. This technology has become much simpler to use over the last few years, and teachers can now create and modify the materials they post with relative ease.

Schools are also purchasing programs that allow them to take advantage of another communication strategy referred to as the **homework hotline** (Berger, 2004). Teachers can make daily recordings of homework assignments and other brief messages intended for either children or parents. Families can call the hotline at any time and listen to the recorded information. Telephone service is the only technology that families need to take advantage of this option.

Visual Communication Tools

Although written communications are an important part of interactions with parents, other options are available for teachers to use. One additional category of communication tools could be called visual displays. Videotapes and bulletin boards (Gestwicki, 2004) are two important types of visual displays discussed here. Many parents would like to know what is happening in their children's classrooms but do not have the chance to drop in on a regular basis. Consider making regular videotapes of the activities in your classroom and then loaning these to parents who want to catch a glimpse of their children's daily activities. Although both children and adults act differently when they know they are being videotaped, before long, normal behavior returns and parents have an accurate picture of what is happening in the classroom.

Bulletin boards are another form of visual communication that can be productively used in working with parents and families. A wide assortment of information can be shared on parent bulletin boards. Upcoming events, classroom activities, samples of children's work, articles on parenting or child development issues, and a wish list of materials parents could collect at home are a sampling of possible items that may be included. A thoughtful parent bulletin board will be read and appreciated by the parents who enter your classroom and have a few minutes to browse (Barbour & Barbour, 2001).

Although bulletin board use has many positive aspects, it is important to mention that bulletin boards do have their limitations. Perhaps the most obvious is the fact that those parents who do not come into your classroom will not be able to see them. Another potential drawback is that bulletin boards do not give parents much opportunity to communicate with the teacher. One-way communications definitely have inherent limitations. Finally, be aware that bulletin boards are time–consuming to create and require periodic updating to make sure the information remains current.

Home Visits

One of the best ways to get acquainted with parents and families is to take time to go out and meet with families in their homes (Gorter-Reu & Anderson, 1998). The teacher sets up an appointment, plans an agenda, and travels to the parents' home to meet and talk with the family. Home visits have been shown to be highly effective in teaching parents skills that they can use in working with their children (Bronfenbrenner, 1974) and for conducting parent–teacher conferences. Perhaps the best way, however, for teachers to get the most from home visits is to use them to get better acquainted with children and their families.

Home visits are an ideal time to casually share with parents a bit about yourself and what you hope to accomplish during the school year.

For more information about home visits, go to the Companion Website at www.prenhall.com/ henniger, select Chapter 7, then choose Web Destinations.

Many preschool teachers attempt to have home visits with all of their families before the school year actually begins. These getting-acquainted visits typically last 30 to 45 minutes and may include a variety of activities. Some teachers take a book or a simple activity with them to break the ice with the children who will be coming into their classrooms. Young children frequently want to lead the teacher on a tour around the house and show off their bedrooms and favorite playthings. Home visits are an ideal time to casually share with parents a little bit about yourself as a person and what you hope to accomplish during the year as a teacher. Sharing in this way often encourages parents to open up to you about their lives as well. Refreshments, casual conversation, and an opportunity to get a feel for home life are other common elements of a getting-acquainted home visit.

If you choose to make home visits, consider the following suggestions (Barbour & Barbour, 2001; Gestwicki, 2004):

- It is essential that you *make an appointment* with parents ahead of time and explain to them the purposes of the visit.

- *Establish a time frame* for the visit (typically 30 to 45 minutes) so that parents know what to expect.

- *Think carefully about what you will wear* on the home visit. Remember that first impressions are important and that you want to appear professional but still approachable by parents or primary caregivers.

- *Avoid note taking* during the home visit itself. Parents generally feel anxious when you do. Drive a few blocks away after the home visit, and then stop to make any needed notes about things you wanted to remember.

Celebrating Play . . .
A Toy Lending Library

Some early childhood teachers are providing parents and families with a valuable service by loaning toys and play equipment from the classroom to use at home. Because teachers only put a small proportion of their total toys and equipment out for play at any one time, they have a great many others that are not in use much of the time. Teachers rotate toys and equipment through the classroom centers so that there are always new and exciting options for children to play with (see Chapter 9 for more details). The play materials that are left in storage can then be loaned to families so that children can take advantage of quality toys in the home environment as well. Many families would benefit greatly from having quality play materials available for use in the home.

If at some point in your teaching career you want to consider lending toys to families, you may want to start on a small scale by loaning only one or two toys at a time. Because a large amount of planning and organization is required for a more complete library, starting with one or two toys at a time allows you to implement this strategy with minimal effort. Rather than having a complete lending library, you would then have a "toy of the week" that could be shared with interested parents. If you wanted to create a more elaborate toy lending library, it would probably be most successful if you were to seek the support and

assistance of several other teachers in your school. By sharing the workload, this project can be made more manageable.

Regardless of the size of your toy lending system, you will need to consider several key steps. The first is to develop an easy but effective checkout system. In addition, a simple method of transporting toys to and from school should be developed. Finally, it is important to have a list of guidelines for toy use that can be sent home with the play materials. One simple method for lending a single toy would be to use an old backpack that children could wear home at the end of the day with the play materials inside in a plastic container. Taping guidelines for toy use to the inside of the container lid would be an effective way to make sure they were readily available.

1. In Chapter 5, you learned of the values of childhood play. Knowing of the importance of play, and despite the added work of creating a toy lending system, do you think it would be worth the effort? Why or why not?

2. In what ways would a toy lending system help you educate parents about the values of childhood play?

Parent Meetings

Getting together with parents in group settings is yet another possible communication strategy to be considered (Foster, 1994). A number of meeting types are useful. Some gatherings could simply be social times, when you have a chance to get to know the parents and help them meet other families in the class. The traditional potluck or a family fun night are examples of this meeting type. Many parent meetings are designed to be educational and focus on a topic of interest and importance to a large number of parents. "Helping Prepare Children for Reading" might be one topic that would interest a variety of parents. Some additional parent meetings are needed to organize for a specific task or to deal with the management of the school. These business meetings can frequently be dull and uninspiring, so it may be best to try to combine this task with another more fun event. Finally, some parent meetings provide an opportunity for child performances.

While not appropriate for the preschool and toddler years, a musical program or the presentation of a play can be a very enjoyable experience for primary children and their families.

If you plan on incorporating parent meetings into your collection of communication tools, be sure to plan carefully for them. Parents who give up precious evening time to come into your classroom will want to get a good return on their investment. Make sure the meeting topics are of interest to parents. A simple questionnaire can be used to determine what parents want and need for their group gatherings. Plan a variety of interesting activities that actively involve parents in discussion and learning. Have a planned agenda organized to keep events moving along smoothly. This careful planning will pay big dividends in terms of parent interest and involvement in your meetings.

Parent–Teacher Conferences

For more information about parent–teacher conferences, go to the Companion Website at www.prenhall.com/henniger, select Chapter 7, then choose Web Destinations.

One of the most common communication tools used in early childhood classrooms is the parent–teacher conference (Gestwicki, 2004). Most schools expect teachers to conference with parents at least once each academic year and more commonly twice. A typical pattern is to have conferences fairly early in the fall and again in the spring. In many early childhood settings, schools will set aside one or two regular school days and additional evening times for conferencing.

Parent–teacher conferences have many strengths as a communication tool. An important benefit of the conference situation is that it brings parents into the classroom. For some, this may be the only time they enter the school. When done well, the conference builds positive rapport with parents as the teacher and parent discuss the child's strengths, progress, and possible areas for improvement. Conferences allow for far greater detail to be shared about the child's progress than either a report card or written report can. In addition, when the conference is held in the classroom, the parent can actually see projects the child has completed and get a better sense for the learning experiences occurring there. Although most parent–teacher conferences are pleasant and enjoyable for both the parent and teacher, occasionally issues raised require the teacher to demonstrate quick thinking and tact to avoid possible problems (Koch & McDonough, 1999). The following purely hypothetical excerpt from a conference situation highlights this issue:

> *Margaret is the mother of 5-year-old Louise. During the parent–teacher conference, Margaret announces, "You know, I am suspicious of anything Louise does. She has fooled me too many times. Oh, I have read all the books on child psychology, but it has not helped me much. I really do not know what to do with Louise. There are so many things wrong with her!"*

As Louise's teacher, you want to understand Margaret's concerns and work effectively with her while also helping the parent see the good things Louise does in your classroom—which is not an easy task. Think about how you might respond to this parent.

Another major consideration for the parent–teacher conference is whether or not to include the child in the event (Taylor, 1999). This is often referred to

Into Practice . . .
Checklist for Parent–Teacher Conferences

Parent–teacher conferences are one of the most common and valuable communication tools you will use with parents. It is important to understand what you can do to make them effective. The following checklist is a good starting point:

- **Make an appointment ahead of time for your conferences, and set a time limit for each.** You do not want to be rigid, but a schedule is needed to manage all the parents who will want to talk to you.
- **Be prepared.** Study all available information on all students, and gather samples of their work. You may want to plan an expected agenda for each conference, while realizing that parent comments or concerns may lead you in different directions.
- **Prepare a comfortable place to hold the parent conferences.** It should have adult-sized chairs arranged in such a way that you let parents know

you see them as partners in the educational process. Make sure the place you choose is private as well, because the information you both share is often sensitive.

- **Adjust your pace to that of the parents.** Some of their concerns may be different from yours, but equally important. Be a good listener. Let parents do a significant portion of the communication.
- **Make the conference professional.** That means sharing clear, specific information about each child and her strengths and areas for improvement in your classroom. It also means that you need to respect parents' and children's information as confidential.
- **Be positive.** It is important to begin and end each conference on a positive note. You cannot ignore the problems, but make sure parents know that their children have demonstrated strengths as well and that you notice them.

as a **three-way conference** and has both strengths and possible problems. When children are involved, their anxiety over what is being discussed is eliminated. They can also share their perspectives on conference issues and, along with the parent and teacher, can commit to any plans for improvement. Many times, seeing the interactions between parent and child in the three-way conference is also insightful and provides the teacher with important information about family life.

The three-way conference has potential problems. For example, the teacher or parent may be less comfortable when the child is present. Each may wish to share information about family life or classroom interactions that is just not appropriate or helpful for children to hear. In other instances, the adults may downplay the child's problems when she is present. Adults can also make the child feel that she is an unimportant part of the conference process by talking over and around the child. Some argue that another potential problem with the three-way conference is that younger children may not understand or be ready to participate in the conference.

Despite these potential problems, you should consider including the child as you prepare for parent–teacher conferences. With careful preparation, even the youngest children can benefit from participation in at least part of your interactions with parents.

 Factors Influencing Quality Involvement

Family involvement does not just happen by magic. It requires a great deal of hard work, including frequent, quality communications between home and school. However, other factors help ensure the success of parent involvement in schools. Williams and Chavkin (1989) have identified seven essential elements of parent involvement programs in schools. Although they identified these elements for schools, the concepts can be applied to individual classrooms as well. In addition to the notion of quality two-way communications, the authors found these elements to be essential:

- *Written policies.* These documents legitimize the importance of parent involvement and provide guidelines for ways in which parents can expect to be involved.

- *Administrative support.* When the administration supports the concept, money is made available, materials and physical resources are provided, and people are assigned the task of carrying out the involvement tasks.

- *Training.* Teachers and parents both need training to make involvement a success. This training should occur over time and focus on developing partnerships between home and school.

- *Partnership approach.* Quality programs emphasize the importance of parents and teachers working as partners in the educational process. Each has much to share and much to learn from one another.

- *Networking.* Network promising parent involvement programs with other programs to share ideas, resources, and expertise.

- *Evaluation.* The best programs also take the time to have regular evaluations of parent involvement activities. Changes and improvements can then be implemented to make involvement activities even more successful.

Parent–Teacher Conflicts

While most interactions with parents are positive, the attitudes and experiences of both parents and teachers lead to potential problems in these relationships. Gestwicki (2004) suggests that the barriers to effective parent–teacher relationships can be categorized into three areas:

- *Barriers caused by human nature.* Fear of criticism, fear hidden behind a "professional" mask, fear of failure, and fear of differences all can cause problems in parent–teacher relationships.

- *Barriers caused by the communication process.* Negative reactions to either the parenting or teaching role, letting emotions influence communications, and introverted personalities lead to less than positive communications between parents and teachers.

- *Barriers caused by external factors.* Time constraints, appearing too busy to interact, failure to adjust to changing family structures, administrative policies that discourage involvement, and personal problems can cause additional conflicts between parents and teachers.

While it may be impossible to avoid all of these barriers, knowing they exist and thinking through potential ways of dealing with them can help reduce the conflicts that may arise. For example, knowing that talking to a parent about her child's low score on a standardized reading test may cause the parent to get emotional, you could plan to highlight first the strengths you have seen the child demonstrate in your classroom before talking about the test score. Remaining calm, even if the parent criticizes your teaching, may be another necessary response.

Families of Children with Special Needs

For more information about families of children with special needs, go to the Companion Website at www.prenhall.com/henniger, select Chapter 7, then choose Web Destinations.

Families that have children with special needs are much the same and yet much different from other families. These parents love their children and want the best for them educationally and socially. However, they are concerned about parenting strategies that work, want their children to learn and grow in healthy and safe environments, are thrilled when a new developmental milestone is reached, and worry about what is best for their children. At the same time, families that have children with special needs often face additional burdens and responsibilities that make parenting and family life a real struggle. Shepherd and Shepherd (1984) describe the range of emotions that many families of children with special needs experience. The following is a sampling of these possible feelings:

- It is a little like everything that everyone else has experienced; it is a lot like nothing anyone else has ever experienced.
- It is feeling like you want to kick in the TV screen every time you see the "Take care of your baby before it is born" public service commercial. I took care of myself when I was pregnant, and our child is handicapped.
- It is being afraid to ask for help because you are fearful that you cannot personally cope with any more blame or guilt.
- It is "dying" from the silence and stares of other people when they meet our son. It is wanting to announce to the whole world that you have a handicapped child and also simultaneously wanting to disappear from the face of the earth for a few moments.
- It is being afraid to even think, much less plan, concerning the future.
- It is dying a little when your son does something inappropriate and others laugh and say "You are so funny!"
- It is having three specialists all ask you during the same day if anyone in your family has ever been diagnosed as schizophrenic. (Shepherd & Shepherd, 1984, pp. 88–89)

Teachers and schools working with these parents and families must make every effort to be sensitive to the special needs and feelings of these families. Extra care must be taken to listen carefully, to communicate positively, and to develop good working relationships with these parents. Remembering that each family unit is unique, teachers must work to understand the challenges these families face and stand ready to assist in whatever ways possible. In addition, families that have children with special needs want to feel needed and accepted as a part of the classroom experiences. Make sure they are welcomed with open arms.

Connecting with the Community

This chapter has focused primarily on involving parents and families in the educational process. Although parents are critical to the success of early education, community members can also provide many important benefits. A great many resources can be productively used to benefit young children (Wright & Stegelin, 2003). In terms of human resources, the local firefighter, police officer, or retired volunteer can share much with your class. Material resources also abound in most communities. Scrap paper, wood, and other recyclable materials can be located and used effectively. Community businesses are often generous in their donations of money and materials in support of local educational efforts. When community members are involved in your classroom, they are also more likely to understand and support your program when talking to others. It makes good sense to work toward involving community members along with parents.

Involving the Community in the School

The community can be active in the early childhood school setting in many good ways (Barbour & Barbour, 2001). One possibility is to allow the school building to be used for appropriate community activities. Groups wanting to offer classes in jewelry making or woodworking, recreational activities such as ballroom dancing, or noncredit classes on such topics as health or psychology always need a place to conduct these activities. Community organizations may also need a meeting room and could benefit from a local school's willingness to provide space.

Another important way to involve community members in the early childhood classroom is to seek out and use resource people to strengthen the curriculum (Gestwicki, 2004). Community helpers such as doctors and dentists can come into the classroom and share information with children about good health and dental care. Workers from a variety of occupations can begin the process of career awareness with young children by demonstrating their expertise. Other community members may well be interested in simply volunteering their time and talents to help out in your classroom.

Finally, community members should be involved in the schools as part of the decision-making process. What is taught, who should serve as teachers, and what equipment and supplies should be purchased are all potential issues in which community members should be involved. The Head Start program requires that every local center have representation from parents and the community on its Advisory Board (U.S. Department of Health and Human Services, 2002). These boards make all the major decisions about Head Start activities. Local public schools also are managed by school boards made up of elected community members who agree to oversee the activities of the schools under its control.

Involving the School in the Community

Early childhood educators and children can also benefit from getting out into the local community (Gestwicki, 2004). By doing so, schools avoid the tendency of isolating themselves from the rest of life. Perhaps the most common way in

Having a firefighter visit the school, or taking your class to a fire station, can enrich your lesson on fire safety.

which teachers and classrooms get involved with the community is through the traditional field trip. A well-planned visit to the local bakery could be a wonderful way to help children understand food production and distribution, for example.

With parental support, the community can also become a site for observation and learning separate from classroom events. In some instances, teachers can provide parents and children with specific assignments to go out into the community and gain insights into business and community services. For example, a second-grade teacher could encourage parents and children to interview a local businessperson in preparation for an upcoming social studies unit. In other circumstances, providing parents with information about upcoming community events and services can lead to important opportunities to learn outside the traditional school setting and day.

Another option for involving the school in the community is to consider ways in which parents, children, and school personnel can give back to the community. Getting involved in a community service project such as planting seedling trees during an Arbor Day celebration could be one way to do this. Another possibility is to adopt a community park and spend time there on a regular basis cleaning and maintaining the grounds. Donating clothing and food to the local women's care facility could be yet another chance to help children and families feel that they are contributing to the community in positive ways.

Summary

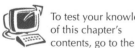

 To test your knowledge of this chapter's contents, go to the Companion Website at www.prenhall.com/henniger, select Chapter 7, then select Study Guide. Also see Chapter Overviews, Reflecting Essay Questions, Multimedia Explorations, and relevant Web Destinations.

Family Life Today

Decreasing numbers of extended families living in close proximity, divorce and single-parent families, blended families, two-career families, parents at older and younger ages, ethnic/cultural diversity, family mobility, and homelessness are all aspects of the diverse families present in America today.

Is Involvement Worth the Effort?

Teachers find that involving parents and community members helps these adults have a greater appreciation for the challenges of teaching, allows teachers to do a better job of teaching, and builds relationships with students and their families. Parents and families find they have more support and ideas for working with their

Observing Development • Parent-Teacher-Child Interactions

Choose one of the age groups within early childhood (infants/toddlers, preschoolers, or primary-age children), *observe* **parent-teacher-child interactions** using the guidelines provided, *reflect* on what you saw and heard, and *apply* the appropriate strategies listed with the children you observed.

Observe	Reflect	Apply
Observe at the beginning of the school day, when parents bring their children into the classroom. Look for specific examples of:	*Think about and respond to the following questions:*	*Consider the following developmentally appropriate strategies for the age group you observed:*
The verbal and nonverbal interactions between parents and teacher (words of greeting, smile, nod, handshake, etc.)	What estimated percentage of parents actually brought their children into the classroom? Was there an attempt on the part of either the parent or the teacher to have meaningful communication as the parent dropped off the child?	Provide independent activities that allow opportunities to greet parents • Infant/toddler: crib toys, play dough, stacking toys • Preschool: Legos, Tinkertoys, books • Primary: Daily math puzzle, writing in journals, silent reading
The verbal and nonverbal interactions between parents and their children (words spoken, facial expressions, holding hands, hugs, kisses, etc.)	What could you infer from what you observed regarding the parent–child relationship? Was the child clinging to the parent or more independent?	Share parenting information • Infant/toddler: start a parent support group so that parents can get together and share ideas and concerns • Preschool: summarize good parenting ideas from magazine articles in weekly newsletter • Primary: inform parents of upcoming community events that focus on parenting skills
The verbal and nonverbal interactions between teacher and children upon arrival (words spoken, pat on the back, high five, facial expressions, etc.)	If you were a child coming into this classroom, would you have felt welcomed by the teacher?	Help each child feel welcome at the start of the school day • Infant/toddler: take a moment to hold or greet each child warmly with a handshake/high five/pat on the back • Preschool: greet each child by name and share something new and interesting in the classroom • Primary: find something positive to say to each child as he or she enters the classroom

children at home. Children benefit with improved school performance, which helps them see the importance of schooling.

Building Strong Two-Way Relationships

The key to working with parents and family members is to build strong two-way relationships through mutual support and communication.

Effective Communication Methods

Communication strategies such as telephone calls, written communications, visual communication tools, home visits, parent meetings, and parent–teacher conferences are essential to the relationship-building process.

Factors Influencing Quality Involvement

Written policies for involvement, administrative support, training in working with families, approaching parent involvement as a partnership, networking with others who involve parents, and systematic evaluation all influence the quality of parent and family involvement.

Parent–Teacher Conflicts

Conflicts with parents or primary caregivers can stem from barriers caused by human nature, the communication process, or external forces.

Families of Children with Special Needs

Families of children with special needs have many of the same needs and interests as others. At the same time, the stress and complications often make parenting more challenging.

Connecting with the Community

Teachers also need planned strategies for involving the community in the school and the school in the community.

Multimedia Explorations and Activities . . .

Getting Parents Involved in Their Child's Education

Over three decades of research have clearly demonstrated the importance of involving parents in their children's education. Active parent participation is an important factor leading to the child's educational success. At Pine Ridge Elementary School, the motto is: "Education is a Family Affair"; that statement is painted boldly on the lunchroom wall. This public school does more than request parent participation; it demands it. As the next video clip shows, teachers and administrators find ways to nurture involvement in every classroom and make it a positive experience for all participants.

Research

While virtually everyone agrees that involving parents in the educational process is critical, many teachers and schools struggle with ways in which this can be accomplished. The purpose of this activity is for you to learn about effective strategies for communicating, interacting, and involving parents and families in the educational process.

1. View the ABC News video segment titled "A Contract to Get Parents Involved in Their Child's Education."
2. Go to the Companion Website at www.prenhall.com/henniger and click on the Multimedia Explorations and Activities button for Chapter 7 for more information on this topic.
3. Talk to a principal or teacher regarding the problems associated with getting parents involved in education and strategies they use to overcome these roadblocks.
4. Talk to a parent of a child in the early childhood range and find out what he or she sees as the benefits and problems associated with involvement.

Reflect

Based on your research of this topic, spend time thinking about each of the following issues:

- Why is parental involvement so critical to your success as a teacher of young children?
- There are obvious benefits to having parents sign a contract committing to involvement in the schools. But could there be problems as well? What might they be?
- What roadblocks did you find that get in the way of parents getting actively involved in schools?
- What creative options for getting parents involved did you find?

Respond

Based on the information and ideas you have found, consider one or more of the following options:

1. Find parents of a young child who have been less involved in their child's education than they would like to be (a teacher may be able to guide you to a good candidate). Spend some time talking with them and listening to what has kept them from getting more involved. Brainstorm with the parents on some creative options for increasing the level of involvement. Spend some time helping the parents implement the strategies you have jointly selected.

2. Work with a teacher of young children to create a list of new options for parent involvement. The teacher you work with should be interested in increasing the level of parent participation. You will first need to learn about current involvement strategies, future needs, and the problems encountered in getting parents involved. Following your initial discussion, create a list of interesting involvement strategies and share them with your teacher. Talk about ways of implementing the agreed-upon options.

DIVERSITY AND YOUNG CHILDREN

In this chapter you will

- Study how young children develop conceptual understandings of diversity.
- Identify ways to encourage acceptance of diverse people.
- Discover methods for integrating diversity topics into the early childhood curriculum.
- Investigate options for working with parents and community members regarding diversity.

*"**What an interesting class** I have!" you think, as you prepare for next week's activities. "These children are unique in so many ways. In my class of 27 third-grade children, I've got quite a mix. There is Dimitri, who comes to us from Russia. His English has improved by leaps and bounds over the last several months. Eduard and Angela are Hispanic and benefit so much from the warmth and support of their extended families. Shantel is African American, and Quen has Asian heritage. Each brings a unique personality to the classroom. Then there is Alex. Despite using a wheelchair from a very early age, he is one of the most active and happy children in the group. To complicate things even further, the class has a higher than normal percentage of boys. It will be even more important than usual to make sure the girls have access to some of the traditionally boy-dominated equipment in the classroom."*

Although the preceding scenario may sound rather unusual, in reality, this level of diversity is often the current norm in many early childhood classrooms. Adults working with children need to be prepared for this situation and be ready to assist children in understanding and appropriately responding to the diversity they will experience.

Diversity as an Essential Element

The topic of diversity is included in this section of the text because it directly influences the other essential elements of early childhood education presented in Chapters 4 through 7. Child development, play, guidance, and working with parents and families are all influenced by diversity. Some examples should help highlight this point:

- *Child development and diversity.* Children with physical disabilities (such as problems with hearing and eyesight) acquire oral and written language differently; boys and girls have variations in their gross and fine motor development (Schickedanz, Schickedanz, Forsyth, & Forsyth, 2001).

- *Play and diversity.* Children who live in cultures that value competition play more competitive games (Sutton-Smith & Roberts, 1981); children with autism seldom engage in symbolic play (Atlas & Lapidus, 1987); boys and girls have different toy preferences (Nash & Fraleigh, 1993).

- *Diversity and guidance.* Children with attention deficits often need special guidance regarding instructions (Landau & McAninch, 1993); eye contact is considered impolite in some cultures, thus changing the way in which you guide some children (Hildebrand & Hearron, 1999).

- *Working with diverse parents.* In African American families, it is common for aunts, uncles, grandparents, and other extended family members to informally adopt children, thus creating unique family constellations for the teacher to work with (Olsen & Fuller, 2003); the involvement of men in child care and education has increased and changes the mix of parents that teachers will be working with (National Center for Education Statistics, 2003).

It should be clear from these examples that diversity influences how teachers work with children and families. As American society grows increasingly more diverse, the importance of this topic will continue to expand. A careful study of diversity will add to your understanding of the essential elements of early childhood education.

Attitudes Toward Diversity

An important starting point in the study of diversity is to address the attitudes of children (and adults) toward people who are different from themselves. Without question, children notice the many distinctions that exist. For example, infants as young as 6 months notice skin color differences (Banks, 1993). By the age of 2, children not only notice similarities and differences but also ask questions about their observations. Clearly, children find diversity topics interesting and want to talk about and understand them.

Racial/Cultural Attitudes

To understand children's attitudes about racial and cultural differences, it is necessary to begin with those held by adults. Children are strongly influenced by the comments and actions of the significant adults in their lives.

Teachers should view diversity as a positive aspect of working with young children and their families.

With the passage of the *Civil Rights Act* in 1964, many people assumed that racial discrimination would end relatively quickly and that attitudes about racial and cultural differences would improve greatly. This has not, however, been the case. Although many people accept and value the racial and cultural diversity of American life, others do not. Unfortunately, some adults continue to pass on to children their misconceptions and negative attitudes about people who are different from themselves.

Children who are exposed to these adults begin to absorb these negative attitudes as early as two-and-a-half years of age (Banks, 1993). Through repeated exposure to parents, teachers, neighbors, television, and other media that regularly reinforce this disapproval of people different from themselves, children start to internalize these values. Because both positive and negative attitudes begin to develop early in the young child's life, it is essential for early educators to help guide children in the process of valuing racial/cultural diversity.

Attitudes About Gender

Efforts to provide women with equitable opportunities in all aspects of American life have been only slightly more successful than the results for racial/cultural minorities. Take, for example, gender equity in National College Athletic Association (NCAA) sports. A study by the NCAA indicates that even though equitable funding has been mandated for many years, it will probably be several more years before parity is reached ("Colleges Make Slight Progress," 2003).

The American Association of University Women (1998) has studied gender equity issues for girls in the K–12 educational system. While there has been considerable progress over the last several years, girls still take fewer advanced classes in

It is just as important for boys to be involved in playing "house" as girls since most boys will eventually be fathers and husbands.

mathematics and the sciences than boys. In addition, girls make up only a small percentage of the students in computer science and computer design courses.

Although most people talk about the importance of gender equity, the subtle (and not-so-subtle) behaviors of many adults indicate that women are often given lower status in American society. Children are again exposed to many parents, adults, and media events that promote gender inequities. This can often lead to childhood behaviors and budding attitudes that are less than desirable.

 Mandy, Ariel, and DeForrest are playing in the dress-up area of their preschool classroom. Clothes and equipment are available for playing doctors and nurses. Mandy wants to dress up as a doctor and begins to gear up for her role. "Hey!" calls DeForrest. "You can't be the doctor! Girls have to be the nurses!"

Preschool children's attitudes about gender roles (like the one just expressed) are often overgeneralizations made from their observations of, and interactions with, other adults. These early stereotypic responses can be modified by adults who provide children with more diverse examples of women's roles in society. Young children need early and frequent exposure to pictures, stories, and adult models that demonstrate more equitable opportunities for women in America.

Children with Special Needs

With the passage of Public Law (PL) 94–142 (the *Education for All Handicapped Children Act*) in 1975, children with special needs began to be mainstreamed into American public school classrooms. Children without disabilities began to work and play with students having special needs. Before this time, these groups rarely interacted. In 1986, PL 99–457 mandated mainstreaming for children

For more information regarding attitudes about gender, go to the Companion Website at www.prenhall.com/henniger, select Chapter 8, then choose Web Destinations.

Family Partnerships . . .
Working with Teen Parents

It may surprise you to learn that the number of teen parents in this country is high. While there was an overall decline in teen parents during the last decade of the 20th century, America still has one of the highest teen pregnancy rates among developed countries. Four of every 10 young women in this country become pregnant at least once before their 20th birthday (Annie E. Casey Foundation, 2003). These statistics make it clear that, as a teacher of young children, your partnerships with families will probably include working with teen parents.

Because of these probable connections, it is important for you to be aware of the many challenges faced by very young parents and be prepared to assist them when possible. Teen mothers tend to drop out of school and live in poverty more often than their peers. In addition, they have children with increased health problems, more frequent developmental delays, and a greater likelihood for future difficulties in school (Shore, 2003). As society struggles to reduce the incidence of teen pregnancy, your job will be to work cooperatively and effectively with these very young parents in whatever ways you can.

In addition to interacting with teen parents in your classroom, you will want to be aware of other resources within the schools and local community. Teen parents are receiving services in several important ways:

- **On-site child care.** Many high schools now provide on-site child care so that teen parents can continue their own schooling while their young children receive quality care. These programs are often cooperative schools (see Chapter 3) and teen parents are expected to spend time as aides in the classroom, where they learn parenting skills as they interact with other trained early educators.

- **Parenting education.** Teen parents typically have limited knowledge of what it takes to be a parent and few resources for parenting advice. They need assistance from others about expectations for child development, strategies for parenting, and help in managing complex lives under difficult circumstances. Teachers, schools, and community agencies are stepping in to assist teen parents in these important areas.

- **Alternative schooling.** Because of their life situations, teen parents may find it difficult to be successful in a regular middle school or high school program. Most school districts provide alternative schooling options for teen parents and others that offer learning experiences to better meet their needs.

- **Counseling and career education.** School districts and community agencies also provide teen parents with counseling and career education opportunities to help them cope with challenging life circumstances and take advantage of local resources.

- **Health care.** Because teen parents are often in low-income family situations, they frequently qualify for free or low-cost medical care. Taking advantage of these services can have a major positive impact on the health and well-being of children.

1. Have you had experiences with teen parents in either your family or home community? What do these experiences tell you about the challenges they face?

2. How do you think you will feel about working with teen parents? How will your attitudes and beliefs influence your interactions?

from ages 3 to 5, further encouraging contact between children with special needs and the general population. More recently, PL 101–336 (known as the *Americans with Disabilities Act*) was enacted in 1990. Viewed as a major piece of civil rights legislation (Wolery & Wilbers, 1994), this law requires equal access to public and private services for individuals with special needs. These services include the opportunity to participate in early childhood programs. PL 101–476, known as the *Individuals with Disabilities Education Act (IDEA)*, was also put into law in 1990. This law provided individuals with special needs who were ages 18 to 21 with services and modified the categories of disability to include such things as autism and attention deficit disorder (ADD).

One result of the preceding legislation was that a definition of the different types of special needs eligible for services evolved. Walsh, Smith, and Taylor (2000) list the following categories of individuals with special needs:

For more information about children with special needs, go to the Companion Website at www.prenhall.com/henniger, select Chapter 8, then choose Web Destinations.

- Autism
- Deaf-blindness, hearing impairment (including deafness), visual impairment (including blindness)
- Mental retardation
- Emotional disturbance
- Multiple disabilities
- Specific learning disability
- Orthopedic impairments
- Other health impairments
- Speech or language impairment
- Traumatic brain injury

The opportunity for early and regular contact has led to many benefits for children with and without special needs. Wolery and Wilbers (1994) list the following potential advantages:

Children with special needs:
- Are spared the negative effects of separate, segregated education.
- Receive realistic life experiences that prepare them to live in the community.
- Have opportunities to develop friendships with typically developing peers.

Children without special needs:
- Can develop more accurate views about individuals with special needs.
- Have opportunities to develop positive attitudes about people who are different from themselves.
- Are provided with models of children who succeed despite many challenges.

Evan is a fun and lively 5-year-old with Down syndrome. One characteristic of his special need is lower than normal muscle tone. This lower tone means that Evan's speech is harder to understand and large and small muscle control is delayed. In addition, Evan is slower to develop conceptual understandings and finds it harder than most children to learn new ideas. Despite these challenges, he is actively engaged in learning both at home and in his kindergarten classroom. Evan is one of the most well-liked children in the group.

An important system is now in place that can help young children develop positive attitudes about people with special needs. Early childhood teachers need to take advantage of these naturally occurring interactions to help children grow in their understanding and acceptance of individuals with special needs. By modeling appropriate interactions and encouraging children to do the same, adults can help

Celebrating Play . . . Children with Special Needs and Play

In your future role as an early childhood educator, you will almost certainly be working with children with special needs. As you begin to think about teaching these students, remember that they are people first and only secondarily require special services. Children with special needs are more like their peers than they are different from them. Their needs, interests, and learning styles are often much like every other child in the classroom. These similarities suggest that play should be considered an important vehicle for learning and development in the lives of children with special needs. As is the case for all children (see Chapter 5), play provides opportunities for children with special needs to develop social, emotional, physical, language, and intellectual understandings in unique ways.

In a position paper for the Association for Childhood Education International (ACEI) titled "Play: Essential for All Children", Isenberg and Quisenberry (2002) make a compelling argument for **all** children having the opportunity for quality play experiences:

> Theorists, regardless of their orientation, concur that play occupies a central role in children's lives. They also suggest that the *absence of play* is an obstacle to the development of healthy and creative individuals. *Psychoanalysts* believe that play is necessary for mastering emotional traumas or disturbances; *psychosocialists* believe it is necessary for ego mastery and learning to live with everyday experiences; *constructivists* believe it is necessary for cognitive growth; *maturationalists* believe it is necessary for

competence building and for socializing functions in all cultures of the world; and *neuroscientists* believe it is necessary for emotional and physical health, motivation, and love of learning. (p. 1)

Given this strong statement, it may surprise you to learn that opportunities for play are not always as readily available for children with special needs. Because the traditional focus of most programs has been on more direct instruction for these children, teachers provide numerous structured learning experiences that help children with special needs develop academic and social/emotional skills. One of the consequences of this focus, however, is that there is frequently less time for play. Another problem faced by many young children with special needs is that the materials used in quality play experiences are not easily adaptable for use by children with special needs. It is impossible, for example, for a child in a wheelchair to use a creative playground structure that is not equipped with a ramp for wheelchair use.

1. Go to the ACEI web site (www.udel.edu/bateman/ acei/playpaper.htm) and read the position statement in its entirety. Based on the arguments presented, do you agree that play is essential for *all* children?

2. Should children with special needs be provided with the toys and equipment they need to engage in quality play experiences?

ensure the development of healthy attitudes. The "Observing Development" feature at the end of this chapter considers children with special needs you might observe in your classrooms, reflects on how these children may impact their classmates, and offers specific applications to increase and improve interactions.

Encouraging an Acceptance of Diversity

It should be clear that teachers and caregivers must actively help children develop appropriate attitudes about diversity. The negative opinions children encounter through many hours of television viewing and interactions with prejudiced adults require careful and frequent effort to overcome. This process should begin with the youngest children and continue throughout the early childhood years. Research indicates that many attitudes are firmly entrenched by 9 years of age and may be difficult to change after that time (Aboud, 1988).

Begin with Self-Analysis

An excellent place to begin this active process of influencing children's attitudes is with self-analysis. Because you will be one of the most influential adults in the life of the child, an understanding of your personal attitudes and behaviors is important (Howard, 1999). Although most of us would like to think that we are not prejudiced against those different from ourselves, careful reflection often uncovers many areas that could be improved. One method for developing more accurate self-awareness is through individual reflection and journal writing. The support and assistance of a small group is strongly encouraged. A sampling of activities that could be useful in this process follows:

- Think about how you would describe or define your racial/ethnic identity. Write about or discuss with others what you find important/not important about this aspect of yourself. Describe how you feel about your racial/ethnic identity.

- Repeat the preceding activity two more times, focusing first on your gender identity and next on differences in physical abilities.

- Think about and share either in writing or with a small group your views on race, ethnicity, gender, and ableness compared with those of your parents.

- Write down lists of acceptable and unacceptable behaviors for boys and girls, men and women. Discuss these lists with others (Derman-Sparks, 1989; Derman-Sparks & Phillips, 1997).

Again, these self-awareness activities are most effective when combined with a support group to help its members discuss and deal with the issues uncovered in this analysis. Often, the feelings encountered are painful and difficult to deal with. Help from others may be needed to work successfully through these concerns.

Talk About Differences

Good early childhood educators have always been effective in recognizing and building on children's natural interests. As captivating topics are identified by children, the creative teacher takes the opportunity to discuss them in detail. Through spontaneous dialogue and additional planned activities, children build important understandings of these issues.

Children recognize and want to know more about the differences between people. Whether during a trip through the grocery store, a church activity, community events, or an experience at school, children are aware of racial, gender, and ableness issues to which they are exposed. Again, the insightful teacher or caregiver recognizes these experiences as opportunities for natural and effective discussion times regarding diversity.

Talk About Similarities

In all likelihood, young children will recognize and talk about the differences they notice in others. The similarities between diverse peoples, however, may be less obvious to them. Teachers should make an effort to point out to children the similarities that exist between all peoples.

Individually and with groups of children, teachers should discuss physical similarities, common interests, daily activities that are similar (like playing and school), similarities in games, and toys that are similar across cultures. Two tools that may be helpful to the teacher in dealing with these issues are:

For more information about books on diversity topics, go to the Companion Website at www.prenhall.com/henniger, select Chapter 8, then choose Web Destinations.

- *Books.* Many good books exist to help children explore both the similarities and differences between diverse groups of people (Marshall, 1998). While most were written to highlight the differences, the alert teacher can also build in a discussion of similarities.
- *Persona dolls.* Another technique that is equally effective in discussing both similarities and differences is the persona doll (Derman-Sparks, 1989). Using dolls that are diverse in appearance for storytelling activities allows the teacher to build pretend personalities and lives that are both similar to and different from those of children in the classroom.

Expose Children to Diversity

Engaging children in discussions about diversity is too important to be left to chance. Early childhood educators must plan for a variety of experiences with diversity that become a natural part of the daily activities of young children. Many toys, materials, pictures, books, and experiences can be woven into the curriculum to challenge children to question, compare, and contrast people and experiences different from themselves. An awareness of the need to plan for these options makes it much more likely that children will develop healthy understandings of diversity.

Inappropriate Responses to Diversity

Before discussing positive ways of addressing diversity in the early childhood classroom, it is important to address two ineffective strategies that are commonly seen. Each has been used by teachers to avoid meaningful discussions of human differences with young children.

Ignore Diversity

One clearly inappropriate response to diversity is to deny that it exists. A typical comment from a teacher ignoring diversity would be: "This multicultural education business does not make sense for my classroom. My class is all White, and anyway, kids do not notice differences at this age." Clearly, this approach is misguided. Children do recognize and talk about the differences they see. Teachers need to weave diversity topics into the curriculum during the early years.

The Tourist Approach

Another ineffective strategy employed by teachers to study cultural differences is to engage in what has been called a tourist-multicultural curriculum (Derman-Sparks, 1994). These well-meaning adults engage in a simplistic, often stereotypic look at different cultures by taking quick little curriculum visits to other parts of the world before returning to the more important European American focus for the majority of time. Boutte and McCormick (1992) describe the tourist approach as follows: "cooking ethnic foods, examining Native American artifacts at Thanksgiving or discussing African American achievements during Black History

Into Practice . . .
Resources for Diversity Materials

Many toy and equipment companies are beginning to include materials that address diversity issues. Other smaller companies have been created specifically to provide toys and equipment that represent multicultural and special needs populations. Some examples of the latter are provided here.

Asia for Kids
4480 Lake Forest Dr., Suite 302
Cincinnati, OH 45242–3726
(800) 765–5885
www.asiaforkids.com/

Sells books, dolls, and games that are representative of Asian cultures.

People of Every Stripe
P.O. Box 12505
Portland, OR 97212–0505
(503) 282–0612

Offers a wide selection of fabric dolls from around the world and dolls with disabilities.

Roots and Wings
P.O. Box 19678
Boulder, CO 80308–2678
(800) 833–1787
www.rootsandwingsbooks.com/

Sells a collection of children's books with multicultural themes and some puppets and stuffed animals from around the world.

Smithsonian Folkways Recordings
414 Hungerford Drive, Suite 444
Rockville, MD 20850
800–410–9815
www.folkways.si.edu/

Offers an extensive collection of CDs and cassette tapes with ethnic, folk, jazz, and children's music from around the world.

month. Certainly, these lessons have merit; however, since they are often isolated and discontinuous, they are actually 'pseudomulticultural' activities" (p. 140).

Although this approach introduces children to aspects of different cultures, it does so in ways that lead children to believe that the European American perspective is the most important and that other cultures are only tangentially significant. Often, these brief visits lead to stereotypic perceptions of other cultures and therefore sabotage the true goals of studying diversity (Irvine, 2003).

The tourist approach to multicultural education tends to disconnect content learned in the quick trips from the main curriculum. The unintended outcome is to trivialize the contributions of different cultural groups. The unconscious thinking of children could be described as follows: "How can this content we are studying be important? It is only a small add-on to the main topics we are discussing. Studying differences cannot be that important if that is all we are going to do to address it." Clearly, this is not the message we want children to receive through the study of multicultural issues.

Obviously, the tourist approach can also be used by well-meaning teachers to address gender and ableness issues. When either topic is treated as tangential to the main curriculum, students get the message that these are less important concerns. If diversity in general is to be a meaningful component of the early childhood classroom, this quick-fix strategy must be avoided.

Integrating Diversity Throughout the Curriculum

To make diversity topics valuable additions to the curriculum, a more complex and thoughtful strategy than the tourist approach must be implemented. Issues relating to cultural differences, gender, and ableness must be made an integral part of the daily activities in the early childhood classroom (Derman-Sparks, 1999). Rather than brief diversions into interesting but less important areas, the curriculum must be infused with materials, activities, and people that provide regular opportunities for young children to come in contact with meaningful diversity issues.

The Antibias Curriculum

Louise Derman-Sparks (1989) suggests an appropriate title for a program that integrates diversity throughout the curriculum: the **antibias curriculum.** She states that, although specific techniques are associated with this approach, each teacher must take the general principles presented and create an appropriate program for their specific group of children and families. The philosophy undergirding the antibias curriculum is value-based: "Differences are good; oppressive ideas and behaviors are not." The antibias curriculum "sets up a creative tension between respecting differences and not accepting unfair beliefs and acts" (Derman-Sparks, 1989, p. x). This approach requires careful planning, self-assessment, and communication with others to implement. It takes dedication and commitment but provides many rewards for children and adults alike.

Teachers interested in implementing an antibias curriculum should take a five-step approach (Derman-Sparks, 1989; Derman-Sparks & Phillips, 1997) to ensure success:

Step 1. *Make a personal commitment.* To make this curriculum a reality, teachers must spend considerable time and energy. Diversity issues must be a high priority.

Step 2. *Organize a support group.* The perspectives and feedback from peers are essential for rethinking the teaching of diversity.

Step 3. *Do consciousness-raising (self-analysis) activities.* Self-analysis was described earlier in the chapter. Teachers need to become aware of their own feelings toward cultural, racial, sexual, and ableness differences.

Step 4. *Make a plan for implementing the curriculum.* Through an evaluation of the physical environment, a critique of current activities, and observations of children, teachers can make plans for implementing antibias activities.

Step 5. *Move slowly and carefully.* Integrating diversity into the curriculum is hard work and requires careful planning. Moving more slowly helps ensure success.

Using Toys That Promote Diversity

 For more information about toys that promote diversity understandings, go to the Companion Website at www.prenhall.com/henniger, select Chapter 8, then choose Web Destinations.

One important way to encourage an acceptance of diversity in the early childhood classroom is through the provision of toys and equipment that portray similarities and differences between people. Swiniarski (1991) suggests that toys are excellent ways to introduce young children to global education. As children play

This puppet show, which includes puppets with physical disabilities, helps children recognize and discuss similarities and differences among people. (Note: The Kids on the Block is an educational company that uses puppets to teach children about disabilities, differences, and social concerns. Created in 1977, the educational puppet curriculums are in use worldwide by more than 1,700 community-based troupes. For information, call 1-800-368-KIDS.)

with these materials and notice their similarities and differences across cultures, many opportunities for natural multicultural learning take place.

> *Four-year-old Natalie is playing with a plastic replica of a giraffe in the block area. This is her first experience with the toy giraffe, so as the teacher stops to observe block play, Natalie asks about this animal. Where does it live? What does it eat? How big is it? Her curiosity leads to the teacher finding some picture books and other materials that describe the habitat of giraffes. Natalie is gaining understanding of a place with people and animals that are different from herself and her surroundings.*

A variety of toys are common worldwide (Swiniarski, 1991). They include

- Dolls
- Toy animals
- Musical instruments
- Puzzles
- Construction toys
- Movement toys (cars, trucks, planes)
- Puppets

The cultural uniqueness of these toys is generally in their presentation or decoration. By including toys from around the world as part of the play materials children can use in the classroom, children have many important opportunities to recognize and discuss their similarities and differences. Cultural discussions and understandings become a natural part of the day.

In addition to culture-specific toys, options are available for providing children with playthings that allow them to explore aspects of ableness. Dolls with disabilities, for example, are available through some toy vendors. Wheelchairs (both toy and real) are another possibility for the early childhood classroom. Other options are sure to present themselves to the teacher who is actively looking for these diversity options.

Toys and materials can also be purchased to encourage discussion and thinking regarding gender issues. One of the best examples of this is the variety of puzzles that are available depicting women in nontraditional work roles. Female doctors, police officers, and airline pilots are representative of this option. Some flannelboard sets and dolls provide additional opportunities for a discussion of gender differences and roles.

Diversity Through Games

Like the toys just described, many games from around the world can be used to enhance young children's understanding of different cultures. As with toys, games played by children around the world have more similarities than differences (Kirchner, 1991). Whether engaged in running and tag activities, ball games, or manipulative and guessing games, children play in very similar ways throughout the world. For example, the game Kick the Can, which has its origins in Canada, is played with slight variations in India (where it is called *Esha Desai*), Holland (*Burkuit*), Sweden (*Paven Bannlyser*), and Japan (*Kankai*) (Kirchner, 1991).

 For more information about games around the world, go to the Companion Website at www.prenhall.com/henniger, select Chapter 8, then choose Web Destinations.

These games, in addition to being fun ways to spend time, provide opportunities for children to play out aspects of different cultures. For example, in the game Antelope in the Net (appropriate for 7- to 10-year-olds), which originated in the Congo, one child is chosen to be the antelope, and the rest form a circle (the net) around the antelope. Children forming the net hold hands and chant "Kasha Mu Bukondi! Kasha Mu Bukondi!" ("Antelope in the net"). The antelope tries to break out of the net by crawling under, climbing over, or running through the tightly held hands. If the antelope is caught, the child who traps him or her becomes the new antelope (Hatcher, Pape, & Nicosia, 1988). In playing this type of game, children are naturally exposed to aspects of another culture and can begin to appreciate both the similarities and differences.

Quality Children's Literature

Books for young children can be wonderful options for addressing diversity issues in the early childhood classroom. A good book can captivate the interests of children while introducing people and events that are new to them. Many times, books can lead to in-depth discussions and activities that help children understand the complexities of diversity topics (Marshall, 1998; National Association for the Education of Young Children, 1993).

For example, to introduce the topic of diverse abilities, the book *Someone Special, Just Like You* (Brown, 1991) could be read and then discussed by young children. This book is a collection of photographs depicting children with special needs engaged in a variety of activities. The situations children have encountered

Into Practice...
Diversity Through Pictures

Teachers of young children collect many different things that will be useful to them in the classroom. One such collection is often a picture file. When put on the walls in centers or used as discussion starters for small- or large-group activities, pictures can help young children develop important insights about diversity. If you create a picture file, be sure to also include nonstereotypic people of color, pictures of individuals with special needs, and examples of men and women in nontraditional roles. Some potential sources of good photos for a diverse picture file include the following:

- Magazines such as *Life, Ms.,* or *Ebony* can provide many good pictures when carefully selected.

- Calendars made by organizations dealing with diversity may have excellent pictures that can be collected.
- Photographs of children and families in your classroom or community and photos from your travels may also be useful.
- UNICEF greeting cards often portray diverse peoples and can be saved for a picture file.
- Posters from organizations focusing on children and families (such as the National Association for the Education of Young Children or the Council for Exceptional Children) are useful.

will naturally lead to further discussions and activities, thus increasing awareness and understanding of this aspect of diversity.

When selecting books on diversity, consider the following:

- Try to find books that represent children in your class.
- Look for books that introduce new information and ideas to children.
- Make sure to balance your selections to ensure that children are introduced to a variety of topics (Yokota, 1993).

The Visual-Aesthetic Environment

Another excellent way to increase opportunities to discuss diversity in the early childhood classroom is to use pictures and posters to decorate the room. These visual accessories should include people from different cultures and individuals with special needs engaging in real-world, everyday activities. Reproductions of artwork from around the world can also be used to decorate the early childhood classroom. All of these visual options can help children see that diversity is a natural part of their lives and can open new opportunities for discussing these important topics.

Artifacts from different cultures may also be used as visual displays to stimulate interest in discussing similarities and differences between people around the world. For example, a traditional African doll purchased by a parent during a recent visit could be introduced at group time and used to discuss dolls in different cultures. While these items may be too fragile or special to be put in a play center, using artifacts for group time experiences and then placing them on display can be a productive use of these materials.

Music is yet another way in which children can be introduced to cultural similarities and differences. Simply playing a variety of musical styles during the day can be a good way of introducing children to an aspect of diversity. Discussing these musical pieces at group time may stimulate further understandings of people around the world.

Meaningful Diversity Experiences

Taking advantage of the cultural, gender, and ableness differences that exist within your classroom and community is an effective way to build meaningful experiences into the curriculum. By bringing diverse people into the classroom and having children interact with them, awareness is heightened, and discussions of similarities and differences increase. These natural interactions can occur while adults read children a book, assist with their math problems, or build in the block corner. They can be important and meaningful steps in understanding diversity.

Informal interactions can be combined with other more focused activities to add meaningful diversity experiences to the curriculum. Having a parent whose first language is something other than English come in to tutor children in her native language is one example of this more organized approach. Another option could be to have a community member help the class prepare a favorite meal that exemplifies his cultural heritage. When teachers locate people in their classrooms or communities who can add these experiences to the curriculum, everyone benefits.

Celebrating Diversity...
Holidays

The traditions surrounding holidays valued by different people are important opportunities for children to learn about diversity. At the same time, however, it is often difficult to choose which holidays to celebrate and how to respect the cultures and religious perspectives represented by each of the children in your group. The National Association for the Education of Young Children (1996) provides the following suggestions:

- Parents and teachers need to ask why children should learn about this holiday and whether it is developmentally appropriate.
- Celebrations should be connected to specific children and families within the group.
- Children should be encouraged to share their feelings and information about the celebrations they have.

- Every group (but not every holiday) represented within the classroom should be honored through celebration of a holiday.
- Activities should demonstrate respect for the customs of different cultures.
- Parents and teachers need to work together in planning these special events.

1. Do holidays celebrated by different cultures and religious groups constitute meaningful diversity experiences as described in this chapter? Why or why not?

2. How do you feel about celebrating holidays that conflict with your religious/cultural heritage? Discuss these feelings with others.

Individuals with Special Needs

Despite attempts over the last 20 years to include children with special needs in pre–K through grade 12 classrooms, individuals with special needs are often misunderstood and are only reluctantly accepted in classrooms by teachers and students alike. Much has yet to be done to more adequately integrate individuals with special needs into American society. Early childhood educators must take important first steps in their classrooms to help this process along.

Develop Inclusive Environments

For more information about inclusion, go to the Companion Website at www.prenhall.com/henniger, select Chapter 8, then choose Web Destinations.

While many of the techniques, methods, and materials used with children who do not have special needs are effective with children with special needs as well, other strategies are often needed. The following four guidelines (Wolery & Wilbers, 1994) can help teachers of young children more effectively design the physical space for children with special needs:

1. *When needed, help children learn to play with toys and materials.* Some young children with special needs may benefit from initial adult assistance in playing with typical early childhood materials. With sensitive guidance, these children, like children without special needs, can greatly benefit from these play experiences.

2. *Select toys and materials that appeal to students.* Through careful observation, teachers can learn what play materials students with special needs enjoy. These should be provided on a regular basis to encourage creative play experiences.

3. *Provide play materials that engage children in playing, interacting, and learning.* When possible, toys and materials for children with special needs should be selected to promote learning identified in their Individualized Education Plans (IEPs).

4. *Adapt toys and materials where needed.* Some toys and materials cannot be manipulated because of physical limitations. Adaptations such as battery-powered toys that can be manipulated with switches and wheelchair-accessible sand play areas outdoors help ensure that all children benefit from quality play experiences.

Strengthen Social Interactions

Creating a physical space that provides quality play experiences for all children is an important step in an inclusive classroom. Equally valuable are the social interactions that are encouraged. Adults must first be aware of the ways in which they relate to children with special needs. Many techniques, such as observing, supporting, facilitating, and expanding children's play and interactions with others, are useful with all students. Other more specialized techniques may be needed with some children. One adult interaction that is useful when teaching students with special needs is the use of **prompts.** A prompt can be defined as help given to assist a child in engaging in specific skills (Wolery & Wilbers, 1994). Prompts can be verbal, gestural, modeled, or used for physical assistance.

Interaction between children with special needs and their typically developing peers is another dimension that teachers must work to enhance. Two important reasons support encouraging these exchanges. First, these social interactions help

The passage of the Education for All Handicapped Children Act (PL 94–142) in 1975 promoted mainstreaming children with special needs into public school classrooms.

children understand one another better while establishing effective relationships that can grow with time. Second, when children with special needs interact with others, they have peers who model appropriate and adaptive behaviors.

These interactions between children with special needs and other children do not simply happen, however. Teachers must support and encourage these exchanges. One strategy teachers can use is to encourage children to engage in social interactions in small-group, rather than large-group, settings. Whenever possible, children with special needs should be placed in small groups that contain peers who are especially competent in growth areas identified on the IEP.

Collaborate with Other Professionals

Joley is 4 years old and uses a wheelchair. Her mother is a single parent, so Joley spends almost 9 hours each day in the Sunshine Child Care Center. In addition to the teachers she works with in the program, Joley spends time with a physical therapist twice a week. In addition, a psychologist works with her on anger control issues biweekly, and a school district special education teacher comes to the home once a month to assist her with oral language skills. Although Joley is benefiting from the assistance of a number of professionals, the coordination of these people and services is a challenge.

A variety of professionals frequently are involved in providing services for children with special needs. Wolery and Wilbers (1994) describe the following disciplines as regular collaborators in caring for young children with special needs:

- Special education
- Psychology
- Speech/language pathology

- Occupational therapy
- Social work
- Nutrition
- Nursing
- Audiology
- Medicine

The collaboration of people within these professions to provide support for young children with special needs has been mandated by legislation for many years. The IEP is one key area that requires this collaboration. Few teachers and other professionals, however, are prepared for the complexities of the interactions required. To succeed, all the professionals involved need to begin these collaborative efforts with an understanding of who should participate, what each professional's role should be, a willingness to communicate often and well, and a desire to adjust roles and responsibilities as needed in the best interests of the child (Hildebrand et al., 2000).

 Issues of Gender Equity

What are the components of gender equity that should concern us in the early childhood classroom? Do these include how we communicate with both sexes? Should we focus on equitable opportunities for boys and girls to participate in activities? What about adult perceptions of gender roles and how they influence interactions with children? Each question defines an important element of gender equity in the early childhood classroom that should be addressed by concerned educators.

Language

The words we use to communicate with children send powerful messages that influence many aspects of development, including attitudes about gender. Take, for example, the seemingly innocuous phrase: "Hey, you guys!" If addressed to a group of boys, there is obviously no problem. But what about using that same phrase to communicate with a mixed-sex group or a gathering of girls? Is there a hidden message here that may be inappropriate? A small thing perhaps, but it is often these finer nuances that children focus on as they make assessments about the relative value of being a boy or girl.

Language has other subtle influences on children. Consistently using words that suggest dependence, weakness, or submission to describe the behavior of girls and other descriptors that imply strength, independence, and dominance in relationship to male behaviors can lead to inappropriate gender definitions by young children. Although most of us try to avoid these categorical descriptions of boys and girls, some of the words we use to talk to young children may be sending a different message. Careful self-assessment is needed to make sure we use appropriate language as we interact with both sexes.

Accessibility Issues

Research on the play behaviors of children in learning centers suggests that certain activities are dominated by boys and others by girls. Boys tend to take on more active/aggressive roles with cars and trucks, construction toys, and blocks. Girls, how-

Into Practice . . .
Gender-Neutral Dramatic Play Activities

One important way in which teachers can encourage both boys and girls to engage in dramatic play is to plan activities that are of interest to both sexes. Selecting these more gender-neutral materials and themes to complement traditional dramatic play activities like dress-up and doll play help make this center more attractive to all children. The following are a few examples of gender-neutral themes and basic materials for creating these centers:

- **Airplane.** Child-sized chairs arranged in rows to simulate airplane seating, headphones from the listening center for pilot headsets, small suitcases, simulated plane tickets, and a large photograph or poster of the cockpit of an airplane provide the basic ingredients for this theme.

- **Camping.** A small tent, sleeping bags, flashlights, lantern, camp stools, and a pretend campfire can be used to create a camping theme.
- **Post office.** Junk mail, mailboxes, postal carriers' bags, envelopes, pretend stamps, stamp pad, paper, writing utensils, and some pictures of postal carriers and post offices will get children started on this exciting play theme.
- **Boating/fishing.** A small inflatable rubber raft, sticks with string for fishing poles, magnets for the string ends, paper "fish" with paper clips attached, blue colored paper cut to represent the water, and pictures of boats and people fishing will attract many children for this dramatic play theme.

ever, often are involved in dress-up activities, artwork, and housekeeping activities (Hughes, 1999). These gender differences are hardly surprising to most of us.

Although much of this natural interest among boys and girls can lead to productive play and learning, children should be encouraged to move out of their comfort zone to engage in other activities. For example, it is important for boys to be involved in doll play and housekeeping activities. Eventually, most will become fathers and need to learn appropriate nurturing behaviors. Similarly, girls need experiences with blocks so that they can begin developing a foundational understanding for learning mathematics and science (Chaille & Silvern, 1996).

Without conscious adult intervention, however, most children will continue doing what they find comfortable. The early childhood teacher can help break children out of their comfort zones in three major ways:

1. *Encourage children to try new activities.* Making suggestions, pointing out interesting options, and redirecting children to play activities not normally chosen are effective for many children.

2. *Provide novel materials* that are more likely to attract children to areas not usually chosen. For example, marble painting or gluing and painting wood sculptures may be two activities that would encourage boys to play in the art center.

3. *Model nontraditional play as an adult.* Female teachers can spend time building with blocks, while males could engage in housekeeping roles, for example.

Attitudes

Adult attitudes about gender are a complex mix of formal and informal learning experiences. Parental values, influential adult role models, experiences

For more information about changing attitudes toward diversity, go to the Companion Website at www.prenhall.com/henniger, select Chapter 8, then choose Web Destinations.

throughout the growing-up years, and the media all have a significant impact on the development of gender identity. Unless adults are particularly introspective, it is hard to identify their true attitudes. Yet, it is important to do so for the sake of young children. Our feelings about gender issues will strongly influence those we teach. Thus, a key starting point is to raise our own consciousness about attitudes toward gender. Although some may be obvious, others are much more subtle. As emphasized earlier, it is helpful to work with a support group to discuss these issues. For example, you might read the books *What Is a Girl?* and *What Is a Boy?* (Waxman, 1976a, 1976b) and then discuss your reactions with others. These books contain photos that show the anatomic differences between boys and girls and discuss problems associated with gender stereotyping. Would you feel comfortable reading these books to young children? Why or why not? As this kind of reflection takes place, you can begin to understand your own attitudes toward gender issues at a deeper level.

Working with Families and the Community

Knowing that the early childhood years are extremely important in the development of attitudes toward diversity, it is essential to work with parents and gain their assistance in promoting equity. Similarly, communities provide many resources that can be useful in dealing with diversity issues.

Family Involvement and Diversity

Without question, parents play a major role in the attitudes children develop toward people who are different from themselves. If parents accept diversity and verbalize their feelings, young children are much more likely to develop positive attitudes themselves (Swick, Boutte, & van Scoy, 1995). Problems occur, however, when parents either do not address diversity topics or actively denigrate people because of their race, sex, or ableness. Teachers need to work hard to help parents understand the importance of discussing diversity and need to provide opportunities for changing inappropriate parental attitudes. Several strategies may be useful in this regard:

- *Parent education.* Teachers can help educate parents about diversity in many ways. Holding meetings about its importance, creating a lending library of books, and getting parents of different cultures and beliefs to interact either in the classroom or at school-sponsored events are some examples of this type.

- *Parent support.* Supporting families in their efforts to find resources and activities that encourage pride in their diversity can be a positive step for many parents.

- *Parent-teacher partnerships.* Parents can take an active role in the planning and implementation of a diversity curriculum. They can share their own experiences and family traditions and work to create a classroom atmosphere that is accepting of the differences between people (Swick et al., 1995).

Changing Attitudes

As teachers begin to work with parents whose attitudes toward diversity are problematic, it can be easy to become frustrated and give up on changing these deeply held beliefs. Parents may either openly or indirectly subvert your efforts to help children develop an attitude of acceptance toward diversity. The natural tendency is to become defensive and either angry or aloof in your relationship with those parents. It may be helpful to remember that these parents' inappropriate

Observing Development • A Child with Special Needs

Choose one of the age groups within early childhood (infants/toddlers, preschoolers, or primary-age children), *observe* **a child with special needs** using the guidelines provided, *reflect* on what you saw and heard, and *apply* the appropriate strategies listed with the children you observed.

Observe	Reflect	Apply
Before observing, find out as much as you can about the disability of the child you will be observing. When you observe, look for specific examples of:	*Think about and respond to the following questions:*	*Consider the following developmentally appropriate strategies for the age group you observed:*
The social interactions between the child you are observing and others (eye contact, verbalizations, playing beside other children, nonverbal actions, etc.)	Do you think that the child's disability had an impact on her/his social interactions with others? Why or why not?	Create situations that increase social interactions • Infant/toddler: take a child by the hand or bring him or her to an activity area where children with special needs are playing • Preschool: suggest a game or activity that children can do together • Primary: have two or more children work cooperatively on the computer
The behaviors and attitudes of the child you are observing that are like others in the group (play activities, responses to the teacher, food preferences, expressed interests, etc.)	Was the child you observed more like others in the group in terms of behaviors and attitudes or were there significant differences between this child and the rest of the class?	Treat children with special needs much like you treat all children • Infant/toddler: hold, cuddle, talk to children with special needs just as you would others • Preschool: whenever possible, use the same guidance strategies (see Chapter 6) • Primary: have high expectations for all children, including those with special needs
The behaviors and attitudes of the child you are observing that are different from others in the group (speech impediment, physical activities that are challenging, emotional outbursts, etc.)	Did the differences in behaviors and attitudes cause distractions or problems for other children in the classroom? How did the teacher respond to the differences you observed?	Provide materials and activities that support the child with special needs • Infant/toddler: teach sign language as an additional communication tool for those who struggle with speech • Preschool: make the sand table wheelchair accessible • Primary: provide appropriate assistive technology so that all children can successfully use the computer

beliefs have developed over long periods of time and through many experiences. Changing them will take patience and time. If teachers can take a longer-term view toward changing attitudes, it may be helpful. Perhaps all a teacher can expect is to lay the groundwork for someone else to make progress in changing a parent's attitudes. Belief systems change slowly, despite our best efforts and careful planning.

Summary

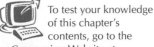 To test your knowledge of this chapter's contents, go to the Companion Website at www.prenhall.com/henniger, select Chapter 8, then select Study Guide. Also see Chapter Overviews, Reflecting Essay Questions, Multimedia Explorations, and relevant Web Destinations.

Diversity as an Essential Element

Diversity should be considered an essential component of early childhood education because of its importance to understanding development and learning, play, guidance, and working with parents and families (described in Chapters 4 through 7).

Attitudes Toward Diversity

Effectively addressing diversity in the classroom begins with an understanding of attitudes about race/culture, gender, and people with special needs.

Encouraging an Acceptance of Diversity

Teachers in the early childhood classroom should understand their own attitudes toward diversity, spend time discussing similarities and differences between people with children, and provide opportunities for children to interact with diverse people.

Inappropriate Responses to Diversity

Two inappropriate responses to diversity are to ignore it or try to teach about diversity using what has been called the tourist approach.

Integrating Diversity Throughout the Curriculum

Teachers can integrate diversity throughout the curriculum by using techniques proposed in the antibias curriculum, by including toys and games that promote diversity, by presenting diverse children's literature, by including diversity in the visual-aesthetic environment, and by providing meaningful diversity experiences.

Individuals with Special Needs

Teachers must prepare inclusive environments, assist with social interactions in the classroom, and collaborate with other professionals working with children with special needs.

Issues of Gender Equity

While progress has been made in providing girls with equitable educational opportunities, teachers of young children must continue their efforts to make this a reality. Language issues, accessibility issues, and attitudes about gender equity are important for the early childhood teacher to understand.

Working with Families and the Community

Working with parents and community members to understand and accept diversity is an important way to help bring about positive change. Parents can be closely involved in slowly changing attitudes about diversity.

Multimedia Explorations and Activities...

Tools for Tolerance

A six-year-old girl with cerebral palsy sits alone in the lunchroom while at a nearby table of children makes fun of the way she eats. . . a four-year-old boy wants to join a game of kickball at recess but he's told "We don't want no lazy Mexicans on our team!" . . . a three-year-old African American boy is not interested in story time—the books never show any kids or families that look like him or the people he loves . . . the dress-up area in a preschool contains only female clothing and when a two-year-old boy enters the area to join two girls who are dressing up, the teacher tells him to "leave the girls alone."

Research

Children during the early childhood years need to be given tools to assist them in becoming more tolerant during their school years and as adults. This activity is designed to get you involved in dealing with this important topic.

1. Go to the Companion Website at www.prenhall.com/henniger and click on the Multimedia Explorations and Activities button for Chapter 8 for more information on this topic.
2. Talk to an early childhood teacher about diversity. What issues does this person face and how is he/she responding to those challenges?
3. Go to a children's section in a library or bookstore and randomly browse through 20 picture books. Do you see diversity represented in the characters, settings, and illustrations? Do you see diversity issues (culture, acceptance, teasing, fear of differences, etc.) represented in the story lines?

Reflect

Following your research on diversity issues, reflect on the following issues:

- What should the goal of an early childhood educator be—to help students accept differences, celebrate differences, or tolerate differences? Think of some specific actions that an educator could do to meet that goal.
- What are some do's and don'ts for people working with young children if they want to create a climate of belonging for all children?

Respond

Dealing with diversity issues will be an important part of what you do as a future teacher. Consider responding in one or more of the following ways:

1. Create a questionnaire that will help early childhood educators assess how they deal with diversity issues themselves. Find a child care center or early childhood center that is willing to distribute these to their employees.
2. Plan an activity for a small group of young children that would introduce them to an aspect of diversity. Real-life, hands-on experiences are always best. Using knowledge from your research, think creatively and then implement your plan with children.
3. Participate in a college or community-based awareness activity related to diversity and share what you learned with your classmates.

PLANNING THE PHYSICAL ENVIRONMENT: INDOORS

In this chapter you will

- Address basic issues related to planning an indoor environment for young children.
- Learn about the typical centers found in an early childhood classroom and the materials available in each.
- Investigate the indoor environments of infants/toddlers, preschoolers, and primary-age children.
- Understand criteria for selecting equipment and materials for the early childhood classroom.
- Study health and safety issues for young children.

It's planning time once again, and you are thinking through the past week with your 4-year-old students in preparation for next week's activities. As usual, the children have engaged in many creative play scenarios in the different classroom centers. The block area has been home to the toy dinosaur collection, and children have been building fences and enclosures to hold their favorite creatures. After discussing block play with the assistant teachers, you decide to leave the dinosaurs out for another week. Interest is strong, and the toys are stimulating imaginative play.

It is early in the school year, so the dramatic play center still contains fairly basic materials, including shirts, hats, dresses, and shoes for dressing up. A mirror, stuffed chair, and chest of drawers are the major pieces of furniture in the center. For next week, you decide to add some jewelry, hair clips, and neckties for accessories.

The library center contained several books on dinosaurs over the past week. You have read them at group time and then made sure children could browse through them on their own. You will add two new books and a flannelboard story for the coming week.

In the manipulative center, three puzzles will replace others that the children have not used recently. You will put away the Legos for a while and make Tinkertoys available. One of your assistants has agreed to make a new batch of play dough for this center as well.

The planning in the preceding scenario exemplifies the efforts of early childhood teachers in their indoor environments. A major role of adult caregivers is to carefully and thoughtfully prepare the classroom for developmentally appropriate play. Because of the importance of child-initiated and child-directed activities, young children need play spaces that stimulate creative experiences.

Planning Guidelines

Quality environments for young children do not just happen. They require careful planning and considerable work. To understand the complexities of creating quality environments, a good place to begin is with an understanding of the fundamentals of room organization.

Basic Considerations

 For more information about furnishing the learning environment, go to the Companion Website at www.prenhall.com/henniger, select Chapter 9, then choose Web Destinations.

The most basic factor in room organization is the physical space available. The National Association for the Education of Young Children (1998) suggests providing a minimum of 35 square feet of indoor space for each child in a preschool or primary classroom. In addition to the square footage available, the window placement, heating and cooling vents, doors, floor coverings (carpeting and vinyl), and other fixed elements influence your planning for children's indoor play spaces. Each of these elements has significant implications for the organization of the classroom. For example, the placement of doors for the room defines natural corridors for entrance and exit. These spaces must be left open for ease of use and safety. Teachers must consider these fixed aspects of the environment, particularly in the initial planning of play spaces.

A second basic consideration is the availability of resources in the classroom. The tables, chairs, room dividers, and storage cabinets strongly influence room design. Additional resources such as unit blocks, table toys, computers, and dramatic play equipment also impact the overall planning of the physical space.

Jamie is getting her kindergarten classroom ready for the coming school year. She has good storage units for the unit blocks, plenty of dividers for sectioning off space for centers, and enough chairs and tables for her expected enrollment. Dramatic play equipment is scarce; she will need to locate a toy microwave oven and child-sized sink. In addition, as she looks through the manipulative toys available to her, it becomes obvious that she will need to carefully plan the use of puzzles. With only 10 sets, she will need to rotate puzzles in and out regularly to maintain interest. However, Jamie has an abundance of different construction sets like Legos. Her students will have many options available for this play type throughout the year.

Teachers also need to consider program goals before beginning plans for the indoor environment (Mitchell & David, 1992). If, for example, a top program priority is the development of fine and gross motor skills, then equipment, materials, and centers need to promote these activities. Similarly, an emphasis on recognizing and appropriately responding to feelings leads to very different materials and planning of the physical space.

Incompatible Centers

As much as possible, teachers should physically separate incompatible activities. Some centers promote active, noisy play, while others encourage quieter times. Typically active/noisy centers include

- Blocks
- Music

- Housekeeping/dramatic play
- Woodworking
- Sand/water play

Centers that tend to stimulate quieter play are

- Art
- Books/library
- Computers
- Writing

Whenever possible, centers from these two categories should be separated. Having a noisy center like the block area near the library area creates unnecessary distractions for children. The banging of blocks and the creative discussion that often accompany the construction process may prevent a child who is concentrating on a book from becoming deeply involved in the story. It would be better to put the block area next to the dramatic play center, for example. These activities are more compatible in most early childhood classrooms.

Similarly, some indoor areas should be kept dry while others are wet/messy centers. The areas that need to be dry should be separated from those that require water and other liquids. The art center—with paints, glue, marking pens, crayons, and other messy activities—needs to be placed away from the library corner, for example.

Spaces for Varying Group Sizes

Another factor in planning indoor environments is the provision of spaces to accommodate gatherings of different numbers of children. Generally, teachers set aside one area for whole-class meetings. In early childhood classrooms, this is usually referred to as *circle time*, which requires an area large enough for children and teachers to gather together in a circle formation, with everyone sitting on the floor (Fisher, 1998). Often, this space is used for other activities, such as music and movement, outside of group times.

Small-group space is needed for many different activities in the early childhood classroom. For example, many programs have a snack time in the mid-morning and again in the afternoon. The most common format for these food breaks is to have children gather together at tables, in groups of three to five, to enjoy a nutritious snack with an adult (Catron & Allen, 2003). When the early childhood classroom is set up in centers, teachers also create several small-group spaces that accommodate two to six children for various center activities.

The environment itself often gives children clues about the number of participants allowed in small-group activities. An art center, for example, with a table and five chairs effectively limits the number of children who can participate there at any given time. Another option is to have a chart posted at the entrance to each center with the number of students allowed pictured in some way. A kindergarten math center chart with three smiley faces tells children the expected capacity for that area.

Indoor space also should make solitary activities a possibility for young children (Readdick, 1993). Teachers tend to overlook this necessary element when

An indoor sandbox provides opportunities for individual and small-group play.

planning classroom space. Healthy child development includes having many opportunities for social interactions with peers and adults. In addition, however, solitary time allows children the chance to reflect and regroup at different times during the day, before returning to the important tasks of socializing with others.

Although students tend to create their own solitary spaces, it is also useful for the classroom teacher to plan for this important activity. Some materials that are useful include

- Large pillows
- Clawfoot bathtub
- Reading loft
- Large cardboard boxes
- Beanbag chairs
- Child-sized stuffed chairs

By combining these materials with room dividers or placing them in strategic spots, adults can create cozy areas for children to get away from the busy activities in the rest of the classroom.

Personal Spaces

Both teachers and children also need to have areas that they can call their own. These personal spaces need not be large or complex but help create a home for individuals' materials (Dodge, Colker, & Heroman, 2002). At the prekindergarten level, a cubby for coats, boots, and classroom projects is a common element. At the primary level, desks provide an area for more personal items. As children mature, the perceived importance of this private area increases. If desks are unavailable or undesirable, teachers should create other personal spaces for children. Teachers also need a spot for themselves for things like lunches, coats, purses, and umbrellas. Pictures of family members, a favorite coffee mug, and other personal items help create a more inviting work environment for adults. A desk or other work space can also be put to effective use in or near the early childhood classroom.

Assessing the Physical Space

One final consideration in planning the physical space is the need for assessment techniques to evaluate environmental quality. One option (Kritchevsky & Prescott, 1969) is to evaluate the complexity of the play units. The "Observing Development" feature at the end of this chapter provides you with an opportunity to assess the physical space used by young children, reflect on how the types of units described here facilitate play and learning, and apply that knowledge in specific ways as you think about constructing a quality indoor play space. Kritchevsky and Prescott have identified three different complexities in units:

- *Simple unit.* This play material or piece of equipment has only one use, and it is obvious to children. A toy truck or a stacking toy is an example of a simple unit.
- *Complex unit.* This play option has subparts, or different materials, that the child can manipulate. A sand table with digging equipment is a complex unit.
- *Superunit.* A superunit has three or more play materials juxtaposed. A block center that includes two different kinds of blocks and accessories such as toy trucks is a superunit.

Although all three unit types are valuable in the early childhood classroom, the more complex units are most attractive to children and hold their interest longest. Kritchevsky and Prescott (1969) suggest that by assigning a value of one to simple units, four to complex units, and eight to superunits, you can determine the total number of play spaces available in an indoor environment. Dividing that total by the number of children gives the number of options available to each child. Having two play options per child is considered highly desirable.

Harms and Clifford (1980) developed a second, more extensive, environmental assessment procedure. This well-respected rating scale has been recently revised (Harms, Clifford, & Cryer, 1998). Called the **Early Childhood Environment Rating Scale,** this assessment tool is organized into seven separate subcategories that allow the teacher to evaluate classroom space from inadequate (1) to excellent (7). The seven categories are:

- *Personal care routines.* All routines that relate to children's health, comfort, and safety.
- *Furnishings and display for children.* Furniture, storage shelves, and display space to facilitate child growth and development.
- *Language-reasoning experiences.* Experiences, materials, and interactions to facilitate basic reasoning discussion among children about such things as cause and effect.
- *Fine and gross motor activities.* The use of small muscles in the hands and the larger muscles in the arms and legs.
- *Creative activities.* Open-ended activities and materials available in centers such as art, block, and dramatic play.
- *Social development.* Positive self-concepts and interaction skills.
- *Adult needs.* The needs of adults for a comfortable and efficient space for teaching.

With training and practice, the Early Childhood Environment Rating Scale can be an effective tool for assessing the indoor classroom. It can help identify both the strengths and limitations of the physical space.

A third way in which classroom space can be evaluated is in terms of its **spatial density.** Johnson, Christie, and Yawkey (1999) define spatial density as the amount of space per child in a play setting. It can be calculated by measuring the total area of the indoor setting, subtracting the unusable space (things like the teacher's desk, spaces too small for play, or areas that are off-limits for some reason), and then dividing that area by the number of children using the space. If the spatial density is less than 25 square feet per child, the play area is too crowded. Research indicates there will be less gross-motor activity and more aggression in these settings (Smith & Connolly, 1980).

The Centers-Based Classroom

Early childhood classrooms are often very individualized for the ages of children served and the educational setting. However, as described earlier in this chapter, classroom space is often defined by centers. Using low dividers, tables, child-sized furniture, and an assortment of storage units, caregivers create small areas within the room that children use for specific play- and work-oriented tasks. At the kindergarten level and below, classrooms are often completely centers-based. Quality first- through third-grade environments can be partially or fully organized around centers. Although not all of the areas described next are found in every early childhood classroom, these centers are common to many indoor play spaces for young children.

Art Center

The art center is essential for the early childhood classroom. Located near a water source for easy clean-up, this area ideally should have a vinyl floor covering or other similar surface. Furniture typically includes a child-sized table and chairs, storage shelves for art supplies, and an easel. A quality art area includes materials such as crayons, markers, and paper of various types that are available daily

Into Practice...
The Art Center

Free exploration of materials in the art center provides many excellent opportunities for creative expression. Teachers should include fixed materials for young artists and other materials that change regularly:

Fixed materials	Materials that change
Easel(s)	Scrap paper for collages
Scissors	Watercolors
Crayons	Fingerpainting materials
Rulers	Screen painting
Staplers	Sponge painting
Scrap paper	Tissue paper for collages
Washable marking pens	Wood scraps, glue, paint

Some children will spend a large percentage of their choice time in art activities. Providing consistency and change at the same time makes this an inviting center for children.

Celebrating Play . . . Puzzles in the Preschool Classroom

Puzzles are a traditional and important part of learning in the preschool classroom. The first puzzles for children were produced in 1760 by John Spilsbury, an Englishman (Maldono, 1996), and have been part of teaching and learning since that time. However, what is the attraction of these manipulatives for young children? When you watch them working with puzzles, children are often intensely focused and will often complete the same puzzle over and over again. Maldono (1996) explains it this way:

> Children are interested in puzzle making because they can be active as observers, problem solvers, and learners, with little or no assistance from adults and others. The intrigue involved in puzzle making is that fragments come together to complete an image. Through puzzle making, young children experience satisfaction by putting things together where they belong. Contentment is achieved by the mere fact that things that look broken are fixed. (p. 4)

Good puzzles should have the following characteristics (Maldono, 1996):

1. *Puzzles should match the child's developmental abilities.* For example, most 2-year-olds need puzzles that have knobs and depict a single whole object like a car. In contrast, 4-year-olds are typically ready for knobless puzzles of 12 to 18 pieces.

2. *Puzzles should be attractive and durable.* They should be colorful and include clearly recognizable items. Because of high usage, they also must be sturdy.

3. *Puzzles should reflect items that are familiar to children.* They should be of items that children have seen or had experiences with, such as foods, vehicles, and animals.

4. *Puzzles should be solvable.* While being challenging, they should be something the child is motivated to complete and be successful with. Some children may be ready for more complex puzzles of 100–150 pieces (Barron, 1999), while others are more typically challenged by puzzles with fewer pieces.

---

1. Do you enjoy doing puzzles as an adult? If so, what do you find attracts you to this activity?

2. Take the time to read one of the two articles referenced in this feature. In terms of overall development, what can children potentially learn from puzzle use?

(Catron & Allen, 2003) and other materials that change regularly. This combination of consistency and change helps make the art center a popular place for play.

Manipulative Center

The manipulative center, also called *table toys*, usually consists of a table and chairs, open shelves for storage, and an assortment of materials that children can use for construction and manipulation. Small baskets or plastic storage units are available for ease of movement to and from the play table. If a separate space for a computer is unavailable, computer activities are compatible with the activities in the manipulative center.

Developing fine motor skills, enhancing early mathematical understanding, and encouraging creative expression are typical goals for this center. Dodge, Colker, & Heroman (2002) identify four categories of toys found in manipulative areas:

- *Self-correcting toys* fit together in a way that lets children know when they have used the materials correctly. Puzzles are good examples of this type of toy, as are most Montessori materials.

Celebrating Diversity . . .
Children's Books About Diverse Cultures

There is a large and growing collection of books for children that provide wonderful stories about diverse children and their families. As a future teacher of young children, you will want to either start your own collection of quality books or keep an annotated bibliography so that you can use these books in your own classroom some day. Here are some good examples of books about diverse cultures (Braus & Geidel, 2000):

So Much by Trish Cooke is a picture book for young children that shows a series of members from an African American extended family arriving home to hug and love a young baby.

Abuela by Arthur Dorros is a story about Rosalba and her grandmother (Abuela) who take a walk in New York City. The inclusion of Spanish words adds further learning opportunities to this story.

The First Strawberries by Joseph Bruchac is a Cherokee story about the first man and woman on earth. When the man gets angry at the woman and she runs away, he asks the sun god to put something in her way to get her to stop running. The sun god creates strawberries, which she stops to enjoy.

Hush by Mingfong Ho is a lullaby describing the author's childhood memories of falling asleep in her native Thailand to the sounds of green frogs, water buffalo, monkeys, and more.

1. Are you aware of other good examples of children's books depicting diverse cultures? What do you like about these books?

2. In what ways do children's books about diverse cultures help young children understand and accept differences between people?

- *Open-ended toys* are unstructured in their use. Creative exploration is stimulated. Legos, Lincoln Logs, and Bristle Blocks all fit this category.

- *Collectibles* are scrounged materials that children use in open-ended ways. Parents, children, and teachers can save plastic bottle caps, buttons, and old keys for sorting, matching, and comparing activities.

- *Cooperative games* engage children in pairs or small groups in simple activities that de-emphasize winning and losing. Lotto games, concentration activities, and matching toys provide additional opportunities for quality play in this center.

Book/Quiet Center

A library center should be a quiet oasis for children to engage in early reading and writing experiences. The main ingredients for this area include comfortable spots for children to sit and read or be read to, storage/display shelves for books, a table, and a collection of quality children's literature. In addition to books, an assortment of emergent literacy activities such as flannelboard story figures, a listening center (with head sets), and magnetic board letters help stimulate the language arts (Fisher, 1998).

The teacher can rotate a variety of book types in and out of the library area to maintain involvement among all children:

Picture books (no words)

New award-winning books

Classic books

For more information about the book/quiet center, go to the Companion Website at www.prenhall.com/henniger, select Chapter 9, then choose Web Destinations.

Nursery rhymes and poetry

Homemade children's books

Books addressing multicultural and diversity issues

Content-oriented books that complement themes

Other materials can be added to provide meaningful experiences with written language. Notebooks with lined paper, chalkboards, magnetic boards with letters, and flannelboard materials are common options. When combined with quality books, this center can entice children to sit and read, be read to, or engage in early writing activities.

Block Center

Blocks have tremendous potential for creative play and learning. This center is an essential for every early childhood classroom, including primary education (Harris, 1994). The basic elements needed for this area are a set of wooden unit blocks, a collection of large hollow blocks (often constructed of wood), a carpeted floor for building, low shelves for organized storage of blocks and ease of access, and accessories such as toy trucks or animals that the teacher rotates in and out of the center regularly.

Although children use unit blocks imaginatively by themselves, the accessories help stimulate further creative play in this area. The teacher should rotate these added props in and out of the center weekly to encourage play related to the current classroom theme. Some examples of accessories that are often used include

For more information about block centers, go to the Companion Website at www.prenhall.com/henniger, select Chapter 9, then choose Web Destinations.

- Toy farm animals
- Transportation toys (trucks, airplanes, etc.)
- Small wooden or plastic people/figures
- Dollhouse furniture
- Zoo animals
- Hats (construction, police, etc.)
- Play money
- Writing materials (for signs)

Housekeeping Center

As the name implies, the housekeeping center is designed for young children to engage in dramatic play focused on home themes (Dodge, Colker, & Heroman, 2002). Typically, the housekeeping area contains materials such as a child-sized sink, stove, refrigerator, microwave, china cupboard, table and chairs, toy dishes, silverware, pots and pans, a telephone and/or cellphone, and a small broom and dustpan set. The teacher can rotate accessories such as pretend foods (empty cans/boxes or plastic food), pictures of people engaged in housekeeping tasks, and additional cooking utensils in and out of this area to create new interest in playing here.

Younger children (ages 4 and below) are particularly attracted to the housekeeping center, and including it as a permanent option with little change to the basic equipment makes good sense. If space is limited or children are somewhat older, the housekeeping area may be effectively combined with the dramatic play center.

Into Practice . . .
Unit Blocks

Unit blocks are generally made from smooth, sanded hardwood and come in sizes that are proportional in length and width to the basic unit, which is $5\frac{1}{2} \times 2\frac{3}{4} \times 1\frac{3}{8}$ inches. Every other block has a mathematical relationship to this basic unit. This proportionality allows for creative building and the learning of many math and science concepts. Some of the typical shapes found in a quality set of unit blocks are shown here:

Square or half-unit

Unit

Double-unit

Quadruple-unit

Pillar

Half-pillar

Small triangle

Large triangle

Small column or cylinder

Large column or cylinder

Small switch

Large buttress

Unit arch and half-circle

Half-roman arch

Small-buttress

Large-switch

Gothic door

Ellipse

Curve

Quarter-circle

Ramp

Intersection

Side road

Roof boards

Dramatic Play Center

The importance of imaginative play has been clearly documented (Singer & Singer, 1990), and this type of play needs to be incorporated into the early childhood classroom at every opportunity. Although imaginative play can be found in any center, a separate space devoted to dramatic activities is crucial. When located next to, or combined with, the housekeeping center, an imaginative play area is a popular addition to the early childhood classroom. Teachers often begin the school year with a few dress-up clothes, a mirror, dolls and doll beds, a chest of drawers, and a coat rack as the staples for this area. Gradually new accessories such as jewelry, hats, and a child-sized briefcase can be added to stimulate more interest; later, thematic materials can be presented.

A common practice for teachers of young children is the creation of prop boxes of materials needed for specific dramatic play themes (Myhre, 1993). Because these boxes are portable, teachers can organize materials that children can easily use either indoors or outside. Some examples of prop box themes include

- Supermarket
- Shoe store
- Repair shop
- Office
- Camping
- Airplane

The Music Center

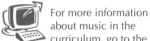

For more information about music in the curriculum, go to the Companion Website at www.prenhall.com/henniger, select Chapter 9, then choose Web Destinations.

Musical experiences are important learning opportunities for young children and create a more pleasant environment (Hildebrandt, 1998). Group times that include singing, movement to music, and the use of instruments are common in most classrooms. In addition, however, it is important to encourage other experiences with music. A center can often be incorporated into the classroom for this purpose. A tape/CD player; an open, carpeted area; storage shelves; an assortment of music-making materials; and a piano are common items found in this area. It is best to start the year with one or two instruments on the shelf and gradually add more as the year progresses. Many teachers stock the group-time area with music materials so that these are available for circle activities in addition to free choice options.

Music-making experiences are an important part of the early childhood curriculum.

As with every center, the teacher should move instruments and musical options in and out of the area to maintain interest and use. Materials that teachers can rotate through this center include

- Rhythm sticks
- Cymbals
- Triangles
- Bells
- Drums
- Autoharp
- Scarves (for movement to music)

Discovery/Science Center

A discovery area provides opportunities for young children to develop important science understandings (Catron & Allen, 2003). Children can use a small table

Into Practice...
Dramatic Play Prop Boxes

Prop boxes are a convenient way to organize the materials needed for dramatic play themes. When sturdy boxes of consistent size are used, the props can be easily stored when not in use. Tape a list of needed materials on the inside lid of the box so that a quick check can be made for missing items before using the box. Here are some sample ideas for specific prop boxes (Myhre, 1993):

Office prop box

Telephone

Typewriter/keyboard

Pads of paper

Desk accessories

Paper

File folders

Envelopes

Repair shop box

Clipboard

Wrenches and screwdrivers

Safety glasses

Nuts and bolts

Toolbox

Scrap wood

Workbench

Beach party prop box

Beach towels

Sunglasses

Straw hats

Water bottles

Life preserver

Air mattresses

Picnic accessories

Grocery store prop box

Cash register

Plastic foods

Play money

Empty food containers

Grocery bags

Grocery cart

Baskets

with displays of interesting materials to learn basic scientific principles and concepts. Additional storage space for other science-oriented materials is useful in this center as well. Materials to consider for the discovery area include

- Plants
- Rocks
- Shells
- Magnifying glass
- Balance scales
- Aquarium
- Animal/insect cages
- Small appliances to take apart and explore

Other Creative Centers

Although the preceding areas are considered essential in the early childhood classroom, several other possibilities can be incorporated as well. These centers provide many play opportunities that cannot be easily duplicated in other ways. Space limitations are the most common reason for not including them.

Woodworking Center. Real, child-sized saws and hammers, wood, nails, safety goggles, a woodworking table with built-in vises, and hand drills are the basic ingredients for the woodworking center (Huber, 1999). Additional accessories could include an old stump for simple nailing practice, glue, c-clamps, and wood rasps. For younger children, or just for a change, styrofoam can be substituted for wood.

Some teachers prefer to have this activity take place outdoors, but with enough space and proper supervision, it can be effectively managed indoors. Also, the noise, mess, and potential safety issues tend to frighten some teachers of young children away from providing woodworking activities. With preparation and careful adult supervision, however, this center can be an exciting and safe place for children.

 For more information about sand play, go to the Companion Website at www.prenhall.com/ henniger, select Chapter 9, then choose Web Destinations.

Sand/Water Play Center. The attraction of natural materials such as sand and water is strong with prekindergarten children. The sensory nature of the experience and the flexible uses of these materials make them popular in the early childhood classroom. Sand and water play should be considered essential for the outdoor setting and, if space permits, are important options indoors (Dodge, Colker, & Heroman, 2002).

Child-sized sand/water tables are available commercially to hold either sand or water. A vinyl floor (or protective covering), water-repelling smocks, and accessories for mixing and pouring sand or water complete this center. Sample accessories include

- Funnels
- Measuring cups
- Waterwheel
- Spoons
- Small buckets
- Hand trowels
- Basters
- Pitchers

Writing Center. Providing many opportunities for early writing experiences is essential for the literacy development of young children. Having writing materials in the art, block, dramatic play, and library centers greatly increases the likelihood that children will incorporate writing into their play (Christie, Enz, & Vukelich, 2003). In addition, older children should have a separate center that focuses specifically on writing activities.

The materials needed for a writing center are relatively simple: a variety of writing instruments, such as pencils, pens, crayons, and markers; recycled paper for rough drafts; lined paper; and heavier-weighted paper for book covers. Children could also productively use a dictionary or word file, staplers, an old typewriter, or the classroom computer.

For more information about the computer center, go to the Companion Website at www.prenhall.com/henniger, select Chapter 9, then choose Web Destinations.

Computer Center. Although some controversy surrounds computer use for young children (see Chapter 17), most early educators feel that when properly used, computers can be an important activity for the early childhood classroom for children age 3 and above (Haugland, 1999). With quality, play-oriented software, children can learn a great deal and have fun at the same time (Haugland & Shade, 1994).

Probably the biggest drawback to computer use is the high cost of the hardware. Many prekindergarten programs in particular have very limited budgets, and committing $1,500 or more to a quality computer system is difficult. Despite their many benefits, computers should not be a higher priority than an ample collection of unit blocks, for example.

Family Partnerships . . .
A Place for Parents and Family Members?

Space in most early childhood classrooms is at a premium. It is often difficult to find room for every desired option. Despite this major problem, if teachers of young children want to help parents and other volunteers feel welcome in the classroom, having a parent corner makes good sense. Consider some creative options such as making your desk and surrounding space available as a parent corner during the day. Or, create a small parent-gathering spot just outside the classroom door with equipment that could be moved back into the classroom at the end of the day. Another option would be to use a space such as a snack table or circle-time area for volunteers during parts of the day when they are not needed by children. The parent corner might also be used as a break area for teachers, enhancing its usefulness during other times during the day and providing opportunities for volunteers and teachers to interact informally in this setting.

The items needed for a parent area vary according to the age of the children and the flexibility of your classroom space. Furniture could include a comfortable chair, a desk, or a small couch with an end table. A parent bulletin board, with information on current classroom activities, a copy of the class newsletter, and articles of interest to families is a nice way to use wall space in this corner and provide parents with valuable information. A small library of parent education books would be another idea for the parent area. Finally, if possible, include a hot water dispenser or a coffeemaker so that volunteers can make coffee and tea when they come into the classroom. When you combine as many of these ingredients as possible into a parent space, you will create a welcoming environment for visiting adults.

1. What sorts of things make you feel welcome in a new place? Are there similar items that you could potentially include in a parent corner?

2. In addition to a parent area/corner, what else could you do to your future classroom space to make it a more welcoming environment for family members?

To provide maximum benefit from a computer, the teacher should place the computer in the classroom (rather than in a separate computer room shared by the entire school). The computer should be available to children as another choice during center time. With two or three chairs at the computer, several children can use it cooperatively.

Age-Related Considerations

Although most of the centers described here can be found in classrooms for children throughout the early childhood age range, teachers need to be aware of special considerations needed in planning these indoor spaces for each age. This section discusses these issues.

Infant/Toddler Classrooms

Figure 9–1 provides an example of the elements in an infant/toddler classroom. Because most infants and toddlers learn a great deal by putting things in their mouths, significant issues for this age are the safety and cleanliness of play materials (Lowman & Ruhmann, 1998). Teachers must not supply toys that may break or splinter when chewed or that are small enough to swallow. Because regular cleaning is necessary as well, equipment should be durable enough to withstand frequent washing.

Much of a young child's day is spent in routines. Eating, sleeping, and toileting activities are significant parts of the curriculum. Special areas for routines are important in infant/toddler programs (Catron & Allen, 2003). A changing area with a table and access to water, for example, is a necessity. Separating it from the eating and play centers also makes good sense. Establishing similar spaces for sleeping and eating that can be used throughout the day are also necessary.

Comfortable adult seating should also be a part of the infant/toddler classroom. The importance of holding and cuddling at this age cannot be overstated. Children need frequent touch for healthy emotional development (Delisle, 1994; Montagu, 1978). Rocking chairs, couches, and comfortable adult chairs help encourage this important activity.

Infants and toddlers are in what Piaget calls the *stage of sensorimotor intelligence* (see Chapter 4). These young children learn about their world through sight, sound, taste, smell, and touch. Sensory materials that these children can easily manipulate are important.

In addition to sensory experiences, young children learn about themselves and their environment through physical movement. Infant/toddler programs need materials that stimulate motor development. Climbing, crawling, walking, and stacking activities address the developmental interests of this age.

Children 3 Through 5

Figure 9–2 diagrams a typical classroom for preschool and kindergarten children. As discussed earlier, play is a primary vehicle for learning during these years. Almost without exception, classrooms for this age are organized around centers. These classrooms include areas for art, books/quiet activities, blocks, manipulatives, housekeeping, and dramatic play (Dodge, Colker, & Heroman, 2002). They also regularly include sand/water play, music, and discovery centers. Children have regular opportunities for spending large blocks of time in play activities that they select in these centers.

Figure 9–1 *Infant/Toddler Classroom*

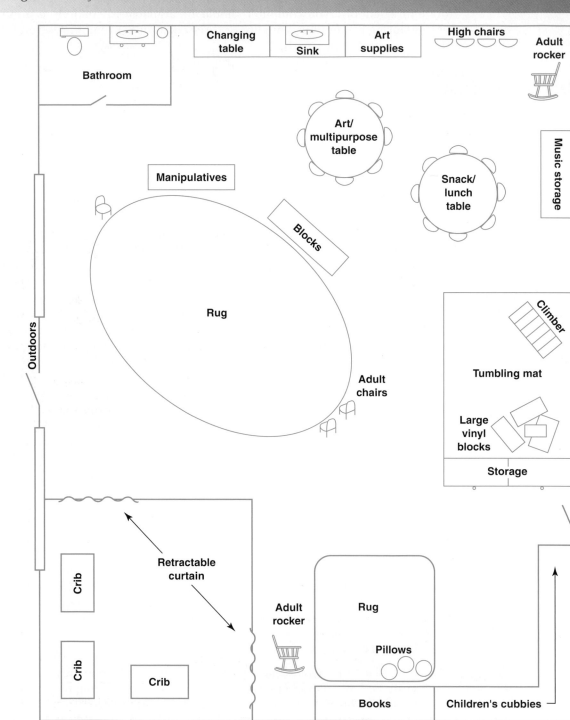

Figure 9–2 *Preschool/Kindergarten Classroom*

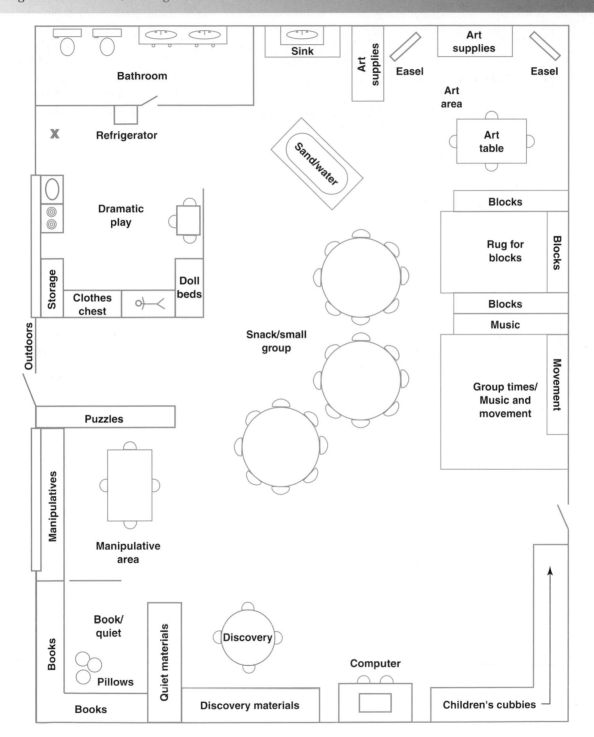

As children move toward greater and greater autonomy, classroom experiences and materials must allow for increasing independence (Mitchell & David, 1992). For example, child-sized pitchers allow children to pour their own juice, and a drying rack for artwork located at child level encourages independent behavior in that center. Materials that are self-correcting, such as puzzles, also require fewer adult interventions. Too much change can be stressful for all children, including those from age 3 to 5. One simple strategy to help reduce stress from change is to have consistency in the environment. Although accessories should change weekly, the general layout of the classroom and the basic structure of each center often remain unchanged (Dodge, Colker, & Heroman, 2002). For example, the block area contains low shelves to store the unit blocks. This shelving and the positioning of blocks on them often remain consistent, while the accessories (like toy trucks) change each week.

Children often begin to engage in pretend activities at about 2 years of age. This important play type is stimulated by realistic materials that clearly resemble the real-world item. With additional experience, more ambiguous toys are effective in stimulating quality dramatic play. Children at age 3 to 5 often need both realistic and ambiguous types of equipment, because of their different developmental abilities.

Primary-Age Children

Figure 9–3 gives an example of a good indoor space for primary-age children. It combines some centers with more traditional work space for this age. A quick

Into Practice...
Infant/Toddler Toys

Toys for children at the infant/toddler age need to be appealing to the senses, safe, and durable. Because of the importance of routines, teachers should provide materials for play in cribs, during diapering, and during general playtime. The following is a sampling of toys that can be valuable in an infant/toddler program:

Crib toys

Beads (large, bright, on sturdy cord)
Clutch balls (large, with finger holds, soft material)
Cradle gyms (things to push, pull, manipulate)
Mobiles
Rattles
Squeeze toys

Play equipment

Large soft blocks for stacking and climbing
Pull toys
Stacking toys
Mirrors
Musical toys
Sorting toys
Peg-Board with large pegs
Interesting smells (cut flowers, spices, etc.)
Texture balls

Figure 9–3 *Primary Classroom*

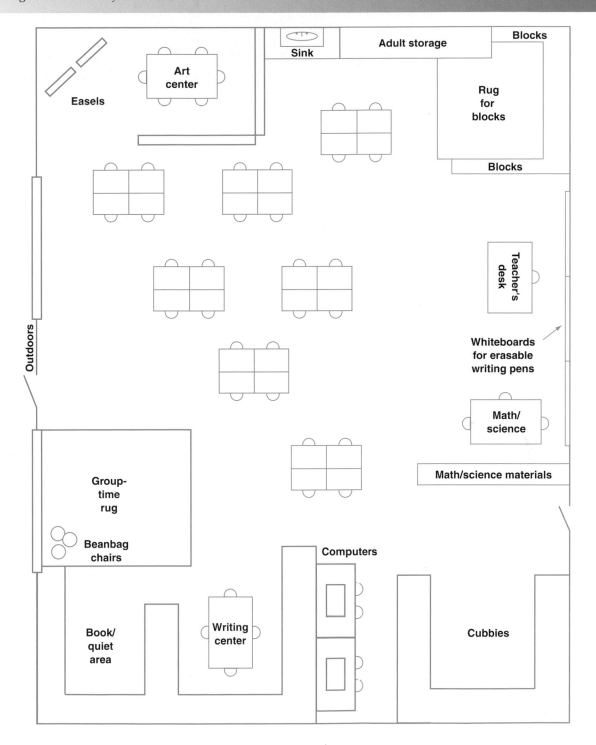

look at most first- through third-grade environments indicates that centers are not in widespread use. One or two areas at most may be available for free choice activities. Many teachers, administrators, and parents of children at this level are yet to be convinced of the learning potential inherent in centers and playful experiences. Children, however, benefit significantly from these opportunities (Wasserman, 2000), and teachers need to slowly add centers to their classrooms. This process (which may take several years to complete) allows for careful preparation of each area and time to educate other adults about the benefits of centers and play.

A good starting point for centers in a primary classroom is to provide activities that allow children to practice academic skills. Mathematics, library, and writing centers can be readily linked to the elementary school curriculum and provide children with quality play experiences that extend their understanding in these important areas (Fisher, 1998). Center use can then be expanded to include equally important centers such as blocks, dramatic play, art, and music.

The primary classroom also needs spaces for cooperative learning and small-group activities. Clustering four to six desks together or using child-sized tables that seat four to six students is a practical arrangement for teachers who want their children to engage in frequent small-group work (Wortham, 2002). With these small groups in the central portion of the classroom, the centers can be on the periphery, and children can use the centers when not engaged in large- and small-group activities.

Selecting Equipment and Materials

An important role of the early childhood teacher is the selection of appropriate equipment and materials for center activities. The combination of many choices and limited budgets makes it essential for adults to make good decisions about play materials for the classroom.

For more information about selecting toys, go to the Companion Website at www.prenhall.com/henniger, select Chapter 9, then choose Web Destinations.

Criteria for Selection

Each center in the early childhood classroom requires specialized materials that the teacher can make or purchase commercially. Community Playthings (1990) has developed broad principles for materials selection to assist in this process:

- *Simplicity of detail.* Particularly as children mature, the amount of detail needed to stimulate quality play decreases. Good play materials keep detail to a minimum.

- *Versatility in use.* Equipment that allows children to explore/use it in open-ended ways is best. More creativity is possible, and children tend to use the materials longer.

- *Easy to use and understand.* Quality materials require little or no explanation by adults to use. They are also of appropriate size for the ages of the children playing with them.

- *Involve the child in play.* Good toys are so inviting and interesting that children cannot resist playing with them. Good toys stimulate the use of imagination, language, cognition, and both large and small muscle movement.

- *Encourage cooperative play.* Because one of the goals of early education is to stimulate social learning, most play materials should promote interaction among small groups of children.

- *Materials look and feel good.* Play is more likely when children have equipment that is attractive to look at and feels good to the touch.

- *Durability.* Classroom materials receive frequent use and must be durable enough to withstand frequent cleaning and the banging, dropping, and general wear-and-tear by young children.

- *Safety.* Teachers should not purchase toys made of toxic materials, toys that can splinter or break, equipment that can pinch or cut, and materials that easily catch fire.

- *Value-priced.* With limited budgets, most early childhood teachers are interested in equipment that provides the best play value at the lowest cost.

Commercial Materials

Many different commercial companies produce toys and equipment for use in the early childhood classroom. They can be categorized as general purpose, specialty, and multicultural companies.

General Purpose Companies. Companies that produce and sell equipment for every center in the early childhood classroom are general purpose companies. Their catalogs are extensive and provide many selections. Examples of this type are Lakeshore Learning Materials, Constructive Playthings, and Kaplan Companies (see Figure 9–4).

Figure 9–4 *Companies Producing Materials for Early Childhood*

General purpose companies	
Lakeshore Learning Materials	(800) 421–5354
Constructive Playthings	(800) 448–4115
Kaplan Companies	(800) 334–2014
Specialty companies	
Nienhuis Montessori USA	(800) 942–8697
Creative Educational Surplus	(800) 886–6428
Cuisenaire Company of America	(800) 237–0338
Judy/Instructo	(800) 321–3106
Playtime Props	(800) 782–8697
Multicultural companies	
Asia for Kids	(800) 765–5885
People of Every Stripe	(503) 282–0612
Remo, Inc.	(818) 983–2600

Into Practice...
A Teacher-Made Game

An example of a teacher-made game that could be used effectively in the early childhood classroom is a concentration game. You may remember this option from your own childhood. Typically, a concentration game has sets of matching cards made from cardboard that are often about 2 or 3 inches on each side. The game generally has 15 to 20 matching pictures, shapes, words, or math problems and solutions. The teacher can use pictures from magazines, hand-drawn shapes, or printed words/math problems to personalize the game for a specific classroom of children and concepts to be learned. To play the game, two children place the cards face down on the floor or table, mix up the cards, and then take turns picking two cards in an attempt to get a match. If the cards do not match, they go back in the same positions, face down. When a match is found, the player gets to keep the cards in her pile. The game continues until all matches are made. This simple game is relatively easy to construct and can be modified for many potential uses in the early childhood classroom.

Specialty Companies. Companies that produce materials that either fit a specific approach to early childhood education or focus on limited aspects of the curriculum are specialty companies (see Figure 9–4). An example of the former type is Nienhuis Montessori USA, which produces materials for the Montessori classroom. Other companies that specialize in aspects of the early childhood curriculum include Creative Educational Surplus (surplus materials that can be used in art and construction activities), Cuisenaire Company of America (hands-on math and science materials), Judy/Instructo (puzzles and other manipulatives), and Playtime Props (play frames to stimulate dramatic play).

Multicultural Companies. Some relatively new companies focus their energies on promoting multicultural play materials for the early childhood classroom. These companies are generally smaller but provide many unique options for play equipment. Some examples include Asia for Kids (books, dolls, games), People of Every Stripe (dolls of all sorts), and Remo, Inc. (multicultural musical instruments). See Figure 9–4.

Teacher-Made Equipment

To save money, many early childhood teachers make their own materials. Teacher-developed equipment can also be more closely matched to the developmental needs and interests of a specific group of children. Ideas for these options come from a variety of sources:

- Imitations of commercial equipment
- Ideas from other teachers
- Curriculum books for early childhood education

Although teachers are generally the source of ideas for noncommercial play materials, parents and other volunteers can be a big help in the actual construction of these items. Using carefully planned instructions, these adults can work on projects for the classroom in their spare time and greatly reduce the teacher's time commitment.

Children with Special Needs

 For more information about spaces for children with special needs, go to the Companion Website at www.prenhall.com/ henniger, select Chapter 9, then choose Web Destinations.

Raymond is an outgoing 4-year-old who uses a wheel chair. He loves his preschool friends and enjoys his play opportunities there. At times, however, Raymond becomes frustrated with the indoor environment. The wheel chair makes it difficult for him to move in and out of some centers and get play items off the shelves. His teachers are working to make the classroom more usable for Raymond.

Teachers need to plan the indoor environment so that it accommodates children with special needs.

As increasing numbers of early childhood programs include children like Raymond, it is important to consider the accommodations necessary for creative play experiences. Winter, Bell, and Dempsey (1994) identify three fundamental elements for true inclusion of children with special needs.

The first element is accessibility. Every child should be able to physically enter each center in the early childhood classroom and use the materials found there. For example, a child in a wheelchair should be able to enter the block center and have easy access to its materials.

A second important component is the ability to engage in activities within each center. Having access to the art center is not enough. Special tools and equipment may be needed, for example, if a child with cerebral palsy is to succeed in using art materials. Children with special needs must have the opportunity to take an active part in the art projects provided there.

A third fundamental component of an inclusive play environment is developmental appropriateness. While materials provided in centers may be age appropriate, they may not be effective in meeting the individual needs of some children with special needs. A broader range of materials can better assist children with varying abilities to enjoy quality play experiences.

Changing the Physical Environment

Children's play can be characterized as fluid and changing. It mirrors the interests, developmental needs, and growth of those engaging in play. Sensitive early childhood teachers continually plan for changes in the indoor environment to facilitate these important experiences for individual children. Each week, adults should critique the uses of existing play equipment and make decisions about what should be kept out or put away and about whether any new materials should be added. By carefully observing children at play, teachers can plan centers that are stimulating and developmentally appropriate.

Balancing Consistency and Change

This planning process for young children's play environments must include careful thought about the need for both consistency and change. A consistent classroom gives young children a sense of security and comfort (Dodge, Colker, & Heroman, 2002). In their home away from home, they need to experience a familiar routine and activities that are interesting without being overwhelmingly different: the younger the child, the greater the need for consistency.

Teachers create this familiar, comfortable environment in the following ways:

- Consistency in the general arrangement of furniture in each center
- Some materials that are always available to children (e.g., basic art materials in the art center)
- Routines for use and storage of play materials that are well-defined and known to children (e.g., blocks stored in clearly marked places on shelves that children can reach)
- Consistent blocks of time for daily creative play experiences

Although it is important to create a consistent environment for children, early childhood educators must also provide for variety and change (Van Hoorn et al., 2003). This helps maintain interest in and enthusiasm for the play environment. Teachers maintain children's involvement by the following:

- Discuss new toys and equipment at group times.
- Engage in play with children, using materials that have been overlooked or underutilized.
- Give children ideas about how to use toys or materials in their play.
- Casually leave materials out at the beginning of an activity period to remind children of their availability.

Rotating Materials Through Centers

Providing for change in the early childhood classroom also means adding new play materials each week and removing other items that have served their current purposes (Dodge, Colker, & Heroman, 2002). Teachers often meet weekly to discuss each center and make decisions about equipment changes. Some guidelines for determining toy needs for each center include the following:

- Make sure materials are available in centers to challenge each child in the classroom to higher levels of development.
- Provide options that build on student interests.
- Change approximately a third of the materials available in each center weekly.
- Make sure equipment and toys match the curricular goals and themes established for the classroom.

Observe and Listen to Children

To effectively plan play environments for young children, adults need to carefully observe what children are doing as they interact with toys and each other (Van Hoorn et al., 2003). In the dramatic play center, for example, which clothes and accessories are the children using? What play themes are the children enacting? What are the children saying as they play? This information is invaluable to teachers in making decisions about toys and equipment to add or put away. If children are playing out travel themes in the dramatic play center, the teacher could put out props like suitcases and travel brochures to further stimulate this play type.

Adults working with a group of children meet regularly to discuss the play experiences observed before planning for the next week. This sharing of information can be very beneficial in selecting center materials and activities. Specifics about individual children and general patterns of behavior become more obvious and make curricular decisions easier.

Health and Safety Issues

For more information about health and safety concerns, go to the Companion Website at www.prenhall.com/henniger, select Chapter 9, then choose Web Destinations.

The health and safety of children are essential for optimal development, and teachers must consider these when planning the indoor environment (Marotz, Cross, & Rush, 2001). By taking responsibility for these issues, adults free children to actively interact with the people and objects around them.

Planning a Healthy Environment

When considering materials for the early childhood classroom, teachers must avoid any materials that would pose potential health risks. For example, many infant/toddler programs substitute cornmeal or rice for sand because of the tendency for children of this age to put everything into their mouths. Similarly, nontoxic markers and crayons should be used. Lead poisoning from old paint (prior to 1977), contaminated drinking water, and certain pieces of imported dishware are potential health problems for young children that can be prevented by adults' planning (Marotz et al., 2001).

Providing a sanitary environment for young children is also important in minimizing health-related diseases in the classroom. The more common problems such as colds and influenza can be better controlled with regular cleaning of the physical environment and careful handwashing techniques. Other communicable diseases such as hepatitis and pinworm infestation also require attention to good hygiene for successful management. Concerns over dealing with children infected with human immunodeficiency virus/acquired immune deficiency syndrome (HIV/AIDS) (Seidel, 1992) have led to the use of disposable gloves and careful handwashing when dealing with children's body fluids.

Safety Concerns

The organization of the physical environment can assist in accident prevention. Due to limited experiences and developing physical skills, children need a carefully prepared classroom (Catron & Allen, 2003). Electrical outlets, stoves, air-circulating fans, and climbing equipment are some examples of equipment that require planning and education for effective use. Medicines, cleaning agents, and insecticides are other materials that teachers must store out of the reach of children or outside the classroom to avoid accidental poisonings.

In many circumstances, adults need to demonstrate or teach children safe use of equipment. For example, assisting children in holding and properly using a sharp knife in a cooking activity helps promote safety. Providing safety goggles for the woodworking bench and demonstrating good sawing techniques will also help prevent accidents in that area. Although this advanced preparation will not prevent all problems from occurring, it helps create an environment where children can explore and experiment with greater freedom.

Summary

To test your knowledge of this chapter's contents, go to the Companion Website at www.prenhall.com/henniger, select Chapter 9, then select Study Guide. Also see Chapter Overviews, Reflecting Essay Questions, Multimedia Explorations, and relevant Web Destinations.

Planning Guidelines

Planning a stimulating indoor environment for young children is a complex process. The teacher should separate active/quiet areas and dry/wet spaces, include areas for different sizes of groups, and evaluate the quality of the physical space.

The Centers-Based Classroom

The indoor environment typically includes an art, manipulative, book/quiet, block, housekeeping, dramatic play, music, and discovery/science center. Each of these areas must be carefully planned by the teacher.

Age-Related Considerations

There are many considerations in planning for infant/toddler, preschool, and primary-age classrooms. The needs, interests, and abilities of children, safety and

Observing Development • Assessing the Physical Space

Choose one of the age groups within early childhood (infants/toddlers, preschoolers, or primary-age children), **assess the physical space** using the guidelines provided, *reflect* on what you saw and heard, and *apply* the appropriate strategies listed with the children you observed.

Observe	Reflect	Apply
Look for specific examples of:	*Think about and respond to the following questions:*	*Consider the following developmentally appropriate strategies for the age group you observed:*
Simple units as defined on page 223 of this chapter	What kinds of play were being exhibited by children using simple units in the classroom?	Provide many simple-unit options • Infant/toddler: Most toys and equipment such as balls, rattles, mobiles, and cradle gyms will be simple units. • Preschool: Puzzles, toy trucks, stacking toys, Montessori materials, and sequence cards are typically simple units. • Primary: Simple play units such as story sequencing cards are less commonly found at this level, and when they are children may well use them in more creative ways.
Complex units as defined on page 223 of this chapter	What are the play advantages of complex units over simple units?	Rotate complex units in and out of the classroom • Infant/toddler: Duplo bricks with toy cars, replaced in a week with foam blocks with people figures. • Preschool: Tinkertoy set replaced in a week with Lincoln Log set. • Primary: Math Blaster software replaced in a week with the Oregon Trail software.
Superunits as defined on page 223 of this chapter	Using the formula provided in the text on page 223, how many play options were available to each child?	Modify superunits to maintain interest • Infant/toddler: Basic art materials such as crayons and markers replaced with colored chalk in the art center. • Preschool: In the book corner, change the books, add new flannelboard stories, include different listening center materials. • Primary: In the block corner, add new accessories such as tape measures, rulers, and paper for recording dimensions of "buildings" constructed.

movement through the classroom, and teacher needs should all be planned for in each setting.

Selecting Equipment and Materials

Several commercial resources are available for quality equipment and materials needed for the early childhood classroom. Teachers can also make inexpensive materials and equipment to meet the needs and interests of children.

Children with Special Needs

Teachers of young children must adapt materials, equipment, and activities so that children with special needs can be effectively included in the classroom.

Changing the Physical Environment

Moderate change of the toys and equipment used by children in the classroom should be planned for and implemented on a regular basis. This change helps stimulate child interest and engagement by providing variety and novelty.

Health and Safety Issues

Teachers must also consider health and safety issues for the early childhood classroom and eliminate unnecessary health and safety hazards. When the physical environment is made safe, children can explore their classroom more freely.

Multimedia Explorations and Activities . . .

Kids Test Products and Disprove Child Resistance

Home is not always a safe place for young children to be. There are numerous dangers, including potential fires, poisons, and hazardous medicines. Despite attempts by manufacturers to make products that are difficult for children to get into, there are still many examples of youngsters managing to cause themselves harm. For example, lighters with a safety catch that forces the user to take one extra step before a flame is possible are still being operated by young children. And we are all familiar with the child-resistant tops to most medicines, where you must push down and twist simultaneously to open. While many of these devices are difficult for adults to use, young children are figuring out ways to get into and use dangerous products. These so-called child-proof packaging options are not stopping young children as often as they should.

Research

Child health and safety are significant issues for early childhood teachers and parents. This activity is designed to make you more aware of the major concerns you will face.

1. View the ABC News video segment titled "It's a Snap: Kids Test Products and Disprove Child Resistance."

2. Go to the Companion Website for this text at www.prenhall.com/henniger and click on the Multimedia Explorations and Activities button for Chapter 9 for more information on this topic.

Reflect

Based on your research, think about the following issues:

- What do you see as the most significant safety concerns facing parents and families in the home environment? How should parents deal with these issues?

- As a teacher of young children, what are the major safety problems you will face? How will you manage these concerns?

- How will you educate parents about health and safety concerns?

Respond

Having investigated health and safety concerns for young children, consider responding in one or more of the following ways:

1. Do your own testing of child-resistant packaging with a young child. Find out what she can or cannot open. Share the results of your testing with others via the message board on the Companion Website accompanying this text.

2. Create a list of important safety concerns for the home. For each item identified, suggest one or two easy solutions. Share your list with a parent.

3. Identify strategies you will use in the classroom to deal with the safety issues you expect to find. Share your strategies with others via the message board on the Companion Website accompanying this text.

10

PLANNING THE PHYSICAL ENVIRONMENT: OUTDOORS

In this chapter you will

- Gain knowledge about the importance of outdoor play.
- Get ideas for planning the outdoor play environment.
- Develop a rationale for stimulating a variety of play types outdoors.
- Address the teacher's role in preparing for outdoor play.
- Review information related to playground health and safety.

Marika and Nikky are excited about spending some time outdoors today and are ready to get started. These eager third graders have been planning to do some gardening activities for several days. The story about growing things and the visit from an expert gardener seem to have stimulated their interest. During project time over the past week, they have been formulating their plans. After reading portions of several books on gardening, they drew a map to scale of the portion of the garden area assigned to them and indicated the vegetables they will grow. Marika wrote a list of procedures for the planting and care of their vegetables, while Nikky gathered from her gardening parents all the seeds they will use and identified the proper planting depths for each. With shovels, trowels, row markers, and seeds in hand, they are ready to begin. It is exciting to see how children's interests can become the basis for playful learning opportunities in the outdoor setting.

Given opportunities to do so, most young children eagerly engage in creative experiences outdoors. The chance to explore the natural wonders found outside the classroom—combined with opportunities to run, jump, climb, and shout—makes this setting a valuable learning environment for children. Early educators need to be sensitive to the importance of this environment and plan for creative play experiences there.

Importance of Outdoor Play

Think about a favorite play experience you remember from your own childhood. What were you doing? Were you playing alone or with others? Were you indoors or outside? In a study of college students, over 75 percent remembered favorite play experiences that occurred outdoors (Henniger, 1994). What makes outdoor play experiences so memorable for many adults?

A variety of possible explanations may help us to understand this finding. The sensory experiences associated with playing outdoors are certainly one possible explanation. Sights, sounds, smells, and textures found outside are attractive to children and make that setting more interesting to them. The greater sense of freedom associated with the outdoors is another possible reason many of us remember outdoor play experiences so vividly (Rivkin, 1995). Running, jumping, shouting, and getting involved in messy activities can be accomplished outdoors with minimum adult involvement. A third possibility is that outdoor play gives children more opportunities for risk taking. Smith (1990) suggests that this is one of the main reasons that children play outdoors. Risk taking is exciting and motivates many children to play.

In addition to children's interests in this setting, there are other reasons for promoting outdoor play. The NAEYC emphasizes the importance of outdoor play as an integral part of developmentally appropriate practices for young children. Daily outdoor play experiences are considered essential for all children from birth through age 8. They provide opportunities to use large and small muscles, learn from materials outdoors, and experience the freedom only the outdoors can allow (Bredekamp & Copple, 1997).

Arturo and Cindy are swinging side by side on their preschool playground. As they move back and forth, Cindy talks of her new baby brother. Mandy joins them, and as they swing, the children decide to pretend to be a mom, dad, and baby out for a picnic in the park.

For more information about the importance of outdoor play, go to the Companion Website at www.prenhall.com/henniger, select Chapter 10, then choose Web Destinations.

These and other outdoor activities provide many opportunities for learning and development. A creative, well-planned playground can stimulate a wide variety of positive play experiences for young children (Frost, Wortham, & Reifel, 2001). Swings, slides, and wide-open spaces encourage sensori-motor play outdoors and provide opportunities for aerobic activities to strengthen young hearts and lungs. A sandbox with digging tools and accessories can stimulate creative construction activities, and children can use an old boat for a variety of sociodramatic play themes. In fact, every aspect of the child's development can be enhanced when adults develop quality outdoor play spaces (Isenberg & Jalongo, 2001). With careful planning and preparation of the playground, children have rich and memorable experiences there.

Planning Guidelines

If outdoor play is to live up to its potential, however, teachers must commit time and energy to planning and preparing this space (Frost, Wortham, & Reifel, 2001). The playground should be viewed as an extension of the indoor classroom and must be an important part of the teacher's planning efforts (Esbensen, 1987).

Basic Guidelines

Several considerations help make the outdoor play space a quality one for young children. These guidelines provide the basic ingredients children need for positive playground experiences:

- The playground should be located next to the classroom.
- Playgrounds should provide at least 100 square feet of outdoor space for each child.
- A balance of sunny and shady areas will help the play yard appeal to the greatest number of students.
- Large, grassy areas should be included for children's games and large muscle activities.
- A tall, sturdy fence helps children feel safe and secure in the outdoor setting.
- A covered area provides opportunities for play during very hot or rainy weather.
- Playgrounds should have areas encouraging group activities and private places for when children need time to themselves.

Fixed Equipment

Playgrounds contain a variety of equipment and materials to stimulate children's play. The most commonly found structures on playgrounds today are pieces of fixed equipment such as swings, slides, and climbers (Frost, Bowers, & Wortham, 1990). These larger pieces of equipment are designed to be permanent and immovable and add important play opportunities for children. An ideal playground environment should include a variety of fixed equipment that children can use in creative ways. Swings, slides, climbers, a sandbox, dramatic play structures, and permanent storage facilities are all important pieces of fixed equipment needed for exciting outdoor play.

Swings provide children with many opportunities to practice coordinating large muscle movements as they pump vigorously with arms and legs. The exhilarating experience of moving back and forth on a swing as fresh air blows briskly over the child's face adds excitement and pleasure to this activity. When more than one swing is available, children will often gather at the swing set to talk and enjoy good friendships as they glide through the air. For other children, swinging can be an opportunity to separate themselves from the crowd and spend time thinking or regaining composure following a difficult experience elsewhere.

Slides and climbers are found on most playgrounds and provide many play opportunities for children.

 Dottie has just reached the top of the largest climber on her elementary playground for the first time. She cannot wait to tell her older brother, who has been "bugging" his first-grade sister to "climb the mountain," about her accomplishment.

The challenge of moving step by step to the top of an imposing structure and then looking down at the rest of the world is an important one for the young child and can give a sense of power and accomplishment. Many modern playground structures provide children with several different ways to reach the top of the slide and challenge children to try them as they build confidence in their climbing

For more information about playground equipment manufacturers, go to the Companion Website at www.prenhall.com/henniger, select Chapter 10, then choose Web Destinations.

abilities. Sliding itself provides other risk-taking opportunities and sensory experiences that are pleasurable for children.

The sandbox is another traditional piece of fixed equipment found on most playgrounds that adds important play options for children. In the sandbox, children spend many happy hours building, tearing down, and building again using simple child-sized tools and accessories such as spoons, scoops, and sifters (Baker, 1966). The joy of digging in the dirt, mixing sand and water, and creating a child-sized world of hills and valleys or a pretend lunch of molded sand is often a richly rewarding experience for children. The sandbox tends to draw children together and encourages them to play near or with others in creative ways. It allows the shy child opportunities to engage in parallel play in preparation for more social activities in the future.

Fixed equipment that encourages children to engage in dramatic play is also valuable on the playground. A playhouse stocked with child-sized furniture is one example of a creative piece of equipment that is useful in stimulating dramatic play. An old boat or small car that has been carefully prepared by adults could also provide children with many happy hours of dramatic play. Although not as commonly found on playgrounds for young children (Frost, Wortham, & Reifel, 2001), these dramatic play structures help stimulate the important play types that can and should occur outdoors.

Another essential piece of fixed equipment needed on playgrounds for young children is the storage shed. A lockable building at least 10×12 feet is needed. If the outdoor environment is to reach its true potential, there must be some way of storing loose parts (Isenberg & Jalongo, 2001). Making the outdoor environment an extension of the classroom requires storage spaces similar to those found indoors. The following items can be effectively stored outdoors for children's use:

- Construction materials (large and small)
- Dramatic play props
- Sand toys and digging equipment
- Materials for children's games
- Wheeled toys
- Art materials

A storage shed allows the teacher to change the materials available to children so that the new items stimulate increased interest and involvement.

Movable Equipment

Although the previously fixed playground equipment described provides many valuable options for children, movable materials are also needed. Remember how children learn during their early years. Hands-on manipulation of toys and equipment in their world provides young children with many opportunities for growth and development (Kamii & DeVries, 1978). When teachers of young children plan for learning indoors, they create centers that are rich with materials children can manipulate (see Chapter 9). Similar opportunities for manipulating toys and equipment are needed outdoors so that children can learn from these experiences as well.

Gordy, Brianna, and Meghan are busily moving lightweight sections of plastic rain gutter to create a series of ramps to roll their tennis balls through. These children are learning basic physics properties as they manipulate this outdoor equipment.

Into Practice...
Playing in the Gutters

Sue Dinwiddie (1993) suggests a simple and creative way to provide children with quality materials that they can move and manipulate outdoors. For her preschool program for children 2½ to 5, teachers introduced children to plastic rain gutters. After purchasing three 10-foot segments of gutter at their local lumberyard, Dinwiddie cut these pieces into different lengths with a hacksaw:

- Two 5-foot sections
- Three sections approximately 3½ feet in length
- One section 7½ feet long, and the remaining piece 2½ feet long

Initially, the teachers set up the gutters ahead of time in such a way that the gutters sloped down to the sandbox and the water table. The teachers placed pitchers, pots, and buckets near the gutters for children to use. The children were then free to experiment with pouring sand and water down the gutters.

As you might expect, this activity attracted many children and held their interest for extended periods. They experimented with different slopes for the gutters and tried a creative assortment of materials such as balls and boats to send down the gutters. This inexpensive, durable option is an excellent example of a type of movable equipment that young children can use productively.

Although most playgrounds for young children currently have limited options for manipulation (Frost, Wortham, & Reifel, 2001), these materials can and should be added. In addition to the tricycles, old tires, and sandboxes typically found on playgrounds, children can effectively use other materials such as child-sized cable spools, commercially produced outdoor blocks, and gardening tools.

The **Adventure Playgrounds** of Europe provide other examples of movable equipment that children can effectively use outdoors (Frost, Wortham, & Reifel, 2001). A trained play leader guides children in their Adventure Playground experiences. They play with scrap lumber, bricks, tires, rope, hammers, nails, saws, a fire pit, and animals (for petting, feeding, and care). Through playful experiences in which they move, manipulate, and build, children gain valuable insights into the world around them.

 For more information about Adventure Playgrounds, go to the Companion Website at www.prenhall.com/henniger, select Chapter 10, then choose Web Destinations.

Variety of Play Options

Traditional playgrounds were designed to stimulate physical/motor play (Frost & Wortham, 1988). Although this is an important goal, playgrounds can encourage many other play types. Research on children's playground behaviors indicates that this environment, when properly prepared, can stimulate a wide assortment of play types (Rivkin, 1990). The "Observing Development" feature at the end of this chapter highlights several playground options within early childhood, reflections on how the playground equipment encouraged children to interact in challenging and creative ways, and methods to promote additional development through playground adjustments.

In addition to active physical/motor play, the outdoor environment can allow for many other play opportunities. For example, solitary play can be encouraged through the use of cardboard and wooden boxes (that children can crawl inside), barrels, and natural plantings that create a small space for individual children. Construction play can also take place when the teacher provides a variety of building materials. In addition, the teacher can take outdoor prop boxes containing dress-up materials and toys for dramatic play to the playground to stimulate imaginative play themes. Games with rules can also be encouraged for children who are ready for this play type by providing any needed equipment. For example, balls of various sizes and types can be made available for primary-age children's games.

Outdoor Play Areas

Many educators view the playground as an outdoor classroom. These teachers carefully organize this environment to provide children with the best possible play experiences. Just as the indoor classroom is divided into centers to encourage different play types, the playground can be similarly organized. Esbensen (1987) suggests organizing the outdoors into seven play zones: transition zone, manipulative/creative zone, projective/fantasy zone, focal/social zone, social/dramatic zone, physical zone, and natural element zone. The playground areas identified next are modifications of the play zones defined by Esbensen.

Transition Area

 Shawna has just walked out the classroom door and is slowly scanning the playground to see what others are doing. She often needs time to warm up to the idea of playing outdoors.

As children leave the relatively quiet indoor environment to engage in more active outdoor play, a transition area helps many children adjust. This area could include quieter activities such as painting and water play (Esbensen, 1987). If possible, the transition area should be covered (making it more usable in poor weather conditions) and have child-sized tables and chairs for sit-down activities.

Manipulative/Construction Area

Another important space on the early childhood playground is the manipulative/construction area. Fine motor development can be enhanced by providing puzzles, small blocks, beads, and other manipulative materials typically found indoors. The addition of a woodworking bench and other building materials also encourage construction play in this area. Creative materials such as play dough, clay, and art activities can stimulate other important play experiences (Esbensen, 1987).

Storage is an important concern for this outdoor area in order to keep materials safe when they are not in use. A shed can be effectively used for many of these items, or an already existing piece of outdoor equipment may have a handy corner that could be used as a storage nook. Another possibility is to store construction materials indoors and bring them outside in boxes or crates when needed.

Dramatic Play Area

 Trentin and Tessa are excitedly playing commuter on the preschool playground. After filling their trikes with gas from the toy gas pump, they both motor over to the playhouse to end their busy workdays and play with their families.

Physical/motor play is an important option for all young children.

While dramatic play occurs spontaneously on the playground, providing creative props will stimulate even higher levels of this important play type. Boys, in particular, seem to engage in more pretend play in this setting when quality materials are available. A permanent structure such as a playhouse can serve as a valuable gathering spot for the dramatic play area. If possible, this structure should also have storage space to accommodate the many props needed for creative dramatic play. Other structures, such as a small stripped car body or a steering wheel mounted in a wooden box, also encourage imaginative play experiences for young children.

Physical Area

The development of large muscles can be encouraged outdoors in many ways. Mounds, hills, grassy areas, asphalt or concrete surfacing, and winding, figure-eight tricycle paths challenge children to use their large muscles in new and interesting ways (Esbensen, 1987). Tricycle paths should be a minimum width of 4 feet to allow children to pass each other as they meet. Open spaces for running, skipping, and simple games are useful. Climbers, slides, and swings all help develop physical skills as well. This area should allow risk taking by children and challenge them with a variety of options and levels as they physically mature. When making decisions about where to locate this area, be sure to separate it from the quieter activities found elsewhere.

Sand/Water Play Area

The sandbox has been a traditional and important part of early childhood playgrounds. From Margaret McMillan's Open-Air Nursery (Braun & Edwards, 1972) in the 19th century to the present time, sandbox play has been encouraged outdoors. This area should be large enough to accommodate several children at the same time. A variety of digging, mixing, and pouring utensils enrich the play experiences

For more information about sand and water play, go to the Companion Website at www.prenhall.com/henniger, select Chapter 10, then choose Web Destinations.

Into Practice...
Sand and Water Play

Sand and water are two natural materials that young children are attracted to and thoroughly enjoy. They should be made available for play in both the indoor and outdoor settings. Yet, in order for children to fully explore and enjoy these elements, other props and tools should be provided to stimulate creative play. As with all areas in the early childhood classroom, these materials should be rotated regularly to increase interest and novelty. For ease of use, you may choose to store different collections of props and tools in separate baskets or storage bins so that you can pull them out quickly and easily for use in sand and water play activities. The following examples are intended to give you ideas about materials to collect for use with either sand or water:

Props	Tools
Miniature toy people	Tin cans of various sizes
Toy boats, cars, airplanes	Plastic cups, bowls, measuring cups
Toy animals, water creatures	Metal spoons and forks of various sizes
Plastic dolls	Hand shovels, trowels, rakes
Toy dump trucks, tractors	Plastic milk jugs
Sticks, branches, rocks	Funnels

children can have there. Other accessories such as toy trucks, boats, plastic animals, and human figures add to the creative play potential of the sandbox. A permanent cover for the sandbox helps protect this area from animal use during nonplay periods. Ideally, the sandbox should also be near a water source so that children can combine these two elements for messy but thoroughly enjoyable play experiences.

Natural Areas

After several weeks of spring rains, today is a beautiful, sunny day. Awesta and Chrissy are skipping joyfully across the open grassy area of the playground, laughing and talking along the way. The dew on newly budding leaves sparkles in the sunlight, while the fragrant aromas of spring fill the air.

Part of the wonder and joy experienced by children outdoors comes from the natural elements found there (Rivkin, 1995). The sights, smells, and textures of this environment are unique and exciting for children. To enhance this aspect of outdoor play, adults should provide a variety of trees, bushes, and plantings. Taking care to choose flowering shrubs and trees for spring blooms, other trees for shade in the warmer seasons, and yet other plantings for vivid fall colors will help make the outdoor setting of continued interest throughout the year. An assortment of natural materials also allows children to experience different textures, leaf sizes, colors, and smells throughout the growing season. Rather than a single, large grouping of natural plantings in one area, several smaller groupings of trees and plants throughout the play yard can add interest and beauty to this environment. Parents and interested community members may assist in planning, planting, and caring for these natural elements. A garden/digging spot that is separate from the sandbox can also be included in the natural area. Child-sized shovels, rakes, and gardening tools allow children to dig, plant, and care for an assortment of in-

Water play is an enticing activity throughout the early childhood years.

teresting plantings. Young children can enjoyably grow a variety of flowers, fruits, and vegetables in a garden plot.

Developmental Considerations

Just as indoor environments reflect the developmental abilities and interests of children, playground planners must consider these important characteristics in their planning as well. An infant/toddler playground will look much different from a play space created with 4- and 5-year-old children in mind. Similarly, before children with special needs can engage in outdoor play, the playground planner must understand their physical conditions and must alter equipment and space to allow equitable access.

Infant/Toddler Play Spaces

You may be surprised to learn that outdoor time is important for children even at the infant/toddler stage. Recently, educators have begun to focus on outdoor play environments for infants and toddlers and have discovered that children this age find the outdoor setting richly rewarding (Lowman & Ruhmann, 1998). Because infants and toddlers learn a great deal through the use of their senses, the playground provides many new opportunities for extending learning. Figure 10–1 provides a sample design for an infant/toddler playground.

Developmentally, infants and toddlers are growing daily in their locomotor skills. They perfect sitting, crawling, standing, and walking as they interact with people and objects in their environment. Socially, these very young children are becoming aware of others and beginning to interact with them. They are developing language and intellectual skills through playful exchanges with adults, other children, and playthings. Although indoor settings certainly enhance these developing abilities, the outdoors is another rich opportunity for growth.

Figure 10–1 *Infant/Toddler Playground*

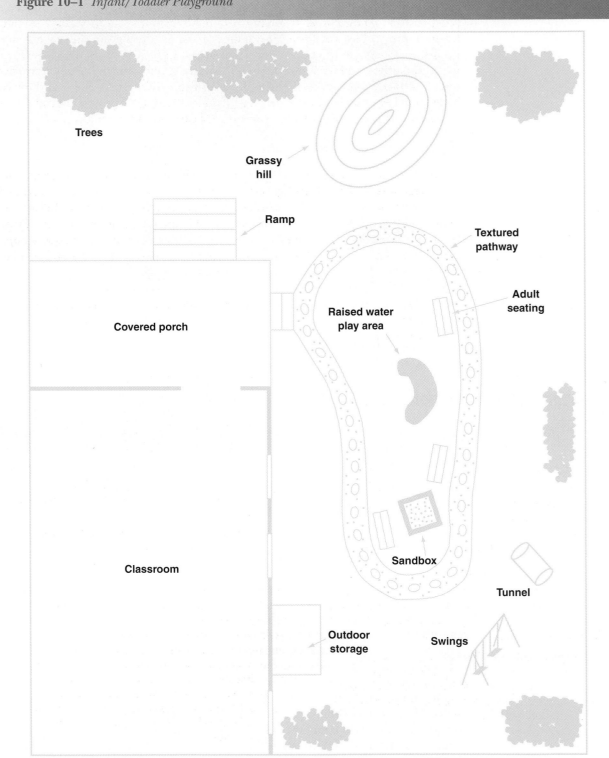

Trees

Grassy hill

Ramp

Textured pathway

Adult seating

Covered porch

Raised water play area

Classroom

Sandbox

Tunnel

Outdoor storage

Swings

Outdoor play environments for the infant and toddler should not be simply scaled-down versions of the complex play structures found on playgrounds for older children (Lowman & Ruhmann, 1998). Many simple additions can be made to the natural elements found outdoors for use by this age group. Small hills, ramps, low steps, and tunnels may all be useful in facilitating physical development. A pathway with different textures to walk on and touch is another creative option. Infants and toddlers often select push toys, riding toys, dolls, and toy vehicles that help stimulate creative play (Winter, 1985). Children this age also productively use sand—or an edible substitute for the youngest children.

Children 3 Through 5

During the preschool and kindergarten years, children are developing greater social awareness and increasingly want to interact with their peers. Playground equipment for this age should help facilitate social skills by bringing children together for play experiences. A complex, multifunctional superstructure (Frost, Wortham, & Reifel, 2001) that includes steps, slides, suspended bridges, ramps, and climbers can be useful for this purpose. Figure 10–2 provides a sample playground design for children 3 through 5 years of age.

Darren is a typical 4-year-old. He loves running, climbing, and swinging activities on the playground. Darren also spends large blocks of time in the sandbox and riding tricycles.

Into Practice . . .
Woodworking Outdoors

While it is probably more common to have woodworking activities indoors, there are good reasons for conducting these important learning experiences on the playground. Hammering and sawing are both rather noisy and messy, so working outdoors makes good sense for these reasons. In addition, playgrounds provide more space so that children are less likely to injure themselves with an inadvertent swing of a saw or hammer.

If finding storage space for a quality woodworking table is a problem, consider the following simple alternatives for productive woodworking activities outdoors:

- Find a larger cable spool and use it as an outdoor woodworking bench that can be left out in the wind and rain. These durable wooden spools, available from your local telephone company, will survive several years of hard use outdoors.

- A play crate or toolbox can be used to store woodworking tools, wood, and safety goggles indoors when not in use.

- Smaller tree stumps create wonderful hammering experiences for young children and can be left outdoors without storage. When the stumps are filled with nails (use large-headed roofing nails approximately 1 1/4 inches long), you can use a chain saw to cut off the top portion and let the children begin again (Leithead, 1996).

- Use other materials for hammering and sawing. For example, children can easily manipulate larger Styrofoam chunks and use them much like wood for hammering and sawing. Another option would be to use heavy-duty cardboard tubes (one source for such tubes would be your local newspaper for the center tubes that hold rolls of newsprint) for sawing and nailing activities.

Figure 10–2 *Preschool Playground Design*

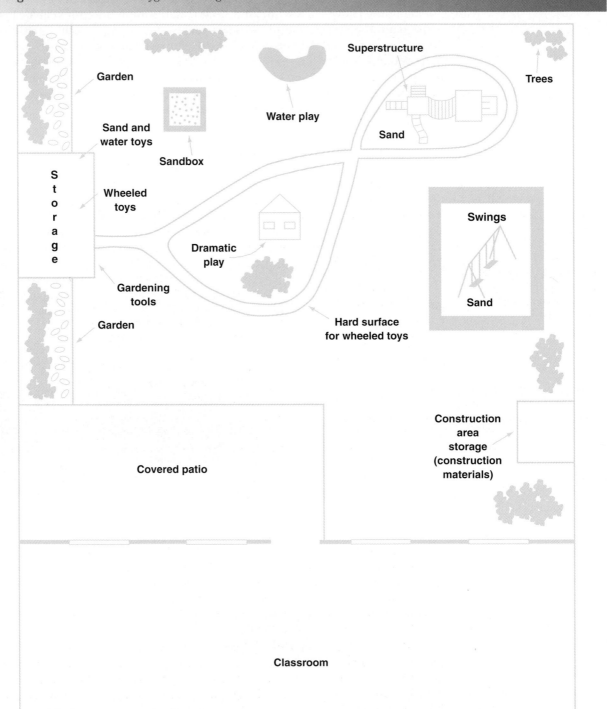

Garden

Trees

Superstructure

Water play

Sand

Sand and water toys

Sandbox

Storage

Swings

Wheeled toys

Dramatic play

Sand

Gardening tools

Garden

Hard surface for wheeled toys

Construction area storage (construction materials)

Covered patio

Classroom

Celebrating Play . . .
The Social Values of Recess

Up through their time in kindergarten, most children have many opportunities for socializing with their peers in the early childhood classroom. As they engage in play activities in various centers, children have time to talk to and interact with others. Beginning in the first grade, however, the opportunities for extended socialization are often limited. Time on the playground is one of the few chances primary children have to interact with their peers. The following quotations are designed to get you thinking about the potential benefits of this time outdoors:

Recess encourages all areas of children's development. As children interact, they use language and nonverbal communications: they make decisions and solve problems, and they deal with the emotional trials and tribulations of their interactions (Jambor, 1994b, p. 18).

Recess is one of the few times during the school day when children are free to exhibit a wide range of social competencies—sharing, cooperation, negative and passive language—in the context that they see as meaningful. Only at recess does the playground become one of the few places where children can actually define and enforce meaningful social interaction during the day (Pelligrini & Glickman, 1989, p. 24).

Unfortunately, as the general level of academic expectations have risen in American schools, there has been a corresponding decrease in the amount of time children spend on the playground. In fact, more and more schools have abandoned recess times altogether. If children are going to experience the previously described social values of recess, parents and school boards will need to be convinced of its value. Jambor (1994b) suggests several strategies for promoting recess time:

- Educate administrators by providing them with articles about the importance of recess.
- Help parents and other teachers understand the importance of recess by describing the social and cognitive benefits.
- Provide in-class recesses to give students more time for play and socialization.
- Write letters and opinion pieces for the local newspaper, school board members, legislators, and others. Don't be afraid to speak out often for the importance of recess.

---

1. Read an article about the importance of recess, and list the benefits cited.

2. Watch children at play on an elementary playground. Describe the kinds of social interactions you observed. Do you think recess provides valuable opportunities for developing social skills?

 For more information about designing playgrounds for young children, go to the Companion Website at www.prenhall.com/henniger, select Chapter 10, then choose Web Destinations.

Physical skills during the preschool years are developing rapidly. These children need equipment that challenges their abilities in running, climbing, and complex tasks such as throwing a ball. Three- to 5-year-old children need a variety of equipment choices that encourage them to expand their skills to a new level. Equipment that can be adjusted or that has built-in varying levels of physical challenge are best suited for this age group.

Preschool and kindergarten children are actively engaged in pretend play sequences, and materials that encourage dramatic play themes are important to include. A variety of materials to stimulate this play behavior are essential. Children this age can creatively use fixed equipment such as an old boat or car body. Smaller props such as dress-up clothes and theme-related toys can also promote valuable dramatic play. Dramatic play prop boxes (see Chapter 9 for more information) can be stored indoors and used periodically for outdoor play.

Primary children continue to benefit from quality outdoor experiences that enhance physical/motor development.

Primary Children

Although many primary-age children are beginning to show interest in other play activities, growing evidence indicates that children this age still need, and should be encouraged to engage in, dramatic play experiences (Smilansky & Shefatya, 1990). This is particularly true for children from low-income families where dramatic play skills often develop at later ages. The materials and equipment described previously for dramatic play should also be available for the primary-age child. Figure 10–3 gives an example of a playground for children 5 through 8 years of age.

> *Carla is an active second-grade child who loves to play jump-rope games and hopscotch and to create her own challenges while twirling on the bars during outdoor time. When some props for camping were made available, she also spent long periods of time engaged in dramatic play around this theme.*

Piaget suggests that primary children are transitioning into the stage of concrete operations. As this process takes place, children become more interested in, and more able to play, games with rules (Piaget, 1962). Teachers can effectively introduce traditional team games such as soccer, baseball, and basketball, especially if competition is minimized. With an emphasis on skill building and enjoyment of the game, many children can benefit from these more structured play events. More spontaneous games that have entertained children for generations can also be productively introduced to young children during the primary grades. Multicultural games from around the world can open up additional playful alternatives for children (Kirchner, 1991).

Children with Special Needs

Teachers of young children should also prepare the outdoor environment to accommodate those with special needs. Playground experiences are important for these children as well. Two basic considerations should be kept in mind for this group.

First, the teacher must be aware that his involvement and assistance are essential when working with children with special needs (Karnes, 1994). Although these children can playfully engage in activities outdoors that stimulate their physical, intellectual, and social/emotional development, they often need more modeling, encouragement, and reinforcement than other children. The teacher should provide this helping hand to ensure that children with special needs get the most out of their play situations.

Figure 10–3 *Sample Primary Playground*

Hard surface for games

Storage for construction toys

Construction area

four-square

Quiet area (surrounded with bushes)

Storage for balls, games, jump ropes

hopscotch

Water

Dramatic play

Garden

Swings

Protective surface (wheelchair accessible)

Classroom

Storage

Superstructure

Covered patio

Celebrating Diversity . . .
Outdoor Play for Children with Special Needs

All children, including those with special needs, benefit from playing outdoors. An essential first step in facilitating their natural interests is to provide quality playground equipment and materials that are accessible to them. In addition to providing the best and most accessible equipment, teachers who have children with special needs in the classroom will also need to think about ways in which they can facilitate quality play experiences. The following list of suggestions (Karnes, 1994) may help in planning quality outdoor play experiences for these children.

Do

Talk with children's physical therapists about making the playground safe and appropriate for each child.

Provide choices of materials based on children's abilities and interests.

Prepare children with special needs to use the play area before they encounter it with other children.

Make sure that children with special needs understand safety rules.

Don't

Expect that all children with special needs will play spontaneously. They may need ideas and assistance.

Make play choices for children with special needs. Let them make decisions for themselves.

Overprotect children with special needs. They are capable of taking an active part in outdoor play.

---

1. Take a look at a playground for young children. What did you see that would indicate accommodations for children with special needs? Share your findings with classmates.

2. What special safety issues may you face with children with special needs on the playground? How would you handle these safety concerns?

Second, the child with special needs must be able to use the available equipment. Many playground surfaces, for example, make it very difficult for children in wheelchairs to get near enough to use the equipment. Sand is a great shock-absorbing material under and around the swings, but it makes it very difficult for a student in a wheelchair to use them. Depending on the nature of the disabilities, other playground modifications may be necessary if we are to make the outdoor environment truly accessible to children with special needs.

Selecting Equipment and Materials

Because playgrounds are typically used by several classrooms in the same school or child care center, teachers are rarely able to make decisions on their own regarding new additions of equipment and materials. Teachers need to make their preferences known to administrators so that positive changes can be made for this setting.

As opportunities arise for adding equipment to the outdoor environment, teachers should consider several options. Commercial materials, donated items, and adult-made equipment all can enhance the play value of the outdoor setting.

Commercial Equipment

Commercial equipment for outdoor gross motor play is readily available for early childhood settings. Many playground companies provide large permanent structures that cost from $4,000 to $20,000 or more. If you purchase all of your materials through commercial providers, the playground will be an expensive area to equip. When estimating costs for commercial structures, make sure to include the cost of the structure itself, installation costs (typically, 35 to 40 percent of the purchase price), and surfacing costs for the material placed under and around the equipment for safety purposes. In addition to the larger permanent play structures, commercial companies also sell some smaller movable equipment such as metal climbers, plastic interlocking panels, and tricycles.

Donated Materials

For more information about parachute play, go to the Companion Website at www.prenhall.com/henniger, select Chapter 10, then choose Web Destinations.

Even if your budget for outdoor equipment is small, you should not let the expense of commercial options stop you from creating an exciting playground for children. Other free or inexpensive options exist. With some creative thinking, you can locate and have donated to your program quality materials for outdoor play. Some commonly found materials that can be effectively used on the playground include old car and truck tires, boards, small cable spools (the kind that hardware stores use to hold chain and rope before sale), PVC pipe and connectors, and lumber for woodworking projects (Frost, Wortham, & Reifel, 2001). Other larger items could include large tires from earth-moving equipment, wooden pallets used for storing materials in warehouses, an old parachute, and cargo netting from overseas shipping activities. Creative adults who get excited about the possibilities of outdoor play can undoubtedly come up with a much longer list than this. The key is to think imaginatively about the materials in your community that could be effectively used by young children on the playground and then get the community involved in providing them for your playground.

Adult-Made Equipment

Many of the materials that businesses and others may wish to donate to your early childhood program can be used to construct low-cost equipment that can serve the same purposes as the more expensive commercial playground structures. For example, a simple tire swing can be constructed from donated materials and have just as much play potential as the more expensive options available through commercial companies (Marston, 1984). More complicated structures like a slide/fort can be constructed with the assistance of knowledgeable parents and community members (Hewes, 1975). Movable equipment can also be constructed by interested parents and others with skills in metal and/or woodworking. Such items as wooden boxes of different sizes, cleated boards to connect smaller pieces of equipment, a steering wheel mounted in a wooden box, and 55-gallon barrels with stands are a few examples of simple equipment that most parent or school groups can effectively design and build.

Hewes (1975) suggests a five-step approach when building your own equipment for outdoor use:

1. Consider the site for the playground equipment. What equipment could be constructed to complement the natural elements and the currently existing options?

2. Once you have commitments for donated materials, determine the amount of money you have for purchasing materials that have not been donated.

3. After resources have been determined, develop a construction plan. The more detailed and accurate the plan, the more likely it will be that the rest of your project will unfold smoothly.

4. Select materials that are durable and safe for young children so that the structures constructed will stand the test of time.

5. Finally, involve children, parents, and community members in the process of actually building your structure.

Planning for Change in the Outdoor Environment

Kate Ortega is a committed, hard-working kindergarten teacher. She understands the importance of planning for creative play and takes time each week to change her centers indoors to stimulate student interest. Recently, she realized that the outdoor environment also required change. Kate now includes time to plan special materials and activities for use on the playground as well.

If we are to make the outdoor setting an integral part of the educational environment, we must plan and prepare the playground with the same care and concern used on the indoor setting. Teachers must change outdoor material and equipment on a regular basis so that children approach playing outdoors with the same sense of excitement and joy as they do indoor explorations (Frost, Wortham, & Reifel, 2001).

For example, when preparing for classroom play in the manipulative center, teachers decide which new puzzles and manipulative materials to place on the shelves so that children can have new and interesting opportunities on a regular basis. Other items can then be put away until later in the school year.

This same planning process must occur for the outdoor setting as well. The provision of outdoor prop boxes, teacher-movable equipment, and child-movable materials that change regularly help create the newness and challenge that are so important to a quality playground.

Outdoor Prop Boxes

A prop box (also referred to as a *play crate*) is a collection of materials organized around a chosen theme to stimulate creative play. The selected props are typically put in a sturdy box that can be easily stored when not in use (Odoy & Foster, 1997). Prop box themes and materials are limited only by the imaginations and creativity of the adults doing the planning. Jelks and Dukes (1985) describe prop boxes for the outdoor setting. Prop boxes can have important benefits when used on the playground:

• The additional props stimulate more dramatic play outdoors.

• Prop boxes make it easy to add change to the outdoor setting.

• They are versatile and can be used effectively both indoors and outdoors.

Hatcher, Nicosia, and Pape (1994) make several suggestions for planning and constructing prop boxes for use in the early childhood classroom, and

Into Practice...
Ideas for Outdoor Prop Boxes

As you consider the possibility of prop boxes for the playground, you may wish to think about several alternatives. First, many of the themes and materials you plan for indoor prop boxes can be productively used on the playground as well. In addition, it is important to realize that the topics for prop boxes may well come from the children themselves. If they show an interest in pet grooming, for example, creating a prop box with that theme makes excellent sense. Finally, remember that the outdoor setting is particularly attractive for certain play themes. Since "real" camping experiences are outdoor activities, for example, having a camping prop box makes excellent sense. With these thoughts in mind, here are some possible outdoor prop box themes and some basic materials that you may wish to collect for each:

Post Office. This prop box could be productively used either indoors or on the playground. With paper, writing utensils, junk mail envelopes, and holiday stickers for stamps, children could write their own letters and then use a canvas bag to deliver their mail around the playground. Shoe boxes could be decorated for mailboxes, tricycles could serve as delivery vans, and the playhouse could be converted to a post office with the use of a few key signs.

Pet Shop. If children were to show an interest in caring for pets, you could collect several stuffed animal "pets," add some old hairbrushes, combs, sponges for "bathing," animal collars, leashes, a toy cash register, and paper money to create a pet shop at an outdoor table. A pet care book with photos would also help stimulate creative play with these materials.

Fishing. For children who have experienced fishing trips or had stories about fishing read to them, a fishing prop box can provide hours of fun. Fishing pole sticks with strings for fishing line and magnets attached to the string end can be used to "catch" laminated fish (with paper clips attached). A playground structure can also be decorated like a boat and a pretend campfire with frying pan set up to add further elements to the play.

Camping. Make sure to read stories about camping experiences for those that have not been camping themselves, and then provide a piece of plastic or a small tarp that can be used to construct a tent-like structure outdoors. Some possibilities for this prop box include a canteen and compass for hikes, materials for a pretend campfire, cooking utensils, and some empty food containers.

Gas Station. A gas station sign attached to an outdoor table or on the side of a play structure (or building wall) near the tricycle path can be the start of a gas station area. From there you can add a cash register, paper money, sections of hose, and some cleaning supplies to generate some creative play with existing tricycles that have suddenly been transformed by children into automobiles.

these also apply to outdoor prop boxes. The box itself should be clearly labeled on the outside to help the teacher locate the needed materials. A theme-related picture attached to the outside of the box can help stimulate children's thinking regarding the topic, just as pictures on the walls in the classroom give children ideas about play in early childhood centers. Inside the lid, an itemized list of props and ideas for setup and use can be included. This can be particularly helpful when prop boxes are shared between several classrooms in larger programs. To aid in storage, all the props should fit in the box and all boxes should be of a uniform size and shape. Finally, making the prop boxes accessible to children and easy to move in and out of designated play areas will make it possible for children to determine their own themes and select the needed play materials.

Children need opportunities to manipulate play materials outdoors.

Teacher-Movable Equipment

When planning for indoor play, teachers consider the physical arrangement of the larger equipment and make periodic adjustments to ensure that children change and have interesting new play options on a regular basis. The sand table may be emptied and refilled with water, for example. This same philosophy can be implemented on the playground; at least some of the materials and equipment can be moved by adults (Henniger, 1993). Placing aluminum climbing equipment in an interesting arrangement near a fixed piece of playground equipment can encourage new interest in this play area. Making a woodworking table and related materials available will stimulate more construction play activities. Moving a portable set of large wooden boxes to a new location on the playground and rearranging them in an interesting pattern can create a quiet space for one or two children for another play option. Rearranging these movable materials will increase the creative play potential outdoors.

Child-Movable Equipment

In addition to larger, adult-movable equipment, it is important to have smaller pieces that children can manipulate (Frost, Wortham, & Reifel, 2001). Commercial options are available through various providers. Outdoor blocks, larger building sets (often plastic for durability and weather resistance), tricycles, and wheeled toys are examples of these materials. Children also can move donated materials such as small cable spools, used tires, and cardboard boxes. For example, when tires are available on the playground, children can use them to roll, sit in, or wash, or as part of their pretend play themes.

By moving equipment themselves, children gain important understandings of their world and see themselves as more competent and capable. Children begin to feel in charge of this environment, just as they do when they manipulate materials indoors. This sense of power and accomplishment is very important in the child's development and must be encouraged as much as possible throughout the curriculum of the early childhood classroom.

Health and Safety on the Playground

> *The elementary school nurse has been working overtime to patch up children's scrapes and bruises from playing outdoors. A kindergarten girl fell and scraped the palms of both hands on the asphalt. Another child cut her head on a metal brace while running under the slide. A third-grade boy sprained his ankle when he slipped and fell off the climber and landed on a log border around the structure.*

For more information about playground safety, go to the Companion Website at www.prenhall.com/henniger, select Chapter 10, then choose Web Destinations.

Despite the many potential health and safety hazards found on most playgrounds, the preceding scenario does not occur regularly. Yet, if the outdoor setting is to meet its potential for stimulating creative play, it not only must be rich with materials and equipment but also must be constructed and maintained to protect children from unnecessary health and safety problems (Catron & Allen, 2003). Currently, many outdoor play spaces for young children fail miserably in this category. Playground injuries and health-related problems are common. As adults become more aware of the issues and change playground construction, many of the following problems can be avoided.

Playground Injuries

The federal government first became concerned about playground injuries in the mid-1970s. The Consumer Product Safety Commission (CPSC) coordinated studies of playground safety (Frost & Henniger, 1979) and found a variety of problems that needed correction. By far the biggest problem then and now is the surfacing under and around play equipment. Large numbers of children across the nation are falling from playground equipment onto hard-packed surfaces and receiving injuries that range from scrapes and bruises to concussions (and worse). Another finding was that equipment on many playgrounds was not appropriate to the developmental abilities of children. Injuries often result when children attempt to use slides, climbers, and swings designed for older students. Equipment design problems in which exposed bolts, sharp edges, and pinch/crush points caused unnecessary injuries were common. Early studies also found that placing pieces of equipment too close together was causing injuries as children moved around the playground.

Unfortunately, statistics indicate that playground injuries today are similar in number to those from the 1970s. Frost, Wortham, and Reifel (2001) indicate that almost a quarter million children are treated in hospital emergency rooms each year for injuries associated with playgrounds. Continued efforts clearly must be made to further reduce these preventable injuries on the playground. Table 10–1 provides information on how to reduce the most serious problem—falls onto hard surfaces.

Safety Guidelines

Because of the just-described injuries, the CPSC developed a set of safety guidelines for equipment on playgrounds. These guidelines, which have gone through several revisions (Consumer Product Safety Commission, 1997), are designed to assist playground equipment manufacturers and concerned adults in creating outdoor environments that are safer places for children to play. Although these guidelines are

| Table 10–1 *Protecting Against Falls* |

Shock-absorbing materials under and around play equipment help prevent injuries from falls. Typical options include wood chips, sand, and pea gravel. But how much is needed to protect against falls of different heights? The following statistics from the Consumer Product Safety Commission provide some initial guidelines. The commission's manual (1997) provides more specifics.

Material	Uncompressed Depth of Material		
	*6 inches	*9 inches	*12 inches
Wood chips	6 feet	7 feet	12 feet
Fine sand	5 feet	5 feet	9 feet
Fine gravel	6 feet	7 feet	10 feet

*Protects falls up to this height.

Note: From *Handbook for Public Playground Safety* by the Consumer Product Safety Commission, 1997, Washington, DC: Consumer Product Safety Commission.

voluntary, equipment manufacturers and others are strongly encouraged to follow them. To date, compliance has been mixed (Frost, Wortham, & Reifel, 2001). Equipment that is less than ideal in terms of safety is still being produced and used on playgrounds for children (Frost & Sweeney, 1996).

Health Considerations

In addition to creating playgrounds that are free from unnecessary safety hazards, planners must consider health-related issues. One such potential problem is the use of toxic materials on the playground (Frost, Wortham, & Reifel, 2001). Chemicals sprayed on plants and coatings on wood surfaces are two examples of problem areas. Poisonous plants are also more common than might be expected and should be excluded from playgrounds. Consult an expert in your area for specific information on plants to avoid. Another consideration is to provide regular maintenance of the playground. Picking up trash and litter will help prevent unwanted injuries and infections from these materials. Standing water can attract insects and disease agents and should be removed from the play yard. Sandbox areas should be covered when not in use to protect them from animal droppings. Regular cleaning of the sand can also protect children from potential health hazards.

The Teacher's Role

Teachers have an important role to play in assisting children on the playground. When actively involved in facilitating outdoor play, teachers can substantially reduce potential injuries. The following list outlines some important considerations in creating a climate for quality outdoor play:

- *Allow plenty of time* for outdoor play. Thirty minutes or more are needed for creative play experiences.
- *Plan with children* for creative playground use. Talk to them about how the equipment can be used.

- *Take time to prepare the outdoors* for children. This will mean that more acceptable and new options will be available to children on a regular basis.
- *Let children know what are acceptable and unacceptable behaviors outdoors.*
- *Periodically inspect equipment* for needed repairs and safety hazards.
- *Spend time interacting with children* in this setting.

Parent and Community Involvement

After the school-wide meeting last night on the condition of the playground, several parents expressed their interest in helping improve the play options outdoors. Marcus's dad is a building contractor and is willing to coordinate the construction of playground structures. Two other families own businesses that can donate some construction materials. The Parent-Teacher Association (PTA) is looking for fund-raising projects and agreed to discuss the playground situation at its upcoming meeting. Perhaps there is hope after all for the much-needed improvements that have been discussed for the playground.

Parents and community members can play an important role in planning and preparing the outdoor environment (Hewes, 1975). A big challenge, however, is to first convince them that this is a valuable activity for children. Can something so uninhibited and joyful as outdoor play also be a quality learning experience?

Family Partnerships...
Encouraging Outdoor Play at Home

A sad fact of life today for many young children is that they have few opportunities for outdoor play at home. One reason for this is the high level of television viewing, video game playing, and computer use by young children. Youngsters who used to run outside and play when they were bored are now plopping down in front of their favorite electronic device and spending much of their free time there. This problem is compounded by the fact that many well-meaning parents are scheduling activities such as youth sports, music lessons, and dance classes to fill up the rest of a young child's waking hours. Despite the undisputed value of these and other activities, many young children simply have very little "free time" in which to get involved in outdoor play. Potential safety issues also make it difficult for many parents to send their children outdoors for extended periods of unsupervised time. Finally, finding handy playmates for outdoor activities is another potential cause for the decrease in outdoor play.

Regardless of the reasons for the decline, parents need to be strongly encouraged to provide their children with quality outdoor play experiences. One thing you could do is to help parents remember the exciting times they had outdoors as children. At a parent meeting designed for this purpose, ask parents to remember a favorite play experience and then to share it with a small group of four or five others. Then, as a large group, discuss how many of these favorite play experiences occurred outdoors and why they were so memorable. Conclude with a discussion of ways in which parents could safely and easily provide similar stimulating outdoor play experiences for their own children.

1. What are your thoughts on the importance of outdoor play for young children? Why do you feel the way you do?

2. Can you think of other strategies you might use to help parents get their children more involved in outdoor play at home?

Teachers need to convince the doubters that the outdoor setting is indeed a rich opportunity for growth. Research and writing supporting the importance of outdoor play for young children are limited. Therefore, concerned teachers will need to provide time for adults to observe and/or discuss this option before many will feel comfortable supporting play outdoors.

Once convinced of its importance, parents and community members can be invaluable in helping prepare a quality playground environment for young children. Through donations of money, materials, and time, major improvements in the outdoor play equipment available to children can be made (Jambor, 1994a). With careful planning, this option can provide safe, durable, and creative play options at a fraction of the cost of commercial equipment.

When thinking of parent and community support, it is also helpful to remember that extra pairs of hands are valuable outdoors as well. Woodworking experiences, for example, frequently require that an adult be present or nearby for safety reasons. These projects are less likely to be available if the teacher is alone outdoors. Consider the benefits of having an adult assist with the garden area. A parent with a special interest in plants and gardening could share this important talent with children in the outdoor classroom. Parent and community support can clearly strengthen the curriculum outdoors, just as in the classroom.

Committing to the Outdoor Environment

Playgrounds should be an extension of the indoor environment. With proper equipment and planning, play outdoors can stimulate all aspects of children's development and be a valuable opportunity for learning. If this perspective is to become a reality, teachers of young children must set aside much of their traditional thinking about playgrounds and begin viewing the outdoors differently. Although fixed equipment is useful, it should be considered secondary in importance to the movable options described throughout this chapter. Children learn best by physically manipulating the materials and equipment in their environment, and these options should be readily available to them outdoors.

This new way of thinking about playgrounds can be easily and inexpensively implemented. Educators, with the help of parents and community members, can construct simple pieces of playground equipment from materials available in their local communities. Locating and using additional donated materials will encourage further creative play experiences. If educators think creatively about what is available to children indoors and bring those materials or similar ones outdoors, they will add diversity to the outdoor play options. Finally, the purchase of movable commercial equipment can support additional play options for children. When educators take these steps, children can have a play space outdoors that truly stimulates all aspects of child development (see Chapter 4) and provides children with a rich and varied playground experience.

This rethinking of the outdoor space also must include a further commitment by teachers to planning and facilitating play in this setting. Teachers must plan each week for new and interesting play options outdoors. This means spending additional time regularly organizing and changing this play space. Already-busy teachers must find the time needed to creatively plan for outdoor play just as they do for the indoor setting. Likewise, teachers must also spend time outdoors with children, committing to the interactions needed to ensure that outdoor play experiences are facilitated in much the same way as indoor play.

Observing Development • Playground Options

Choose one of the age groups within early childhood (infants/toddlers, preschoolers, or primary-age children), *observe* **playground options** using the guidelines provided, *reflect* on what you saw and heard, and *apply* the appropriate strategies listed with the options you observed.

Observe	Reflect	Apply
Look for specific examples of:	*Think about and respond to the following questions:*	*Consider the following developmentally appropriate strategies for the age group you observed:*
Equipment and spaces that stimulate large muscle-use (climbers, swings, large grassy areas, etc.)	Do you think that the equipment and spaces you saw challenged children to build and extend their large-muscle skills without undue risk?	Provide change and novelty outdoors • Infant/toddler: change accessories available for sand and water play • Preschool: add a new board ramp or a rope climber to a stationary piece of playground equipment • Primary: change balls and equipment available for sport-like activities
Equipment and materials that encourage children to engage in construction play (sandbox with accessories, woodworking activities, loose parts for manipulating, etc.)	Were any of the construction materials objects children could move and change on their own in creative ways?	Add child-movable materials • Infant/toddler: take some manipulative materials (like Tinkertoys) outside for children to use • Preschool: collect small cable spools and boards for use in construction projects • Primary: bring a large cardboard box for children to use for constructing a play structure of their choice
Equipment and materials for pretend play (parts of equipment that could be used for pretending such as a steering wheel mounted on a piece of equipment, a dramatic playhouse, an old boat or car, etc.)	Did you find evidence that teachers had planned for pretend play outdoors?	Create dramatic play options • Infant/toddler: bring out toy cars and trucks for use in or near the sandbox • Preschool: create a prop box and bring it outdoors • Primary: have two or three puppets that children could use near one piece of stationary playground equipment

This is by no means a small task. Teachers who decide to move in this direction must realize the commitment they are making in terms of time and energy. Yet, this is one area of the early childhood curriculum that has been significantly undervalued and has the potential for being a rich part of children's lives. The benefits to children are great, and enriching outdoor play experiences will pay many dividends in terms of healthier, happier children.

Summary

To test your knowledge of this chapter's contents, go to the Companion Website at www.prenhall.com/henniger, select Chapter 10, then select Study Guide. Also see Chapter Overviews, Reflecting Essay Questions, Multimedia Explorations, and relevant Web Destinations.

Importance of Outdoor Play

Outdoor play is often devalued in early education. In this chapter, however, you learned of its importance to the health and well-being of children.

Planning Guidelines

In addition to understanding general guidelines for planning quality playgrounds for young children, it is important to know about the value of fixed equipment, movable equipment, and the importance of having a variety of play options outdoors.

Outdoor Play Areas

Children benefit from having different outdoor play spaces such as a transition area, manipulative/construction space, dramatic play, physical area, sand/water play, and a natural area.

Developmental Considerations

Teachers should design the playground to meet the developmental needs of those playing there: infants/toddlers, preschool children, primary-age students, and children with special needs.

Selecting Equipment and Materials

Quality playgrounds for young children may well include commercial equipment, donated materials, and adult-made equipment.

Planning for Change in the Outdoor Environment

Just as with classroom centers indoors, regular change in the outdoor play environment is stimulating for children, and teachers should plan for these changes to maintain student interest.

Health and Safety on the Playground

Teachers and playground planners need to be aware of health and safety issues such as standing water on the playground and the surfacing under and around playground equipment, and must be prepared to eliminate them.

Parent and Community Involvement

Once convinced of its importance, parents and community members can enrich playground activities by helping to build a creative outdoor environment for children and provide assistance with activities such as gardening.

Committing to the Outdoor Environment

Teachers must be convinced that outdoor learning experiences are highly valued and then work to educate parents and community members about the need for renewed commitment to outdoor activities for young children.

Playgrounds

A surprising number of American playgrounds are hazardous places for children. In one report, over 1,000 lawsuits were pending in California courts because of playground injuries. In the state of Colorado, a study of playgrounds found that approximately 95 percent had unnecessary hazards. The litany of problems often cited include protruding bolts and sharp edges that injure unsuspecting children, sandboxes that are used by local cats as litter boxes, equipment placed too close to other structures so that children are swinging or slamming into others, and poorly maintained playground equipment. The issue of playground safety is one that must be addressed.

Research

For the most part, playgrounds are wonderful places for young children. One problem area, however, is the concern over playground safety. Most of these problems can be prevented once they are identified. The purpose of this activity is to get you involved in finding and eliminating unnecessary safety hazards on playgrounds for young children.

1. View the ABC News video segment titled "Playgrounds."

2. Go to the Companion Website at www.prenhall.com/henniger and click on the Multimedia Explorations and Activities button for Chapter 10 for more information on this topic.

Reflect

Now that you have a better idea of the problems associated with playground safety, consider the following issues:

- How would you define the most significant problems associated with playgrounds for young children and what can be done to remedy them?

- What information would you want to share with parents regarding playground safety?

- Is there such a thing as a playground that is too safe? Why or why not?

Respond

Armed with the results of your investigations, consider one or more of the following options:

1. Examine a local playground for safety concerns. Look critically for safety problems such as hard surfacing under and around equipment, placement of equipment, and developmental appropriateness. Report any problems found to the appropriate community agency.

2. Identify strategies for educating parents and children about the potential hazards of playground use. Share your thoughts with a teacher of young children.

3. Write a brief position paper on the importance of having some level of danger/risk on the playground and share it with others via the message board on the Companion Website for this text.

ACTIVITY PLANNING AND ASSESSMENT

In this chapter you will

- Study the components of developmentally appropriate curriculum.
- Understand the importance of observations in planning and assessment activities.
- Learn about activity and lesson planning.
- Identify elements of an integrated curriculum and the project approach.
- Read about scheduling issues and the curriculum.
- Clarify the important elements of assessment in the early childhood classroom.

Mary Beth's mother just finished talking to you following the Open House. She is concerned about allowing children time for project learning in your second-grade classroom. The curriculum has so many required components that taking major blocks of time for child-selected, playful learning just does not seem right to her. This conversation is no surprise to you as the classroom teacher. Having recently modified your activities to provide a more developmentally appropriate curriculum, you expected this response from some of your parents. The letter you sent home before the school year began emphasized this shift and encouraged parents to come in to see the learning that was taking place. Although several did drop in, others still needed to be convinced. Tonight's discussion on developmentally appropriate practice seemed to help others understand as well. Time and more positive communications appear to be needed before this issue can be fully resolved.

Creating a more child-directed, playful curriculum will probably generate the kind of response just described. Parents, other teachers, and administrators often need to be convinced that an approach to teaching and learning that includes freedom of choice, manipulation of real-world materials, and child-directed learning is appropriate for young children. This is particularly true at the primary level. When the more traditional curriculum is replaced with one that actively engages children in learning through hands-on manipulation of materials in their environment, adults unfamiliar with this approach must learn more before they can accept it as valuable for young children.

Creating a Developmentally Appropriate Curriculum

Although preparing a play-oriented, developmentally appropriate curriculum may appear rather simple, it is actually a challenging task requiring a clear understanding of children and their development. Earlier chapters in this text have outlined important components in this process.

Understanding child development and learning (Chapter 4), the importance of play (Chapter 5), effective guidance and discipline (Chapter 6), working with parents (Chapter 7), and diversity (Chapter 8) are all essential considerations when planning a developmentally appropriate curriculum. In addition, the "Observing Development" feature at the end of this chapter highlights specific examples of materials, equipment, and activities that challenge children at various ages within early childhood, reflections on how the materials were used to create intellectual development, and ways to apply that learning through problem-solving tasks.

Guidelines for the Developmentally Appropriate Curriculum

For more information about developmentally appropriate practice, go to the Companion Website at www.prenhall.com/henniger, select Chapter 11, then choose Web Destinations.

The National Association for the Education of Young Children (NAEYC) has identified nine guidelines for a developmentally appropriate curriculum:

- The curriculum provides for all aspects of the child's development (physical, social, emotional, and cognitive).
- The curriculum for young children is intellectually interesting and meaningful to them.
- New knowledge is built upon already existing understandings and abilities.
- Much of the time, traditional subject-matter areas are integrated, rather than taught separately, to help children make more meaningful connections and develop richer concepts.
- Although learning concepts and skills is important, the early childhood curriculum should also emphasize the development of problem-solving skills and an interest in lifelong learning.
- An age-appropriate curriculum for early childhood education also has intellectual integrity. It challenges children to use the concepts and tools of the different disciplines.
- While supporting the child's home culture and language, a quality curriculum also strengthens the ability to participate in the shared culture.
- Goals for the curriculum are reasonable and attainable for most children.
- Technology used in the early childhood classroom is physically and philosophically integrated into the classroom curriculum (Bredekamp & Copple, 1997).

Due to the unique makeup of each child and the diverse mix of children found in every early childhood classroom, it is not possible to simply pick up a teacher's guide and begin teaching in developmentally appropriate ways. The developmentally appropriate curriculum must be tailored to the needs and interests of the children involved. Although this is a more difficult way to teach,

Into Practice . . .
Coping with Tragedy Through Art

Young children encounter tragedy in many different ways. World events like the September 11, 2001, World Trade Center disaster, wars, and famine are regularly viewed by young children on television programs. A death in the local community, a serious illness of a schoolmate, and the loss of a family member are additional examples of tragedies faced by young children. Teachers need to provide ways in which children can process this difficult information. Gross and Clemens (2002) describe how 2- to 5-year-olds used their artwork to respond to the tragedy of September 11:

> On September 12, 2001, when five-year-old Joshua drew a picture of a hurricane, I asked him, "Tell me about your drawing." Joshua replied, "It's a hurricane." I wondered if his violent image arose from seeing frightening images on television, and I

The airplane is flying and it is almost about to crash.

Isabelle, age 4

Four-year-old Isabelle dealt with her emotions after viewing the television images of World Trade Center terrorist attacks by drawing this picture and relating what she saw to her teacher.

used a neutral question to let him say what was on his mind: Toni (teacher): "What's happening in your hurricane?" Joshua: "It hurts people. It knocks down towers." (p. 44)

A few minutes after my discussion with Joshua, four-year-olds Emma and Emily began a quarrel in the dramatic play area. I saw Emily crying. Toni (teacher): "What's happening with you?" Emily: "I don't *want* to be the girl who is burning!" Toni: (turning to Emma) "Do *you* want to be the girl who is burning?" Emma: (drawing back) "No!" Toni: (noticing that both children look frightened) "Maybe this play is too scary. Maybe you'd like to paint this story?" (p. 45). (Emma went directly to the art center and painted what she was feeling; Emily took nearly two weeks before she could do so.)

In both instances, young children who were faced with a very difficult tragedy expressed their feelings through artwork. For many children, this can be a very useful tool in working through the conflicting feelings and difficult emotions surrounding a tragedy. Gross and Clemens (2002) suggest several steps you can take to prepare yourself and children for dealing with tragic events:

- Make sure to find people who can discuss with you (the teacher) practical ideas for dealing with tragedy.
- Have children who have expressed an idea in one art medium share it again in other art forms. Taken together, these different pieces provide even greater validation of what the child is feeling.
- Make sure that children have access to open-ended art materials daily so that they are used to expressing themselves with these items.
- Let children know that freely expressing themselves through their artwork is fully accepted by you as the teacher. Foster relationships in the classroom that encourage this same attitude among children.
- Use neutral language and open-ended questions that help children talk more deeply about the works they have created.

the end result is a classroom in which active, excited learners are growing to their fullest potential.

Developmental Considerations

In addition to the preceding guidelines, early childhood teachers must base their planning on specific developmental characteristics of children. Activities and lessons will vary markedly between infant/toddler, preschool, and primary classrooms because of these developmental differences.

Caregivers at the infant/toddler level need to know, for example, that children are learning a great deal through the use of their senses. The environment should be richly furnished with materials that engage the child's sight, touch, hearing, taste, and smell. Colorful crib hangings, pictures of human faces, mirrors, and cheerful room furnishings all help create an exciting visual environment. Similarly, toys that infants and toddlers can shake, drop, squeeze, and push are effective tactile stimulants. By actively exploring these and other sensory materials, children are learning a great deal about their ever-expanding world.

Although developmental considerations are different during the preschool years, they are equally important in curriculum planning. For example, an understanding of emotional development at this age should influence the selection of books read to children. Reading and discussing books like *William's Doll* (Zolotow, 1985) and *Girls Can Be Anything* (Klein, 1973), for example, should be helpful to children as they struggle with stereotypic expectations.

During the early elementary years, curriculum planning is strongly influenced by local school district and state guidelines. At the same time, however, teachers at this level must develop lessons and use materials that match the developmental abilities and interests of these children. For example, primary-age children are developing the basic physical skills needed for games such as baseball and basketball. While many children at this age show an interest in these activities, they often become frustrated with the competitive element. The creative adult can teach the physical skills needed while encouraging children to play noncompetitive versions of these sports. Through an understanding of both the physical and emotional aspects of typical primary-age children, the teacher can successfully introduce traditional sports activities.

For more information about developmental abilities of primary children, go to the Companion Website at www.prenhall.com/ henniger, select Chapter 11, then choose Web Destinations.

Observation as a Curriculum Tool

Teachers who want to develop curricula based on student interests must find effective strategies for determining these preferences. Observing children as they work and play provides adults with many opportunities to gain these insights.

As Juanita and Sharena play in the dress-up area in their preschool classroom, they are talking about Sharena's mom, who is pregnant and expecting a new baby in a few months. After listening to their conversation for a few minutes, you realize that this issue is important to both these girls and several other children in the class. Raul has a new baby sister, and Maggie's mom just mentioned the other day that she was going in for a pregnancy test. Perhaps this topic could be part of the focus for the upcoming discussion on families.

Although teachers use many different types of observation techniques, the **anecdotal record** may be the most useful for curriculum planning. These brief written notes should include when the observation was made (date and time), who was observed, what the children were doing, and what was said. Despite the short time available for making good observations, the teacher should make every effort to provide as much detail as possible to clarify what was occurring. It is also important to separate what is actually seen and heard from your interpretation of events (Wortham, 2001). One simple way to do this is to include insights that go beyond the actual behaviors in parentheses. These techniques require considerable effort to do well. Brief, specific notes should be made throughout the day to identify what children are learning:

> *8/29/03, 9:30 AM, Pat and Marcie (both age 3), Block Area*
> *On the rug in the block area, Pat says: "Let's make a barn and pasture for our horses! Then we can play farm." (The class went on a field trip to a farm last week.) Marcie replies, "What about all the other animals? Where will the pigs and cows and chickens go?"*

Taking time to make observations of children in your classroom is never an easy task. Preparing for each activity, assisting children who need your help, and teaching both large and small groups leaves little time for anything else. Yet, teachers frequently mention that observation is an essential element of the teaching/learning process. By carrying writing materials around throughout the school day and jotting brief but accurate notes about behaviors observed and comments made, teachers can develop a much clearer understanding of children's interests. It may also be useful to tape record or videotape children's activities to document more completely what is being observed. These activities are helpful in curriculum planning because they focus the curriculum on children's preferences.

Curriculum Goals

In addition to knowing general guidelines for developmentally appropriate practice, creating a strong curriculum for young children requires a clear sense of what you are trying to accomplish. **Curriculum goals** are broad learning outcomes that identify the key results anticipated from the educational process. Goals are often created as part of a school-wide mission statement identifying the philosophy and values of the program. Because the goals are general, however, your personal interpretation of these goals may differ somewhat from those of other teachers with whom you work. It is important to stop and reflect on these broad learning outcomes and make decisions about how they can be implemented in your early childhood classroom.

In a developmentally appropriate program for young children, the curriculum goals should include all aspects of child development. The following are examples of common expectations in programs for young children:

- Physical goals (2-year-olds)
  1. Scribble using large crayons or other similar art materials.
  2. Develop the ability to engage in running activities for short distances.

- Social goals (4-year-olds)
  1. Learn to control nonproductive impulses such as hitting and taking things without asking.
  2. Listen when others are speaking, take turns talking, and use other conventions of communication.
- Emotional goals (5-year-olds)
  1. Use words to describe and deal with feelings experienced.
  2. Develop a sense of competence at school-related tasks.
- Cognitive goals (8-year-olds)
  1. Use the scientific method to explore materials presented.
  2. Know and use the arithmetic operations of addition, subtraction, multiplication, and division.

Planning Activities and Lessons

The starting point for an effective early childhood curriculum is the physical setting itself. Developmentally appropriate activities require careful planning and preparation of the indoor and outdoor environments. Chapters 9 and 10 address these important topics.

Once these settings are prepared, however, much remains to be done in developing specific events for each day. The teacher should create **long-term plans** to give a sense of direction for several weeks, months, or even the entire school year. Because they are general plans, they provide a flexible framework for building a more specific curriculum as the year progresses. The teacher then prepares **short-term plans** weekly and daily to identify the activities in which children will

Preparing a visually appealing and texture-rich crib area is an important part of developmentally appropriate practice for infants.

be engaging. Whenever possible, the teacher should base these activities on children's interests.

Adam, a 4-year-old child in your preschool classroom, has just shared his rock collection during show and tell. Students were attentive and asked him many good questions about his specimens. You have decided to add some books about rocks to the library next week and see if Adam would be willing to have his rock collection available for observation at the science table.

For more information about planning for preschoolers, go to the Companion Website at www.prenhall.com/henniger, select Chapter 11, then choose Web Destinations.

After identifying student interests, the teacher must make decisions about procedures to be followed and materials needed. Hildebrand and Hearron (1999) suggest that teachers begin by brainstorming possible pathways to investigate the topics selected. For example, an interest in the postal service by 7-year-olds could be studied in many different ways, including the following:

- Read written information about mail carriers and the postal service.
- Invite a postal employee into the classroom to talk about her work.
- Set up a post office in the classroom where children can create and send mail to one another.
- Visit a local post office to tour the facilities and see how mail is sorted and moved.
- Take a neighborhood walk to notice the different mailboxes that families use for their mail.

Once activities have been selected, the teacher must then plan times during the week when they can be implemented, organize the materials, schedule guests and field trips, and identify specific procedures for each activity. Experienced teachers accomplish this portion of their planning by making relatively brief notes to themselves. New teachers, however, may find that more detailed written plans are necessary for successful activities. The next two sections of this chapter describe options for creating effective activity and lesson plans.

Activity Planning

Ryan and Amy are building together in the block area of their kindergarten classroom. Following a recent field trip to a local dairy farm, the play during center time has focused on this theme. Amy and Ryan are no exception. They are busily constructing a fenced pasture and barn for their dairy herd. It is clear from the conversation that much has been learned from the field trip, and the play theme is allowing them both to consolidate their understandings of this topic.

Because play opportunities like those of Amy and Ryan are such an important part of the early childhood curriculum, planning for these experiences is a high priority. It should be clear, however, that because play is open-ended and child-directed, the activity plans themselves must take into consideration this important element. Flexibility is a key component of these plans.

Into Practice . . .
Planning for Guidance Strategies

As you learned in Chapter 6, much of the guidance in the early childhood classroom consists of your efforts as a teacher to prevent problems from occurring in the first place. You should plan ahead by defining potential problems you may encounter as children engage in activities and work to prevent these problems from happening. For example, a cooking activity can get out of hand quickly if you leave partway through the process to gather some forgotten ingredients or needed utensils. Sharp knives or tempting taste treats may be too much for children while you are away. So, as you plan for activities, take the time to also consider things you can do to prevent problems from occurring as children proceed through the activities. Consider the following:

- **Gather all needed materials.** As in the previous cooking example, having all the materials needed for planned activities together and ready to go can prevent many problems from occurring in the first place.
- **Consider space needs.** Some activities have specific space needs for safety and freedom of expression. For example, woodworking activities often involve hammers and saws, and cramped spaces can lead to inadvertent accidents when children move with these relatively dangerous tools. Another enjoyable activity for young children is movement to music with colorful scarves. To move freely and creatively, however, requires considerable space for each child.
- **Provide several popular toys.** When setting up a creative play center, be sure to include more than one of the same popular toy so that there are fewer problems with sharing. For example, having two or three popular trucks in the block center makes it possible for several children to engage in similar play themes.
- **Think about potential conflicts.** Part of your planning should include thoughts about potential conflicts that might occur between children and ways in which these conflicts can be resolved. In the computer area, for example, you may have several children wanting to use a new software program at the same time. You could set a time limit (a timer that buzzes when time is up is a good option) or set up two or three chairs at the computer so that several children can work together using the same software.
- **Plan for clean-up time.** Although many activities are highly exciting for young children, cleaning up the messes made can be a less attractive component of the task. Cleaning up a creative fingerpaint activity, for example, could be facilitated by assigning different roles to children. Some could be responsible for hanging up wet paintings, others could put away paints, and a third group would be responsible for wiping the table clean.

Teachers use many different formats for written activity plans, each of which has its own strengths and limitations. The essential elements include

- Purposes for the activity
- Materials and preparation needed
- Procedures to follow
- Variations that may be introduced
- An evaluation component

Figure 11–1 provides an example of a mathematics activity plan for a second-grade classroom.

Initially, new teachers find that developing detailed activity plans like the one in Figure 11–1 is necessary to ensure successful learning experiences for children.

Figure 11–1 *Mathematics Activity Plan for a Second-Grade Classroom*

Purposes

1. Identify the geometric shapes of square, triangle, and parallelogram.
2. Use the tangram shapes to build a pattern matching those on accompanying cards.

Materials and Preparation

1. Tangram puzzle pieces (three sets). Each set consists of seven geometric shapes that fit together to form a square.
2. Pattern cards.
3. Select pattern cards of varying difficulties to challenge ability levels of different children.

Procedures

1. Discuss tangrams at group time, describing how they can be used to create patterns illustrated on accompanying cards.
2. Place tangram sets and pattern cards in the mathematics center for children to use during choice time.
3. Observe the mathematics center for tangram use, assisting children as needed.

Possible Variations

1. Encourage interested students to create their own pattern cards that others can use with the tangram sets.
2. Consider having some children work in pairs to solve puzzle patterns. Joint problem solving may be an important confidence booster for some students.

Evaluation

1. Observe students working with the tangram sets to see if they are enjoying the task and using effective problem-solving strategies as they work.
2. Discuss tangrams at group time to see if students use appropriate terminology for shapes and to determine if pattern cards are at an appropriate level of difficulty.

Every piece of play material found in the early childhood classroom should have a specific purpose, and the teacher should clearly understand procedures for effective use. However, with several centers and perhaps hundreds of options available to children, writing detailed plans for each experience is clearly overwhelming for the full-time teacher. Taking these planning steps while learning to be a teacher makes it possible to succeed with more mental planning later.

Lesson Planning

Group time is the next scheduled event for your group of 4-year-olds. Today, after singing two or three songs, a story is planned, followed by a movement activity, a brief discussion of growing plants, and more singing. This is a busy, but typical agenda.

To make group times positive experiences, teachers of young children must carefully plan and be well organized. Lesson planning can help ensure success.

Figure 11–2 *Group-Time Lesson Plan for 4-Year-Olds*

Objectives

1. Students will participate in songs, listen to the story, and be involved in the movement activity.
2. Children will be able to identify the root system, stems, and leaves in three drawings of plants.

Introduction

1. "I brought a special living thing from my home today to share with the class. It is hidden in this brown grocery bag. It sits on my window sill at home. I water it once a week. Can anyone guess what it is?"
2. After giving children an opportunity to guess the bag's contents, remove the plant, and discuss its roots, stems, and leaves.
3. "Today at group time, we are going to spend time talking about plants and how they grow. Let's begin by singing a new song."

Content

1. Introduce a new song about flower gardens. Sing two familiar songs.
2. Read a story about plants.
3. Perform a movement activity to music.
4. Discuss plants.
5. Sing concluding songs.

Methods and Procedure

1. Sing "Flower Garden" from *Piggyback Songs* and one or two other student choices for songs.
2. Read *In the Garden* by Eugene Booth.
3. Play "Over in the Meadow" by Raffi (*Baby Beluga* tape), and have children move to the music.
4. Use plant drawings to discuss the root system, stems, and leaves of plants.
5. Sing concluding songs chosen by children.

Closure

1. Put a plant and drawings of plants out in the science area for children to use during free-play time.
2. Have bean seeds, pots, and soil available outdoors for students interested in growing their own plants.

Resources and Materials

1. Plant from home, book, audiotape, and plant drawings
2. Bean seeds, pots, and soil for planting activity

Evaluation

1. As children discuss plant components during group time, can they accurately identify them?
2. Do children spend time observing the plant and drawings placed in the science center? Do they use appropriate terminology in describing what they observe?

Although similar to the previously described activity plans, lesson plans tend to be more structured in identifying procedures, questions, and comments. Although still flexible, lesson plans often focus more on specific learning and predetermined procedures. A typical lesson plan includes objectives, introduction, content, methods and procedure, closure, resources and materials, and evaluation (Moore, 2001). A sample plan for a preschool group time appears in Figure 11–2.

The Integrated Curriculum

Mariah and Jasmine are working intently at the kitchen table in Mariah's home. These second-grade children recently returned from the local community's Fourth of July ceremonies. Intrigued by the concept of Independence Day, they researched the topic via the Internet and became fascinated with the clothing from the colonial period of American history. After making a list of interesting tidbits gleaned from web sites, they are now busy sketching out some articles of clothing they hope to make for their dolls. With some adult assistance, this interest could become a long-term project with considerable learning potential. Language, mathematics, and social studies are just a few of the naturally occurring curriculum elements built into this experience. Mariah and Jasmine are engaging in an integrated learning experience at home.

Why Implement an Integrated Curriculum?

For more information about an integrated curriculum, go to the Companion Website at www.prenhall.com/henniger, select Chapter 11, then choose Web Destinations.

One important reason for using an integrated curriculum is evident from the preceding example: It is a natural way of learning that matches what children and adults do outside the classroom. Krogh (1995) describes buying a car as an example of integrated adult learning in the real world. Reading ads and brochures, computing payments, investigating fuel efficiency and engine power, considering the car's aesthetic appeal, and negotiating with the salesperson require language, mathematics, science, art, and social studies learning. This is definitely an integrated (and complicated) real-world educational experience. Clearly, the lives of both children and adults are full of these naturally occurring integrated learning times.

Integrated learning makes the curriculum more relevant (Catron & Allen, 2003). Mathematics, for example, can be taught as a series of procedures and rote memorization tasks. Unfortunately, this approach fails to make mathematics meaningful and interesting to children. However, when adults demonstrate the usefulness of mathematics in real-life situations, such as computing the time it will take to save allowances to buy a pair of roller blades, children can see the relevance of their learning and get excited about mathematics. Similarly, reading has little value until these skills can be applied to written topics that are of interest to children.

The integrated curriculum also takes advantage of the child's natural way of learning (Isenberg & Quisenberry, 2002). That is, hands-on manipulation of materials is more likely in an integrated approach. Typically, this curriculum is organized around themes of interest to children. For example, a theme or unit on birds for a second-grade classroom could emphasize activities that include reading, mathematics, science, and social studies learning, all of which involve children in reading, talking about, and manipulating materials.

For more information about the values of integrated learning, go to the Companion Website at www.prenhall.com/henniger, select Chapter 11, then choose Web Destinations.

A quality program based on integrated learning also allows for more in-depth study (Stone, 1995) of the themes chosen. Because all content areas are considered in the planning of thematic units, longer blocks of time can be spent engaging in these learning activities. Rather than breaking the afternoon into half-hour segments for the study of mathematics, reading, social studies, and science, a first-grade teacher could plan and present an exciting thematic unit on community helpers using a larger block of time each day. Students use graphing

Hands-on manipulation of materials is an important part of an integrated curriculum.

skills, for example, to chart the number of fires in the community within the last year. Children read and discuss books on community helpers. A trip to the police station helps children learn more about their community. Letters of thanks to visiting community helpers provide opportunities for writing experiences. This type of integrated learning experience gives children more time to develop deeper and more relevant understandings of the concepts being learned.

Planning and Preparation

At first glance, the planning needed for integrated learning may seem easier and less complicated than for a more traditional curriculum. After all, it is a natural way for learning outside the classroom, and little preparation is needed for those experiences. Why can't we just gather some good materials and then turn children loose with them and see what they come up with?

Unfortunately, planning an integrated curriculum is not that simple. This approach is definitely more complicated and demanding for the classroom teacher than a more traditional curriculum. More planning and preparation are required rather than less. For one thing, no how-to manuals clearly and specifically lay out a strong integrated curriculum for young children. Although good books are available (see, e.g., Mitchell & David, 1992) that provide effective guidance for the planning process, they are, of necessity, general in their focus. Because integrated learning should be based on student interests and abilities, themes selected and activities used will vary from one classroom to the next.

The starting point for planning an integrated curriculum is to select appropriate themes. The teacher should base the choice of topics primarily on the needs and interests of children, which will vary from one group of children to the next. Children in coastal Alaska, for example, would probably be interested in the life cycle of salmon, whereas those in Arizona would be more likely to find a study of cacti

Celebrating Play . . . Reinventing Mathematics

Constance Kamii and Georgia DeClark (1985), a researcher and primary teacher, respectively, wrote *Young Children Reinvent Arithmetic,* a book describing the benefits of young children reinventing their mathematical understanding. Based on the theories of Jean Piaget, this book presents a detailed account of children constructing arithmetic understanding through play. The authors developed a complete first-grade mathematics curriculum based entirely on group games and activities that focus on everyday events in the lives of children. Some examples of activities and games of this type include the following:

Voting

In DeClark's first-grade classroom, she strongly encouraged voting on many issues throughout the day. This allowed children to use arithmetic skills in meaningful ways. For example, children had a chance to vote on the number of times they needed to practice writing letters in their journals. One child suggested six times on each line, and a second child thought nine times was more appropriate. Children then voted on which option they preferred, with 20 preferring six times, and 5 wanting the nine repetitions. On this occasion, after the votes were recorded, one child wanted to change his vote from nine repetitions to six. This allowed the class to discuss the results of adding one vote to the first column and removing one from the second. Meaningful mathematics was being practiced.

Group Games

DeClark and Kamii used some common card games to promote additional arithmetic practice in more fun ways for first-grade children. The card game War is one example. Children use a deck of cards and split them into equal piles (one for each child playing). Each child turns the top card up in her stack, and the child with the card having the highest value wins that set of cards. Tic-tac-toe is an example of a board game that DeClark encouraged as well. Although this activity does not build arithmetic skills, it helps children decenter (see things from another's perspective), which is important to growth in intellectual functioning.

1. What do you see as the strengths and limitations of reinventing mathematics or any other curriculum area through play?

2. Why is play critical to this approach to learning? What is the role of play in the reinvention process?

more relevant. Although childhood needs and interests are the most important factors in selecting themes, it is also valuable to consider your own interests as a teacher. You will be spending large blocks of time and energy in preparing the materials and activities needed for the themes chosen. If the topic is something you can get excited about as an adult, the children are much more likely to do the same.

After selecting an appropriate theme, Dodge, Colker, and Heroman (2002) suggest the following steps in thematic planning:

- Learn about the topic selected.
- Find and organize materials related to the theme.
- Reflect on what you want the children to learn.
- Identify open-ended questions to encourage inquiry.
- Plan activities and lessons related to the theme.
- Invite parent participation.
- Determine a closing event or activity.
- Evaluate the theme and what children have learned.

To learn about the chosen topic, the teacher becomes a student and reads books and related written materials, explores field trip possibilities, talks to others who are more expert on the subject, and engages in some of the same activities that children may later explore. This process should be an exciting one—an opportunity to learn and grow as an adult while preparing for children's learning.

Finding and organizing materials is time–consuming but important in thematic planning. Because understanding during the early childhood years is best gained through hands-on manipulation of materials, finding objects that enhance learning about the chosen topics is essential. Books, puzzles, props for play, and pictures are all examples of materials that the teacher can collect and use for specific themes. Resource books such as those by Mayesky (2002) are useful at this point in the planning process to help locate appropriate materials.

Reflecting on what you want children to learn brings focus to the thematic planning. What is it, specifically, that you want children to gain from the activities you are planning? Once this question has been answered, the activities themselves are more easily identified. Time should also be spent at this point identifying the relationships between this specific theme and the overarching goals and objectives for the school year. The objectives should clearly fit with your overall plan.

The process of *identifying open-ended questions* for inquiry often begins with the children themselves. Ask children what they already know about the upcoming theme. What do they need clarified? Are there questions they want answered? Obviously, younger children will need more assistance with this discussion, but beginning in the preschool years, this planning step can provide much helpful information in developing the theme.

Planning lessons and activities for a chosen theme usually starts with a process called *webbing.* Basically, webbing is a brainstorming technique that provides a visual overview of the content to be emphasized in a unit. The teacher begins by writing the theme title in the middle of a page and drawing curriculum spokes for each area to be addressed. Typically, language, mathematics, science, art, music and movement, and social studies are each represented as a spoke (Petersen, 2003). For each of these areas, then, the teacher identifies as many activities as possible that address the separate curricular domains. Other teachers, resource books, and the Internet are all useful in adding items in this brainstorming effort. A major advantage of the webbing process is that it quickly identifies areas of the curriculum that are either over- represented or underrepresented. At this point, it is easy to add or delete items to better balance the curriculum.

After creating the curriculum web, most teachers then develop a written overview of the thematic unit. This unit overview identifies the major activities planned for each week. If the classroom is set up in centers, this summary sheet briefly describes thematic activities found in each area. This overview usually includes group-time experiences, daily snacks, and outdoor activities as well.

Finally, the teacher creates lessons and activities using the planning strategies discussed earlier in this chapter. New teachers generally find that they need more written planning for successful efforts, while those with more experience do much of this step mentally. In either case, having a clear understanding of the specific procedures and materials needed for productive learning experiences is a critical step.

It is also important to *invite parent participation* in the planning, preparation, and teaching of thematic activities (Dodge, Colker, & Heroman, 2002). Collecting materials at home, helping organize a field trip, assisting in the classroom, and making suggestions for activities and events are all tasks that parents can do to help. Not only will parent participation make your job as teacher easier, but it increases the likelihood that what is learned in school will be reinforced at home. When parents are involved in some way in curriculum planning and teaching, children benefit.

Deciding on a closing event or activity brings a positive ending to the unit of study. For the theme of pets, for example, the teacher might plan a pet show as a closing event. Children and parents could bring pictures, videos, and pet accessories to share with the rest of the class. In addition to being an enjoyable event, the closing activity allows children to summarize what they have learned and get ready to move on to the next theme. It brings closure to the unit activities.

The final step in planning for thematic learning, which should actually be ongoing throughout the teaching and learning activities, is to *evaluate the theme and what children have learned*. The teacher can collect written observations of children and samples of their work and use these to assess the successes and areas for improvement in the unit. The teacher can share these materials with parents and others to document the students' growth through thematic teaching.

The Project Approach

Over the last several years, many teachers of young children have become interested in involving children in group projects. This trend has been strongly influenced by the impressive results of project work done by young children in prekindergarten programs in Reggio Emilia, Italy, described in Chapter 3 (see also Hendrick, 2004). Although this approach to teaching is not new, it is currently receiving considerable attention by many educators.

Computers with Internet access provide a wealth of information for project work.

For more information about the project approach, go to the Companion Website at www.prenhall.com/henniger, select Chapter 11, then choose Web Destinations.

A **project** can be described as an in-depth study of a topic of interest to children (Katz & Chard, 1989). Typically, a group of children within a class undertakes a project that springs from a desire to find answers to questions about the topic. The following situation is an example of how children become interested in a subject, which can then lead to an in-depth investigation:

> One day after a rainstorm, 5-year-old children noticed a large puddle in the schoolyard and asked to go outside to play. As they explored the puddle, stamping their boots, floating leaves, and making circles by casting pebbles, they noticed that their reflections were upside down. This discovery surprised them and led them to pose many questions and hypotheses. (Edwards & Springate, 1993, p. 9)

Edwards and Springate (1993) describe how teachers took advantage of the interests of these children to create a project that led in many different directions. Children wondered what would happen if everything in the world was upside down. This concept was then discussed and explored. The rainy day also got students thinking about where water goes after the storm. They began a study of the underground areas of city streets. Each new insight led to further questions and new areas for investigation as the project continued to expand, grow, and change. At all times, the students' interests and questions provided direction for the project, while teachers helped focus their efforts and suggested materials and activities to explore the issues raised.

Katz and Chard (1989) describe three phases of a project. Phase one is called **getting started** and is the time when children and their teacher spend several discussion periods selecting and refining the topic to be investigated. Phase two, **field work,** is the direct study of the project selected and may include field trips, activities, careful observations, drawings, models of the concept being studied, and discussions of findings. The final phase, **culminating and debriefing events,** consists of concluding activities that help children summarize their new learning.

It should be clear from this discussion that project learning parallels the thematic approach described earlier. The major difference is that in project learning, the activities chosen and new directions taken are not clearly defined before beginning the study but rather are based on questions children pose along the way. Careful planning is still needed, but it is done daily and weekly to keep pace with children's changing interests and needs.

For examples of projects, go to the Companion Website at www.prenhall.com/henniger, select Chapter 11, then choose Web Destinations.

Scheduling Issues

In addition to carefully planning lessons and activities for young children, it is important to think about how all these events fit together to form a daily schedule, as shown in Figure 11–3. Teachers should consider several important issues as a schedule is created:

- *Length of the school day.* As the school day lengthens, teachers must plan rest/nap times, snacks/meals, outdoor options, and playtimes to accommodate the longer time span.
- *Large blocks of time.* When teachers plan a play-oriented, theme-based curriculum, children need large blocks of time. Thirty- to 60-minute periods both indoors and outdoors make quality experiences possible.

Figure 11–3 *Daily Schedules*

The sequence of events for an early childhood classroom varies from one room to the next, but sample schedules for full-day programs at both the prekindergarten and primary level follow:

4-Year-Old Program		*Second-Grade Classroom*	
7:00 AM	Arrival, breakfast, limited centers	8:45 AM	Arrival, greetings
8:30 AM	Opening group	9:00 AM	Opening group time
8:45 AM	Indoor centers	9:15 AM	Center planning time
10:00 AM	Toileting, snack	9:30 AM	Learning centers
10:30 AM	Outdoor time	10:30 AM	Outdoor play
11:30 AM	Lunch	11:00 AM	Reading
Noon	Group-time story	11:45 AM	Lunch/outdoors
12:30 PM	Quiet time	12:30 PM	Story time
2:00 PM	Center time	1:00 PM	Mathematics
3:00 PM	Snack	1:45 PM	Library/music/physical education
3:30 PM	Physical education/outdoors	2:30 PM	Silent, sustained reading
4:15 PM	Limited centers	2:50 PM	Closing group
5:00 PM	Departure	3:15 PM	Departure

- *A balance of active/quiet times.* Schedule planning must also take into consideration the need to have periods of both high physical activity and calmer, quieter times. These should be mixed throughout the program day.

- *Meeting children's needs.* The physical needs of young children require scheduled times as well. Teachers must consider time for snacks and meals, planned toileting opportunities, and rest/nap/quiet times.

- *Smooth transitions.* Younger children often struggle with transitions. Planning consistent times during the day for transitions helps make these times less stressful. The schedule should include times for arrival, departure, and cleanup after play.

- *Consistent sequence of events.* During the early childhood years children are just beginning to understand time; thus, beginning center activities each day at 9:15 is less important for this age than the fact that this experience follows group time. When activities follow a consistent sequence, children are more secure and content with the day. This de-emphasis on rigid starting and ending points for activities provides additional flexibility to the day and enhances learning.

 **Assessment**

The theme-based, project-oriented approach to the curriculum described in this chapter can best be evaluated using a variety of techniques. While the more traditional standardized tests commonly found in school settings serve important purposes, other techniques must be used to appraise most aspects of student

Celebrating Diversity . . .
Closing the Achievement Gap

Throughout the history of American schooling, a troubling phenomenon has been the disparity in performance between many African American and Hispanic students and their more privileged White peers. While the former score at the lower end of the performance scale, their White counterparts typically do considerably better. One indicator of this achievement gap comes from statistics published by the National Black Caucus of State Legislators (2001). They state that while 30 of every 100 White kindergartners continue their schooling through college, only 16 of every 100 Black children earn a college degree. There are many factors cited for this achievement gap. Three of the most significant factors are:

- **Standardized tests.** Standardized tests have been criticized for many things, including the very real possibility that they discriminate against students from non-White cultures. Kohn (2000) states it this way: "For decades, critics have complained that many standardized tests are unfair because the questions require a set of knowledge and skills more likely to be possessed by children from a privileged background" (p. 46).
- **Low household income.** Children who are raised in a low-income family typically have fewer educational resources at home and poorer health care and nutrition. These children tend to have

lower academic performance in schools (National Center for Education Statistics, 2003).
- **Underfunded inner-city schools.** Because a large proportion of minority students live in inner-city environments, they attend schools in their local community. These schools are typically underfunded and, consequently, students generally receive a poorer quality of education (Carey, 2003).

Regardless of the causes, teachers at all levels must commit time and energy to ensuring that all children have equitable opportunities to learn and grow in the classroom. If we truly want "no child left behind," teachers, families, and communities must work together to meet the needs and interests of children from all cultures and socioeconomic backgrounds.

1. Have you had direct experience with students who have achieved at lower rates because of their ethnicity or socioeconomic status? What could have been done to assist these students in being more successful?

2. Read one or more of the articles referenced in this feature. Based on this reading, are you willing to commit to meeting the educational needs of all children, regardless of ethnicity and socioeconomic status? What do you see as the challenges you will face with this commitment?

---

progress in the early childhood classroom. Observations of children have proven effective in both assessment and curriculum development. Portfolios, which often include observations, are another major tool for evaluation in the early childhood classroom.

Using Standardized Tests

For more information about standardized tests, go to the Companion Website at www.prenhall.com/henniger, select Chapter 11, then choose Web Destinations.

Standardized tests are carefully developed by professional designers to accurately measure a child's performance compared to other children or in relation to some standard or objective (Wortham, 2001). **Norm-referenced tests** are standardized tests that provide information on how an individual child compares with the performance of others. **Criterion-referenced tests** assess how the child performed in relation to a defined standard or objective.

Some examples of norm-referenced tests used with preschool and primary children include:

- *Wechsler Preschool and Primary Scale of Intelligence* (Wechsler, 1967). This test can be used to identify children with learning disabilities or qualify others for gifted programs.
- *Peabody Picture Vocabulary Test—Revised* (Dunn & Dunn, 1981). This test is used to assess the hearing vocabulary and receptive knowledge vocabulary of children.
- *Boehm Test of Basic Concepts* (Boehm, 1971). This norm-referenced test evaluates the child's understanding of basic concepts needed for success in the first few years of school.

Two examples of criterion-referenced tests commonly used with young children are:

- *Denver Developmental Screening Test—Revised* (Frankenburg, Dodds, Fandal, Kajuk, & Cohr, 1975). This test is frequently used by pediatricians and other medical personnel to identify children from birth to age 6 with serious developmental delays.
- *California Achievement Test* (California Achievement Test, 1977). This test is designed to show which educational objectives have been met by the child and identify others that need further instruction.

While standardized tests have their place in educational settings, they are often misused or difficult to use with young children. For example, in many instances the results of standardized tests are used to place children in special education programs even though the test designers never intended the results to be used in this manner (Wortham, 2001). At other times, standardized tests are misused because they are either too difficult to administer to young children in some situations or it is challenging to accurately measure some aspects of the young child's development. As this discussion indicates, standardized tests should be used and interpreted by trained professionals who understand the purposes and limitations of these methods of evaluation.

The No Child Left Behind Act of 2001 has led many educators and others to have additional concerns about standardized tests. This federal law mandates that all states test student performance in reading and mathematics annually in grades 3 to 8 (*Assessment*, 2003). Many states are using these test results to make critical decisions about students and schools:

> Certain uses of achievement test results are termed "high stakes" if they carry serious consequences for students or for educators. Schools may be judged according to the school-wide average scores of their students. Low school-wide scores may bring public embarrassment or heavy sanctions. For individual students . . . low scores may result in students being held back in grade or denied a high school diploma. (American Educational Research Association, 2000)

The Role of Observation in Assessment

As mentioned earlier, observation is an important tool in determining student needs and interests for curriculum planning. It is an equally valuable technique

Taking time to observe children as they work and play can pay big dividends.

for assessment purposes. Because the physical space plays such an important role in early childhood education, observations of how children use their environment are an important aspect of evaluation. Do children avoid some areas or use other areas too often? Can children move easily from one center to the next? Which materials are children using? These are questions that need to be answered through careful observations of the environment.

An emphasis on developing the whole child provides an additional rationale for using observations of children in assessment. Identifying physical skill development, listening to oral language children are using as they play, and studying social interactions are all examples of important evaluation strategies that teachers can implement. Observations are often the best techniques to use in assessing these aspects of the child's development.

 Raylynn is a cheerful first grader who is having difficulty learning to read. She tries hard, seems interested in books, and comes from a home that emphasizes the importance of school. Yet, her progress is agonizingly slow and difficult. Some careful observation may be needed to help determine the problems she faces. After several observations in the book corner, the teacher has decided to refer Raylynn for a vision test. She seems to have difficulty clearly seeing the printed letters and words.

Early childhood classrooms have many children like Raylynn. They struggle with some aspect of learning or development, but the specific cause is not easily determined. Observations can again be useful in identifying the root problems and helping guide the teacher in choosing effective strategies for intervention.

A major reason we engage in evaluation experiences is to document the progress children are making in our programs. Parents, other teachers, administrators, and community members all want to know what skills children are learning through their efforts and ours. When children engage in hands-on learning, observation is again one of the best choices for assessing this progress. When observations are objective and detailed, they provide excellent records of what children have accomplished. The **anecdotal record** described earlier in this chapter is one of the best observation tools to use for assessment purposes. A good anecdotal record should

- Include necessary identifying information (names of children observed, date and location of observation).
- Provide a continuous, detailed description of student behavior.
- Record only observed behavior during the observation time.
- Provide interpretation later than, and separate from, what was actually observed (Gallagher, 1998).

Making good observations is a skill that requires considerable time, energy, and practice. Often, early attempts at observation are very general and not useful for planning purposes (Cohen, Stern, & Balaban, 1997). Another common problem is that observers have difficulty distinguishing between what is actually being observed and their interpretation of the events taking place. Using a tape recorder or videotape to record children's activities and comparing these tapes with written observations may help improve the quality of teachers' beginning observation attempts.

A second observational technique that provides many insights is the **checklist.** Although published checklists are available for teacher use, many times teachers need to develop an appropriate form. Wortham (2001) identifies four steps in creating a checklist:

1. Identify the skills to be included.
2. List separately the behaviors to be observed.
3. Sequence the checklist in order of complexity or difficulty.
4. Develop a simple system of record keeping.

Figure 11–4 provides an example of a teacher-developed checklist. To use, the teacher merely places a check beside the items observed during the day. When used consistently, the checklist can be an effective method of monitoring specific behaviors or equipment use.

The Portfolio and Its Use

Portfolios are important assessment tools used by teachers to compile and organize information about individual children (McAfee & Leong, 2002). Although the use of portfolios in education is a relatively new assessment technique, the concept has been around for a long time. Artists and photographers, for example, have long used collections of their best work to demonstrate their abilities to others. DeFina (1992) presents seven assumptions about portfolios:

For more information about portfolio assessment, go to the Companion Website at www.prenhall.com/henniger, select Chapter 11, then choose Web Destinations.

- *They represent a systematic effort to collect meaningful student works.* Selecting and updating the best materials for a portfolio require considerable planning and preparation by both the student and teacher.

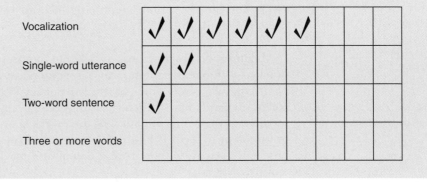

Figure 11–4 *Observation Checklist*

Teachers can develop checklists to record occurrences of nearly any type of child behavior. Infant/toddler caregivers could use the following example to record observations of oral language development.

Child's Name Meghan   **Parent(s)** Anita Smith

Observer Adrienne   **Birth Date** 9/10/03

Directions: Mark the appropriate category each time you observe one of the following verbalizations from the targeted child.

- *Students should be actively involved in selecting pieces to include in the portfolio.* Because students create many of the materials found in their portfolios, they need to be major participants in choosing items to include.
- *Portfolios can contain materials from teachers, parents, peers, and school administrators.* Including items from a variety of sources adds important dimensions to this assessment tool.
- *Portfolios should reflect the actual daily learning activities of children.* Portfolios should measure what students have accomplished in day-to-day experiences.
- *Portfolios demonstrate the students' progress over time.* Growth is best documented over a longer period. Ideally, portfolios should follow students from one year to the next.
- *Portfolios may have subcomponents.* Some students may want to separate finished projects from works that are still in progress. Having sections for notes about items in the portfolio, activities in progress, and best works may help the organization of the portfolio.
- *A variety of media can be used.* Written work, art projects, audiotapes, and videotapes are examples of the different media that may be found in portfolios.

Shores and Grace (1998) suggest a 10-step approach in the development of portfolios:

1. *Establish a portfolio policy.* Before actually beginning to use portfolios, teachers need to create a brief set of guidelines defining what will be saved and how these materials will be used.

Into Practice...
Organizing Portfolios

To be useful as an assessment instrument, portfolios need to be systematic and organized. Wortham (2001) suggests organizing portfolios by developmental category. By dividing the portfolio into separate sections for motor development, social and emotional development, language development, and cognitive development, the teacher and student can collect and organize works that represent the child's abilities in all areas. Some examples of materials that may be assembled for two aspects of development for a 6-year-old child follow:

Cognitive Development (Mathematics, Science, and Social Studies)

- Photographs of child building with blocks
- Child's record of mathematics games played
- Work samples demonstrating number concept understanding
- Child-developed graphs summarizing observations of plant growth
- Written account of community helpers project
- Teacher observations of child's activity during math and science time
- Taped interview documenting problem-solving strategies with child-initiated problem
- Computer-generated listing of time spent and activities on the computer

Personal and Social Development

- Teacher observations that document interactions between children in classroom settings and on the playground
- Child's response to questionnaire on friendships in the classroom
- Child's story about family life
- Notes from meetings with parents

2. *Collect work samples.* Following decisions about the materials to be saved, both the teacher and student should participate in collecting samples of work efforts to place in the portfolio either temporarily or for the longer term.

3. *Take photographs.* An effective portfolio should also include photographs of children's activities in the classroom. Photos document efforts that cannot easily be placed in the portfolio (a block construction or an outdoor play activity would be examples of this type).

4. *Conduct learning log conferences.* A learning log is written by the teacher and student and includes records of the plans and accomplishments of individual children. Teachers meet regularly with each student to talk over recent activities.

5. *Conduct interviews.* Interviews are extensions of learning log conferences and allow the teacher to gain deeper insights into what individual children know and can do.

6. *Make systematic records.* In this step, teachers use observations to collect data on specific issues concerning growth and development. For example, a teacher may wish to know if a 4-year-old child can skip. She can plan to observe that child on the playground for evidence of this ability.

7. *Make anecdotal records.* As part of the portfolio process, teachers must also recognize important spontaneous events that occur in the classroom and take the time to make brief, clear written records of these activities to include in the portfolio.

Family Partnerships...
Curriculum Nights

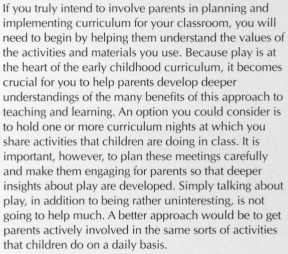

If you truly intend to involve parents in planning and implementing curriculum for your classroom, you will need to begin by helping them understand the values of the activities and materials you use. Because play is at the heart of the early childhood curriculum, it becomes crucial for you to help parents develop deeper understandings of the many benefits of this approach to teaching and learning. An option you could consider is to hold one or more curriculum nights at which you share activities that children are doing in class. It is important, however, to plan these meetings carefully and make them engaging for parents so that deeper insights about play are developed. Simply talking about play, in addition to being rather uninteresting, is not going to help much. A better approach would be to get parents actively involved in the same sorts of activities that children do on a daily basis.

A kindergarten teacher, for example, might use the following format for an evening meeting about curriculum:

6:45–7:00 Greetings, name tags, coffee and cookies

7:00–7:15 Overview of classroom centers, format for evening's events

7:15–7:45 Parents "play" in at least two classroom centers, using the directions provided by the teacher for each center

7:45–8:15 Question and answer session regarding the curriculum and the values of play

Another possible format for a curriculum night would be to focus on only one or two centers, have parents play with materials typically found in these centers, and then engage in a more in-depth conversation about the center activities and the values of play for those centers. This would obviously mean that more than one curriculum night would be needed to share with parents the full spectrum of the curriculum in your class. Whether you follow the first or second formats for a parent meeting, getting parents actively involved in playing in classroom centers will help them develop valuable insights about centers-based learning and play. Please realize that it may take more than one such meeting for parents to recognize the values of a curriculum based on play and center activities. This is a major shift in thinking for most parents to make and will require some time and patience on your part.

1. It should be clear that planning a curriculum night like the ones previously described will take a good deal of effort. Can you see yourself engaging in the planning needed to hold a successful parent meeting in which centers and play are discussed? Why or why not?

2. Do you think it is important for parents to learn about, and be supportive of, the curriculum you will be using in your future classroom?

8. *Prepare narrative reports.* These reports can be viewed as something like a "report card" summarizing an individual child's progress during a specified period of time.

9. *Conduct three-way portfolio conferences.* Children participate in these parent-teacher conferences where the entire portfolio is reviewed to demonstrate progress in all aspects of development since the last reporting period. Many educators consider this process of student reflection on past performance and future directions essential (Smith, 2000).

10. *Use portfolios in transitions.* As the child moves from one classroom to the next, a smaller representative sample of materials from the full portfolio should be passed along to the new teacher. This pass-along portfolio can then be used for making initial curriculum and activity planning decisions for this child.

Observing Development • Developmentally Appropriate Curriculum

Choose one of the age groups within early childhood (infants/toddlers, preschoolers, or primary-age children), *observe* **developmentally appropriate curriculum** using the guidelines provided, *reflect* on what you saw and heard, and *apply* the appropriate strategies listed with the children you observed.

Observe	Reflect	Apply
Look for specific examples of:	*Think about and respond to the following questions:*	*Consider the following developmentally appropriate strategies for the age group you observed:*
Materials, equipment, and activities that are intellectually interesting and meaningful to children (evidenced through their play and communications with others)	What did you see or hear that led you to believe that children were intellectually interested in the materials, equipment, and activities presented and found them meaningful?	Provide materials based on the interests of children • Infant/toddler: sensory materials like mirrors, rattles, texture balls • Preschool: dramatic play materials such as dress-up clothes • Primary: living things in nature such as insects, animals, and plants
Materials, equipment, and activities that provide an integrated curriculum (cognitive, language, physical, and emotional learning included)	Is it possible or necessary to integrate all aspects of learning into every material, piece of equipment, and activity?	Emphasize the integrated learning found in every activity • Infant/toddler: talk about sounds as infants shake rattles • Preschool: count objects in stories that you read to children • Primary: talk about emotions as you discuss world events of interest to children
Materials, equipment, and activities that encourage problem solving (children engage in problem-solving tasks as they use the materials and equipment and engage in the prepared activity)	Is problem solving an important life skill that all children should learn? What leads you to take this stance?	Give children opportunities to problem solve • Infant/toddler: allow child to experiment extensively with putting puzzle pieces together • Preschool: encourage children to get dressed on their own • Primary: give children the opportunity to work out their own disagreements without your intervention

Involving Parents

While teachers are responsible for planning and implementing curriculum, parents have an important role to play in the process. First, they should have a clear understanding of the teacher's short- and long-term plans. When parents understand and support the curriculum, they can be important allies (Dodge, Colker, & Heroman, 2002). Families are also valuable resources for finding and collecting materials, planning and preparing activities, assisting in the classroom, and extending learning options at home. For a unit on friends, for example, parents could collect and organize pictures from home that include friends, tape-record an oral story about a close friend, help their child write a letter to a friend, and assist in the classroom with planned activities on friendships.

When parents are left out of the planning process, difficulties are sure to follow. Parents often misunderstand the use of learning centers and play-oriented activities. Parents' experiences in school settings were frequently quite different, which is likely to result in many misinterpretations. If parents have not been involved in creating the curriculum, they are much more likely to question this approach. You can educate parents regarding these issues by helping them to get involved. They will then see firsthand the importance and value of these tasks.

Summary

To test your knowledge of this chapter's contents, go to the Companion Website at www.prenhall.com/henniger, select Chapter 11, then select Study Guide. Also see Chapter Overviews, Reflecting Essay Questions, Multimedia Explorations, and relevant Web Destinations.

Creating a Developmentally Appropriate Curriculum

Several general guidelines can help teachers begin the process of creating a developmentally appropriate curriculum. Teachers must also understand the roles of child development, observation, curriculum goals, and planning in creating a developmentally appropriate program for young children.

The Integrated Curriculum

The integrated curriculum is a natural way of learning that makes the curriculum more relevant for children and allows for more in-depth study.

The Project Approach

The work of the Reggio Emilia programs in Italy has heightened interest in group project work for children. Projects are topics of interest to children that are studied in-depth.

Scheduling Issues

By carefully planning a schedule that meets the needs of young children, more effective learning can take place in the classroom.

Assessment

Student observations and the development of portfolios are important assessment alternatives to the traditional standardized test in most early childhood classrooms.

Involving Parents

Whenever possible, teachers should inform and involve parents in curriculum and assessment issues.

Multimedia Explorations and Activities...

Wild About Learning

Some teachers have got it all wrong. They think learning for young children should follow the patterns they experienced as children. Learning for these teachers takes place only when children are sitting quietly and listening to the teacher share knowledge with them. Bev Bos, the popular speaker and preschool teacher featured in this video, thinks very differently about how teachers engage children in learning. She believes both kids and teachers should be passionate about their learning. Rather than sitting passively while listening to the teacher, children should be moving, doing, and creating. Thinking about teaching and learning in this way allows children to develop the skills they will need to become creative, problem-solving adults.

Research

Active, exciting classroom and playground experiences where young children get "wild about learning" are the goal of every good early childhood teacher. This multimedia exploration will help you better understand what it takes to make these opportunities a reality.

1. View the ABC News video segment titled "Wild About Learning."

2. Go to the Companion Website at www.prenhall.com/henniger and click on the Multimedia Explorations and Activities button for Chapter 11 for more information on this topic.

Reflect

With the information you have now collected, reflect on the following issues:

- What new insights did you gain about what it means to have a developmentally appropriate curriculum?

- How do you instill in young children a "zest for learning"? Why does this often disappear in older students and adults?

- Is it possible to allow children to have too much freedom in their learning? Why or why not? Try to identify specific examples to support your position.

Respond

Consider one or more of the following responses to the issue of creative and developmentally appropriate classroom teaching and learning:

1. Spend some time in an early childhood classroom observing children to determine their interests and developmental abilities. Plan a creative and developmentally appropriate activity for a small group of students. Actually do the activity, critique its success, and share your results with others via the message board on the Companion Website for this text.

2. Create a newsletter article for parents describing the characteristics and importance of developmentally appropriate practice. Work to get your article published in a local newsletter.

3. Visit an early childhood classroom and evaluate it for evidence of developmentally appropriate practice. Without using names, share your results with others.

12

ENHANCING PHYSICAL
DEVELOPMENT

In this chapter you will

- Learn about the components of physical development.
- Study the role of the teacher in facilitating children's physical development.
- Understand the role of toys and play in enhancing gross and fine motor skills.
- Gain insight regarding the importance of outdoor activities in physical development.
- Read about health and safety issues in early childhood.

Friday afternoon, at last! *It has been a busy, exciting week in your first-grade classroom. The cool, crisp weather of fall seems to be reflected in the children's active behaviors. As you sit down to plan for the coming week, you are reminded of the difficulties children had in staying on task this past week—too much sitting and listening for many of your students. To make the classroom day more manageable and enjoyable for children, you decide to add more active class involvement. This will also help provide new opportunities for building physical development activities into your curriculum. Several ideas come to mind. Perhaps it is time to bring out the math manipulatives. In addition to their usefulness in teaching mathematical concepts, the Cuisenaire Rods and Unifix cubes give children opportunities to develop fine motor skills. Another option is to provide art materials for times when children have finished other projects. The easel and art activity table will give students additional play options that also enhance small muscle development. Songs like "Head, Shoulders, Knees and Toes" can add some spice to your group-time activities. An obstacle course in the gym for rainy day play can supplement the outdoor play that is so important to the development of large muscle skills. It certainly makes a difference when plans for the next week include fun, active participation. Combining learning and physical activity makes good sense.*

Throughout the early childhood years, children need to spend much of their classroom days moving and doing. Not only is this a major way of learning about the world at this age, but it is also an important way to break up those necessary times of sitting and listening that young children experience in the school setting. Furthermore, movement activities promote the child's physical development. Although many teachers fail to carefully plan for motor skill development, it is an important component of the early childhood curriculum.

The Importance of Motor Skills

From the first days of life, children begin using their bodies to learn about the world around them. Piaget (1950) suggests that sensory and motor experiences are the basis for all intellectual functioning for approximately the first 2 years of life. As children continue to mature, their reliance on physical interactions with people and objects remains strong. Motor skills are an essential component of development for all children. Gallahue (1993) puts it this way:

> Movement is at the very center of young children's lives. It is an important facet of all aspects of their development, whether in the motor, cognitive, or affective domains of human behavior. To deny children the opportunity to reap the many benefits of regular, vigorous physical activity is to deny them the opportunity to experience the joy of efficient movement, the health effects of movement, and a lifetime as confident, competent movers. (p. 24)

Social Skills and Physical Development

For more information about developing social skills on the playground, go to the Companion Website at www.prenhall.com/henniger, select Chapter 12, then choose Web Destinations.

Movement activities are especially well-suited to helping children develop social skills (Pica, 2004). As children participate in group tasks that require movement, they learn that their efforts are critical to the success of the group. Coordinating the movements of the group in parachute play, for example, allows children to create a dome overhead and sit inside at the same time. Simple games like this for young children also require cooperation and positive social skills.

Motor Activities and Emotions

Physical activity has long been viewed as a positive way to release the pent-up energy generated from strong emotions. Vigorous physical activity such as running outdoors is generally considered an acceptable way to get rid of angry feelings. Such activities are far more positive than aggressive interactions with other children.

More subtle, perhaps, is the use of art materials for emotional release. Children painting at the easel or molding with play dough or clay may well be playing out their feelings in a socially acceptable way. This behavior, which Freud labeled **sublimation** (Thomas, 1985), provides children with positive ways to work through emotions using physical activity. Bunker (1991) reminds us that children acquire self-confidence and self-esteem in part through successful physical activities. As children master and refine basic motor skills, they see themselves as more competent and capable. The preschool child who has mastered the monkey bars and exclaims for all the world to hear, "Hey, look at me!" is feeling good about himself and his accomplishment.

Connections to Cognitive Development

Early childhood education is rooted in the belief that learning through doing is fundamental for young children. For example, infants beginning to crawl are working hard to master a physical skill that will enable them to explore more fully the home or school environment. At a slightly older age, walking allows toddlers

Celebrating Play...
Play and Risk-Taking

Smith (1990) suggests that a major attraction of playing outdoors is the opportunity to take risks. It is exciting to engage in play that might lead to accident or injury. Children do not want to be injured, but the possibility makes play more fun. This attitude is certainly contrary to what most adults want children to experience. That may be one reason why adults are frequently absent when children engage in their favorite play experiences outdoors. Kids want to take risks; adults prize safety in play.

When teachers allow risk-taking to take place, children are challenged to extend themselves both physically and emotionally in their motor play. By providing a safe play environment in which children are free to explore and stretch their skills, they gain confidence in their abilities and want to spend more time in building them further. Because of the decline in active play and the resulting lack of physical fitness in many children, teachers should seriously consider this issue of risk-taking and work to balance healthy risk-taking with safety needs. In this way, children can explore more freely and spend the time they need in physically active play.

1. Think back to your favorite play experiences and try to remember any that had elements of risk-taking. Do you think that the risks you took were an important reason why you enjoyed this play so much?

2. Do you think playgrounds and indoor-play environments for young children should include risk-taking opportunities? If you do, what could you provide or do to allow this to take place?

to have even greater opportunities for touching, manipulating, and creating with the objects around them. During the preschool years, building with a set of blocks allows young children to learn about such mathematical concepts as proportionality and number.

Finally, the refinement of fine motor skills in play makes it possible for children to succeed with writing tasks in the primary classroom. Physical competence is fundamental to cognitive development during early childhood. Montessori (1967) stated that, for learning to reach its full potential, it must be directly connected to physical movement for the young child. This unity of mental and physical activity is at the heart of the Montessori method of education. When the motor skill is directly related to the task being learned, children can understand concepts more completely and quickly. For example, a Montessori material called the Pink Tower is a collection of pink cubes of differing sizes that are designed to be stacked from largest on the bottom to the smallest on top. As children practice this physical task, they learn about *seriation* (ordering from largest to smallest), which is a concept essential to later mathematical understanding.

 For more information about movement and cognitive development, go to the Companion Website at www.prenhall.com/henniger, select Chapter 12, then choose Web Destinations.

Foundation for Physical Fitness

Although educators of young children traditionally have not thought of physical fitness as a major concern, mounting evidence indicates that teachers should encourage their young students to be more active. Poest, Williams, Witt, and Atwood

It is important to encourage fitness activities during the early childhood years.

(1990) identify the following issues as a rationale for engaging young children in fitness activities:

- The first signs of arteriosclerosis (hardening of the arteries) are appearing as early as age 5.
- Young children are not engaging in the intense physical activity needed to increase cardiovascular fitness.
- Of every hundred children, at least 16 are obese.
- Over the last 30 years, obesity has significantly increased.

 For more information about fitness for young children, go to the Companion Website at www.prenhall.com/henniger, select Chapter 12, then choose Web Destinations.

Little research has been done in the area of early childhood fitness. One early study of motor development in preschool children found that free play was not as effective as planned motor activities in improving large muscle development (Miller, 1978). This indicates that more structured motor activities are needed to overcome the problems in the preceding list (Gallahue & Ozman, 2002). With careful planning, these motor activities can effectively complement the natural movement that is a part of children's free play.

The Components of Physical Development

Katie, age 5, has just lost her first tooth.

Armondo, age 3, needs your help cutting paper.

Keneesha, age 7, can dribble and pass a soccer ball.

George, age 4, is learning to move to music at group time without bumping into other children.

Lee, age 8, has shown interest in running for fitness and fun. He can run several laps around the school track without stopping.

Each of these very different scenarios exemplifies an aspect of physical development that is important to understand. Physical growth, gross and fine motor skills, and perceptual-motor development are all important to the early childhood teacher. An understanding of each will provide a foundation for physical education at these ages.

Physical Growth

Knowing how children physically develop can give the teacher many important insights for teaching in the early childhood classroom. Child development experts (Schickedanz et al., 2001; Trawick-Smith, 2003) suggest the following generalizations about physical growth:

- Early childhood is the period of most rapid growth.
- Development proceeds in spurts rather than at an even pace.
- Large muscles develop before smaller ones.
- Both heredity and environment play important roles in physical development.
- Physical development proceeds in a sequence from the top of the child's head to the toes. This is referred to as **cephalocaudal development.**
- A second sequence seen in physical growth is the development from the center of the body outward to the extremities. This is called **proximodistal development.**

Different components of the child's physical self develop at varying rates during childhood. Figure 12–1 describes these patterns for brain, height and weight, and sexual growth. As these growth curves emphasize, the early years are a time of rapid development. It is important for teachers to be aware of these trends and use them in planning appropriate experiences for the early childhood classroom.

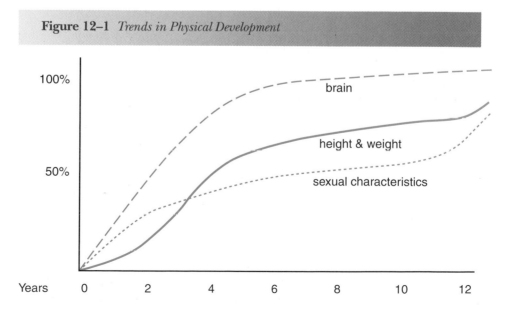

Figure 12–1 *Trends in Physical Development*

Physical development influences the ways in which adults interact with children. As toddlers become more mobile, adults generally give them more freedom of movement and greater opportunities to explore their world. When a young child stands 5 inches taller than any of her classmates, adults unconsciously think of the child as being older and may treat the child as though she is more emotionally or intellectually mature. A physically attractive child will probably receive better treatment from his teachers than would an unattractive peer. In these examples, physical characteristics of children affect the adult-child relationship.

Gross Motor Development

Gross motor activities involve moving the entire body or the large muscles of the neck, arms, and legs. These large muscles are the first to come under the control of young children. For example, starting with walking, infants and toddlers become increasingly able to manipulate their leg muscle movements and move from unsteady toddling to confident walking to more complex tasks such as running, hopping, skipping, and jumping. Coordination and use of arm muscles follow a similar pattern of refinement. By the end of the early childhood years, children have mastered basic gross motor skills.

Into Practice . . .
A Mud Center?

Do you have any fond memories of playing outside with mud, making mud pies, mud sandwiches, or other interesting concoctions? It is a sensory experience that many people fondly remember. For a large number of children today, however, this is a rare opportunity at best (Jensen & Bullard, 2002). Apartment life, city existence, and even growing up in rural areas today just do not seem to be as compatible with the messy joys of mud play. Early childhood teachers should consider setting up a mud center either in the classroom or on the playground. With careful planning, children can again experience this valuable play experience.

Jensen and Bullard (2002) identify the materials they used to set up a mud center on their school playground. They include:

- **An old stove.** Some sort of discarded stove or oven that can be left outdoors as the focal point for mud play is essential. A box made to look like a stove could also be used.

- **Dirt and water.** Some containers are needed for the supply of dirt that is needed to make mud, along with a water source. If a hose or faucet is not close by, be sure to have several buckets of water for mixing and clean-up.
- **Cooking utensils.** One of the key dramatic play themes generated by this center will be cooking activities, so having pots and pans, items for stirring and mixing, empty containers of spices and condiments, and dishes available helps stimulate this theme.
- **Smocks.** Because of the mess, it is best to have several smocks that children can put over their clothes so that they can avoid getting dirty.
- **Writing materials.** A recipe box, recipe cards, and writing utensils help stimulate literacy-related activities in this center as well.
- **Table and chairs.** Providing a spot where "meals" can be served adds yet another fun element to the dramatic play in this center.

Miller (1999) suggests that during the early childhood years, children master basic movements needed for later, more complex physical activities. **Fundamental movement skills** are those needed for basic locomotion, manipulative or ball skills, and balancing (Benelli & Yongue, 1995). Examples for each category follow:

Basic Locomotion	Ball Skills	Balancing
Walking	Throwing	Bending
Running	Kicking	Stretching
Jumping	Striking	Twisting
Hopping	Bouncing	Swinging

Fine Motor Skills

Fine motor development involves the small muscles of the body, primarily the hands and feet. The educator's main concern is for development of the hand muscles necessary for such skills as eating, dressing, writing, and making artwork. Beginning in infancy and following the development of larger muscles, the young child refines use of these small muscles. This process continues well beyond the early childhood years. The "Observing Development" feature at the end of this chapter provides an opportunity to observe the fine motor skills of young children, reflect on how the classroom environment contributes to these skills, and consider strategies to further develop these skills through applicable activities.

Using small muscles in the hands allows children to gradually develop skill in the use of a variety of tools (Trawick-Smith, 2003). Infants learning to grasp are practicing an early fine motor skill that will allow them to use a simple tool such

Small muscles are developed as children manipulate toys and equipment.

as a rattle to make a noise. During the preschool years, children are refining small muscle control and can use such cooking utensils as potato mashers and spoons in food preparation. In the primary grades, students can use pencils and crayons as tools to write and communicate with others.

Phases of Motor Development

Gallahue (1993) suggests that children move through phases in their gross and fine motor development, much as they do in cognitive and social/emotional development. He has identified four specific phases of motor development. During the **reflexive movement phase,** children in the first year of life gradually replace reflexive movements such as the sucking and rooting reflex with more voluntary muscle movements. The **rudimentary movement phase**—when grasping, sitting, standing, and walking become possible for the young child—begins during the first year of life and predominates during the second year. From approximately 2 to 7 years of age, children are in the **fundamental movement phase.** Children are mastering basic skills such as jumping, running, throwing, catching, and kicking. During the **specialized movement phase,** starting at approximately age 7, children begin to combine fundamental movements with other skills to develop specialized movements such as the lay-up shot in basketball.

Teachers during the early childhood years need to be aware of these developmental phases and assist children in refining the movements defined here. Although many children need little direct instruction, others will benefit from adult guidance. If children do not master these skills during their early years, it will be more difficult for them to do so later (Gallahue & Ozman, 2002).

Perceptual-Motor Development

Children also learn to take in information from the environment, process it, and respond motorically. Perceptual-motor development is generally thought to include body, time, spatial, directional, visual, and auditory awareness (Payne & Isaacs, 2002). **Body awareness** is the child's ability to locate, name, and correctly describe body part functions. Moving to a steady beat, making coordinated movements, and increasing or decreasing rates of movement are aspects of **time awareness.** A child's ability to control his body as it moves through space exemplifies **spatial awareness. Directional awareness** includes the child's capacity to understand relational concepts such as *up, down, in, out, over,* and *under.* Skill in seeing and copying demonstrated movements is referred to as **visual awareness.** Finally, a child's capacity to focus on verbal directions and distinguish between different sounds is called **auditory awareness.**

Teaching Physical Development

Although children rather naturally engage in physical activity, it is necessary for the teacher to incorporate activities and periodically teach the skills needed for healthy motor development (Miller, 1999). By planning for and encouraging physical skills during play and by teaching developmentally appropriate motor activities, the early childhood teacher can assist children in an important aspect of their development.

Into Practice...
Guiding Violent Play

One thing you have undoubtedly discovered by now is that young children love to imitate significant others. Unfortunately, many of the role models for young children come from the television programs and movies they watch. Many of these programs include violent characters such as those in *Star Wars: Attack of the Clones* and adult action heroes like Arnold Schwarzenegger. It should come as no surprise, then, that we sometimes find even very young children engaged in play of a violent nature. Although children typically do not intend to hurt one another, the end result of violent play is often just that. In addition, it is important for young children to learn better strategies than violence for dealing with disagreements. Consider the following strategies for guiding children away from violence in their play:

- **Avoid pretend weapons.** Make sure no toys resembling weapons are brought from home. Suggest nonviolent uses for sticks and other neutral objects that children pretend are weapons.

- **Redirect play themes.** If children are playing out a cartoon theme such as *"Dragonball Z"* and becoming violent, try to redirect the play without entirely changing the theme. Having some knowledge of the characters being imitated would help with this task.
- **Rehearse verbal responses.** Be prepared with simple, direct responses to violent play. "I won't let you play in that way. Someone might get hurt." "You need to find another way to play Teen Titans so that no one gets hurt."
- **Remain calm, but firm.** Your responses to violent play will impact how children accept your intervention. Make sure to use a calm but firm voice.
- **Model appropriate behavior.** In some situations, it may be effective to actually join in the play and through your actions show children more appropriate ways to interact.
- **Seek parental support.** Make sure to share with parents both the importance of intervening in violent play and the strategies you are using in school so that parents can support you at home.

Basic Considerations

Regardless of the skill being learned or the ability levels of individual children, teachers can use several general guidelines to promote physical development (Benelli & Yongue, 1995; King & Gartrell, 2003; Pica, 2004):

- Create time in the daily schedule for children to engage in both play-oriented and teacher-directed movement activities.

- Plan for physical pursuits both indoors and outdoors.

- Make sure all children get involved in a variety of motor activities.

- Evaluate your responses to both boys and girls to ensure equitable opportunities for physical movement.

- Identify your expectations for children's motor development. Consider these goals as you plan your curriculum.

- Establish clear rules for children as they engage in movement activities. Two basics: Respect one another's personal space, and keep noise to a minimum.

- Identify for children the boundaries for physical activities. Where are they allowed to play the game, toss the ball, or move to music?

For more information about teaching children about their bodies, go to the Companion Website at www.prenhall.com/henniger, select Chapter 12, then choose Web Destinations.

- Integrate physical development activities into all aspects of the curriculum. Mathematics, science, art, and music are just some of the possibilities for integration.
- Careful observation of children as they engage in physical activity is essential in determining strengths and areas for improvement. It should also form the basis for future planning.
- The materials and equipment for physical development should be developmentally appropriate and meet the diverse needs and abilities of children.
- Remember that children need repeated opportunities for practice as they learn new skills.

Instructional Strategies for Physical Education

Pica (2004) describes three teaching methods for early childhood physical education. The direct approach, guided discovery, and exploration are all effective in different situations for teaching motor skills. Some physical activities are best taught through the *direct approach*. The Hokey Pokey is a traditional dance activity that young children thoroughly enjoy. Through description, modeling, and imitating the necessary steps, children can readily learn this task. This approach has the advantage of allowing the teacher to quickly discover if any children are having trouble following the directions or producing the desired movement. *Guided discovery* is a child-centered approach that allows for inventiveness and experimentation as the teacher guides children toward an appropriate solution to a problem. For example, the teacher can use a series of questions to lead children to discover the skills needed for a forward roll. Guided discovery gives children an important role in learning the physical skill being taught. Also referred to as divergent problem solving, the *exploration approach* should be used as much as possible. When children explore, they produce a variety of responses to each challenge. For example, asking children to balance on two body parts should result in many different responses from a group of students. Extending and refining children's initial responses to a specific challenge give them many opportunities for practicing skills.

Physical Development and Play

Play is critical to a child's overall development. Childhood play enhances every aspect of growth, including physical development. As the teacher plans for motor development, it is essential to consider ways in which play can be used to encourage movement skills. Careful planning of the indoor and outdoor environments (see Chapters 9 and 10) and the teacher's comments and questions are both important.

Teachers should select play equipment to stimulate gross and fine motor development and perceptual-motor skills. Toys and equipment that could be used include the following:

Gross Motor	Fine Motor	Perceptual-Motor
Climber	Water play	Rhythm instruments
Digging area	Blocks	Dance scarves
Large balls	Crayons	Pattern blocks
Wheeled toys	Legos	Body part puzzles
Tumbling mats	Sand play	Sound cylinders

When quality toys and equipment are available to young children, they will use these materials in play to naturally develop motor abilities.

During free-play time, the teacher's primary role is to serve as facilitator. By asking the right questions, making appropriate comments, and redirecting children to more positive options, early educators assist in overall development. When the focus becomes physical development, teachers' verbalizations help facilitate these skills in children:

- "Suzanna, where should you put your hands so that you can reach the next level on the climber?"

- "Adrianne, your handwriting has improved so much lately! You have learned how to make *b*s and *d*s correctly and are printing so much clearer now. Congratulations!"

- "Eddie, let me show you how I use a saw to cut a board. Watch how I push and pull the saw blade across the wood."

By actively facilitating physical skills during play, the teacher can help emphasize these important abilities throughout the school day.

Organized Physical Activities

Although infants and toddlers benefit most from play-oriented activities for the development of motor skills, teachers can productively introduce more teacher-directed tasks during the preschool and primary years. These activities should be fun for children, should include specific guidance on how to perform various skills, and should also allow for many opportunities to practice newly learned movements (Benelli & Yongue, 1995; Pica, 2004).

- *Throwing activities.* Children can learn to step forward with the opposite foot when throwing. Use of a target, such as a decorated sheet, helps ensure success. Beanbags and smaller soft balls are better for throwing tasks. Verbal cues help the child learn appropriate motions.

- *Catching activities.* A bright, colorful ball helps the younger child follow it visually. Yarn balls, balloons, and beach balls are good beginning items for catching.

Organized physical activity can help children develop more complex movement skills.

If the person throwing can toss at a consistent speed and height, children will have more success in catching.

- *Striking activities.* As in throwing, children will be more successful in striking an object when they step forward with the leg closest to the target. A soft ball, placed on a batting tee at waist level, creates an easier target for preschool and early primary children. A bat made from a plastic 2-liter bottle and a dowel rod is helpful for many young children.

- *Kicking skills.* Targets help children improve their kicking skills. A large sheet or plastic 2-liter bottles set up like bowling pins make good targets. Children should be told to step beside the ball as they kick it with their dominant leg. Watching the ball also helps improve success rates with kicking.

- *Balancing tasks.* These activities can initially be practiced on the floor. Walking forward and backward on a line drawn on the floor, and then using an uneven surface such as a rope or hoop, will help children develop the skills needed to walk on a balance beam.

- *Jumping activities.* Jumping off low platforms is an enjoyable event for most young children. Providing safe, stable alternatives for jumping is a good beginning here. This can be followed by having children practice jumping vertically and horizontally.

- *Spatial awareness.* Children need to practice moving, dodging, balancing, and stopping without invading the personal space of others. Music and movement activities provide many opportunities for spatial awareness.

- *Fitness activities.* Although young children tire easily from vigorous activity, it is important to encourage walking, running, and jumping for fitness. Make sure to have fun, and downplay the competitive element. The important thing is to get children engaged in aerobic movement.

Enhancing Physical Development Indoors

As teachers of young children plan for organized physical activities indoors, they need to balance the many different categories listed previously. By identifying key curriculum resources (see, e.g., Pica, 2004) and building ideas for involvement around student needs and interests, teachers can implement a strong motor skills program. The following is a sampling of more specific tasks that may be adapted for use in the early childhood classroom.

Organized Games and Activities: Indoors

For more information about indoor physical activities, go to the Companion Website at www.prenhall.com/henniger, select Chapter 12, then choose Web Destinations.

- *Magical Marching.* Having children march to music, swinging their arms and raising their knees, can be a fun fitness activity. A variety of musical recordings are available that encourage a range of marching speeds. Accompanying the music with a drumbeat can be helpful for younger children. Either pretending to play a musical instrument as children march or actually including simple rhythm instruments can add variety and interest to this task. Allowing children to assume special pretend roles such as drum major, baton twirler, and flag bearer add further opportunities for playfulness.

- *The Bunny Hop.* Children love to pretend, and animals are a favorite theme. Why not combine these interests with physical movement? Children can pre-

Into Practice...
Integrating Curriculum Through Movement and Music

One popular and effective strategy for developing an important part of an integrated curriculum is to combine movement and music. Each complements the other in supporting learning and development. In addition, children find this combination of activities particularly enjoyable. The following examples highlight the benefits of this approach:

- **Signing and singing the ABC Song.** The small muscle skills needed to sign the alphabet challenge young children and also motivate them to learn the ABCs while doing an enjoyable task. It is also a good way to introduce children to an important aspect of life for deaf and hard-of-hearing children.

- **Head, Shoulders, Knees and Toes.** Children learn body parts, practice coordinated movements, and have fun singing this traditional song.
- **Silk scarves and movement to music.** Many children love the combination of free flowing movements to music while holding colorful billowing silk scarves. Creative movement, balance, and timing are all being practiced when this activity is encouraged.
- **The Eensy Weensy Spider.** In addition to practicing fine motor skills, very young children experience a simple story sequence that fascinates them over and over again. They are developing a deeper understanding of an important early literacy skill.

tend to be rabbits and hop across the rug. Remind students to avoid leaping into another child's path. Then consider other hopping creatures. Frogs and kangaroos are two other possibilities. Keep students actively involved yet under control for some exciting hopping experiences. Other animals may be the starting point for additional movement possibilities (horses? crabs? elephants?).

- *Quick, Freeze!* Movement and music go together very well in early childhood. Play an instrumental piece of music, and ask children to move any way they like until the music stops. They must then "quick, freeze" in the position they were in when the music stopped. Use a variety of musical styles and rhythms to encourage different movements and to add interest to the activity. Make sure to stop the music at unexpected times so that children must be careful listeners as well as creative movers. Props such as scarves and streamers help self-conscious students focus more on the prop and move more productively to the music.

- *Hit the Bull's-Eye.* Beanbags make great initial throwing instruments for young children. They are easy to grasp, weighted for good distance, and soft enough to be safe when the toss is off target. Paint a large bull's-eye on an old donated sheet and cut a hole in the center for the beanbags to be tossed through, attach it securely by one edge to the ceiling, and have children practice tossing the beanbags at the target. Tape on the floor at varying distances from the target can add further challenges for children as they become more accurate in their tosses.

- *Finger Frolics.* Young children love to engage in activities that involve their fingers and hands. A variety of finger plays and action songs are available (see Chapter 16 for more specifics) that allow children to practice fine and gross motor skills. "Five Little Speckled Frogs," "The Eensy Weensy Spider," and "Head, Shoulders, Knees and Toes" are well-known examples of fine and gross motor activities combined with games and singing. Make sure to repeat them often, because children enjoy them even more with practice.

- *Catch Me If You Can.* The eye-hand coordination needed for a young child to catch a ball or other object is higher than might first be expected. Begin by having children catch their own bounced ball. Next, try having an adult who is an accurate tosser throw a beach ball or other large, soft object for catching. Mastering tossing an object into the air and catching it is yet another step in the process. Catching tends to be more difficult than tossing activities for many children. They may be afraid of being hit by whatever is being tossed. Be sensitive to this as you introduce the activity.

- *Balancing Circus.* Balance activities can follow a sequence from fairly simple to more complex. A good beginning for young children is to have them pretend to be circus high-wire performers and walk on a line taped to the floor. Next, they can walk on a small rope secured to the floor. Have children walk forward, placing one foot in front of the other. Later, they can practice moving sideways along the rope and then backward. Older children can use the same procedures with a low balance beam as they gain skill and confidence in moving and balancing.

Enhancing Physical Development Outdoors

The outdoor environment provides children with many opportunities for motor skill development. The wide-open spaces and fewer restrictions beckon children to move. Outdoor free play activities are full of large and small muscle movement that may be particularly enticing to young boys (King & Gartrell, 2003). The classroom teacher can also organize events to encourage further practice in movement.

Rough-and-Tumble Play

Bobbie and D. J. are two very active first-grade students. On the playground, they love to wrestle and chase each other across the grass. This type of vigorous activity is referred to as *rough-and-tumble play* (Pelligrini & Perlmutter, 1988). Wrestling, play fighting, chasing, and fleeing behaviors are common when children engage in this play. Although at first glance this activity may seem to lead to more aggressive behavior, research indicates that rough-and-tumble play has positive educational and developmental value, especially for boys, and should be encouraged (Pelligrini, 1987).

This play type is clearly valuable in getting children to engage in high-energy activity that stimulates cardiovascular fitness and large muscle use (Sutterby & Frost, 2002). As such, it is an important element in physical development activities in the early childhood classroom. Teachers need to carefully observe as children engage in rough-and-tumble play to make sure the activity remains positive. Intervention may be needed to redirect the play in new ways.

Organized Games and Activities: Outdoors

The outdoor setting is an ideal place for teachers to lead children in organized physical development activities. The larger spaces and reduced noise restrictions make the outdoors valuable for the development of motor skills. There are many good resources for children's games and activities that can be effectively used with young children outdoors (see, e.g., Kamii & DeVries, 1980; Kirchner, 1991; Orlick, 1978). With careful selection and planning, these games and activities will be popular with children and provide many opportunities for growth. Good games for young children should have simple rules, include all children who want to participate, and be noncompetitive (Isenberg & Jalongo, 2001).

The children in your second-grade classroom have been struggling at recess to implement a game of kickball. They are arguing over how to choose teams, and they have hurt feelings regarding winning and losing. Rather than discourage their obvious interest in this active game, you decide to plan for this activity later in the week. After discussing the problems with competition at group time, you take children out to recess, arbitrarily assign students to teams, and then show them how they can play the game and de-emphasize the competitive element. The next week, you notice that several children have spontaneously chosen your modified game and are actively and happily involved during recess.

Gardening is a wonderful outdoor experience that combines physical activity with many learning opportunities.

This example highlights one of the biggest problems with organized games for young children: competition. Piaget (1965) suggests that until about 7 or 8 years of age, children are often not cognitively or emotionally ready for games with rules, many of which contain significant amounts of competition. Losing is difficult for young children and should be downplayed in games (Rivkin, 1995). With creativity and thought, teachers can modify most games so that competition is reduced or eliminated. Orlick (1978) identifies many new noncompetitive game options and describes traditional competitive games that have been made more cooperative. An example of each follows:

- *Fish Gobbler.* In a large grassy area with enough space for all the children to spread out, the caller (known as the Fish Gobbler) says, "Ship," and children run to a designated spot on the playground. When the caller announces, "Shore," children run to a second location. When the caller says, "Fish Gobbler," children drop quickly to the grass. While lying on their stomachs, students link arms, legs, or bodies together so that the Fish Gobbler cannot come by and gobble them up. Later, the teacher can add other directions such as "Sardines" or "Crabs," and children can respond with appropriate motions.

- *Nonelimination Musical Chairs.* Even though chairs are removed when the music is stopped, as in the traditional version, the object of this game is to keep everyone involved. Children simply come up with creative ways to share the remaining chairs. They must work together to make sure the game can continue.

- *Tug of Peace.* Rather than playing the traditional game of tug of war, where children compete in teams and pull against each other, introduce children to the tug of peace. In this game, children cooperate by working together with a rope to meet a specific objective. For example, in small groups, children can create a geometric pattern such as a triangle or rectangle. They can also create different letters of the alphabet as another cooperative task. Small groups can then be combined to form larger groups for more complex tasks.

Although many of the ideas presented earlier for indoor use can be effective on the playground, the additional options presented here provide a larger sample of appropriate outdoor physical activities for children during the early childhood years.

- *The Road Runner.* After discussing the "Road Runner" cartoon and how fast he runs, encourage children to practice being road runners on the playground. A poster mounted in the classroom with the designated trail and decorated with individual road runners who have made the trip may encourage others to try it as well. Praise individuals (avoid comparing children to downplay competition), and have students challenge themselves to run longer distances as the year progresses.

- *The Bumblebee.* Children enjoy pretending and can creatively move to music or a drumbeat. Combine these interests into a playground movement activity. Talk about how a bumblebee travels through the air and what body parts children could move to imitate the bee. Question them about what body parts they can move slowly or quickly. Give students plenty of room, and have them pretend to be bumblebees. This activity can be expanded by asking children to suggest other things they could imitate. They will probably come up with a long list. Discuss the movements required, and then have children practice different rates of speed by pretending to be the creatures they have suggested.

- *Mountain Climbing.* Using an obstacle course is a fun way for children to develop their physical skills outdoors. A combination of movable climbers, ladders, boards, wooden boxes, tires, cable spools, and barrels can challenge children to climb over, crawl under, and step through the skills course. Encourage pretending by discussing mountain climbing/hiking at group time and suggesting that the obstacle course is actually a mountain trail that the children can explore. After several days of exploring the trail, change the trail and give it a new name, such as the jungle or the forest.

- *La Piñata.* A favorite multicultural celebration can also be a good introductory striking experience for young children. A piñata attached to a rope and hung from a stationary piece of outdoor equipment makes a large target for this age. Depending on children's abilities, the piñata can remain at a fixed height for younger children, or it can be raised and lowered to increase the challenge for older students. The bat should be light enough for children to swing easily and wide at the striking end to ensure success in hitting the target. Choose a piñata that can be broken by children, fill it with healthy treats, and give each child a chance to strike away.

- *Traffic Jam.* Wheeled toys like tricycles and wagons help young children develop leg muscle coordination. Pretend city streets laid out by adults on the playground can be a fun way to encourage children to pedal and steer in and around various obstacles. Stop signs, turn indicators, a simple ramp to drive over, traffic cones, and a pretend gas pump can stimulate good exercise that children will enjoy for many days. Changing the traffic patterns every few days will help maintain interest in this activity.

- *Parachute Play.* Group activities with a parachute can help promote cooperation and allow for both large and small muscle use. Begin by demonstrating

Celebrating Diversity . . .
Movement Activities for Children with Special Needs

Although physical skills may present many challenges to children with special needs, the benefits of involvement include:

- Better coordination
- Improved listening skills
- Enhanced expressive abilities

Although these are important reasons for including children with special needs, perhaps the most significant reason is improved self-concept (Gallahue & Ozman, 2002). Many disabilities make it harder for children to participate in physical tasks, or when they do get involved, the outcome is different from that of other children. This can lead to a distorted body image. Involving children with special needs in successful movement activities can help them feel good about themselves.

Here are some planning considerations for including children with special needs (Flynn & Kieff, 2002; Pica, 2004):

- Make sure that all children can succeed with the tasks you include.
- Consider modifying movement activities or materials to make them positive experiences.
- Include music as an important component that can help improve response, motivation, and enjoyment.
- Consult with parents and special educators for other insights in planning for physical activities.

1. Take a look at playground equipment for young children. What adaptations would be needed (or were made) to make them accessible to children with special needs?

2. Talk to a physical education teacher to find out the benefits and problems of involving children with special needs in movement activities.

how to grip the parachute: either palms down, palms up, or alternating. Children can use the parachute to create waves by using different large arm movements to make it go up and down. Experiment with different positions (sitting, kneeling, standing) and a variety of motions as children gain confidence in manipulating the parachute. For a more advanced activity, place a lightweight ball on the parachute and have children keep it bouncing.

Teaching Children to Care for Their Bodies

Helping children develop motor skills is an important part of physical development during the early childhood years. In addition, it is important for educators to promote an understanding of health-related issues and safety concerns. Young children develop patterns of behavior during these years that often last a lifetime. Teaching respect and care for one's body is an essential element of the early childhood curriculum.

Health Education

The soaring costs of medical care and a growing realization that it is easier to avoid problems than to cure them have led to positive changes in the health care professions (Marotz, Cross, & Rush, 2001). The focus is now on preventive health. For young children, issues that can be addressed include

• Good dietary habits
• Physical fitness
• The importance of medical and dental care
• Personal hygiene
• Stress reduction

Nutritional status clearly influences the young child's behavior. A good **diet** helps children be more alert, attentive, and active in the early childhood classroom. Poor nutrition will generally have the opposite effects and may lower the child's resistance to illnesses. Overeating and malnutrition also contribute to many problems in childhood, and early childhood educators need to address these issues.

Educators can teach good dietary habits through modeling them in the early childhood classroom. Teachers should carefully plan snacks and meals, with an emphasis on balanced nutrition. Discussion of what makes a good diet can then occur naturally as children eat the foods prepared for them.

Cooking experiences are another common and fun way to help teach young children good nutrition. For example, a fruit salad is easy and fun for young children to prepare and provides a healthy alternative to high sugar or fatty cooking projects.

The issue of **physical fitness** is growing in importance for the early childhood years. As increasing numbers of young children are classified as overweight (Sutterby & Frost, 2002) and their activity levels decrease, teachers must work to counter this trend. Although it is essential to downplay competition and remember that short periods of vigorous activity are best, young children can benefit from simple fitness activities (National Association for Sport and Physical Education, 1998). For example, teachers can encourage running and walking in playful ways to increase cardiovascular health.

Although good **medical and dental care** are commonplace in many households, other children and families do not have adequate coverage. Low-income families and those without medical and dental insurance may be unable to afford these services. Many schools for young children therefore provide information about the importance of good care and referrals to low-cost alternatives.

Educators must also be alert to health problems that could lead to later difficulties for children. Providing for vision, hearing, and speech screening is a common first step that schools can take to help identify potential health problems. Careful observation by the teacher can also be helpful in discovering other concerns.

You have overheard Rachel complaining of headaches for the last several days in your third-grade classroom. With the school's annual standardized tests scheduled for tomorrow, Rachel's headaches may be related to stress. You decide to call her parents to discuss the problem further.

A final component of health education during the early childhood years is an emphasis on **personal hygiene.** When teachers integrate good health habits into classroom activities, young children can learn and practice these important routines. Handwashing before eating and after toileting is an example of this emphasis. Hair grooming, brushing teeth, and caring for a runny nose are other aspects of good personal hygiene.

For more information about childhood fitness, go to the Companion Website at www.prenhall.com/henniger, select Chapter 12, then choose Web Destinations.

For more information about personal hygiene, go to the Companion Website at www.prenhall.com/henniger, select Chapter 12, then choose Web Destinations.

Safety Issues

 Amelia, a 4-year-old, knows she can explore the materials on the shelves in her preschool classroom. She is encouraged to take the blocks and build with them or create art projects from the many options available in that center. But what about under the sink near the snack area? As she opens the cupboards to investigate, she finds two different cleaning agents among the sponges and rags. Luckily, her teacher notices Amelia's inquisitiveness and redirects her to more appropriate areas. Furthermore, Mrs. Abbot decides to bring up the issue of storing cleaners in a more secure area at the next staff meeting.

Young children are naturally interested in everything around them and work hard to learn through hands-on exploration of their environment. Adults need to prepare the indoor and outdoor settings so that harmful materials are out of reach and potential accidents and injuries are minimized (King & Gartrell, 2003; Sutterby & Frost, 2002). As much as possible, children should be able to unleash their curiosities in environments that are free from unnecessary hazards. For example, the classroom should not include toys and equipment that break easily or are hard to clean. In addition, small objects that infants and toddlers can put in their mouths are hazardous. With common sense and an understanding of child development, the teacher of young children can create an atmosphere that is supportive of the child's natural ways of learning.

Family Partnerships . . .
Organized Sports for Young Children

If you have spent any time around youth sports activities, you know that parents are enrolling children as young as 3 or 4 years of age in a variety of organized sports. Baseball, soccer, basketball, and football are all being played by young children, with eager parents providing encouragement to their young charges. With proper leadership and parental support, these activities can provide some positive social outlets and enjoyable fitness experiences for young children.

David Elkind (2001), however, reminds us that most children during the early childhood years are not ready for highly competitive sports and games. He suggests that parents who push their children into early competitive activities are hurrying them to grow up too quickly and adding extra stress to their lives. Underwood (1981) puts it this way:

> To visit on small heads the pressure to win . . . is indecent. To dress children up like pros in costly outfits is ridiculous. In so doing, we take away many of the qualities that competitive sports are designed to give to the growing process. (p. 73)

Many well-meaning parents create unnecessary structure in their children's lives by introducing them to early competitive sports. Although these activities for young children are improving, with more appropriate coaching and fewer fanatical parents shouting from the sidelines, most young children benefit at least as much from more unstructured, vigorous play activities rather than organized sports. Parents need to hear this message repeatedly from a variety of experts so that they can stand up to the pressure from others to get their children involved in too many organized sports activities at an early age.

1. Do you think David Elkind is right in saying that early organized sports place unnecessary stress on the lives of young children? Why or why not?

2. What can or should you do in your work with parents to share your ideas about the values and/or problems with organized sports for young children?

Working with Parents and Families

Parents can be major contributors to every aspect of their child's growth, including physical skills. Teachers can assist in this process by providing families with information and activities that support motor development. This parent education effort should build upon the positive things parents are already doing and take minimal effort for families to implement.

Understanding Physical Growth

Parents know a great deal about their individual children but often know little about how typical they are. "Is it normal for Aletha to be so clumsy at age 7?" "Mike's first-grade writing assignments are so hard to read. How does he compare to other children his age?" Parents benefit from information that clearly describes how children develop large and small muscle skills. Teachers can informally share this information with parents as issues arise or include it in written materials such as newsletters. Some parent groups may be interested in an evening meeting at which physical skill development is discussed.

Importance of Active Play

Although early childhood educators view childhood play as critical to development, most parents see play as a fun, but trivial, part of children's lives. To counter this widely held perspective, teachers should give parents many opportunities to learn about the importance of play for all aspects of child development. This includes information about its role in physical development. Teachers can share brochures, videos, and articles in early childhood journals to help parents understand the impact of play on learning, fine and gross motor skills, and childhood fitness.

Nutrition Information

For more information about nutrition information for parents, go to the Companion Website at www.prenhall.com/henniger, select Chapter 12, then choose Web Destinations.

With few exceptions, parents want the best for their children. In many instances, however, they need guidance in knowing what can be done to encourage healthy development. Without putting parents on the defensive or making them feel like they are failures, teachers need to help them learn about good nutrition and diet for young children. While many families do well in this area, others eat foods high in fat, sugar, salt, and preservatives. Providing resources (see, e.g., Marcon, 2003; Wanamaker, Hearn, & Richarz, 1979) for simple, nutritious alternatives to fast foods and communicating with parents about the importance of healthy diets will make a difference in the overall physical development of young children.

Summary

The Importance of Motor Skills

Motor skills have a significant influence on the development of social, emotional, and cognitive skills. Therefore, teachers must emphasize motor development during the early years.

Foundation for Physical Fitness

It is becoming increasingly important for teachers of young children to promote physical fitness for overall health and well-being.

Observing Development • Fine Motor Skills

Choose one of the age groups within early childhood (infants/toddlers, preschoolers, or primary-age children), *observe* **fine motor skills** using the guidelines provided, *reflect* on what you saw and heard, and *apply* the appropriate strategies listed with the children you observed.

Observe	Reflect	Apply
Look for specific examples of:	*Think about and respond to the following questions:*	*Consider the following developmentally appropriate strategies for the age group you observed:*
Typical fine motor skills of children in the group (grasps with whole hand, uses pincer grasp [thumb and index finger], holds a writing instrument between thumb and index finger, cuts on a line, can print legible alphabet letters)	What did the classroom teacher do to help students develop their fine motor skills?	Plan to assist each child in developing fine motor skills • Infant/toddler: help the child grasp smaller objects using the pincer grasp • Preschool: place your hand over the child's and guide fingers as she cuts a piece of paper • Primary: make sure children are holding their pencils properly as they engage in writing activities
Range of fine motor skills (children who are either far beyond the typical children in the group or who are considerably behind—be specific in identifying differences)	What are some of the potential reasons for the differences in fine motor skills that you observed?	Provide a range of activities based on the ability levels of children • Infant/toddler: texture balls for grasping, dried peas for pincer grasp • Preschool: different sizes of paintbrushes at the easel • Primary: activities for practicing drawing letters, opportunities for writing stories
Materials available for children to use in developing fine motor skills (balls to grasp, rattles, writing utensils, small paintbrushes, puzzles, etc.)	Was there any evidence that the teacher had planned for activities and materials to encourage fine motor skills?	Intentionally plan for fine motor activities • Infant/toddler: rolling a ball back and forth • Preschool: cutting activity in the art center • Primary: having students write up the results of a science experiment

Into Practice . . .
Nutritious Snacks and Meals

It is important that snacks and meals for young children be healthy and nutritious. In addition to the obvious physical benefits to children, these healthy food options model for parents some positive alternatives to the high salt and sugar foods that are found in many homes. By selecting easy-to-prepare foods that children like to eat, parents can be shown that good nutrition is easy, inexpensive, and enjoyable for all involved. In the classroom, simple options also mean that children can benefit from being involved in the actual food preparation itself for additional learning experiences.

The following ideas should get you started thinking about healthy options for young children:

Banana Smoothie. Combine two peeled bananas, two cups of strawberries or other fruit, one cup of milk, and a cup of plain yogurt and place the mix in a blender. Blend until smooth.

Ants on a Log. On 2- to 3-inch pieces of cleaned celery, spread a layer of peanut butter and then top with a row of raisins.

Fruit Salad. Wash, clean, and peel the fruits of your choice. Be sure to have a good variety of seasonal alternatives. Chop fruit into small pieces and mix together in a large bowl.

Yummy Bagel Sandwich. Cut bagels of your choice in half lengthwise (an adult task unless you have a special bagel cutter), add a slice of cheddar cheese, a round slice of apple (green is best), and a dash of cinnamon. Bake 5 to 10 minutes at 350 degrees.

To test your knowledge of this chapter's contents, go to the Companion Website at www.prenhall.com/henniger, select Chapter 12, then select Study Guide. Also see Chapter Overviews, Reflecting Essay Questions, Multimedia Explorations, and relevant Web Destinations.

The Components of Physical Development

Overall physical growth patterns, gross motor development, fine motor skills, the phases of motor development, and perceptual-motor development are all important parts of physical development that early educators must know about.

Teaching Physical Development

An understanding of basic considerations, the importance of play in physical development, and the role of organized physical activities will help teachers be successful with this important part of the curriculum.

Enhancing Physical Development Indoors

It is important for teachers to plan for organized games and activities indoors to enhance physical development.

Enhancing Physical Development Outdoors

While it is important to provide many opportunities for free play outdoors, young children can benefit from organized games and activities in that setting as well.

Teaching Children to Care for Their Bodies

Information about good nutrition, the importance of physical fitness, adequate medical and dental care, personal hygiene, and safety should be shared with young children.

Working with Parents and Families

Families often need to understand the general trends for physical growth, the importance of active play, and information about good nutrition for the healthy physical growth of their children.

Multimedia Explorations and Activities . . .

They Are What They Eat

Offering a variety of foods at an early age sets the
stage for life-long healthful eating habits.

(American Dietetic Association)

Research

This activity is designed to make you more aware
of the issues involved in helping young children
develop healthy eating patterns.

1. Go the Companion Website at
   www.prenhall.com/henniger and click
   on the Multimedia Explorations and
   Activities button for Chapter 12 for more
   information on this topic.
2. Talk to the parents of a young child to
   get their perspective on childhood
   nutrition. What do they typically eat and
   drink on an average day? What won't
   they eat? Why?
3. Walk through a grocery store, focusing
   on what is placed on shelves at a child's
   eye level. How and why are children
   attracted to certain products? Are these
   products healthy for children? What
   words could be misleading to a parent
   who is trying to make healthy choices for
   their children (e.g. "all natural")?

4. View the ABC News video segments titled
   "They Are What They Eat" and "Carol
   Porter: Feeding Hungry Children."

Reflect

After you complete your research, think about the
following issues:

- Why are growing numbers of children
  overweight? What do you see as the top two or
  three reasons?
- Should educators be concerned about this
  issue? What is the role of an educator in
  responding to this problem?
- What can parents do to improve the eating
  habits of young children? What could early
  childhood educators do to encourage these
  behaviors?

- What about children who are dealing with
  hunger or poor nutrition issues? How could an
  educator help a family dealing with these issues?

Respond

Based on your reflections, consider one or more
of the following responses to the issue of
childhood nutrition:

- Find a child care center, early childhood
  education center, or elementary school that is
  willing to have you evaluate the snacks they
  provide to children. Create a report card
  where you can give them feedback and
  suggestions for improvement.
- Find a family with young children that is willing
  to have you look through their kitchen to
  evaluate the food choices they are making.
  Create a report card from which you could give
  them feedback and suggestions for improvement.
- Many families living in poverty make poor food
  choices for their children because they say they
  can't afford to feed their children a nutritional
  diet. Create a flyer that compares the costs of
  nutritional food choices versus junk food costs.
  Aim to persuade the reader that it is possible to
  provide a healthy diet for even less money than
  it costs to feed a child fast food and junk food.
  Find a child care center, early childhood
  development center, preschool, or elementary
  school that is willing to copy and distribute the
  flyer to their students' families.
- Contact a local parenting group such as a
  school PTA to arrange a presentation about the
  importance of providing healthy food choices
  for their children. Make sure your presentation
  addresses how their children are persuaded to
  make unhealthy food choices (via advertising,
  grocery store food displays, and peers). Provide
  ways that parents can combat those negative
  influences and make eating nutritional foods
  fun for kids.
- Volunteer with a local organization that provides
  food for young children or families with young
  children. Share what you learned with your class.

13

SUPPORTING SOCIAL AND EMOTIONAL DEVELOPMENT

In this chapter you will

- Review the components of social competence.
- Study the social development curriculum.
- Gain understanding in helping children deal with their feelings.
- Recognize the impact of stress on social and emotional development.
- Focus on developmental issues and their relationships to growth in these areas.

Andrea has changed over the past few weeks from an excited, busy 5-year-old in your kindergarten classroom to a withdrawn and anxious child. Her life was turned upside down recently with the sudden death of her father. It is affecting her ability to relate to other children and has led to a short attention span as well as lackluster play experiences.

Some other children in the group, although not experiencing the same dramatic loss, live in single-parent homes and have limited contact with their fathers. They are wrestling with their own related problems.

You have decided to provide materials and activities in your classroom that can assist children in working through these stressors. Many excellent children's books are available that deal with living in single-parent homes, and you can add some to the library corner. A puppet family is another good possibility for the dramatic play area. In addition, now may be the time for that unit on families that you have been planning to introduce.

The problems of separation and loss are only two of many issues that young children and their families face today. Combine these stressors with the more normal challenges of social and emotional development, and it becomes clear that the curriculum of the early childhood classroom must address these important topics. A quality program for young children recognizes the value of guiding the growth of social skills, emotional development, and the coping strategies necessary to deal with the stress of modern life.

Toward Social Competence

The process of **socialization** begins at birth and continues throughout childhood. It involves learning to relate to a variety of people in many different circumstances (Kostelnik, Stein, Whiren, & Soderman, 2002). For example, relating to parents is different from interacting with teachers, grocery clerks, strangers on the street, and peers. Children also must learn that different environments call for varying social skills. It is generally okay to shout, run, and get dirty outdoors; the classroom tends to be a somewhat quieter environment. Similarly, churches, drugstores, and swimming pools each have their own environmental requirements for social interactions.

Historically, early educators have placed a heavy emphasis on encouraging positive social development (Braun & Edwards, 1972). More recent research helps substantiate the value of this emphasis. Hartup (1992) states:

> Indeed, the single best childhood predictor of adult adaptation is *not* IQ, *not* school grades, and *not* classroom behavior, but, rather the adequacy with which the child gets along with other children. Children who are generally disliked, who are aggressive and disruptive, who are unable to sustain close relationships with other children, and who cannot establish a place for themselves in the peer culture are seriously "at risk." (p. 2)

For more information about developing children's social skills, go to the Companion Website at www.prenhall.com/henniger, select Chapter 13, then choose Web Destinations.

Given the importance of quality social skills, it is helpful to have a list of positive attributes to encourage in the early childhood classroom. McClelland and Katz (1997) provide a checklist of social skills as a guide for teachers:

- Approaches others positively
- Expresses wishes and preferences clearly
- Asserts personal rights and needs appropriately
- Is not easily intimidated by bullies
- Expresses frustrations and anger in positive ways
- Easily joins others in work or play
- Participates in discussions and makes contributions to activities
- Is able to take turns
- Shows an interest in others
- Can negotiate and compromise in interactions with others
- Accepts and enjoys people of diverse ethnic groups
- Uses appropriate nonverbal communication such as smiles and waves

Building a Sense of Self

Social and emotional development strongly influence one another in childhood, as exemplified through the relationship between a child's self-concept and social development. **Self-concept** can be defined as how people feel about themselves and is generally considered a component of emotional development. It has three dimensions (Kostelnik et al., 2002):

- *Competence.* The belief that you can accomplish tasks and achieve goals
- *Worth.* A person's sense of being valued by others
- *Control.* The degree to which people feel they can influence events around them

Into Practice...
Enhancing Self-Concept

Teachers can strengthen students' self-concepts in two major ways. The first is through their daily interactions with children. Dreikurs, Grunwald, and Pepper (1982) call this *encouragement*; it is the teacher's efforts to let children know she trusts and believes in them. The second method of building self-concept is through *planned activities*. Examples of each type follow.

Encouragement

Although every child reacts differently to adult interactions, children often view these behaviors as encouraging:

- Smiling, a pat on the shoulder, a hug
- Spending time finding out about a child's weekend
- Praise for work well done
- Pointing out a child's strengths
- Displaying a child's work
- Attending an after-school sports event

Planned Activities

Planned events, while contrived, are still very productive in helping children feel good about themselves. The titles for these activities are meant to be playful descriptors of their intent.

- **I Like . . . .** Choose one member of the class each day, and have students share things they like about that person. With younger children, come prepared with several things you like about the targeted child so that many examples can be presented. Make sure that every student eventually has a chance to be the center of attention for this activity.
- **V.I.P. (Very Important Person) of the Week.** Give every child in the class a week when he or she is the V.I.P. Special privileges can be granted, such as leading the flag salute or being first in line for music. A bulletin board created by family members and the child can include pictures and other highlights. The teacher can also invite family members to the classroom.

For more information about self-concept, go to the Companion Website at www.prenhall.com/henniger, select Chapter 13, then choose Web Destinations.

Self-concept is seen as a significant factor in emotional development, but it also plays a role in the socialization process (Kostelnik et al., 2002). Children with strong self-concepts think of themselves as competent and likable. They look forward to the challenges of social interactions, and expect to do well. Individuals with low self-concepts, however, often feel inadequate in social situations and fear rejection.

Obviously, we want to promote positive self-concepts in the classroom and need to engage children in activities and interactions that enhance conceptions of themselves. Canfield and Wells (1994) suggest the following principles for building self-concepts:

- Teachers can either positively or negatively influence self-concept. Learn and use the positive strategies.
- Building a strong self-concept is not easy. It takes time and considerable energy.
- Although they are harder to change, try to influence central beliefs, such as feelings about academic ability, social skills, or attractiveness.
- Relate the successes and strengths you observe in children to one another. This enhances those central beliefs.
- All the little things you do—such as calling students by their names and complimenting them for positive interactions—help build strong self-concepts. When these interactions are sincere, specific, and occur regularly, children see themselves as more competent.

Into Practice . . .
Building Teacher–Student Relationships

When teachers focus on strengthening students' self-concepts, relationships are also enhanced. Jones and Jones (2004) present the following guidelines for building effective relationships:

- **Engage in an open, appropriate dialogue.** Honest and open communication about the lives of students and the teacher can create a climate where caring relationships develop. Without getting overly involved in students' lives, the teacher must demonstrate a willingness to talk about and help with much more than just academics.
- **Maintain a high ratio of positive to negative statements.** Although it is necessary to deal with the inappropriate words or actions of children, teachers must commit to interacting much more often with students when they engage in positive behaviors.
- **Communicate high expectations.** Teachers have high expectations for children who see themselves as more competent and know that adults care about them. Teacher–student relationships are strengthened.
- **Take time for personal communications.** Showing an interest in students' activities, occasionally eating lunch with children, joining in childhood play from time to time, and sending students a birthday card are some examples of this type of personal communication.

Teacher–Student Relationships

Teachers in the early childhood classroom are an important factor in the development of children's social skills. Their efforts to relate effectively with students, the classroom climate that teachers create, and the strategies used to deal with problems are all significant in this process.

Without question, teachers are models of behavior that young children imitate (Bandura, 1989). Children listen to the words that teachers use to communicate with others and then try them out in their own speech. Students use polite comments like "please" and "thank you" far more often in classrooms where teachers regularly use them. Children imitate smiles, eye contact, and physical touch when they see adults using these nonverbal skills. Children also observe and imitate the techniques adults use to resolve problems with children and other adults.

The classroom climate that the teacher creates is another important factor influencing children's developing social skills. Glasser (1990) calls this building a friendly workplace and identifies several strategies that are helpful to teachers in this process:

- Avoid becoming adversarial in relationships with students.
- Create an atmosphere where courtesy prevails.
- Show an interest in students' lives, and share some information about yourself as a person.
- Ask students for advice and help whenever you can.
- Develop close, caring work relationships with students.

The way a teacher organizes and decorates the physical environment also influences the overall classroom climate. For example, a comfortable child-sized couch or several throw pillows create an inviting space for reading or other quiet activities. Decorating the walls with children's artwork and creative writing also delivers an important message that this work is valued by those who work and play there. Careful attention to these details in the beginning of the school year can pay big dividends later.

The intervention strategies that the teacher uses to deal with socialization problems that come up throughout the day also strongly influence the skills children develop.

 Margaret is an active, busy 4-year-old in your child care program. She is a natural leader, and others in the group often follow her direction. Margaret is playing in the block center and decides that she wants to use the dump truck Deforrest is filling with blocks. She says "Deforrest, if you let me use the truck, I'll play with you later." New to the group and naturally shy, he reluctantly agrees rather than cause conflict.

How should the teacher intervene in this situation to help both children learn better strategies for interacting? Deforrest needs to develop positive ways to stand up for himself while at the same time becoming more a part of the group. Margaret has to learn she cannot always have her own way and needs to channel her leadership abilities in more positive directions. One possible response is, "Margaret, Deforrest is using the truck right now. When he is finished, I hope you will ask him again to play with you." The intervention strategies the teacher uses to deal with this situation and others will help determine how effectively both children learn to relate in social settings.

Peer Interactions

For more information about peer interactions, go to the Companion Website at www.prenhall.com/henniger, select Chapter 13, then choose Web Destinations.

Relationships with teachers and other adults help children develop social skills; interactions with peers are the proving ground for these unfolding abilities. Developing peer relationships is an important step for children and one that is difficult to accomplish. Infants and toddlers spend most of their time interacting with adults and only gradually move toward the more challenging task of socializing with peers.

One of the reasons children struggle with peer relationships is their level of cognitive development. Piaget suggests that young children are **egocentric** (Flavell, 1963). They have difficulty seeing issues from the perspective of others. More recent research (see, e.g., Newcombe & Huttenlocher, 1992) suggests that children may be less rigid in their perspective taking than Piaget originally believed; however, it is only gradually and through repeated interactions with peers in play and work situations that children consistently recognize that others may have opinions, attitudes, and needs that are separate from their own.

Play, both indoors and on the playground, is one of the best settings for the development of social skills (Van Hoorn, Nourot, Scales, & Alward, 2003). Most play sequences include several children and require effective communication, compromise, leaders, and followers in order to be successful. Children have many opportunities to practice all aspects of their developing social skills as they engage in play themes. Jambor (1994b) suggests that for school-age children, recess time on the playground is unfortunately one of the few opportunities they have to engage in meaningful social experiences.

Developing friendships and learning to interact with peers is an important element of early learning.

As children engage in play activities and other interactions with peers, they develop important social skills:

- *Making friends.* The essentials of friendship are commitment and reciprocity between two people who are fairly equal in power. Early friendships often set the stage for making and keeping friends later in life (Hartup & Moore, 1990).

- *Sharing and helping.* Taking turns with toys, helping with a puzzle, and sharing food at snack time are examples of behaviors that children engage in regularly when encouraged to do so. Practicing these skills helps develop caring adults who support and encourage one another.

- *Cooperation.* When children willingly and without coercion by an authority figure support and assist one another, they are engaging in cooperative activity. Play provides many opportunities for cooperation.

- *Respecting rules.* Rules or conventions for appropriate conduct are an important part of all social interactions. Listening when another is speaking is just one of these rules that children must learn to follow if they want to participate effectively in social interactions.

- *Problem solving.* Social interactions often lead to disagreements that must be resolved. Children learn problem-solving strategies to deal with these conflicts.

- *Expressing feelings.* Although children often express their feelings in inappropriate ways with others (hitting, kicking, biting, name calling), they also quickly learn that these approaches get in the way of friendships and being part of a group. More appropriate ways of communicating feelings are needed.

For more information about expressing feelings, go to the Companion Website at www.prenhall.com/henniger, select Chapter 13, then choose Web Destinations.

The Social Development Curriculum

In many instances, the curriculum for developing social skills occurs spontaneously as children need assistance in interacting with peers or other adults. Quietly assisting a child in finding alternatives to hitting as an expression of anger is one such example. Yet, in addition to these teachable moments, many opportunities to plan for social skill development arise.

The Environment and Materials

The physical setting in which children interact is an important element of the socialization process. Careful planning of the space helps make positive interactions more likely. The following suggestions should be considered in organizing space:

For more information about helping children play together, go to the Companion Website at www.prenhall.com/henniger, select Chapter 13, then choose Web Destinations.

- *Space to be social.* The physical space should invite children to interact with one another. Clusters of desks or child-sized tables and chairs, centers designed for small groups of students, large throw pillows, and open spaces for gathering are examples of this type.

- *Access to work and play spaces.* If teachers want children to interact spontaneously with their peers and others on a regular basis, they need to provide ready access to the classroom spaces available to them (Hubbard, 1998). Children who are free to explore their environment for major parts of the school day will naturally have more social interactions with others.

- *Pictures that depict social activities.* When selecting pictures to decorate the walls in the different centers, try to find ones that show adults and children engaging in prosocial behaviors.

- *Materials that foster cooperation.* A mural for an art project, computer software that takes two or more to play, and noncompetitive board games are examples of materials that children can productively use to strengthen social skills.

- *Fewer options to encourage sharing.* Having just one piece of popular equipment (e.g., a special dump truck) for children may lead to major conflicts. Having too many pieces, however, eliminates the opportunity to practice sharing. The best option is to have fewer pieces than children would like so that some sharing is needed.

- *Books dealing with social skills.* A variety of children's books deal with socialization issues. One such example is *A Friend Is Someone Who Likes You* (Anglund, 1983). The teacher should rotate these books in and out of the library/book center throughout the school year.

The daily schedule of events also influences the development of social skills. When teachers provide adequate time for children to work and play in small groups or as a class more productive interactions take place (Hubbard, 1998). It is critical to remember that short time blocks are seldom effective for socialization and may in fact be counterproductive.

Children need time to warm up to the idea of working or playing with others, time to plan what they are going to do, additional opportunity to engage in the activity, and a cooling-off period. Even for primary-age children, these blocks of time are seldom productive if they are shorter than 20 or 30 minutes.

Puppets are popular with young children, and teachers can use them to model appropriate social interactions.

Activities and Themes

Planning the social curriculum should also include activities that promote the developmental skills emphasized in the early childhood program. Teachers can choose from a rich assortment of options. A sampling of ideas for activities follows:

- *Songs.* Singing and music are wonderful learning tools for all areas of the curriculum. Social development is no exception. Some songs are appropriate for every age within the early childhood range. Examples that fit this category from a songbook by Warren (1983) titled *Piggyback Songs* include "Helping," "Friends," "Be My Friend," and "Here We Are Together."

- *Games.* Games for children this age should be noncompetitive. Many excellent board games are available to promote positive social interactions. For example, the ChildsWork ChildsPlay Corporation sells The Kindness Game and Sleeping Grump, both of which promote cooperation and kindness in young children.

- *Community workers.* An important aspect of social development is learning about and effectively relating to people in the community. Having construction workers, firefighters, doctors, and others as guests in your classroom allows children opportunities to better understand and interact with these people.

- *Discussions.* Reading a good book about social relationships or using a similar discussion starter can help generate a productive dialogue with children about social skills. When the discussion includes topics being experienced by children, meaningful communication can take place.

- *Cooperative learning.* For primary-age children, the teacher can assign group projects that require children to work together to complete tasks. These cooperative learning experiences help build social skills and are quality educational opportunities (Ellis & Whalen, 1990).

Celebrating Diversity...
Through the Use of Dolls

The toys we have available to children tells them a great deal about what we value as teachers. If we provide colorful, inviting options that encourage children to explore and experiment, we are telling them that we value these attributes. Similarly, if we value diversity in our classrooms, it is important to provide toys that demonstrate this commitment. One important option that should be considered is to have dolls of all types available for children to play with in the classroom. For example, there are several manufacturers that currently produce high-quality dolls with skin tone differences and clothing options that are representative of African American, Native American, and Asian cultures. When these dolls are placed in the classroom, Caucasian children can play out events in which multicultural children participate in natural ways. Children of color unconsciously see their ethnicity respected and valued through the provision of quality dolls. All children are more likely to engage in productive dialogue about diversity when these multicultural dolls are available.

In addition to the multicultural dolls just described, several companies are also producing dolls with special needs that teachers are purchasing for use in the classroom. A doll without a leg and equipped with crutches, or a doll in a wheelchair, can be a useful toy in any classroom. These toys may be particularly valuable in classes in which there are no children present with these special needs. When dolls with special needs are made available, children can play out their understandings of disabilities and be reinforced by either the teacher or other children when they are correct and learn from others when they have misunderstandings. Again, all children benefit as conversations and play themes focus more directly on issues related to children with special needs.

A more controversial option available for teachers and classrooms is the provision of anatomically correct dolls for use in play. Several companies are producing boy dolls complete with penis and testicles and girl dolls with vaginas. The intent is to let young children naturally explore these sexual differences in their play. By asking direct questions, young children receive matter-of-fact responses from teachers about sexual differences and the reasons for them. As you might expect, this early introduction of sexual topics is not always well-received by parents and others. Despite the good intentions of this approach, many parents see this as an infringement upon the family's responsibility for addressing this issue.

1. Do you think a diverse collection of dolls can help young children develop deeper understandings of both the similarities and differences among people? Why or why not?

2. How do you feel about including anatomically correct dolls in the early childhood classroom? Give a rationale for your response.

Thematic teaching can also be used to stimulate social learning. The topic of cooperation is one example of a theme that teachers can productively use in the early childhood classroom to build social skills. The following examples of center materials and activities outline some of the content of a unit on cooperation:

- *Pictures* in centers showing adults and children cooperating help create the right atmosphere for the theme.
- *Cooperative block building* can be encouraged verbally and by providing a large map of a city that children can use as the foundation for creating their own city.
- *Difficult puzzles* in the manipulative center can be completed by two or more children.

Into Practice...
Games and Socialization

Sports and competitive games have long been viewed as valuable ways for people to develop abilities to work effectively with others. However, many suggest that, for the early childhood years, the emphasis should be on cooperation rather than competition. Games focusing on cooperative interactions develop stronger social skills and better prepare children for the competitive situations they will face later in life. A variety of good resources are available for those who are interested in using cooperative games:

Kamii, C., & DeVries, R. (1980). *Group games in early education.* Washington, D.C.: National Association for the Education of Young Children. In this classic book, Kamii and DeVries suggest that group games should: "(1) suggest something interesting and challenging for children to figure out how to do; (2) make it possible for children themselves to judge their success; and (3) permit all players to participate actively throughout the game" (p. 3). They present numerous examples of

games which meet these criteria and downplay the element of competition.

Orlick, T. (1978). *The cooperative sports and games book: Challenge without competition.* New York: Pantheon. This is probably the best-known and most widely used book on cooperative games and sports. More than 100 options provide children of all ages with many enjoyable activities.

Orlick, T. (1982). *The second cooperative sports and games book.* New York: Pantheon. This book presents an additional 200 games that can be used with children of all ages, including toddlers. The games emphasize imagination as well as cooperative skills.

Sobel, J. (1984). *Everybody wins: 393 non-competitive games for young children.* New York: Walker and Company. The cooperative games in this book are specifically designed for children from 3 to 10 years of age. The author also selected games that promote feelings of self-worth and confidence.

- *Cooperative sand structures* can be part of the outdoor activities. Teachers can give pairs or small groups of children their own tools for building.

- *Mural art projects* allow children to work on a common art activity.

- *Group fingerpainting* is another art project that encourages children to work together.

- *Post office* props in the dramatic play area help children cooperate as they take different roles related to writing, sending, and receiving mail.

- *Books* on cooperation such as *Sharing* by Newman (1990) support the theme.

- *Commercial music recordings* such as Fred Rogers' *Let's Be Together Today* or Marlo Thomas's *Free to Be You and Me* can be available for use in the music center.

Helping Children with Emotional Development

Emotional development in young children consists of a gradual growth in the ability to recognize, label, and appropriately respond to their feelings. Each of these steps is important to emotional health and must be learned through repeated interactions with others. The "Observing Development" feature at the end of this chapter highlights ways to observe children expressing emotions, reflect on how these emotions impact the classroom, and apply strategies to identify and accommodate these emotions.

What Are Emotions?

For more information about understanding childhood fears, go to the Companion Website at www.prenhall.com/henniger, select Chapter 13, then choose Web Destinations.

Emotions are feelings that come in response to other people, experiences, or circumstances. Stimuli from the environment cause physiological responses in the body that lead to feelings such as anger, fear, sadness, or surprise (Kostelnik et al., 2002).

> *Seven-year-old Kimberly was severely bitten by a pit bull at age 3 and has since been fearful around dogs of all sorts. When she sees a dog, her heart rate goes up, and she literally begins to shake as she runs to her father for protection. Although not all emotional responses are as clearly defined as Kimberly's, we each have our own physical reactions to stimuli. These feelings are real and must be recognized and dealt with in positive ways.*

Researchers who have studied emotional development suggest that young children are genetically programmed with **core emotions** that include joy, anger, sadness, and fear (Plutchik, 1980). These intense, relatively pure emotions serve as the foundation for the later emergence of more **complex emotions** such as frustration, annoyance, jealousy, and boredom.

Dealing with Feelings

Young children have much to learn about their feelings. Because it is very difficult to change our emotional responses to situations and people, it makes more sense to help children respond appropriately to their feelings.

Recognizing and Labeling Feelings. Before responding appropriately to emotions, children need to successfully recognize that they are having an emotional reaction and need to give it a name. Through most of the early childhood years, teachers and other adults will need to help children with this task. When the adult sensitively recognizes the emotional signs and gives them a label, children gradually develop the ability to do the same.

> *Six-year-old Ara is playing with a car in the block corner, and he briefly leaves the area to get a drink of water. Upon his return, Ara sees that Adrienne has taken the car he was using. With a loud scream, Ara rushes into the center, grabs his vehicle, and violently kicks down the block structure Adrienne has constructed. The teacher enters the area, takes Ara by the hand, and leads him away to a quiet corner of the room. She gets down at the child's level and says, "I can tell by your scream and kicking that Adrienne made you very angry when she took the car you were using." The teacher needs to continue her discussion with both Ara and Adrienne, but these initial comments make it clear that she has provided a label for Ara's feelings.*

Accepting Feelings. The emotions children experience can often be powerful and seem almost overwhelming to them. Children need to know that it is normal

Children's emotions are often clearly observable in their facial expressions and body language.

to have strong feelings and that it is important to accept them as a natural part of life. Unfortunately, many adults have not learned this lesson and try to deny their own feelings or those of children. Often, they make comments to children such as: "You're okay. There is nothing to be afraid of!"

The words adults use in communicating with children about emotions help them accept their feelings. The teacher dealing with Ara in the preceding example could add the following to her initial comment: "It's okay to be angry. Everybody gets angry sometimes." This will help Ara accept the strong emotion he experienced.

Appropriate Responses to Emotions. As children learn to recognize, label, and accept their feelings, they also need assistance in developing prosocial responses. Although hitting, kicking, crying, or withdrawal may be the natural reaction for many children, they must learn to use words to more effectively deal with emotions.

The teacher dealing with Ara in the preceding example could finish her discussion with him by saying:

"Ara, even though you are angry, I can't let you scream or kick playthings in the classroom. Can you think of a better way to let Adrienne know that you are angry?" If the child is unable to come up with another option, the teacher can then suggest acceptable alternatives.

Materials and Activities for Emotional Development

As the preceding example with Ara indicates, many teachable moments for emotional development are spontaneous and come from the lives of children themselves. In addition, however, teachers can use a variety of materials and activities in the early childhood classroom to help children learn about dealing with feelings. The following materials are effective in allowing children to express their feelings in positive ways:

- *Art materials.* Clay, play dough, and paints (including fingerpaints) are all examples of materials that many children use regularly to express their feelings. Playing with a lump of play dough or painting a picture can be a healthy release for many children.

- *Dramatic play props.* Dolls, puppets, dress-up clothes, and housekeeping materials can also encourage children to act out the experiences that lead to strong

Celebrating Play...
Play as Therapy

In a classic study on children and play, Brown, Curry, and Tittnich (1971) describe the reactions of several kindergarten children to the following situation:

> On September 26, 1968, the children at the Arsenal Family and Children's Center witnessed a tragic accident outside the play yard. In this accident a man, who had been working on lights 20 feet above the ground, was catapulted from the bucket of his crane-like machine onto the concrete below. Because he did not have his safety helmet on, his head was severely injured. All this occurred only a few feet from the kindergarten playground which was occupied by 12 observant children. (p. 27)

You can imagine the scene: children standing around excitedly watching the man working high up in the air changing lights, followed by hushed silence as the man falls and strikes his head on the concrete. At that point, the teacher decides to let the children stay outdoors because she wants the children to see that people who get hurt receive aid quickly. In all likelihood, all 12 children remain glued to the fence until the ambulance comes to take the injured man away to the hospital. Still dazed and confused, the children are then taken indoors where they are encouraged to talk about what they have seen.

The authors go on to describe the longer-term reactions of these children to the accident they observed. With encouragement from their teachers, these children began to play both indoor and outdoor themes that included falling, injuries, and others coming to provide assistance. These play sequences were repeated over and over again for a period of several months with small modifications as children explored new aspects of the situation. For example, at one point they pretended they were wearing safety helmets and thus avoiding serious injury. After this extended period of play, children were eventually able to work through their anxieties and move on to other play themes. For these children, play was a therapeutic tool that allowed them to work through the difficult situation they observed.

1. Can you remember any therapeutic play sequences that either you or your friends engaged in? If so, describe them.

2. Do you think play can serve as an important therapeutic tool to help children work through many, if not most, of the stressors they face? Why or why not?

emotions. By playing them out, they can understand their feelings better and gradually work to set them aside.

- *Books.* Many excellent children's books are available that address children's emotional issues. The story lines of these books bring up difficult issues (e.g., divorce or death) or the more normal emotions we all experience, thereby helping children begin to deal with the feelings involved.

- *Sand and water activities.* Play with sand and water has a definite therapeutic value. When this play is combined with small figurines and dramatic play props, children can once again play out their emotional concerns. Some professional therapy techniques use sand to encourage disturbed youngsters to play out their severe emotional traumas (Yawkey & Pellegrini, 1984).

- *Music.* Tapes and CDs are available that either provide a calming background for classroom activities or address specific emotional issues. An example of the latter is Rosey Greer's "It's All Right to Cry" (in Marlo Thomas, *Free to Be You and Me*).

Stress as a Factor in Social and Emotional Development

When we think about stress, we generally associate it with adult life rather than childhood. Over the last few decades, however, more and more people have been concerned about the levels of stress that even young children experience. David Elkind (2001) has been the most visible and well-known spokesperson for this issue.

Stress has always been a part of childhood. Making friends, going to grandma's house, learning about the world around them, and living in a family are all examples of the normal stresses of growing up. But what Elkind and others are concerned about are the additional stressors children face today. Divorce, violence and sexual themes on television, and the increased pressures of schooling are examples.

This combination of both normal and extra stress is making it difficult for many children to deal successfully with aspects of their social/emotional development. If stress is allowed to build, almost every child reaches a point of feeling overwhelmed, and developmental progress suffers. For example, a common response from children of divorce is that they feel responsible for their parents' breakup (Elkind, 2001). These feelings can then cause children to devalue themselves as individuals and may negatively affect not only their overall self-esteem but their social development as well.

For more information about helping children cope with stress, go to the Companion Website at www.prenhall.com/henniger, select Chapter 13, then choose Web Destinations.

Stress Factors

What are the major factors causing children stress? Some have been mentioned briefly here, but the following list helps clarify the most significant issues.

Family Circumstances. The most common stressor faced by today's children is divorce. However, remarriage, two-career families, and gay parents are other examples of family situations that can cause children stress. For example, a young child in a two-career family may experience what Elkind (2001) calls *change overload* from being shuttled between early morning care, school, and late afternoon supervision.

Early Pressure to Excel. Many well-meaning parents inadvertently put stress on their children by involving them in too many extracurricular activities. While some young children benefit from early musical experiences, competitive sports programs, and computer camps, more often these experiences add stress to their lives. A more specific example of early pressure to excel comes from the writings of Glenn Doman (1961). Through his book, *Teach Your Baby to Read,* and parent workshops, Doman has been encouraging parents for approximately 40 years to teach their infants and toddlers to read. Although it is possible to teach some children to read at very early ages, there is no research to indicate that this approach has any long-term value for these early readers. For most children, this activity only adds to their stress level.

Media Stress. For a variety of reasons, television is a stressful media experience for children (Center for Communication Policy, 1997). One reason for this stress is that young children have difficulty separating fact from fantasy and therefore

It is difficult for young children to appropriately process televised violence.

struggle to understand and cope with the violence and sexual themes they regularly encounter. Television advertising has also been criticized because of the unhealthy foods and low-quality toys promoted and the conflicts that arise in interactions with parents (Notar, 1989). Movies, popular music, and even some children's books (e.g., see Carlsson-Paige & Levin, 1986) have also been cited for their stressful impact on children.

Child Abuse and Neglect. Parents and families under stress may react in very inappropriate ways to children. Physical abuse in the form of beatings, sexual relations between family members, and blatant neglect may result (see Figure 13–1). The Child Abuse Prevention and Treatment Act, originally enacted by the federal government in 1974 and most recently reauthorized in 1996, requires mandatory reporting of suspected cases of child abuse. All 50 states have passed similar legislation requiring teachers and selected other professionals to report cases of child abuse to the proper authorities. Make sure you know the specific legal regulations for the state in which you plan to teach.

Growing Up Too Quickly. Elkind (2001) suggests that many children today are being pressured by society to grow into adulthood too quickly. He calls these children "hurried" and sees this push to grow up as a pervasive element in American society. Consider, for example, the clothing we now buy for our children. There is virtually no distinction between adults and children in the clothes we wear. When youngsters are dressed like adults, we expect them to engage in adult-like behavior. In many small ways like this, children are being hurried into adulthood.

Helping Children Cope

Clearly, children need adult assistance in working through both the normal stresses of development and the added complications of living in modern American society. Several good strategies are available to help children deal with stress (Elkind, 2001; McCracken, 1986):

- *Be aware of the times we hurry children.* This recognition is the first step in helping children deal with their stress.
- *Analyze the distinctive effects of stress on each child.* The temperament, age, developmental level, and individual child's perception of the stress all influence the impact of stress. Some children seem to have an incredible ability to manage

Figure 13–1 *Symptoms of Abuse*

	Physical Indicators	Behavioral Indicators
Physical abuse	Unexplained bruises	Self-destructive
	Unexplained burns	Behavioral extremes (withdrawn/aggressive)
	Unexplained fractures, lacerations, abrasions	Uncomfortable with physical contact
		Arrives at school early and stays late (afraid)
		Complains of soreness or moves uncomfortably
		Wears clothing to cover up body
Sexual abuse	Torn, stained, bloody underclothing	Withdrawn, chronic depression
	Pain, itching genitals	Hysteria, lack of emotional control
	Difficulty walking or sitting	Inappropriate sex play
	Bruises, bleeding in external genitalia	Threatened by physical contact, closeness
Emotional abuse	Speech disorders	Habit disorders (rocking)
	Delayed physical development	Neurotic traits (sleep disorders, inhibited play)
		Passive and aggressive behavioral extremes

Adapted from Bear, T., Schenk, S., & Buckner, L. (1993). Supporting victims of child abuse. *Educational Leadership, 50*(4), 42–47.

seemingly overwhelming circumstances; others struggle unsuccessfully to deal with much lower levels of stress.

- *Eliminate stressors whenever possible.* This is easy to say and much harder to do. However, teachers and parents can work together to reduce stress by doing such things as making sure children eat right, get plenty of rest, slow down, have time to talk about issues and concerns, and avoid inappropriate television programming.

- *Take time to have fun with kids.* When teachers and other adults get to know children better by occasionally eating lunch with them or playing a game for fun, relationships are strengthened and children are fortified to better deal with the next stress to come their way.

Family Partnerships...
Reducing Stress at Home

Stress is an all-pervasive force within our society. We all face it in many different forms. In some instances, the stressors are deeply rooted and difficult to address. The loss of a loved one, for example, causes deeply felt stress that may take years and professional assistance to resolve. Other stressors are more a matter of life-choices and can be resolved with careful thought and effort. For example, lack of sleep causes most people to be irritable and have poor work performance. With careful planning, however, this stressor can be eliminated. As a future teacher, you can help parents address this latter category of stressors. When you do, happier and healthier children are the result.

As you work to assist families in reducing the stress in their lives, it is important to keep the following in mind:

- **Remind without belittling.** "Lecturing" parents about the importance of good nutrition, for example, will have little chance of changing behaviors. You will need to be nonjudgmental as you share useful information with them.
- **Share information from other experts.** Avoid setting yourself up as the expert. First of all, you are probably not, and second, parents will resent your attitude. Find others in the community, state, or nation that can share their knowledge and insight with families.
- **Use a variety of reminders.** There are a number of different ways to send the same message. A parent

meeting, class newsletter, a video or book that parents can check out, or a notice regarding a community event may all be useful tools to share your ideas with parents. By using a variety of approaches, you are more likely to reach a greater number of parents.

- **Avoid a critical attitude.** You will probably never fully know all the problems and stresses faced by each of your families. You will need to avoid being critical of families when your helpful advice goes unheeded. Time and repeated discussions may be needed before a change can take place.
- **Be a good role model.** Even for parents and families, you will need to make sure you model the message you are sharing with them. If you want parents to be aware of the importance of active outdoor experiences as a stress reliever, make sure you are engaging in these activities yourself so that parents can see that you are "practicing what you preach."

1. How effective are you right now in reducing the unnecessary stresses in your life? Is this something you will need to work on before helping families to do the same?

2. At this point, do you think you will be able to commit time and energy as a future teacher to helping families reduce the stress in their lives? Why or why not?

- *Be respectful of children.* Elkind (2001) suggests that showing respect is a simple, direct way to let children know that we value them. Just knowing that adults care is a support to children under stress.

- *Encourage childhood play.* Elkind states, "Basically, play is nature's way of dealing with stress for children as well as adults" (Elkind, 2001, p. 197). When children can repeatedly play out the issues they are struggling to understand, they can make sense of them and gradually be able to set them aside. From the serious problems of a disturbed child (Axline, 1964) to the more mundane struggles of young children everywhere, childhood play is one of the best techniques available to work through stress (Frost, Wortham, & Reifel, 2001).

Teachers' Personal Development

For more information about teacher stress and burnout, go to the Companion Website at www.prenhall.com/henniger, select Chapter 13, then choose Web Destinations.

Just as the stresses of life are often high for students, the same can be said for teachers. The personal lives of teachers mirror those of society in general, with family, financial, and job stressors creating tensions and pressures that can potentially get in the way of quality interactions with children. If left unchecked, these stresses can reach a breaking point and teachers find they can no longer cope.

To maintain the balance needed for effective teaching, adults working with young children need to make sure to preserve their own social/emotional well-being. It is critical for teachers to

- *Eat healthy foods, exercise regularly, and get adequate rest.* Teachers readily encourage children to live a healthy lifestyle but sometimes forget that these same strategies also help adults deal effectively with the stresses they face.

- *Maintain social relationships with other adults.* The social and emotional demands of teaching are draining on adults, making it easy for some teachers to spend less energy on their own social needs. But when this happens, teachers lose valuable opportunities for personal growth and end up shortchanging the children they are trying to serve.

- *Take time for self.* Hobbies, interests, and time to simply reflect and "be" are necessary for healthy emotional development. Teachers who neglect this aspect of life may gradually become overwhelmed by the stresses of life and teaching.

- *Know your limits.* As the role of the teacher continues to expand (Allison, 1999), adults must frequently reassess what they can reasonably expect to accomplish in their work with children and what should be referred to other professionals. Knowing your limits is another important component of personal well-being.

Summary

To test your knowledge of this chapter's contents, go to the Companion Website at www.prenhall.com/henniger, select Chapter 13, then select Study Guide. Also see Chapter Overviews, Reflecting Essay Questions, Multimedia Explorations, and relevant Web Destinations.

Toward Social Competence

Teachers can enhance children's social competence by helping students develop a positive sense of self, by promoting strong student-teacher relationships, and by enabling effective peer interactions.

The Social Development Curriculum

Teachers need to be aware of the environment, materials, activities, and themes for a social development curriculum.

Helping Children with Emotional Development

Children experience a wide range of emotions; teachers can help children deal with their emotions by assisting them in identifying, accepting, and responding appropriately to their feelings.

Observing Development • Childhood Emotions

Choose one of the age groups within early childhood (infants/toddlers, preschoolers, or primary-age children), *observe* **childhood emotions** using the guidelines provided, *reflect* on what you saw and heard, and *apply* the appropriate strategies listed with the children you observed.

Observe	Reflect	Apply
Look for specific examples of:	*Think about and respond to the following questions:*	*Consider the following developmentally appropriate strategies for the age group you observed:*
What is said or done that suggests children are expressing positive emotions (words spoken, facial expressions, hugs, high fives, etc.)	What impact does positive emotion have on the atmosphere of the classroom?	Label and acknowledge positive emotions • Infant/toddler: Establish eye contact, get close, smile, and say, "You're feeling happy right now." • Preschool: "Brian, it is so good to see you excited and happy today." • Primary: "Jasmine, I love your bright smile and happy outlook today."
What is said or done that suggests children are expressing negative emotions (words spoken, facial expressions, hitting, stamping feet, etc.)	Did you observe more children expressing positive or negative emotions? Does this tell you anything about the classroom? Why or why not?	Provide acceptable ways of dealing with negative emotions • Infant/toddler: Make sure infants/toddlers are in a location where they cannot harm themselves or others as they work through negative emotions. • Preschool: Physically guide the child into a new center where he or she can start over in more positive ways. • Primary: Give the child words to express negative emotions to others in a socially acceptable way. ("Tell Javier that you are mad at him for not wanting to be your friend today.")
Reactions of the teacher and other children to the emotions expressed by children (words spoken, facial expressions, hugs, restraining child, etc.)	How often did the teacher respond to the positive emotions expressed in the class as compared to responses to the negative emotions?	Model appropriate responses to emotions • Infant/toddler: Smile, hug, and be playful with children when you are happy. • Preschool: Be calm but firm when you communicate verbally about your anger. • Primary: Verbalize your pleasure when you greet students at the beginning of the day.

Materials and Activities for Emotional Development

Art materials, dramatic play props, books, sand and water play, and music are all possible materials that can be used as part of the emotional development curriculum.

Stress as a Factor in Social and Emotional Development

Family circumstances, early pressure to excel, media stress, child abuse and neglect, and growing up too quickly can all cause young children stress. Teachers should plan strategies to help children cope with the stresses they face.

Teachers' Personal Development

As a future teacher, you will need to maintain your own social/emotional well-being by eating right, exercising regularly, getting adequate rest, maintaining social relationships, taking time for yourself, and knowing your own limits.

Multimedia Explorations and Activities...

Resilience in Children

My father gets drunk. He said he was going to kill my mother and me. My mother put me with friends and ran away. I don't know where she is.

(6-year-old boy)

I have to go to the hospital a lot because I have so many illnesses. I don't know if I will ever get well.

(10-year-old girl)

I saw my father get stabbed by a neighbor who was mad at him.

(6-year-old girl)

I am very short and people tease me at school all the time.

(11-year-old boy)

Children in every corner of the world experience the kinds of stresses described above (Grotberg, 1995, p. 8). Health crises such as AIDS, war, extreme poverty, and natural disasters impact numerous children and their families. In addition, almost all children experience challenges that are less sensational, but still highly stressful events: divorce, remarriage, a new child in the family, a family illness, a fight on the playground, and name calling or bullying by a more powerful child are all relatively common stressors faced by children today. The child's ability to deal with the stresses of life depends, in large part, on his resilience.

Research

For a large number of children, daily encounters with highly stressful events are a reality. Yet, some are able to deal with these difficulties relatively easily and well. These resilient children have been carefully studied so that adults can try to help others under stress be more able to cope. This activity is designed to get you acquainted with the literature on resiliency and get you involved in helping children under stress.

1. Go to the Companion Website at www.prenhall.com/henniger and click on the Multimedia Explorations and Activities button for Chapter 13 for more information on this topic.
2. Talk to a classroom teacher about children who appear to be resilient. While avoiding names, have the teacher describe the student, family situation, and any other relevant information that would help you understand how this child copes with the major stresses in her life.

Reflect

After studying the topic of resiliency, think about the following issues:

- How would you define resiliency? What seem to be the most common characteristics of children who successfully cope with high levels of stress?
- Can anything be done to decrease the levels of stress that children face? What is your role in this process?
- What can you do as a teacher of young children to help them be more resilient?

Respond

Consider responding to the issues surrounding resiliency in one or more of the following ways:

1. Describe in writing several strategies you found that teachers can use to help children who face high levels of stress. Share your strategies with a classroom teacher.
2. Plan a "resiliency workshop" for your classmates. Include information on what it is, strategies for assisting children, and the teacher's role in working with parents regarding this issue. Make sure you actively engage your audience as they learn about this important topic.

14

MATHEMATICS, SCIENCE, AND SOCIAL STUDIES LEARNING

In this chapter you will

- Study the goals for cognitive development in the early childhood classroom.
- Develop an understanding of the constructivist approach to learning.
- Address issues relating to mathematics instruction in early childhood.
- Identify the science curriculum for young children.
- Understand the importance of social studies in the early childhood classroom.

Michael and Eric are fascinated by their discoveries from morning recess. Using the bug catchers from the science center, they have managed to capture a ladybug, two spiders, and several ants. After creating separate homes for each of their bugs with leaves, sticks, and dirt, the boys are off to the computer to see if they can find out what their new friends like to eat. These second graders are learning to navigate the Internet and soon find some sites to explore.

During the afternoon recess, Michael and Eric scour the playground for food for their bug collection and additional materials for the habitats (a term they learned from the web search). Following recess, they record what they have learned in the science center journal. The boys also make plans to describe their bug collection at tomorrow's sharing time. They talk with the teacher about what they want to do and how long it will take.

Eric decides to take home one of the books in the science center to help him prepare for tomorrow's presentation. Michael has agreed to spend some more time browsing the Internet on his family's home computer to gather additional information for sharing time. Both boys leave school flushed with excitement and ready to continue learning about bugs.

In the situation just described, Michael and Eric are engaged in constructivist learning. As they study the living creatures found on the playground, both boys are developing mathematics, science, and language skills. They are engaged in the process of cognitive development.

The word *cognition* has its roots in the Latin word *cognoscere*, which means "to know." **Cognitive development** is the continuing process of learning about the world and all of its many components. Young children come to understand their environment best through manipulating real-world materials and discovering facts, concepts, and relationships. Although this intellectual growth is greatest during the early years, healthy people never stop learning.

Goals of the Cognitive Curriculum

A major role of the teaching profession is to facilitate students' intellectual understandings. Preparing for and teaching mathematics, science, and social studies are central components of education at all levels, including the early years. Therefore, teachers must clearly understand how this part of the curriculum should be taught in the early childhood classroom.

Learning Facts

For more information about learning facts, go to the Companion Website at www.prenhall.com/henniger, select Chapter 14, then choose Web Destinations.

Think back to your elementary school years and the teaching of mathematics, science, and social studies. Unless your experience was unusual, much of your time was spent on learning facts. Mathematics emphasized number facts such as the multiplication tables. Science probably included tasks like studying the parts of a flower. Social studies provided additional opportunities to memorize names and dates associated with important events or people.

How much of this information do you remember today? Most people find that they retain only a small portion of the facts they have learned. Although the instruction may have been both fun and intellectually stimulating at the time, the facts themselves are often forgotten. Does this tell you anything about the value of a cognitive curriculum that places heavy emphasis on the learning of facts?

Make no mistake: *the learning of facts is often an important task.* Could you successfully balance your checkbook without ready recall of addition and subtraction facts? Likewise, a basic knowledge of motor vehicle laws is necessary every time you drive a car. Every adult needs much essential information to function as a productive member of society. However, when facts become the primary focus of the learning process, a child's development suffers.

In many instances, the factual information learned in early childhood settings is secondary to other more important goals. Take, for example, the science experiences of Michael and Eric described at the beginning of this chapter. As they explore the Internet, read books on bugs, and talk to others, they are learning facts. But it is the *process of scientific learning* that is most important and will lead to the greatest long-term benefits.

If the learning of facts should not be the primary focus of the cognitive curriculum in early childhood, what should? Educators have emphasized three goals: (a) fostering critical thinking, (b) encouraging problem solving, and (c) promoting lifelong learning (Bredekamp & Copple, 1997; National Council of Teachers of Mathematics, 2000; Olson & Loucks-Horsley, 2000).

Critical Thinking

Teachers in the early childhood classroom need to recognize the importance of promoting critical thinking in children. Today's citizens are bombarded with information from so many different sources that it is difficult even for adults to make sense of it all. Teachers need to help children develop the ability to examine data critically and determine what is useful in making specific decisions and what is not.

Piaget effectively describes the importance of critical thinking:

> [An essential] goal of education is to form minds which can be critical, can verify, and not accept everything they are offered. The great danger today is of slogans, collective opinions, ready-made trends of thought. We have to be able to

resist individually, to criticize, to distinguish between what is proven and what is not. So we need pupils who are active, who learn early to find out by themselves, partly by their own spontaneous activity and partly through materials we set up for them. (quoted in Elkind, 1981a, p. 29)

Problem Solving

For more information about problem solving, go to the Companion Website at www.prenhall.com/henniger, select Chapter 14, then choose Web Destinations.

A second important goal for the cognitive curriculum is to help children become successful problem solvers. On a daily basis, each of us encounters situations that we must evaluate and deal with. Children need to develop skills in first recognizing and then solving the problems that come their way. The ability to approach issues confidently, identify possible strategies for dealing with them, and then successfully resolve problems requires considerable cognitive skill.

A major tool for encouraging problem solving in the early childhood classroom is the creative play experience. As children engage in play, they naturally encounter many problems that require resolution.

Shauntel and Blythe are playing in the sandbox outdoors. They are trying to create a tunnel connecting their two holes in the sand. Shauntel suggests trying to use sticks from the playground to strengthen the walls of their tunnel. Although the sticks help, both girls are disappointed in the results. Blythe adds a second option when she proposes they try digging their holes deeper and connecting farther down in the sandbox. This option, however, makes it difficult to make the bend needed to join the holes. After talking through their dilemma yet again, they decide to try moistening the sand with water so that it will remain firmer through the digging process. They have found a workable solution.

Because there are no right or wrong answers in play, children can feel free to experiment, explore, and problem solve as Shauntel and Blythe have done. Tegano, Sawyers, and Moran (1989) put it this way:

When playing, young children openly and spontaneously express themselves because they are in a nonthreatening environment. The creative process—defining the problem, generating ideas and solutions, evaluating solutions, converting solutions into outcomes—is enhanced in an open, "psychologically safe" environment. (p. 93)

Lifelong Learning

A third important goal for the cognitive curriculum is to instill in children a love of learning that will help them continue growing intellectually throughout their lives. While young children tend to be naturally curious about the world around them, the schooling process has often been accused of dampening enthusiasm. Albert Einstein (1949) said this about education:

It is in fact nothing short of a miracle that the modern methods of instruction have not yet entirely strangled the *holy curiosity of inquiry,* [emphasis added] . . . . It is a very grave mistake to think that the enjoyment of seeing and searching can be promoted by means of coercion and a sense of duty. (p. 17)

Einstein is implying that when instruction consists of hands-on learning through discovery, children are much more curious and motivated to understand their world. This reinforces once again the importance of play in the early childhood classroom. As children engage in center activities, they are spontaneously and naturally involved in cognitive development and are motivated to learn more. This playful way of knowing is essential in stimulating a positive attitude toward lifelong learning.

The Constructivist Approach

It should be clear from the preceding discussion that traditional educational methods in which the teacher dispenses knowledge to children who are passive recipients are not compatible with the goals described for the cognitive curriculum. A much more effective and developmentally appropriate approach is referred to as **constructivist education.** Grounded in the developmental theories of Jean Piaget (1950) and Lev Vygotsky (1978), this approach to early education promotes the idea that children build or construct their own understanding of the world through activities based on personal interests. As they manipulate real-world objects and interact with the people around them, children create for themselves an understanding of the world.

Chaille and Britain (2003) have identified four characteristics of children that make the constructivist approach the best match for early learning:

1. *Young children are theory builders.* The constructivist position suggests that knowledge is built by children themselves as they make educated guesses about why things work the way they do and then test out their theories in the real world. Children do this naturally and without prompting by adults.

2. *Cognition requires a foundation of physical knowledge.* Children are naturally motivated to understand the physical world around them. This knowledge of how objects and materials such as balls and cubes work lays the foundation for the more abstract understandings that come later.

3. *Children acquire increasing autonomy and independence.* As young children mature, they gradually move from dependence on adults for meeting their needs to more independent functioning. Healthy youngsters have a strong need to experiment, explore, and discover on their own.

4. *Young children are social beings.* Children are naturally social and spend considerable effort planning and interacting with others. These interchanges are an important part of the learning process. Children construct many understandings through their social exchanges with adults and peers.

DeVries and Zan (1995) identify the following strategies for creating a constructivist classroom:

- *Cultivate an atmosphere of respect.* Children need to work and play in a classroom in which they are respected as individuals and encouraged to experiment and explore without fear of poor treatment by adults or peers. This atmosphere allows children to engage in the construction of knowledge as they interact with people and things.

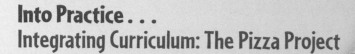

Into Practice . . .
Integrating Curriculum: The Pizza Project

Helm and Beneke (2003) describe a project conducted in a licensed child care center for children from 3 to 5 years of age in which mathematics, science, art, social studies, and early literacy experiences were integrated through the study of pizza. The project began after children identified several topics of interest to them, voted on their priorities, and selected pizza as their first option. Both counting and graphing skills were used in this initial step as sticky notes were used to record children's votes on a large graph on the wall. After having children share what they currently knew about pizza, children were given the opportunity to draw and talk about this topic. A staff member then brought in pizza pans, chef hats, and pizza tools from her part-time job in a pizza parlor and discussed their use prior to putting them in the dramatic play center. Children were encouraged to touch, draw, and label these tools. Additional science and math learning opportunities were integrated when pizza toppings were counted, smelled, cooked, and observed when left without refrigeration.

After this initial phase of exploration, children began a more in-depth investigation of how pizza was made and then delivered by arranging two field trips to a local pizza parlor. One of the teachers created a book of photos to give children ideas about what they could expect to see on their trips. The first visit was used to familiarize children with the general operations. Children took clipboards and had some initial questions they wanted answered. Of special interest on this first visit were the oven and the machine used to grind meat and cheese. During the second field trip, many children sketched and labeled items of special interest and then made their own pizzas using the tools they had been playing with in the classroom. After returning to the classroom, children modified the dramatic play area to make it more like the real pizza parlor, including the construction of a grinder and pizza warmer. Further math, social studies, and early literacy learning was incorporated into these activities. The culminating activity for the project was a pizza party that included a sharing time to help parents see what children had learned from their pizza explorations.

- *Allow children to be active learners.* The best learning occurs when children are allowed to pursue their own interests and physically manipulate the things in their environment. A child's mental functioning is enhanced when physical activity also takes place.

- *Foster social interactions.* When cognitive tasks allow for social interchange, childhood learning is enhanced. Sharing ideas with others helps clarify misunderstandings and provides additional perspectives that enrich the learning experiences.

- *Emphasize self-regulation and reflection.* As adults help children to take responsibility for their learning experiences, children become more independent and self-confident in seeking new knowledge. Encouraging reflection leads to an attitude of questioning that is at the heart of critical thinking.

Mathematics and Young Children

When many of us recall our own early mathematical experiences, memories of rote learning with little connection to real life often predominate. However, mathematics is an exciting, interesting, relevant topic for investigation. With the

Figure 14–1 *Classification by Color*

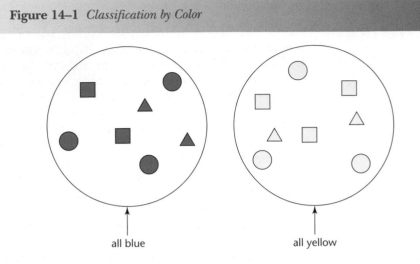

all blue   all yellow

constructivist approach, young children can learn a broad assortment of topics through manipulation and discovery and make mathematical connections to real issues in the world around them.

Classification

During early childhood, children develop cognitive understanding of many mathematical concepts that are essential to future growth in the discipline. One such concept is the ability to classify. Putting objects or ideas with similar characteristics into groups demonstrates **classification** competence (see Figure 14–1).

Although this cognitive ability seems simple for us as adults, children require considerable practice and time to understand classification. For example, a 3-year-old child given a set of colored blocks and asked to "put blocks together that are the same" may playfully organize and reorganize the blocks, not really using any logical thinking in creating his groupings.

Classification skills are fundamental to many mathematical concepts. For example, writing the numeral 43 requires an understanding of the "tens place" and "ones place" as different groupings. In addition, the study of algebraic functions places a heavy emphasis on the ability to classify, for example, "Consider n to be the set of all integers greater than zero."

Teachers of young children can provide many opportunities for practicing an understanding of classification. Mary Baratta-Lorton (1976), in her classic book *Mathematics Their Way,* provides many good ideas for simple materials that can be used for sorting and classifying tasks:

- People in the classroom
- Buttons for grouping
- Old bottle caps
- Natural materials for sorting such as acorns, leaves, rocks, and shells
- Nuts and bolts
- Teacher-directed activities using geoboards (square board with 25 regularly spaced pegs over which rubber bands can be stretched)

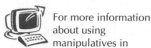

For more information about using manipulatives in mathematics, go to the Companion Website at www.prenhall.com/henniger, select Chapter 14, then choose Web Destinations.

Seriation

Ordering objects from smallest to largest is referred to as **seriation.** This sequencing can be based on height, weight, shades of color, or any other characteristic. This is another important cognitive task for young children to master. It is essential to an understanding of the number system.

Many opportunities to practice seriation are necessary for children to truly make sense of it. Although parts of this cognitive understanding are seen in many children at age 3 or 4, the full development of this concept is often reached as late as age 8 or 9. Piaget spent considerable time studying the growth of this developmental task (Flavell, 1963).

Many excellent commercial materials are available to give children practice with seriation. One well-known example is Montessori's cylinder block. Each rectangular block has several wooden cylinders that fit into holes ordered from smallest to largest in the block. Children practice their sequencing skills by finding the right cylinder for each hole. Another set of materials that can be used for seriation activities are Cuisenaire Rods. These multicolored rods begin with a small cube as the basic unit and grow step by step to the longest rod, which is 10 units in length.

Patterning

Being able to recognize and create visual, auditory, spatial, and numerical **patterns** is another important mathematical understanding. The discipline of mathematics is logical and based on patterns of all sorts. The number system, for example, with groupings of 10 has a clear pattern that children must recognize to truly understand its complexities.

Students must also master patterns in arithmetic, algebra, and geometry. Teachers can provide young children with many meaningful opportunities to engage in patterning activities. Some examples of appropriate materials and activities include:

- Stringing beads in patterns
- Constructing designs with pattern blocks
- Repeating clapping patterns
- Listening to musical patterns
- Building with Unifix cubes (plastic cubes that can be snapped together to form patterns)
- Playing with Cuisenaire Rods

Number Concepts

Children's understandings of number concepts develop rapidly during the early childhood years. While a 3-year-old often is just beginning to understand that "1" is a small number and others are larger, 5-year-olds have typically mastered basic number concepts through "9" (Murray & Mayer, 1988). During the primary years, children develop the ability to count forward and backward, skip count (counting by twos, fives, tens, etc.), and understand numbers into the hundreds (Charlesworth, 2000).

Counting. Much of the preschool child's understanding of number comes from repeated counting experiences. Many songs and finger plays (e.g., "Five Little Speckled Frogs" and "Ten Little Monkeys") give children enjoyable opportunities

Many primary children benefit from using concrete materials in counting activities.

for rote counting experiences. The day-to-day life of the classroom and home provide many other meaningful opportunities to count and understand numbers. Discussing the calendar at group time, counting crackers in the snack bowl, and finding out how many ladybugs were caught on the playground are examples of these natural opportunities for counting.

It is important to remember that primary-age children often use counting as an aid in solving addition and subtraction problems. Although this strategy eventually becomes cumbersome and slow, it helps many children make the transition to more mature arithmetic skills. The use of concrete materials in counting is still necessary for many primary-age children, and teachers should encourage it at this level.

Arithmetic Skills. During the primary years, children develop the ability to understand addition, subtraction, and multiplication. However, part of the problem with the traditional approach to teaching these skills is that not all children are cognitively ready to begin when the teacher starts this instruction. Some may need more counting experience first, while others should spend additional time developing basic number concepts. When the teacher uses a constructivist approach and allows children to manipulate materials and discover arithmetic understandings as they work on real-world problems, children are much more able to set their own pace and conquer this task.

Measurement

Another important mathematical understanding to be emphasized during the early years is the ability to quantify materials in the world. Finding the height, weight, volume, and dimensions of objects are examples of **measurement.** Piaget's work tells us that, until children have reached the stage of concrete operations (around age 7 or 8), they have difficulty measuring using standardized units such as inches, pounds, and liters (Flavell, 1963). Younger children, however, can learn much when given the opportunity to measure with nonstandard units.

The preschool and kindergarten child can engage in the following types of informal measurement activities:

- Use blocks to measure tables, floor space, and other elements of the classroom environment.
- Find out how many plastic cups of sand or water it takes to fill containers in the sand or water play area.
- Use a balance to compare weights of different objects.
- Trace full-body silhouettes of children and have them compare heights.

Children in the primary grades can engage in many of these same activities but with the use of standardized units of measurement. Children this age can use and understand rulers, weight scales, and one-cup containers. Measurement activities should remain meaningful and relevant to the children's lives. To achieve this goal, consider weighing the class guinea pig, measuring the dimensions of playground equipment, and discovering how many liters of water are needed to fill the classroom sink.

Geometry

The study of two- and three-dimensional shapes and how they are related to one another is called **geometry.** Although this topic is often thought of as part of the high school mathematics curriculum, it is highly applicable in the early childhood classroom. The young child's world is filled with interesting shapes to explore and understand.

Young children develop geometric understandings from playing with materials such as unit blocks, pattern blocks, tangrams, and paper for origami. In addition, teachers can help children identify the many shapes that exist in the classroom and outdoors on the playground by casually pointing them out. Books like *My Very First Book of Shapes* (Carle, 1985) can be good discussion starters for this topic.

The Language of Mathematics

Preschool teacher: *(holding up a ball)*	"We're going to talk about shapes today. This ball is a circle."
Kindergarten teacher: *(writing on the chalkboard)*	"This is how we write the number '5'."
Second-grade teacher: *(demonstrating with manipulatives)*	"I have five Popsicle sticks in my right hand and seven in my left. Which hand is holding less?"

In each of these situations, teachers have used inaccurate terms to describe mathematical concepts. In the first, the preschool teacher has used a two-dimensional term to describe a three-dimensional object (sphere). The kindergarten teacher in the second situation should have used the word *numeral* rather than *number* to describe the representation on the chalkboard. In the last situation, the more accurate term is *fewer,* rather than *less.* These common errors that many teachers make daily seem like fairly minor issues. Is it really worth the effort it would take to use more accurate terms?

Tracy (1994) makes a strong case for refining the language we use to teach mathematics. Language directly influences the concepts children develop. Because mathematics is such a precise field of study, teachers need to use accurate language with children. Not only do they understand concepts more easily when precise language is used, but children also enjoy using the more interesting terms. *Rhombus, ellipse, cube, rectangle,* and *numeral* are all words that children can learn and enjoy. Teachers should refine the language they use by first recognizing the terms that may cause misunderstandings and then work to identify and consistently use more appropriate words to describe the mathematical concepts being presented. Although this is not an easy task, the benefits to children are worth the effort.

Science Learning

Just as mathematical concepts are an important part of the early years, the science curriculum surrounds young children in their daily lives. What makes some things float and others sink at the water table? How does a flower grow? What does an ant eat? What makes a person grow? How do fish breathe? Why does a magnet pick up some things but not others? When teachers prepare an environment that allows children to manipulate and discover the answers to these and other important questions, the science curriculum will be a major success.

Science consists of three main components: content, process, and attitudes (American Association for the Advancement of Science, 1999). **Content** is the actual body of knowledge developed over time by the scientific community. The **scientific process** consists of the methods that scientists use to gather information and solve problems. In this context, the term **attitudes** refers to the way a person approaches a scientific problem. Each of these components is described in the following sections.

Scientific Content

Conceptually, science content is often divided into the **physical sciences** (which include physics, chemistry, geology, and astronomy) and the **biological sciences** (biology, botany, and zoology). At first glance, these topics may seem more appropriate for the high school curriculum than the early childhood classroom. However, teachers can find many opportunities to build developmentally appropriate science content into their work with young children. The following examples should help clarify this point.

Early Physics Experiences. **Physics** can be defined as "the science of matter and energy and of interactions between the two" (Chaille & Britain, 2003, p. 76). When we provide children with opportunities to discover the

Cooking is an important science activity.

physical properties of objects, they are learning physics concepts. Sprung (1996) provides three examples of appropriate physics activities:

- *Ramp experiments* provide materials that allow children to roll objects down ramps that they construct. Children learn about the properties of inclined planes.
- *Water experiments* provide materials that allow children to explore the properties of water. For example, funnels of different sizes allow children to experiment with the rate at which water moves through varying diameters.
- *Tinkering experiments* allow children to tinker with objects to see how they work. For example, children can take apart and put back together old appliances that adults have made safe.

For more information about cooking with kids, go to the Companion Website at www.prenhall.com/henniger, select Chapter 14, then choose Web Destinations.

Early Chemistry Experiences. **Chemistry** is defined as the study of substances and what happens when they are combined or come in contact with one another. Here are a few examples of chemistry activities for young children:

- *Cooking activities.* When mixing ingredients and cooking foods, teachers and children can observe and discuss the changes that are taking place in the materials used.

Into Practice . . .
Gardening with Young Children

Digging in the dirt is unquestionably a favorite activity for many young children. When combined with planting and growing vegetables, herbs, flowers, and other plants in a garden bed, young children have many wonderful opportunities for science learning. Clemens (1996) describes four different types of gardens that teachers can effectively use with young children:

Container Gardens. By using small containers such as milk cartons or purchased pots, teachers can convert nearly any spot into a small garden area for children. Each container can hold a different type of plant, or each child can have his own container garden.

Square-Foot Gardens. Another option is to mark off a small area that can be considered the garden spot for a specific class. Because each garden is small, more classrooms can participate in the fun of gardening. It does not take much space to enjoy creative gardening activities.

Conventional Gardens. Having a somewhat larger space where vegetables and flowers can be planted in

traditional rows can be another good option. It requires more upkeep but is workable if the space is available.

Raised Gardens. A raised garden bed is created by using some sort of wood or rock border that builds the garden bed up several inches above the ground. This arrangement makes the bed easier to plant and weed and can allow for the addition of soil amendments to aid in growing. Additionally, the soil warms earlier in the spring for planting.

Gardening has great potential for helping children learn science concepts and strategies. Children can predict, experiment, draw conclusions, observe patterns, and understand interactions between plants, insects, and birds. They can learn about the growth process of plants and how it varies between species. Children can study and understand the effects of rain, drought, wind, and sun. The opportunities for constructivist learning are virtually unlimited.

- *Mixing liquids of different viscosities.* Mix liquid corn oil and water, for example, and observe the results. To add an element of ecology, mix motor oil and water, and then try to figure out ways to separate the two liquids.

- *Engage in bubble-making activities.* The process of making bubble solutions can be a fun chemistry project. It often takes some effort to get the best solution. Using different items to blow bubbles adds an element of physics to the project.

Early Zoology Experiences. Zoology is the study of animals. Children love the opportunity to feed, hold, and learn more about all sorts of living creatures. Guinea pigs, rabbits, mice, hamsters, turtles, frogs, lizards, and gerbils are examples of animals that teachers can bring into the early childhood classroom for children to study as part of the zoology curriculum. Field trips to the zoo or a local farm can provide additional opportunities for learning about animals.

The examples presented here illustrate that scientific content does not have to be mysterious or foreign to young children. Teachers can develop similar methods for teaching geology, astronomy, and botany concepts to young children. Strong early childhood programs have been presenting children with op-

Celebrating Play . . .
Block Play and Science

Although there are many materials in the early childhood classroom that can be used for hands-on science learning, unit blocks are among the best alternatives for all ages. Mary Moffitt (1996), in a classic book on block play, says it this way:

> (S)cience content is better learned through the development of processes of inquiry, such as observing, comparing, classifying, predicting, and interpreting. Block building is a medium that is particularly well adapted for children to use these processes. Children's scientific thinking is stimulated as they discover and invent new forms, compare and classify different sizes and shapes, test ideas of "What will happen if. . . ?," or learn to use clues to predict outcomes because they have become familiar with the properties of the blocks with which they build. (p. 27)

She describes how children who play with blocks learn about their properties, such as size, shape, and weight, and then use this knowledge as they construct during their play. As they build, children are learning about their block structure as a system and the importance of the various elements to that system, which are both important scientific concepts. They are also learning about the interaction of forces within a system. Gravity, for example, influences such things as equilibrium, balance, and stability. In block play, children are also learning about space as they build up or create a pattern on the floor. Beginning measurement skills are practiced as they compare the length, height, and depth of block structures. Children develop basic understandings of architectural forms as they create tunnels, build bridges, and add ramps to their block structures. Because block building is an open-ended activity, children have many opportunities for engaging in creative thinking and scientific reasoning.

1. Finish reading this section of the chapter on science learning in the early childhood classroom. Then think about the possibilities for teaching important science concepts through the use of unit blocks. Do you think blocks are a useful tool in science learning?

2. Although not commonly found in the primary classroom, do you think blocks could be effectively used for science learning at that level? Why or why not?

portunities such as these to study scientific content since the beginning of this century (Sprung, 1996).

The Scientific Process

The processes used to study science are even more important than the content. Early childhood specialists need to promote the same techniques that scientists themselves use in their inquiries. This process consists of the following steps:

1. *Identify a problem for investigation.* Scientists must first recognize that a situation needs to be studied. Teachers can help young children identify problems through the use of simple questions or statements like, "Abby, do you know what a spider eats?"

2. *Collect data.* Once a problem is identified, a scientist works to collect information that may be useful in solving the problem. For young children, practicing good observation techniques is a primary way to collect data.

3. *Generate possible solutions to problems.* Following the collection of data, scientists formulate several hypotheses or solutions for the problems they face. Likewise, play situations provide many opportunities for children to generate answers to the problems they face.

4. *Test solutions.* Some potential solutions simply will not work, while others are only partially successful. The only way to work through a problem is to keep trying until success is achieved. Adults can help children know that it is normal to fail many times before finding an option that works.

5. *Draw conclusions and share with others.* Once the testing has taken place, the scientist summarizes his findings and shares the results of his investigations with others.

Developing Scientific Attitudes

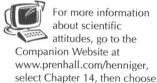

For more information about scientific attitudes, go to the Companion Website at www.prenhall.com/henniger, select Chapter 14, then choose Web Destinations.

Scientists approach problems with attitudes or ways of thinking that help them succeed. These approaches do not come easily to young children, and they will need assistance in using them. Teachers can model these attitudes while providing the guidance necessary to ensure that children use these approaches themselves. Wolfinger (1994) identifies five qualities that are essential to scientific investigations:

- *Objectivity.* This is perhaps the most difficult attitude to model and encourage in children. Basically, objectivity is the ability to look at all sides of an issue before making a decision. Many adults struggle with being objective. Children, because of their egocentrism during the early childhood years, also find this difficult. Adults must work hard to model appropriate objectivity as they work with children.

- *Willingness to suspend judgment.* A scientist waits until all of the evidence is in before making a decision. The adult must again be a good model by demonstrating a willingness to suspend judgment in problems encountered with children.

- *Skepticism.* Although this word often carries a negative connotation, the skeptic is one who questions all things. Rather than simply accepting the first idea that comes to mind, the scientist questions, searches for additional information,

Celebrating Diversity . . .
Helping All Children Learn Math and Science

Because of the importance of mathematics and science in today's world, all children must have the opportunity to succeed in these fields. Unfortunately, however, statistics indicate that this currently is not the case. For example, although women represent 45 percent of the total workforce, only 13 percent are scientists and engineers (Shaw & Blake, 1998). In mathematics performance, White students have consistently achieved higher scores than their Black or Hispanic peers, and Asian American students perform better than Whites (Viadero, 2000).

What can be done to improve this situation? Although attitudes change slowly, and it will be difficult to improve conditions quickly, the following two ideas can be important first steps.

Equal Opportunities to Participate

Most teachers intuitively feel that they encourage boys, girls, all cultures, and all socioeconomic groups to participate at the same level in science and math activities. However, research suggests this is not the case (American Association for the Advancement of Science, 1999). For example, consider the way teachers usually set up a block center. The accessories are typically those that interest boys: trucks, airplanes, zoo animals, and so on. When the block center includes materials more attractive to girls, both genders will use it to learn important math and science concepts. Teachers also need to become more aware of how

effectively they are verbally encouraging children to engage in science and math activities. Either videotaping or audiotaping a portion of the day can help uncover problem spots.

Get the Support of Parents

Parents play a significant role in all of child development. They make a big difference in how children perceive the importance of science and mathematics. If parents support the value of these subjects, assist with simple learning experiences around the home, and encourage play and reading activities to replace unregulated television viewing, children will be much more successful in mathematics and science. Unfortunately, this role is often hard for many parents who were themselves low achievers in these subjects. Thoughtful parent education and involvement are needed to correct this difficult situation.

---

1. Spend some time working with a young child who is struggling in science or math. Try to find ways to make the child feel (s)he can succeed.

2. Talk to a teacher about ways she tries to encourage children to engage in math and science activities.

3. Based on your previous work, do you think that helping all children learn math and science will be a significant issue for you as a future teacher? Why or why not?

and critically evaluates the available data. The teacher can guide children through this process as they approach science activities.

-   *Respect for the environment.* Scientific inquiry should never be damaging to any part of the natural environment. Taking fallen leaves on a nature walk rather than stripping live ones from a tree, keeping insects alive for observation and study rather than killing them, and using organic methods for controlling insects in a garden bed are all examples of environmentally friendly approaches to science activities.

-   *Positive approach to failure.* When students make predictions for solutions to a problem, many will prove to be wrong. However, much is learned from failure. It helps refine an understanding of the problem and may lead to a future solution. Adults need to work hard to let children know that it is perfectly acceptable to make predictions that are wrong and should help children learn from their misperceptions.

Young Children and Social Studies

An understanding of self begins during the first year of life.

For more information about the content of social studies, go to the Companion Website at www.prenhall.com/henniger, select Chapter 14, then choose Web Destinations.

Social studies help children understand relationships between people and environmental factors that influence their lives. In the adult world, this broad topic includes the disciplines of history, psychology, economics, sociology, anthropology, geography, and political science. Young children are constantly engaged in the process of learning about human relationships and the factors that influence them.

Developmentally, children begin their lives learning to relate to their primary caregivers. Crying, smiling, touching, staring, and vocalizing are early attempts to understand and communicate with parents and significant others. Gradually, children begin to expand their sphere of learning about people, relationships, and the environment. Developing an understanding of self and family, relating to friends and relatives, and developing relationships in school are all examples of this growing interest in broader social studies learnings. The "Observing Development" feature at the end of this chapter provides opportunities to observe the child's understanding of self and others, reflect on how to help children achieve this understanding, and apply strategies to create an environment that supports this aspect of development.

Understanding Self

The young child's social studies interests begin with an understanding of self. Although this is a lifelong process for each of us, it is during the early childhood years that children become aware of their physical, emotional, and intellectual selves and begin to understand how they are similar to and different from others. Much of this learning about self is informal and comes from interactions with parents, teachers, peers, and others. At the same time, more structured experiences help children learn about themselves. Hamilton, Flemming, and Hicks (1990) suggest the following categories for this study of self:

This is my body.

I belong to someone.

My family is special.

I can change by growing.

I can change by learning.

I can change by dressing differently.

I can change by getting sick/well.

I can change by acting differently.

Some things I cannot change.

A closer look at one of these categories may help clarify the kinds of planned events that help children develop a sense of self. A study of children's physical selves (the first category mentioned) might include the following activities:

- *Create body art.* In the art center, children can create their own handprints and footprints and can have an adult trace their bodies on large sheets of paper for decoration.
- *Take photos.* Take photographs of children in the class, discuss similarities and differences at group time, and then mount the pictures on a bulletin board so that children can study them in more detail. Or use a digital camera to create a computerized bulletin board for study and sharing with others.
- *Read stories.* Collect several books that talk about children's physical selves, and read them at group time. Two examples are *Teach Me About Series: My Body* (Berry, 1986) and *Bodies* (Brenner, 1970). Make the books available during center time for children to browse.
- *Sing songs.* Many songs help children understand their physical selves. Some examples include "Head, Shoulders, Knees and Toes," "You Are Special" (Mr. Rogers), and "Getting to Know Myself" (Hap Palmer).

Understanding Others

Throughout the early years, children are expanding their knowledge of human relationships as they interact with parents, teachers, peers, and others. Understanding relationships within the family is an important starting point for this growing knowledge base. Families influence almost every aspect of the young child's early development and generate much interest as a topic of discussion in the classroom. Some ideas for the study of families include:

- *Family of the week.* Make sure each family in your classroom has a special week when they can share with others elements of their lives at home. Invite parents/caregivers and siblings into the classroom; have the family create a bulletin board, family scrapbook, or videotape that helps others know about them; encourage parents/caregivers to share occupations, hobbies, and family traditions.
- *Holiday celebrations.* Every family is shaped by their cultural roots, and this can be celebrated through the sharing of special holiday traditions. Take advantage of the diversity of families within the classroom to learn about similarities and differences between cultures.
- *Family volunteers.* Encouraging parents, relatives, and older siblings to spend time helping out in the classroom can be an effective way for children to learn about family differences through casual interactions.
- *Family foods.* Have families sign up to provide special snack foods that are popular in the home. Food is a great socializer and can be another way to initiate conversations about similarities and differences among families.
- *Family jobs.* Parents/caregivers can share with the class their work responsibilities. A photo essay, videotape, field trip, or personal sharing time (with appropriate work props) can be a productive way to learn more about families.

A second important component of understanding others is the study of community relationships. A frequent starting point for this discussion is learning

Into Practice...
Constructivist Social Studies

One interesting way to involve children in valuable social studies experiences is to provide them with handmade cloth dolls with no facial features. Wien, Stacey, Keating, Rowlings, and Cameron (2002) describe the 6-month constructivist curriculum they developed with children from 27 months to 3½ years. After teachers noticed that many of the children were frequently taking dolls and washing, feeding, combing, and carrying them around the classroom, each child in the program was offered a handmade cloth doll without any distinguishing facial features. "Art consultant Rhonda Wakely-Fortin designed and constructed the dolls in a resplendent variety of skin tones and body shapes, from skinny mahogany to plump peach. She also devised simple shapes for facial features and hairpieces, which she enclosed in plastic zipper bags" (p. 33). The intent behind these dolls was to create a sense of surprise and mystery in very young children and give them opportunities to think about and discuss what they saw.

This project, based on the Reggio Emilia approach (see Chapter 3), began with teachers audiotaping the conversations of children as they were presented with the dolls. Without exception, the first thing children noticed and discussed was the lack of eyes, making comments like "My doll cannot see you" (p. 34). Children began a rather lengthy study of their own eyes. They then made decisions about the color of eyes their own dolls should have and glued on appropriate colors of felt pieces. A field trip to a local optometrist provided additional opportunities to discuss eyes and eyeglasses. After several weeks, the discussion and resulting activities moved on to the topic of hair. Children were invited to come along when one of their teachers got a haircut at a local hair salon. A book was later created from photographs, drawings, and children's comments about the visit. With permission, a lock of hair from each child was cut and placed on laminated index cards and added into the book. Hairpieces from the art consultant were also placed on a table for children to glue onto their dolls. As the project continued, further investigations included a study of noses and mouths and the construction of doll beds. Throughout this experience, these very young children were constructing new knowledge about themselves and others through the use of their handmade dolls.

about community helpers. What does a police officer do? How does a firefighter control a burning building? Why does the doctor listen to my chest with her stethoscope? Children are fascinated by these issues and many more. Taking a field trip to these community work sites or inviting these workers into the classroom makes for exciting social studies learning.

Many aspects of community relationships remain hidden to children unless we take the time to point them out. Where does the garbage go once the truck picks it up? How do grocery stores work? Who fixes the city street when it needs repair? Children are curious about these issues and more. Adults should make sure that the early childhood program has many opportunities to address the complexities of community relationships.

Integrating Cognitive Learning Throughout the Curriculum

It should be obvious at this point that cognitive development occurs throughout the day as children interact with adults, peers, and materials in their environment. Intellectual understanding is not limited to specific topics taught at set times. Rather, all that the child does, hears, and sees provides the raw material for cognitive growth.

Every center within the early childhood classroom and in the outdoor environment encourages intellectual development. Playing with blocks, painting in the art center, digging in the garden, and reading books in the library center are all examples of activities that can lead to cognitive growth. As the teacher prepares each of these centers, he needs to plan for developmentally appropriate materials and activities that enhance learning opportunities for young children. These preparations will vary with the ages and developmental abilities of the children in the program.

Infant/Toddler Materials and Activities

For more information about infant/toddler learning, go to the Companion Website at www.prenhall.com/henniger, select Chapter 14, then choose Web Destinations.

Piaget (Ginsburg & Opper, 1969) describes the infant/toddler's cognitive functioning as sensorimotor intelligence. By this he means that children at this age are learning about their world through sensory and motor exploration. Sights, sounds, tastes, and physical manipulation provide many opportunities for intellectual growth.

To integrate cognitive learning throughout the infant/toddler environment, caregivers need to provide materials and activities that children can experience through sensory/motor activity. Some examples follow:

- Mobiles in cribs, pictures of human faces around the room, and picture books to stimulate visual exploration
- Blocks, stacking toys, and push-pull toys for physical manipulation
- Balls made of different materials, texture sheets, water play activities; cornmeal, rice, or dried peas in a dishpan; food experiences that include a variety of textures for tactile stimulation
- Talking to and holding children to develop relationships and communicate caring
- Music-making materials, sound discrimination toys for auditory stimulation, and recorded music

Children 3 Through 5

As discussed in Chapters 9 and 10, most preschool and kindergarten classrooms are organized into centers with schedules that allow children to spend large blocks of time playfully exploring the indoor environment and playground. Teachers should provide materials for each center that enhance children's cognitive understandings. Examples for each center follow.

Block Center. Unit blocks are among the best materials in the early childhood classroom for cognitive learning. Counting, shape recognition, understanding stability and balance, and developing beginning mapping skills are just a few of the many learning opportunities (Hirsch, 1996). In addition, the accessories added can help facilitate other learning. For example, the teacher can place multicultural family figures in the center to help children realize that families are diverse. With the assistance of the teacher, children can begin to discuss and understand these diversity issues.

Art Center. Providing paints of different textures and colors and a variety of brushes and applicators allows children to explore the properties of the art materials and how they can be used to create different paintings. Conceptually, children learn to recognize patterns, identify colors and shapes, and develop an understanding of symmetry as they playfully explore these materials (Schirrmacher, 2002).

Manipulative Center. Legos, Bristle Blocks, Tinker Toys, puzzles, simple matching games, and most of the typical materials found in the manipulative area help children develop concepts of color, size, and shape. Children practice patterning, one-to-one correspondence, and counting skills as they work with manipulatives as well.

Book Center. The pictures and text in any good children's book have great potential for stimulating conceptual growth. Understanding relationships, specific information on science and mathematics topics (e.g., different types of birds), and books addressing feelings are just a few of the possibilities for learning. Providing a variety of books that focus on specific themes and are changed regularly will stimulate many learning opportunities.

Dramatic Play/Housekeeping Center. As children play out themes in these centers, they learn properties of real-world materials through the use of toys (e.g., a toy stethoscope), grow in their understanding of roles (doctors, nurses, and other health workers), and gain information from other players ("Hey, doctors don't do it that way, they . . . ").

Music Center. Play with musical instruments can be useful in building conceptual knowledge. Striking a xylophone, for example, and then discussing what causes the sound can be an excellent learning opportunity. Many songs (e.g., "Five Little Speckled Frogs") also contain conceptual information that children learn as they sing.

Discovery Center. The science materials in this center have clear potential for stimulating cognitive development. Examining, classifying, and reading about different rocks is one example. Measuring a plant's growth and charting it on a graph are other possible learning activities for this center.

The Primary Grades

Although interest in other options is growing, the traditional elementary school curriculum tends to teach cognitive subjects in isolation from one another. That is, mathematics, science, and social studies are each taught at a distinct time during the school day. This more-segmented approach is in direct conflict with the constructivist approach. The child in the constructivist classroom learns through manipulation and discovery, which is much more open-ended in terms of outcomes. Any given task generally provides opportunities for cognitive growth in many different areas.

One highly appropriate technique that engages children in constructivist learning is called the *project approach*. Children who have decided to pursue a particular subject in more depth form a small group to take on a project (see Chapters 3 and 11 for more detailed descriptions). Katz (1994) describes a project involving an investigation of balls. For this project, a kindergarten teacher asked the children to collect from home, friends, relatives, and others as many old balls as they could. She developed a study web by asking what the children might like to know about the balls. The children collected 31 different kinds of balls, including a gumball, a cotton ball, a globe of the earth, and an American football (which led to a discussion of the concepts of sphere, hemisphere, and cone).

The children then formed subgroups to examine specific questions. One group studied the surface texture of each ball and made rubbings to represent

Project learning allows children to study topics in depth and learn from their peers.

their findings; another measured the circumference of each ball with pieces of string; and a third tried to determine what each ball was made of.

As children engaged in their study of balls, new questions arose, groups shared information, and the children learned concepts of science, mathematics, and social studies. Excited children learned rapidly from this project.

Although not all experiences in the primary classroom can be organized around projects, this option clearly works well and leads to important conceptual growth. By beginning with student interests and assisting children as they construct their projects, exciting learning opportunities can take place.

 Parental Roles in Cognitive Development

Parents are children's first and best teachers. They play crucial roles in cognitive development. Parents need to support the importance of intellectual growth, assist in classroom learning, and engage children at home in cognitive tasks.

Supporting the Importance of Cognitive Development

Parents, teachers, and community members generally agree about the importance of learning mathematics, science, and social studies concepts and readily concede the values of cognitive development. Achievement in these areas is a major factor needed for success in work and life.

The content and process of this learning, however, are less often agreed upon. Many of these differences of opinion come from the parents' own experiences as

Family Partnerships...
IFSP and IEP Meetings

As a future teacher of young children, you will need to participate in creating either an Individualized Family Service Plan (IFSP) or an Individualized Education Plan (IEP) for each of the children with special needs in your classroom. By federal law, every child identified with special needs must have a detailed learning plan developed and revised annually through group meetings between the classroom teacher, the special education teacher, other educational specialists (such as a speech therapist, occupational therapist, psychologist, physical therapist), and parents. Because of the critical role of families in early development, children under 3 and their families receive an IFSP (Bruder, 2000). After age 3, planning for children with special needs is usually in the form of an IEP.

Families are strongly encouraged to participate in the finalization of either the IFSP or IEP. While in many cases these meetings are friendly and collegial, other situations exist in which they are marked by considerable tension. These tensions can stem from a variety of sources. In some instances, school personnel fail to understand the heavy physical and emotional burdens families bear as they provide 24-hour care for their child with special needs.

Consequently, a relatively simple request from educational personnel for assistance from home can be met with anger or helplessness on the part of parents. Another source of tension comes when teachers and schools are unable to provide services that are either expected by parents or mandated by federal law. Due to limited funding and a lack of qualified personnel, many schools find it difficult to fully meet the needs of children with special needs. When this happens, educational personnel tend to get defensive while parents may experience frustration as the needs of their children go unmet. Careful planning and an understanding attitude can help reduce the tensions in these stressful meetings.

1. Choose a special need of interest to you and take some time to learn more about family stresses associated with that special need. What did you learn that could be shared with others?

2. You are more likely to resolve problems when they are addressed in a strong relationship. What could you do to strengthen your relationships with families that have children with special needs?

---

children. If social studies learning, for example, focused on the memorization of names, dates, and significant historical events, many parents might feel this is appropriate for their own children. "It worked for me," they think, "so why shouldn't it work for my kids?"

The past approaches focusing on rote learning, however, have proven to be ineffective for many children. The constructivist approach described earlier in this chapter is a much more positive technique for encouraging cognitive development (DeVries & Kohlberg, 1987; Kamii & DeVries, 1978). Because it is new to many parents, teachers need to spend time helping parents understand this approach. As they see constructivist learning in action, discuss the approach with others, read about its benefits, and observe the results of these efforts, parents can become strong advocates of this alternative to rote learning.

Assisting with Classroom Learning

Parents who can spend time helping out in the classroom are assisting with cognitive development. Reading to children, helping individual children with mathematics projects, and going on class field trips are examples of this support. More

 For more information about getting parents involved in mathematics learning, go to the Companion Website at www.prenhall.com/henniger, select Chapter 14, then choose Web Destinations.

mundane tasks like preparing materials for an art project or constructing a game help free up the teacher's time for more direct assistance in cognitive learning. The parents' presence in the classroom also sends children the message that their own work is important and motivates them to do their best.

Parents who are unavailable during the school day can help out at home by gathering the ingredients for the upcoming science project, saving materials for mathematics manipulatives, or making telephone calls for the field trip next week. These kinds of tasks give parents important roles to play when they cannot come into the classroom.

Home Learning Tasks

Parents have many unique opportunities to promote cognitive understanding outside the school environment. Often, however, parents do not take advantage of these opportunities because they fail to recognize the value of the many informal learning experiences they have. Setting the table for dinner, for example, gives young children the chance to count and practice one-to-one correspondence (one fork, spoon, and knife for each person) as they assist with a household chore. Likewise, a trip to the grocery store can be a great time to practice money concepts and discuss the rationale for buying some foods but not others.

Many teachers send parents lists of simple activities that can be built into daily life to promote cognitive development. These home learning tasks should be easy to prepare for and fun to do. Berger (2004) suggests many good ideas for home learning activities, including:

- *Cooking activities.* Have children help with cooking. It can teach number concepts, fractions, measurement, and much more.
- *Backyard science.* Encourage exploration outdoors for insects, leaves, and rocks. Plant seeds and bulbs in the garden. Children engaged in these kinds of activities are classifying, observing, and experimenting with variables as they play with the materials outdoors.
- *Play games with children.* Children, for example, can learn to discriminate between size, shape, and color as they play simple card-matching games. Parents often need suggestions for making competitive games more cooperative.
- *Visit museums.* Take time to explore the resources within the community, including museums of interest to children. When these experiences include things children can touch and manipulate, the interest will be greater. While providing many opportunities for learning, museums are wonderful opportunities for children to have meaningful experiences learning about history.

Summary

Goals of the Cognitive Curriculum

The goals of the early childhood mathematics, science, and social studies curricula include an emphasis on critical thinking, problem solving, and lifelong learning rather than an overemphasis on the learning of facts.

Observing Development • Understanding of Self and Others

Choose one of the age groups within early childhood (infants/toddlers, preschoolers, or primary-age children), *observe* **understanding of self and others** using the guidelines provided, *reflect* on what you saw and heard, and *apply* the appropriate strategies listed with the children you observed.

Observe	Reflect	Apply
Look for specific examples of:	*Think about and respond to the following questions:*	*Consider the following developmentally appropriate strategies for the age group you observed:*
Evidence that children are working on developing a better understanding of self (looking at self in the mirror; practicing use of arms, hands, legs, and body; language used; pictures drawn; play activities chosen; stories dictated or written; etc.)	How important is an understanding of self to overall development for young children? For people of all ages?	Verbalize aspects of self as you work with young children • Infant/toddler: "Yolanda, you have two beautiful brown eyes!" • Preschool: "Andre, you are really enjoying painting lately. It is good to see you in the art center." • Primary: "Jolene, your writing has improved so much since the beginning of the year. I appreciate all your hard work."
Evidence that children are working on developing a better understanding of others (observing others, language used, pictures drawn, play activities chosen, stories dictated or written, etc.)	Did you notice differences between children regarding their interest in understanding others? What might be the reasons for these differences?	Give children opportunities to interact with others • Infant/toddler: place two infants on the rug with similar play materials • Preschool: encourage two or more children to work on the same block structure, paint a mural, etc. • Primary: assign children to small groups for some activities each day
Equipment, materials, or activities that facilitate an understanding of self or others (mirrors, books, song such as "Head, Shoulders, Knees and Toes")	Are the equipment, materials, and activities available in an early childhood classroom an important part of how children learn about themselves and others?	Plan the environment so that children have opportunities to understand themselves and others better • Infant/toddler: read books like *More, More, More Said the Baby* that address issues related to self and others • Preschool: play a CD that provides music from different cultures • Primary: cluster the desks in groups of three or four so that children are naturally seated in small groups for much of the school day

To test your knowledge of this chapter's contents, go to the Companion Website at www.prenhall.com/henniger, select Chapter 14, then select Study Guide. Also see Chapter Overviews, Reflecting Essay Questions, Multimedia Explorations, and relevant Web Destinations.

The Constructivist Approach

While other instructional methods have value, the constructivist approach to mathematics, science, and social studies learning is emphasized in the early childhood classroom. Children typically learn best when they build their own knowledge of the world through manipulating real-world objects and interacting with other people.

Mathematics and Young Children

Mathematics learning for young children includes classification, seriation, patterning, number concepts, measurement, geometry, and problem-solving experiences.

Science Learning

An understanding of scientific content, process, and attitudes is essential to the science curriculum. When addressed in developmentally appropriate ways, the physical and biological sciences are all appropriate topics for discussion in the early childhood classroom.

Young Children and Social Studies

The social studies curriculum helps young children understand relationships between people and environmental factors that influence their lives. Knowledge of self and others are the two key elements of the early childhood social studies curriculum.

Integrating Cognitive Learning Throughout the Curriculum

It is important to integrate cognitive learning with other components of the early childhood curriculum at the infant/toddler, preschool, and primary-age levels.

Parental Roles in Cognitive Development

Parents play important roles in cognitive development during the early childhood years. Teachers must help them understand the important learning opportunities that exist at home and provide ideas for facilitating growth in cognitive development.

Multimedia Explorations and Activities . . .

Discovery Van: Learning Experience for Caregivers and Kids

Lawrence, Massachusetts, is a small town much like many others across America. Parents with young children who work in this community do not have many options for child care. Children are most often taken care of in child care homes, where one mother ends up caring for several children in the neighborhood. While providing good basic care, these settings frequently do not have the resources needed for creative learning experiences. The solution to this dilemma for Lawrence was the creation of a Discovery Van that travels throughout the community and provides art activities, a hands-on museum, and books for lending. Funded by local unions and employers, this van delivers to child care homes a rich assortment of materials that can be used for creative activities by caregivers and young children.

Research

Approximately 5 million American children are cared for in family child care homes. While many of these programs provide excellent care, they have access to limited resources and materials to use with young children. This activity is designed to give you exposure to creative options available in early childhood settings to enhance cognitive learning.

1. View the ABC News video segment titled "Discovery Van: Learning Experience for Caregivers and Kids."

2. Go to the Companion Website at www.prenhall.com/henniger and click on the Multimedia Explorations and Activities button for Chapter 14 for more information on this topic.

Reflect

Based on the research you previously conducted, consider the following issues:

- What materials and experiences are best for stimulating cognitive learning in young children? What makes them so useful in this regard?

- What materials and experiences in your community can teachers of young children use for free or at a minimal cost to stimulate thinking and learning?

- If you were a family child care home provider, in addition to costs, what issues would you need to consider before taking advantage of community resources for cognitive development?

Respond

Having learned more about creative options for stimulating cognitive development, consider implementing one or more of the following options:

1. Create a list of free field trips in your community that young children would enjoy and that stimulate mathematics, science, or social studies learning. For each option, give a paragraph description of the possible experiences children could have there. Share the results of your efforts with a teacher of young children.

2. Plan several creative activities for math, science, or social studies that require no expenditures and use materials found in any home. Share your ideas with others via the message board on the Companion Website for this text.

3. Identify community people who are willing to come into the classroom to stimulate children's cognitive understanding. An example would be a police officer. Share your list of specific names (also include a paragraph describing the things they are willing to do) with others in your class.

chapter

15

LANGUAGE AND LITERACY LEARNING

In this chapter you will

- Investigate the development of language in young children.
- Differentiate among the many linguistic systems children must master to understand language.
- Study techniques for facilitating language learning.
- Develop an understanding of the young child's emerging reading and writing skills.
- Review effective techniques and materials for language and literacy learning.

Your class of 4-year-olds is playing during their free choice time indoors. For the moment, children are productively interacting with peers and play materials, so you have time to step back and observe what is taking place. With a notepad in hand, you focus your attention on the play themes unfolding around you.

Blake and Abby are in the art center, involved in the fingerpainting activity there. "Ooo, ooo, ooo. Goo, goo, goo!" chimes Blake as he smears the shaving cream mix in large circular motions on his tray. "Boo, hoo, hoo. You're full of moo!" responds Abby as she looks up from her painting. Both children giggle and then return to their art project.

Terrance and Stuart pretend to be shopper and grocery clerk in the store set up in the dramatic play area. As Terrance brings his groceries up to Stuart for bagging, he says, "Say, you got any peanut butter? Ah love my peanut butter!" "Sorry," replies Stuart, "We're out. How about some beans?" "Nah, beans and me don't get along too well," responds Terrance. "I'll buy what I've got." They continue to dramatize their play theme while chatting.

Tina is in the book corner with a parent volunteer, and the two of them are absorbed in reading the book Mike Mulligan and His Steam Shovel (Burton, 1939). They have read the story once and are just beginning a second reading at Tina's request. This time, she stops the parent periodically to ask questions about the steam shovel and Mike Mulligan. Tina is fascinated by the story.

The children in the class previously described are engaged in language and literacy learning. No direct instruction is taking place, but as they play and communicate, children are intuitively learning how language works, practicing its many nuances, and gaining insights into the meanings of written language.

Language and literacy competence are at the heart of the human experience. The ability to communicate with others enables us to learn and grow, while enriching our lives. Adults working with children during the early childhood years need considerable knowledge about language and literacy learning so that they can facilitate these important experiences.

Language and literacy learning, though clearly related, are generally thought of as complementary processes. **Language** can be defined as either oral or hand-signed communication between humans. Every culture arbitrarily assigns meaning to sounds. Then people within the culture use combinations of these basic units to create words and sentences that communicate messages to others. Rules govern the ways in which sounds are used to form words and how words are combined to form sentences. Speakers of the language intuitively (but usually not consciously) understand these rules.

Literacy concerns language in written form. Literate people are those who can read and write the language of their culture. Cultures arbitrarily assign meaning to written symbols and construct systems to organize these symbols on the written page. Literacy is the ability to interpret the intended message of these symbols (reading) and to use them to communicate information to others (writing).

Language Learning

The process of learning language may appear effortless, but in reality it is a major undertaking for young children. Those who study language acquisition have considerable difficulty even explaining it. This section should help you understand how children learn language and the strategies adults can use to assist in the process.

Theoretical Perspectives

Theorists have proposed three different views of how children learn language. **Behaviorists** argue that children acquire language through the same stimulus-response connections that influence learning in all areas (Skinner, 1957). Children hear language spoken by parents and others, imitate that speech, and are rewarded for their efforts. This positive reinforcement encourages them to communicate more.

While behaviorist theory helps explain some aspects of language learning, other perspectives add further insight into how children develop linguistic competence. The **maturationist** theory suggests that every child, regardless of culture, intellectual ability, or socioeconomic status, inherits the genetic capability for language. When children are exposed to language, this innate ability, or **language acquisition device (LAD),** allows them to gradually make sense of the rules for oral communication (Chomsky, 1965).

A third view of language learning is the **interactionist** approach. Proponents of this theory suggest that language acquisition combines an innate ability with environmental influences. Both factors interact in complex ways as children learn language. The writings of both Piaget (1959) and Vygotsky (1962) support the interactionist view.

Language Development

Children vary in the rate at which they learn language, but eventually almost every child masters the complex linguistic system in which she is immersed. This process begins in infancy and continues throughout the early childhood years.

For more information about language development, go to the Companion Website at www.prenhall.com/henniger, select Chapter 15, then choose Web Destinations.

Infancy. Even newborn infants work to communicate with others and are beginning to learn about their linguistic system (Kuhl, 1993). Crying is the earliest form of infant communication, and parents quickly learn the many different messages children send in this way: "I'm wet." "Feed me!" "I'm sleepy."

At the same time, infants are attending to the oral language of caregivers and others. They notice changes in sounds, rhythm, and intonation. At about 3 or 4 months of age, children start to coo and babble. Gradually, infants start to recognize and babble the sounds of the specific language they must eventually master (Kuhl, 1993).

Near the end of the first year of life, children begin to speak words. To the great thrill of their parents, "mama" or "dadda" are often the earliest words spoken. Many infants have expanded their initial vocabulary to about a dozen words by their first birthday.

Celebrating Diversity...
Supporting English Language Learners

Growing numbers of young children come to the early childhood classroom speaking languages other than English at home. Data from the U.S. Census Bureau (2000) indicate that nearly one in five American families speaks a language other than English at home, with Spanish, Chinese, Tagalog (Filipino), Korean, Vietnamese, Arabic, Hindi, and Russian being the most common (Banks, 2002). Teachers of young children must be prepared to support these English Language Learners as they work to master a new language.

Lake and Pappamihiel (2003) identify four main components of a developmentally appropriate language environment for young English Language Learners (ELL):

1. *Conversation.* Teachers must make time to engage English Language Learners in direct conversation to stimulate their understanding and use of oral language. While avoiding overcorrecting and judging these children, regular and natural conversations help children practice and build confidence in their English speaking abilities.

2. *Understanding and acceptance.* Much has been written about the process of second language acquisition, and teachers will need to understand and accept the additional steps children must take. Lake and Pappamihiel (2003) emphasize that even though young children take only 1 to 2 years to develop basic interpersonal communication skills, it often requires 5 to 8 years to reach the point where they have the language competence needed for academic success.

3. *Experience.* As with all children, English Language Learners need meaningful experiences that they can then use as the basis for productive oral language communications. Teachers should plan a variety of meaningful experiences with these English Language Learners in mind.

4. *Children's literature.* Quality children's literature that values the differences between children can help young English Language Learners feel good about themselves and stimulate oral language learning. A collection of books like *Someone Special, Just Like You* (Brown, 1991) will add important insights for the whole class.

---

1. Think about the positive aspects of having English Language Learners in the classroom. How will these children enrich your life and the lives of other children?

2. Read an article about English Language Learners and then think about the implications for your future teaching. What changes will you need to make in how you teach when you have English Language Learners in your room?

Toddlerhood. Toddlers proceed rapidly in their acquisition of language. By the end of the second year of life, children have expanded their vocabularies up to as many as 50 words. Many of these words carry much more meaning than the adult equivalent. This is referred to as **holophrastic speech.** For example, "More!" may well mean "Give me more milk right now! I'm still hungry!"

As toddlers mature, they begin the process of stringing two words together to form simple sentences. A toddler who wants to go in the car with Daddy, for example, may say, "Me go!" Often referred to as **telegraphic speech** because of limited word usage, these two-word sentences are a major step forward in the young child's use of language.

The Preschool Years. The language understanding of children during the preschool years continues to rapidly expand. Vocabulary increases at an amazing rate, with new words added almost daily. Sentences move quickly beyond the two-word stage to more complex combinations. These young children are refining their understanding of the rules of communication and becoming more proficient at holding a conversation with others.

The Primary Grades. Growth in vocabulary and sentence complexity continues throughout the primary grades. By this time, children have mastered most of the grammar needed for oral language communication. They are adding the finer nuances of linguistics: learning about humor, multiple meanings for words and phrases, and the importance of intonation in communications.

Linguistic Systems

When adults study language, it is generally divided into five main elements or systems. Children must master each of these systems to become competent in communicating with others. Without any direct instruction, youngsters learn about phonology, morphology, semantics, syntax, and pragmatics (Kostelnik, Soderman, & Whiren, 1999; McNeil, 1970; Seefeldt, 1999).

Phonology is the system of sounds used to make up words in a specific language. Cultures assign arbitrary meaning to these sounds, and speakers use consistent rules to combine these sounds into words. Phonology also includes an understanding of the intonations used to add meanings to combinations of sounds.

A second linguistic system is referred to as **morphology.** Language learners must understand the rules for combining sounds to form words within a specific language. The rules for creating plurals (*apples*) and tense (*went* for past tense; *will go* for future tense) are examples of morphology. This system is complex and varies within a single language as well as from one language to the next.

The **semantics** of language is a third system children must master. This involves the meanings given to words. For some words like *hat*, this is a relatively simple task; other words vary in meaning depending on the context. How many different meanings, for example, exist for the word *nurse?* Because of the literalness of young children, many words or phrases are difficult to comprehend. "I've got a frog in my throat" may actually be a frightening concept to a 3-year-old struggling to understand the semantics of this statement.

A fourth linguistic system is called **syntax** and refers to the procedures for combining words into phrases and sentences. Even nonsense words acquire some meaning when placed in phrases and sentences. "The crog slagged zuppily across the waggor" contains many nonsense words, but even young children can find meaning in this sentence because of the syntax, or placement of the words.

The final linguistic system is **pragmatics;** it consists of the understandings necessary for adapting language to different social situations. A 5-year-old learns that talking to a baby is different from interacting with peers, for example. Recognizing that "please" and "thank you" are expected in many social interactions is another aspect of pragmatics. Children gradually learn that certain words, phrases, and styles of communication are appropriate in some situations and not in others.

Facilitating Language Learning

Maria Montessori (Lillard, 1972) promoted the idea of **sensitive periods** in the child's life. During these blocks of time, children have a keen interest in certain aspects of their development. The early childhood years are generally considered the sensitive period for language; therefore, adults should do all they can to assist children in the development of linguistic competence.

There are many opportunities for informal conversations throughout the school day.

Informal Conversations. During the early childhood years, one important way for adults to help children develop communicative competence is through informal conversations. These interchanges do not need to be long or carefully planned ahead of time, but when teachers use opportunities to engage in casual interactions, children can learn a great deal about language and the world around them. Some suggestions for making these conversations more productive follow:

- *Show interest by listening carefully to what the child has to say.* Give the child your full attention as he speaks. This will encourage further discussion by the child.

- *Use open-ended questions to get the child to elaborate on what has already been said.* In response to "Grammy's in Vermont," you could say, "That sounds like fun. What is she doing there?"

- *Build language into routines.* Toileting, eating, and sleeping activities are significant components of the day for very young children. Adults should take advantage of these times to talk positively with the child as they assist in meeting the child's needs.

- *Model good communication by speaking courteously and using good grammar and proper word choice.* Make sure both the verbal and nonverbal messages you send do not contradict one another.

- *Build on the child's interests as you communicate.* This will help make conversation attractive to the child. For example, a simple response to a child interested in insects might be, "Janet, I found a new book on insects yesterday in the school library. Would you like to look at it during silent reading?"

- *Expand vocabulary by using words that children may not know but that are relevant to their lives.* Labeling the emotions children express, using precise terms for science and math concepts, and identifying occupations within the community are examples.

Celebrating Play . . .
Developing Language Skills Through Physical Activity

When playful physical activities are combined with language training, young children benefit. Connor-Kuntz and Dummer (1996) studied children 4 to 6 years of age in special education, Head Start, and typical preschool classes. They provided some of these students with guided physical activities and gave the rest both the guided physical activities and additional language skills training.

Children in the latter group received natural opportunities to learn language concepts related to their physical activities such as

- Around
- Over and under
- Front and behind
- Above and below
- Distance
- Height
- Shape

Children receiving these additional language experiences, including those with impaired cognitive and language abilities, showed improvements in their language skills. Furthermore, these children showed equivalent gains in their motor skills to those receiving the physical training alone.

1. Which of the theories presented in this book would support the results of this study? Review Chapters 2 and 3 and then discuss this with your classmates.

2. Do the results of this study make sense to you? Why should playful physical activities combined with adult-led language enrichment lead to improved language skills? Discuss this with others.

- *Be sensitive to children.* Listen when that is needed, lead the conversation when it is appropriate to do so, and try to avoid interrupting productive play time or interactions with peers to engage in conversation.

Play. Childhood play provides numerous opportunities for language learning. Garvey (1990) describes how children engage in playing with language. As they vocalize, children explore how to combine sounds, learn about syntax, and experiment with fantasy and nonsense. Garvey shares the following example of two 5-year-olds playing with language:

> Girl 1: Mommy, Mommy, I got new friends called Dool, Sol, Ta.
>
> Girl 2: Dool, Sue, and Ta? (both girls laugh)
>
> Girl 1: Those are funny names, aren't they?
>
> Girl 2: No, its Poopi, Daigi, and Dia . . . Diarrhea. (both laugh again) (Garvey, 1990, p. 71)

Language is also an important part of the play experience itself. Children use **metacommunication** statements to structure and organize the play. Designating the make-believe properties of an object ("Let's pretend this stick is a fishing pole."), assigning roles ("You be the daddy, I'll be the baby."), and planning the story line ("First, we'll cook dinner, and then we'll sit down and eat.") are all examples of metacommunication statements for enacting play sequences.

The language used in play provides additional opportunities for developing linguistic competence. The conversation necessary to engage in pretend play is one good example of this language usage: "Hush baby! Mommy is on the telephone." Children must communicate in other types of play as well. Two girls constructing a block tower, for example, use language to discuss their intent and rationale for placement of blocks, ask each other for feedback as they proceed, and discuss alternatives while they build.

For more information about good books to read aloud, go to the Companion Website at www.prenhall.com/henniger, select Chapter 15, then choose Web Destinations.

Language-Rich Experiences. The motivation to expand vocabulary and communicate with others is greatly enhanced when children have adventures that excite them in some way. Teachers can provide children with a diversity of experiences to assist in language development. Good books can be that kind of opportunity for many children. By touching on issues that are meaningful or interesting to children, books become a starting point for further investigation and communication.

Field trips also have the potential to spark children's interests in a topic. Traveling to a nearby pond to collect tadpoles, insects, and underwater plant life could be an excellent starting point for a science unit and a great way to generate individual and group discussion on these topics. Every community has many potentially beneficial sites for field trips.

Taking advantage of people and events in the community may be yet another language-rich experience for young children. For example, a retired volunteer who is good at storytelling could come into the classroom and talk about his experiences as a child. Participating in a community-sponsored musical concert or going to see a play or puppet show for young children can provide other experiences that children can talk about at home or in the classroom.

Into Practice...
Group Storytelling

Once children have experienced quality storytelling by the teacher, Whaley (2002) suggests that group storytelling can help motivate young children to engage in this experience themselves. She provides several ideas for group storytelling:

1. *Round-robin or sentence stories.* Select story topics that are familiar to young children (animal stories and fables are good choices), begin a story, and then ask children to determine what will come next. Depending on developmental abilities, it may be best to begin with children deciding the next steps as a group and later have individual children add a sentence at a time to the story.

2. *Theme stories.* Have children choose the theme for the story (e.g., a story about monkeys) and then proceed to create your own story as a teacher, focusing on the identified theme.

3. *Descriptive stories.* Once children have gained confidence in round-robin storytelling, help them expand their language through the use of more descriptive words to tell their stories. Instead of "The cow walked across the street," you could encourage them to say, "The brown and white cow walked slowly across the busy street as cars honked their horns in anger."

4. *Picture stories.* Children can choose photographs, or pictures from magazines, to be the starting point for their stories. As they describe what they see and think is happening, their story unfolds.

5. *Grab bag stories.* Prepare a bag full of familiar objects. Have children take one from the bag to tell their own story or add to a group story already in progress.

For more information about facilitating language learning through storytelling, go to the Companion Website at www.prenhall.com/henniger, select Chapter 15, then choose Web Destinations.

The Power of Storytelling. Storytelling is an important tool for language and literacy learning that should be an integral part of the teaching/learning process for young children. Isbell (2002) states:

> The experience of hearing a story told is more personal and connected to the listener. The *storyteller* can maintain eye contact and adapt the telling of the story to specific listeners. . . . Listeners, regardless of their language skills or reading abilities, can understand the story because it is communicated through words, vocal intonation, gestures, facial expressions, and body movement. . . . Storytelling promotes expressive language development—in oral and written forms—and presents new vocabulary and complex language in a powerful form that inspires children to emulate the model they have experienced. (p. 26)

Almost any book can be told as a story, but the best options typically include repetitive phrases, unusual words, and actions that the teacher can incorporate into the story. Teachers can also make up their own stories or tell children about some of their own or others' interesting life experiences. With practice, storytelling can be an easy and enjoyable part of the day for early educators. Raines and Isbell (1999) and Isbell and Raines (2000) provide tips for storytelling and provide over 30 stories for teachers who are interested in using storytelling with young children.

Language Learning Materials

Virtually every toy and piece of equipment in the early childhood classroom can lead to language learning. Some options, however, are particularly important in stimulating linguistic exploration. One such material is the flannelboard story. For younger children, having a board covered with flannel material and figures that relate to popular books helps them to retell familiar story lines. Older children can benefit from a collection of flannel pieces that they can use to tell their own stories. Teachers can either make or purchase commercial flannel pieces to use in the classroom.

Another material closely related to the flannelboard is the magnetic board. As the name implies, pieces stick to a metal board rather than flannel. Using magnetic strips, adults can create figures that children can manipulate to tell familiar or invented stories.

Puppets are another versatile material that children use for extensive language experiences. Handmade and commercial puppets stimulate increased verbal interactions in the classroom. Many quiet children end up being much more verbal with a puppet on their hand.

Dramatic play props create additional opportunities for language development. As children use the props and play out themes, they engage in many linguistic interactions. Some examples of useful props include

- Restaurant props
- Camping materials
- Doctor's office
- Grocery store
- Barber/beauty shop

For more information about dramatic play props, go to the Companion Website at www.prenhall.com/henniger, select Chapter 15, then choose Web Destinations.

Into Practice...
A Trip to the Post Office

Mrs. Riley's first-grade class is off for a field trip to the community post office. With the help of several parent volunteers, the children arrive safely at mid-morning and are greeted by postal workers who have prepared a tour of the facilities. Children see where the mail arrives in big trucks and how it is unloaded, sorted, and prepared for delivery. They also see how mail on its way to other cities is prepared for shipping. Students watch postal workers assist customers who need stamps and their packages mailed. It is a busy morning.

Upon returning to the classroom, children spend time as a large group talking with Mrs. Riley about what they saw. She records their comments on the overhead projector. Later, she will combine this written record with student illustrations to construct the monthly newsletter for parents.

Mrs. Riley has set up the dramatic play center as a post office with pretend stamps, envelopes, paper, writing instruments, and mailboxes for each member of the class. Children can spend free time writing, sending, and reading their mail. The center is buzzing with activity throughout the day.

The library corner has three new books with mail-related themes: *What's It Like to Be a Postal Worker?* (Matthews, 1990), *The Postman's Palace* (Henri, 1990), and *Here Comes the Mail* (Skurzynski, 1992). Mrs. Riley introduced these books at group time, and children are eagerly browsing through them with the parent volunteer. In the process, they recognize many of the procedures that they saw earlier at the post office.

Bookmaking is the theme of the writing center, and several children spend time there working on tales about the trip to the post office. They draw pictures of remembered events and then dictate stories to the parent volunteer. Children add their finished books to the library corner and read them to other interested children.

Literacy Learning

As stated earlier, language and literacy learning are related but not identical processes. Although almost all children learn oral language, many find reading and writing more difficult. Illiteracy is a burden that some adults carry with them throughout their lives. The impact on self-esteem and job status is strong.

As with oral language development, the early childhood years are pivotal times for learning to read and write (Snow, Burns, & Griffin, 1998). Children who have good literacy experiences during these years are much more likely to become literate adults. Teachers need to understand the theory behind these aspects of development and work to prepare materials and activities that facilitate growth in reading and writing (Fields & DeGayner, 2000).

Literacy Development

As with the development of speech, literacy awareness and learning begin in infancy. The 8-month-old child who cuddles up on her father's lap to look at a picture book is developing early literacy understandings. The 18-month-old scribbling on a piece of paper is preparing for writing in later childhood. Through these and other early experiences, very young children slowly learn literacy concepts such as beginning in the front of the book and moving sequentially to the back, reading each line of print from left to right, and being aware that print has meaning (Bobys, 2000).

Traditional View. The idea that even infants are engaged in meaningful literacy learning is relatively new. The more traditional view has been that language and literacy development are different (Christie, Enz, & Vukelich, 2003). While language learning occurs naturally, the traditional view held that formal reading and writing instruction should begin around age 6, when children have developed the mental and physical maturity needed for these tasks. Furthermore, this traditional view promoted the idea that children be taught reading and writing through the use of basal readers, worksheets, and handwriting practice.

Emergent Literacy. The idea that learning to read and write has much in common with oral language development is called **emergent literacy** (Sulzby & Teale, 1991). This approach promotes the idea that children begin learning about reading and writing in infancy. With appropriate materials and supportive adults, young children construct knowledge about print and gradually become more literate (Yaden, Rowe, & MacGillivray, 2000). By immersing the child in a print-rich environment and providing guidance during the discovery process, adults help children grow into readers and writers.

Formal Literacy Instruction. Although children continue to construct their own understanding of reading and writing during the primary grades, classroom teachers also implement formal literacy instruction. For the last several decades, literacy experts have debated the relative merits of **phonics instruction** (teaching the relationships between sounds and sound combinations to their written counterparts) and **whole language learning** (helping children construct reading and writing understandings from meaningful literacy activities). While early educators tend to lean toward the whole language approach, many current researchers and writers are suggesting that reading instruction must integrate both phonics instruction and the whole language approach to be successful (National Association for the Education of Young Children, 1998; Snow, Burns, & Griffin, 1998).

Assisting with Emergent Literacy

The emergent literacy perspective means that early childhood educators working with prekindergarten children need to get involved in providing experiences that lead to discoveries about reading and writing. It also changes the approaches that primary teachers should use with this age range. Teachers need to find alternatives to the traditional basal readers, worksheets, and handwriting exercises so often found in the primary grades.

Print-Rich Environments. Teachers at all levels within the early childhood range need to provide children with meaningful written materials that can lead to literacy learning. The most obvious of these are books. Beginning in infant/toddler programs (Kupetz & Green, 1997), adults should provide children with access to a wide variety of books and should read to individual children or small groups.

Christie et al. (2003) describe several key elements of a print-rich environment:

- *A variety of materials for reading.* In addition to books, classrooms should have many types of print that serve real-life functions (labels on food items, restaurant menus, road signs, etc.).

For more information about emergent literacy, go to the Companion Website at www.prenhall.com/henniger, select Chapter 15, then choose Web Destinations.

Into Practice . . .
Integrating Curriculum Through Story Songs

Shelly Ringgenberg (2003) provides good evidence that music can be used as an important tool for language learning. She experimented with both conventional storytelling and what she calls story songs where well-known stories are matched with a simple tune and sung with children. Ringgenberg found that children not only remembered more words from the story songs, but also found them to be very popular with all ages of children in her preschool class.

Ringgenberg (2003) suggests three graduated steps in the creation of story songs:

1. *One musical phrase.* Take a story familiar to children and create a musical phrase to use with a repeating portion of the story. For example, in the story *Brown Bear, Brown Bear* the phrase "Brown Bear, Brown Bear, what do you hear?" is repeated several times. By creating a simple melody (or using a melody from a well-known song such as "Mary Had a Little Lamb"), you can tell the story and then sing the repeating phrase with children.

2. *Melody for an entire story.* The next step is to try creating a song for an entire story. Again, choose a story that you and the children both know well, one that includes repetition and rhythm, and set it to a tune you create or to a familiar tune. For example, you could use the tune of "Frére Jacques" to sing the story *I Went Walking*. To make the story and song match, repeat each line: "I went walking, I went walking. What did you see? What did you see? I saw a black cat. I saw a black cat. Looking at me. Looking at me."

3. *Create your own story songs.* A third type of story song is one you create totally on your own. Write your own story about people and events that are meaningful to you and children, create a tune (or use a well-known favorite), and put them together for a creative experience with young children. The nice thing about children is that they accept your efforts without criticism and simply enjoy your creation along with you. You do not have to be an accomplished musician to have fun with this option.

- *Diverse writing materials.* A well-equipped writing center should be the focus of these activities, with materials available throughout the classroom that encourage children (or adults) to record important written communications (title of artwork, description of block structure, story to accompany flannelboard figures, etc.).

- *Displays of children's written products.* Teachers help children see the importance of writing by displaying their stories, books, and letters to friends and families.

- *Integrated printed materials.* Written materials should be connected with ongoing activities in the classroom. Gardening activities outdoors could be connected to teacher-recorded stories of children's gardening experiences, labeling of plant rows, recordings of plant growth, and books in the library center about aspects of gardening.

- *Literacy as part of routines.* Literacy activities can be highlighted during the routines of the school day. The attendance charts, hot and cold lunch counts, daily schedule, Pledge of Allegiance, and weather chart can be used for meaningful reading and writing experiences.

Children's artwork may be the basis for a language experience story.

Making the Oral and Written Language Connection. Young children need meaningful opportunities to grasp the connections between oral and written language. Understanding that what is said can be written down, as well as understanding that printed information can be spoken orally, are important steps during the early childhood years.

An important technique that many early childhood teachers use to help children make these connections is the **language experience** approach. Children dictate information about personal experiences while an adult writes them down. The adult can then read the story back to children and encourage them to practice reading their dictated work. Christie et al. (2003) describe three language experience options:

- *Group experience stories.* Following a shared group experience such as a field trip to the bakery, the class can discuss the highlights of the event and together create a story about the activity. As the class dictates the story, the teacher writes it down. The teacher can then reread the completed story and ask children to join in choral reading. Group experience stories can be duplicated and sent home to give parents further information on school activities and provide opportunities for reading at home.

- *Individual experience stories.* These stories come from individual children, who dictate them to the teacher. An example of this type is a child creating a picture book of his family's trip to the zoo with space at the bottom of each page for the dictated story.

- *Classroom newspaper.* First, children share interesting things that have happened to them. The teacher then records these experiences and compiles them into a newspaper to share with parents. Teachers who have an overabundance of news items may limit the number of students sharing, making sure that all the children eventually have a chance to have their stories recorded.

Literacy Learning Through Play. Many different play types can effectively stimulate literacy understandings. Dramatic play, for example, can lead to early reading and writing experiences.

> *Liam, Jerome, and Erika are playing in their preschool classroom's restaurant. Liam is the cook, Jerome is the waiter, and Erika is the customer. Erika pretends to read the menu and gives her order to Jerome, who pretends to write it down by making scribbles on his notepad and takes it to the cook. As these children engage in dramatic play, they are dealing with many beginning literacy concepts.*

Construction play in the block area can also lead to reading and writing opportunities.

> *Chad and Marshall, two third graders, have just completed building a castle based loosely on a book they recently read in the library center. Now they are interested in writing their own story about medieval times and life in a castle. They plan to spend time on the Internet collecting more information about castles before engaging in their literary efforts.*

Each center in the early childhood classroom should be equipped with literacy-related materials that children can use in their play. Pencils and paper for writing, signs created by parents/teachers/children, magazines, newspapers, and an old typewriter are examples of options to include (Rybczynski & Troy, 1995).

Reading to Children. Many experts consider reading young children books and other printed materials the most important way to develop early literacy skills in young children. The Commission on Reading (Anderson, Hiebert, Scott, & Wilkinson, 1985) states, "The single most important activity for building the knowledge required for eventual success in reading is reading aloud to children" (p. 23). This process should begin in infancy and continue throughout the early childhood years, both at home and in school.

Kupetz and Green (1997) provide the following guidelines for reading to children:

- Read to children when they are in the mood for it.
- Choose a book appropriate to the age of the children.
- Read stories that are of interest to you as well.
- Have special reading times as part of the routine of the day.
- Allow the children to assist you in the reading process.
- Use your voice to show interest and help tell the story.

Preparing a comfortable center where children can go to read with others is an essential component of the early childhood classroom. In addition to displaying plenty of reading options, this area should invite children to participate in the wonder of books. You should provide children with a cozy pillow to lie on, comfortable chairs, and good lighting. Take extra care in preparing this corner of the classroom.

Family Partnerships . . .
Involving Parents in Reading

KINDERGARTEN NE

One of the most important things you can do as an early childhood teacher is to develop ways to successfully involve parents in reading aloud to their children at home. The research indicates that this is the single most important activity needed for success in reading (National Association for the Education of Young Children, 1998). While this may seem to be a simple task, it actually requires careful planning and constant effort. Parents and families lead busy lives and often forget (or do not realize) that this effort is critical to success in reading.

While the following list of suggestions is not complete, it should get you thinking about what you can do to increase the likelihood of parents and children sitting down together to read.

- **Provide a rationale for reading.** Because of their busy lives, parents need to be highly motivated to spend some of their precious time reading to children. Collect research and writing that supports this position and send home regular reminders in newsletters or other written communications summarizing the views expressed.
- **Suggest good children's literature.** There are literally thousands of books available to children of all ages and reading abilities. Parents need guidance about what books might be appropriate for their children and where they might be found. Send home lists periodically (you may wish to tie them to the concepts you are teaching in class) so

that parents will consistently know about quality literature they can read.
- **Prepare reading backpacks.** Prepare one or more backpacks, each equipped with a good children's book, a note to the parents explaining what they should do and why, and some possible extensions of the reading task into other activities. At the end of each school day, send a backpack home with a child for use overnight. Make sure every child regularly has the opportunity to take home the backpack.
- **Conduct parent meetings.** It may be useful to have parents come together for an evening meeting in which you explain the importance of reading aloud to children and provide some examples of quality children's literature and where it can be found. Discussing this topic with other parents may also encourage "reluctant parent readers" to get involved in this important task.

1. Talk to an early childhood teacher about parental involvement in reading to their children. From your discussion, do you think most parents believe that reading to their own children as infants, toddlers, and preschoolers is an important task? Why or why not?

2. Do you enjoy reading for pleasure? How will you work to instill this attitude in the children you teach?

For more information about children's books, go to the Companion Website at www.prenhall.com/ henniger, select Chapter 15, then choose Web Destinations.

Children's Books

Every early childhood classroom should have an excellent collection of books to entice children into the library corner. The International Reading Association (1998) suggests that a classroom library for elementary children should have a minimum of five books for every child. Some of these books can remain in the center throughout the year, but most books should be rotated in and out of the classroom on a regular basis.

Over the course of the school year, early childhood teachers may literally need hundreds of children's books for their library centers. Although teachers can check books out from school and public libraries, developing a collection of your own books also makes good sense. Christie et al. (2003) suggest the following resources for building your own classroom library:

- Commercial publishers (expensive but important resources)
- Used bookstores
- Garage sales
- Public library sales
- Parent donations

Selecting Books. Machado (2003) provides several criteria for selecting books for young children. First, does the book match the *attention span, maturity, and interests of the children* with whom it is to be used? These characteristics vary widely across the early childhood range. For example, even within a homogeneous age group, attention spans vary greatly. Books chosen should reflect this diversity.

Adults working with young children should also select books that help *develop broad literary and artistic tastes.* Texts from each of the categories presented here, books by a variety of authors, and ethnically and culturally diverse writers and illustrators encourage breadth in children's literature.

Is the author's *writing style interesting* to young children? The vocabulary and story sequence should be appropriate for the targeted children. Repetition of words, actions, or rhymes makes the book more enjoyable to young children. Humor and silliness that children can understand can add to the attractiveness of an author's writing.

Books can be selected in part based on their *educational value.* Does the content of the book add to the child's knowledge of the world? Books that add new vocabulary to areas of childhood interest should be considered. Are the issues faced by characters in the books the same ones that children and their families encounter? Are the solutions presented workable ones for real-world problems?

Selecting good books for children is a difficult task, as hundreds of quality books have been published since the 1940s. Furthermore, each year approximately 500 new books for children are added, many of which are excellent options to consider. However, busy parents, teachers, and librarians have limited time to spend reading new books.

Since 1975, the Children's Book Council and the International Reading Association have helped make this selection process easier by publishing a list of books that children enjoy reading. Every fall, children's most popular choices are published in *The Reading Teacher* with a brief summary of each book's content.

The **Children's Choice Awards** list books that are appropriate for children throughout the early childhood and elementary/middle school years. Approximately 10,000 children participate in the selection process each year, helping ensure that the books chosen will have wide appeal. These awards, although not the only source for book ideas, help make it easier for adults to select good literature for children to read.

Two other ways to recognize quality children's literature are through the **Newbery** and **Caldecott awards.** The Newbery is awarded for the year's most distinguished new book for children. The Caldecott is awarded for the best illustrated book of the year.

Books for Infants and Toddlers. It is never too early to integrate literacy experiences into young children's lives. Adults can share books with infants and toddlers so that the wonder and excitement of print communications can be a part of their lives. Kupetz and Green (1997) describe five types of books that are appropriate for this age:

- *Rhythmical language books.* Books with rhymes and lullabies (e.g., *Mother Goose*) are some of the first to interest very young children.

- *Point-and-say books.* Containing pictures or photographs of familiar animals, toys, family members, and the like, these books allow the adult to point to pictures and say their names. Eventually, children can do the pointing and become more involved in the reading.

- *Touch-and-smell books.* Children are presented with different textures to touch and/or a variety of smells to get them actively involved in exploring these books.

- *Board books.* These durable books are made of board-like materials that withstand the banging and chewing of young children. Children can thus spend more time independently exploring these books.

- *Early picture storybooks.* Many toddlers are ready for books with simple story lines and clear illustrations that help tell the story.

Books for Preschool and Primary Children. Neuman and Roskos (1993) suggest the following categories of books for preschool and primary children:

- *Action books.* These books contain mostly pictures and have pop-ups, pull tabs, and other movable parts to encourage active child participation.

- *Informational books.* Books that share specific content on topics of interest to young children through words and pictures fit this category. A story about how milk is produced (Carrick, 1985) or the life of a squirrel (Lane, 1981) are examples.

- *Picture books.* Books of this type contain mostly pictures and have limited print. Young children can learn many of the conventions of reading books (e.g., reading each page from left to right and top to bottom) while enjoying the pictures.

- *Predictable books.* These books have repetitive patterns that make it easy for children to predict what comes next. Many of the Dr. Seuss books (see, e.g., Seuss, 1960) fit this category.

- *Storybooks.* Although containing pictures on most pages, these books also provide children with an interesting story line to follow. *Leo the Late Bloomer* (Kraus, 1971) is an example of this type.

- *Wordless books.* Children can use the pictures in these books to tell their own stories. An example is *Frog Goes to Dinner* (Mayer, 1974).

- *Beginning chapter books.* These books are more adult-like. They have limited pictures, complex plots, and are organized into chapters. Parents or teachers often read these books to primary-age children. Judy Blume's (1970) book *Freckle Juice* is a popular example of this type.

For more information about supporting children's writing, go to the Companion Website at www.prenhall.com/henniger, select Chapter 15, then choose Web Destinations.

Writing Tools

Just as children's books are important tools for emerging readers, certain materials are particularly helpful in fostering early writing experiences. The following items provide playful ways for children to experiment with producing written language:

- *Magnetic boards.* When used with a set of magnetic letters, the magnetic board provides children with unlimited ways to combine letters into words. Without actually needing to draw letters with their own hand, children can experiment with writing.

- *Paper and writing instruments.* Teachers should stock each center with paper and writing materials of all types for children to manipulate. Children can effectively use lined paper, unlined paper, recycled paper, notepads, notebooks, pencils, pens, marking pens, crayons, and so on for writing activities.

- *Child-sized chalkboards.* The unique feel, shape, and smell of chalk make it an inviting writing instrument. Child-sized chalkboards allow children to sit comfortably and work on their own writing tasks. In addition, chalk is easy to erase, allowing children to change what they have written.

- *Tracing materials.* Montessori (Lillard, 1972) developed a set of shapes that children can trace around with a writing instrument. These and similar materials help develop the fine motor skills necessary for writing.

- *Typewriter.* Young children are fascinated with how things work. An old manual or electric typewriter not only gives them a chance to see a machine at work but also encourages children to write something—or pretend to do so. Preschool children, in particular, can benefit from this option.

Language and literacy skills can be enhanced with the use of quality word processing software.

- *Computer.* Computers have made word processing a much easier and more enjoyable process for everyone, including young children. Several software designers have created excellent programs that help primary children engage in quality writing experiences. In addition, younger children can benefit from having a computer in the classroom to simply type letters and words on the screen.

Writing Instruction

Do you remember how you were taught to write? For many students, the teacher assigned the topics that were used to practice writing skills. At the beginning of the school year, a popular tactic was to ask children to write about events that occurred over summer vacation. Or perhaps you remember story starters like, "The sun was going down over the dusty plains. Exhausted from the day's travels, the riders dismounted from their horses and. . . . " While children can learn from these experiences, it is much better to teach writing (Harwayne, 1992) and then allow children to choose their own topics.

Christie et al. (2003) and many others are now promoting teaching the behaviors of good writers. Good writers think about what they want to write (prewrite); read and reread what they are drafting; revise their drafts through adding, deleting, and reorganizing; and edit for spelling, grammar, and punctuation problems. This process is often referred to as teaching the writing workshop way. This relatively new approach includes the following:

- Children need to choose their own topics for writing.
- Writing should be done for real audiences (peers, parents, and others) rather than imaginary audiences.
- Initially, writing should focus on what the writer wants to tell others. Once that is achieved, the writer should polish the grammar, spelling, and punctuation.
- Children should have the opportunity to do many drafts so that they can create a quality piece of writing.
- In addition to needing plenty of time, children need the chance to talk to the teacher and peers about their writing.
- Teachers should provide opportunities to engage in a variety of writing categories (narrative, persuasive, informative).

Formal Reading Instruction

For more information about formal reading instruction, go to the Companion Website at www.prenhall.com/henniger, select Chapter 15, then choose Web Destinations.

As with many issues in education, there has been a tendency in reading instruction to emphasize either phonics or whole language learning rather than including both as important elements of the reading curriculum. In a joint position statement of the International Reading Association and the National Association for the Education of Young Children (National Association for the Education of Young Children, 1998), leading educators in both fields strongly advocate for reading instruction that includes both phonics and whole language learning. Since there is great diversity in student abilities and experiences, this integrated approach is likely to be the most effective for all children. The "Observing Development" feature at the end of this chapter provides opportunities to observe children's early literacy experiences, reflect on how adults and books impact literacy, and apply methods to encourage children to maintain their interest in reading.

The reading curriculum should include the following elements (National Association for the Education of Young Children, 1998):

- *Daily reading experiences.* Children should be read to and allowed to engage in independent reading activities.
- *Systematic code instruction.* Phonics instruction should be included as a part of meaningful reading experiences.
- *Daily writing experiences.* Because reading is an integral part of the literacy experience, students gain additional insights into this task as they engage in teacher-supported writing experiences.
- *Small group work.* Both instruction and interaction in small groups allow children to become better readers.
- *Challenging curriculum.* By providing an overall curriculum that is exciting and challenging, children expand their knowledge of the world and increase their vocabularies.
- *Individualized instruction.* For those children who are advanced and those needing additional assistance in learning to read, teachers must work to individualize the reading instruction so that motivation and progress remain strong.

Encouraging Parent Involvement

While parents play significant roles in all aspects of the young child's development, none are more critical to academic success than the promotion of language and literacy learning. Parents who create an environment in the home that stimulates positive communications and demonstrates the importance of written language provide their children with an invaluable asset that is difficult to duplicate.

For many parents, one of the most difficult hurdles to overcome is the belief that what they do in the home really does not make a difference in language and literacy development. Parents need to be educated about the importance of their role. Articles from professional journals, workshops for parents on language and literacy learning, and informal discussions with individual parents are some potential ideas that teachers can use to help promote this concept.

Taking Advantage of Daily Living

At the same time that parents are being convinced of their important role in language and literacy development, many need specific ideas about how they can assist in this process. Numerous activities that parents and children engage in daily are excellent opportunities for encouraging oral and written language understandings. Machado (2003) gives examples of these natural learning opportunities:

- Spend some time each day giving individual attention to each child in the family. Talk about your life or what is happening in the child's day; make it a pleasant time of sharing.

- Try to extend the child's vocabulary by adding new and interesting words to your communications.

- Take time to point out meaningful print in the child's world such as names on food containers and road signs.

- Make trips to the grocery store (and similar chores) learning opportunities by talking about the things being purchased and pointing out and discussing labels and brand names.

- Become a skilled questioner to promote thinking and effective communication.

- Be a good conversationalist. Listen carefully to what the child has to say, and try to build on his comments in your responses.

- Model the importance of reading by taking time to read yourself. Share what you read about with your child.

Simple Home Learning Tasks

The natural opportunities for language and literacy learning just described make a big difference, but other more specific tasks are also valuable. These should be easy to prepare for and require a limited time commitment by the parent. The following examples highlight the diversity of these simple home learning tasks:

- Read, read, and read some more to your child. These times should be enjoyable for both the parent and child. Reading one or more books before bed each night is an excellent habit to develop.

- Construct a writing center in the home with paper and writing instruments that the child can use to create her own stories and books.

Parents and teachers need to take advantage of the many opportunities for meaningful print experiences.

Observing Development • Early Reading Experiences

Choose one of the age groups within early childhood (infants/toddlers, preschoolers, or primary-age children), *observe* **early reading experiences** using the guidelines provided, *reflect* on what you saw and heard, and *apply* the appropriate strategies listed with the children you observed.

Observe	Reflect	Apply
Look for specific examples of:	*Think about and respond to the following questions:*	*Consider the following developmentally appropriate strategies for the age group you observed:*
Children initiating experiences with print (looking at a book, interest in words on bulletin boards/signs/labels in the classroom, etc.)	Were the adults you observed reading to individual children or groups? Did the adults and children seem to be enjoying the experience?	Encourage children to explore materials in print • Infant/toddler: offer books and other print materials as play choices • Preschool: suggest the book corner when children need a play option • Primary: praise children who select print materials during choice time
Adults reading to children (a book, words on chalkboard/overhead/signs, assignments, etc.)	What did adults do when children were engaged in experiences with print? Did they intervene in some way or simply sit back and observe?	Model interest in reading • Infant/toddler: focus your energy on the child and the print materials you are reading • Preschool: use inflection and modulation to show children you are reading with enthusiasm • Primary: have your own reading materials to use when children are engaged in their own silent reading
Materials and equipment to stimulate reading (books, computer games, stories on the computer, labels in the room, listening center with books on tape, etc.)	Did the classroom contain a variety of materials for children to read? Were children able to use these materials at their convenience?	Provide a variety of reading materials • Infant/toddler: rotate new books in and out of the classroom on a weekly basis • Preschool: label common objects in the classroom (chair, table, desk, coat rack, etc.) • Primary: allow children to bring in reading materials that are of interest to them

- Make books with young children. If needed, the parent can write down the child's story and then the child can illustrate it.

- Do things together as a family: visit the zoo, browse through museums, spend time at the public library, and attend musical concerts. Spend time talking and writing about these special events after returning.

- Encourage children to write thank-you cards, birthday messages, and letters to friends and relatives. Make sure children see you doing the same.

- For families with computers and Internet access, parents can help children send e-mail messages to friends and family members.

Summary

 To test your knowledge of this chapter's contents, go to the Companion Website at www.prenhall.com/henniger, select Chapter 15, then select Study Guide. Also see Chapter Overviews, Reflecting Essay Questions, Multimedia Explorations, and relevant Web Destinations.

Language Learning

To assist with oral language development, educators need to understand different theoretical perspectives, the developmental patterns associated with growth in verbal communications, the adult's role in facilitating language learning, and appropriate materials for language learning.

Literacy Learning

Supporting literacy learning requires an understanding of literacy development, the importance of print-rich environments in learning to read and write, recognition of the role of play in literacy learning, and the critical importance of reading to children. It is important to select quality books for young children that match their interests and developmental abilities. Teachers need to include materials in the classroom that support children's early writing efforts.

Encouraging Parent Involvement

Parents need to be educated about their critical roles in language and literacy learning. They can take advantage of daily living experiences and be involved in simple home learning tasks to assist in language and literacy learning.

Multimedia Explorations and Activities...

Books and Young Children

Much has been written about the value of books. Reading books and being read to at an early age develops literacy, enhances vocabulary and grammar skills, instructs the reader about the world close at hand and far away, and encourages creativity and imagination. Being read to establishes a never-to-be-forgotten sense of security in providing a ritual, a period of time during which a child and reader sit together and attend to a story.

(Hermes, 1995, p. 6)

Research

There is much to be learned about books for young children. Your teacher preparation program may require you to take an entire course on the subject so that you will know more about the benefits of using children's literature in the early childhood classroom, selecting good books for young children, encouraging parents to read to young children, and building children's literature into the curriculum. This activity is designed to help you begin to understand the critical importance of reading quality books to young children.

1. Go to the Companion Website at www.prenhall.com/henniger and click on the Multimedia Explorations and Activities button for Chapter 15 for more information on this important topic.
2. Talk to a professor who has specialized in children's literature and find out what she recommends you consider as essential to know and do regarding books for young children.

Reflect

Based on your research results, reflect on the following issues:

- What are the characteristics of a good book for young children? How will you make decisions about which books you will use in your classroom?

- Why is it so important for adults to begin reading to children from a very early age? What tips help make this reading experience more enjoyable and productive for both the adult and the child?

- How can you integrate good children's literature into the various subjects you will teach in the early childhood classroom?

Respond

Consider one or more of the following options as a response to the issue of quality children's literature:

1. For the age/grade you hope to teach, construct an annotated bibliography of 10 to 20 children's books that you consider excellent books for that age. Give a rationale in your annotations for each selection. Share your list with others by posting it on the message board found on the Companion Website for this text.

2. Write an article for a parent newsletter describing the values of reading to young children and strategies that help make this activity successful. Work to get your article published in a local early childhood education newsletter.

3. Based on your new knowledge of children's literature, give yourself a small budget and see if you can purchase several good used books for your future classroom. Consider used bookstores, garage sales, parents of young children, and other sources for purchasing your books.

4. Go to your local community library and review their collection of children's literature. Compare what you found there with the guidelines and ideas you gathered from your web search. Talk to a library official about suggested improvements.

16

USING THE CREATIVE ARTS TO SUPPORT DEVELOPMENT AND LEARNING

In this chapter you will

- Define creativity as it applies to young children in the early childhood classroom.
- Clarify the importance of art and music in child development and learning.
- Understand the teacher's role in facilitating the creative arts.
- Identify creative art and music activities for children from birth to age 8.

Your kindergarten classroom has just begun its morning schedule. Children gather at circle time for opening activities, two or three familiar songs, a movement activity using silk scarves and selected music, and a discussion of the activities available in the classroom centers. You explain that a fingerpainting activity will be available in the art center in addition to the regular art supplies.

As children wander off after group time, you watch as Jaylani and Amanda head straight to the art corner to get involved in fingerpainting. They are tentative at first as they get their hands covered with the gooey paint and shaving cream mix. Soon, however, they are happily weaving intricate patterns on the tabletop. They spend nearly 20 minutes exploring this activity before moving on to another center.

Matt and Karen have discovered some new materials in the music center and are busily exploring the music-making potential of these new instruments. The shallow drum and homemade stringed instrument are the main attractions. As they pluck and tap, they sing their newly created song about the Eensy Weensy Tadpole.

This is just a small sampling of the musical and artistic activities that your students regularly experience. Each day many new activities are available for children to explore.

Quality early childhood programs are full of opportunities for creative expression. Like the children in the class just described, young people want and need a wide variety of outlets for their creativity. When they are given the right materials and allowed the freedom to explore in their own special ways, children delight in art and musical experiences.

The Association for Childhood Education International (ACEI) recommends that all children be able to express themselves through the arts. The association developed a position paper that states the following:

> The creative process, contrary to popular opinion, is socially supported, culturally influenced, and collaboratively achieved. In taking this position, ACEI acknowledges that several challenges must be addressed by educators throughout the world. First, we need to redefine creative teaching and confront misconceptions about creative thinking. Second, we need to provide students with role models of motivation and persistence in creative thought, and arrive at more capacious ways of assessing creative processes and products. Finally, educational institutions and the larger societies in which they exist need to reflect deeply on what they hope children will become. We need to do more than prepare them to become cogs in the machinery of

commerce. The international community needs resourceful, imaginative, inventive, and ethical problem solvers who will make a significant contribution, not only to the Information Age in which we currently live, but beyond to ages that we can barely envision. (quoted in Jalongo, 2003, p. 218)

What Is Creativity?

Before looking specifically at art and music, a discussion of the concept of creativity itself is necessary. Creative expression takes place throughout the day in the early childhood classroom. E. Paul Torrance, a leading researcher and writer in this area, suggests the following as a rather whimsical description of creative activity:

Creativity is digging deeper.

Creativity is looking twice.

Creativity is crossing out mistakes.

Creativity is talking/listening to a cat.

Creativity is getting in deep water.

Creativity is getting out from behind locked doors.

Creativity is plugging in the sun.

Creativity is wanting to know.

Creativity is having a ball.

Creativity is building sand castles.

Creativity is singing in your own way.

Creativity is shaking hands with the future. (quoted in Edwards, 2002, p. 27)

Defining Creativity

For more information about creativity, go to the Companion Website at www.prenhall.com/ henniger, select Chapter 16, then choose Web Destinations.

Clearly, the activities that Torrance includes under the broad umbrella of creativity are many and varied. Defining the term, therefore, is difficult. In general, however, definitions of creative activity have two common criteria: novelty and appropriateness (Starko, 1995).

To be creative, an idea or product must be *new*, or *novel*. The key question that must be asked, however, is novel to whom? Does the idea or product need to be new to humankind? If so, very, very few of us are creative. Creative acts would be limited to the Mozarts and Einsteins of the world. However, if ideas or products are new to the person who produced them, then most people engage in creative activity. This latter description makes the most sense when working with children.

The second criterion for judging an act as creative is *appropriateness*. For adults, this means that activities are creative when they are acceptable and useful by some set of criteria. These criteria vary from one culture to the next and between groups of adults. Whereas some might view an adult's photo essay of migrant farm workers as creative, others could see it as meaningless and therefore not appropriate.

Once again, the lines blur as we apply the criterion of appropriateness to children. Using adult standards of appropriateness to evaluate children's artwork or musical productions, for example, makes little sense. We cannot expect beginning artists and musicians to produce creative materials rivaling those of adults. Rather, when children's efforts are meaningful to them, they are appropriate.

Take, for example, 7-year-old Shawnna, who spent the past 30 minutes in the art center painting at the easel. Shawnna has been intently creating a picture of her home and front yard, carefully choosing colors and creating a good representation of that environment. Are her efforts novel and appropriate as defined earlier? From Shawnna's perspective, it is a new activity that she finds meaningful and useful. Adults should view her efforts as a creative activity.

Characteristics of Creative Individuals

The list of characteristics associated with creative individuals is lengthy and varies from one researcher to the next. Torrance (1962) describes the following seven characteristics of highly creative young children:

- *Curiosity.* Creative children have a healthy curiosity; they consistently ask meaningful questions and manipulate materials in the environment.
- *Flexibility.* Creative children are flexible. When one approach to a problem does not work, they simply try something else.
- *Sensitivity to problems.* Creative children can sense missing elements and quickly identify problem situations.
- *Originality.* Creative children commonly have unusual ideas and create original products.
- *Independence.* Creative children are comfortable in working alone as they play with ideas or materials. Creative individuals often work with others, but they can accomplish much on their own.
- *Redefinition.* Creative children combine ideas or materials in new and unusual ways.
- *Penetration.* Creative children gain much insight from spending time thinking deeply about ideas and problems.

Assisting with the Creative Process

It is counterproductive to think about formally teaching children to be creative, but teachers and parents nonetheless have important roles to play in facilitating creativity. Several key ingredients are needed for children to be creative individuals. One such element is to have adults who value creativity. Children need to know that the creative process is important in the adult world and that it enriches each of our lives. In addition to the unquestioned value of the ideas and products of highly creative adults, new solutions to the everyday problems faced by adults also help make life more enjoyable and pleasant. By valuing originality with our words and actions, we can help children grow into more creative adults.

Teachers can promote creative activity by establishing low-risk classroom environments. As children solve problems, explore, and experiment, they need to know that failure is acceptable and normal. Wasserman (1992) puts it this way: "Inventions of the new do not come from duplicating what is already there. They come from minds that are unafraid to take risks to try" (p. 135). Creativity is only possible when teachers encourage children to experiment with ideas that may not work. They learn from these failures and come back with even better, more creative solutions.

Teachers also need to create an environment in which children have the freedom to explore. Children need large blocks of time for exploration and experimentation if creativity is to take place. Children must also be free to choose the activities that interest them and to mess around with materials in their own unique ways. Although these activities are often noisy and messy, this freedom to explore will pay big dividends in terms of creative activity.

A rich assortment of open-ended materials provides children with increased opportunities for creative expression. Interesting art materials, such as colorful paints and a variety of paper textures, help children produce imaginative works that express their unique personalities and developmental abilities.

Creativity and Play

During group time today, your 4-year-olds requested "The Eensy Weensy Spider" once again for music. Then Adam suggested a variation he called "The Eensy Weensy Caterpillar." It was a big hit. Following group time, Adam and Marika stayed on the rug and spent another 10 minutes creating their own playful modifications to "The Eensy Weensy Spider." They developed words and hand movements for "The Eensy Weensy Frog" and "The Eensy Weensy Bird."

Celebrating Play . . .
For the Fun of It

Throughout this text there has been an emphasis on the learning potential associated with childhood play. Children enhance physical, social, emotional, linguistic, and intellectual knowledge as they engage in creative play experiences. Educators need to understand these many benefits and be prepared to share them with parents, administrators, and concerned others.

While strongly supporting the many benefits of play, David Elkind (2003) makes a case for simply allowing children to play for the sheer fun of the activity. He believes that while childhood is an important time for developing skills for the future, it should also be enjoyed in the present through play. He justifies this position in the following way:

I first recalled Freud's response when asked what was necessary to lead a happy and productive life. He replied, "*Lieben und Arbeiten*" (loving and working). With all due respect to Freud, I believe he should have added a third activity, namely, *Speilen* (playing). I believe that play is

as fundamental a human disposition as loving and working. We play because we are programmed to play; it is part of human nature, and of animal nature as well. (p. 46)

Take a moment to consider the importance of play in adult lives. Although the play of adults may be different from that of children, is it not equally true that adults need to engage in playful activities to have balanced and meaningful lives? Doesn't "all work and no play" make for a dull adult existence? Healthy adults, just like healthy children, consistently take time for play "just for the fun of it."

1. What do you think of this perspective on childhood play? Should we allow children time to play for the sheer fun of the activity? Are there dangers in this approach?

2. Do you believe that adults need play for a healthy lifestyle? Are you taking the time needed to have playful experiences as an adult?

Open-ended art materials provide many opportunities for creativity and play.

For more information about creativity and play, go to the Companion Website at www.prenhall.com/henniger, select Chapter 16, then choose Web Destinations.

Perhaps you have noticed already that many of the concepts discussed earlier about childhood play (see Chapter 5) also apply to creativity. In fact, play and creativity are closely linked. Although it is possible to play and not be creative, or for creativity to occur outside of the play experience, the two often take place together.

Highly creative adults, for example, often describe their creative acts as playing around with ideas or materials. Goertzel and Goertzel (1962) describe the lives of famous people such as the Wright brothers, Frank Lloyd Wright, Thomas Edison, and others as filled with playful explorations and discoveries. Wasserman (1992) quotes Richard Feynman, a Nobel Prize winner in physics, as saying this about his playfulness:

> Why did I enjoy doing it [physics]? I used to play with it. I used to do whatever I felt like doing. It didn't have to do with whether it was important for the development of nuclear physics, but instead whether it was interesting and amusing for me to play with. (p. 139)

This ability to simply play around with physics concepts eventually led to a discovery that won Feynman the Nobel Prize.

Play probably will not lead most of us to this level of creativity, but lives are clearly enriched when children and adults alike engage in quality play experiences. Albert Einstein (1954), considered one of the greatest thinkers of the 20th century, clearly felt that play was necessary for creative thinking when he stated, "Play seems to be the essential feature in productive thought" (p. 26).

The Young Artist

Art and music are not the only ways for young children to express their creative talents; however, they are important options in the early childhood classroom. The foundation laid in these early years often determines whether or not individuals enjoy the creative arts throughout their lives.

Why Include Art?

Historically, most Americans have viewed the creative arts as less important than the teaching of more academic subjects. Consequently, at all levels of public education, when budgets or time became tight, the art and music programs were often the first to be cut or de-emphasized. This attitude has influenced many parents and teachers at the prekindergarten level as well.

Recently, however, the creative arts have been recognized as central to the curriculum for the 21st century. For example, the Arts Education Partnership (2004), which was founded in 1995, includes over 100 national organizations that have joined forces to promote the arts as essential components of the subject matter that students must master in public school if they are to succeed in later life.

Family Partnerships...
The Art Docent

Because of budget cutbacks and the higher priority of academic subjects such as mathematics and reading, many schools and school districts have chosen to do without trained art educators. While understandable from a fiscal standpoint, this approach leaves regular classroom teachers with the responsibility for carrying on this important component of the curriculum with very little background or training in the arts. The result is that many young children get little or no exposure to art on a regular basis.

One way in which some schools are attempting to keep the art education curriculum alive and well in difficult financial times is to seek and train volunteers to serve as art docents. The word *docent* comes from the Latin word *docere,* which means "to teach" or "to lead." After receiving training from an art professional, docents travel from classroom to classroom to share an art education curriculum that would otherwise not be taught.

Parents and community members with a passion for art are accepting the challenge and assisting with art education activities in the classroom. They may lead a field trip to a local museum to view important works on display, prepare activities that help students understand the different styles of famous artists, or share techniques for using different art media (such as watercolors and chalk). By sharing their excitement and expertise in art, art docents help young children begin to develop an interest in art that can be strengthened through later school and life experiences.

1. What do you see as the strengths and limitations of having art docents deliver the art curriculum to young children?

2. How high a priority should art education be in the early childhood classroom? Is it of equal or lesser importance than the more academic subjects? Give reasons for the position you take.

The Task Force on Children's Learning and the Arts (Bruce, 1998) says this about early education and the arts:

> The arts motivate and engage children in learning, stimulate memory and facilitate understanding, enhance symbolic communication, promote relationships, and provide an avenue for building competence. The arts are natural for young children. Child development specialists note that play is the business of young children; play is the way children promote and enhance their development. The arts are a most natural vehicle for play. (p. v)

Ernest Boyer (1987) has identified three main reasons for including the creative arts as significant parts of the curriculum:

For more information about the benefits of the arts, go to the Companion Website at www.prenhall.com/henniger, select Chapter 16, then choose Web Destinations.

- The arts help children express feelings and ideas that are difficult to share using words.
- Teachers can integrate the generally splintered academic world of students through the arts. Seeing connections and finding patterns across disciplines can be accomplished through the arts.
- The arts provide the child with a universal language that is useful in communicating with others.

Misconceptions About Art

Jalongo (1995) suggests that many people have misconceptions about art, and educators need to take actions to counteract them. She identifies five misconceptions that we should actively work to overcome:

- *Art is a nonessential element of the curriculum.* This misconception is widespread and needs to be carefully addressed by teachers. First of all, communicating to others through the medium of art is an essential element of our humanity and cannot be taken lightly. Second, children practice considerable higher-level thinking skills as they engage in art activities. Art needs to be considered an essential component of education rather than an unnecessary frill.
- *Discovering talent is the goal.* Our job as teachers of young children is *not* to discover the next Picasso or Monet. Every child should be encouraged to participate in art. Teachers should emphasize the process, not the product.
- *Teachers must have performance skills in art to teach it.* It is most important to share with children an enthusiasm for art and its production. This does not require strong performance skills. When teachers communicate excitement, provide materials for creative art experiences, and facilitate children's efforts, a rich curriculum in art is ensured.
- *Creative teaching is teacher-centered.* Although it is possible to assist children in their creative efforts (see information on Reggio Emilia in this chapter), the process of creative thinking and expression must come from within the child. Making an art pattern for children to cut out and decorate is not helpful in stimulating creativity. Shidler-Lattz and Ratcliff (1998) make it clear that when

we force children to "color within the lines," we end up with frustrated students who are likely to avoid art altogether.

- *The teacher is uninvolved.* While the teacher cannot directly teach creative art, much can be done to ensure quality experiences. In addition to providing quality materials, the teacher needs to ask appropriate questions, make helpful comments, and guide the creative efforts of young children.

Developmental Trends in Art

Rhonda, at 18 months, is a very busy young girl. At her child care center, she is particularly interested in playing with paper and pencils. Rhonda has been fascinated with her older sister's pictures and stories and spends several minutes each day creating her own artful scribbles. To the untrained eye, they appear to be simply scratch marks on paper. But to Rhonda, they are important first steps in communicating with others.

As children mature both physically and mentally, their progress in art moves from rather random scribbles during the infant/toddler years to more recognizable art during the primary grades. Many researchers, including Rhoda Kellogg (1969), have carefully studied these developmental trends. Kellogg's collection of children's paintings and drawings from the United States and other countries around the world totals over a million samples.

Schirrmacher (2002) summarizes the research of Kellogg and others and identifies the following stages in children's art:

- *Scribbling and mark-making stage (birth to about age 2).* Kellogg (cited in Schirrmacher, 2002) identified 20 basic scribbles that young children use as the foundation for future art activities. These change from simple dots and lines to the more complex motions needed to create an imperfect circle. Children begin by making random marks and gradually move to more controlled and purposeful scribbling.

- *Personal symbol and design stage (approximately 2 to 4 years of age).* During this period, children make scribbles and marks in specific areas on their paper to create personal symbols and designs. For example, a large imperfect circle with four lines protruding at odd angles might become an early symbol for the human figure. The young child includes whatever features he views as important and omits those elements that he considers insignificant.

- *Attempts at public representation (approximately 4 to 7 years of age).* At this point, children modify their personal symbols and gradually produce art that is more recognizable to others. They include more details, as accurate representation becomes increasingly important to children. For example, if a child is drawing his mother, who has brown hair and blue eyes, the drawing will contain these details.

- *Realism stage (late primary years and up).* Children at this point strive hard to include even the smallest of realistic details as they create their artwork. This attempted photographic realism emphasizes size, placement, proportion, and other elements in attempts at reproducing replicas of people, places, and things the child has experienced.

Time and appropriate materials lead to creative art experiences for young children.

The Early Childhood Art Curriculum

For more information about early childhood art, go to the Companion Website at www.prenhall.com/henniger, select Chapter 16, then choose Web Destinations.

The content of the art program for young children may appear straightforward; however, many experts suggest that it is more than just the production of art using a variety of media. Opportunities for making art are only one part of the larger curriculum young children need to explore.

Schirrmacher (2002) identifies four central elements in a strong art program:

- *Sensing and experiencing.* When children use their senses and engage in meaningful experiences, these experiences form the foundation for creative expression. Art is an expression of these events to others.

- *Making art.* Children need to express themselves by making art with diverse art media.

- *Learning about art, artists, and their styles.* The natural interest of young children in learning about community helpers can be extended to include artists. Local artists using a variety of styles and media can tell their stories and share works with children.

- *Aesthetics.* Aesthetics is the study of beauty in color, form, and design. With assistance, children can come to appreciate beauty in different artworks and in the natural world around them.

Another recent approach to the art curriculum in early childhood education is referred to as **discipline-based art education.** The Getty Center for Education in the Arts (Alexander & Day, 1999) has been a major proponent of this approach. Designed for children in the primary grades and beyond, this perspective promotes developing the technical skills needed in art production, plus the

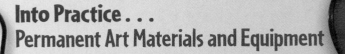

Into Practice...
Permanent Art Materials and Equipment

Teachers of young children should give careful consideration to the materials and equipment provided for art activities in the classroom. A well-stocked art center will attract considerable interest from young children. Many art centers contain two distinct categories of materials and equipment: those that remain in the area on a permanent basis and those that are changed regularly (generally every week). The following are examples of typical materials and equipment that are a permanent part of the early childhood art center.

Materials

Paper (scrap, recycled, colored, etc.)
Color crayons, marking pens, pens, and pencils
Scissors, hole punches, and staplers
Rulers, protractors, and compasses (for older children)
Glue, glue sticks, and rubber cement

Equipment

Easel (having two is preferable)
Child-sized table and chairs
Shelves for storage of materials
Trays for holding paper
Drying space/spots for completed projects

teaching of four disciplines that help children create, understand, and appreciate art:

- Art production
- Art history
- Art criticism
- Aesthetics

The Teacher's Role in Art Experiences

Teachers can facilitate creative art experiences in the early childhood classroom in many ways. An important first step is providing a variety of appropriate materials for children to explore. Tempera paints, watercolors, chalk, and clay are all examples of diverse art materials that children can use productively during the preschool and primary years. By rotating exciting materials in and out of the art center, teachers provide children with experiences using different materials, which maintains a high level of interest in making art. Chapter 9 describes additional materials for the art center.

Another way in which teachers support quality art experiences is to value creativity. Unfortunately, many well-meaning adults can permanently damage the creative abilities of young children with their comments and interactions. Rather than shutting down the creative expressiveness of young children, we need to let children know, both through our words and actions, that we value their unique uses of art materials. That kind of emotional climate will keep children motivated to engage in art activities. The "Observing Development" feature at the end of this chapter provides opportunities to observe children's creative behaviors in play, art, and music, reflect on these aspects of childhood creativity, and apply strategies to enhance creativity in the early childhood classroom.

During center time, Mrs. Duncan's first-grade students are engaged in a variety of activities, including art. Aletha is using the colorful cloth scraps to create an intricate design on her paper. Mrs. Duncan takes a moment to carefully observe Aletha at work and then says, "Aletha, I'm impressed with the variety of colors you are using and the wonderful designs being created. Very interesting!" Mrs. Duncan is showing Aletha that she values her creative efforts in art.

Children also benefit when adults describe and/or demonstrate appropriate uses for art tools and materials. When an early childhood teacher casually describes how positioning a paintbrush allows the artist to make different strokes, she is providing young children with valuable art instruction. And because children learn in different ways, some will find it more helpful to watch the teacher demonstrate how to use some materials rather than listening to a verbal description. In both instances, children can benefit from this one-on-one assistance in using art tools and materials.

It is critical, however, that these demonstration efforts avoid the use of models. Models that the teacher constructs have no place in the early childhood classroom. They send children the message that their art is of poor quality because it can never look as good as the teacher's example. Models also say to children that there is a right way to use these materials. When adult interactions say to children that there is a correct way to paint or construct with art items, their creativity and motivation are diminished.

Teachers of young children also need to emphasize the process of art rather than the product. Creative acts occur when children have plenty of opportunities to explore and experiment. This means that many of the products will be the result of messing around with materials. Although it is important to teach children specific art techniques, an emphasis on the product makes it less likely that the much-needed experimentation will take place. Edwards (2002) and Szyba (1999) suggest that teachers of young children:

- Put away patterns, ditto masters, and premarked papers.
- Throw out coloring books.
- Avoid cookbook art activities.
- Enjoy the freedom that basic materials provide.

Talking about art with children is yet another important way in which teachers can guide the developing artist's work. The wrong questions and comments can be damaging to children. Although well-meaning, questions such as "What is it?" may be difficult to answer and emphasize the product rather that the process of art.

Making appropriate comments and asking the right questions require thoughtfulness and insight. Engel (1996) suggests that adults must learn to look more carefully at children's art so that they can respond in positive ways. She identifies six questions that teachers can ask themselves as they prepare to talk with children about art:

- What is it made of (size, tools, medium)?
- What does the adult see (lines, angles, shapes, symmetry, colors, overlaps)?
- What does it represent (design, story, scene, symbol)?
- How is it organized (perspective, composition, action, view, completion)?
- What is it about, what is the nature of involvement (violence, peace, love, sadness, persuasion, information)?
- Where does the idea come from (imagination, observation, literature, imitation, TV, messing around)?

When teachers respond enthusiastically and with these kinds of questions, children get excited about producing art that is meaningful to them.

Finally, teachers need to display children's art in the classroom. The message adults must convey is that art is a means of expression for all, not just something for a select few who demonstrate special talent. Displaying artwork from each child helps both parents and children value the creative activities of each classmate. The teacher should place art at the child's eye level and rotate it regularly to make sure children fully appreciate the artwork of their peers.

The Art of Reggio Emilia

The model preschool program known as Reggio Emilia is well known for its artwork. Seefeldt (1995) describes it as having rather amazing results:

> Stunning displays of art surround you. Brightly colored drawings and paintings, surrealistic in appearance and depicting all kinds of animals— giraffes, zebras, horses, lions, and tigers—decorate the walls. A mural of children playing in a field of red poppies hangs from the ceiling. Shelves and pedestals hold sculptures. (p. 39)

This is not a description of what most preschool teachers in the United States regularly experience. What makes the artwork of children in the Reggio Emilia approach so astonishing? The maturity and complexity of the productions are truly amazing. Certainly, the children are no different from those in preschool programs in the United States. So, where do the differences come from?

Seefeldt (1995) argues that in Reggio Emilia teachers consider art *serious work.* They organize the art program around three principles:

- *Understanding cognitive theories of art.* A basic premise of cognitive theories is that art is an important form of communicating ideas and feelings to others. Art becomes a language of expressing cognitive understandings to others.
- *Motivating children to produce art.* Children who are provided with quality experiences can be motivated to express their learning to others through art. Deeply meaningful experiences can lead to amazing art.

• *Selecting teaching strategies.* Teachers in the Reggio Emilia program are actively involved in teaching young children the skills they need to succeed in art. This is done individually as the child demonstrates a need for instruction. Modeling appropriate techniques, physically assisting the young child from time to time, and providing specific verbal feedback are all used to teach art to young children.

Music and the Young Child

Just as art provides many opportunities for young children to express themselves, music draws others into creative activities in the early childhood classroom. When adults carefully prepare the environment with appropriate materials and encourage musical experiences, children become willing participants in a variety of musical activities.

The Importance of Music in Early Childhood

For more information about the importance of music in early childhood, go to the Companion Website at www.prenhall.com/henniger, select Chapter 16, then choose Web Destinations.

The technical quality of musical productions at this age shows that children are just beginning to develop their skills. However, most children are genuinely interested in and enjoy musical experiences. Just as with the child's developing art abilities, the foundations for later musical production and enjoyment are built during the early childhood years. Ball (1995) cites longitudinal research that reveals that musical aptitude (the potential to learn music) becomes stabilized by age 9. The clear implication is that if we want to help children develop the basic

Celebrating Diversity . . .
Early Musical Talent

Many parents of very young children are enrolling them in formal musical instruction in either violin or piano as early as age 2. The Suzuki method (Wilson, 2004), begun in Japan in 1928, is now a popular approach for early musical training in the United States. While not specifically designed for gifted and talented children, the program often attracts parents who believe their children are highly capable.

The Suzuki method assumes that just as young children learn language early and well by being immersed in a language-rich environment, they can learn music by listening, repeating, and practicing until they have mastered simple tunes such as "Twinkle, Twinkle, Little Star." Parents are an essential part of the Suzuki approach, encouraging their children to spend time each day listening to the music being learned and practicing their musical skills. In a relatively short time, many young children using the Suzuki method can

play very complex music. By emphasizing perfection in form and production, the Suzuki method has helped a large number of very young children develop the skills they need to perform complex musical pieces that often astound adult listeners. While not all children continue to develop their musical skills after their early successes, some do become truly gifted musicians.

1. Do you have any personal experience with the Suzuki method? Has a family member or friend been involved in this approach? What was the experience like?

2. Go back and reread the sections in Chapter 13 on stress and young children. Do you think parents who enroll their children in Suzuki music programs are pushing them too hard and creating stress for young children? Why or why not?

skills necessary for musical expression later in life, they need many opportunities to experience music during the early childhood years.

There are many reasons for including music in the curriculum. Isenberg and Jalongo (2001) have identified the following benefits of music for child development:

- *Psychomotor skills.* As children strike the xylophone, tap their rhythm sticks, beat a drum, or move to music, they are refining their control over large and small muscle movements.

- *Perceptual skills.* Recognizing a familiar tune and imitating it or tapping out a rhythmic pattern are examples of how music allows children opportunities to develop perceptual abilities.

- *Affective development.* Music naturally leads to emotional responses and provides many children with important and appropriate ways to express their feelings.

- *Cognitive growth.* Musical experiences have been found to enhance the reasoning abilities of young children. Children develop higher-level thinking skills and memory through musical activities.

- *Social skills.* Many musical experiences encourage participation, sharing, and cooperation. These important social skills need constant reinforcement in the early childhood classroom in natural and meaningful ways.

- *Cultural understandings.* Multicultural musical experiences help familiarize children with an important aspect of different cultures. This can lead to meaningful discussions of the similarities and differences between cultures. Children also identify with music from their own culture and react positively when teachers include this music in the classroom.

Musical Development

John and Astra are sitting on the circle time rug and singing along with their favorite music tape by Raffi. These busy 3-year-olds then decide to add some music-making of their own to the activity. John takes a drum off the shelf, while Astra locates a triangle to use for her rhythm instrument. They restart the tape and sing along while keeping a reasonably accurate beat with their instruments. John and Astra are progressing normally in their musical development.

Researchers who have studied the development of musical abilities in young children (e.g., Bayless & Ramsey, 1991) generally describe their results in terms of typical performance at different ages rather than identifying stages of development. The following abilities are milestones in musical development (see also Figure 16–1).

- *Infants* respond to the loudness and softness of sounds; react to the human voice, particularly the primary caregiver's; and express lively reactions to action songs and more subdued responses to lullabies.

- *Toddlers* discriminate among sounds and may try to approximate them; listen to music, enthusiastically responding to certain songs while repeating repetitive phrases; enjoy making sounds with musical instruments or common household items; and may sing or hum casually as they play.

- *Three-year-olds* develop better voice control and can master simple songs; many have favorite tunes they recognize; they can play rhythm instruments with a basic understanding of beat.

- *Four-year-olds* can learn basic musical concepts such as pitch, duration, tempo, and loudness; are able to classify musical instruments by sound, shape, size,

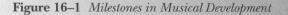

Figure 16–1 *Milestones in Musical Development*

Infants	Toddlers	Three-year-olds	Four-year-olds	Five-year-olds	Six-, Seven-, Eight-year-olds
React to loudness, softness, human voice	Listen to music, repeat some phrases, enjoy making music	Better voice control, master simple songs	Can learn basic musical concepts, sing complete songs from memory	Maturing sense of pitch, rhythm, and melody	Singing voices approaching maturity, enjoy silliness and word-play

and pitch; sing complete songs from memory with improving rhythm and pitch; and have an average singing range of five notes.

- *Five-year-olds* have a maturing sense of pitch, rhythm, and melody; like longer songs with predictable elements; reproduce a melody in an echo song; and extend their singing range to six notes.

- *Six-, 7-, and 8-year-olds* have singing voices that approach maturity; can sing in tune with up to 10 notes; are beginning to develop a sense of harmony; enjoy silliness and wordplay in songs; have a greater awareness of printed music and its role; often have well-established musical preferences; and may show an interest in playing a musical instrument.

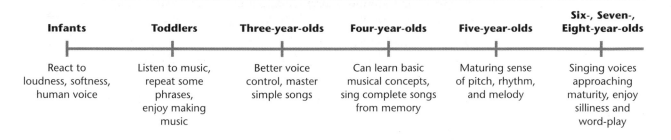

Into Practice...
Music for the Nonmusician

Does all this discussion about music make you nervous? Would you consider yourself below average in musical abilities? If you have not had any musical training, the thought of encouraging young children to engage in these activities may seem daunting. The good news is that you really do not need to be highly proficient musically to have a strong program for young children. Jalongo (1996) suggests five ways the nonmusician can use recorded music to create quality experiences for young children:

- **Choose music that is at a comfortable pitch.** Young children's voices are still maturing, and music that has a high pitch is harder to sing. Singers such as Raffi and Ella Jenkins have many recordings that are easy for children (and adults) to sing along with because of the lower pitch.
- **Expand your musical repertoire.** Try to avoid sticking to only familiar music. Borrow some recorded music from the library or other teachers, and work on

expanding your musical horizons. This helps ensure that students are getting richer musical experiences.

- **Become familiar with the best music available for young children.** Several musical awards are presented regularly for children's music, such as the Parent's Choice Seal of Approval. Professional journals also review recordings, and these can be helpful in selecting quality options. Talking to other teachers and music specialists provides additional insight for selection.
- **Provide a wide range of musical styles, including ethnic music.** Recordings of songs sung in different languages and others that use culturally specific instruments can be excellent additions to the early childhood classroom.
- **Arrange many opportunities for quiet listening.** Teachers can set up a cassette player with headphones and a basket of tapes for listening times. Background music at different times during the day can provide another productive listening experience.

The Music Curriculum for Young Children

The early childhood music curriculum has four components (Bayless & Ramsey, 1991; Edwards, 2002). Listening to music is the first of these elements. Teachers may lead a group activity in which they play recordings of different musical styles, instruments, or old favorites and help children listen more carefully to the elements of the music. Individual children can put on headphones and listen to taped music during free time. Finally, some teachers play music at different times during the day to create a pleasant atmosphere in the classroom. In all these instances, children are refining their musical listening skills in an enjoyable setting.

A second element of the early childhood music curriculum is responding to music through movement. Young children have an almost irresistible urge to move to the music they hear. Adults can encourage this through modeling, group movement and music activities, and the provision of materials and space for movement. Many songs for young children also include hand motions; adults can teach these, and children can use them when singing. Teachers can also create a marching band with musical instruments and a lively recording. Children can use scarves and streamers in the music corner as they move to music during free play.

A third important component of the music curriculum is that children must have many opportunities to make music. Singing enjoyable songs is one way to have fun making music. Many excellent songbooks and recordings (see Flohr, 2004, for example) can provide children with a variety of singing experiences. Playing different musical and rhythmic instruments gives great pleasure to young children as well. Rotating these options in and out of the classroom adds further interest to this aspect of music-making.

Making music is an important way for children to engage in creative expression; teachers should encourage them to create new verses for familiar songs and develop their own musical and rhythmic expressions.

For more information about play and music, go to the Companion Website at www.prenhall.com/henniger, select Chapter 16, then choose Web Destinations.

Many songs for young children also include hand and body movements.

The final element of the early childhood music curriculum is to help children begin to understand music and music-making. For example, children need to acquire a vocabulary that helps them describe musical experiences. Children can learn and use musical terms such as *pitch, duration, tempo,* and *loudness* to help them describe both their own and others' musical experiences. Teachers can also present the appropriate names for musical instruments and simple explanations for how each makes music. Learning that music communicates feelings and helping children to identify the emotions generated by specific pieces is yet another way to begin developing a cognitive understanding of music.

Facilitating Musical Experiences

Adults play important roles in facilitating quality musical experiences. Having positive attitudes about music and taking the time needed for adequate planning and preparation can help ensure exciting adventures in this aspect of the curriculum. The following guidelines identify specific strategies that teachers can use.

- *Prepare the classroom environment.* Careful planning and preparation are the essential starting points for good musical experiences. Thoughtful selections of songs to sing, music to play, and instruments for children to use will strengthen the music curriculum (Achilles, 1999). While children love to repeat favorite songs and enjoy the opportunity to thoroughly explore musical instruments, it is also important to have new materials and songs to maintain interest.

- *Encourage creative expression.* Teachers need to allow young children the freedom to experiment and explore with music. When adults value creative musical expression, children's performances blossom. As they make up songs or new verses to familiar tunes and create their own rhythmic expressions, children are truly making music in meaningful ways.

- *Emphasize enjoyment.* The quality of musical expression should *not* be the focus of the early childhood music curriculum. Children have yet to develop the skills needed for quality performance. Rather, the emphasis should be on enjoying a variety of musical experiences. Developing a love of music during the early years can help maintain interest and involvement in later life.

- *Make music fun.* Teachers have a major role to play in making musical experiences fun for young children. It is important, for example, to demonstrate to children your own excitement. If the teacher is animated and involved, children will be, too. Active participation in musical experiences increases the likelihood that children will find them fun. Adding props to songs, selecting motivating music, and providing quality musical instruments also help make these activities more fun for children.

- *Carefully observe.* Observations serve several purposes in the early childhood music curriculum. They allow teachers to determine which music materials are being used and when change is needed. Observations help adults recognize who is participating and what can be done to get others involved. Children's musical understandings can also be assessed through observation and activities planned to meet deficits.

Into Practice . . .
Singing Songs with Young Children

Singing should be an integral part of the curriculum in early childhood. Songs can strengthen conceptual understandings, make more routine activities such as clean-up time more pleasant, and add an enjoyable interlude to the day. If you enjoy singing, so will young children. You can even make up songs that can be sung to familiar music and create your own music curriculum.

Singing to Strengthen Conceptual Understanding

Many songs allow children to learn while they sing. The following is an example for mathematics:

> **Four Little Horses**
> Four little horses, galloping through town
> Two are white and two are brown
> Two gallop up and two gallop down
> Four little horses galloping through town.

You can create your own tune for this song and, using fingers for horses, merrily sing about four, six, eight, or even five little horses.

Singing During Routines

Songs are a good way to alert children to the start of routines like snack, clean-up, and outdoor time. An example of this type is:

> **Brushing Teeth**
> (Sing to the tune of "Mulberry Bush")
> This is the way we brush our teeth,
> brush our teeth, brush our teeth.
> This is the way we brush our teeth
> so early in the morning
>
> > (Herr & Libby-Larson, 2004, p. 189)

Singing for Fun

Songs with hand motions or full-body involvement are often popular with young children and are frequently requested. "The Eensy Weensy Spider" and "Head, Shoulders, Knees and Toes" are two traditional favorites.

Activities in Art and Music

Many idea books are available to assist teachers of young children in planning creative art and music activities. Herr and Libby-Larson (2004) and Silberg and Schiller (2003) are two good examples of resource guides that are useful in planning for art and music. Teachers should take care to adapt the suggestions of these or other idea books to meet the needs and interests of specific children. Similarly, the ideas that follow may need modifications to succeed with children you know.

Activities for Infants/Toddlers

Programs for infants and toddlers spend much time and effort dealing with the routines of young children's lives (Watson & Watson, 2003). Toileting, bathing, eating, and sleeping activities consume much of the day. An art and music curriculum at this age should be integrated with these activities whenever possible. Some possibilities include the following:

- Adults can place artwork within the view of infants and toddlers as they participate in various routines.
- Adults can playfully sing to young children while diapering, feeding, or preparing them for naps.
- Playing background music during the routines of the day introduces infants and toddlers to pleasant musical experiences.
- Adults can place rattles and other noisemakers within reach of young children for playful exploration during diaper-changing times.

During the rest of the day, adults can give infants and toddlers additional opportunities to explore art and music. Infants and toddlers can use simple (and safe) drawing materials for scribble art, for example. Teachers can encourage toddlers to move to music by providing a space and some lively music. Edible play dough is another enjoyable art alternative for this age.

Art and Music for Preschoolers

The preschool child's blossoming skills allow for a much-expanded art and music curriculum. Teachers should include old favorites like crayons and easel painting for art and classic songs like "The Eensy Weensy Spider"; children also need the chance to experience new creative arts activities.

Art Ideas. The following are selected examples of creative art experiences for preschool children:

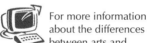
For more information about the differences between arts and crafts, go to the Companion Website at www.prenhall.com/henniger, select Chapter 16, then choose Web Destinations.

- *Mural painting.* This can be a fun outdoor activity for young children. Tape a large sheet of butcher paper to any exterior wall, and let children collectively paint to their hearts' content. Alternatively, provide children with buckets of water and paintbrushes of different sizes and encourage them to paint the walls and other structures with water.
- *Straw painting.* Provide children with glossy paper and straws. Children put small amounts of fairly runny paint on the paper and then blow through the straws to create interesting images and a mixing of paints. Be sure to instruct younger preschoolers to blow out rather than suck up through their straws.
- *Crayon rubbings.* Using items with a definite texture, such as leaves, coins, or sandpaper, place a piece of newsprint on top and have children rub the flat side of the crayon over the paper. Let children experiment with objects of their own choosing to make rubbings.
- *Working with clay.* Although clay is more difficult for young children to work with than the more traditional play dough, it can be an enjoyable experience with careful preparation. It may be possible to create finished fired pottery, but those products are not necessary for children to have a meaningful experience with clay.

Playdough provides young children with many opportunities for creative experiences.

- *Attend an art show.* Preschool children can benefit from spending some time viewing the artwork of older students. These older artists can talk to preschool children about the art they have created.

Music Ideas. Many different types of musical experiences can be valuable for preschool children. The following suggestions provide a beginning point for this level:

- *Scarves.* Collect silky scarves from parents, and use these to help young children move to music. Have the scarves available in the group time area with music to fit the mood you want to encourage. Help children realize that they need to avoid collisions with others, and simply turn them loose. This is a favorite activity for many children.
- *"I Know an Old Lady."* This classic song about an old lady who swallows a fly (and much more) is often sung with primary-age children. But with props for the flannelboard, this song has considerable appeal for younger students. The catchy tune, combined with much repetition, makes it a hit.
- *Marching band.* With a good collection of rhythm instruments—such as cymbals, bells, and drums—children can practice making music by marching around the classroom (or outdoors) in time to a good piece of music with a clear beat. The addition of hats and a band leader (the teacher initially) makes the activity even more attractive to young children.
- *Music appreciation.* Choose several pieces of music that create different moods for you as an adult. Have children close their eyes and listen to each piece, imagining that they are doing something as they listen. Talk about what children imagined and how the music created that mood. Add your own insights.

Into Practice...
Multicultural Musical Instruments

Teachers can productively use a diverse collection of multicultural musical instruments in the early childhood classroom. Although it is important to avoid being stereotypic, presenting traditional instruments can open up a productive dialogue about the similarities and differences between cultures. In addition, the musical experiences can be very rewarding for children. Here are a few examples of instruments that you may want to consider as part of the music curriculum:

- **Rain stick.** This instrument comes from Chile and is made from a long, cylindrical, dried cactus, with the spines pounded inward and sealed with small pebbles inside. Tipping the stick allows the stones to bounce off the cactus spines and create a pleasant tinkling sound.
- **Ocarina.** This instrument is also called a vessel flute and originated in South America. Made from clay, it has a small built-in mouthpiece and several holes for making different musical notes. More appropriate for primary-age children, this instrument requires careful handling and cleaning between players.

- **Drums.** No one culture holds a monopoly on drums. They seem to come from many different places and make a wide range of sounds. African, Chinese, Brazilian, and Native American cultures all have diverse drums for use in the early childhood classroom. Children enjoy trying out the many different varieties and talking about similarities and differences.
- **Guiro.** This traditional rhythm instrument originated in Mexico and is a favorite for all ages. Shaped somewhat like a shortened, hollow baseball bat with grooves running horizontally around the instrument, the player taps or rubs a short stick over the grooves on the exterior of the guiro to keep time with the music.
- **Shakeree.** This rhythm instrument comes from Africa and consists of a large gourd with seeds strung over its exterior in an intricate pattern. Shaking the gourd causes the seeds to make a rattling sound similar to maracas.

The Primary Years

The continued development of motor skills and cognitive understanding makes it possible for teachers to plan and implement increasingly complex art and music activities for primary-age children. The following examples are designed to get you thinking about the possibilities for this level.

Art Suggestions. Schirrmacher (2002) has many good suggestions for primary-age children. He reminds us that the young artist at this age is still eager to mess around with materials, exploring their properties and enjoying the process of art. Providing plenty of paper, glue, scissors, crayons, and paint for basic exploration remains important. Adding new materials like chalk and pastels is also useful. Although messy, these give children the opportunity to blend colors in beautiful combinations. Light chalk on dark paper, wet chalk, and pastels on heavy paper are possibilities.

Using crayon shavings to make art projects is another option for this age. The teacher can scrape old broken crayons with a dull knife to create the shavings needed for the project. To create attractive designs, the children place the shavings on a piece of waxed paper and put another sheet of waxed paper on top. The teacher presses these with a warm iron, through a protective sheet of plain paper. Before adding the second piece of waxed paper, children can include other items, such as glitter, bits of ribbon, or tissue paper, to individualize their creations.

Some children at the primary level begin to show an interest in drawing or sketching. Simple sketches of each other, objects in the room, or things at home may be attractive options for many primary-age children. Brookes (1986) provides excellent ideas for helping children develop their creative drawing abilities.

Making stars and snowflakes is another fun activity for winter-time art. Coffee filters (flat-bottomed rather than conical) are just the right shape, size, and thickness for creating individually designed stars or snowflakes. By folding the filters into quarters, snipping off small pieces, and carefully unfolding the paper, children can easily construct and then display their efforts on classroom windows.

Music Activities. The musical experiences of primary-age children should include many different ways to make music. Children this age can productively use more complex instruments. The autoharp is an excellent example that both teachers and children can use. When the autoharp has clear markings for chords, children who have learned songs the teacher has previously played can recreate the appropriate chords by reading a song card. Orff instruments, designed by the German composer Carl Orff, are other examples of more complex instruments that produce beautiful musical tones. The metallophone, for example, is like the traditional xylophone, but produces rich alto and bass tones on bars of thick metal.

Primary-age children can enjoy listening to and discussing classical music. Edwards (2002) suggests the following for young children:

Mozart, Symphony no. 39 in E Flat and Symphony no. 41 in C

Chopin, Sonata no. 3, op. 58

Beethoven, String Quartet no. 3 in D Major and String Quartet no. 4 in C

Bach, Brandenburg Concerto no. 106

Singing songs remains a high priority for children at this age. With increasing musical abilities, children can enjoy singing songs in rounds. A classic example is "Row, Row, Row Your Boat." Silly songs with child-oriented humor are also very popular. Take, for example, "Fried Ham":

Fried ham, fried ham

Cheese and bologna

After the macaroni

We'll have more fried ham, fried ham, fried ham!

Children enjoy singing this silly song using a variety of unusual voices, such as underwater, robot, and baby. It is great fun and provides many opportunities for creative expression.

Primary-age students can also benefit from listening to a live concert. Having a middle school or high school band come to play would be one option. Taking a field trip to listen to a live performance is another possibility.

For more information about multicultural songs, go to the Companion Website at www.prenhall.com/henniger, select Chapter 16, then choose Web Destinations.

Observing Development • Creative Behavior

Choose one of the age groups within early childhood (infants/toddlers, preschoolers, or primary-age children), *observe* for **creative behavior** using the guidelines provided, *reflect* on what you saw and heard, and *apply* the appropriate strategies listed with the children you observed.

Observe	Reflect	Apply
Look for specific examples of:	*Think about and respond to the following questions:*	*Consider the following developmentally appropriate strategies for the age group you observed:*
Creative behavior in play (using a toy in an unusual way, solving a problem encountered in play, making up words, etc.)	What is the role of play materials or equipment in the creative play of young children?	Provide open-ended materials for play • Infant/toddler: water-play table and materials • Preschool: dress-up clothes and accessories around a theme (doctor's office, fire station) • Primary: set of unit blocks
Creative behavior in art (an art creation that is new and interesting to the child, expressing feelings through art, etc.)	Were the creative art experiences you observed limited to a small number of children or did most engage in creative expression through art?	Reinforce children's creative art expressions • Infant/toddler: "You're having fun mixing the red and blue fingerpaints." • Preschool: "Tell me about your picture. It interests me." • Primary: "That's the third drawing you've done today. I really appreciate your efforts."
Creative behavior in music (using musical instruments to create music, making up words to a familiar song, dancing to music, etc.)	What criteria did you use to determine the creative elements of the musical experiences you observed?	Model creative musical experiences • Infant/toddler: playfully move to the music while holding an infant/toddler • Preschool: bring musical instruments to group time and demonstrate their use, then have children try them out • Primary: make up a song to go along with a familiar tune and sing it to the class

Summary

 To test your knowledge of this chapter's contents, go to the Companion Website, at www.prenhall.com/henniger, select Chapter 16, then select Study Guide. Also see Chapter Overviews, Reflecting Essay Questions, Multimedia Explorations, and relevant Web Destinations.

What Is Creativity?

An understanding of the creative process is central to the teaching of art and music. Studying definitions of creativity, the characteristics of creative individuals, the most helpful ways for adults to assist with the creative process, and the relationships between play and creativity provides the foundation needed to understand this complex process.

The Young Artist

Although some consider art education less important than other parts of the curriculum, there is a strong rationale for including art in the early childhood classroom. Understanding developmental trends in art, the content of the early childhood art curriculum, and the adult's role in art experiences allows teachers to create appropriate and interesting art experiences for young children.

Music and the Young Child

Music is another important element of the early childhood curriculum. When teachers understand the developmental patterns children follow in their musical growth, create appropriate content for the music curriculum, find ways to facilitate musical experiences, and include appropriate materials and activities for young children, they can implement exciting musical experiences for young children.

Activities in Art and Music

There are many good resources for creative art and music activities for young children. Teachers should plan on including them as an integral part of infant/toddler, preschool, and primary-age education.

Multimedia Explorations and Activities . . .

The Benefits of Art and Music

A close look at what constitutes the best kind of experience for infants and young children leads quickly to the arts. From a baby's first lullaby, to a three-year-old's experimentation with finger paint, to a seven-year-old's dramatization of a favorite story, developmentally appropriate arts experience is critical. For all children, at all levels, the arts play a central role in cognitive, motor, language, and social-emotional development. The arts motivate and engage children in learning, stimulate memory and facilitate understanding, enhance symbolic communication, promote relationships, and provide an avenue for building competence. The arts are natural for young children. Child development specialists note that play is the business of young children; play is the way children promote and enhance their development. The arts are a most natural vehicle for play.

(Bruce, 1998, p. v)

Research

Due to well-meaning efforts to strengthen the academic potential of young children, many early childhood programs are feeling pressures to limit the arts experiences provided so that more time can be spent on activities designed to strengthen intellectual and language development. While these latter areas are clearly critical, so too are the arts. This activity is designed to make you more aware of the benefits of art and music in the early childhood classroom.

1. Go to the Companion Website at www.prenhall.com/henniger and click on the Multimedia Explorations and Activities button for Chapter 16 to find more information on this topic.

2. Interview an art or music educator for his or her perspective on the values of the arts in early childhood education.

Reflect

Based on your research, consider the following issues:

- Why should the arts be considered a basic element of the early childhood curriculum?

- What interest groups are discouraging an emphasis in the arts, and how can their arguments be overcome?

- Which decision-makers need to be convinced that the arts are essential in the classroom? What evidence will they need to be persuaded of their importance?

Respond

Consider one or more of the following options as responses to your commitment to arts education:

1. Develop a rationale for arts education that would help convince parents about its importance in the early childhood classroom. Share the rationale with a teacher of young children for inclusion in a newsletter to parents.

2. Call or write a local official who has influence on the curriculum for young children. Work to convince this person that arts education should be a central component of the curriculum.

3. Summarize the key findings of research on the benefits of either art or music to young children and post it on the message board of the Companion Website for this text. Include bibliographic references so that others can review these works as well.

USING TECHNOLOGY TO SUPPORT DEVELOPMENT AND LEARNING

In this chapter you will

- Study the impact of television on young children.
- Learn about the relationships between technology and play.
- Investigate characteristics of developmentally appropriate software for the early childhood classroom.
- Identify the teacher's role in technology use.
- Clarify strategies for communicating with parents about technology.

Navin and Mark are playing at the computer in their preschool classroom. Like the rest of their classmates, these 4-year-old children fearlessly experiment with the computer as they navigate through the art program they are using. As they draw and paint on the computer screen, Mark and Navin talk about their creation. "Let's try the stamps" insists Navin as they change the background color from white to green. "Okay, I want butterflies in our picture, and they have some in the stamp part," Mark says. The two children work to negotiate additional elements of their project as play continues over the next 15 minutes. Once the picture is complete, they print it out, show it to two interested classmates, and then take off for the block corner to engage in additional play.

The scene just described is becoming more and more common in the early childhood classroom. Teachers and parents recognize the value of computer use for young children and opportunities to use computers on a regular basis are expanding. Children are enthusiastically using the computer as an effective tool for exploration, learning, and play.

Until fairly recently, however, many adults questioned the value of computers in the early childhood classroom. During the 1980s, as computers became more accessible to children in prekindergarten–12 education, some early educators voiced concerns about developmental readiness (Barnes & Hill, 1983), lack of social interactions (Heller & Martin, 1982), and the move away from concrete, real-world materials (Cuffaro, 1984) associated with computer use by young children.

Writing and research from the 1990s to the present have generally been supportive of computer use by young children. Socialization issues (Baron, 1991), concerns over software options (Shade, 1992), and developmental appropriateness (Clements & Sarama, 2003) have been addressed to the satisfaction of many early educators.

This chapter demonstrates the appropriateness of computers and other forms of technology as learning tools in the early childhood classroom beginning at age 3. Although there are a growing number of technology options for infants and toddlers being produced and marketed, particularly to families, many early childhood specialists consider these alternatives developmentally inappropriate (Galley, 2000). Although this equipment can be misused by older children as well, with careful selection and planning, activities involving technology can successfully complement the other more traditional activities of young children.

Television and Young Children

Television is one form of technology that has been available to parents and teachers for many years. Much has been written about the problems young children encounter as they interact with this technology. Time spent viewing, the content of programming, and advertising issues have all been concerns voiced about television viewing. Despite these valid criticisms, limited television viewing in the early childhood classroom may be useful. In this section, we will look at both the limitations and potential for effective television viewing.

Time Spent Viewing

For more information about problems associated with TV viewing, go to the Companion Website at www.prenhall.com/henniger, select Chapter 17, then choose Web Destinations.

One major concern voiced about television use is the large amount of time children spend viewing. Miller (1997) states that children in the United States watch an average of 3 to 5 hours of television daily. One study also indicates that 30 percent of children from birth to 3 and 43 percent of 4- to 6-year-olds have a television in their bedroom (Rideout, Vandewater, & Wartella, 2003). By the time young adults graduate from high school, they have spent more time watching television than doing any other activity except sleeping (Cohen, 1994). Even if all the programming being watched was excellent, spending this much time in front of the television significantly decreases the child's opportunities for other valuable experiences. For children during the early childhood years, the activity that television is most likely to replace is play.

Let's create a typical day in the life of a 5-year-old child to see the potential impact of an average level of television viewing:

7:00 AM	Wake up, dress, breakfast, television
8:30 AM	Leave for kindergarten
2:30 PM	After-school care (with 1 hour of TV viewing)
5:00 PM	Home, television (½-hour), dinner
6:30 PM	Television (1½ hours)
8:00 PM	Prepare for bed

Too much television and inappropriate programming can cause problems for young children.

Family Partnerships . . .
Alternatives to Television

While many parents understand at some level that they and their children probably watch too much television, they may need to understand the rationale for cutting back on their viewing and have good alternatives to implement that are easy to organize and pleasurable for both parents and children. As a teacher of young children, you will need to remind parents regularly of creative and fun alternatives to television. Perhaps including a column in each edition of your newsletter or holding a parent meeting to discuss this topic would work best for you. Whatever method you choose, be ready with a long list of good alternatives to TV viewing. Here are a few ideas to get you started:

- **Family reading time.** Encourage parents to set aside time each evening for reading. Even 15 or 20 minutes can be valuable in motivating interest in reading. Children need to see their parents engaged in reading, and children can benefit greatly from being read to. Be sure to provide lists of quality children's literature and possible locations so that it will be easy for parents to find good selections.
- **Game night.** Taking one evening a week for a short game can be an enjoyable alternative to television viewing. Once again, parents can benefit from some information about good game options (see Chapters 5, 9, and 12 for resources and ideas for developmentally appropriate games). You might send home a description of a simple game that you

played in school and that families might enjoy playing together.

- **Family play time.** Many families have gotten out of the habit of playing together. With regular reminders and simple suggestions, this can be another important addition to family routines. Things like singing and acting out "Row, Row, Row Your Boat" with infants and toddlers, building block structures with preschoolers, and helping a primary-age child construct a "fort" using an old blanket are examples of things you could share. When they are relatively short and simple to prepare, parents will be more likely to commit to this activity.
- **Getting outside.** Going for a walk around the neighborhood, visiting a local park, or planting a small garden are all options that get both parents and children out of the house and engaged in fun activities together. Parents often need reminders to get involved in these enjoyable tasks as well.

1. Are you a good model for reasonable television viewing? Will you be able to speak from experience when you talk about alternatives to television?

2. How do you feel about this role in working with families? Will you be comfortable in suggesting alternatives to television? Why or why not?

It does not take much imagination to see that this child has little time for anything other than the regular routine and about 3 hours of television viewing. The TV has crowded out most of the opportunities for socializing with others, being read to, or playing.

Sex, Violence, and Advertising

A careful analysis of television programming during prime time also shows considerable content that is inappropriate for young children. Sexual themes and acts of violence are often cited as problem areas (Cortes, 2000; Huston & Wright, 1996; Thornton, 2002). Children are viewing a variety of adult-oriented sexual situations and many different acts of violence on a daily basis. Their ability to make sense of these situations is limited, at best, and leads to considerable confusion and misunderstanding among children. If something is on television, does that mean it is acceptable in the real world? Young children are struggling to define the borders between reality and fantasy. Unfortunately, television often blurs this already unclear distinction. The results are painfully evident in the inappropriate behaviors of young children.

Another problem area associated with television viewing is the advertising to which children are exposed. It is estimated that the average child sees approximately 20,000 commercials a year, many of them specifically targeting children as consumers (Clearinghouse on Elementary and Early Childhood Education, 1990). The majority of foods advertised for young children have high sugar content. Similarly, the toys being promoted tend to be less creative than other products available to young children. Many parent-child conflicts over toys to buy can be traced to the advertising seen on television.

Redeeming Aspects?

The preceding discussion suggests that television viewing has a strong negative impact on the lives of young children. Although research supports this perspective, other evidence indicates that children can benefit when they spend time watching quality programming. Educational programs like *Sesame Street* and *Between the Lions* are receiving good reports in terms of their impact on preparing children for school. Regular viewing of these programs has helped improve early literacy and mathematics skills (Rath, 2002; St. Clair, 2002; Wright & Huston, 1995). Although many television programs have limited value, educational programming may be a positive experience for many young children.

Guidelines for Parents

For more information about television guidelines, go to the Companion Website at www.prenhall.com/henniger, select Chapter 17, then choose Web Destinations.

Perhaps the most universal piece of technology found in American homes is the television. Very few are without at least one, and most have two or more. Many families provide little guidance and supervision for young children's viewing. The following ideas may help parents deal more effectively with the television:

- *Collect articles* from professional literature that provide information about the problems and benefits of television viewing. The articles discussed in this section are all good examples of articles for your collection.

- *Encourage parents to limit television viewing* by suggesting alternatives that are healthier for the child's overall development. When provided with specific suggestions for simple play experiences, parents can take the difficult step of turning off the television for at least part of the child's free time.

- *Suggest that parents discuss* what the children are watching. Whenever possible, parents can view programming along with children and talk about the negative aspects that are being presented. This can help children be better consumers of the programs they watch.

- *Move the television* to a room not in the center of family life. This will help encourage other more valuable activities when family members gather.

The Video Game Dilemma

> *Matt and Alan rush home from their second-grade classroom and head straight to the video game shelf. They select a favorite game, plug it in, and spend the next 45 minutes deeply engrossed in manipulating their joysticks. Their animated conversation and intense focus show that Matt and Alan are definitely excited about the game.*

Many children like Matt and Alan find video games highly motivating, and the number of homes with these games continues to grow. In a study of low-income families, approximately 75 percent of the homes had video games for young children (Wright & Huston, 1995). In one study of 4- to 6-year-olds who have video games, girls spent an average of 53 minutes a day of daily use while boys averaged an hour and 8 minutes (Rideout, Vandewater, & Wartella, 2003).

The Debate over Value

Although children typically spend less time playing video games than watching television, many adults are concerned about video game use. Fantasy, violence, and autonomous action rather than cooperation are frequently cited as problem areas (Funk, 1993; Rideout, Vandewater, & Wartella, 2003). For some children, another issue is the large amount of time spent playing these games. Again, this leaves little time to engage in other more important activities such as vigorous physical activity and creative play.

However, some adults feel that video games offer benefits over television viewing. While TV is a passive activity, video games may increase a child's eye-hand coordination and improve attention to detail. Others suggest that these games can be a nonthreatening way to introduce children to computers. Finally, many children also gain a sense of accomplishment from playing (Cesarone, 1994).

One influential writer, Seymour Papert (1993), suggests that video games give insight into the potential power of computers to transform the way children learn. He states that parents and teachers should try to understand why video games captivate children. "Any adult who thinks one of these games is easy need only sit down and try to master one. Most are hard, with complex information—as well as technique—to be mastered" (p. 4). Video games, according to Papert, allow children to explore and experiment in situations with predetermined rules and to learn a great deal from these experiences. Papert wants computers to provide similar types of playful interactions for children.

For more information about children's video games, go to the Companion Website at www.prenhall.com/henniger, select Chapter 17, then choose Web Destinations.

Parental Roles

Many of the issues parents face regarding video games are similar to those discussed earlier for television viewing. One major concern is the amount of time some children spend playing video games. Parents should be encouraged to help their children find other activities when they spend too much time manipulating a joystick. Another significant issue is the concern over the level of violence portrayed in some video games. Many children are negatively influenced by the violence they see (Funk, 1993). The NAEYC (1997) identifies the following problems associated with violence:

- Children who view violence tend to see it as an acceptable way of resolving conflict.
- Children become less sensitive to the suffering of others.
- Anxieties may increase in some children. They may be more fearful of the world around them.

Selection of video games should be carefully made after thorough review of the content of the games.

Can Computers Be Used in Developmentally Appropriate Ways?

When NAEYC first published its description of developmentally appropriate practice in 1987, it did not mention computers (Bredekamp, 1987). At that time, fewer computers were being used by young children, and there was considerable disagreement among leaders in the field (Mageau, 1993) regarding their appropriateness. After much discussion, however, NAEYC approved and published a position statement describing effective technology use in the early childhood classroom (NAEYC, 1996). This document emphasizes the following points:

For more information about developmentally appropriate computer use, go to the Companion Website at www.prenhall.com/henniger, select Chapter 17, then choose Web Destinations.

1. The teacher must exercise professional judgment to ensure that each opportunity for computer use is age appropriate, individually appropriate, and sensitive to cultural diversity.
2. When implemented properly, technology can stimulate children's cognitive and social skills.
3. Computers should be integrated into the classroom environment and used by children as simply another learning option.
4. All children should have equitable access to computers in the schools.
5. Software selected for use should avoid stereotyping any group of people and avoid the use of violence as a problem-solving strategy.
6. Teachers and parents should work cooperatively to advocate for quality hardware and software options for young children.
7. Early childhood educators need training in appropriate computer use, including its implementation as a tool for working with other professionals.

Computers and Play

As discussed in Chapter 5, a key element of developmentally appropriate practice is allowing children to interact playfully with the materials and people in the environment. Play is a primary means for learning in the early childhood classroom. If the computer is to become an important option for young children, it must also encourage playful behaviors.

The "Observing Development" feature at the end of this chapter provides opportunities to observe children's use of computer hardware and software, reflect on the role computers play in enhancing child development, and apply strategies to encourage technology use.

Celebrating Play . . .
The Computer's Impact on Play

While there are those who believe that technologies such as computers have no place in the early childhood classroom, there is a growing body of evidence that suggests young children can benefit from appropriate technology use (Clements & Sarama, 2003). With the availability of quality technology products and appropriate preparations by the classroom teacher, benefits include social and emotional growth as well as language and cognitive learning. Still, there are those who harbor lingering doubts about the impact of computer use on childhood play. Some worry that technology will replace other play activities in the classroom. Others are concerned about the potential for social isolation. A third concern is that technology will take away opportunities for creative expression that are so prevalent in play.

Fischer and Gillespie (2003) addressed these concerns and others after carefully observing a typical Head Start classroom in rural Iowa. First, they found that when a variety of creative learning centers (such as blocks, art, dramatic play, and technology) are made available to children, they spend time among each of the options rather than focusing only on computer use. The technology center simply becomes one of several good choices within the classroom and children continue to take part in the more traditional play experiences. Second, they discovered that children engage in considerable social interaction as they use technology in the classroom. They felt that the portability of laptop computers helped facilitate these social exchanges. Finally, observations led them to conclude that creativity can prosper when open-ended developmentally appropriate software is made available to young children. Fischer and Gillespie concluded that technology can have a positive impact on play and the young child's development.

1. Based on what you have read in this chapter, what is the impact of computers on childhood play?

2. Should preschool programs include a technology center as one option for children during playtime? Why or why not?

The software available to children is the key ingredient to playful computer use. When it is designed to be used creatively by children, the potential for playful interactions is greatly enhanced. Many companies produce software for the early childhood age range. Some, however, have been more actively involved in creating playful products for young children. As a future teacher, you will need to review potential software carefully to be sure that it is developmentally appropriate and playful.

When characteristics of play are discussed in relation to computer use, we can see that while much of the software available for young children is of low quality, some options can be used to facilitate playful interactions in the early childhood classroom (Henniger, 1994):

- *Play is active.* Rather than being a passive event, play is generally associated with physical activity. Yet, the level of physicalness varies from one play event to the next. Puzzles, for example, require small muscle movements similar to those needed for manipulating a computer mouse and keyboard.

- *Play is child selected.* Good play experiences are chosen by the child from a variety of available options. When teachers place computers in the classroom and make them available to children during choice time, playfulness is enhanced.

- *Play is child directed.* Children can engage in quality play events with limited adult intervention. Independent use of the computer requires careful software selection, because much of what is currently available requires considerable adult assistance.

- *Play is process oriented.* In play, the process is more important than any product the child may create. Computers should allow children to enjoy the process of exploring and experimenting without emphasizing an end product.

- *Play stimulates imagination and creativity.* Many play experiences allow children to use their imaginations and be creative in their interactions with people and things. Drill-and-practice software (discussed later in this chapter, in the section entitled "Selecting Computers and Software Programs") discourages these important characteristics. There is only limited availability of more creative software options.

- *Play is a low-risk activity.* Play provides an opportunity for children to experiment and explore with little risk of failure. Software that is difficult for children to use independently or that requires specific responses makes it more likely that children will fail. Drill-and-practice software again receives low marks in this category.

As the preceding discussion indicates, the key ingredient in developmentally appropriate computer use is the software selected. Out of the hundreds of op-

Into Practice . . .
Lapware for Infants and Toddlers?

Computer software programs designed for infants and toddlers are often referred to as lapware because they are designed to be used with the young child sitting in the lap of a parent or caregiver. With titles such as Jump Start Baby, Baby and Me, and Reader Rabbit: Playtime for Baby (Galley, 2000), these products have developed into a multimillion-dollar business. While parents are the primary purchasers of these products, some early childhood programs for infants and toddlers are also including this option.

Most early childhood professionals, however, feel that computers should be postponed until approximately age 3. There is no need to rush into computer use; many opportunities will become available in the preschool years and later. Parents and caregivers of infants and toddlers should spend their time doing other things such as:

- **Encouraging play with sensory materials.** Learning at this age takes place primarily through sensory

experiences with real-world materials. Curiosity, independence, and conceptual understanding are stimulated through their use. Lapware provides limited opportunities for developing these same attributes.

- **Playing with children.** Adults should be spending time playing simple games like "Patty Cake" and "This Little Piggy" that develop initial socialization skills along with cognitive understanding, rather than sitting in front of a computer screen with young children.

- **Reading to children.** The single most important activity for developing early literacy skills in young children is to read to them (see Chapter 15). This process should begin with children as soon as they can sit up and enjoy a book on an adult's lap. A good book is the only "lapware" needed for infants and toddlers.

tions being marketed, excellent software is available. However, much of what is offered has limited play value. Teachers need to examine each piece of software carefully to ensure that young children have quality computer experiences.

Social Interactions

 For more information about computers and social interactions, go to the Companion Website at www.prenhall.com/henniger, select Chapter 17, then choose Web Destinations.

An early concern about computers was that they would isolate children, thereby discouraging the social experiences that are essential to development. When we think about how adults use computers, this concern seems justified. To accomplish tasks on the computer, most adults need to shut out other distractions and focus their energies on manipulating the keyboard and mouse. It becomes a solitary activity.

Yet, with children, this problem can be easily overcome. By simply putting more than one chair out at each available computer and encouraging children to help each other as they work their way through various software programs, teachers can significantly enhance social exchanges. Research indicates that in at least some instances, computer use can be more social than other more traditional activities for young children (Clements & Sarama, 2003).

Developmental Abilities

Another frequently cited concern related to young children and computers is the issue of developmental readiness. Do children have the cognitive skills needed to understand and manipulate the computer? Early detractors suggested they do not. Barnes and Hill (1983) argued that developmentally, children need to be in Piaget's stage of concrete operations (approximately age 8) before they are ready to use the computer. At that point, they suggest, children can more effectively manage the symbol world of the computer. Similarly, Cuffaro (1984) was concerned that preschool children should use concrete, real-world materials rather than the more abstract, symbol-oriented computer.

With proper preparation, computer use can be a social activity.

Although young children need many opportunities to manipulate objects in the real world, they can use symbols in their play from an early age. Consider the following situation:

> *Aletha and Selena (both age 4) are playing in the dress-up area of their preschool classroom. Following their recent trip to the fire station, they have decided to dress up as firefighters and pretend to put out a fire. Aletha describes the scene: "Let's say the wall is the apartment building on fire. It has three stories, and there are people hollering for us to quick, put out the fire! You hold the hose, and I'll get the water started!"*

Clearly, these two girls are using a wealth of symbols in their pretend play. They are envisioning complex situations that are not physically present, and they are manipulating these symbols successfully in play.

Young children can manage the symbol world of the computer, although it is one step removed from real objects and interactions (Clements & Sarama, 2003). When computers are one of many choices, they can provide quality experiences that expand, rather than detract from, the young child's learning opportunities.

The Child with Special Needs

Computers and technology are potentially powerful tools for assisting children with special needs. For example, computers help some children with attention deficits focus more effectively on their learning tasks; children with autistic tendencies may improve their interactions with peers as they use the computer together (Haugland & Wright, 1997). Teachers can consult experts in the field to locate software and hardware that meet the needs of children with special needs.

Some children need specialized hardware to take advantage of the computer. Touch screens, trackballs, and simplified keyboards are just a few of the options that are available to make the computer more accessible to children with special needs. When teachers combine this hardware with appropriate software, children can move from dependent to more independent learning (Mulligan, 2003; Snider & Badgett, 1995).

Computers in the Classroom

If children are to use computers in developmentally appropriate ways, teachers need to incorporate computers physically into the classroom space. When technology is readily accessible on a daily basis, it becomes just another tool that students can use to further their knowledge about the world. Computers become integrated into the learning experiences that take place. This natural connection helps make technology developmentally appropriate for young children (NAEYC, 1996).

To integrate computers effectively into the early childhood classroom, teachers should consider the following:

- Set up a computer center, with open access during designated times during the school day.
- Place the screen and keyboard at appropriate heights for the children using them.

For more information about a computer center, go to the Companion Website at www.prenhall.com/henniger, select Chapter 17, then choose Web Destinations.

Teachers play an important role in effective computer use.

- Organize each computer with at least two chairs to encourage more than one child to use the computer at a time.
- Make sure that the teacher can easily observe children working at the computer so that she can help as needed.
- Develop activities and lessons that make it more likely that children will use the computer as a regular part of their school day.

Interacting with Children Using Computers

Davis and Shade (1994) suggest three key roles for teachers as they interact with children using computers:

1. *Teacher as instructor.* When the computer is brought into the early childhood classroom, the teacher will need to help children learn how to use the technology.

2. *Teacher as coach.* As children become more comfortable with the computer, the teacher becomes more of a facilitator by providing assistance as needed and guiding children into appropriate use of the technology.

3. *Teacher as model.* Children should see the teacher using the computer as well. Recording children's oral stories, creating charts and signs for use in the classroom, and incorporating computers into small-group activities are some examples of this type of teacher modeling.

   In addition to making good decisions about the software available to children, teachers must also be prepared to restrict access to inappropriate Internet sites. Unfortunately, many Internet sites contain materials that are harmful to children. Teachers and parents need to monitor student use of the Internet to make sure children are making appropriate web site choices.

Celebrating Diversity...
Assistive Technology

Public Law 100–407, The Technology-Related Assistance for Individuals with Disabilities Act, was passed in 1988 to ensure that children with special needs and their families have access to technology resources. Children benefit significantly from having this technology in their early childhood classrooms (Mulligan, 2003). Roblyer, Edwards, and Havriluk (1997) identify two major benefits:

- **Improved motivation and self-concept.** Children with special needs spend more time on instructional tasks and have improved self-confidence when provided with assistive technology.
- **Enhanced communication and interaction with others.** Technology also helps children with special needs express themselves more effectively in their communications with others.

Recently, many tools have been designed to make technology more useful to children with special needs. Some examples follow:

- **Alternate input devices.** Some students with physical disabilities find it difficult to use the keyboard and mouse to enter information into the computer. Touch screens, alternative keyboards, and voice-controlled devices are examples of hardware available to help these students.
- **Substitute output devices.** Children with visual impairments need mechanisms such as enlarged computer images, speech devices that tell what the program is doing, or printers that produce Braille to assist them in productively using a computer.
- **Equipment to assist deaf learners.** Captioned video that provides subtitles for television and other video presentations is one example of this type.

---

1. Visit an early childhood program that includes children with special needs. Review the assistive technology available for use.

2. Observe a child with special needs using technology. What benefits can you see from your observation? Discuss this with others.

Selecting Computers and Software Programs

For more information about selecting children's software, go to the Companion Website at www.prenhall.com/henniger, select Chapter 17, then choose Web Destinations.

One of the major challenges facing early educators who want to use computer technology in their classrooms is to choose appropriate hardware and software. Numerous options are available, and new products are regularly being developed; therefore, it is difficult for even the experts to keep up with all the choices. A variety of monitors, hard drives, multimedia options, CD-ROM and DVD drives, printers, and hundreds of software options make selections mind-boggling for many. Although each of these decisions is personal, some guidelines may help make the process more manageable.

Hardware Options

First, the latest hardware is not always necessary for effective computer experiences. Preschool children can benefit from even the oldest computer with a monochrome monitor and little software. Just becoming comfortable with the technology and being able to type and print are valuable experiences for this age. Donations of this older hardware by parents or community members are common and can be an easy way to get started using technology in the classroom.

Having said this, however, if you are serious about computer use, it makes sense to consider having the following basic hardware for your classroom:

- *Color monitor.* Color makes most software programs come to life and will motivate young children to explore.

- *Hard drive.* A hard drive allows the computer to be used without handling floppy disks. It is a simpler, quicker way for children to access software.

- *Sound capabilities.* Although sound can be a distracting feature (see section on software selection), it adds another dimension to computer use and should be included. External speakers will offer better sound quality than those built into most computers. The sound option can be turned off when it is too distracting.

- *CD-ROM or DVD drive.* This option greatly expands the software options available. Many of the new programs run most effectively from the CD-ROM or DVD drive.

- *Color printer.* The costs of color printers have dropped significantly over the last few years. This is now an affordable option that increases the ability of children to create pictures and stories on the computer and then print them out.

- *Modem.* Most newer computers come equipped with a modem, which allows Internet access when used in conjunction with an Internet provider such as America Online (AOL).

The best way to evaluate computer software is to spend time using it.

Selecting Computer Software

Many software options are available for young children, and their numbers are growing rapidly. More than 4,000 titles are reviewed in a current book on children's software (Buckleitner, Orr, & Wolock, 2002). Although many programs provide children with positive experiences, numerous others are inappropriate and should be avoided. The teacher's most important task, therefore, is to select the best software from the hundreds of options available.

The following characteristics should be evident in the software before teachers consider it for use in the early childhood classroom (Henniger, 1994):

- *Minimal adult instruction and interaction.* Materials in a good early childhood classroom have a significant characteristic in common: They can all be used with little or no adult instruction or assistance. Good software should have this same quality. It should be simple enough to use that the teacher can install the software on the hard drive and turn children loose to explore its possibilities.

- *Easy to enter and exit.* Quality programs should also allow children to enter the software and later exit without assistance. This seemingly small characteristic can make a big difference in the child's confidence level in approaching and using the computer. When software is user friendly, children will be more likely to try it out and have greater success along the way.

Into Practice...
Drill-and-Practice Software

Estimates indicate that nearly three-fourths of all software being produced for young children is drill-and-practice. The computer prompts the user to respond in a specific, predesigned way to problems it poses.

Despite the fact that these programs can be used less creatively by children (much like the *self-correcting toys* described in Chapter 9), some drill-and-practice software does make rote learning experiences more interesting. As long as it is not the only type of software available, teachers can productively use some drill-and-practice software programs in the early childhood classroom. The following examples highlight some effective uses of this type of software:

- **Learning arithmetic/number facts.** Most of us can remember the traditional flash cards used to teach basic arithmetic facts. This approach, although

effective in many ways, is not exciting. Several software companies have produced much more motivating ways to learn these basic facts. Math Rabbit by The Learning Company and the Math Blaster series by Knowledge Adventure are good examples.

- **Spelling.** Another rather routine task faced by children in the primary grades is the learning of appropriate spelling of words. The Spelling Blaster by Knowledge Adventure presents more interesting activities for children.

- **Prereading and reading activities.** Letter recognition and phonics activities can be effective supplements to the whole language approach to reading. Knowledge Adventure, Disney Interactive, and The Learning Company all produce software program that help with these tasks.

Into Practice...
Classroom Homepage Connections

Charland (1998) presents an exciting technology option for communicating with parents and community members. She suggests creating a homepage on the Internet to inform parents and others about the activities in your classroom. This electronic bulletin board can be used for many purposes, including

- Sharing discipline procedures
- Identifying homework and grading policies
- Discussing home learning tasks (see Chapter 7)
- Asking for assistance in the classroom or at home
- Providing parenting information
- Sharing the calendar of classroom events for the week or month

- Opening a dialogue with parents on a variety of topics relevant to the classroom, such as issues surrounding television viewing

Creating a homepage sounds like a difficult task, but newer software makes this project manageable for those with average computer skills. Charland (1998) also suggests that getting students involved can help make the experience educational for them as well. If you choose this option, be sure to share the same information in other ways so that families without Internet access can still be informed.

- *Verbal instructions.* Because most children in the early childhood years are either nonreaders or beginning readers, the instructions that are necessary for software use should be verbal or pictorial rather than written.

- *Child manipulated.* Good software allows children to experiment, explore, and manipulate the program as they see fit. They then take control and use the software in ways that are interesting and developmentally appropriate. Children will spend more time with these options and learn more along the way.

- *Stimulates imagination and creativity.* When children play, they frequently use their imaginations as they creatively work through roles and situations. Quality software should also encourage these important qualities.

- *Simple in design, complex in use.* The best play materials for children are simple in design, yet can be used in virtually unlimited ways. Blocks are a good example of this concept. Without overwhelming the young child with too many choices, a good software program should allow the child to manipulate and explore for long periods of time. Imaginative, creative experiences are often the result.

Much of the software available for young children does not meet these criteria. Haugland and Shade (1994) estimate that approximately 70 percent of the software developed for young children has limited value. One type of program that should be used less often, drill-and-practice software, requires children to respond with one right answer to closed-ended questions and leaves little opportunity for independent, creative manipulation. Although some drill-and-practice software has value in teaching early math and reading skills, this option should comprise only a small portion of the programs in the early childhood classroom.

Good software can be organized into several categories. Although not all programs in these areas are developmentally appropriate, they tend to be better options for young children. These categories include the following:

- *Storyboard software.* Shade (1995) states that these programs allow children to build a story by first picking a background and then adding their own choices of objects and people, much like the more traditional flannelboard stories children create.

- *Draw/paint programs.* Some software programs allow children to use the computer much like an electronic easel. Children can draw pictures, paint, use electronic stamps, and utilize a variety of other options to create an art project on the computer screen.

- *Electronic books.* With the growth of CD-ROM software, many stories have been computerized, with excellent graphics and sound capabilities that allow the computer to read to the child.

- *Writing/publishing software.* Several good programs are available for children to write and publish their own stories. They are designed for children in the primary grades and above and often allow children to illustrate their creations as well.

With the hundreds of titles available, it is difficult for most teachers to find the time to adequately review software in preparation for purchase. Fortunately, good resources can help narrow the list of options down to a manageable size:

 For more information about Children's Software Review, go to the Companion Website at www.prenhall.com/henniger, select Chapter 17, then choose Web Destinations.

- *Children's Software and New Media Review.* This bimonthly newsletter reviews children's software and other new media. Edited by Warren Buckleitner, Ann Orr, and Ellen Wolock, this publication evaluates more than 100 software titles and new media in each issue. Call (800) 993-9499 for more information.

- *The Complete Sourcebook on Children's Interactive Media.* With over 5,000 reviews of software titles and other interactive media for young children, this is perhaps the most comprehensive resource for teachers of young children. Published annually by the Children's Software Review, this book can be obtained by calling (800) 993-9499.

Helping Parents to Select Software

With the hundreds of software titles being sold for young children, it is difficult for parents to choose the software that will best meet their children's needs and interests. Perhaps the most useful assistance that teachers can provide is to share with parents resources for rating software quality. Having some of the best options available in the classroom and letting parents see and try out these programs are also helpful. Identifying the limitations of drill-and-practice software is also beneficial for parents. Finally, differentiating between quality playful software and those that are just entertaining may provide parents with additional insights for software selection.

Observing Development • Computer Usage

Choose one of two age groups within early childhood (preschoolers or primary-age children), *observe* **computer usage** after considering the guidelines provided, *reflect* on what you saw and heard, and *apply* the appropriate strategies listed with the children you observed.

Observe	Reflect	Apply
Look for specific examples of:	*Think about and respond to the following questions:*	*Consider the following developmentally appropriate strategies for the age group you observed:*
Independent use of computer hardware (turns computer on/off, selects computer software, manipulates mouse, navigates independently through software, etc.)	Are all preschool and primary-age children developmentally ready to independently manipulate computer hardware?	Encourage independent computer use • Preschool: provide pictorial directions/instructions for computer use • Primary: give children group instruction (as needed) for computer use
Software choices (names and purposes of the software used by individual children)	Were the software options you observed children using oriented toward drill-and-practice or more creative and open-ended experiences?	Provide open-ended software options • Preschool: purchase a draw/paint program like KidPix • Primary: use a writing/publishing program such as Children's Publishing and Writing Center
Tasks completed when using the computer (play a game, computer "reads" a story, writing/word processing task, etc.)	Do computers provide unique opportunities for learning and development in young children?	Help children make good software choices • Preschool: suggest/guide software choices to help children develop skills/understandings they need • Primary: purchase management software that allows you to track the computer usage of each child

Summary

To test your knowledge of this chapter's contents, go to the Companion Website at www.prenhall.com/henniger, select Chapter 17, then select Study Guide. Also see Chapter Overviews, Reflecting Essay Questions, Multimedia Explorations, and relevant Web Destinations.

Television and Young Children

Television has a significant impact on young children's lives. They spend a large amount of time viewing TV, often watching programs with sexual themes, violence, and misleading advertising. Parents play an important role in helping children make sense of what they see on television.

The Video Game Dilemma

Both strengths and weaknesses are associated with children's use of video games. Again, parents can assist young children in their use of these games.

Can Computers Be Used in Developmentally Appropriate Ways?

Educators have expressed concerns about the developmental appropriateness of computers and problems associated with solitary computer use. With the selection of playful computer software and careful organization of the computer in the early childhood classroom, however, these problems can be overcome.

Selecting Computers and Software Programs

It is important to select hardware and software that can be playfully explored by children. Because of the huge number of software options available, teachers must carefully select the best quality programs after a thorough review process.

Multimedia Explorations and Activities . . .

Navigating the Internet with Children

Children have important tasks to accomplish during their early years to build a solid base for future learning. Used appropriately, technology can be a positive factor in a child's learning process. But the use of computers and other technology must be thoughtfully planned to provide for their learning needs. Two important questions need to be considered when introducing young children to anything new, including technology:

- Is it developmentally appropriate—is it consistent with how a child develops and learns, and with the child's current developmental stage?
- Will the activity benefit the child, or will it replace some other, more meaningful learning activities?

(Northwest Educational Technology Consortium, 2004)

Research

One of the difficulties with the rapidly growing number of technology options available for young children is the challenge of determining which are developmentally appropriate. This is especially true in the area of Internet resources. This activity is designed to provide you with information to evaluate the many Internet sites available for young children.

1. Go to the Companion Website at www.prenhall.com/henniger and click on the Multimedia Explorations and Activities button for Chapter 17 for more information on this topic.

2. Talk to a parent of a young child who has Internet access. Find out strategies used in monitoring web sites visited and how those sites are selected.

Reflect

- At what age does it make sense to encourage children to spend time on the Internet? Why?
- If you were a parent of a young child, what criteria would you use in selecting sites for your child to use?
- What are the advantages and disadvantages of Internet use when compared with software designed for young children?

Respond

Based on your activities in this section, consider one or more of the following options:

1. Create a list of 10 to 20 Internet sites for young children that you feel would provide valuable experiences for them. Give a brief rationale for your selection of each site. Share your list with a teacher of young children.

2. Make a case either for or against the use of the Internet by children younger than age 5. Post it on the message board of the Companion Website for this text. Would you feel the same way if the ages were 5 to 8? Share your reasoning on the message board.

REFERENCES

Aboud, F. (1988). *Children and prejudice.* London: Basil Blackwell.

Achilles, E. (1999). Creating music environments in early childhood programs. *Young Children, 54*(1), 21–26.

Adherents.com. (2002). *Largest religious groups in the United States of America.* Retrieved from www.adherents.com/rel_USA.html

Administration for Children and Families. (2001). *Child Care Bureau: FFY 2001 CCDF data tables and charts.* Retrieved March 29, 2003, from www.acf.dhhs.gov/ programs/ccb/research/01acf800/chldser1.htm

Administration for Children and Families. (2002). *A descriptive study of Head Start families.* Retrieved November 29, 2003, from www.acf.hhs.gov/programs/ core/ongoing_research/faces/technical_report/tech_title.html

Ainsworth, M. (1973). The development of infant and mother attachment. In B. Caldwell & H. Ricciuti (Eds.), *Review of child development research* (Vol. 3, pp. 121–143). Chicago: University of Chicago Press.

Alexander, K., & Day, M. (Eds.). (1999). *Discipline-based art education: A curriculum sampler.* Los Angeles: J. Paul Getty Trust.

Allison, J. (1999). On the expanded role of the teacher. *Childhood Education, 75*(5), 258–259.

American Association for the Advancement of Science. (1999). *Dialogue on early childhood science, mathematics, and technology education.* Washington, DC: Author.

American Association of University Women. (1998). *Gender gaps. Where schools still fail our children.* Washington, DC: Author.

American Educational Research Association. (2000). *High stakes testing in pre–K–12 education.* Retrieved October 23, 2003, from www.aera.net/about/policy/stakes.htm

American Psychological Association. (2003). *Gay and lesbian parenting.* Retrieved November 29, 2003, from www.apa.org/pi/parent.html

Anderson, R., Hiebert, E., Scott, J., & Wilkinson, I. (1985). *Becoming a nation of readers: The report of the Commission on Reading.* Washington, DC: National Academy of Education.

Anglund, J. (1983). *A friend is someone who likes you.* San Diego, CA: Harcourt Brace Jovanovich.

Annie E. Casey Foundation. (2003). *Kids count data book.* Baltimore, MD: Author.

Aries, P. (1962). *Centuries of childhood.* New York: Vintage Books.

Arts Education Partnership. (2004). *Strategic plan 2004–2006.* Retrieved January 8, 2004, from aeparts.org/ PDF%20Files/AEPStratPlan.pdf

Assessment (2003). *Education Week.* Retrieved December 15, 2003, from www.edweek.org/context/topics/issuespage.cfm?id=41

Atlas, J., & Lapidus, L. (1987). Patterns of symbolic expression in subgroups of the childhood psychoses. *Journal of Clinical Psychology, 43,* 177–188.

Axline, V. (1947). *Play therapy.* Boston: Houghton Mifflin.

Axline, V. (1964). *DIBS: In search of self.* Boston: Houghton Mifflin.

Baker, K. (1966). *Let's play outdoors.* Washington, DC: National Association for the Education of Young Children.

Ball, W. (1995). Nurturing musical aptitude in children. *Dimensions of Early Childhood, 23*(4), 19–24.

Bandura, A. (1989). Social cognitive theory. *Annals of Child Development, 6,* 1–60.

Banks, J. (1993). Multicultural education for young children: Racial and ethnic attitudes and their modification. In B. Spodek, (Ed.), *Handbook of research on the education of young children* (pp. 236–250). Upper Saddle River, NJ: Prentice Hall.

Banks, J. (2002). *An introduction to multicultural education* (3rd ed.). Boston: Allyn & Bacon.

Baratta-Lorton, M. (1976). *Mathematics their way.* Menlo Park, CA: Addison-Wesley.

Barbour, C., & Barbour, N. (2001). *Families, schools, and communities: Building partnerships for educating children* (2nd ed.). Upper Saddle River, NJ: Merrill/Prentice Hall.

Barnes, B., & Hill, S. (1983). Should young children work with microcomputers—Logo before Lego? *The Computing Teacher, 10*(9), 11–14.

Baron, L. (1991). Peer tutoring, microcomputer learning and young children. *Journal of Computing in Childhood Education, 2*(4), 27–40.

Barron, M. (1999). Three- and four-year-olds completing 150-piece puzzles? Impossible! *Young Children, 54*(5), 10–11.

Bayless, K., & Ramsey, M. (1991). *Music: A way of life for the young child* (4th ed.). Upper Saddle River, NJ: Merrill/Prentice Hall.

Bear, T., Schenk, S., & Buckner, L. (1993). Supporting victims of child abuse. *Educational Leadership, 50*(4), 42–47.

Benelli, C., & Yongue, B. (1995). Supporting young children's motor skill development. *Childhood Education, 71*(4), 217–220.

Berger, E. H. (2004). *Parents as partners in education* (6th ed.). Upper Saddle River, NJ: Merrill/Prentice Hall.

Berk, L. (1994). Vygotsky's theory: The importance of make-believe play. *Young Children, 50*(1), 30–39.

Berry, J. (1986). *Teach me about series: My body.* Danbury, CT: Grolier.

Bloom, B. (1964). *Stability and change in human characteristics.* New York: John Wiley & Sons.

Blume, J. (1970). *Freckle juice.* Scarsdale, NY: Bradbury.

Bobys, A. (2000). What does emerging literacy look like? *Young Children, 55*(4), 16–22.

Boehm, A. (1971). *Boehm test of basic concepts.* New York: Psychological Corp.

Boutte, G., & McCormick, C. (1992). Authentic multicultural activities. *Childhood Education, 68*(3), 140–144.

Bowlby, J. (1969). *Attachment and loss: Vol. I. Attachment.* New York: Basic Books.

Boyer, E. (1987, January). Keynote address to the National Invitational Conference sponsored by the Getty Center for Education in the Arts, Los Angeles.

Braun, S., & Edwards, E. (1972). *History and theory of early childhood education.* Belmont, CA: Wadsworth Publishing.

Braus, N., & Geidel, M. (2000). *Everyone's kids' books.* Brattleboro, VT: Everyone's Books.

Bredekamp, S. (Ed.). (1987). *Developmentally appropriate practice in early childhood programs serving children from birth through age 8.* Washington, DC: National Association for the Education of Young Children.

Bredekamp, S. (1993). Reflections on Reggio Emilia. *Young Children, 49*(1), 13–17.

Bredekamp, S. (1996). 25 years of educating young children: The High/Scope approach to preschool education. *Young Children, 51*(4), 57–61.

Bredekamp, S., & Copple, C. (Eds.). (1997). *Developmentally appropriate practice in early childhood programs* (rev. ed.). Washington, DC: National Association for the Education of Young Children.

Brenner, B. (1970). *Bodies.* New York: Dutton.

Bright Horizons. (2003). *About Bright Horizons.* Retrieved on November 17, 2003, from www.BrightHorizons.com

Bronfenbrenner, U. (1974). *Is early intervention effective?* (Vols. 1 & 2). Washington, DC: U.S. Government Printing Office.

Bronfenbrenner, U. (1979). *The ecology of human development.* Cambridge, MA: Harvard University Press.

Brookes, M. (1986). *Drawing with children: A creative teaching and learning method that works for adults, too.* New York: G. P. Putnam's Sons.

Brown, N., Curry, N., & Tittnich, E. (1971). How groups of children deal with common stress through play. In N. Curry & S. Arnaud (Eds.), *Play: The child strives toward self-realization* (pp. 26–38). Washington, DC: National Association for the Education of Young Children.

Brown, T. (1991). *Someone special, just like you.* New York: Holt, Rinehart & Winston.

Bruce, C. (1998). *Young children and the arts: Making creative connections.* Washington, DC: Arts Education Partnership.

Bruder, M. (2000). *The individual family service plan (IFSP).* ERIC Digest #E605. Retrieved February 23, 2004, from http://ericec.org/digests/e605.html

Bruner, J. (1960). *The process of education.* New York: Vintage Books.

Bruner, J. (1966). *Toward a theory of instruction.* Cambridge, MA: Harvard University Press.

Bruner, J. (1972). The nature and uses of immaturity. *American Psychologist, 27,* 687–708.

Buckleitner, W., Orr, A., & Wolock, E. (2002). *The complete sourcebook on children's interactive media* (vol. 10). Flemington, NJ: Active Learning Associates.

Bunker, L. (1991). The role of play and motor skill development in building children's self-confidence and self-esteem. *The Elementary School Journal, 91*(5), 467–471.

Burton, V. (1939). *Mike Mulligan and his steam shovel.* Boston: Houghton Mifflin.

California Achievement Test. (1977). *Test coordinator's handbook, forms C and D.* Monterey, CA: McGraw-Hill.

Campbell, B. (1992). Multiple intelligences in action. *Childhood Education, 68*(4), 197–201.

Canfield, J., & Wells, H. (1994). *100 ways to enhance self-concept in the classroom* (2nd ed.). Boston: Allyn & Bacon.

Carey, K. (2003). *The funding gap: Low-income and minority students still receive fewer dollars in many states.* Retrieved from www2.edtrust.org/NR/rdonlyres/EE004C0AD7B8-40A6-8A03-1F26B8228502/0/funding2003.pdf

Carle, E. (1985). *My very first book of shapes.* New York: Harper & Row.

Carlsson-Paige, N., & Levin, D. (1986). The butter battle book: Uses and abuses with young children. *Young Children, 41*(3), 37–42.

Carrick, D. (1985). *Milk.* New York: Greenwillow.

Castle, K. (1990). Children's invented games. *Childhood Education, 67,* 82–85.

Catron, C., & Allen, J. (2003). *Early childhood curriculum* (3rd ed.). Upper Saddle River, NJ: Merrill/Prentice Hall.

Center for Communication Policy. (1997). *The UCLA television violence monitoring report.* Retrieved December 22, 2003, from The University of California at Los Angeles website: www.ccp.ucla.edu/pages/VReports.asp

Cesarone, B. (1994). Video games and children. *ERIC Digest,* EDO-PS-94-3. Urbana, IL: ERIC Clearinghouse on Elementary and Early Childhood Education.

Chaille, C., & Britain, L. (2003). *The young child as scientist: A constructivist approach to early childhood science education* (3rd ed.). New York: Longman.

Chaille, C., & Silvern, S. (1996). Understanding through play. *Childhood Education, 72*(5), 274–277.

Charland, T. (1998). Classroom homepage connections. *T. H. E. Journal, 25*(9), 62–64.

Charlesworth, R. (2000). *Experiences in math for young children* (4th ed.). Albany, NY: Delmar.

Charlesworth, R. (2004). *Understanding child development* (6th ed.) Albany, NY: Delmar.

Chattin-McNichols, J. (1992). Montessori programs in public schools. *ERIC Digest,* EDO-PS-92-7. Urbana, IL: ERIC Clearinghouse on Elementary and Early Childhood Education.

Children's Defense Fund. (1999). *The state of America's children: Yearbook 1999.* Washington, DC: Author.

Children's Defense Fund. (2002). *The state of children in America's union: A 2002 action guide to leave no child behind.* Washington, DC: Author.

Chomsky, N. (1965). *Aspects of a theory of syntax.* Cambridge, MA: MIT Press.

Christie, J., Enz, B., & Vukelich, C. (2003). *Teaching language and literacy—Preschool through the elementary grades* (2nd ed.). New York: Longman.

Chronicle of Higher Education. (2003). Colleges make slight progress toward gender equity in sports. *Chronicle of Higher Education,* July 25, 18.

Clark, P., & Kirk, E. (2000). Review of research: All-day kindergarten. *Childhood Education, 76*(4), 228–231.

Clearinghouse on Elementary and Early Childhood Education. (1990). Guidelines for family television viewing. *ERIC Digest,* EDO-PS-90–3. Urbana, IL: ERIC Clearinghouse on Elementary and Early Childhood Education.

Clemens, J. (1996). Gardening with children. *Young Children, 51*(4), 22–27.

Clements, D., & Sarama, J. (2003). Young children and technology. What *does* the research say? *Young Children, 58*(6), 34–40.

Cohen, D. (1994). Building the better playground. *Education Week, 13*(21), 33–35.

Cohen, D., Stern, V., & Balaban, N. (1997). *Observing and recording the behavior of young children* (4th ed.). New York: Teachers College Press.

Coleman, J. (1966). *Equality of educational opportunity.* Washington, DC: U.S. Government Printing Office.

Comenius, J. (1896). *School of infancy.* Boston: Heath.

Community Playthings. (1990). *Criteria for play equipment.* Rifton, NY: Author.

Connor-Kuntz, F., & Dummer, G. (1996). Teaching across the curriculum: Language-enriched physical education for preschool children. *Adapted Physical Activity Quarterly, 13*(3), 302–315.

Consumer Product Safety Commission. (1997). *Handbook for public playground safety.* Washington, DC: Author.

Cortes, C. (2000). *The children are watching: How the media teach about diversity.* New York: Teachers College Press.

Cuffaro, H. (1984). Microcomputers in education: Why is earlier better? *Teacher's College Record, 85,* 559–567.

Damon, W. (1983). *Social and personality development: Infancy through adolescence.* New York: W. W. Norton.

Davis, B., & Shade, D. (1994, December). Integrate, don't isolate! Computers in the early childhood curriculum. *ERIC Digest,* EDO-PS-94-17. Urbana, IL: ERIC Clearinghouse on Elementary and Early Childhood Education.

DeFina, A. (1992). *Portfolio assessment.* New York: Scholastic Professional Books.

Delisle, J. (1994, September 21). Reach out—But don't touch. *Education Week,* 33.

Derman-Sparks, L. (1989). *Anti-bias curriculum: Tools for empowering young children.* Washington, DC: National Association for the Education of Young Children.

Derman-Sparks, L. (1994). Empowering children to create a caring culture in a world of differences. *Childhood Education, 70*(2), 66–71.

Derman-Sparks, L. (1999). Markers of multicultural/antibias education. *Young Children, 54*(5), 43.

Derman-Sparks, L., & Phillips, C. (1997). *Teaching/learning anti-racism.* New York: Teachers College Press.

DeVries, R., & Kohlberg, L. (1987). *Constructivist early education: Overview and comparison with other programs.* Washington, DC: National Association for the Education of Young Children.

DeVries, R., & Zan, B. (1995). Creating a constructivist classroom atmosphere. *Young Children, 51*(1), 4–13.

Dewey, J. (1929). *Democracy and education.* New York: Macmillan.

Dinwiddie, S. (1993). Playing in the gutters: Enhancing children's cognitive and social play. *Young Children, 48*(6), 70–73.

Dodge, D., Colker, L., & Heroman, C. (2002). *The creative curriculum for early childhood* (4th ed.). Washington, DC: Teaching Strategies.

Doman, G. (1961). *Teach your baby to read.* London: Jonathan Cape.

Dreikurs, R., Grunwald, B., & Pepper, F. (1982). *Maintaining sanity in the classroom* (2nd ed.). New York: Harper & Row.

Dunn, L., & Dunn, L. (1981). *Peabody picture vocabulary test—revised.* Circle Pines, MN: American Guidance Service.

Dunn, M. (2002). Is Ritalin the answer? *American Journal of Nursing, 102*(12), 22.

Eck, D. (2001). *A new religious America: How a "Christian country" has become the world's most religiously diverse nation.* San Francisco: Harper.

Edwards, C., Gandini, L., & Forman, G. (Eds.). (1998). *The hundred languages of children: The Reggio Emilia approach to early childhood education* (2nd ed.). Norwood, NJ: Ablex.

Edwards, C., & Raikes, H. (2002). Extending the dance: Relationship-based approaches to infant/toddler care and education. *Young Children, 57*(4), 10–17.

Edwards, C., & Springate, K. (1993). Inviting children into project work. *Dimensions of Early Childhood, 22*(1), 9–12, 40.

Edwards, L. (2002). *The creative arts: A process approach for teachers and children* (3rd ed.). Upper Saddle River, NJ: Merrill/Prentice Hall.

Einstein, A. (1949). Autobiographical notes. In P. A. Schilpp (Ed.), *Albert Einstein: Philosopher and scientist.* Evanston, IL: The Library of Living Philosophers.

Einstein, A. (1954). *Ideas and opinions.* New York: Crown Publishers.

Eisenberg, L. (1990). *What's happening to the American family?* (PS 019 149). Paper presented at the annual meeting of the American Academy of Pediatrics, Boston. (ERIC Document Reproduction Service No. ED 325 222)

Eli Lilly and Company. (2003). *Life at Lilly.* Retrieved September 12, 2003, from www.lilly.com/careers/ benefits/personal-life.html

Elkind, D. (1981). *Children and adolescents* (3rd ed.). New York: Oxford University Press.

Elkind, D. (2001). *The hurried child: Growing up too fast too soon* (3rd ed.). Boulder, CO: Perseus Books.

Elkind, D. (2003). Thanks for the memory. The lasting value of true play. *Young Children, 58*(3), 46–50.

Ellis, M. (1973). *Why people play.* Upper Saddle River, NJ: Prentice Hall.

Ellis, S., & Whalen, S. (1990). *Cooperative learning: Getting started.* New York: Scholastic Professional Books.

Engel, B. (1996). Learning to look: Appreciating child art. *Young Children, 51*(3), 74–79.

Epstein, J. (1995). School/family/community partnerships: Caring for the children we share. *Phi Delta Kappan, 76*(9), 701–712.

Erikson, E. (1963). *Childhood and society* (2nd ed.). New York: W. W. Norton.

Erikson, E. (1968). *Identity: Youth and crisis.* New York: W. W. Norton.

Erle, J., Adams, G., & Tout, K. (2001). *Who's caring for our youngest children?* Washington, DC: Urban Institute.

Esbensen, S. (1987). *An outdoor classroom.* Ypsilanti, MI: High/Scope Press.

Fields, M., & Boesser, C. (2002). *Constructive guidance and discipline: Preschool and primary education* (3rd ed.). Upper Saddle River, NJ: Merrill/Prentice Hall.

Fields, M., & DeGayner, B. (2000). Read my story. *Childhood Education, 76*(3), 130–135.

Fischer, M., & Gillespie, C. (2003). One Head Start classroom's experience. Computers and young children's development. *Young Children, 58*(4), 85–91.

Fisher, B. (1998). *Joyful learning in kindergarten* (2nd ed.). Portsmouth, NH: Heinemann.

Flavell, J. (1963). *The developmental psychology of Jean Piaget.* New York: D. Van Nostrand.

Flohr, J. (2004). *The musical lives of young children.* Upper Saddle River, NJ: Prentice Hall.

Flynn, L., & Kieff, J. (2002). Including everyone in outdoor play. *Young Children, 57*(3), 20–26.

Forum on Child and Family Statistics. (2003). *America's children: Key national indicators of well-being.* Washington, DC: Author.

Foster, S. M. (1994). Successful parent meetings. *Young Children, 50*(1), 78–81.

Frankenburg, W., Dodds, J., Fandal, A., Kajuk, F., & Cohr, M. (1975). *Denver developmental screening test: Revised reference manual.* Denver, CO: LADOCA Foundation.

Freeman, N., Feeney, S., & Moravcik, E. (2003). Ethics and the early childhood teacher educator: A proposed addendum to the NAEYC Code of Ethical Conduct. *Young Children, 58*(3), 82–86.

Freud, S. (1938). *An outline of psychoanalysis.* London: Hogarth.

Froebel, F. (1886). *Education of man* (J. Jarvis, Trans.). New York: Appleton-Century-Crofts.

Froebel, F. (1906). *Mother-play and nursery songs.* New York: Lothrop, Lee, & Shepard.

Fromberg, D. (2002). *Play and meaning in early childhood education.* Boston: Allyn & Bacon.

Froschl, M., & Sprung, B. (1999). On purpose: Addressing teasing and bullying in early childhood. *Young Children, 54*(2), 70–72.

Frost, J., Bowers, L., & Wortham, S. (1990). The state of American preschool playgrounds. *Journal of Physical Education, Recreation, and Dance, 61*(8), 18–23.

Frost, J., & Henniger, M. (1979). Making playgrounds safe for children and children safe for playgrounds. *Young Children, 34*(5), 23–30.

Frost, J., & Sweeney, T. (1996). *Cause and prevention of playground injuries and litigation.* Washington, DC: Association for Childhood Education International.

Frost, J., & Wortham, S. (1988). The evolution of American playgrounds. *Young Children, 43*(5), 19–28.

Frost, J., Wortham, S., & Reifel, S. (2001). *Play and child development.* Upper Saddle River, NJ: Merrill/Prentice Hall.

Funk, J. (1993). Reevaluating the impact of video games. *Clinical Pediatrics, 32,* 86–90.

Furman, R. (1995). Helping children cope with stress and deal with feelings. *Young Children, 50*(2), 33–41.

Gallagher, J. (1998). *Classroom assessment for teachers.* Upper Saddle River, NJ: Merrill/Prentice Hall.

Gallahue, D. (1982). *Understanding motor development in children.* New York: Wiley.

Gallahue, D. (1993). Motor development and movement skill acquisition in early childhood education. In B. Spodek (Ed.), *Handbook of research on the education of young children* (pp. 24–41). Upper Saddle River, NJ: Prentice Hall.

Gallahue, D., & Ozman, J. (2002). *Understanding motor development: Infants, children, adolescents, adults.* (5th ed.). New York: McGraw-Hill.

Galley, M. (2000, May 10). Computer companies give birth to 'lapware' for babies. *Education Week,* 5.

Gandini, L. (1993). Fundamentals of the Reggio Emilia approach to early childhood education. *Young Children, 49*(1), 4–8.

Gardner, H. (1983). *Frames of mind: The theory of multiple intelligences.* New York: Basic Books.

Gardner, H. (1993). *Multiple intelligences: The theory in practice.* New York: Basic Books.

Gardner, H. (1999). *Intelligence reframed.* New York: Basic Books.

Garvey, C. (1990). *Play* (enlarged ed.). Cambridge, MA: Harvard University Press.

Gesell, A., & Ilg, F. (1949). *Child development: An introduction to the study of human growth.* New York: Harper & Brothers.

Gestwicki, C. (2004). *Home, school and community relations* (5th ed.). Albany, NY: Delmar.

Ginott, H. (1972). *Teacher and child.* New York: Macmillan.

Ginsburg, H., & Opper, S. (1969). *Piaget's theory of intellectual development.* Upper Saddle River, NJ: Prentice Hall.

Glasser, W. (1969). *Schools without failure.* New York: Harper & Row.

Glasser, W. (1990). *The quality school.* New York: Harper & Row.

Goertzel, M., & Goertzel, R. (1962). *Cradles of eminence.* Boston: Little, Brown.

Gordon, T. (1974). *Teacher effectiveness training.* New York: Wyden.

Gorter-Reu, M., & Anderson, J. (1998). Home kits, home visits, and more! *Young Children, 53*(3), 71–74.

Griffith, M., Kauerz, K., & McMaken, J. (2003). How states fund full-day kindergarten. Denver, CO: Education Commission of the States. Retrieved November 17, 2003, from www.ecs.org/clearinghouse/45/60/4560.htm

Gropper, N., & Froschl, M. (1999, April). The role of gender in young children's teasing and bullying behavior. Paper presented at the American Educational Research Association Annual Meeting, Montreal, Quebec.

Gross, T., & Clemens, S. (2002). Painting a tragedy. Young children process the events of September 11. *Young Children, 57*(3), 44–51.

Grossman, S. (1999). Examining the origins of our beliefs about parents. *Childhood Education, 76*(1), 24–27.

Grotberg, E. (1995). *A guide to promoting resilience in children: Strengthening the human spirit.* The Netherlands: Bernard Van Leer Foundation.

Guimps, R. (1890). *Pestalozzi: His life and work* (J. Russell, Trans.). New York: Appleton.

Hallahan, D., & Kauffman, J. (2003). *Exceptional learners: Introduction to special education with casebook* (9th ed.). Boston: Allyn & Bacon.

Hamilton, D., Flemming, B., & Hicks, J. (1990). *Resources for creative teaching in early childhood education* (2nd ed.). San Diego, CA: Harcourt Brace Jovanovich.

Harms, T., & Clifford, R. (1980). *Early childhood environment rating scale.* New York: Teachers College Press.

Harms, T., Clifford, R., & Cryer, D. (1998). *Early childhood environment rating scale (ECRS)* (rev. ed.). New York: Teachers College Press.

Harris, T. (1994). The snack shop: Block play in a primary classroom. *Dimensions of Early Childhood, 22*(4), 22–23.

Hartup, W. (1992). Having friends, making friends, and keeping friends: Relationships as educational contexts. *ERIC Digest,* EDO-PS-92-4. Urbana, IL: ERIC Clearinghouse on Elementary and Early Childhood Education. (ERIC Document Reproduction Service No. ED 345 854)

Hartup, W., & Moore, S. (1990). Early peer relations: Developmental significance and prognostic implications. *Early Childhood Research Quarterly, 5*(1), 1–18.

Harwayne, S. (1992). *Lasting impressions.* Portsmouth, NH: Heinemann.

Hatcher, B., Nicosia, T., & Pape, D. (1994). *Interested in inviting and sustaining play behaviors? Prop boxes offer promise!* Paper presented at the Annual Conference of the Association for Childhood Education International, New Orleans, LA.

Hatcher, B., Pape, D., & Nicosia, T. (1988). Group games for global awareness. *Childhood Education, 65*(1), 8–13.

Haugland, S. (1999). What role should technology play in young children's learning? Part I. *Young Children, 54*(6), 26–31.

Haugland, S., & Shade, D. (1994). Software evaluation for young children. In J. Wright & D. Shade (Eds.), *Young children: Active learners in a technological age* (pp. 17–24). Washington, DC: National Association for the Education of Young Children.

Haugland, S., & Wright, J. (1997). *Young children and technology.* Needham Heights, MA: Allyn & Bacon.

Heidemann, S., & Hewitt, D. (1992). *Pathways to play: Developing play skills in young children.* St. Paul, MN: Redleaf Press.

Heller, R., & Martin, C. (1982). *Bits 'n bytes about computing.* Rockville, MD: Computer Science Press.

Helm, J., & Beneke, S. (2003). *The power of projects: Meeting contemporary challenges in early childhood classrooms.* New York: Teachers College Press.

Hendrick, J. (Ed.). (1997). *First steps toward teaching the Reggio way.* Upper Saddle River, NJ: Merrill/Prentice Hall.

Hendrick, J. (2003). *Total learning: Developmental curriculum for the young child* (6th ed.). Upper Saddle River, NJ: Merrill/Prentice Hall.

Hendrick, J. (Ed.). (2004). *Next steps toward teaching the Reggio way: Accepting the challenge to change.* Upper Saddle River, NJ: Merrill/Prentice Hall.

Henniger, M. (1993). Enriching the outdoor play experience. *Childhood Education, 70*(2), 87–90.

Henniger, M. (1994). Software for the early childhood classroom: What should it look like? *Journal of Computing in Childhood Education, 5*(2), 167–175.

Henri, A. (1990). *The postman's palace.* New York: Macmillan Children's Book Group.

Hermes, J. (1995). Read me a story: 101 good books kids will love. *U.S. Catholic,* October, 6–15.

Herr, J., & Libby-Larson, Y. (2004). *Creative resources for the early childhood classroom* (4th ed.). Albany, NY: Delmar.

Hewes, J. (1975). *Build your own playground.* Boston: Houghton Mifflin.

Hildebrand, V., & Hearron, P. (1999). *Guiding young children* (6th ed.). Upper Saddle River, NJ: Merrill/Prentice Hall.

Hildebrand, V., Phenice, L., Gray, M., & Hines, R. (2000). *Knowing and serving diverse families* (2nd ed.). Upper Saddle River, NJ: Merrill/Prentice Hall.

Hildebrandt, C. (1998). Creativity and music in early childhood. *Young Children, 53*(6), 68–74.

Hirsch, E. (Ed.). (1996). *The block book* (3rd ed.). Washington, DC: National Association for the Education of Young Children.

Hohmann, C. (1996). *Foundations in elementary education: Overview.* Ypsilanti, MI: High/Scope Press.

Hohmann, M., & Weikart, D. (1995). *Educating young children: Active learning practices for preschool and child care programs.* Ypsilanti, MI: High/Scope Press.

Honig, A., & Wittmer, D. (1996). Helping children become more prosocial: Ideas for classrooms, families, schools, and communities. *Young Children, 51*(2), 62–70.

Howard, G. (1999). *We can't teach what we don't know: White teachers, multiracial schools.* New York: Teachers College Press.

Hubbard, R. (1998). Creating a classroom where children can think. *Young Children, 53*(5), 26–31.

Huber, L. (1999). Woodworking with young children: You can do it! *Young Children, 54*(6), 32–34.

Hughes, F. (1999). *Children, play, and development* (3rd ed.). Boston: Allyn & Bacon.

Hunt, J. (1961). *Intelligence and experience.* New York: Ronald Press.

Huston, A., & Wright, J. (1996). Television and socialization of young children. In T. M. MacBeth (Ed.), *Tuning in to young viewers: Social science perspectives on television* (pp. 37–60). Thousand Oaks, CA: Sage.

Hymes, J. (1978). *Living history interviews.* Carmel, CA: Hacienda Press.

International Reading Association. (1998). Learning to read and write: Developmentally appropriate practices for young children. A joint statement of the International Reading Association (IRA) and the National Association for the Education of Young Children (NAEYC). *Young Children, 53*(4), 30–46.

Irvine, J. (2003). *Educating teachers for diversity.* New York: Teachers College Press.

Isbell, R. (2002). Telling and retelling stories. Learning language and literacy. *Young Children, 57*(2), 26–30.

Isbell, R., & Raines, S. (2000). *Tell it again 2.* Beltsville, MD: Gryphon House.

Isenberg, J., & Jalongo, M. (2001). *Creative expression and play in early childhood* (3rd ed.). Upper Saddle River, NJ: Merrill/Prentice Hall.

Isenberg, J., & Quisenberry, N. (2002). *Play: Essential for all children.* A position paper of the Association for Childhood Education International. Retrieved December 3, 2003, from www.udel.edu/bateman/acei/playpaper.htm

Itard, J. (1962). *The wild boy of Aveyron* (G. Humphrey & M. Humphrey, Trans.). New York: Appleton-Century-Crofts. (Original work published 1801 and 1806)

Jalongo, M. (1995). Awaken to the artistry within young children! *Dimensions of Early Childhood, 23*(4), 8–14.

Jalongo, M. (1996). Using recorded music with young children: A guide for nonmusicians. *Young Children, 51*(5), 6–14.

Jalongo, M. (2003). The child's right to creative thought and expression. *Childhood Education, 79*(4), 218–228.

Jambor, T. (1994a). A playground raising: Context for intergenerational relationships. *Dimensions of Early Childhood, 22*(2), 31–36.

Jambor, T. (1994b). School recess and social development. *Dimensions of Early Childhood, 23*(1), 17–20.

Jelks, P., & Dukes, L. (1985). Promising props for outdoor play. *Day Care and Early Education, 13*(1), 18–20.

Jensen, B., & Bullard, J. (2002). The mud center. Recapturing childhood. *Young Children, 57*(3), 16–19.

Jensen, M., & Hannibal, M. (2000). *Issues, advocacy, and leadership in early education* (2nd ed.). Boston: Allyn & Bacon.

Johnson, J., Christie, J., & Yawkey, T. (1987). *Play and early childhood development.* Glenview, IL: Scott, Foresman.

Johnson, J., Christie, J., & Yawkey, T. (1999). *Play and early childhood development* (2nd ed.). New York: Longman.

Jones, V., & Jones, L. (2004). *Comprehensive classroom management: Creating communities of support and solving problems* (7th ed.). Boston: Allyn & Bacon.

Kameenui, E., & Darch, C. (1995). *Instructional classroom management.* White Plains, NY: Longman.

Kamii, C., & DeClark, G. (1985). *Young children reinvent arithmetic: Implications of Piaget's theory.* New York: Teachers College Press.

Kamii, C., & DeVries, R. (1978). *Physical knowledge in preschool education.* Upper Saddle River, NJ: Merrill/Prentice Hall.

Kamii, C., & DeVries, R. (1980). *Group games in early education.* Washington, DC: National Association for the Education of Young Children.

Kamii, C., & Ewing, J. (1996). Basing teaching on Piaget's constructivism. *Childhood Education, 72*(5), 260–264.

Karnes, M. (1994, May/June). Outdoor play for children with special needs. *Scholastic Early Childhood Today*, 55.

Katz, L. (1994). The project approach. *ERIC Digest*. EDO-PS-94-6. Urbana, IL: ERIC Clearinghouse on Elementary and Early Childhood Education.

Katz, L., & Chard, S. (1989). *Engaging children's minds: The project approach*. New York: Ablex.

Kellogg, R. (1969). *Analyzing children's art*. Palo Alto, CA: Mayfield Publishing.

King, M., & Gartrell, D. (2003). Building an encouraging classroom with boys in mind. *Young Children, 58*(4), 33–36.

Kinsey, S. (2001). *Multiage grouping and academic achievement*. ERIC Digest ED448935. Champaign, IL: ERIC Clearinghouse on Elementary and Early Childhood Education.

Kirchner, G. (1991). *Children's games from around the world*. Dubuque, IA: William C. Brown.

Klein, N. (1973). *Girls can be anything*. New York: Dutton.

Koch, P., & McDonough, M. (1999). Improving parent-teacher conferences through collaborative conversations. *Young Children, 54*(2), 11–15.

Kohn, A. (2000). Standardized testing and its victims. *Education Week*, September 27, 46–47, 60.

Kostelnik, M., Soderman, A., & Whiren, A. (1999). *Developmentally appropriate programs in early childhood education* (2nd ed.). Upper Saddle River, NJ: Merrill/Prentice Hall.

Kostelnik, M., Stein, L., Whiren, A., & Soderman, A. (2002). *Guiding children's social development* (4th ed.). Albany, NY: Delmar.

Kowalski, T. (2004). *Public relations in schools* (3rd ed.). Upper Saddle River, NJ: Merrill/Prentice Hall.

Kraus, R. (1971). *Leo the late bloomer*. New York: Windmill.

Kritchevsky, S., & Prescott, E. (1969). *Planning environments for young children: Physical space*. Washington, DC: National Association for the Education of Young Children.

Krogh, S. (1995). *The integrated early childhood curriculum* (2nd ed.). New York: McGraw-Hill.

Kuhl, P. (1993). *Life language*. Seattle, WA: University of Washington.

Kupetz, B., & Green, E. (1997). Sharing books with infants and toddlers: Facing the challenges. *Young Children, 52*(2), 22–27.

Lake, V., & Pappamihiel, N. (2003). Effective practices and principles to support English Language Learners in the early childhood classroom. *Childhood Education, 79*(4), 200–203.

Landau, S., & McAninch, C. (1993). Young children with attention deficits. *Young Children, 48*(4), 49–58.

Lane, M. (1981). *The squirrel*. New York: Dial.

Leithead, M. (1996). Happy hammering . . . a hammering activity with built-in success. *Young Children, 51*(3), 12.

Lewis, R. (1994, March 16). Hands-on nurturing: Teaching children how to care. *Education Week*, 46.

Lillard, P. (1972). *Montessori—A modern approach*. New York: Schocken Books.

Lillard, P. (1996). *Montessori today: A comprehensive approach to education from birth to adulthood*. New York: Schocken Books.

Lowman, L., & Ruhmann, L. (1998). Simply sensational spaces: A multi-"s" approach to toddler environments. *Young Children, 53*(3), 11–17.

Machado, J. (2003). *Early childhood experiences in language arts* (7th ed.). Albany, NY: Delmar.

Mageau, T. (Ed.). (1993). Early childhood and school success. *Electronic Learning, 12*(5), 23.

Maldono, N. (1996). Puzzles: A pathetically neglected, commonly available resource. *Young Children, 51* (4), 4–10.

Marcon, R. (2003). Growing children. The physical side of development. *Young Children, 58*(1), 80–87.

Marion, M. (2003). *Guidance of young children* (6th ed.). Upper Saddle River, NJ: Merrill/Prentice Hall.

Marland, S. (1972). *Education of the gifted and talented*. Washington, DC: U.S. Government Printing Office.

Marotz, L., Cross, M., & Rush, J. (2001). *Health, safety and nutrition for the young child* (5th ed.). Albany, NY: Delmar.

Marshall, C. (1998). Using children's storybooks to encourage discussions among diverse populations. *Childhood Education, 74*(4), 194–199.

Marshall, C., Morrison, K., & Davis, R. (2000). Passion, politics, and collaboration: Changing early childhood teacher preparation and certification. *Journal of Early Childhood Teacher Education, 21*(1), 13.

Marston, L. (1984). *Playground equipment*. Jefferson, NC: McFarland.

Maslow, A. (1968). *Toward a psychology of being*. Princeton, NJ: Van Nostrand Reinhold.

Matthews, M. (1990). *What's it like to be a postal worker?* Mahweh, NJ: Troll Associates.

Mayer, M. (1974). *Frog goes to dinner*. New York: Dial.

Mayesky, M. (2002). *Creative activities for young children*. Albany, NY: Delmar.

McAfee, O., & Leong, D. (2002). *Assessing and guiding young children's development and learning* (3rd ed.). Boston: Allyn & Bacon.

McClellan, D., & Katz, L. (1997). *Fostering children's social competence: The teacher's role*. Washington, DC: National Association for the Education of Young Children.

McCracken, J. (Ed.). (1986). *Reducing stress in young children's lives*. Washington, DC: National Association for the Education of Young Children.

McMillan, M. (1919). *The nursery school*. New York: E. P. Dutton & Co.

McNeil, D. (1970). *The acquisition of language: The study of developmental psycholinguistics*. New York: Harper & Row.

Miller, D. (2004). *Positive child guidance* (4th ed.). Albany, NY: Delmar.

Miller, S. (1978). *The facilitation of fundamental motor skill learning in young children.* Unpublished doctoral dissertation, Michigan State University, East Lansing.

Miller, S. (1997). Family television viewing—How to gain control. *Childhood Education, 74*(1), 38–41.

Miller, S. (1999). Balloons, blankets, and balls. *Young Children, 54*(5), 58–63.

Mitchell, A., & David, J. (Eds.). (1992). *Explorations with young children.* Mt. Rainier, MD: Gryphon House.

Mitchell, E., & Mason, B. (1948). *The theory of play.* New York: Barnes.

Moffitt, M. (1996). Children learn about science through block building. In E. Hirsch (Ed.), *The block book* (3rd ed.). Washington, DC: National Association for the Education of Young Children.

Montagu, A. (1978). *Touching: The human significance of the skin* (2nd ed.). New York: Harper & Row.

Montessori, M. (1965). *Dr. Montessori's own handbook.* New York: Schocken Books.

Montessori, M. *The absorbent mind.* New York: Dell Publishing. (Original work published 1949)

Moore, K. (2001). *Classroom teaching skills* (5th ed.). New York: McGraw-Hill.

Mulligan, S. (2003). Assistive technology. Supporting the participation of children with disabilities. *Young Children, 58*(6), 50–51.

Murray, P., & Mayer, R. (1988). Preschool children's judgements of number magnitude. *Journal of Educational Psychology, 80,* 206–209.

Myhre, S. (1993). Enhancing your dramatic-play area through the use of prop boxes. *Young Children, 48*(5), 6–11.

Nash, A., & Fraleigh, K. (1993, March). *The influence of older siblings on the sex-typed toy play of young children.* Paper presented at the Biennial Conference of the Society for Research in Child Development, New Orleans.

National Association for the Education of Young Children. (1993). Enriching classroom diversity with books for children, in-depth discussion of them, and story-extension activities. *Young Children, 48*(3), 10–12.

National Association for the Education of Young Children. (1996). NAEYC position statement: Technology and young children—Ages three through eight. *Young Children, 51*(6), 11–16.

National Association for the Education of Young Children. (1998a). *Accreditation criteria and procedures of the National Association for the Education of Young Children—1998 Edition.* Washington, DC: Author.

National Association for the Education of Young Children. (1998b). Learning to read and write: Developmentally appropriate practices for young children. *Young Children, 53*(4), 30–46.

National Association for the Education of Young Children. (1998c). *Media violence and young children: A guide for parents.* Washington, DC: Author

National Association for the Education of Young Children. (2001). *NAEYC standards for early childhood professional preparation—Initial licensure programs.* Washington, DC: Author.

National Association for the Education of Young Children. (2003). *NAEYC standards for early childhood professional preparation—Associate degree programs.* Washington, DC: Author.

National Association for the Education of Young Children. (2004). *Celebrating holidays in early childhood programs.* Retrieved January 21, 2004, from www.naeyc.org/resources/eyly/1996/18.asp

National Association for Sport and Physical Education. (1998). *Physical activity for children: A statement of guidelines.* Reston, VA: Author.

National Black Caucus of State Legislators. (2001). *Closing the achievement gap: Improving educational outcomes for African American children.* Retrieved from www.nbcsl.com/news/pdf/cag.pdf

National Center for Education Statistics. (2003). *The condition of education 2003.* Washington, DC: U.S. Government Printing Office.

National Coalition for the Homeless. (2001). Homeless families with children. Retrieved November 29, 2003, from www.nationalhomeless.org/families.html

National Council of Teachers of Mathematics. (2000). *Principles and standards for school mathematics.* Reston, VA: Author.

Neuman, S., & Roskos, K. (1993). *Language and literacy learning in the early years.* Ft. Worth, TX: Harcourt Brace Jovanovich.

Newcombe, N., & Huttenlocher, J. (1992). Children's early ability to solve perspective-taking problems. *Developmental Psychology, 28*(4), 635–643.

Newman, N. (1990). *Sharing.* New York: Doubleday.

No Child Left Behind. (2002). Retrieved September 26, 2003, from www.ed.gov/legislation/ESEA02/pg1.html#sec101

Northwest Educational Consortium. (2004). *Early connections: Technology in early childhood education.* Taken from the World Wide Web at: http://www.netc.org/earlyconnections/index1/html, March 18, 2004.

Notar, E. (1989). Children and TV commercials: Wave after wave of exploitation. *Childhood Education, 66,* 66–67.

Nourot, P., & Van Hoorn, J. (1991). Symbolic play in preschool and primary settings. *Young Children, 46*(6), 40–50.

Odoy, H., & Foster, S. (1997). Creating play crates for the outdoor classroom. *Young Children, 52*(6), 12–16.

Olsen, G., & Fuller, M. (2003). *Home-school relations: Working successfully with parents and families* (2nd ed.). Boston: Allyn & Bacon.

Olson, L. (2000, September 27). Children of change. *Education Week,* 30–41.

Olson, S., & Loucks-Horsley, S. (Eds.). (2000). *Inquiry and the National Science Education Standards: A guide for teaching and learning.* Washington, DC: National Academies Press.

Orlick, T. (1978). *The cooperative sports and games book: Challenge without competition.* New York: Pantheon.

Orlick, T. (1982). *The second cooperative sports and games book.* New York: Pantheon.

Owocki, G. (1999). *Literacy through play.* Portsmouth, NH: Heinemann.

Paintal, S. (1999). Banning corporal punishment of children. *Childhood Education, 76*(1), 36–39.

Papert, S. (1993). *The children's machine. Rethinking school in the age of the computer.* New York: Basic Books.

Parris, P. (2001). *Child Development Associate national credentialing program.* Retrieved from www.nncc.org/ Evaluation/cdacb.html

Parten, M. (1933). Social play among preschool children. *Journal of Abnormal and Social Psychology, 28,* 136–147.

Paulsell, D., Nogales, R., & Cohen, J. (2003). *Quality child care for infants and toddlers: Case studies of three community strategies.* Washington, DC: National Center for Infants, Toddlers, and Families.

Payne, G., & Isaacs, L. (2002). *Human motor development: A lifespan approach* (5th ed.). New York: McGraw-Hill.

Pelligrini, A. (1987). Elementary school children's rough-and-tumble play. *Monographs of the Institute for Behavioral Research.* Athens: University of Georgia.

Pelligrini, A., & Glickman, C. (1989). The educational benefits of recess. *Principal, 62*(5), 23–24.

Pelligrini, A., & Perlmutter, J. (1988). Rough-and-tumble play on the elementary school playground. *Young Children, 43*(2), 14–17.

Pepler, D., & Ross, H. (1981). The effects of play on convergent and divergent problem solving. *Child Development, 52,* 1202–1210.

Petersen, E. (2003). *A practical guide to early childhood curriculum* (2nd ed.). Boston: Allyn & Bacon.

Piaget, J. (1950). *The psychology of intelligence* (M. Piercy & D. Berlyne, Trans.). New York: Harcourt, Brace.

Piaget, J. (1959). *The language and thought of the child* (M. Gabain, Trans.) (3rd ed.). London: Routledge & Kegan Paul.

Piaget, J. (1962). *Play, dreams, and imitation in childhood* (C. Gattegno & F. Hodgson, Trans.). New York: W. W. Norton.

Piaget, J. (1965). *The moral judgement of the child* (M. Gabain, Trans.). New York: Free Press.

Piaget, J., & Inhelder, B. (1969). *The psychology of the child* (H. Weaver, Trans.). New York: Basic Books.

Pica, R. (2004). *Experiences in movement, birth to age eight* (3rd ed.). Albany, NY: Delmar.

Piirto, J. (1999). *Talented children and adults: Their development and education* (2nd ed.). Upper Saddle River, NJ: Merrill/Prentice Hall.

Plutchik, R. (1980). *Emotion: A psychoevolutionary synthesis.* New York: Harper & Row.

Poest, C., Williams, J., Witt, D., & Atwood, M. (1990). Challenge me to move: Large muscle development in young children. *Young Children, 45*(5), 4–10.

Powell, D. (1998). Reweaving parents into the fabric of early childhood programs. *Young Children, 53*(5), 60–67.

Raikes, H. (1993). Relationship duration in infant care: Time with a high ability teacher and infant-teacher attachment. *Early Childhood Research Quarterly, 8,* 309–325.

Raines, S., & Isbell, R. (1999). *Tell it again.* Beltsville, MD: Gryphon House.

Rankin, B. (1993). Curriculum development in Reggio Emilia: A long-term curriculum project about dinosaurs. In C. Edwards, L. Gandini, & G. Forman (Eds.), *The hundred languages of children.* Norwood, NJ: Ablex.

Rath, L. (2002). Using *Between the Lions* to support early literacy. *Young Children, 57*(2), 80–86.

Readdick, C. (1993). Solitary pursuits: Supporting children's privacy needs in early childhood settings. *Young Children, 49*(1), 60–64.

Reynolds, E. (2001). *Guiding young children. A child-centered approach* (3rd ed.). New York: McGraw-Hill.

Rideout, V., Vandewater, E., & Wartella, E. (2003). *Zero to six: Electronic media in the lives of infants, toddlers and preschoolers.* Menlo Park, CA: The Henry Kaiser Family Foundation. Taken from the World Wide Web at: http://www.kff.org

Rimdzius, T. (2003). *Third national Even Start evaluation: Program impacts and implications for improvement.* Washington, DC: U.S. Department of Education.

Ringgenberg, S. (2003). Music as a teaching tool: Creating story songs. *Young Children, 58*(5), 76–79.

Rivkin, M. (1990). Outdoor play—What happens here? In S. Wortham & J. Frost (Eds.), *Playgrounds for young children: National survey and perspectives* (pp. 191–214). Reston, VA: American Alliance for Health, Physical Education, Recreation and Dance.

Rivkin, M. (1995). *The great outdoors: Restoring children's right to play outside.* Washington, DC: National Association for the Education of Young Children.

Roblyer, M., Edwards, J., & Havriluk, M. (1997). *Integrating educational technology into teaching.* Upper Saddle River, NJ: Merrill/Prentice Hall.

Roopnarine, J., & Johnson, J. (Eds.). (2000). *Approaches to early childhood education* (3rd ed.). Upper Saddle River, NJ: Merrill/Prentice Hall.

Rousseau, J. (1979). *Emile* (A. Bloom, Trans.). New York: Basic Books. (Original work published 1762)

Rybczynski, M., & Troy, A. (1995). Literacy-enriched play centers: Trying them out in "the real world." *Childhood Education, 72*(1), 7–12.

Saracho, O., & Spodek, B. (1998). *Multiple perspectives on play in early childhood education.* Albany, NY: SUNY Press.

Schickedanz, J., Schickedanz, D., Forsyth, P., & Forsyth, G. (2001). *Understanding children and adolescents* (4th ed.). Needham Heights, MA: Allyn & Bacon.

Schirrmacher, R. (2002). *Art and creative development for young children* (4th ed.). Albany, NY: Delmar.

Schunk, D. (2004). *Learning theories: An educational perspective* (4th ed.). Upper Saddle River, NJ: Merrill/Prentice Hall.

Schweinhart, L. (1993). Observing young children in action: The key to early childhood assessment. *Young Children, 48*(5), 29–33.

Schweinhart, L. (2003, April). Benefits, costs, and explanation of the High/Scope Perry Preschool Program. Paper presented at the Meeting of the Society for Research in Child Development, Tampa, Florida.

Seagoe, M. (1970). An instrument for the analysis of children's play as an index of socialization. *Journal of School Psychology, 8,* 139–144.

Seefeldt, C. (Ed.). (1990). *Continuing issues in early childhood education.* Upper Saddle River, NJ: Merrill/Prentice Hall.

Seefeldt, C. (1995). Art—A serious work. *Young Children, 50*(3), 39–45.

Seefeldt, C. (1999). *The early childhood curriculum: Current findings in theory and practice* (3rd ed.). New York: Teachers College Press.

Seguin, E. (1907). *Idiocy and its treatment.* Albany, NY: Press of Brandow Printing Co.

Seidel, J. (1992). Children with HIV-related developmental difficulties. *Phi Delta Kappan, 74,* 38–40, 56.

Seuss, Dr. (1960). *Green eggs and ham.* New York: Random House.

Shade, D. (1992). Computers and young children: Software with the appeal of blocks. *Day Care and Early Education, 19*(3), 41–43.

Shade, D. (1995). Storyboard software: Flannel boards in the computer age. *Day Care and Early Education, 22*(3), 45–46.

Shaw, J., & Blake, S. (1998). *Mathematics for young children.* Upper Saddle River, NJ: Merrill/Prentice Hall.

Shepherd, T. R., & Shepherd, W. L. (1984). Living with a child with autistic tendencies. In M. Henniger & L. Nesselroad (Eds.), *Working with parents of handicapped children* (pp. 85–106). Lanham, MD: University Press of America.

Shidler-Lattz, L., & Ratcliff, N. (1998). Coloring in the lines: A tale of two children. *Young Children, 53*(1), 68–69.

Shore, R. (2003). *Kids Count indicator brief: Preventing teen births.* Retrieved December 1, 2003, from www.aecf.org/kidscount/indicator briefs/teen pregnancy.pdf

Shores, E., & Grace, C. (1998). *The portfolio book. A step-by-step guide for teachers.* Beltsville, MD: Gryphon House.

Silberg, J., & Schiller, P. (2003). *The complete book of activities, games, stories, props, recipes, and dances for young children.* Beltsville, MD: Gryphon House.

Singer, D., & Singer, J. (1990). *The house of make-believe.* Cambridge, MA: Harvard University Press.

Skeels, H. (1966). Adult status of children with contrasting early life experience. *Monographs of the Society for Research in Child Development, 31*(3, Serial No. 105).

Skinner, B. (1957). *Verbal behavior.* New York: Appleton-Century-Crofts.

Skinner, B. (1974). *About behaviorism.* New York: Knopf.

Skurzynski, G. (1992). *Here comes the mail.* New York: Macmillan Children's Book Group.

Smilansky, S. (1968). *The effects of sociodramatic play on disadvantaged preschool children.* New York: Wiley.

Smilansky, S., & Shefatya, L. (1990). *Facilitating play: A medium for promoting cognitive, socio-emotional and academic development in young children.* Gaithersburg, MD: Psychosocial and Educational Publications.

Smith, A. (2000). Reflective portfolios: Preschool possibilities. *Childhood Education, 76*(4), 204–208.

Smith, P., & Connolly, K. (1980). *The ecology of preschool behavior.* Cambridge, England: Cambridge University Press.

Smith, S. (1990). The riskiness of the playground. *The Journal of Educational Thought, 24*(2), 71–87.

Snider, S., & Badgett, T. (1995). I have this computer, what do I do now? Using technology to enhance every child's learning. *Early Childhood Education Journal, 23*(2), 101–105.

Snow, C., Burns, S., & Griffin, P. (1998). *Preventing reading difficulties in young children.* Washington, DC: National Academy Press.

Sobel, J. (1984). Everybody wins: 393 non-competitive games for young children. New York: Walker and Company.

Sprung, B. (1996). Physics is fun, physics is important, and physics belongs in the early childhood curriculum. *Young Children, 51*(5), 29–33.

St. Clair, J. (2002). Using *Between the Lions* in a kindergarten classroom. *Young Children, 57*(2), 87–88.

Standing, E. (1962). *Maria Montessori: Her life and work.* Fresno, CA: Academy Guild Press.

Starko, A. (1995). *Creativity in the classroom: Schools of curious delight.* White Plains, NY: Longman.

Steiner, G. (1976). *The children's cause.* Washington, DC: Brookings Institution.

Stone, S. (1995). Wanted: Advocates for play in the primary grades. *Young Children, 50*(6), 45–54.

Sulzby, E., & Teale, W. (1991). Emergent literacy. In R. Barr, M. Kamil, P. Mosentahl, & P. Pearson (Eds.), *Handbook of reading research* (Vol. 2, pp. 82–97). New York: Longman.

Sutterby, J., & Frost, J. (2002). Making playgrounds fit for children and children fit for playgrounds. *Young Children, 57*(3), 36–41.

Sutton-Smith, B., & Roberts, J. (1981). Play, games, and sports. In H. C. Triandis & A. Heron (Eds.), *Handbook of cross-cultural psychology: Vol. 4. Developmental psychology* (pp. 223–241). Boston: Allyn & Bacon.

Swick, K., Boutte, G., & van Scoy, I. (1995, March). Family involvement in early multicultural learning. *ERIC Digest*, EDO-PS-95-2. Urbana, IL: ERIC Clearinghouse on Elementary and Early Childhood Education.

Swiniarski, L. (1991). Toys: Universals for teaching global education. *Childhood Education, 67*(3), 161–163.

Szyba, C. (1999). Why do some teachers resist offering appropriate, open-ended art activities for young children? *Young Children, 54*(1), 16–20.

Taylor, J. (1999). Child-led parent/school conferences—In second grade? *Young Children, 54*(1), 78–82.

Tegano, D., Sawyers, J., & Moran, J. (1989). Problem-finding and solving in play: The teacher's role. *Childhood Education, 66*(2), 92–97.

Thomas, R. (1985). *Comparing theories of child development* (2nd ed.). Belmont, CA: Wadsworth.

Thornton, K. (2002). From our president. Exporting TV violence—What do we owe the world's children? *Young Children, 57*(2), 6, 74.

Torrance, E. (1962). *Guiding creative talent.* Upper Saddle River, NJ: Prentice Hall.

Tracy, D. (1994). Using mathematical language to enhance mathematical conceptualization. *Childhood Education, 70*(4), 221–224.

Trawick-Smith, J. (2003). *Early childhood development: A multicultural perspective* (3rd ed.). Upper Saddle River, NJ: Merrill/Prentice Hall.

Underwood, J. (1981, February 23). A game plan for America. *Sports Illustrated,* 64–80.

U.S. Census Bureau. (1999). *Who's minding the kids? Child care arrangements: Spring 1999.* Retrieved from www.census.gov/population/www/socdemo/child/ppl-168.html

U.S. Census Bureau. (2000). *Census 2000.* Washington, DC: Government Printing Office.

U.S. Department of Education. (2001). *Twenty-third annual report to congress on the implementation of the Individuals with Disabilities Education Act.* Washington, DC: Author.

U.S. Department of Education. (2003). *No child left behind: A desktop reference.* Retrieved September 3, 2003, from www.ed.gov/offices/OESE/reference/1a.html

U.S. Department of Health and Human Services. (2002). *Program performance standards for the operation of Head Start programs by grantee and delegate agencies.* Washington, DC: Author.

U.S. Department of Health and Human Services. (2003). *Head Start performance standards and other regulations.* Washington, DC: Author. Retrieved September 3, 2003, from www.acf.hhs.gov/programs/hsb/performance/index.htm

Van Hoorn, J., Nourot, P., Scales, B., & Alward, K. (2003). *Play at the center of the curriculum* (3rd ed.). Upper Saddle River, NJ: Merrill/Prentice Hall.

Vandenberg, B. (1980). Play, problem-solving and creativity. *New Directions for Child Development, 9,* 49–68.

Viadero, D. (2000, March 22). Lags in minority achievement defy traditional explanations. *Education Week, 1,* 18–22.

Vygotsky, L. (1962). *Thought and language.* Cambridge, MA: M.I.T. Press.

Vygotsky, L. (1978). *Mind in society: The development of higher psychological processes* (M. Cole, V. John-Steiner, S. Scribner, E. Superman, Eds.). Cambridge, MA: Harvard University Press.

Waelder, R. (1933). The psychoanalytic theory of play. *Psychoanalytic Quarterly, 2,* 208–224.

Wallis, C. (1994, July 18). Life in overdrive. *Time,* 43–50.

Walsh, V., Smith, B., & Taylor, R. (2000). *IDEA requirements for preschoolers with disabilities.* Retrieved March 23, 2003, from www.ideapractices.org

Wanamaker, N., Hearn, K., & Richarz, S. (1979). *More than graham crackers: Nutrition education and food preparation with young children.* Washington, DC: National Association for the Education of Young Children.

Ward, C. (1996). Adult intervention: Appropriate strategies for enriching the quality of children's play. *Young Children, 51*(3), 20–25.

Warren, J. (1983). *Piggyback songs.* Everett, WA: Warren Publishing.

Wassermann, S. (1992). Serious play in the classroom—How messing around can win you the Nobel Prize. *Childhood Education, 68*(3), 133–139.

Wassermann, S. (2000). *Serious players in the primary classroom. Empowering children through active learning experiences* (2nd ed.). New York: Teachers College Press.

Watson, J. (1924). *Behaviorism.* New York: W. W. Norton.

Watson, L., & Watson, M. (2003). *Infants and toddlers curriculum and teaching* (5th ed.). Albany, NY: Delmar.

Waxman, S. (1976a). *What is a boy?* Los Angeles: Peace Press.

Waxman, S. (1976b). *What is a girl?* Los Angeles: Peace Press.

Weber, E. (1984). *Ideas influencing early childhood education.* New York: Teachers College Press.

Wechsler, D. (1967). *Wechsler preschool and primary scale of intelligence: Manual.* New York: Psychological Corporation.

Weikart, D., Rogers, L., Adcock, C., & McClelland, D. (1971). *The cognitively oriented curriculum.* Washington, DC: National Association for the Education of Young Children.

Whaley, C. (2002). Meeting the diverse needs of children through storytelling. *Young Children, 57*(2), 31–34.

Wiechel, J. (2003). From our president. Advocates face immense challenges. *Young Children, 58*(3), 6.

Wien, C., Stacey, S., Keating, B., Rowlings, J., & Cameron, H. (2002). The doll project. Handmade dolls as a framework for emergent curriculum. *Young Children, 57*(1), 33–38.

Williams, D. L., & Chavkin, N. F. (1989, October). Essential elements of strong parent involvement programs. *Educational Leadership, 47,* 18–20.

Wilson, A. (2004). *The Suzuki method.* Retrieved January 19, 2004, from www.japanfile.com/arts and entertainment/music/features/Suzuki1.shtml

Winter, S. (1985). Toddler play behaviors and equipment choices in an outdoor playground. In J. Frost & S. Sunderlin (Eds.), *When children play* (pp. 129–138). Wheaton, MD: Association for Childhood Education International.

Winter, S., Bell, M., & Dempsey, J. (1994). Creating play environments for children with special needs. *Childhood Education, 71*(1), 28–32.

Wittmer, D., & Honig, A. (1994). Encouraging positive social development in young children. *Young Children, 49*(2), 4–12.

Wolery, M., & Wilbers, J. (Eds.). (1994). *Including children with special needs in early childhood programs.* Washington, DC: National Association for the Education of Young Children.

Wolfinger, D. (1994). *Science and mathematics in early childhood education.* New York: HarperCollins.

Wortham, S. (2001). *Assessment in early childhood education* (3rd ed.). Upper Saddle River, NJ: Merrill/Prentice Hall.

Wortham, S. (2002). *Early childhood curriculum: Developmental bases for learning and teaching* (3rd ed.). Upper Saddle River, NJ: Merrill/Prentice Hall.

Wright, J., & Huston, A. (1995). *Effects of educational TV viewing of lower income preschoolers on academic skills, school readiness, and school adjustment one to three years later.* Lawrence, KS: Center for Research on the Influences of Television on Children.

Wright, K., & Stegelin, D. (2003). *Building school and community partnerships through parent involvement* (2nd ed.). Upper Saddle River, NJ: Merrill/Prentice Hall.

Yaden, D., Rowe, D., & MacGillivray, L. (2000). Emergent literacy: A polyphony of perspectives. In M. Kamil, P. Mosenthal, P. Pearson, & R. Barr (Eds.), *Handbook of reading research* (Vol. III). Mahwah, NJ: Erlbaum.

Yawkey, T., & Pellegrini, A. (Eds.). (1984). *Child's play and play therapy.* Lancaster, PA: Technomic Publishing.

Yokota, J. (1993). Issues in selecting multicultural children's literature. *Language Arts, 70,* 43–50.

Zero to Three Policy Center. (2003). *The national evaluation of early Head Start: Early Head Start Works.* Washington, DC: Author. Retrieved from www.zerotothree.org

Zolotow, C. (1985). *William's doll.* New York: Harper & Row.

AUTHOR INDEX

AUTHOR INDEX

Subject Index